DIRECTORY OF SOCIAL AGENCIES

NEW YORK 1921

DIRECTORY OF SOCIAL AGENCIES NEW YORK 1921

HOW TO USE THIS DIRECTORY

If you know the title *of the agency you are looking for, you will find it without the aid of an index or page numbers, by alphabetical sequence, being guided by the key words at the top of pages.*

If you do not *know the title of the agency you are looking for but do know the nature of its work, you will find it by consulting the Subject Index at the front of the book. In this index all agencies are classified according to their functions.*

If you are looking for a church, *you must turn to the Denominational Division of the Church List section, following the Alphabetical List. Institutional churches are entered both in the Alphabetical and the Church lists. See also the Subject Index.*

If you know people *who are prominent in social service, church or other related work, but do not know their connections, you will be able to locate them by using the Name Index at the back of the Directory.*

DIRECTORY
OF
SOCIAL AGENCIES

FORMERLY THE

NEW YORK CHARITIES DIRECTORY

THIRTIETH EDITION

1921

A REFERENCE BOOK OF SOCIAL SERVICE

IN OR AVAILABLE FOR
GREATER NEW YORK

BY
LINA D. MILLER

Published by the
CHARITY ORGANIZATION SOCIETY
IN THE CITY OF NEW YORK
105 EAST 22D ST.

Price, $2.00

THE
CHARITY ORGANIZATION SOCIETY
1882-1921

FORM OF BEQUEST

I devise and bequeath to "THE CHARITY ORGANIZATION SOCIETY OF THE CITY OF NEW YORK," incorporated under Chapter 139 of the laws of 1882 of the State of New York, to be applied to the benevolent uses and purposes of said Society, and under its direction (*insert description of the money or property given*).

FOREWORD

HE new title for this book, the Directory of Social Agencies, will satisfy many objectors to the word "Charities" in the old name, "New York Charities Directory," of which this is the 30th edition. That we should have outgrown our name, and have been obliged to make a change in order to be properly descriptive, is one of the signs of the coming of a new day. There is in it a harbinger of new growth and added responsibility. We welcome it.

During the past year a very marked impulse toward social welfare work was obvious among the churches; more clergymen and church workers having felt the need of the Directory. In this age of wider horizons, charity springing from religion and touching more and more of humanity in its broadening course embraces social service in all its phases. It is coming to be recognized as an inevitable responsibility, a natural part of the Church's work. Following such recognition a many-sided outlook on the material as well as the spiritual aspects of life becomes at once a fundamental necessity. The Directory is a finger-post with many arms indicating the social resources of the entire city.

Inclusion in the Directory of any agency must not be taken to mean approval by the Charity Organization Society. We have excluded any agency known to us to be actually fraudulent. The omission of any agency, however, does not mean that it has been found unworthy.

Many changes are constantly taking place, new organizations are forming while others cease to be active or become amalgamated under new titles.

The statements have been compiled with the co-operation of the agencies listed, and the information is current and authoritative so far as diligence and care can make it. Where an asterisk (*) appears before the name of an agency, the entry is based on the statement in the previous edition or reports by the agency during the year. The asterisk indicates that current information from such organization has not been received in response to our inquiries for this edition.

The apparent reduction in size of the book is due to the use of thinner paper. Nothing has been omitted and we have added in the Index of this volume a general list of all the churches which had been indexed heretofore under denominational headings only.

We welcome and appreciate constructive suggestions wherever users of the Directory may see opportunity for its improvement. The Charity Organization Society thanks the societies and individuals who have cooperated with it in compiling this edition. For help on the Church List of their respective denominations, special mention is due Mr. J. F. E. Nickelsburg, of the American Lutheran Publicity Bureau, the Rt. Rev. Mgr. Dunn, and the Rt. Rev. Mgr. O'Hara.

L. D. M.

"HOW TO USE THIS DIRECTORY"

(*See page facing title*)

SUBJECT INDEX

NOTE: *In this Index the agencies are classified under headings that are descriptive of their objects or the nature of their work. When looking up an agency of which you already know the title, you do not need the Index; simply proceed as when using a dictionary or encyclopedia, following the alphabetical sequence in the body of the book, guided by the running heads, until you come to the agency you are looking for. Where the work of the agencies is definitely confined within the several borough boundaries of the city, the lists are separated under their respective borough headings.*

A

Children's Hospitals.

Churches.

City Departments.

Civic, Economic, etc.

Friends, Religious Society of.

G

Gardens. See AGRICULTURE.

General Relief. (Food, Clothing, Money, Fuel, etc.).

Manhattan and Bronx

H

Naturalization and Colonization.

Negroes.

Manhattan and Bronx

"HOW TO USE THIS DIRECTORY"

(*See page facing title*)

ALPHABETICAL LIST

This is the encyclopedic list of all agencies, including those churches having some form of social service as a part of their program. For the complete Church List see following the Alphabetical List.

A

Abbott E. Kittredge Club for Girls, The (est. 1889), 440 East 57th St., N.Y.C. (tel. Plaza 342). Maintains an evening clubhouse, with educational classes, social evenings, dances, lectures, shower baths, library, roof garden, etc. Self-governing and partly self-supporting.

Officers: Wm. H. Hamilton, pres.; Edward W. Harris, treas.; James F. Longley, secy.; Mrs. Ida Seymour Hutchinson, supt.

Abby House. See BRONX DAY NURSERY.

Academy of Design, National. See NATIONAL ACADEMY OF DESIGN.

Academy of Medicine. See AMERICAN ACADEMY OF MEDICINE; also, NEW YORK ACADEMY OF MEDICINE.

Accounts, Commissioner of. City of New York. 12th floor, Municipal Bldg. (tel. 4315 Worth); David Hirshfield, Comr.

Actor's Fund of America, The (incorp. 1882), Columbia Theatre Bldg., Broadway and 47th St. (tel. 1396 Bryant). Grants relief to sick and needy actors, singers, stage-dancers, and others interested and concerned in the management of, or who earn a living from, any theatre or reputable place of amusement. Supported by funds annually collected, donations and benefit performances at theatres throughout the United States, and dues from members. Has under its jurisdiction:

THE ACTOR'S FUND HOME, West New Brighton, S. I. Established for the purpose of providing, under proper restrictions, a home for the aged and worn-out actor.

Officers: Daniel Frohman, pres.; Sam A. Scribner, treas.; Gus Hill, sec.; W. C. Austin, asst. secy., to whom address communications.

Adirondack Cottage Sanitarium. See TRUDEAU SANATORIUM.

Admission Bureau. See TUBERCULOSIS HOSPITAL ADMISSION BUREAU.

African M. E. Church Parent Home and Foreign Missionary Society. See HOME AND FOREIGN MISSIONARY DEPARTMENT AFRICAN METHODIST EPISCOPAL CHURCH.

After-care Home for Crippled Children, 142 Bruce Ave., Yonkers, N. Y.

Agudath Achim Chessed Shel Emeth (org. 1888, incorp. 1889), 245 Grand St. A free burial association for poor Hebrews. In January, 1901, the United Hebrew Charities discontinued this branch of benevolence, and this society, which is composed of members paying annually three dollars or more, assumed the duty of attending to deceased poor Hebrews of Greater New York.

The society maintains cemeteries at Mt. Richmond and Silver Lake, S. I., and two sections in Bayside Cemetery, L. I. Number of deceased Hebrews given burial in 1919, 652; grand total for the 31 years, 31,579. There are no salaried officers except the secretary.

Officers: B. Friedman, pres.; L. Michalisky, Max Tarshes and Morris Levinsky, vice-prests.; Marks Silver, treas.; H. E. Adelman, secy.

***Ahawath Chessed Shaar Hashomayim Sisterhood of Personal Service** (incorp. 1892), 126 East 101st St., N.Y.C. Headquarters for relief, 192 East 125th St. Maintains classes for Americanization, sewing, domestic science, etc.

A. Jacobi Hospital for Children Social Service, Inc. (incorp. 1918). Associated with Lenox Hill Hospital, 112 East 77th St., N.Y.C. (tel. Rhinelander 3600). For after-care of the

** Current information not received.*

children of the hospital. Hours 9 to 10 A. M., and 1 to 2 P. M. Supported by voluntary contributions.

Officers: Mrs. Joseph Plaut, pres.; Mrs. Roland Monroe, treas.; Mrs. B. S. Rosenbaum, secy.; Dr. A. L. Goodman, consulting director; Jean Grey Long, R.N., Social Service worker.

Aldermen, Board of, City of New York. Clerk's office: 2d floor, Municipal Bldg. (tel. 4430 Worth). President's office: City Hall (tel. Cortlandt 6770).

Alfred Corning Clark Neighborhood House (opened 1899), cor. Cannon and Rivington Sts., N.Y.C.

Staff of workers: Mary S. Brewer, manager; Charles H. Warner, director of boys' work; H. C. Yoxall, director of gymnasium; Maud I. Purnell, director of girls' work; Adeline M. Tipple, director of Italian work; Jean Allison, director of Montessori and kindergarten; Lucy Jones, head of domestic science department.

All Angels' P. E. Church, West End Ave. and 81st St. Maintains guilds and gymnasium classes in the parish house, 251 West 80th St. See also under PROTESTANT EPISCOPAL CHURCHES in the Church List.

All Saints' P. E. Church, Henry and Scammel Sts. Social clubs, pool and printing room. Rev. Dr. K. S. Guthrie, Vicar; Miss Anna Erwin Tait, Missionary, 292 Henry St.

See also under PROTESTANT EPISCOPAL CHURCHES in Church List.

All Souls' P. E. Church, St. Nicholas Ave., between 114th and 115th Sts., maintains

EDWARD WHITNEY HOUSE, 88 St. Nicholas Ave. for guilds and societies; also the residence of parish workers.

All Souls' Unitarian Church, Fourth Ave. and 20th St. Rev. William Lawrence Sullivan.

PARISH HOUSE, 104 East 20th St.

SOCIETY FOR THE EMPLOYMENT AND RELIEF OF POOR WOMEN (org. 1844; incorp. 1874); New York Flower and Fruit Mission (org. 1870); All Souls' Mission Sewing-School (opened 1865); Frances Hackley Memorial Kindergarten; Country Home, Spring Farms, Green Farms, Conn.

See also under UNITARIAN CHURCHES, in the Church List.

Alliance Israelite Universelle (est. 1860). To help establish civil and religious rights for Jews throughout the world and to ameliorate their conditions whenever they may be oppressed or in distress. The Alliance maintains 200 educational institutions in Turkey, Persia, Morocco, Egypt, etc.

NEW YORK BRANCH, 108 East 31st St., Nissim Behar, American Representative; Julius J. Dukas, pres.; Meyer Levy, treas.; M. F. Behar, secy.

Allied Loyalty League, 103 Park Ave., N.Y.C. Promotes Americanism and friendly understanding between the allied countries.

Officers: James M. Beck, pres.; Harris A. Dunn, treas.; Emily H. Chauncey, exec. secy.

Ambulance Service, Board of, City of New York, 10th floor, Municipal Bldg. (tel. Worth 748). This board is composed of the Police Commissioner, Commissioner of Public Charities, the President of the Board of Trustees of Bellevue and Allied Hospitals, and two members appointed by the Mayor. It has supervision over the ambulance service in Greater New York and may itself establish and maintain ambulance stations in districts not provided with adequate ambulance service.

Any citizen may call an ambulance.

Emergency calls may be made without charge; tell the operator that an ambulance is wanted, giving address.

Emergency ambulances maintained by the public hospitals do not make any charge for their service. Free ambulances are operated by the Department of Health for the transfer of cases of contagious diseases.

The following hospitals have an emergency ambulance service:

MANHATTAN AND BRONX

BELLEVUE HOSPITAL, foot of East 26th St. (tel. Madison Sq. 8800-4397-4398).

BROAD STREET HOSPITAL, Broad and South Sts. (tel. Broad 17).

FLOWER HOSPITAL, Eastern Boulevard (Ave. A), between 63d and 64th Sts. (tel. Plaza 5506).

FORDHAM HOSPITAL, Crotona Ave. and Southern Blvd. (tel. Fordham 5000).

GOUVERNEUR HOSPITAL, Gouverneur Slip, 42 Front St. (tel. Orchard 4430).

HARLEM HOSPITAL, Lenox Ave., 136th to 137th St. (tel. Harlem 5000).

KNICKERBOCKER, Amsterdam Ave. and 131st St. (tel. Morningside 63).

LINCOLN HOSPITAL AND HOME, East 141st St. and Concord Ave., west of Southern Blvd. (tel. Melrose 4100).

NEW YORK HOSPITAL, 7 West 15th St. (tel. Chelsea 8700).

RECEPTION HOSPITAL, Dept. of Public Charities, foot of East 70th St. (tel. Plaza 2622).

ST. LAURENCE HOSPITAL, 163d St. and Edgecomb Ave. (tel. Wadsworth 5065).

ST. VINCENT'S HOSPITAL, 11th and 12th Sts. and Seventh Ave. (tel. Chelsea 4050).

VOLUNTEER HOSPITAL AND DISPENSARY, Beekman and Water Sts. (tel. Beekman 42).

BROOKLYN

BETH MOSES, Stuyvesant Ave. and Hart St. (tel. Bushwick 7007).

BRADFORD STREET HOSPITAL, 113 Bradford St., East New York (tel. East New York 240).

BROOKLYN HOSPITAL, Raymond St. and De Kalb Ave. (tel. Nevins 2900).

BUSHWICK HOSPITAL, Howard Ave., cor. Putnam Ave. (tel. Bushwick 5400).

CONEY ISLAND HOSPITAL, Ocean Pkway. and Ave. Z, Coney Island (tel. Coney Island 1141).

CUMBERLAND ST. HOSPITAL, Cumberland St., near Myrtle Ave. (tel. Prospect 1300).

GREENPOINT HOSPITAL, Kingsland Ave. and Bullion St. (tel. Greenpoint 4431).

HOSPITAL OF THE HOLY FAMILY, 155 Dean St. (tel. Main 103).

JEWISH HOSPITAL, Classon and St. Mark's Aves. (tel. Prospect 3900).

KINGS COUNTY HOSPITAL, Clarkson St., Flatbush (tel. Flatbush 4000).

LONG ISLAND COLLEGE HOSPITAL, Henry, Pacific, and Amity Sts. (tel. Main 9800).

METHODIST EPISCOPAL HOSPITAL, 6th St. to 7th St., Seventh Ave. to Eighth Ave. (tel. South 123).

NORWEGIAN LUTHERAN DEACONESSES' HOME AND HOSPITAL, Fourth Ave. and 46th St. (tel. Sunset 4200).

ST. CATHARINE'S HOSPITAL, Bushwick Ave., between Ten Eyck and Maujer Sts. (tel. Stagg 1061).

ST. JOHN'S HOSPITAL, Atlantic and Albany Aves. (tel. Lafayette 2060).

ST. MARY'S HOSPITAL, St. Mark's

Ave., between Rochester and Buffalo Aves. (tel. Lafayette 6500).

SWEDISH HOSPITAL, Rogers Ave. and Sterling Pl. (tel. Prospect 7561).

WILLIAMSBURGH HOSPITAL, Bedford Ave. and South 3rd St. (tel. Greenpoint 2290).

WYCKOFF HEIGHTS HOSPITAL, St. Nicholas Ave., Stanhope and Stockholm Sts. (tel. Evergreen 3200).

QUEENS

FLUSHING HOSPITAL AND DISPENSARY, Parsons and Forest Aves., Flushing, L. I. (tel. Flushing 2000).

JAMAICA HOSPITAL, New York Ave. (tel. Jamaica 87).

MARY IMMACULATE HOSPITAL, Shelton Ave., Jamaica (tel. Jamaica 199).

ROCKAWAY BEACH HOSPITAL, Hammels, L. I. (tel. Hammels 70).

ST. JOHN'S LONG ISLAND CITY HOSPITAL, 12th St. and Jackson Ave., Long Island City (tel. Hunters Point 2816).

ST. JOSEPH'S HOSPITAL, Central Ave., Far Rockaway (tel. Far Rockaway 520).

RICHMOND

STATEN ISLAND HOSPITAL, Castleton Ave., New Brighton, S. I. (tel. Tompkinsville 1160).

ST. VINCENT'S HOSPITAL, Bard Ave., West New Brighton, S. I. (tel. West New Brighton 740).

Amelia Relief Society, The (org. 1896), 113–115 East 101st St. (tel. 3374 Lenox). Provides a social center for the community, conducts classes, clubs, etc., and does relief work in co-operation with the United Hebrew Charities (q. v.). Mrs. S. M. Bondy, chrm.

American Academy of Medicine (org. 1876, incorp. 1913). Object, the study and publication of studies on subjects connected with "Social Medicine."

Dr. T. W. Grayson, secy., Jenkins Arcade, Pittsburgh, Pa.

American Artists' Committee of One Hundred, 215 West 57th St., N.Y.C. Relief fund for the families of French soldier-artists and especially for the support of orphan children of French artists killed in the war. The American Committee will continue its work until October, 1922. It co-operates with La Fraternité des Artistes, Paris, M. Leon Bonnat, pres., which distributes funds raised by itself and contributed from the American Committee. Cash only is sent by the American Committee. Total amount of Relief Fund to October 1, 1920, $61,726.02.

William A. Coffin, N.A., chrm.; Hon. Pres. of the Fraternité des Artistes; William Bailey Faxon, A.N.A., treas. and gen. secy.

American Association for Community Organization. An association of financial federations, councils of social agencies and similar community groups for the exchange of material and information.

Sherman C. Kingsley, pres.; Elwood Street, secy., 652 S. 4th St., Louisville, Ky.

American Association for the Hard of Hearing, Inc., 126 East 59th St., N.Y.C. To act in the national and international fields of social work for the deafened; to encourage the founding of local organizations; to properly carry on national propaganda in the interests of the deafened and in the prevention of deafness.

Officers: Wendell C. Phillips, M.D., pres.; Mrs. N. Todd Porter, Jr., treas.; Miss Annetta W. Peck, cor. secy.

American Association of Hospital Social Workers, University Hospital, Philadelphia. Works toward improvement and development of standards of social work in hospitals and dispensaries.

Officers: Edna G. Henry, pres.; Harriet Gage, treas.; M. A. Cannon, secy.

American Association for International Conciliation (est. 1906, incorp. 1908). Object: to promote in all practicable ways mutual understanding and good feeling between nations.

Officers: Nicholas Murray Butler, pres., Columbia University; Robert A. Franks, treas., 522 Fifth Ave.; H. S. Haskell, secy., 407 West 117th St.

American Association for Labor Legislation (1906), 131 East 23d St. (tel. Gramercy 2589). To investigate conditions underlying labor legislation and to collect and disseminate information leading to the enactment and efficient enforcement of laws for the promotion of the comfort, health, and safety of employees.

Officers: T. L. Chadbourne, pres.; Adolph Lewisohn, treas.; John B. Andrews, secy.

American Association for Organizing Family Social Work (est. 1911), 130 East 22nd St. (tel. Gramercy 6781). To promote the organization and development of family social work societies (Associated Charities) throughout the country. Through field secretaries it offers assistance in the work of organizing and reorganizing societies, as well as in the maintenance of programs of work.

Officers: Mrs. John M. Glenn, chrm.; Henry H. Bonnell, treas., Philadelphia, Pa.; David H. Holbrook, exec. director; Francis H. McLean, field director.

American Association of Social Service Exchanges, 69 Schermerhorn St., Brooklyn (tel. Main 8200).

Aaron A. Lopez, secy.

American Association for the Study of the Feeble-Minded (org. 1876). To discuss all questions relating to the feeble-minded and to consider their training and education. Membership open to all interested. Annual conference held.

Dr. B. W. Baker, secy., Laconia, N. H.

American Association for Study and Prevention of Infant Mortality. See AMERICAN CHILD HYGIENE ASSOCIATION.

American Baptist Education Society. See BOARD OF EDUCATION OF THE NORTHERN BAPTIST CONVENTION.

American Baptist Foreign Mission Society, The (org. 1814). National headquarters: 276 Fifth Ave., N.Y.C.

Officers: Hon. Carl E. Milliken, pres., Augusta, Maine; George B. Huntington, treas.; William B. Lipphard, rec. secy.

American Baptist Home Mission Society, The (org. 1832, inc. 1843) 23 East 26th St., N.Y.C. Purpose: evangelization of North America. Maintains schools for Negroes and Indians. Has benevolent loan fund to help erect church edifices on promising but needy fields.

Officers: Charles R. Brock, pres.; Samuel Bryant, treas.; Charles L. White, exec. secy.

***American Baptist Publication Society, The** (org. 1824, incorp. 1845), New York office: 23 East 26th St.; National office: 1701 Chestnut St., Phila., Pa.

American Bible Society, The (org. 1816, incorp. 1841), Bible House (tel. Stuyvesant 4800). To encourage a wider circulation of the Holy Scriptures without note or comment. Issues only Bibles and portions of the Bible, and supplies them by sale at cost and by gift. Unsectarian; interdenominational. Conducts work in the United States and in foreign lands. Prints Scriptures,

* *Current information not received.*

in four styles for the blind. Co-operates with missionary societies. Its operations are strictly benevolent; its sales of Scriptures yielding no profit.

The Society was organized on May 8, 1816, in the City Hall of New York, and celebrated its Centennial in the same room of the same City Hall, on May 9, 1916.

Receipts for the Calendar Year 1919, including legacies, gifts from individuals and churches, gifts from Auxiliaries, sales and income from trust funds, were $866,758.86. Disbursements were $858,-348.52.

During the Calendar Year 1919, 3,732,309 volumes of Scripture were issued. Of these 1,734,864 were issued abroad and 2,017,445 volumes were issued in America, a total of 137,903,939 volumes in 104 years.

Officers: Churchill H. Cutting, pres.; James Wood, pres. emeritus; Gilbert Darlington, treas.; Rev. Wm. I. Haven, D.D. and Frank H. Mann, gen. secretaries; Rev. L. B. Chamberlain, rec. secy.

American Bible Society, EASTERN AGENCY, 137 Montague St., Brooklyn. The work of this branch is to distribute Bibles, and raise funds therefor in Brooklyn and New York State generally.

Advisory Committee: L. D. Mason, M.D.; Rev. W. H. Hendrickson, W. W. Kouwenhoven, Rev. Joseph G. Snyder, George M. Blauvelt, Rev. Samuel C. Benson, Agency secy.

American Board of Commissioners for Foreign Missions, The (org. 1810, incorp. 1812), 105 East 22d St. National headquarters: Boston, Mass. Conducts foreign missionary work for the Congregational Churches of the United States. Supported by voluntary contributions of church and legacies. Income last year, $1,666,834.

Officers: Frederick A. Gaskins, treas., Boston; Rev. Edw. Lincoln Smith, D.D., cor. secy., N.Y.C.

American Central Committee for Russian Relief. See RUSSIAN ST. NICHOLAS CATHEDRAL.

American Child Hygiene Association (formerly American Association for Study and Prevention of Infant Mortality) (org. 1909). Headquarters: 1211 Cathedral St., Baltimore, Md. To study child hygiene in all its phases. To stimulate and encourage measures for promoting the health of children from the prenatal period through school age and adolescence.

American Church Building Fund Commission, The (incorp. 1880), Church Missions House, 281 Fourth Ave., N.Y.C. Makes loans, gifts, and grants of money to aid in erecting churches and other parish buildings for the use of the Protestant Episcopal Church. Permanent fund, $665,554.24.

Officers: Rt. Rev. Charles S. Burch, D.D., pres.; Charles A. Tompkins, treas.; Rev. C. L. Pardee, D.D., cor. secy.

American Church Institute for Negroes, 281 Fourth Ave., N.Y.C. (tel. Gramercy 3012). To supervise and further religious education in the Negro schools connected with the Protestant Episcopal Church in the United States.

Officers: Rt. Rev. Thomas F. Gailor, D.D., pres.; Rt. Rev. Edwin S. Lines, vice-pres.; Louis J. Hunter, treas.; George Foster Peabody, LL.D., asst. treas.; Rev. Robert W. Patton, D.D., special representative; Mrs. Isabel M. Carter, secy.

American Civic Association (org. 1904), 914 Union Trust Bldg., Washington, D. C. For the cultivation of higher ideals of civic beauty in America; the promotion of town and neighborhood improvement; the preservation of landscape, and the advancement of outdoor art. Membership, $5, $10, $50, and $200. Various publications on civic improvement and industrial towns.

Officers: J. Horace McFarland, pres.; Eleanor E. Marshall, secy. and acting treas.

American College for Girls at Constantinople, Turkey. See CONSTANTINOPLE COLLEGE.

American Committee of the Argonne Association, 140 West 58th St., N.Y.C. Maintains model boarding-out system and vocational training for French war orphans.

Officers: E. V. Frothingham, pres.; Dr. Haven Emerson, treas.; Dr. Royal Haines, secy.

American Committee for Devastated France, 16 East 39th St., N.Y.C. (tel. Murray Hill 3863). Established in four Cantons of the Department of the Aisne, normal population 50,000. Supported by voluntary contributions. The object is to assist the inhabitants of the devastated villages to become again self-supporting by supplying implements of trade and to feed and educate the children who have suffered the horrors of war for five years.

Officers: Hon. Myron T. Herrick, pres.; Miss Anne Morgan, chrm.; Dr. Alexander C. Humphreys, treas.

American Committee for Relief in the Near East. See NEAR EAST RELIEF.

American Defense Society, Inc., 116 East 24th St., N.Y.C. To promote an adequate national defense of free institutions in the United States.

Officers: J. Raymond Tiffany, pres.; Robert Appleton, treas.; Frances Tilghman, exec. secy.

American Economic Association (est. 1886). For the encouragement of economic research; the issue of publications on economic subjects; the encouragement of perfect freedom of economic discussion. Supported by membership dues $5 a year.

Prof. Ray B. Westerfield, Yale Station, New Haven, Conn., secy.-treas.; Prof. Davis R. Dewey, 222 Charles River Road, Cambridge, Mass., managing editor, American Economic Review.

American Federation for Sex Hygiene. See AMERICAN SOCIAL HYGIENE ASSOCIATION.

American Female Guardian Society and Home for the Friendless (org. 1834, incorp. 1849), 936 Woodycrest Ave., near Jerome Ave. and 161st St. (tel. Jerome 811). Receives in the Home destitute children, boys 3 to 12 years, and girls 3 to 16 years of age, committed by the Bureau of Dependent Children, and, when legally surrendered, places them in approved homes for adoption. The Home also cares for children temporarily until their parents are able to remove them, provided application is made to conform with dates of admission. The Home accommodates 210 children. Supported by a small appropriation from the city, children's board, and voluntary contributions.

Maintains a School in the Home, and four Industrial Schools outside, which receive children who are not eligible to the public schools. Number registered, 5,690. These schools are located as follows:

Home School, 936 Woodycrest Ave.

Industrial School, No. 1, 303 East 109th St.

Industrial School, No. 7, 243 East 103d St.

Industrial School, No. 8, 222 East 148th St.

Industrial School, No. 12, 2247 Second Ave.

Summer Home (Wright Memorial) at Oceanport, N. J., where children from the home are cared for during July and August.

Officers: Miss Selena M. Campbell, pres.; Mrs. H. G. Mendenhall, treas.; Mrs. C. H. Brown, cor. secy.

American Free Milk and Relief for Italy, Inc. Vanderbilt Hotel, N.Y.C. Distributes dried milk in Italy for relief of children under four years.

Mrs. John A. Drake, pres.; Walter Meacham, treas.

American Friends Service Committee, The. Head office, 20 S. 12th St., Philadelphia, Pa. Represents all the different groups of the Society of Friends (Quakers) in America. It has been engaged for four years in relief of war victims in Europe; during 1917, 1918 and 1919, it maintained a large relief and reconstruction unit in France, and until the Soviet revolution, a relief unit in Russia. It is now rendering an extensive service of relief and reconstruction in France, Austria, Germany, Serbia, Poland and Russia. While in some places its representatives are doing anti-typhus work, rendering medical relief or doing agricultural reconstruction, its most important work is feeding the undernourished children of Germany and Austria, and distributing supplies to children's institutions in Russia.

Wilbur K. Thomas, exec. secy.

American Home Economics Association (org. 1908, incorp. 1909), 1211 Cathedral St., Baltimore, Md. To improve conditions of living in the home, the institutional household, and the community. Publishes "Journal of Home Economics."

Miss Lenna Cooper, secy., Battle Creek, Mich.

American Huguenot Committee. See FEDERAL COUNCIL CHURCHES OF CHRIST IN AMERICA.

American Institute of Criminal Law and Criminology (org. 1909). To further the scientific study of crime, criminal law and procedure, to formulate and promote measures for solving related problems and co-ordinate efforts for the administration of certain and speedy justice.

Edwin M. Abbott, secy., 1028 Land Title Bldg., Philadelphia.

American Jewish Relief Committee (War Relief), 15 East 40th St., N.Y.C. (tel. Vanderbilt 2635). To afford relief to Jewish sufferers in the war zones.

Officers: Louis Marshall, pres., 120 Broadway; Arthur Lehman, treas., 20 Exchange Pl.; Paul Baerwald, asst. treas.; Cyrus L. Sulzburger, secy.; Henry H. Rosenfelt, director.

American Lutheran Publicity Bureau (est. 1915), Hartford Bldg., 22–26 East 17th St., N.Y.C. (tel. Stuyvesant 3015). To acquaint the American people with the teachings, principles, practices and history of the Lutheran Church. Information Bureau for the Lutheran Churches and Institutions. Official organ, "The American Lutheran," published monthly.

Officers: T. H. Lamprecht, pres., 230 Fifth Ave., N.Y.C.; Arthur C. Rauf, treas., 1910 Wallace Ave., N.Y.C.; Rev. F. H. Lindeman, secy., 881 East 167th St., N.Y.C.; J. F. E. Nickelsburg, business manager.

American Medical Association (1847), 535 North Dearborn St., Chicago, Ill. To promote the science and art of medicine and to unite the medical profession of the U. S. for fostering the growth and diffusion of medical knowledge. Constituent associations in states. Component societies in counties. Dr. George H. Simmons, editor and gen. mgr.; Dr. Alex. R. Craig, secy.

American Medico-Psychological Association (1844). Discussion of medical topics, chiefly relating to the care of the insane. Holds annual meetings usually in the spring of the year.

Officers: Owen Copp, M.D., pres., Philadelphia, Pa.; Sanger Brown, M.D., vice-pres., Kenilworth, Ill.; H. W. Mitchell, M.D., secy. and treas., Warren, Pa.

American Memorial Hospital, Inc. (founded by American Fund for French Wounded), 61 Broadway, N.YC. Building endowed hospital for women and children in Rheims.

Officers: Edith Bangs, chrm.; Charles M. Chapin, treas.; Daniel T. Peirce, secy.

American Missionary Association, The (org. 1846, incorp. 1862), 287 Fourth Ave. (tel. Gramercy 3622). The work of the Association reaches throughout the United States, continental and insular. Missions are established in the lowlands and in the highlands of the South, among the Indians, Mexicans and Spaniards in the West, the Chinese, Japanese and Hindus in the Pacific States, and in Porto Rico and Hawaii. The scope of the work includes the farm, the shop, the home, the school, and the church.

BUREAU OF WOMEN'S WORK, Mrs. F. W. Wilcox, secy.

Form of bequest: "I give and bequeath the sum of ...... dollars to The American Missionary Association, incorporated by Act of Legislature of the State of New York."

Officers: Irving C. Gaylord, treas.; George L. Cady, D.D., cor. secy.; Rev. Samuel Lane Loomis, assoc. secy.; A. F. Beard, editor, American Missionary Association Department in "The American Missionary."

American Museum of Natural History, The (incorp. 1869), Central Park West, 77th St. and Columbus Ave. (tel. Schuyler 7700). Founded in 1869 for the purpose of establishing and maintaining a Museum and Library of Natural History; of encouraging and developing the study of Natural Science; of advancing the general knowledge of kindred subjects, and to that end of furnishing popular instruction. The Museum is under the control of a self-perpetuating Board of Trustees, which has the entire direction of all its activities as well as the guardianship of all the collections and exhibits. The Trustees give their services without remuneration. The building is erected and largely maintained by the City through the Department of Parks. The City also makes an annual appropriation to the corporation which is devoted to the heating, lighting, repair and supervision of the building and the care of the collections. The funds which enable the Trustees to purchase specimens, to carry on explorations and various forms of scientific work, to prepare and publish scientific papers and to enlarge the library are raised by contributions from the Trustees and other friends. The annual income is derived from four sources: (1) the Endowment Fund, (2) City Maintenance Appropriation, (3) Membership Fund, (4) voluntary subscriptions.

The exhibits of the Museum include the life of the land and sea from all regions of the earth; birds, fishes, mammals, insects, reptiles, woods of North America, native races of men and their art, minerals, fossils. The Museum maintains a free public scientific refer ence library of more than 100,000 volumes. Among the exhibits of note are the Habitat Groups of North American Birds; the Morgan Collection of Gems and Precious Stones, the gift of the late J. Pierpont Morgan; the Jesup Collection of North American Woods; the finest collection in the world illustrating the Evolution of the Horse; extensive series of dinosaur remains; Habitat Groups of North American Mammals; Habitat Groups of Amphibians; extensive collections from the Indians of North America, and unique groups and models showing marine life.

The Museum supplies Nature Study Collections to the public schools of the City. Courses of lectures are delivered to the pupils of the public schools; free lectures to the public are given on Tuesday and Saturday evenings, October to April, inclusive, under the auspices of the Board of Education of New York City. Several courses of lectures are given to Members of the Museum during the year. The exhibition halls are open free to the public every day in the year. Hours: Week-days, including legal holidays, from 9 a. m. to 5 p. m.; Sundays, from 1 to 5 p. m.; Tuesday and Saturday evenings from 7 to 10.

The contribution of $50,000 constitutes a Benefactor; $25,000 constitutes an Associate Founder; $10,000 constitutes an Associate Benefactor; $1,000 constitutes a Patron; $500 a Fellow; $100 a Life Member; the payment of $25 yearly confers Sustaining Membership and the payment of $10 yearly confers Annual Membership.

Officers: Henry Fairfield Osborn, pres.; Cleveland H. Dodge, 1st vice-pres.; J. P. Morgan, 2d vice-pres.; Henry P. Davison, treas.; Adrian Iselin, secy.; Dr. Frederic A. Lucas, Director.

American Museum of Safety. See SAFETY INSTITUTE OF AMERICA.

American Ouvroir Funds, 681 Fifth Ave., N.Y.C. The American Ouvroir Funds is the sole representative in America of ten well established French societies for the care of war orphans. It endeavors chiefly to aid orphans of officers of the French army and navy, also orphans of a certain number of Belgian officers. It supplies photographs and histories of children upon application; has no publicity and no advertising; has sent $1,200,000 in less than four years, expects to continue probably for five years, as it aims specially to give financial and moral assistance for the education of these children.

Mrs. Henry P. Loomis, chrm.

American Parish, The. A federation of Presbyterian agencies under the Church Extension Committee of the New York Presbytery for promoting Christian community life in a polyglot district. Maintains the

NEIGHBORHOOD HOUSE, 324 Pleasant Ave. (tel. Harlem 2267). A center of religious and social work especially among Italians, Magyars and Czecho-Slovaks. Various clubs and classes, athletic, social, musical, civic, and educational are maintained among men, women and children.

CONSTITUENT AGENCIES: Church of the Ascension, 340 East 106th St.; East Harlem Church and First Magyar Church, 233 East 116th St.; Harlem Magyar House, 454 East 116th St.; Church of the Holy Trinity, 253 East 153d St.; Summer Camp, Oak Ridge, N. J.

Rev. Howard V. Yergin, exec. secy., 200 East 116th St., whom address (tel. Harlem 634).

American Peace Society, The (est. 1828, incorp. 1848). Colorado Bldg., Washington, D. C. For the promotion of international peace through justice.

Officers: Hon. Andrew J. Montague,

pres.; George W. White, treas.; Arthur D. Call, secy. and editor of "The Advocate of Peace."

American Prison Association, The (incorp. 1871). To improve the laws in relation to public offences and offenders and the mode of procedure by which such laws are enforced; improvement of penal, correctional, and reformatory institutions throughout the country, and of the government, management, and discipline thereof; care of providing employment for discharged prisoners.

O. F. Lewis, gen. secy., 135 East 15th St., N.Y.C.

American Public Health Association, The (est. 1872), 169 Massachusetts Ave., Boston, Mass. To protect and promote public and personal health.

Officers: M. P. Ravenel, M.D., pres., Columbia, Mo.; Roger I. Lee, M.D., treas., Cambridge, Mass.; A. W. Hedrich, secy., Boston, Mass.

American Red Cross, The (National) (incorp. by Congress, January 5, 1905).

The Act of Congress which incorporated the Red Cross and which is its Charter, defined its purpose as follows: "To furnish volunteer aid to the sick and wounded of armies in time of war," and "to carry on a system of national and international relief in time of peace and apply the same in mitigating the sufferings caused by pestilence, famine, fire, floods, and other great national calamities, and to devise and carry on measures for preventing the same."

The Red Cross is the reserve emergency organization of the American people for community relief in time of disaster, and for the relief of the wounded and distressed in time of war.

National Headquarters: 17th and D Sts., N.W., Washington, D. C.

Officers: Woodrow Wilson, pres.; Robert W. de Forest, and William Howard Taft, vice-prests.; John Skelton Williams, treas.; Stockton Axson, secy.; Frederick C. Munroe, gen. manager; W. C. Lewis, comptroller.

Central Committee. (Appointed by the President of the United States.) Livingston Farrand, chrm.; Robert Lansing, Washington, D. C.; John Skelton Williams, comptroller of the currency, United States Treasury, to represent Treasury Department; Major General Merritt W. Ireland, surgeon-general U.S.A., retired, to represent the War Department; Rear Admiral William C. Braisted, surgeon-general, U.S.N., to represent the Navy Department; Alexander C. King, solicitor general, to represent the Department of Justice.

(Elected by Board of Incorporators.) Miss Mabel T. Boardman, Washington, D. C.; Cornelius N. Bliss, Jr., N.Y.C.; John Bassett Moore, N.Y.C.; Charles D. Norton, N.Y.C.; John D. Ryan, N.Y.C.; George E. Scott, Chicago, Ill.

(Elected by Delegates.) Mrs. August Belmont, N.Y.C.; Franklin K. Lane, N.Y.C.; Mrs. Frank V. Hammar, St. Louis, Mo.; Judge W. W. Morrow, San Francisco, Calif.; Eliot Wadsworth, Boston, Mass.; Henry P. Davison, N.Y.C.

Executive Committee. (Elected by the Central Committee.) Livingston Farrand, chairman ex-officio; Willoughby G. Walling, vice-chairman ex-officio; Maj. Gen. Merritte W. Ireland; Rear Admiral William C. Braisted; Franklin K. Lane; George E. Scott; Henry P. Davison; Eliot Wadsworth; Cornelius N. Bliss, Jr.

National Divisions

The National Red Cross operates through fourteen divisional headquarters as follows:

New England (Maine, New Hampshire, Vermont, Massachusetts, Rhode Island), 73 Newbury St., Boston, Mass.

Atlantic (New York, Connecticut, New Jersey), 44 East 23rd St., N.Y.C.

Pennsylvania-Delaware (Pennsylvania, Delaware), Medical Arts Building, Philadelphia, Pa.

Potomac (Maryland, District of Columbia, Virginia, West Virginia), National Headquarters, Washington, D. C.

Southern (North Carolina, South Carolina, Georgia, Florida, Tennessee), 249 Ivy St., Atlanta, Ga.

Lake (Indiana, Ohio, Kentucky), Plymouth Building, Cleveland, Ohio.

Central (Michigan, Wisconsin, Illinois, Iowa, Nebraska), Pioneer Building, Chicago, Ill.

Mountain (Wyoming, Colorado, Utah, New Mexico), 14th and Welton Sts., Denver, Colo.

Northwestern (Washington, Oregon, Idaho), 315 University St., Seattle, Wash.

Pacific (California, Nevada, Arizona), Civic Center, Hyde and McAllister Sts., San Francisco, Calif.

Southwestern (Kansas, Missouri, Arkansas, Oklahoma, Texas), 901 Equitable Bldg., St. Louis, Mo.

Gulf (Mississippi, Alabama, Louisiana), Washington Artillery Hall, New Orleans, La.

Northern (Minnesota, North Dakota, South Dakota, Montana), 423 Fifth St., South, Minneapolis, Minn.

Insular and Foreign (Hawaiian Consular Territories of United States, all foreign countries), 17th & E Streets, N.W., Washington, D. C.

The Foreign Language Service, furnishes free news service to the foreign language press of Government Department information; gives free information to foreign speaking people on immigration, emigration, naturalization, education, health, passports, etc., furnishes free information to American press, magazines and writers, on immigrant problems.

Covers the following foreign speaking groups. Czechoslovak (Czechs and Slovaks), Danish, Dutch, Finnish, German, Hungarian, Italian, Jewish, Jugoslav (Serbian, Croatians and Slovenes), Lithuanian, Norwegian, Polish, Russian, Swedish, Ukrainian.

American Red Cross in Greater New York. Activities of the Red Cross in Greater New York, under jurisdiction of the Atlantic Division, Howard J. Rogers, manager, 44 East 23rd St., are directed by the New York County Chapter, the Bronx County Chapter, Brooklyn Chapter, Queens County Chapter, Richmond County Chapter and Van Cortlandt Chapter. These activities, in general, consist of mobilizing the volunteer spirit of the men and women of New York for service in the community in accordance with the purposes set forth in its Congressional Charter.

Departments

1. Civilian Relief.
   - (a) Bureau of Case Correspondence and Home Service Standards
   - (b) Bureau of Medical Social Service
     - U. S. P. H. S. District Supervisor's Office
     - U. S. P. H. S. Hospitals
     - Contract Hospitals
   - (c) Liaison Officer with Federal Vocational Board
2. Military Relief.
   - (a) Bureau of Camp Service
     - Army and Navy Hospitals
   - (b) Motor Corps
   - (c) Canteen Service
3. Disaster Relief.
4. Health Service.
   Health Centers and other co-operative service.

(a) Bureau of First Aid
(b) Bureau of Life Saving
(c) Bureau of Social Hygiene

5. NURSING SERVICE.
   (a) Bureau of Public Health Nursing
   (b) Bureau of Nutrition
   (c) Bureau of Instruction in Home Care for the Sick
6. CHAPTER PRODUCTION.
   Production of clothing and surgical dressings on requisition for emergencies, disasters, foreign relief, local and military hospitals and also preparing equipment for the nurses' loan closet and emergency closet, and conservation of material along many lines, etc.
7. JUNIOR SERVICE.
   Is carried on entirely in schools. School Committees are formed through the local Chapter. Helps children in foreign lands, producing garments, toys, etc.
8. INFORMATION SERVICE.
   (a) General domestic and foreign affairs
   (b) Federal and State departmental procedure
   (c) Health and social resources

NEW YORK COUNTY CHAPTER, American Red Cross, 119 West 40th St. (tel. Bryant 9860).

Officers: James H. Perkins, chrm.; Mrs. William Kinnicutt Draper, vice-chrm.; Mortimer N. Buckner, treas.; Henry J. Cochran, asst. treas.; Hon. John Bassett Moore, secy.; Alfred L. Curtiss, asst. secy.

Board of Directors: John S. Ellsworth, chrm.; John G. Agar, Mrs. Austin R. Baldwin, Mrs. August Belmont, George Blumenthal, George S. Brewster, Robert W. de Forest, Homer Folks, Mrs. John M. Glenn, John M. Glenn, Mrs. John A. Hartwell, Walter Jennings, Paul U. Kellogg, Miss Margaret Knox, Mrs. Charles C. Mickle, Dr. James A. Miller, Miss Ruth Morgan, Grayson M. P. Murphy, Miss Mary Parsons, Mrs. Whitelaw Reid, Charles H. Stout, Carl Taylor, George M. Woolsey, Mrs. Leonard Wood, honorary members.

Department of Business Management: John S. Ellsworth, director.

Department of Headquarters Offices: Alfred L. Curtiss, director. Bureau of Office Management; Bureau of Domestic Information; Bureau of Foreign Information; Bureau of Membership; Bureau of Staff Welfare.

Department of Production: Mrs. Charles C. Mickle, director; Mrs. Thomas M. Noyes, asst. director. Workrooms, Civilian, Foreign and Disaster Relief Supplies.

Department of Auxiliary Service: Mrs. Charles C. Mickle, director. Enlistment and placing of volunteers for the services of the Chapter.

Department of Military Relief: John S. Ellsworth, director. Bureau of Canteen Service; Bureau of Transportation; Base Hospital Bureau; Welfare Bureau.

Department of Medical Social Service in the United States Public Health Hospitals. Mrs. William K. Draper, director. Ellis Island, U. S. Public Health Service Hospital No. 43. Polyclinic, U. S. Public Health Service Hospital, No. 38.

Department of Disaster Relief: Director of Supplies other than Food, Miss Mary Parsons.

Department of Nursing Service: Miss Isabel L. Evans, director. Recruiting for Training Schools; Nurses' House; Medical and Nursing Service for Disaster Relief.

Accounting Department: Fred M. Van Valen, director. Bureau of Supplies.

Department of Publicity. Miss Helen C. Denman, director.

Department of Teaching Service: 24 Fifth Ave. (tel. Stuyvesant 1846). Miss Frederika Farley, director. Instruction in Home Hygiene and Care of the Sick, First Aid to the Injured, Home Dietetics, Diet Kitchen.

Department of Home Service. (See statement below.)

Department of Junior Red Cross: 131 Livingston St., Brooklyn, N. Y. (tel. Main 5890). Mrs. S. Q. Cumming, director.

Department of Health Service: 119 West 40th St. (tel. Bryant 9860). George R. Bedinger, director.

Bureau of Public Health Information: A clearing house for information on public health matters.

Bureau of Public Health Education: Assisting health agencies by printing effective health literature.

Bureau of Health Speakers: A clearing house for lecturers on public health.

Red Cross Child Health Stations: In co-operation with Christodora House. 147 Avenue B. (tel. Orchard 7010). Nutritional Classes, Dental Clinic.

Morningside Nutrition and Home-making Center. 100 Lawrence St. (tel. Morningside 4604). In co-operation with Teachers' College and the Home Economics Committee of the Charity Organization Society.

Department of Health Service: In co-operation with Greenwich House, 27 Barrow St. (tel. Spring 9833): Nutritional Classes, Dental Clinic.

Home Service Section, 131 West 38th St., N.Y.C. (tel. Fitz Roy 2100) of the New York and Bronx County Chapters, is concerned with the welfare of those men disabled in the service of this country during the World War, or those discharged from such service less than six months and their families. Included in the above are those who served with the Allies of the United States and whose families are residents of this country.

Its duties in brief are to help maintain the standards of home life of the families while the returned soldiers or sailors are becoming adjusted to civilian life. It works in close conjunction with the War Risk Bureau, the Federal Board for Vocational Education, and the United States Public Health.

Officers: Mrs. John M. Glenn, chrm.; Mrs. George T. Wood, Jr., director; Miss Jessie H. Foster, office manager; Miss Augusta Mayerson, case supervisor.

BRONX COUNTY CHAPTER, 681 East Tremont Ave. (tel. Fordham 8080). The activities include all those already mentioned above operative in the Bronx, and in addition a Health Center at 677 Morris Ave. (tel. Melrose 8878) and Maternity Centers and Pre-Natal Clinics. Central Nurses' Office, 916 Brook Ave. (tel. Melrose 1423).

Officers: Miss Catherine S. Leverich, chrm.; Fred Berry, treas., care Columbia Trust Co., 148th St. & Third Ave.; Mrs. Charles D. Dickey, secy.; Mrs. Grace Keating, office secy.

BROOKLYN CHAPTER, American Red Cross. Headquarters, 165 Remsen St. (tel. Main 3961).

Chapter officers: Adrian Van Sinderen, chrm.; Mrs. Thomas R. French, vice-chrm.; Edward C. Blum, vice-chrm.; Thomas W. Hynes, treas.; G. Foster Smith, asst. treas.; Mrs. William Denny Sargent, secy.; Albert E. Vaughan, exec. secy.

Executive Committee: Edward W. Allen, Edward C. Blum, F. A. M. Burrell, Guy Du Val, James M. Edsall, Mrs. Thomas R. French, Mrs. Otto Heinighe, Thomas W. Hynes, Rev. John H. Lathrop, Mrs. Fred Warburton Leef, Miss Emma C. Low, Edwin P.

Maynard, Mrs. John M. Perry, Mrs. William Denny Sargent, Rev. John Henri Sattig, G. Foster Smith, Mrs. Henry Beale Spelman, Miss Josephine H. Sutphin, William E. Taylor, Adrian Van Sinderen, James S. Waterman, M.D., Alfred T. White, Miss Louise G. Zabriskie.

Business Administration Committee: Edward W. Allen, chrm.; Mrs. T. R. French, vice-chrm.; Thomas W. Hynes, F. A. M. Burrell, Alfred T. White, Mrs. William Denny Sargent, Mrs. John M. Perry, Miss Josephine H. Sutphin, Rev. J. H. Lathrop, Guy Du Val, Adrian Van Sinderen.

Offices, at headquarters for: Military Relief (Canteen, Disaster Relief, Motor Corps, etc.); Speakers Bureau—Health Service Department.

Department of Supplies: 130 Pierrepont St. (Auxiliaries, Surgical Dressings, Production).

Home Service Section, 85 Court St. Civilian Relief.

Educational Department, 160 Montague St., Teaching Center, Home Dietetics, Instruction in First Aid, etc.

Junior Red Cross, 131 Livingston St.

The Fo'castle, 77th St. and Shore Road.

QUEENS COUNTY CHAPTER, Headquarters, Bridge Plaza, Long Island City, N. Y. (tel. Astoria 3060). Now engaged in the post-war activities of the Red Cross, and fulfilling its obligation to the service men.

Officers: Judge James J. Conway, chrm.; Mrs. R. H. E. Elliott, 1st vice-chrm.; Mrs. M. E. Marsden, 2nd vice-chrm.; Mrs. Carl Besch, 3rd vice-chrm.; John G. Embree, treas.; Edward J. Clarry, secy.

The county is divided into the following branches: Bayside, Corona, College Point, Douglaston, Elmhurst, Forest Hills, Flushing, Jamaica, Jackson Heights, Long Island City, Queens Village, Rockaway Peninsula, Ridgewood, Woodhaven - Richmond Hill, Whitestone.

RICHMOND COUNTY CHAPTER, American Red Cross. Headquarters: Borough Hall, St. George, S. I. (tel. Tompkinsville 946). Mrs. Wm. G. Wilcox, chrm.; M. E. Stone, treas.; Mrs. Arthur Kavanagh, secy.

Work-rooms: Dutch Reformed Church Parish House, Richmond Ave., Port Richmond, and Christ Church Parish House, Franklin Ave., New Brighton.

American Relief Administration, (org. 1918), 42 Broadway, N.Y.C. (tel. Broad 7210). Supplies supplementary meal for 3,000,000 children under 16 in Poland, Austria, Czechoslovakia, Hungary, the Baltic Provinces and in Germany through the agency of the American Friends Service Committee. Provides adult relief to individuals and institutions in Austria, Czechoslovakia, Germany, Hungary and Poland through staple foodstuffs delivered on presentation of Food Drafts sold by nearly 5000 American banks. A private organization supported by voluntary contributions and grants by governments interested.

Herbert Hoover, chrm.; Alexander J. Hemphill, treas.

American Relief Committee for German Children, Inc., 14 Pine St., N.Y.C. Raises funds to provide food for German children in co-operation with American Relief Administration European Children's Fund and American Friends Service Committee.

Officers: A. Barton Hepburn, pres.; James Speyer, treas.

American Relief Committee for Hungarian Sufferers, Hotel McAlpin, N.Y.C. Raises funds to provide supplementary meals for Hungarian children in co-operation with American Relief Administration European Children's Fund.

Officers: Bertalan Barna, chrm.; Rudolph Oblatt, treas.; Dr. Frank I. Horn, exec. secy.

American Scenic and Historic Preservation Society (incorp. 1895), Tribune Bldg. (tel. Beekman 1870).

To preserve historic objects or memorable or picturesque places in the United States, to improve cities, and to hold real and personal property in fee or in trust, and to improve the same.

Officers: George F. Kunz, Ph.D., Sc. D., pres.; Edward Hagaman Hall, L.H.D., secy.

American School Citizenship League, (est. 1908), 405 Marlborough St., Boston, Mass. The American School Citizenship League aims to develop an American citizenship which will promote a responsible world democracy and a real co-operation among the nations.

Randall J. Condon (Supt. of Schools, Cincinnati) pres.; Mrs. Fannie Fern Andrews, secy.

American Seamen's Friend Society, The (incorp. 1833), 76 Wall St., N.Y.C. An undenominational, international, and national society for the aid of seamen. The Society helps shipwrecked and destitute seamen, places loan libraries on vessels sailing from New York; publishes the "Sailor's Magazine," maintains the

SAILOR'S HOME AND INSTITUTE, 507 West St., which accommodates 200. Supported by voluntary contributions.

Officers: John B. Calvert, D.D., pres.; Clarence C. Pinneo, treas.; George Sidney Webster, secy.

American Social Hygiene Association, Inc., The (1912), 105 West 40th St., N.Y.C. (tel. Bryant 2434).

Officers: Charles W. Eliot, hon. pres.; Jerome D. Greene, treas.; Donald R. Hooker, M.D., secy.; Wm. F. Snow, M.D., general director; James H. Foster, exec. secy.

American Society for the Control of Cancer (1913), 25 West 45th St., N.Y.C. (tel. Bryant 4174). Objects: To disseminate knowledge concerning the symptoms, diagnosis, treatment, and prevention of cancer, to investigate the conditions under which cancer is found, and to compile statistics in regard thereto.

The Society is organizing and directing a general campaign of education in the United States and Canada to reduce the cancer death rate by bringing about the earlier recognition and treatment of disease. Branch committees are formed and affiliation with existing local organizations is sought. Membership is both lay and medical. The Society is supported by dues and contributions.

Officers: Dr. Charles A. Powers, pres.; Dr. Edward Reynolds, chrm. of Board; Howard Bayne, treas., care of Columbia Trust Company, N.Y.C.; Frank J. Osborne, exec. secy.

American Society for Extension of University Teaching (est. 1890, incorp. 1892), 729–730 Witherspoon Bldg., Philadelphia. Objects: 1. To extend higher education to all classes of people; 2. To extend education through the whole of adult life; 3. To extend thorough methods of study to subjects of every-day interest. For sample syllabus and circulars address William K. Huff, secy.

American Society for the Prevention of Cruelty to Animals. See SOCIETY FOR, etc.

American Sunday School Union, The (incorp. 1845). (Headquarters, Philadelphia). New York office: Room

134, Bible House. Sends missionaries to establish Sunday-schools on the frontier, publishes religious literature. Supported by contributions and legacies.

George J. Becker, secy. for New York and New Jersey, to whom apply.

American Tract Society, The (org. 1825, incorp. 1841), Park Ave. and 40th St. Its work is interdenominational and international in scope, and is commended by all evangelical denominations. It has published the Gospel message in 178 languages, dialects, and characters. It has been the pioneer for work in Latin America and also among the foreign-speaking people in our country.

During the past year it has issued 1,084,200 volumes, periodicals and tracts in Spanish, making the grand total of publications in Spanish and Portuguese 19,216,663 amounting in value to $709,351.41.

Its missionary colporters are making a home-to-home visitation among the spiritually destitute, both in the cities and rural districts, leaving Christian literature, also the Bible or portions of the Scriptures.

Its publications of leaflets, volumes, and periodicals from the home office totals 804,843,750 copies with 5,736 distinct publications in the foreign field. The value of the gratuitous distribution for the past year is $14,739.42 and the grand total is $2,706,797.41, the equivalent of 5,376,220,081 tract pages. Its missionary work is wholly dependent upon donations and legacies.

Officers: William Phillips Hall, pres.; Judson Swift, D.D., gen. secy.; Louis Tag, treas.

American Union Against Militarism, Westory Bldg., Washington. Opposes military training and all forms of militarism. Favors and works for reduction of armaments and eventual disarmament.

Officers: Oswald G. Villard, chrm.; Agnes B. Leach, treas.; Charles T. Hallinan, exec. secy.

American Women's Hospitals, 637 Madison Ave. War and reconstruction relief work at home and abroad, organized by the Medical Women's National Association.

Martha Tracy, M.D., pres., Medical Women's National Association.

Esther Lovejoy, M.D., chrm., American Women's Hospitals.

Angel Guardian Home, Brooklyn. See SISTERS OF MERCY.

Anthony Home, Inc. (incorp. 1913) 119–121 East 29th St. (tel. Madison Square 1881). A home for respectable, self-supporting young women under 40 years of age. Non-sectarian. Capacity 110. Board and lodging, $7.50 double rooms, $9.00 single, a week.

Officers: Mrs. F. W. Vanderbilt, pres.; F. L. Merriam, vice-pres.; Miss Matilda C. Faulhaber, supt. secy. and treas.

Anti-Saloon League of New York, The, entire 16th floor, 906 Broadway, near 20th St., N.Y.C. (tel. Stuyvesant 8490). The object of the League is the extermination of the beverage liquor traffic, for the accomplishment of which it invites the alliance without reference to party or denomination of all who are in harmony with this object. Its preliminary work for the enactment of prohibition covered one generation. Its consummation program: "Enforce prohibition in America—redeem the world from alcohol," will take most or all of another. It will not touch the tobacco question or any other divisive issue which is not an integral part of its main proposition.

In New York State, where over two-thirds of the townships and nearly half of the cities were already dry by local action and where the Federal Amendment was ratified by the State Legislature, the specific issue of the League is to pass enforcement legislation to put New York squarely in line with the National Government on enforcement and then to furnish the expert leadership and the non-partisan, nonsectarian basis of union through which moral public sentiment can effectively support conscientious public officials until they enforce the law.

The Anti-Saloon League has projected and is carrying forward the organization of the "Allied Citizens of America, Incorporated to Uphold American Ideals and the United States Constitution," as a Nation-wide and State-wide system of flexible local organizations which, without dues, assessments or initiation fees, is a mere covenanting together of individuals to co-operate for the enforcement of all law, local, state and national.

Officers: William H. Anderson, State supt. (exec. officer); Maude M. Odell, assistant to the Superintendent; Rollin O. Everhart, editor "The American Issue," New York Edition (official publication); Miss Adella Potter, supt. Organization Department; Rev. L. P. Tucker, D.D., supt. Field Work; Orville S. Poland, Legislative Dept.; Robert G. Davey, counsel and supt. Law Enforcement Department; Rose Weston Bull, supt. Publicity Department.

Metropolitan District: Samuel L. Hamilton, supt.; other districts, Capital, Albany; Central, Syracuse; Western, Buffalo.

Rev. David James Burrell, D.D., LL.D., pres. Board of Trustees; Rev. George Caleb Moor, D.D., secy. of Board; B. H. Fancher, State treas.

Aquarium, The New York, Battery Park. Open free to the public, every day in the year, 9 A. M. to 5 P. M. in summer, 10 A. M. to 4 P. M. in winter. Attendance during the past year, 1,850,575. Exhibits about 5,000 living specimens of fishes and other aquatic animals, representing 200 different species. The Aquarium is under the management of the New York Zoological Society (q. v.). It assists teachers in the City schools in maintaining small aquaria in the classrooms and provides a guide to teachers visiting the Aquarium with their classes.

Charles H. Townsend, director.

Armenian Colonial Association (incorp. 1909), 115 East 24th St. To promote the general welfare of Armenians in America. Provides a circulating library and public reading room, lecture courses, and evening classes, advises, protects, finds employment, etc. No fees charged. Branch in Chicago.

Rev. H. G. Benneyan, director.

Armitage Community House, (formerly Armitage House Settlement) (est. 1917, incorp. 1920). 451 East 121st St., N.Y.C. (tel. Harlem 2946). Carries on the usual settlement activities. Supported by voluntary contributions.

Officers: Mary Ogden White, pres.; Mrs. Henry Villard, vice-pres.; Caroline Caesar, secy.; Henry E. Goericke, treas.; Fanny Fried, asst. treas.; Katharine Fairbairn, Dorothy M. Mueller, workers in charge.

Armory Board, City of New York, 22nd fl., Municipal Bldg. (tel. 594 Worth). C. D. Rhinehart, secy.

Armstrong Association. See HAMPTON ASSOCIATION OF NEW YORK.

Arnold Toynbee House, 311 East Broadway, cor. Grand St., N.Y.C. A neighborhood house affording the usual club activities, a roof garden, which last summer accommodated a play school for anæmic children, kindergarten, gymnasium, auditorium for lectures, concerts and dances, bowling alleys and pool tables for adult recreation. Supported by voluntary contributions.

Miss Rose Gruening, headworker.

Art Commission, City of New York. City Hall (tel. 1197 Cortlandt). No objects of art can be acquired, or buildings constructed, by the City without the Commission's approval.

Art Workers' Club for Women, The (incorp. 1901), 224 West 58th St., N.Y.C. This is an organization founded by Mrs. Ripley Hitchcock, and a group of women painters and sculptors, for the mutual benefit of women artists and models. It provides a club house where entertainments, classes and lectures are held, a restaurant with meals at minimum cost. An employment and costume bureau for members and a circulating library. Capacity, about 800. No limitations as to nationality, race or sect, from 18 years up. Supported by donations and annual dues from members.

Caroline T. Foster, supt. and exec. secy.

Artists' Aid Society (org. 1890), 215 West 57th St., N.Y.C. To assist needy members or their families, whenever possible. The Society also controls a free bed in the Presbyterian Hospital for the use of any artist considered worthy. Supported by voluntary contributions.

Charles L. Hinton, secy., Bronxville.

***Artists' Fund Society of the City of New York, The** (org. 1859, incorp. 1861), 33 West 67th St., N.Y.C. For the relief of sick and disabled members (professional artists) and their families. Has also a Benevolent Fund for artists not members of the Society.

Ascension Memorial P. E. Church, 251 West 43d St., maintains a kindergarten, etc. (See list of PROTESTANT EPISCOPAL CHURCHES.)

Ascension Protestant Episcopal Church, Fifth Ave. and 10th St. Rev. Dr. Percy Stickney Grant, Rector; Rev. James B. Thomas, D.D., Rev. Charles W. Nauman, Rev. Harold A. Lynch, Curates. The Church is open every week day from 8.30 A. M. to 5.30 P. M. (See also under PROTESTANT EPISCOPAL CHURCHES in the Church List.) The various activities include:

THE PARISH HOUSE, 12 West 11th St. Mrs. F. P. Beattie, Parish worker, Miss Norma Thompson, director of Children's work; Miss M. A. Haskins, Parish secy.

THE ALTAR AND VESTMENT COMMITTEE.

WOMAN'S AUXILIARY, Prayer and Service Union, JUNIOR AUXILIARY.

Mothers' Meeting, Young Married Woman's Club, Girls' Friendly Society, Candidates G. F. S. Girls' and Boys' Clubs.

WOMEN'S FEDERATION, includes all the Women's Societies, with a common treasury. General meeting, monthly, first Wednesday at 4 P. M.

SOCIETY FOR THE RELIEF OF THE INDUSTRIOUS POOR.

CONFERENCE OF VOLUNTEER WORKERS: subcommittees, Industrial Branch, Fresh Air, Parish Wardrobe, Placing in Homes, Sales Industrial Branch, Sales of Groceries and Clothing.

PARISH LIBRARY, Sunday-School, Bible Class.

ST. AGNES' DAY NURSERY (opened 1888, incorp. 1890), 7 Charles St. For the care of healthy children from 8 days of age, whose mothers are obliged to work away from home.

THE PUBLIC FORUM (founded 1907, incorp. 1912). To promote the discussion of public questions, etc. Meets every Sunday in the church at 8 P. M. Speakers' Class, Thursdays, 8.15 P. M.

MEN'S CLUB: Fitz John Porter, pres.; Lyman Nichols, secy. Committees: Ushers, General, Social Evenings, Employment, Boys' Work, Neighborhood Co-operation.

Asilo Scalabrini Day Nursery, 8 Downing St., N.Y.C. Cares for children from 3 to 6 years of age, of mothers who are obliged to leave home to work.

Assessors, Board of, City of New York. Eighth floor, Municipal Bldg. (tel. 29 Worth). William C. Ormond, pres.; Andrew T. Sullivan, Maurice Simmons.

Associated Charities of Flushing (incorp. 1914), 64 Main St., Flushing (tel. 1345 Flushing). Works for family rehabilitation and to be a center of intercommunication between the various social service agencies in Flushing. Supported by voluntary contributions and dues.

Officers: Edward M. Franklin, hon. pres.; Harold G. Murray, pres.; Mrs. Viola V. N. Woodruff, vice-pres.; Frank C. Whittelsey, treas.; Miss Flora MacDonald, secy.; Miss Ruth B. Howard, gen. secy.

Associated Out-Patient Clinics of the City of New York (org. 1912), 15 West 43d St. (tel. Vanderbilt 9673). The general aim of the association is the co-ordination of the work of existing dispensaries and out-patient clinics.

Officers: Rev. George F. Clover, pres.; John Winters Brannan, M.D., Howard Townsend, S. S. Goldwater, M.D.. treas.; John W. Fiske, secy.; E. H. Lewinski-Corwin, Ph.D., exec.-secy.

Associated Tuberculosis Auxiliaries (incorp. 1920), 10 East 39th St., N.Y.C. (tel. Murray Hill 7772). 1. For the care and prevention of tuberculosis through the promotion of adequate relief and economic rehabilitation. 2. The study of relief methods. 3. The establishment of an auxiliary in every tuberculosis clinic, and the standardization of the work. 4. The co-ordination of all agencies interested in the care and prevention of tuberculosis. Supported through sale of Christmas Seals.

Officers: Miss Blanche Potter, chrm., 140 East 56th St., N.Y.C.; Mrs. Hermann Biggs, secy. and treas., 39 West 56th St., N.Y.C.; Miss Gretta Jones, exec. secy.

Association for the Aid of Crippled Children (est. 1899, incorp. 1908), Room 901, 105 East 22d St., N.Y.C. (tel. Gramercy 5071). To procure education for crippled children, either through the public schools, or otherwise; to procure medical and surgical aid for them; to provide trained nurses to personally attend in the homes of those in need of aid and advice, and to advance and improve the mental and physical condition of cripples, especially crippled children.

Officers: Mrs. Edgar S. Auchincloss, Jr., pres.; Miss Sofie M. Shippen and Mrs. Charles Fiske Bound, vice-presidents; Thomas S. McLane, treas.; Miss Margaret Armstrong, secy.; Miss Genevieve Wilson, exec. secy.

Association of the Bar of the City of New York, The (incorp. 1871), 42 West 44th St. The Association's Committee on Grievances, receives, examines, and prosecutes complaints against unfaithful and delinquent lawyers (members or others).

Officers: John G. Milburn, pres.; Wilson M. Powell, treas.; Charles H. Strong, secy.; Einar Chrystie, Attorney for the Committee.

Association for Befriending Children and Young Girls. See SISTERS OF DIVINE COMPASSION.

Association of Catholic Charities. See CATHOLIC CHARITIES OF THE ARCHDIOCESE OF NEW YORK; also, LADIES OF CHARITY, etc.

Association of Catholic Day Nurseries of New York, Inc., The. Office, 667 Lexington Ave., N.Y.C. (tel. Plaza 8047). To increase, by organization and co-operation, the usefulness of Catholic day nurseries in the City of New York, and to elevate to a common standard of the highest attainable merit the character of the work done in such nurseries. To establish, promote, develop, encourage, assist and maintain day nurseries for children; to dispense information and advice in respect to the establishment, maintenance, management and administration of such day nurseries; and also to federate and standardize day nurseries for children in the City of New York.

Officers: Mrs. John A. Jackson, pres. and treas.; Miss Anna G. Peck, secy.

Association of Day Nurseries of New York City, Inc., The (org. 1895). Office, R. 42, 289 Fourth Ave. Office hours, 10 to 4 daily. Saturday, 10 to 1. To increase, by organization and co-operation, the usefulness of day nurseries in New York City, and to elevate to a common standard of the highest attainable merit, the character of the work done in these nurseries.

Officers: Mrs. Clyde Furst, pres.; Miss Flora Benjamin, secy.; Miss H. M. Sears, exec. secy.

Association for the Improved Instruction of Deaf Mutes. See INSTITUTION FOR THE IMPROVED INSTRUCTION OF DEAF MUTES.

Association for Improving the Condition of the Poor, The New York (org. 1843, incorp. 1848). Central offices: United Charities Bldg., 105 East 22d St., N.Y.C. (tel. Gramercy 7040). Is non-sectarian and supported by voluntary contributions.

Officers: Cornelius N. Bliss, Jr., pres.; R. Fulton Cutting, Percy R. Pyne, Dwight Morrow and Albert G. Milbank, vice-prests.; Acosta Nichols, secy.; George Blagden, treas.; George W. Wickersham, counsel; Bailey B. Burritt, gen. dir.

Board of Managers: Mrs. A. A. Anderson, Henry G. Barbey, Mrs. Courtlandt D. Barnes, Mrs. August Belmont, George Blagden, Cornelius N. Bliss, Jr., Mrs. C. N. Bliss, Jr., George S. Brewster, Mrs. James A. Burden, Jr., C. C. Burlingham, Thomas Cochran, R. Fulton Cutting, Dr. Haven Emerson, Ernesto G. Fabbri, Homer Folks, Michael Friedsam, Harvey D. Gibson, John Greenough, John Henry Hammond, Samuel S. Keyser, John A. Kingsbury, Franklin B. Kirkbride, Langdon P. Marvin, Albert G. Milbank, Dr. James Alexander Miller, Frederic P. Moore, Miss Ruth Morgan, Dwight W. Morrow, George Murnane, Acosta Nichols, Robert P. Perkins, George B. Post, Mrs. John H. Prentice, Percy R. Pyne, Harry P. Robbins, DeWitt J. Seligman, James Sheldon, William B. Thompson, Miss Ruth Twombly, Dr. Philip Van Ingen.

DEPARTMENT OF FAMILY WELFARE, William H. Matthews, director. This department has under its direction the work of the Association which deals directly with individual families.

DEPARTMENT OF SOCIAL WELFARE, John C. Gebhart, director. This department is charged with the responsibility of the preventive work of the Association dealing with the community as a whole, as distinguished from work with particular families. It works through the various activities of the A. I. C. P. and also in co-operation with official and other private organizations.

BUREAU OF FAMILY REHABILITATION

AND RELIEF, Mrs. Helene Ingram, supt.; Miss Halle D. Woods, Miss Alice C. Mayer, Miss J. T. Gardner, Miss Helen Givin, Mrs. Isabel Myers, supervisors.

The work of the bureau is (1) to relieve at once immediate distress and suffering; (2) to acquaint itself with facts as to the needs and extent to which charitable relief is required; (3) to maintain for the family relief and treatment to enable it to return to a condition of normal self-support.

THE CRAWFORD SHOPS, 505 East 16th St., conducted to give work to people who because of age or other handicaps are unable to work in regular industries.

JOINT APPLICATION BUREAU, 105 East 22nd St., open until midnight daily, maintained jointly with the Charity Organization Society, cares for homeless men and women and receives personal applications for assistance.

BUREAU OF EDUCATIONAL NURSING AND FRESH AIR, Miss Rita Rearwin, acting supt. This work is carried on by a staff of nurses whose duty is the overseeing of the health of the families. The bureau makes a specialty of preventive work, particularly with children. Prenatal instruction is given to all expectant mothers and overseeing of mother and child continued until the child is under the care of a milk station. The bureau has a specially trained group of nurses for tuberculosis work. Besides this staff, several nurses give their entire time to work in connection with children's clinics.

NUTRITION BUREAU, Miss Lucy H. Gillett, supt. A bureau of education and research in food and nutrition problems. It trains individual families under the care of the Association in economical purchases and suitable preparation of foods essential to their continued health and efficiency. It provides special care for undernourished children both through nutrition classes and through work in the home. It publishes pamphlets, charts and other material of a general educational character.

CAROLINE REST at Hartsdale, N. Y., Miss Christina Mackenzie, supt., a convalescent home and school for mothers convalescing after childbirth, with a capacity of about 100 and open during all the year.

NEW SEA BREEZE, Woods of Arden, Staten Island. New Sea Breeze takes the place of the former Sea Breeze Home of the A. I. C. P. at Coney Island. It has an entirely new plant that will accommodate approximately 350 people. Convalescent women, children and babies are taken to this institution for an average period of two weeks. During the Summer of 1920, 2,407 Mothers and children were cared for at Sea Breeze Home. New Sea Breeze will accommodate approximately the same number in 1921.

GREY MOUSE FARM at Saugerties, N. Y., girls between ages of 6 and 16, capacity 50.

BOYS' CAMP, Southfields, N. Y. For boys between ages of 8 and 16, capacity 180.

SUNSET LODGE, North Germantown on the Hudson, where special provision for outings is made for old people and those needing convalescent care.

VICTORIA APARTMENTS, Miss Helen Millrea, supt., located at 315 East 158th St., is a dwelling house into which families are admitted where one or both of the parents and children are suffering from tuberculosis in an early stage.

MULBERRY COMMUNITY HOUSE AND HEALTH CENTER, 256 Mott St. Miss Mary A. Frasca, director of civic and recreational activities. Miss Anne Sutherland, supervisor of public health nursing. Miss Reba Reed, supervisor of nutrition work. Dr. DeLane Kinney, supervisor of dental work. The following activities which have for their aim the improvement of the health and social condition of this community have their headquarters in this building. Pre-natal and post-natal examination and care for mothers; thorough medical examination for children from infancy to adulthood; intensive follow-up work with families to secure the removal of physical defects; intensive care for undernourished children; a preventive dental service which provides prophylactic treatment for all children in the first five grades of school and corrective treatment for dental defects among children between 6 and 9 years; civic and social clubs; library; gymnasium; play rooms and story telling for children; civic and English classes for foreign born; a community paper "The Mulberry News" and many other recreational and civic activities.

THE WET WASH LAUNDRY, Richard E. Taylor, Jr., supt., 325 East 38th St., the first quasi-public wet wash laundry in America, with equipment for doing work for 2,000 families weekly on a basis of self-supporting service. The plant is used as a demonstration of efficiency in organization, sanitary protection, machine guarding, etc.

THE PUBLIC KITCHEN COMMITTEE, Mrs. James A. Burden, Jr., chrm.; the first kitchen established February, 1915, at 29th St. and Tenth Ave., serving three meals a day on a self-supporting basis to two or three hundred people.

Association of Neighborhood Workers of New York. See UNITED NEIGHBORHOOD HOUSES.

Association of Practical Housekeeping Centers (incorp. 1906). Office 62 Washington Sq. (tel. 6832 Spring). Demonstration and Training for Home-making, 226 Henry St.; 101 Thompson St.; 525 West 47th St.; 88 Ridge St.; P. S. No. 7, Chrystie and Hester Sts.; 188 Clinton St.; 204 East 70th St. For teaching school children and working women the applied science and arts requisite for conducting orderly family life.

Mabel Hyde Kittredge, pres.; Irving K. Taylor, secy. and treas., 29 Broadway.

Association for the Prevention and Relief of Heart Disease, Inc. 325 East 57th St., N.Y.C. (tel. Plaza 1306). Pioneer in the National Movement to control the increase of Heart Disease and the resulting suffering and economic loss sustained by the individual and the community. Maintains a central office and clearing house, gathers and publishes information on methods of prevention and relief. Provides occupations for cardiacs. Promotes establishment of special cardiac clinics, institutions for convalescents and incurables. Seeks to co-ordinate all agencies dealing with the various phases of the cardiac problem.

Lewis A. Conner, M.D., pres.; Robert H. Halsey, M.D., secy.; M. L. Wougher, exec. secy.

Association to Promote Proper Housing for Girls (est. 1915). 108 East 30th St., N.Y.C. (tel. Mad. Sq. 4825). To maintain a bureau of rooming and boarding houses for girls; to investigate conditions of rooming and boarding houses and work for their standardization; to organize Girls' Community Clubs in rooming house sections and to establish model rooming houses in connection with the clubs; to secure co-operation of non-commercial houses for girls. Supported by subscriptions and donations.

Officers: Miss Cornelia E. Marshall, pres.; Miss Ethel L. McLean, 1st vice-pres.; Mrs. Frederick Nathan, 2nd vice-pres.; Mrs. James D. Pell, treas.; Miss Mary S. Van Winkle, secy.; Mrs. F. L. Berthoud, exec. secy.

Bureau of Rooming and Boarding Houses for Girls, 108 East 30th St., N.Y.C. (tel. Mad. Sq. 4825). Hours: daily 10 A. M. to 8 P. M.; Saturdays, 10 A. M. to 5 P. M.; keeps a list of investigated houses and information as to their prices and vacancies. No fee is charged to those securing a room for $6.00 or under; to others 25 cents.

House Mothers' Round Table (est. 1915). An organization of managers of the non-commercial houses for girls; meets monthly to discuss the problems of such houses.

Landladies' Conferences (est. 1915). Meets monthly for discussion of problems of rooming house management.

Girls' Community Club, 109 East 30th St. (tel. Mad. Sq. 10219). Has a room reserved for the accommodation of girls' and women's organizations desiring to have luncheon served separately. Mrs. George S. Hornblower, chrm.; Miss E. R. Tompkins, director.

Girls' Community Club, 94 Macdougal St. Mrs. Alexander V. Roe, chrm.; Mrs. E. Allison, director.

Room $5.00 to $6.50 per week. Board $5.50 per week including two meals daily and three on Sundays and holidays. Club fee $1.50. Only girls under thirty and earning not more than $35 per week are admitted to membership. A cafeteria is open daily in each Club from 11.45 A. M. to 2 P. M. for the business girls and students in the neighborhood; rest rooms and a large garden in each Club.

Association for the Relief of Respectable Aged and Indigent Females in the City of New York, An (incorp. 1815), 104th St. and Amsterdam Ave. Maintains a home for gentlewomen of the class indicated in the title. None received who have lived as servants. Applicants must be 65 years of age or more and furnish satisfactory testimonials as to character and conduct. Those admitted must pay an entrance fee of $300, and make over to the Association all their real and personal property which at their death reverts to the Association. Capacity, 120. Supported by subscriptions and interest on permanent fund. Visitors admitted daily except Sundays.

Apply to the Committee for Receiving Applications at the Home, on the third Thursday of each month at 11 A. M., except during June, July, August, and September.

Officers: Mrs. W. Emlen Roosevelt, 1st directress; Miss M. G. Janeway, 2nd directress; Miss Blanche Potter, secy.; Wm. Parkin, treas.; Miss E. W. Muller, secy., Application Committee.

Association of Tuberculosis Clinics, The, 10 East 39th St., N.Y.C. (tel. Murray Hill 7772). To organize dispensary control of pulmonary tuberculosis in New York City and to develop a uniform system of operation of such dispensaries as are organized for this purpose; to maintain patients under observation until they are satisfactorily disposed of, and to prevent their drifting from one dispensary to another; to facilitate the attendance of patients at the dispensary most convenient to their homes; to facilitate the work of visiting nurses in the homes of patients; to provide for each patient requiring it, assistance by special funds or through benevolent organizations; to provide proper hospital, sanatorium, or dispensary care; and to co-operate with, and assist as far as possible the Department of Health in the supervision of tuberculosis.

Officers: James Alex. Miller, M.D., pres.; John S. Billings, M.D., secy.; Josephine L. Toering, R.N., exec. secy.

The CLINICS connected with the Association are:

Manhattan

Bellevue Hospital Dispensary (1), 419 East 26th St. Daily, 1 to 3 P. M. Friday, 7 to 9 P. M. Children, Tuesday, 1.30 to 3 P. M. Saturday, 10 A. M. to 12 M. District bounded by 42d St. from Park Ave. to Third Ave.; to 44th St., to First Ave. to 34th St., to East River; to 14th St., to Fourth Ave. and Park Ave., to 42d St.

Lenox Hill Hospital Dispensary (2) 76th St. and Park Ave. Monday, Wednesday, Thursday, Saturday, 11 A. M. to 12 M. Children, Saturday, 9.30 to 11.00 A. M. District bounded by 91st St. from Fifth Ave. to Third Ave., to 89th St., to East River, to 79th St., to Third Ave., to 76th St., to Fifth Ave. to 91st St.

Gouverneur Hospital Dispensary (3), Gouverneur Slip. Daily, 2 to 4 P. M. Children, daily except Saturday, 2 to 4 P. M. Saturday, 10 A. M. to 12 M. District bounded by Division St., from Catherine to Grand, to Cannon St., to Rivington St., to East River, to Catherine St., to Division St.

Harlem Hospital Dispensary (5), 136th St. and Lenox Ave. Daily, 2 to 4 P. M. Thursday, 8 to 9 P. M. Children, Tuesday, 2 to 4 P. M., Saturday, 10 A. M. to 12 M. District bounded by Harlem River to Third Ave., to 119th St., to Fifth Ave., to 110th St., to Eighth Ave., to Harlem River.

Health Department—Chelsea Clinic (6), 307 West 33d St. Daily, 2 to 4 P. M. Thursday, 8 to 9 P. M. Children, Saturday, 10 A. M. to 12 M. District bounded by West 42d St. from Hudson River to Park and Fourth Aves.. to 28th St., Sixth Ave. to 22d St. to Tenth Ave., to 26th St., to Hudson River.

Health Department—Corlears Clinic (7), 331 Broome St. Daily, 2 to 4 P. M. Thursday, 7.30 to 9 P. M. Children, Saturday, 10 A. M. to 12 M. District bounded by 3d St. from Bowery to Avenue D and Columbia St., to Rivington St., to Cannon St., to Grand St., to Division St., to Bowery, to 3d St.

Health Department—Jefferson Clinic (8), 341 Pleasant Ave. Daily, 10 A. M. to 12 M. Tuesday, Thursday, Saturday, 2 to 4 P. M. Tuesday, 8 to 9 P. M. Children, Saturday, 10 A. M. to 12 M. District bounded by Harlem River, East River to 99th St., to First Ave., to 104th St., to Third Ave., to Harlem River.

Health Department—Riverside Clinic, 481 West 145th St. Daily, 2 to 4 P. M. Thursday, 8 to 9 P. M. Children, Saturday, 10 A. M. to 12 M. District bounded by Ship Canal to Harlem River, to Eighth Ave., to West 134th St., to Hudson River.

Health Department—Stuyvesant Clinic (9), 540 East 13th St. Daily, 2 to 4 P. M. Tuesday, Thurdsay, Saturday, 10 A. M. to 12 M. Thursday, 8 to 9 P. M. Children, Saturday, 10 to 12 M. District bounded by 14th St., from Fourth Ave., to East River, to Rivington St., to Columbia St., and Avenue D, to Third St., to Bowery and Fourth Ave., to 14th St.

Health Department—Washington Clinic (10), cor. Prince and Wooster Sts. Daily, 2 to 4 P. M. Thursday, 8, to 9 P. M. Children, Saturday, 10 A. M. to 12 M. District bounded by 14th St. from Hudson River to Sixth Ave., to Waverly Pl. through Washington Sq., to West Broadway, to West Houston St., to Broadway, to Battery Park, to Hudson River, Greenwich District, formerly known as St. Vincent's, is for the present being covered by this clinic.

Health Department—Yorkville Clinic (11), 439 East 57th St. Daily, 2 to 4 P. M. Wednesday, 8 to 9 P. M. Children, Saturday, 10 A. M. to 12 M. District bounded by 63d St. from Fifth Ave. To third Ave., to 64th St., to East

River, to 34th St., to First Ave., to 44th St., to Third Ave., to 42d St., to Sixth Ave., to 59th St., to Fifth Ave., to 63d St.

Mt. Sinai Hospital Dispensary (12), Madison Ave., and 100th St. Tuesday, and Thursday, 9 to 11 A. M. Children, Saturday, 9 to 11 A. M. District bounded by 119th St. from Fifth Ave. to Third Ave., to 104th St., to First Ave., to 99th St., to East River, to 89th St., to Third Ave., to 91st St., to Fifth Ave., to 119th St.

New York Dispensary (13), 34 Spring St. Monday, Wednesday, Friday, and Saturday, 11 A. M. to 1 P. M. District bounded by West Houston St., from Broadway to the Bowery, to Catherine St., to the East River, to Battery Park, to Broadway, to West Houston St.

New York Hospital Dispensary (14), 8 West 16th St. Monday and Friday, 2 to 4 P. M. Tuesday, 7 to 8.30 P. M. Children, Wednesday, 3 to 5 P. M. District bounded by West 26th St. from Hudson River to Tenth Ave., to 22d St., to Sixth Ave., to 28th St., to Fourth Ave., to the Bowery, to East and West Houston Sts., to West Broadway, through Washington Sq. to Waverly Pl., to Sixth Ave., to 14th St., to Hudson River.

Presbyterian Hospital Dispensary (15), Madison Ave., and 70th St. Daily 1 to 2.30 P. M. Tuesday and Friday, 7.30 to 8 P. M. District bounded by 76th St. from Fifth Ave. to Third Ave., to 79th St., to East River, to 64th St., to Third Ave., to 63rd St., to Fifth Ave., to 76th St.

St. Luke's Hospital Dispensary (16), Amsterdam Ave. and 113th St. Tuesday and Thursday, 1.30 to 2.30 P. M. Friday, 7.30 to 8.30 P. M. Children, Saturday, 9 to 10 A. M. District bounded by West 134th St. from Hudson River to Eighth Ave., to West 86th St., to Hudson River.

Vanderbilt Clinic (17), Amsterdam Ave. and 60th St. Monday, Wednesday, and Friday, 9.30 A. M. to 1.30 P. M. Children, Monday and Saturday, 1 to 2 P. M. District bounded by West 86th St. from Hudson River to Eighth Ave., to 59th St., to Sixth Ave., to 42d St., to Hudson River.

Bronx

Health Department—Mott Haven Clinic (1), 493 East 139th St. Daily, 10 A. M. to 12 M. Tuesday, 8 to 9 P. M. Children, Saturday, 10 A. M. to 12 M. District lying north and east of Harlem River and south of the following line: 161st St. from Harlem River to Morris Ave., to Park Ave., to 160th St. to Cortlandt Ave., to 159th St., to Melrose Ave., to 157th St., to Elton Ave., to 158th St., to German Pl., to 159th St., to Eagle Ave., to 161st St., to Prospect Ave., to Westchester Ave., to Kelly St., to 163d St., to Whitlock Ave., to Bryant Ave., to Garrison Ave., to Bronx River Rd., to West Farms Rd., to Silver St., to Williamsbridge Rd., to Westchester Creek.

Health Department—Tremont Clinic (2), Third Ave. and St. Paul's Pl. Daily, 2 to 4 P. M. Thursday, 8 to 9 P. M. Children, Saturday, 9 to 11 A. M. District lying east and north of Harlem River and north of the above dividing line.

Brooklyn

Health Department—Bay Ridge Clinic (4), 5208 Fourth Ave. Monday, Wednesday, and Friday, 2 to 4 P. M. District bounded by 24th St. from East River to Greenwood Cemetery, southwest boundary of Greenwood Cemetery, to 37th St., to Ft. Hamilton Parkway, to 58th St., to Twenty-second Ave., to 78th St., to Stillwell Ave., to Avenue T, to West 9th St., to Gravesend Basin.

Health Department—Brownsville Clinic (6), 64 Pennsylvania Ave. Daily, 2 to 4 P. M. Children, Saturday, 10 A. M.

to 12 M. District boundary: Granite St. from Borough Line to Broadway, to East New York Ave., to East 91st St., to Clarkson St., to Remsen Ave., to Ralph Ave., to Paerdegat Basin.

Health Department—Eastern District Clinic (1), 306 South 5th St. Daily, 2 to 4 P. M. Children, Saturday, 10 A. M. to 12 M. District bounded by Newtown Creek, to Borough Line, to Flushing Ave., to East River.

Health Department—Bedford Clinic (2), 420 Herkimer St. Daily, 2 to 4 P. M. Children, Saturday, 10 A. M. to 12 M. District bounded by Borough Line to Granite St., to Broadway, to East New York Ave., to Lefferts Ave., to Prospect Park, to Franklin Ave., to Brevoort Pl., to Bedford Ave., to Flushing Ave., to Borough Line.

Health Department—Prospect Clinic (3), Fleet and Willoughby Sts. Daily, 2 to 4 P. M Tuesday and Thursday, 8 to 9 A. M. Children, Saturday, 10 A. M. to 12 M. District bounded by Flushing Ave. from East River to Bedford Ave., to Brevoort Pl., to Franklin Ave., to Prospect Park, boundary of Prospect Park, to Greenwood Ave., to Greenwood Cemetery, to 24th St., to East River.

Queens

Health Department—Queens Plaza Clinic (4), 138 Hunter Ave., Long Island City. Tuesday, Thursday, and Saturday, 2 to 4 P. M. District bounded by Bowery Bay Rd. from Bowery Bay, Old Bowery Bay Rd., to Jackson St., to Celtic Ave., to Point Ave., to Van Pelt St., along Calvary Cemetery to Bradley Ave. to Newtown Creek, to East Channel, to East River.

Health Department—Corona Clinic (1), 127 45th St., Corona, L. I. Tuesday, Thursday, and Saturday, 2 to 4 P.M. District bounded on the north by Ditmars Ave. and part of North Beach; on the east by Flushing Bay, south by Walker St. and west by Junction Ave. Includes all of third and part of second ward.

Health Department—Jamaica Clinic (2), 372 Fulton St., Jamaica, L. I. Monday, Wednesday, and Friday, 2 to 4 P. M. Thursday, 8 to 9 P. M. District bounded by Rocky Hill Rd. from City Line, to Boundary Line between Third and Fourth Wards, to Union Ave., to Forest Park, to Elderts Lane, to Ruby Ave., to Spring Creek, through Grassey Bay, to Blank Bank Marsh, to Black Wall Channel, to Jamaica Bay, including Rockaway Park, Rockaway Beach, Far Rockaway, to City Line.

Health Department—Ridgewood Clinic (3), 753 Onderdonk Ave., Ridgewood, L. I. Tuesday, Thursday, and Saturday, 2 to 4 P. M. Thursday, 8 to 9 P. M. Children, Saturday, 10 A. M. to 12 M. District bounded by Bowery Bay Rd. from Bowery Bay, Old Bowery Bay Rd. to Jackson St., to Celtic Ave., to Point Ave., to Van Pelt St., along Calvary Cemetery, to Bradley Ave., to Newtown Creek, to Borough Boundary Line, to Cemetery of the Evergreens, to Highland Blvd., to Reservoir, to Cypress Hills Cemetery, to Forest Park, to Linden Rd., to Newtown Rd., to Flushing Creek, to Flushing Bay.

Richmond

Health Department—Richmond, Clinic, Bay and Baltie Sts., Stapleton, S. I. Monday, Wednesday, and Friday, 2 to 4 P. M. District, Borough of Richmond.

B

Babies' Dairy, The (est. 1908, incorp. 1911). Stations: 416 East 65th St.; 511 West 41st St.; 523 East 78th St.; 342 East 116th St. Hours 9 to 12 daily. For feeding sick infants under one year of age. They should be brought to the Dairy once a week for examination by the physician. Supported by voluntary contributions.

Babies' Hospital of the City of New York, The (incorp. 1887), Lexington Ave., cor. 55th St. For the care of poor, sick children under three years of age suffering from non-contagious diseases. Children must be presented for examination at the Hospital between 9 A. M. and 12 M. No mothers are received. Accommodation for seventy-five. The Hospital is open during the entire year. Visitors are welcome Friday from 2.30 to 5 P. M. Supported by voluntary contributions and by city funds. The Hospital employs no collectors.

THE DISPENSARY FOR CHILDREN is on the ground floor of the Hospital. Open daily, except Sunday and holidays, from 1 to 3 P. M.

TRAINING SCHOOL FOR INFANTS' NURSES; young girls of good character between twenty and thirty years of age are taught the management and training of sick and well children, how to prepare their food, bathe, and dress them, and to detect any signs of ill-health. Applications for nurses are to be made to Miss Mary Agnes Smith, supt., at the Hospital.

COUNTRY BRANCH HOSPITAL, at Rumson, N. J.; open during the summer months. Accommodation for fifty.

Officers: John Sherman Hoyt, pres., 511 Fifth Ave.; Oliver G. Jennings, vice-pres., 51 Wall St.; Francis Louis Slade, treas., Permanent Fund, 115 Broadway; Mrs. John B. Calvert, treas., 135 East 55th St.; B. Ogden Chisolm, secy., 66 Beaver St.

Board of Women Managers: Mrs. John J. Knox, hon. pres., Red Bank, N. J.; Mrs. Oliver G. Jennings, pres., 882 Fifth Ave.; Mrs. Roswell Miller, 1st vice-pres., 969 Park Ave.; Mrs. Ira Barrows, 2d vice-pres., 521 Park Ave.; Mrs. Theron G. Strong, rec. secy., 29 East 65th St.; Miss Maud H. Curtiss, cor. secy., 41 East 64th St.

Babies' Shelter, The, St. Johnland, Kings Park, L. I. See HOLY COMMUNION P. E. CHURCH, this list.

Babies' Welfare Federation (org. 1912), Health Dept. Bldg., 505 Pearl St. (tel. Worth 9400). A federation of the various agencies throughout Greater New York which are interested in child welfare work. Its central office acts as a clearing house for information and co-operative work, bringing about uniformity of method and eliminating duplication of effort.

Officers: Dr. Henry Dwight Chapin, pres., 51 West 51st St.; Mrs. Arthur M. Dodge, treas., 563 Park Ave.; Dr. Charles Herrman, secy., 76 West 86th St.; Mary Arnold, exec. secy.

Backyard Playgrounds Association, Inc., 312 East 31st St., N.Y.C. (tel. Vanderbilt 3891). Establishes backyard playground centers in crowded blocks and provides caretakers and play leaders for them; conducts a health centre, a clinic for general ailments on Wednesdays at 4 P. M., and a women's clinic on Thursdays from 11 A. M. to 1 P. M.; clubs for boys, girls and women, classes in housekeeping, cooking, folkdancing, athletics, cobbling, etc.

Other Centers are at 308 East 34th St., 319 East 56th St., 341–7 East 73rd St. and 339 East 37th St.

Officers: Mrs. Robert G. Clarkson, pres.; Charles Loring Brace, treas.

Baptist Church Extension Society of Brooklyn and Queens (incorp. 1887), 215 Montague St., Brooklyn. To plant Baptist churches and Bible-schools, to foster feeble ones, to promote gospel preaching, to aid in erecting meeting houses and mission stations, etc.

Officers: Harry E. Bailey, pres., 1428

56th St., Brooklyn; Howard O. Patterson, treas.; Alexander Tilly, secy.

Baptist Foreign Mission Society. See AMERICAN BAPTIST FOREIGN MISSION SOCIETY.

Baptist Home for the Aged (incorp. 1869, re-incorp. 1886 and 1914). 68th St., between Park and Lexington Aves., N.Y.C. For aged and infirm or destitute members of Baptist churches.

Mrs. F. M. Burr, cor. secy.

Baptist Home Mission Society. See AMERICAN BAPTIST HOME MISSION SOCIETY.

Baptist Ministers' Conference of New York and Vicinity (includes all ministers in good and regular standing of the Baptist, Free Baptist, and Disciplist Churches). Meets every Monday, except the fourth in the month, at 11 A. M. in the Parish Home of the Madison Avenue Baptist Church, 31st and Madison Ave.

Baptist Ministers' Home Society, See MINISTERS AND MISSIONARIES BENEFIT BOARD, NORTHERN BAPTIST CONVENTION.

Baptist Missionary Convention of the State of New York (incorp. 1807), 276 Fifth Ave., N.Y.C. To promote gospel preaching; establish and help to maintain Baptist churches; construct and care for Baptist church properties, etc.

Officers: Rev. W. A. Granger, pres.; Rev. E. B. Richmond, exec. secy.; Rev. C. Wallace Petty and Volney Kinne, vice-prests.; Orrin R. Judd, treas.

Baptist Mission Society, See NEW YORK CITY BAPTIST MISSION SOCIETY.

Baptist Orphanage, Brooklyn. See BROOKLYN BAPTIST ORPHANAGE.

Baptist Publication Society. See BROTHERHOOD AND SOCIAL SERVICE EDUCATION OF THE AMERICAN BAPTIST PUBLICATION SOCIETY.

Barat Settlement House. See NATIVITY, CHURCH OF THE.

Barbour House (opened 1916), 330 West 36th St., N.Y.C. A self-supporting boarding house for business women on small salaries. Accommodates 120. Room with two meals a day and three on Sunday, $6.00 to $10.75 per week.

Officers: Mrs. George Richards, chrm., Board of Directors; Miss Katharine E. Wheeler, treas.; Miss Blanche D. Haley, director of the house.

Barge Office. See UNITED STATES DEPARTMENT OF LABOR.

Baron de Hirsch Fund (org. 1891), Room 1715, 80 Maiden Lane. For the benefit of Russian, Roumanian and Galician Jewish immigrants who have been (except for educational purposes) in this country not longer than two years. To Americanize and assimilate the immigrants with the masses and teach them to become good citizens; and to prevent by all proper means their congregating in large cities. It subscribes to day and night classes for both children and adults in New York and in some places outside of New York, and only when the local authorities or organizations have failed to make ample provision, wherein shall be taught the elementary branches of English, and these shall include the Constitution of the United States and improved sanitary habits.

Officers: Eugene S. Benjamin, pres.; S. F. Rothschild, treas.; Max. J. Kohler, hon. secy.; Bernard A. Palitz, gen. agt.

The Baron de Hirsch Fund maintains also THE BARON DE HIRSCH TRADE SCHOOL, 222 East 64th St., between Second and Third Aves., New York. To prepare Jewish young men to enter one of the following trades as helpers: Carpentry, Plumbing, Machinist, Electrical Work, and House, Fresco and Sign Painting, Operating Engineering, Printing, and Metal Sheeting. Instruction free. J. Ernest G. Yalden, supt.

Co-operates with JEWISH AGRICULTURAL AND INDUSTRIAL AID SOCIETY.

It started a COLONY AT WOODBINE, N. J., which has a population of about 2,800, where immigrant families can rent or purchase farms, which are worked upon modern methods; and such members of the family who are not employed on the farms, work in the factories of the town. There are four schools supported by the Borough of Woodbine, a high school, and one evening school.

AN AGRICULTURAL SCHOOL, at Woodbine, N. J., accommodating 100 pupils, Jewish young men are taught scientifically and practically, agriculture, horticulture, and floriculture, and also such trades as pertain to farming. (Removal of the school to Peekskill, N. Y., to buildings being erected there, is under way.)

Bay Ridge Hospital. See VICTORY MEMORIAL HOSPITAL.

Beacon Light Gospel Hall. See NATIONAL BIBLE INSTITUTE.

Bedford Dispensary and Hospital, 343–345 Ralph Ave., Brooklyn. See OCEAN HILL MEMORIAL DISPENSARY AND HOSPITAL.

Bedford Park Congregational Church, Bainbridge Ave. and 201st St., Bronx, is a social center for young people, providing gymnasium, Boy Scouts, Girl Scouts organizations, etc.

Rev. Ralph L. Peterson.

Bedford Reformatory for Women. See STATE REFORMATORY FOR WOMEN.

Bedford Sanatorium. See MONTEFIORE HOME.

Beekman Hill M. E. Church, 319 East 50th St., N.Y.C. Social Center; Fresh Air Work, etc.

Belgian Bureau (org. 1913), 431 W. 47th St., N.Y.C. (tel. Longacre 372). Affords protection to newly arrived and immigrant Belgians; meets them on steamship docks; assists them at Ellis Island; finds employment for them and renders such services as are needed and possible to Belgians in or outside of New York City. Indigent Belgians desiring relief from the BELGIAN SOCIETY OF BENEVOLENCE (q. v.) should apply to this Bureau. All services are free to immigrants; no fees from employers.

During the seven years of its existence the Bureau has rendered assistance of various kinds to 50,000 Belgians. It is supported by voluntary contributions.

Officers: Rt. Rev. J. F. Stillemans, dir.; Rev. O. A. Nys and Rev. C. C. Roosens, asst. directors; Miss M. Lepesqueur, secy.; Miss M. Van de Casteele, representative at Ellis Island; Henry Lasschaert, representative at S. S. docks and R. R. Stations.

Belgian Society of Benevolence (incorp. 1871), 431 W. 47th St., N.Y.C. Relieves indigent Belgians through the BELGIAN BUREAU (q. v.). Supported by voluntary subscriptions. Total assets, $15,885.95; last year's receipts, $16,384.10; expenditures, $10,721.67.

Officers: Lionel Hagenaers, pres.; Oscar G. Schovaers, treas.; Rev. O. A. Nys, secy.

Belknap Summer Home for Day Nursery Children (incorp. 1901), Far Rockaway, L. I. To provide a summer vacation for day nursery children, primarily those of the Bryson and Sunnyside Day Nurseries. Maintained by annual subscriptions and donations.

Officers: Miss Eleanor de Graff Cuyler, pres., 903 Park Ave.; Mrs. Hugh D. Auchincloss, treas., 33 East

67th St.; Mrs. J. Horace Harding, secy., 955 Fifth Ave.

Bellevue and Allied Hospitals, Board of Trustees of (1902 Chap. XIII of Greater New York Charter, adopted 1901). Consists of seven citizens of the City, together with the Commissioner of Public Charities, ex-officio. Has charge of the following:

BELLEVUE HOSPITAL, foot of East 26th St. (see below).

BELLEVUE TRAINING SCHOOL FOR WOMEN NURSES, 440 East 26th St. See BELLEVUE HOSPITAL.

FORDHAM HOSPITAL (1907), Crotona Ave. and Southern Blvd. (q. v.).

GOUVERNEUR HOSPITAL, Gouverneur Slip, cor. Front St. (q. v.).

HARLEM HOSPITAL (1907), Lenox Ave. 136th to 137th Sts. (q. v.).

NEPONSIT BEACH HOSPITAL FOR CHILDREN (1915), Rockaway Beach, N. Y.

SCHOOL OF MIDWIFERY, 223 East 26th St. See BELLEVUE HOSPITAL.

TUBERCULOSIS CAMP, "John H. Huddleston," East River, foot of Jackson St. See GOUVERNEUR HOSPITAL.

Bellevue Hospital (1816), foot of East 26th St. (tel. Madison Sq. 8800). A general hospital for the destitute, sick and injured of the City and County of New York. No contagious diseases admitted. Patients received at any hour. Capacity 1,654 beds. Visiting days, Mondays, Wednesdays, and Fridays, 6 to 8 P. M.; Tuesdays, Thursdays, Saturdays, and Sundays, 2 to 4 P. M.

Dr. John Winters Brannon, pres.; 48 West 51st St.; John G. O'Keeffe, secy., 31 Gramercy Park; George O'Hanlon, gen. med. supt.; Mark L. Fleming and John J. Hill, asst. med. supts.

AMBULANCE SERVICE (tel. Madison Sq. 8800), covers the district from Houston to 42d Sts., Fourth Ave. to East River, and 42d St. to 59th St. and Fifth Ave. to North River.

OUT-PATIENT DEPARTMENT provides medical and surgical treatment from 9 A. M. to 5 P. M. daily, except Sundays.

TUBERCULAR WARDS, First Ave. and 26th St., admit patients suffering with tuberculosis pending their transfer to some other hospital. Men, women, and children, all classes of cases, are received. Capacity, sixty-nine, all free. Visiting days, Tuesdays, Thursdays, Saturdays, and Sundays, 1 to 4 P. M.; Mondays, Wednesdays, and Fridays, 6 to 8 P. M. Apply to the Tuberculosis Hospital Admission Bureau, 124 East 59th St.

TUBERCULOSIS DISPENSARY. See ASSOCIATION OF TUBERCULOSIS CLINICS.

TUBERCULOSIS DISPENSARY SPECIAL CLASSES (org. 1901) meet Mondays, Tuesdays, and Thursdays at 2 P. M. There are three classes of not more than twenty-five patients each. Patients restricted to those living within the district. The homes of class patients are under the supervision of the nurse attached to the class.

TRAINING SCHOOL FOR NURSES (incorp. 1874), 440 East 26th St. Provides a two-years' and nine-months' course in general professional nursing. Mrs. William Church Osborn, pres.; Mrs. Linzee Blagden, secy.; Miss Carrie J. Brink, gen. supt., to whom apply.

ALUMNAE REGISTRY FOR NURSES, 426 East 26th St. (tel. 8350 Madison Sq.). Provides suitable nurses for the sick.

EDITH'S SUMMER HOME (org. 1890), Belle Island, South Norwalk, Conn. The gift of Mr. O. H. Northcote to the Board of Managers of the Bellevue Training School for Women Nurses, in memory of his wife. For nurses, teachers, or governesses in need of a vacation. Accommodates fourteen. Miss Carrie J. Brink, application agt., Office of Training School.

SCHOOL FOR MIDWIVES, 223 East 26th St. For training and educating women as midwives. Miss A. E. Aikman, Nurse in Charge.

BENJAMIN TOWNSEND LIBRARY of 6,000 volumes, open daily from 9 A. M. to 5 P. M. Rev. E. V. Collins, Chaplain and Librarian.

SOCIAL SERVICE BUREAU (est. 1906), to look after the social needs of the patients of Bellevue and Allied Hospitals. The divisions of work include Convalescent Relief, Child Welfare, Psychopathic, Tuberculosis, etc. Miss Mary E. Wadley, exec. secy., whom address, care of Bellevue Hospital.

WOMAN'S AUXILIARY (est. 1906, incorp. 1916). To assist the Bureau of Social Service to complete by social service care the medical work done for patients in the hospital and dispensary. Supported by voluntary contributions.

Officers: Mrs. William Church Osborn, pres., 40 East 36th St.; Mrs. Elliot S. Benedict, treas., 144 East 56th St.; Miss Blanche Potter, secy., 410 Park Ave.

Bellevue Settlement House (Edith Gibb Kimball Memorial) (est. 1911), 206 East 30th St., N.Y.C. Woman's Auxiliary to the Bellevue Tuberculosis Clinic. For the temporary care of women and girls recommended by the Clinic, pending their entrance to sanatoria. A home offering good food, fresh-air sleeping, and the general comforts required by tubercular persons. Capacity, 20 beds for adults. Nursery for limited number of infants not tubercular themselves but with tubercular parents, is attached with diet-kitchen, outdoor sleeping porch, etc. $4.20 a week is charged for each patient; if unable to pay, the expense is met by the auxiliary or other agencies.

Alice E. Clements, nurse-in-charge.

Benai Berith Home for Aged, Yonkers, N. Y. See INDEPENDENT ORDER, B'NAI B'RITH, etc.

Berkshire Industrial Farm (incorp. 1886), Canaan, Columbia Co., N. Y. New York office, 287 Fourth Ave. A non-sectarian Training School for unruly, disobedient, and delinquent boys, aged eight to fifteen, who are falling into criminal ways. Moral and religious influences, assisted by useful work and good common-school teaching.

Boys are taken, after approval by the Superintendent, by deed of surrender from parents or guardians, by commitment by Magistrate, and by transfer from other institutions.

Supported by voluntary gifts and agreed payments for boys whose parents are able to pay.

Visitors welcomed at the Farm, which can be easily reached from New York via Harlem R. R. to Canaan, thence three miles by carriage procurable at the depot. The Pittsfield Express leaves Grand Central Station about 9 A. M. and 3 P. M.

Officers: Samuel T. Carter, Jr., pres., 111 Broadway, N.Y.C.; Wolcott G. Lane, vice-pres., 80 Broadway; Richard M. Hurd, treas., 287 Fourth Ave., N. Y.C.; James F. Maury, secy., Cotton Exchange Bldg.

Directors: Samuel G. Allen, 30 Church St., N.Y.C.; Edmund Coffin, 46 Cedar St.; Rev. William M. Crane, Richmond, Mass.; Rev. Franklin B. Dwight, Morristown, N. J.; William E. S. Griswold, 26 Broadway; Frank E. Hagemeyer, 17 Battery Pl.; Lorillard Spencer, 50 Madison Ave.; Wm. Van R. Erving, Albany, N. Y.

For information, terms, and conditions, address E. B. Hilliard, supt., at the Farm, or the New York office.

Berwind Free Out-door Maternity Clinic. See JOHN E. BERWIND FREE MATERNITY CLINIC.

Beth David Hospital, 1822-1828 Lexington Ave., N.Y.C. (tel. Harlem 5523). A general hospital, capacity sixty-four beds.

Officers: Israel Sachs, pres., 1956 Crotona Ave.; Samuel Levine, treas., 7 East 107th St.; Jacob Greenberg, secy., 174 East 104th St.; Sol Appel, supt., 753 Jennings St., Bronx.

Beth-El Sisterhood (incorp. 1890), 329-331 East 62d St., New York. District Boundary: North of 42d St., to and including both sides of 70th St., from Fifth Ave. to East River. Conducts a day nursery and kindergarten, open from 7 A. M. to 7 P. M.; also maintains a creche, an employment bureau, school lunches, English classes, sewing classes, religious schools, mothers' meetings, sewing society, game room, working girls' clubs, boys' clubs, gymnasium, classes in basketry, chair caning, cobbling, dancing. Supported by annual dues, voluntary contributions and the Federation for Support of Jewish Philanthropic Societies.

Officers: Mrs. L. Kohns, pres., 550 Park Ave.; Mrs. S. Schulman, vice-pres., 55 East 92d St.; Mrs. M. Young, treas., 43 West 75th St.; Mrs. J. Anspach, secy., 260 West 70th St.

Beth Israel Hospital Association (incorp. 1890), Monroe, Jefferson, and Cherry Sts., N.Y.C. Maintains a hospital for the medical and surgical care of the sick poor in the down-town East side districts, irrespective of race or sect. One hundred and forty free beds, sixteen private beds; 2,489 patients treated during the past year, each remaining in the hospital an average of fifteen days.

The dispensary is free to the sick poor, and open daily, except Sunday, from 1 to 5 P. M.; 68,541 consultations made last year, and 64,743 prescriptions dispensed. Includes, also, a Social Service Department. Supported by voluntary contributions and members' subscriptions. Last year's receipts, $183,084.60; expenditures, $216,096.38.

Officers: Joseph H. Cohen, pres.; Arnold Herrmann, treas., A-16 Produce Exchange; Melville J. Scholle, hon. secy., 5 Nassau St. Apply to Louis J. Frank, supt.

Beth Moses Hospital (incorp. 1916), 402-404 Hart St., Brooklyn, N.Y. (tel. Bushwick 7007). A non-sectarian institution to be conducted under strict Mosaic Dietary Laws.

Officers: Isaac Levin, pres.; Israel Rokeach, treas.; Jacob Carlinger, supt.

Bethany Associates, Inc., 400 East 67th St., N.Y.C. Conduct a fresh-air and convalescent home at Amityville. L.I. Capacity 500, but present equipment provides for 250. Cost of care defrayed by guests, churches or settlements sending same, or from voluntary subscriptions. Especially adapted to Protestant Christians capable of appreciating superior religious advantages and individual care. Well-equipped playground, with wading and bathing in bay which surrounds property. Pure air and good food, but simple living. Accommodations for working girls who are willing to give two hours' services daily in the work of the house.

Address applications to superintendent, A. B. Churchman, 400 East 67th St.

Bethany Congregational Church, Tenth Ave., near 35th St., Rev. James Alexander McCague, Minister (tel. Greeley 6558). Maintains a

READING-ROOM, GYMNASIA for girls, boys and men, CLUBS for girls, boys and men, DAILY KINDERGARTEN.

INDUSTRIAL SCHOOL, FRESH-AIR WORK, and BOY SCOUTS.

See also under CONGREGATIONAL CHURCHES in the Church List.

Bethany Day Nursery, The (org. 1887, incorp. 1910), 402 East 67th St. Cares for children of poor women employed during the day away from home. Fee, 10 to 25 cents per day for each child. Kindergarten. Nursery open daily from 7 A. M. to 6 P. M. Capacity, 150. Daily attendance 100.

Mrs. J. C. Kerr, cor. secy.; Miss Evelyn Clash, supt.

Bethany Deaconesses' and Hospital Society of the East German Conference of the Methodist Episcopal Church (incorp. 1894), 237 St. Nicholas Ave., cor. Bleecker St., Brooklyn (tel. Evergreen 3430). Maintains a home for deaconesses who care for the sick, the poor and the aged, and do general missionary work. Also a hospital where a few free patients are accommodated.

Rev. G. Bobilin, supt., 606 Woodward Ave., Brooklyn, N. Y.

Bethany Memorial Chapel, 67th St. and First Ave. Rev. Arthur B. Churchman, Minister. Maintains

GYMNASIA for boys and for girls; bowling alleys, free baths, reading-room, employment bureau, clubs, and classes. See also under REFORMED CHURCHES in the Church List.

Bethlehem Day Nursery. See INCARNATION P. E. CHURCH, this list.

Bethlehem Orphans' and Half-Orphans' Asylum (incorp. 1886), Ft. Wadsworth, S. I. Evangelical Lutheran. For the care and education of orphan and half-orphan children from three to fifteen years. Capacity 160. Supported by annual subscriptions and donations.

Officers: Theo. Lamprecht, pres., 230 Fifth Ave., N.Y.C.

Better Films Committee. See NATIONAL BOARD OF REVIEW, etc.

Better Times, Inc. (incorp. 1920), 70 Fifth Ave., N.Y.C. Publishers of "Better Times," an illustrated magazine which reports the most important activities of the 2,000 charitable and public welfare agencies in New York City. Ten issues per year. Subscription price, $2.00. A non-commercial enterprise.

Herbert Hoover, chrm. Board of Advisers and Sponsors; George J. Hecht, editor; Arthur P. Kellogg, Harold Riegelman, Gertrude Hill Springer, Kenneth D. Widdemer, associate editors; Gordon Grant, art editor; Lewis L. Strauss, Jr., treas.

Bible and Fruit Mission to the Public Hospitals of New York City, The. Object: To contribute to the comfort, relief, and spiritual uplift of all patients in the public hospitals. Mrs. James Talcott, pres., 7 West 57th St.; Miss S. R. Kendall, vice-pres.; Miss E. S. Hamilton, secy.; Mrs. Raymond S. Clark, asst. treas., Great Neck Station, L. I. See Advertisement.

Bible Society. See AMERICAN; also NEW YORK BIBLE SOCIETIES.

Bible Teachers Training School (1901), 541 Lexington Ave. cor. 49th St., N.Y.C. (tel. Plaza 8521). For the preparation of ministers and Christian workers for service in all lands. Interdenominational. Evangelical. Italian Department. Students (1920–1921) represented twenty-two denominations and fifteen countries. Value of real estate, over $600,000. Supported by voluntary contributions. Catalogue upon request.

Officers: Wilbert W. White, pres.; J. Campbell White, vice-pres.; Orrin R. Judd, treas.; Leslie J. Tompkins, secy.

Bide-A-Wee Home Association, Inc. (founded 1903, incorp. 1905). 410 East 38th St., N.Y.C. and Wantagh, L.I. Is a home for sick, forlorn or deserted animals. It is the only home of its kind in New York City and was the first to operate a free clinic for animals of the poor. During the past 16 years it has operated a country home for animals where thousands of dumb creatures are made comfortable until suitable homes can be found. Through its efforts thousands of animals have been rescued from misery and given happy surroundings. The only support which this humane work receives is from voluntary contributions and membership fees.

Mrs. Harry Ulysses Kibbe, pres., 43 West 58th St., N.Y.C.; Ethel B. Champion, secy., Stapleton, S. I.

Big Brother Movement, Inc. (founded 1904, in New York City), 200 Fifth Ave., N.Y.C. (tel. Gramercy 1204–1205). Since its organization the work has been taken up in over one hundred cities on lines laid down by this office.

There is a staff of paid workers, supplemented by volunteers, lawyers, physicians, merchants, executives, teachers, all busy men selected because of their good will and natural ability to do effective work.

The Little Brothers are boys referred by parents, hospitals, police, courts, by other boys, and by the boys themselves. They are sometimes sons of widows, inebriates, prisoners, of careless or ignorant parents, boys who are largely the victims of their environment.

The task is to ascertain the cause of the boys' trouble, whether it be truancy, stealing, lying, running away from home, etc.; then with the co-operation of parents, through the mediation of the Big Brothers, to build up within the boy a sense of honor and good citizenship.

Every possible agency is employed to secure results, hospitals for examination or operation, the Y. M. C. A., church and settlement gymnasiums, industrial classes and boys' clubs, Boy Scouts, trade schools, camps, and farm schools.

Supported by voluntary contributions and workers.

Officers: Hon. Franklin C. Hoyt, pres.; Luther H. Lewis and Robert L. Gerry, vice-prests.; Ernest K. Coulter, chrm. Executive Committee; Francis J. Danforth, treas.; Charles A. Taussig, secy.; Rowland C. Sheldon, gen. secy.; Miss N. M. Rigby, fin. secy.

Big Sisters, Inc., The, 164 Lexington Ave., N.Y.C. An association of women individually to take, and secure others to take, a friendly interest in children, especially girls, who have been brought before the Children's Court; and in other children whose physical, mental, and moral development has been hindered or endangered because of bad environment or other conditions.

Officers and Directors: Mrs. William K. Vanderbilt, hon. chrm.; Mrs. Willard Parker, Jr., chrm. and treas.; Mrs. Edward Livingston Smith, secy.; Mrs. George Gordon Battle, Mrs. Frederick O. Beach, Mrs. J. Nelson Borland, Mrs. Bernard Carter, Mrs. Franklin Chase Hoyt, Mrs. Charles L. Parmelee, Mrs. Hoffman Miller, Mrs. Charles H. Senff.

Big Sisters of Queensborough, Inc., The, 207 Borough Hall, Long Island City (tel. Hunters Point 5400—Ext. 43). An organization of Protestant, Catholic and Hebrew women, who work in co-operation with the Probation Officers of the Children's Court, and whose object is to help the unfortunate children and young girls of Queensborough, in every way that is necessary.

Officers and Directors: Mrs. Smith Alford, pres., 5 Locust St., Flushing, L. I. (tel. Flushing 2563); Miss Mary L. Lyles, vice-pres.; Miss Anna Hickey, secy.; Mrs. E. J. Weil, treas.; Mrs. H. E. Hendrickson; Mrs. J. J. Kindred; Mrs. Walter Sickles; Mrs. Murray Brown; Mrs. John Demarest; Miss Langfitt; Mrs. J. J. Doyle; Miss Ella Morris.

Bikur Cholem Kosher Hospital and Annex of the Hebrew Ladies of Brooklyn, 830-838 Lafayette Ave. Maintains a hospital and annex for the medical and surgical care of the poor sick of Brooklyn. Also an up-to-date maternity ward. All patients treated irrespective of race or sect, Nurses Training School, 887 Lafayette Ave.

The Dispensary, 84 Cook St., is free to the sick poor and open daily except Saturday, from 2 to 5 P. M. Sunday from 9 to 1. Includes also a Social Service Department. Supported by voluntary contributions.

Officers: Judge Jacob S. Strahl, pres.; Jacob Fink, 1st trustee; Samuel Grolnick, treas.; Solomon Feinman, supt.

Blodgett Memorial Country Home Association. Office: 213 East 115th St., N.Y.C. Maintains a home at Golden's Bridge, N.Y., for the temporary care of children and other persons in need of rest in the country. Conducted by a Board of Trustees from Grace Emmanuel and Holy Trinity Harlem churches, jointly.

Wm. Knight, McGown, pres.

Bloomingdale Clinic. See ST. MICHAEL'S P. E. CHURCH.

Bloomingdale Day Nursery (incorp. 1898), 62 West 97th St. For the care of children from four weeks to seven years of age, whose mothers are obliged to work away from home; also, temporary shelter day and night for babies whose mothers are ill in hospitals. Fee charged.

Officers: Mrs. Thomas Dimond, hon. pres., 20 West 73d St.; Mrs. William H. Browning, pres., 18 West 54th St.; Mrs. C. Valentine Schuyler, 158 West 95th St., Mrs. Andrew W. Rose, 22 East 57th St., vice-prests.; Mrs. Raymond B. Martin, 45 St. Andrews Pl., Yonkers, N.Y., rec. secy.; Mrs. Wm. B. Goodwin, 161 East 79th St., cor. secy.; Mrs. James D'Olier, treas., 20 West 73d St.

Bloomingdale Hospital. See SOCIETY OF THE NEW YORK HOSPITAL.

Blue Anchor Society, Aid for the Shipwrecked, Women's National Association (org. 1880, incorp. 1882, re-incorp. 1909). United Charities Bldg., Room 422, 105 East 22d St. Supplies the coast guard stations throughout the United States with clothing, etc., for the shipwrecked, under requisition from the Coast Guard Headquarters, Washington, D.C. Supported by subscriptions and donations.

Officers: Mrs. Frederic T. Hume, pres., 116 West 85th St., N.Y.C.; Mrs. E. Louise Young, treas., 215 Manhattan Ave.

Blythedale Home (1904), Hawthorne, N. Y. (tel. 13 Pleasantville). A convalescent home for tubercular joint cases. Open all year, with accommodations for thirty-six children, male and female, sent from Orthopedic Hospitals and Clinics in Greater New York. Elementary school, kindergarten; also vocational classes. The Home is maintained solely through voluntary contributions.

Officers: Mrs. Edgar A. Hellman, pres.; Bernard L. Tim, treas., 26 Beaver St., N.Y.C.; Mrs. E. W. Herz, secy.; E. M. Crysler, R. N., matron.

Board of.—NOTE: Agencies which have titles beginning with these words will usually be found listed according to the dominant words or significance of the titles unless they are departments of other organizations.

Board of Censorship of Moving Pictures. See NATIONAL BOARD OF REVIEW OF MOTION PICTURES.

Board of Child Welfare (est. 1915, secs. 148–155 Gen. Mun. Law), Room 2, City Hall, N.Y.C. (tel. Cortland 4127). Grants allowances to widows whose husbands were citizens of the United States and residents of the State of New York at the time of their death. Widows must be in need and proper guardians for their children. Mothers whose husbands have been confined in State Institutions for Insane and mothers whose husbands have been sentenced to five years or more in prison. About 7,000 widows received assistance during 1919.

Members of the Board: Miss Sophie Irene Loeb, pres.; Mrs. William Einstein, Mrs. S. McKee Smith, Mrs. Matthew Figueria, Rev. William A. Courtney, Hon. P. J. Menahan, Hon. Frank P. Cunnion, Mrs. Edgar Smith, Dr. William Irving Sirovich; William L. Kavanagh, exec. secy.

Board of the Church Erection Fund of the General Assembly of the Presbyterian Church in the United States of America. See PRESBYTERIAN CHURCH ERECTION FUND, etc.

Board of Direction of the General Synod of the Reformed Church in America. See REFORMED CHURCH BOARD OF DIRECTIONS.

Board of Domestic Missions of the Reformed Church in America. See REFORMED CHURCH BOARD OF DOMESTIC MISSIONS.

Board of Education. See EDUCATION, BOARD OF.

Board of Education of the Northern Baptist Convention, Dr. F. W. Padelford, exec. secy., 276 Fifth Ave.

Board of Foreign Missions of the Methodist Episcopal Church. See METHODIST EPISCOPAL FOREIGN MISSIONS BOARD.

Board of Foreign Missions of the Presbyterian Church in the United States of America. See PRESBYTERIAN BOARD OF FOREIGN MISSIONS.

Board of Foreign Missions of the Reformed Church in America. See REFORMED CHURCH FOREIGN MISSIONS BOARD.

Board of Home Missions of the Presbyterian Church in the United States of America. See PRESBYTERIAN BOARD OF HOME MISSIONS.

Board of Missions of the Protestant Episcopal Church. See PRESIDING BISHOP AND COUNCIL, ETC.

Board of Parole of the New York Reformatory of Misdemeanants. See CORRECTION, DEPARTMENT OF, City of New York.

Board of Publication and Bible-school Work of the Reformed Church in America. See REFORMED CHURCH PUBLICATION AND BIBLE-SCHOOL WORK.

Board of Trustees of Bellevue and Allied Hospitals. See BELLEVUE AND ALLIED HOSPITALS.

Borough Boundaries of the City of New York.

MANHATTAN consists of Manhattan Island, bounded by the Hudson River and Spuyten Duyvil Creek. Part of the creek is now filled in and the boundary follows the thread of the stream as it formerly existed north of Marble Hill, the Harlem River, the East River (Long Island Sound) and New York Bay, Nuttin or Governor's Island, Bedloe's Island, Bucking or Ellis Island, the Oyster Islands, and also Blackwell's Island, Randall's Island, and Ward's Island, in the East or Harlem Rivers.

BRONX consists of all that portion of

the City of New York lying northerly and easterly of Manhattan Island, between the Hudson River and the East River or Long Island Sound, including the several islands belonging to the municipal corporation heretofore known as the Mayor, Aldermen, and Commonalty of the City of New York not included in the Borough of Manhattan.

BROOKLYN consists of that portion of the City of New York formerly known as the City of Brooklyn, including the former towns and villages known as Williamsburg, Canarsie, Flatlands, Gravesend, New Utrecht, Bay Ridge, New Lots, Flatbush, etc.

QUEENS consists of the territory known as Queens county, and includes the localities formerly known as Long Island City, Astoria, Newtown, Jamaica, Rockaway, and Far Rockaway, Elmhurst, Arverne, Maspeth, Edgemere. Woodlawn, Glendale, Whitestone, Flushing, College Point, Little Neck.

RICHMOND consists of the territory known as Richmond County, also known as Staten Island.

Borough President's Offices, City of New York.

MANHATTAN: 20th floor, Room 2050, Municipal Bldg. (tel. Worth 4227).

BRONX: Third and Tremont Aves. (tel. Tremont 2680).

BROOKLYN: 2d floor, Borough Hall (tel. Main 9100).

QUEENS: 68 Hunters Point Ave., Long Island City (tel. Hunters Point 5400).

RICHMOND: New Brighton, S. I. (tel. Tompkinsville 1000).

Botanical Garden, The New York (incorp. 1891), Bronx Park, N.Y.C. (tel. Fordham 1200). Comprises nearly 400 acres with extensive greenhouses, museums, library, herbarium, laboratories, lecture hall, etc., for the collection and cultivation of plants, flowers, shrubs and trees, the advancement of botanical knowledge and science by investigation and instruction. Open to the public every day in the year without charge. Supported by City appropriation, membership dues, subscriptions, gifts, and income from funds of the Board of Managers.

Officers: W. Gilman Thompson, pres.; Francis Lynde Stetson, Edward D. Adams, vice-presidents; John L. Merrill, treas.; Henry De La Montague, asst. treas.; N. L. Britton, secy.

Bowery Branch, Y. M. C. A. See YOUNG MEN'S CHRISTIAN ASSOCIATION.

Bowery Mission and Young Men's Home (org. 1879, incorp. 1897), 227 Bowery, N.Y.C. Gospel meetings every night at 8 P. M. and on Sundays at 11 A. M.

FREE LABOR BUREAU, 10 to 12 A. M. and 1 to 3 P. M. Free to employers and employees.

WINNER'S CLUB. A home for self-supporting men.

THE BROTHERHOOD, meets every evening at 7.

CONCERTS, Tuesday evenings at 8:00.

BOARD OF EDUCATION LECTURES, Wednesday 8 P. M.

PATRIOTIC MEETING, Thursday evenings at 8.

MOVING PICTURES, Fridays 8 P. M.

Trustees: Rev. J. G. Hallimond, D.D., pres. and supt. of Mission; Dr. George H. Sandison, vice-pres.; Graham Patterson, treas.; Gardner Palmer, Mrs. Mary M. Klopsch and Anson C. Baker, secy.

Bowery Settlement for Girls. See CHINATOWN AND BOWERY SETTLEMENT.

Bowling Green Neighborhood Association, 45 West St., N.Y.C. Aims to foster co-operation among the various social agencies and furnish practical solutions for the social problems of that section of Manhattan lying west of Broadway and south of Vesey St.

Officers: Minor C. Hill, M.D., pres.; Chellis A. Austin, treas.; Edmund Leamy, exec. secy.

Boy Conservation Bureau, The (incorp. 1912), 90 West Broadway. To guide and help homeless and imperiled boys through the character-forming years of their lives chiefly between six and fifteen years, by securing their admittance into industrial and farm schools and private homes in the country. Supported by private voluntary contributions.

Officers: A. B. Leach, pres.; E. R. A. Eschenbach, treas.; C. V. Baker, asst. treas.; E. W. Watkins, exec. secy.

Boy Scouts of America, The (incorp. 1910, Federal Charter granted 1916). National Headquarters, 200 Fifth Ave., N.Y.C. (tel Gramercy 1000). This movement aims to supplement the various existing educational agencies and to help boys to help themselves. Scouting means outdoor life and therefore health, strength, happiness, and practical education. By wholesome, attractive outdoor activities and the influence of the Scout Oath and Law, the movement develops character. Boy Scouts are required to do a good turn daily. Scoutcraft includes instruction in first aid, life saving, tracking, signalling, cycling, nature study, seamanship, campcraft, woodcraft, chivalry, and all of the handicrafts. Any boy twelve years of age or over, of any class or creed, living in any part of this country, may become a scout.

Citizenship training by doing is a fundamental feature of Scouting. Since America's entry in the war the members of the Boy Scouts of America throughout the country have rendered conspicuous service to the Government by their nation-wide participation in civic services in times both of war and peace.

Officers of National Council: Woodrow Wilson, hon. pres.; William H. Taft, Daniel Carter Beard and Wm. G. McAdoo, hon. vice-prests.; Colin H. Livingstone, pres.; Mortimer L. Schiff, Milton A. McRae, Benjamin L. Dulaney, Arthur Letts, and Robert J. Thorne, vice-prests.; Daniel Carter Beard, National Scout Commissioner; George D. Pratt, treas.; James E. West, Chief Scout Executive, at the above address.

Boys' Athletic League. See PUBLIC SCHOOLS ATHLETIC LEAGUE.

Boys' Club, The (org. 1876, incorp. 1887). Main Building, Ave A & 10th St., N.Y.C. (tel. Orchard 2042). A recreation and athletic club for boys of the lower East Side, most of them of foreign parentage or birth. Active membership over 7,000, age limit 7 years and over. District—14th St. to Houston Street.

Gives boys in small self-governing groups, under high grade voluntary leadership, opportunity for athletic and educational development, with incidental training in citizenship and vocational guidance. At present 3,000 boys over 12 are organized in 80 group clubs.

The Club is open from 8.30 A. M. to Public Schools of the neighborhood lacking swimming or gymnasium facilities, caring especially for subnormal and ungraded classes. The Club proper is open from 3 P. M. to 11 P. M. It contains completely equipped gymnasiums, running-track, swimming pool, bowling alleys, game rooms, pool rooms, moving pictures, concert auditorium and theatre, library, restaurant, monthly paper and employment bureau. A visiting physician examines every boy using gymnasium or pool and records of defective cases are followed up by the physical director and corrected at the Club or a nearby hospital. Scholarships in art, music and at universities are maintained by friends of the Club.

Entirely non-sectarian, and supported by voluntary contributors. Visitors every day from 3–9 P. M. Curtis Wheeler, director.

WENDELL BRANCH OF THE BOYS' CLUB (News Boys Foundation) (org. 1920). 225 West 35th St., N.Y.C. (tel. Longacre 2348). In co-operation with the Children's Aid Society, whose building it operates. It offers the same opportunity to the boys of the Hudson River front as The Boys' Club does to the East Side. Louis DeForest Downer, supt.; G. E. Blum, asst. supt.

WILLIAM CAREY CAMP, Jamesport, L. I. (org. 1903). (tel. Jamesport 215-F-2-2-). Open from June 15th to Sept. 10th. 36 acres of land on Long Island Sound, opposite Saybrook, with eighteen completely equipped small dormitories and buildings, accommodating 500 boys. Permitted a two weeks vacation last year to 2,500 Boys' Club members. Operates on the same group principle, taking college men on their summer vacation as leaders. Curtis Wheeler, supt.

Officers: Charles H. Sabin, pres.; W. Averell Harriman, William W. Skiddy, Allan McCulloh, vice-presidents; Eliphalet N. Potter, treas.; Thomas Frothingham and Trowbridge Hall, asst. treas.; H. S. Brooks, secy.

Boys' Club Federation (International), Room 804, 110 West 40th St., N.Y.C. (tel. Bryant 4070). For the purpose of organizing clubs, supplying superintendents, conducting conferences, practical co-operation in building campaigns, and local surveys. Supplies literature bearing on work for boys and invites correspondence on any phase of work with boys.

C. J. Atkinson, exec. secy.

Boys' Welcome Hall Association, (incorp. 1893). 185 Chauncey St., Brooklyn, N. Y. Free to boys from 9 years up of any color, religion, or race. Furnishes games, library, gymnasium, showers, employment bureau and savings fund. Teaches good citizenship, good morals. Supported by voluntary contributions.

Officers: Wesley S. Twiddy, pres.; Miss May E. Day, secy.; G. C. May, treas.; W. R. Shaw, exec. secy.

Brace Farm for Boys, Valhalla, N. Y. See CHILDREN'S AID SOCIETY.

Brace Memorial Home for Boys. See CHILDREN'S AID SOCIETY.

Bradford St. Hospital. See PUBLIC WELFARE DEPARTMENT, CITY OF NEW YORK.

Brearley League Industrial School for Cripples (est. 1908), 350 East 88th St., N.Y.C. (tel. Lenox 5734). Trade classes to teach cripples self-support. Elementary classes, sewing, manual training, advanced manual training, jewelry, and embroidery classes. Supported by voluntary contributions.

Miss Dorothy Bull, pres. of the League, Litchfield, Conn.; Mrs. Carl A. Mead, treas. of Committee on Charities, 310 West 79th St.

Brez Foundation, 37–39 Maiden Lane, N.Y.C. (incorp. 1917). Purpose: To distribute in the City of New York and vicinity the income of its principal for charitable work including hospitals, orphan asylums, relief associations, homes for the aged and the helpless and other charitable institutions as donations which are decided upon and voted for by the Board of Directors. It is self-sustaining and does not solicit contributions.

Jules Racine, president and treasurer.

Brick Presbyterian Church, Fifth Ave. and 37th St. (tel. Greely 2362). Rev. William Pierson Merrill, D.D., and Rev. Theodore A. Greene, 412 Fifth Ave. Affiliated churches:

THE CHURCH OF THE COVENANT, 310 East 42nd St., and CHRIST CHURCH, 336-344 West 36th St. See also under PRESBYTERIAN CHURCHES in the Church List.

The social service of the church includes:

THE BRICK CHURCH NEIGHBORHOOD HOUSE, 11 West 37th St.

NEIGHBORHOOD LUNCH CLUB FOR WOMEN, 11 West 37th St.

NEIGHBORHOOD HOUSE, St. Cloud, N. J.

MEN'S ASSOCIATION; committees on Employment, Legal Aid, and Medical Aid, etc.

SICK CHILDREN'S AID SOCIETY, for the care of poor and sick children and does Fresh-air Work.

WOMEN'S EMPLOYMENT SOCIETIES, provides sewing for poor women and distributes clothing.

WOMEN'S ASSOCIATION.

BARBOUR HOUSE (q. v.), 330 West 36th St. A home for working girls and women.

Bridges, Department of, City of New York. See PLANT AND STRUCTURES.

Brightside Day Nursery and Kindergarten, The (org. 1894), 89 Cannon St., N.Y.C. For children of ten days to seven years of age, of working mothers. Supported by the Federation for Support of Jewish Philanthropic Institutions.

British War Relief Association, Inc. (incorp. 1914), 247 Fifth Ave., N.Y.C. For the purpose of relieving distress caused by the War, and rendering aid to the hospitals and relief stations in England, France, Belgium, and their Allies.

Major Louis L. Seaman, M.D., pres.; Mrs. Oliver Herford, vice-pres.; Henry Clews, treas.

Broad Street Hospital in the City of New York, The, 129 Broad St. (tel. Broad 17). Capacity 100 beds. Supported by voluntary contributions.

Officers: Elisha Walker, 24 Broad St., pres.; Wm. H. Childs, treas., 17 Battery Place; Dr. A. J. Barker Savage, secy. and supt.

Broadway Tabernacle, The, Broadway and 56th St., maintains Young Women's Club, men and women's organizations for social work.

See also in the Church List.

Bronx Branch, Young Women's Christian Association. See YOUNG WOMEN'S CHRISTIAN ASSOCIATION.

Bronx Day Nursery, Abby House (incorp. 1913), 339 East 142d St. (tel. Melrose 914). Care of small children during the day. Capacity, fifty.

Officers: Mrs. J. M. Hodson, pres.; Mrs. N. B. Van Etten, treas.; Mrs. J. L. Wells, secy.; Faith Habbertin, supt.

***Bronx Eye and Ear Infirmary** (incorp. 1902), 459 and 461 East 141st St. For treatment of diseases of eye, ear, nose, and throat.

***Bronx Hospital and Dispensary, The** (incorp. 1911), 1385 Fulton Ave., N.Y.C.

Bronx House (est. 1911), 1637 Washington Ave. bet. East 172nd and 173rd Streets. (tel. Tremont 4686). A Social Settlement and Music School. Maintains clubs and classes, also houses a pre-natal clinic. Provides a good musical education for those who otherwise could not afford it, through its piano, violin, cello and orchestra departments.

Miss Estelle Deutsch, headworker.

* *Current information not received.*

Bronx International Institute, Y. W. C. A. See INTERNATIONAL INSTITUTE.

Bronx Park. See BOTANICAL GARDEN, NEW YORK ZOOLOGICAL GARDEN, and PARKS, DEPARTMENT OF.

Brooklyn Association for Improving the Condition of the Poor, The (org. 1843, incorp. 1864), 104 Livingston St. (tel. Main 6571).

Relieves promptly all cases of destitution. Non-sectarian, supported by voluntary contributions.

THE EXCHANGE AND TRAINING SCHOOL FOR THE BLIND conducts a salesroom where articles made by the blind are sold. Also educational classes for the adult blind, helping them to become self-supporting.

HOUSEKEEPING CENTERS, model apartment, supper club for working girls, classes in cooking, and clubs for girls, visits made in the homes giving instructions in cooking and housekeeping that better homes can be maintained on a more economical basis.

DENTAL CLINIC, also a MAL-NUTRITION CLINIC.

FRESH-AIR WORK. Women and children are given days' and weeks' outings during the summer.

ORTHOPAEDIC CLINIC, contributes to support of clinic for children at Long Island College Hospital.

Officers: Ernest H. Pilsbury, pres.; Frank L. Sniffen, treas.; Miss Jessie M. Hixon, gen. agt.

Brooklyn Auxiliary of the Consumer's League of the City of New York (org. 1895), 3 Pierrepont Pl., Brooklyn (tel. Main 1405). To investigate the conditions of women and children employed in department stores, factories and other industries. It upholds such business houses as conform to the standards of the Labor and Mercantile Laws of New York State. Published in 1917 a handbook of Labor Laws of New York which contains addenda giving laws to date. Supported by annual dues of $1.00 to $5.00 and contributions.

Mrs. Stephen Loines, chrm., 3 Pierrepont Pl.; Miss Elma Loines, treas.; Mrs. Louis Ehrenberg, cor. secy., 1806 Caton Ave., Brooklyn.

Brooklyn Baptist Orphanage, Ocean Ave. and Avenue S, Coney Island. For the care of orphaned children from Baptist Churches and Sunday-schools on Long Island. Capacity 36.

Miss Flora L. Cluff, supt.

Brooklyn Bar Association (1891), 123 Remsen St., Brooklyn. The Committee on Grievances receives and examines complaints against unfaithful and delinquent lawyers having an office for the practice of law or residing in Kings County only. Robert H. Wilson, pres.; Henry S. Rasquin, secy.

***Brooklyn Benevolent Society** (incorp. 1845), 84 Amity St., Brooklyn. For care of Roman Catholic orphans and poor of all ages.

Brooklyn Bible Society. See AMERICAN BIBLE SOCIETY, Eastern Agency.

Brooklyn Brotherhood of Congregational Ministers. Rev. Ernest M. Halliday, pres.; Rev. Charles J. Allen, secy., 1776 Forty-fifth St., Brooklyn.

Brooklyn Bureau of Charities (org. 1878, incorp. 1887; consolidated with the Union for Christian Work of the City of Brooklyn, 1901).

Anyone knowing of a case of distress within the limits of Brooklyn is invited to communicate with this society.

Officers: (1920–1921) Alfred T. White, president emeritus, 14 Wall St., N.Y.C.; Darwin R. James, Jr., pres., 19 West 44th St.; James H. Post, 129 Front St., Frederick P. Pratt, 215

* *Current information not received.*

Ryerson St., Brooklyn, Alex. M. White, 14 Wall St., vice-presidents; Edwin P, Maynard, treas., 177 Montague St., Brooklyn; Thomas J. Riley, Ph.D., gen. secy., 69 Schermerhorn St., Brooklyn; Gordon R. Hall, M.D., medical adviser, 164 Clinton St., Brooklyn; Simeon E. Chittenden, counsellor, 2 Rector St.

CENTRAL OFFICE: 69 Schermerhorn St. (tel. Main 8200). Thos. J. Riley, Ph.D., gen. secy. Office hours, daily 8 A. M. to 6.30 P. M.; Sundays 10 A. M. to 12 M.

Objects: To promote the welfare of the poor, suffering and friendless. Specific objects and methods include: To relieve distress and suffering of all kinds; to rescue the poor from hunger and want and to restore them to self support; to teach the blind; to aid the crippled; promotion of co-operation among benevolent societies, churches and individuals; maintenance of a body of visitors to the poor; encouragement of thrift, self-dependence and industry; temporary employment and industrial instruction; collections and diffusion of knowledge on charitable work; maintenance of free library of information on these subjects; prevention of imposition; diminution of vagrancy and pauperism; provides temporary employment in industrial agencies (work rooms, laundries, woodyards); maintains day nurseries for children under 6; secures legal advice when required; employs mendicancy officer to cooperate with police department for suppressing begging; conducts Social Service Exchange; maintains committees for the prevention of tuberculosis and for the improvement of housing conditions; serves as an institutional member of the National Red Cross for Long Island; assists in maintaining ferryboat Rutherford, located at ft. of No. 2d St., Bkln., and the Medford Sanatorium, Medford, L. I., both for patients suffering from incipient tuberculosis; has committee to deal with court questions.

ADMINISTRATION AND FINANCE, 69 Schermerhorn St. (tel. Main 8200). Thomas J. Riley, Ph.D., gen. secy.; Aaron M. Lopez, asst. to the gen. secy.; Theo. W. Hanigan, fin. secy.; Edwin Madvig, auditor; Miss M. K. Willard, cashier.

SERVICE AND RELIEF DEPARTMENT, 69 Schermerhorn St. (tel. Main 8200). Miss May Harding, supt.; Mrs. M. Hammel, Homeless Department.

DISTRICT OFFICES: Hours 9 A. M. to 5 P. M., except Sundays. Saturdays, 9 A. M. to 1 P. M.

District	Office	Secretary
Bedford,	1660 Fulton St.,	H. Tibbetts, acting.
Bushwick,	723 Hart St.,	Miss M. Allen.
East New York,	141 Pennsylvania Ave.,	Miss G. Hubbard.
East Williamsburg,	255 Division Ave.,	Miss L. Gilman.
Flatbush,	876a Flatbush Ave.,	Miss D. Ihlsing.
Fort Greene,	506 Grand Ave.,	Miss M. Van Wycke.
Gowanus,	321 Ninth St.,	Mrs. E. Harding.
Greenpoint,	182 Franklin St.,	C. Boylston.
Navy Yard,	322 Jay St.,	Miss E. Germain.
Red Hook,	419 Clinton St.,	Miss M. Reid.
St. Marks,	1660 Fulton St.,	Mrs. N. Sturdevent.
Southern,	5704 Fourth Ave.,	Miss J. Dawson.
Williamsburg,	255 Division Ave.,	Miss J. Birdsall.

DAY NURSERY COMMITTEE, 69 Schermerhorn St. (tel. Main 8200). Maintains two day nurseries where day's care is provided for the children of working mothers, Central Day Nursery, 69 Schermerhorn St.; Williamsburg Day Nursery, 255 Division Ave., Mrs. J. B. Creighton, chrm.; Aaron M. Lopez, secy.

LAUNDRIES, 1660 Fulton St. (tel. Decatur 123). Maintains a commercial laundry equipped to do first-class work for the public, its object being to teach women laundry work so that they may be able to become self-supporting; maintains a laundry at 1660 Fulton St. and also provides a neighborhood laundry at 255 Division Ave. where women may do their washing. Geo. M. Galloway, supt.

WOODYARD, 1660 Fulton St. (tel. Decatur 123). The Woodyard is a self-supporting industry where opportunity is provided for men to earn a living while seeking to secure a permanent position. Geo. M. Galloway, supt.

COMMITTEE ON CRIPPLED CHILDREN, 69 Schermerhorn St. (tel. Main 8200). Provides transportation to clinics for those children in need of same; furnishes summer outings, co-operates in securing of education through the public schools and otherwise looks after the welfare of all crippled children in the boroughs of Brooklyn. James H. Post, chrm.; Miss Ethel Evans, secy.

COMMITTEE ON THE BLIND, Headquarters for the Blind, 289 Schermerhorn St. (tel. Main 8200). Instruction in basketry, raffia, rug and linen weaving, sewing, music, massage, typewriting, switch-board operation, etc. A salesroom is maintained at 306 Livingston St., where orders for special work are received. Trained teachers provide home instruction for the blind, unable to attend at headquarters. Adrian Van Sinderen, chrm.; Aaron M. Lopez, secy.; Miss H. Beatrix Griswold, director.

CONFIDENTIAL SOCIAL SERVICE EXCHANGE, 69 Schermerhorn St. (tel. Main 8200). A central bureau or clearing house which aims to co-ordinate the work of all the agencies in Brooklyn and Queens so as to best serve the family. Supported in part by other agencies that use it. Aaron M. Lopez, secy.; Dorcas Campbell, asst. secy.

REGISTRY, 69 Schermerhorn St. (tel. Main 8200). Has charge of the records of all families cared for or under the care of this Society; gives reports to other Societies and individuals entitled to same concerning work done by this Society for a family. Aaron M. Lopez, secy.; Miss A. Edwards, registrar.

COMMITTEE ON PREVENTION OF TUBERCULOSIS, 69 Schermerhorn St. (tel. Main 8200). This Committee endeavors to educate through exhibitions, pamphlets, and lectures; encourage increase of facilities for the care of tubercular patients; carry on investigations which will lead to the betterment of health conditions; maintains health centers in congested sections. Frederic B. Pratt, chrm.; Nels A. Nelson, secy.

HOUSING COMMITTEE, 69 Schermerhorn St. (tel. Main 8200). The Committee has been especially active in the abolition of dark rooms and betterment of sanitary conditions. It encourages the passage of legislation which will strengthen the Tenement House Law and co-operates with the Tenement House Department in the enforcement of existing regulations. W. F. Atkinson, chrm.; Robert Stuart, secy.

COURTS COMMITTEE, 69 Schermerhorn St. (tel. Main 8200). Questions concerning the Children's Court, Domestic Relations, Night Court, Probation, Buildings, Law and Legislation are considered by this Committee. Ralph K. Jacobs, chrm.; Louis H. Pink, secy.; Mendicancy Officer, John D. Godfrey.

Brooklyn Children's Aid Society, The (incorp. 1866), 72 Schermerhorn St. (tel. Main 6278–6279). For the protection, care, and shelter of homeless youth. The departments of work include:

A BUREAU OF COUNCIL, RELIEF, AND INVESTIGATION.

A SHELTER DEPARTMENT FOR CHILDREN, providing a temporary shelter for homeless children.

THE WORKING BOYS' HOME.

PLACING-OUT AND BOARDING-OUT DEPARTMENTS.

SEASIDE HOME FOR MOTHERS AND CHILDREN, Far Rockaway.

SEASIDE HOSPITAL FOR BABIES, Far Rockaway, extending the work of Seaside Home. Full hospital equipment of 60 beds.

HERRIMAN FARM SCHOOL, Monsey, Rockland Co., N. Y.

EDGECLIFF CONVALESCENT HOME, Englewood Cliffs, N. J. For crippled children; pre-operative and post-operative cases.

FRESH-AIR WORK in co-operation with the "Tribune" Fresh-air Fund.

FREE MILK supplied at the Department of Health milk stations.

Officers: Howard O. Wood, pres., 831 St. Mark's Ave.; Thornton Gerrish, treas., 166 Montague St.; Arthur E. Wakeman, gen. secy.

Brooklyn Children's Court. See CHILDREN'S COURT.

Brooklyn City Dispensary (incorp. 1850), 11 Tillary St. Brooklyn (tel. Main 1062). Dental clinic, Mondays, Wednesdays, and Fridays from 2 to 5 P. M.; chiropody clinics evenings.

Maternity Center, and Social Service Department.

Brooklyn City Mission and Tract Society, The (incorp. 1865), 44 Court St., Brooklyn. Represents the united effort of the Evangelical Protestant Churches of Brooklyn to extend Christian care and teaching to all uncared for by other religious organizations. See also WOMAN'S BRANCH.

Officers: Hon. Charles H. Fuller, pres,; Frank H. Parsons, treas.; Rev. U. G. Warren, D.D., supt.

Brooklyn Deaconess Home and Training School of the Methodist Episcopal Church, 238 President St., Brooklyn. For deaconesses who are parish workers, pastors' assistants, or teachers in industrial classes. Capacity twenty.

Officers: Rev. W. A. Layton, D.D., pres.; Mrs. Edward McIntyre, treas.; Mrs. Lillian H. Welday, supt.

Brooklyn Eastern District Dispensary and Hospital. See WILLIAMSBURG HOSPITAL.

Brooklyn E. D. Homeopathic Dispensary Association (incorp. 1872), 194 South 3d St. (tel. Greenpoint 1319). Hours 2–4 P. M. For medical and surgical treatment to the sick poor.

Officers: George M. Schaedel, pres., 144 Devoe St.; Roy M. Hart, treas., 32 Court St.; R. T. Johnston, M.D., 615 Eastern Parkway, secy.

Brooklyn Eye and Ear Hospital (incorp. 1868), 94 Livingston St. and 71–79 Schermerhorn St. (tel. Main 6940–6941). For diseases of the eye, ear, nose, and throat. No charge for medical or surgical treatment. Clinic 1 to 3 P. M. daily.

H. R. Baker, supt.

Brooklyn Federation of Jewish Charities (incorp. 1909), 12 Graham Ave. Organization for the collection and distribution of funds for affiliated charitable and philanthropic institutions.

Officers: Alexander H. Geismar, pres.; Elias Reiss, treas.; Max Abelman, exec. director.

YOUNG MEN AND WOMEN'S SOCIAL SERVICE AUXILIARY.

Brooklyn Female Employment Society (incorp. 1854), 93 Court St., Brooklyn, N. Y. To provide fine and coarse sewing for self-supporting women. Conducts a school to train children for needle work.

Officers: Mrs. W. A. Putnam, pres., 70 Willow St.; Mrs. F. H. Davol, treas., 75 Remsen St.; Mrs. R. M. Montgomery, Jr., secy., 41 Remsen St.

Brooklyn Free Kindergarten Society (incorp. 1896), 67 Schermerhorn St., Brooklyn, N. Y. (tel. Main 1928). Capacity seventeen kindergartens. Children from three to six years of age; no sex, nationality, race or sect limitations. Supported by voluntary subscriptions.

Officers: Rev. J. Clarence Jones, pres., 230 Classon Ave.; Frederick B. Pratt, treas., Pratt Institute; Miss Alice H. Dahm, secy., 141 Lafayette St.; Miss Gertrude E. Skinner, supervisor, 84 Remsen St.

Brooklyn Guild of Deaf-Mutes (org. 1892). Assists destitute deaf; holds lectures, debates, and entertainments; meets the first Thursday each month in the parish building of St. Mark's Church, Adelphi St., near De Kalb Ave. Sunday Services at 3 P. M. Rev. John Chamberlain, Pastor, 511 West 148th St., N.Y.C.; Archibald J. McLaren, pres., 199 Franklin St., Brooklyn; Mrs. Harry Liebsohn, secy., 8645 17th Ave., Bath Beach.

Brooklyn Hebrew Free Loan Association, The (Gemilath Chasodim), 19 Park St., Brooklyn (tel. Stagg 967). Loans to poor people from $5 to $300 without charge and without interest to be repaid in weekly payments.

Nathan Tremsky, pres., 906 Eastern Parkway.

Brooklyn Hebrew Home and Hospital for the Aged, Howard and Dumont Aves., Brooklyn. Capacity, 165. Strict dietary laws are observed; there are two kitchens. All modern conveniences.

Officers: Mrs. Charles Rosenthal, pres.; Mrs. M. Sabt, treas.; Mrs. Berger, cor. secy.

Brooklyn Hebrew Orphan Asylum Society (incorp. 1878), 373 Ralph Ave., Dean and Pacific Sts., Brooklyn (tel. Decatur 6376). For the care and education of Jewish orphans from four to sixteen years of age. Maintains a boarding-out bureau for its youngest wards. Provides industrial training. Emphasizes after-care work. Present number of wards about 800.

Officers: Louis L. Firuski, pres.; Moses B. Schmidt, vice-pres.; A. N. Bernstein, teas.; Mrs. Otto Kempner, pres. Women's Auxiliary; A. L. Jacoby, supt.

Brooklyn Home for Aged Colored People (incorp. 1891), 1095 St. Johns Pl. (tel. Bedford 701). Non-sectarian. For men and women over sixty-five years of age.

Officers: Mrs. Peter Bogert, pres., 8649 Bay 15th St.; Mrs. Charles J. Search, treas., 453 Franklin Ave.; Mrs. D. M. Staebler, rec. secy., 690 Macon St.; Mrs. Cora Dame, matron.

Brooklyn Home for Aged Men and Couples, The (incorp. 1878), 745 Classon Ave. (tel. Prospect 1464). For respectable aged Protestant men and couples. Male applicants must be at least sixty-eight years, and females sixty years of age, and residents of Brooklyn at least five years previous to admission.

Brooklyn Home for Blind, Crippled, and Defective Children (incorp. 1908), Port Jefferson, N. Y. Office: 4 Court Sq., Brooklyn (tel. Main 2645). A Roman Catholic Home for the support, care, education, medical, and surgical treatment of blind, crippled, and defective children. The territory in which its operations are to be principally conducted is in the counties of Kings, Queens, Nassau, and Suffolk of the State of New York. Accommodates 350 children, both sexes, two to fourteen years of age. Application for admission and discharge should be made at the office.

Officers: Rt. Rev. Charles E. McDonnell, D.D., Bishop of Brooklyn, pres.; Rev. Mother Theresa, treas.; John C. York, secy.; George F. Shiebler, gen. agt., whom address.

Brooklyn Home for Consumptives (incorp. 1881), 240 Kingston Ave. (tel. Bedford 6061). Capacity, 113. A number of beds subsidized by Department of Charities. All classes of cases and ages taken. Negroes admitted. Non-sectarian. Visiting days and hours: Wednesdays and Sundays, 2 to 4.

Officers: Mrs. T. W. Wardell, pres., 168 Hicks St.; Mrs. Frank Reynolds, treas., 44 Remsen St.; Mrs. Charles H. Adams, cor. secy., 420 West End Ave., N.Y.C.; Miss Caroline D. Camp, rec. secy.; Mrs. Clifford, supt.

Brooklyn Hospital, The (incorp. 1845), Raymond St. and DeKalb Ave. (tel. Nevins 2900). A general hospital for the free care of the sick; also has private rooms and wards for pay patients. Capacity, 306 beds. Chronic or contagious cases not admitted. Maintains a

DISPENSARY (org. 1868), for the treatment of medical, surgical, orthopedic, and gynecological cases. Open daily, 12.30 to 2 P. M., except Sundays and holidays.

TRAINING SCHOOL FOR NURSES (org. 1881), offers a three years' course in the profession of nursing.

Officers: Harold I. Pratt, pres., 26 Broadway, N.Y.C.; Edwin P. Maynard, treas., 151 East 18th St.; Bayard S. Litchfield, 16 Remsen St., Brooklyn, secy.; Miss Kate Madden, directress of nurses; Dr. W. G. Nealley, supt.

Brooklyn Industrial School Association and Home for Destitute Children (incorp. 1854), 217 Sterling Pl., between Flatbush and Vanderbilt Aves., Brooklyn (tel. Prospect 41). Maintains a Home for unfortunate children who attend the public schools.

Children are received in the Home free, or at a low rate of board, after investigation by a committee; some are committed by the Commissioner of Public Welfare or City magistrates. The Home provides also a Nursery accommodating fifty-eight children between three and six years of age; kindergarten instruction is given. A Hospital with fifty-eight beds, and two contagious Wards is thoroughly equipped with all modern appliances for care of the sick. All children of the Association enjoy the benefit of different Recreation Funds.

The Association is supported by subscriptions from churches, receipts from annual donation reception, interest on investments, and sundry donations, board of children, and City appropriation.

Officers: Miss L. G. Zabriskie, 878 Flatbush Ave., pres.; Mrs. Henry E. Ide, 161 Henry St., 1st vice-pres.; Miss Clara L. Kimball, 2d vice-pres.; Miss Florence English, treas., 141 Lincoln Pl.; Miss Rosamond Roberts, asst. treas., 20 Cambridge Pl.; Miss Nellie T. Lazell, cor. secy., 69 Livingston St.; Mrs. Louis C. Cummings, asst. cor. secy., 52 Montgomery Pl.; Mrs. B. A. Conolly, supt., 217 Sterling Pl.

Brooklyn Junior League. See JUNIOR LEAGUE OF BROOKLYN.

Brooklyn Juvenile Probation Association (incorp. 1906), Children's Court Bldg., 102 Court St. (tel. Main 5364). To assist and extend juvenile probation work by co-operating with the Children's Court and Correctional Institutions. It co-ordinates and supervises all volunteer effort done in connection with the Court and is the clearing-house for Big Brother and Big Sister Work.

Officers: Hon. Robert J. Wilkin, pres.; David H. Lanman, treas., 177 Montague St.; Miss Gertrude Grasse, exec. secy.

Brooklyn Labor Lyceum Association (incorp. 1882), 949–957 Willoughby Ave. Maintains a kindergarten, day school, art school, and gymnasium. Conducts lectures on economics and on political questions.

John H. Hofmann, manager.

Brooklyn and Long Island Church Society of the Methodist Episcopal Church, The, 246 Lafayette Ave., Brooklyn (tel. Prospect 4174). Object: Mission and church extension work in Brooklyn and Long Island.

Brooklyn Maternity. See PROSPECT HEIGHTS HOSPITAL.

Brooklyn Methodist Episcopal Church Home, The, Park Pl., cor. New York Ave., Brooklyn (tel. Bedford 407). Cares for the aged and infirm men and women of the Methodist churches of Brooklyn and Long Island who are over sixty-five years of age and have no means of support for them. Admission fee $300.

Mrs. Chas. A. Lent, treas., 518 Putnam Ave.; Mrs. H. C. M. Ingraham, rec. secy., 444 Clinton Ave.

Brooklyn Music School Settlement (incorp. 1912), 126 St. Felix St., Brooklyn, N. Y. (tel. Prospect 5833). Gives musical instruction of high standard in all branches at a price to those who could not otherwise obtain it.

Officers: Mrs. Charles J. McDermott, acting pres.; G. Foster Smith, treas.; Mrs. Walter Hammitt, secy.; Kendall K. Mussey, director.

Brooklyn Neighborhoods Association, 176 Nassau St. An organization of Brooklyn settlements and individuals interested in social work and the improvement of social conditions in Brooklyn.

Officers: Seymour Barnard, pres.; Miss Florence L. Drinker, treas., 122 Pierrepont St.; Herman Brickman, secy., 564 Hopkinson Ave.

Brooklyn Nursery and Infants' Hospital (incorp. 1871), 396–410 Herkimer St., Brooklyn. To aid and nurture needy and friendless infants None received over four years of age. Capacity of nursery, 100; of hospital, 100. Mothers received with young infants.

Brooklyn Presbyterian Home for the Aged (incorp. 1916). Not yet established. A. G. Van Cleve, secy., 280 Washington Ave.

Brooklyn Society of the New Church, 104–8 Clark St., Brooklyn. Maintains a Neighborhood Club, library, etc.

Robert Alfred Shaw, pres.

Brooklyn Society for the Prevention of Cruelty to Children, The (est. and incorp. 1880), 105 Schermerhorn St., Brooklyn (tel. 5490 Main). Office hours, 8.30 A. M.–10 P. M. daily; shelter open continuously; capacity eighty-five; annual admissions to shelter, 4,000. Jurisdiction: Borough of Brooklyn and County of Nassau. Protects and aids children under sixteen years of age, both sexes, regardless of race, color, or creed.

Main lines of work: Investigates complaints of abuse, neglect, and improper exposure of children. Rescues children from unfit surroundings and aids them in securing a fresh start in life. Provides temporary care for homeless, mistreated, and delinquent children in Society's shelter. Improves home conditions and compels parents to treat their children properly. Compels parents to allow children to receive needed medical or surgical attention. Studies needs of individual children and aids them in various practical ways, both directly and through co-operation of charitable, medical, reformatory, and other agencies. Investigates applications for release of children from institutions, to which they have been committed for no proper guardianship. Prosecutes adult offenders against children, and enforces laws relating to children in theatres, saloons, and other places where their welfare might be endangered. Has charge of detention quarters in children's court of Brooklyn. Collects payments for the city from fathers for the support of their children in institutions. Studies child welfare needs. Acts as a bureau of information and advice.

Supported both by voluntary gifts and by public funds. Annual expenses, $120,000. Deals with 8,000 families a year, involving about 20,000 children. Officers: James A. Smith, pres,; John J. William, treas.; Arthur W. Towne, supt.

Brooklyn State Hospital, Clarkson and Albany Aves. (tel. Flatbush 4100). For the care and treatment of mental diseases in the Borough of Brooklyn. Capacity, 1043. Maintains also a training school for nurses.

I. G. Harris, med. supt.

Brooklyn Sunday School Union (org. 1816), Bryant Bldg., 23 Flatbush Ave To encourage and assist those engaged in Sunday-school work; to improve the methods of teaching;. and to unite evangelical denominations in this benevolent enterprise.

Officers: H. B. Shaen, pres.; Edgar B. Van Buskirk, rec. secy., 132 Herkimer St.; William M. Cartwright, treas., Rev. Walter I. Southerton, field secy.

Brooklyn Training School and Home for Young Girls, The (incorp. 1889), 1483–1489 Pacific St., Brooklyn. To aid and protect friendless girls between the ages of nine and sixteen, teaching them to be self-supporting. Protestant. Supported by money from the City for commitment cases; in few instances money received from parents, and by private contributions.

Officers: Mrs. J. J. Roberts, pres., 841 President St.; Miss C. Murton Walker, treas., 407 Washington Ave.; Mrs. Eugene W. Sutton, cor. secy., Hotel Mohawk, Washington Ave., Brooklyn; Mrs. Hanna L. Gray, supt.

Brooklyn Urban League (incorp. 1917), 105 Fleet Place, Brooklyn, N. Y. For social service among Negroes.

Mrs. Thomas L. Leeming, chrm.; William H. Baldwin, treas.; Mrs. Edwin F. Horne, secy.; Robert J. Elzy, exec. secy.

Brooklyn Young Men's Christian Association (incorp. 1869), General Office, 55 Hanson Pl. (tel. Prospect 1603). The Association provides educational classes, entertainments, reading rooms, lectures, religious meetings, gymnasia, swimming pools, summer athletics, summer camps, dormitories, and conducts employment agencies and restaurants. Membership, 16,906.

John W. Cook, gen. secy.; J. C. Armstrong, assoc. gen. secy.; H. W. Northcott, Army secy.; R. P. Walker, industrial secy.; C. G. Brooke, industrial physical director; A. R. Keemer, boys' work secy.; J. Howard Field, accountant.

Officers of the Board of Directors: Frank C. Munson, pres.; Edwin Packard, William McCarroll, Herbert L. Pratt and Edwin P. Maynard, vice-prests.; Clinton D. Burdick and Frank H. Parsons, comptrollers; Edward A. Richards, rec. secy.

Officers of the Board of Trustees: James H. Post, chrm.; John T. Underwood, vice-chrm.; Herbert K. Twitchell, secy.-treas.

The work is conducted at

CENTRAL BRANCH, 55 Hanson Pl., Charles W. Dietrich, secy.

EASTERN DISTRICT BRANCH, Marcy Ave. and South 9th St., Frank J. Slater, secy.

BEDFORD BRANCH, Men's Bldg., 1121 Bedford Ave., Boys' Bldg., 420 Gates Ave., Halsey Hammond, secy.

PROSPECT PARK BRANCH, 357–365 9th St., Lawson H. Brown, secy.

HIGHLAND PARK BRANCH, 125 Logan St., W. H. Waechter, secy.

LONG ISLAND RAILROAD BRANCH, 45 Borden Ave., Long Island City, A. K. Hicks, secy.

ARMY BRANCHES, FORT HAMILTON, John H. Berry, secy.; FORT TOTTEN, L. W. Draper, secy.

FORT TILDEN, C. E. Schuyler, secy.

COLORED MEN'S BRANCH, 405 Carlton Ave., R. M. Meroney, secy.

GREENPOINT BRANCH, 99 Meserole Ave., W. D. Miller, secy.

BUSH TERMINAL BRANCH, Second Ave. and 40th St., A. E. Chamberlain, secy.

BETHELSHIP SEAMEN'S BRANCH, 56 Sullivan St., Carl Brandt, manager.

LONG ISLAND CITY INDUSTRIAL BRANCH, 426 Jackson Ave., A. W. Walch, secy.

NEW UTRECHT BRANCH, 1841 84th St., Earl H. Burritt, secy.

JAMAICA COMMUNITY BRANCH, J. O. Arroll, secy.

NAVAL BRANCH (affiliated), 167 Sands St., W. L. Tisdale, secy.

Broome Street Memorial Church. See NEW YORK CITY MISSION SOCIETY, this list.

***Brotherhood of St. Andrew, The** (org. 1883). National headquarters, Church House, Philadelphia, Pa. Object: the spread of Christ's kingdom among men and boys. Official organ, "St. Andrews Cross," published monthly.

***Brotherhood and Social Service Education of American Baptist Publication Society, Department of** (1912), 1701 Chestnut St.; Philadelphia, Pa. Purpose: To study social conditions and report findings to the churches; to prepare and publish social service literature and studies for churches, Sunday-schools and study groups; to organize and enlist men of the churches in definite lines of social work; to promote temperance and social purity; to co-operate with other social agencies.

Samuel Z. Batten, secy.

***Brownsville Day Nursery,** 453 Hopkinson Ave., Brooklyn.

Brownsville and East New York Hospital (est. 1910, incorp. 1914), Rockaway Parkway and Ave. A, Brooklyn. To maintain a hospital for the people of Brownsville and East New York.

H. J. Moss, M.D., supt.

Bryant School for Stammering. See NEW YORK SCHOOL FOR STAMMERING.

* *Current information not received.*

***Bryson Day Nursery** (incorp. 1897), 149 Avenue B, N.Y.C. For the care of babies and children from one month to seven years old, at a charge of ten cents per day for each child. Montessori classes at 9 A. M. and 1 P. M. daily. Open from 7 A. M. to 6 P. M.

Bureau of Advice and Information of the Charity Organization Society, The, 105 East 22d St., N.Y.C. (tel. Gramercy 4066). Offers general information to all inquirers, and to members of the Society and of certain affiliated organizations special reports on work done by social agencies soliciting funds in New York City.

Mrs. Gertrude Hill Springer, secy.

Bureau of Boarding Houses for Girls. See ASSOCIATION TO PROMOTE PROPER HOUSING FOR GIRLS.

Bureau of Deportation. See STATE HOSPITAL COMMISSION.

Bureau of Educational Experiments, The (incorp. 1917), 16 West 8th St., N.Y.C. The Bureau is organized to conduct experiments in education; to collect and distribute information regarding educational experiments; and to prepare and issue reports dealing with the newer ideas in education.

Bureau of Industrial Research, The (est. 1918). 289 Fourth Ave., N.Y.C. Office hours: 9 A. M. to 5 P. M. Devoted to the dissemination of facts and methods in the field of industrial relations and personnel management.

Staff: Robert W. Bruère, Heber Blankenhorn, Mary D. Blankenhorn, Arthur Gleason, Leonard Outhwaite, Ordway Tead, Savel Zimand.

Bureau of Industries and Immigration. See STATE INDUSTRIAL COMMISSION.

* *Current information not received.*

Bureau of Institutional Inspection. See PUBLIC WELFARE, DEPARTMENT, CITY OF NEW YORK.

Bureau of Jewish Social Research, The, 114 Fifth Ave., N.Y.C. (tel. Watkins 6998). An organization for investigation and research; a center for information on Jewish philanthropic activities, serving the Federation for the Support of Jewish Philanthropic Societies and Jewish communities in America at large. This Bureau is a merger of the former Bureau of Philanthropic Research, of the Bureau of Statistics of the American Jewish Committee and of the Field Bureau of the National Conference of Jewish Charities. It is supported by the Federation, the New York Foundation, the American Jewish Committee and by private contributions. With its staff of research workers it is in a position to undertake important community surveys.

Officers: Adolph Lewisohn, chrm., 61 Broadway; David M. Heyman, treas., 14 Wall St.; Cyrus L. Sulzberger, chrm. of exec. com., 354 Fourth Ave.; Dr. Lee K. Frankel, chrm. of the advisory committee, 1 Madison Ave.; Morris D. Waldman, secy., 80 Wall St.; Dr. Ludwig B. Bernstein, exec. dir.

Bureau of Municipal Research (incorp. 1907), 261 Broadway, N.Y.C. (tel. Barclay 5860). Purposes: To promote efficient and economical government; to promote the adoption of scientific methods in the transaction of public business.

Luther H. Gulick, secy. Board of Trustees.

Bureau of Philanthropic Research. See BUREAU OF JEWISH SOCIAL RESEARCH.

Bureau of Public Buildings and Offices. See PUBLIC BUILDINGS, BUREAU OF.

Bureau of Public Improvements. See PUBLIC IMPROVEMENTS BUREAU.

Bureau of Social Hygiene, Inc., 105 West 40th St., N.Y.C. (tel. Bryant 2434). Established for the study, amelioration and prevention of those social conditions, crimes and diseases which adversely affect the well-being of society, with special reference to prostitution and the evils associated therewith.

Directors: John D. Rockefeller, Jr., chrm.; Starr J. Murphy, secy. and treas.; Charles O. Heydt, Katharine Bement Davis, gen. secy.

Associates: Abraham Flexner, Raymond B. Fosdick.

Bureau of Social Investigations. See PUBLIC WELFARE, DEPARTMENT, CITY OF NEW YORK.

Bureau of Vocational Information, 2 West 43rd St., N.Y.C. (tel. Vanderbilt 1848). A clearing house of vocational information for women. Cooperates with trained and experienced women in all professions and in business in the collection of occupational information. Co-operates with colleges and schools in the distribution of this information among students and prospective workers. Publishes vocational bulletins.

Officers: Mrs. Wendell T. Bush, pres.; Mrs. Frederick H. Cone, treas.; Miss Mabel Foote Weeks, secy.; Miss Emma P. Hirth, director.

Bureau of War Risk Insurance. See WAR RISK INSURANCE.

Bureau of Workmen's Compensation. See STATE INDUSTRIAL COMMISSION.

Burke Relief Foundation, The Winifred Masterson (incorp. 1902). Office, 170 Broadway, N.Y.C. Convalescent Home, White Plains, N. Y. Admission office, 325 East 57th St. For men and women convalescent after illness, or discharged from hospitals; or other unfortunates in need of temporary assistance. Supported by income from endowment.

Bush Terminal Hospital (est. and incorp. 1916), 4012 Second Ave., Brooklyn. For treatment of industrial accidents and diseases.

Sophie E. Moyer, R.N., supervisor.

Bushwick Avenue—Central M. E. Church, Bushwick Ave. and Madison St., Brooklyn. Provides a social center, gymnasium, etc. Rev. George E. Bishop.

Bushwick and East Brooklyn Dispensary (incorp. 1878), Myrtle and Lewis Aves. Furnishes medical supplies and relief to the sick poor. Open at 2 P. M. daily, except Sundays and holidays; Saturdays at 11 A. M.

Officers: Eugene F. Barnes, pres.; David Morehouse, treas.; Sidney L. Rowland, secy.; 685 Myrtle Ave., Fred H. Wagner, supt.

Bushwick Hospital (incorp. 1890), 41 Howard Ave., Brooklyn (tel. Bushwick 5400). No contagious cases taken. Capacity, ninety beds. Visiting days to the wards, Tuesdays, Thursdays, and Sundays, 2–4 P. M. Maintains an Ambulance Service and the

JEWETT TRAINING SCHOOL FOR NURSES, REGISTERED. Supported by voluntary contributions and board from patients.

Margaret L. Fisher, R.N., supt.

C

Caledonian Hospital of the City of New York, The (est. 1916), 53 Woodruff Ave., Brooklyn. A general hospital. Capacity, twenty beds.

D. D. Sinclair, pres., 11 East 24th St., N.Y.C.; Howard Wood, treas., 316 Clifton Pl., Brooklyn; Nora E. Young, supt.

Calvary P. E. Church, Fourth Ave. and 21st St., Rev. Theodore Sedgwick, D.D., Rev. Raymond S. Brown and Rev. Wolcott Cutler. Maintains

CALVARY PARISH HOUSE, 102–106 East 22d St. Reading rooms; clubs, mothers' meetings; Girls' Friendly Society; lunch room for working women open from 12 M. to 2 P. M.

RELIEF DEPARTMENT, 104 East 22d St.

FREE READING ROOM FOR MEN, 344 East 23d St. Open 4.30 to 9.30 P. M. Sundays, 11 A. M. to 10 P. M.

INDIA TEA DIVAN, 344 East 23d St.

OLIVE TREE INN, Lodging House for Men, 338–340 East 23d St.

Camp Dixon. See HAARLEM HOUSE.

Camp Fire Girls (incorp. 1912), 31 East 17th St., N.Y.C. A national self-supporting and self-governing organization of girls over twelve years of age. Using the home as its basis, the object is to add the power of organization and the charm of romance to daily life and to promote team work. Local Camp Fires, under authorized Guardians, follow a program of activities designed to secure the broadest opportunity for the development of every girl and to bring the out-of-door spirit into everyday life. Woman's work is divided into seven crafts and each craft subdivided into many separate tasks to show that work is a collection of definite units rather than an endless chaos. Being thus measured it is compensated for and given social status by means of honors based upon definite achievement. The ranks are Wood Gatherer, Fire Maker, Torch Bearer. The Minute Girls is the service order of the Camp Fire Girls, with a reconstruction program comprising conservation of health, thrift, home-making, citizenship and Americanization.

Officers: Robert Garrett, acting pres.; J. A. Potter, treas.; Lester F. Scott, secy. and national executive.

Canadian Society of New York, The (org. 1897), Fred W. Shibley, pres., 16 Wall St., N.Y.C. (tel. Rector 8900). To foster cordial social relations amongst Canadians in New York and vicinity and to keep alive memories of Canada; also to assist indigent Canadians.

Cancer Hospital. See NEW YORK SKIN AND CANCER HOSPITAL.

Canton Christian College, Trustees of the (incorp. in State of New York). Office: 156 Fifth Ave., N.Y.C. (tel. Chelsea 9604). Maintains an American College in Canton, China, for Chinese. Supported by voluntary contributions, chiefly from Americans.

Carnegie Foundation for the Advancement of Teaching (est. 1905, incorp. 1906), 522 Fifth Ave. (tel. Vanderbilt 9958). Provides for retiring allowances for university and college professors and conducts educational inquiries. Supported by endowment.

Officers: Henry S. Pritchett, pres.; Robert A. Franks, treas.; Clyde Furst, secy.

Caroline Country Club, Hartsdale, N. Y. Miss Florence Hardy, pres. For persons engaged either professionally or as volunteers in social work and for nurses. Its object is recreation, rest, and social enjoyment. The club house is comfortably equipped to accommodate members over night, over weekends, or for longer periods. Address inquiries regarding membership to secretary, Caroline Country Club, 105 East 22nd St. (tel. Gramercy 7040).

Caroline Rest. See ASSOCIATION FOR IMPROVING THE CONDITION OF THE POOR.

Carry-On Association, Inc., 271 Madison Ave., N.Y.C. Maintains homes for disabled soldiers receiving vocational re-education.

Officers: Mrs. Wendell Phillips, chrm.; Edwin S. Schenck, treas.; Parker Sloane, secy.

Casa Maria (Sociedad: Centro Maria, Inc. incorp. 1920). 215 West 14th St., N.Y.C. A Spanish settlement and home for working girls under the patronage of the Augustinian Fathers of the Assumption, for the temporal, social, mental, moral and religious welfare of young women and Spanish speaking people in general. It is self-supporting. Maintains an employment bureau.

M. de Choiseul, directress.

Catharine Mission (incorp. 1888), 22-28 Catharine Slip (tel. Orchard 1504). Maintains a reading room, mothers' meetings, kindergarten, day nursery, and industrial classes. Also supplies free medical treatment for women and children.

Cathedral of St. John the Divine, The, Amsterdam Ave. and 112th St. Maintains the

St. Ambrose Italian Mission, 236 East 111th St.

St. John's Club for Colored Boys, 39 West 131st St.

Colored Working Girls' Home (q. v.).

Fresh Air Association (incorp. 1905), maintains a Fresh Air House at Tompkins Cove, Rockland Co., N. Y. Clergy desiring to send needy children and mothers may apply to the Rev. Dr. George F. Nelson, Diocesan House, 416 Lafayette St.

Catholic Big Brothers League (est. 1915), 1 Madison Ave., N.Y.C. (tel. Gramercy 1575). Befriending and care of boys; general development, promotion and advancement by the individual and collective efforts of the members for the general welfare, moral, mental, and physical condition of the male youth of the city.

Catholic Boys' Clubs. See Ozanam Association.

Catholic Center for the Blind, 119 West 70th St., N.Y.C. A home for blind working girls, under the supervision of the Sisters of St. Dominic.

Catholic Charities of the Archdiocese of New York, The (incorp. 1920). Central Office: Grand Central Palace, 11 floor, 114 East 47th St., N.Y.C. (tel. Vanderbilt 3420). Most Rev. Patrick J. Hayes, D.D., Archbishop of New York, pres.; Rev. Robert F. Keegan, A.M., Secretary for Charities to the Archbishop, secy.

Central Organization. It provides a center to which people can go for advice and information concerning every Catholic social and charitable activity in the Archdiocese. It re-arranges and co-ordinates the functions of various activities in order that they may serve more people and serve them better. It points out weaknesses in existing organizations, and helps overcome them by supplementing their resources, giving expert advice and encouraging higher standards. It promotes the extension or establishment of agencies to cover fields where Catholic interests are at present neglected. It presents reports of their work to the general public and represents them at conferences. It serves, while leaving special works autonomous, to unify Catholic charities.

Division of Families. The work of this division is: 1. To relieve at once acute distress and suffering. 2. To supervise, co-ordinate and improve the standards of Catholic agencies and organizations in the Archdiocese doing relief or family rehabilitation work.

John Philip Bramer, director.

Division of Children. The work of this division is to supervise, co-ordinate, improve and extend the work of Catholic agencies and organizations engaged in child care.

Rev. Bryan J. McEntegart, A. M., director.

DIVISION OF HEALTH. The work of this division is to supervise, co-ordinate and improve all Catholic agencies and organizations engaged in health activities.

Rev. John F. Brady, M.D., D.D., director; Rev. Joseph S. O'Connell, assistant director.

DIVISION OF PROTECTIVE CARE. The duty of this division is to supervise, co-ordinate and improve the work of agencies, organizations, institutions and societies engaged in Protective, Probation and Parole Work.

Rev. Thomas J. Lynch, S.T.B., director; Rev. Arthur Avard, assistant director.

DIVISION OF SOCIAL ACTION. The work of this division is carried on in two departments:

1. Department of County Activities. This work looks to the improvement of all Catholic charitable activities in Westchester, Dutchess, Putnam, Ulster, Sullivan, Orange and Rockland Counties.

2. Department of Social Activities. This department supervises, co-ordinates, improves and extends Catholic agencies, societies and organizations engaged in recreational and social activities.

Rev. John J. McCahill, director; Rev. John A. White, in charge of Boy Scout Work.

DIVISION OF FINANCE. The work of this division is to formulate and set up organization in order to facilitate the payment and collection of pledges made in the Catholic Charities Enrollment Campaign.

Rev. Edward A. Hayes, director.

Catholic Charities Bureau of the Diocese of Brooklyn, The, 4-5 Court Sq. (org. 1913). Its object is to supervise, direct, and encourage all the Catholic Charitable Institutions of the Diocese.

Very Rev. Mgr. Francis J. O'Hara, chrm.

Catholic Guardian Society, The (incorp. 1913), 139 East 17th St., N.Y.C. (tel. Stuyvesant 7058). To care for orphan, friendless or destitute children, and to place them in family or other homes and for that purpose to receive such children by surrender, commitment or otherwise; and for the after-care of children from Catholic institutions. Five thousand children under the supervision of the Society during the present year.

Rev. Samuel Ludlow, exec. secy.

Catholic Guardian Society of the Diocese of Brooklyn, The (incorp. 1914), 4-5 Court Sq., Brooklyn. To place in proper homes orphan and destitute children, and to supervise such children when they are discharged from Catholic child-caring institutions of Brooklyn Diocese.

Very Rev. Francis J. O'Hara, pres.

Catholic Home Bureau for Dependent Children (org. 1898, incorp. 1899), 289 Fourth Ave., N.Y.C. To place destitute, dependent, or neglected Catholic children in Catholic family homes.

During the year ending September 30, 1920, 146 children were placed in free family homes and 29 were transferred to new homes. Number of children under supervision at close of year 1575.

Officers: Charles F. McKenna, pres.; Alfred J. Amend, vice-pres.; James F. Boyle, treas.; William C. Daly, secy.; Edmond J. Butler, exec. secy.

Catholic Institute for the Blind, 222d St. and Eastchester Rd., Bronx (tel. 816 Olinville). For the education and care of Catholic blind children. Capacity 45. Under the direction of the Sisters of St. Dominic. Supported by private and city funds.

Officers: Stephen Farrelly, pres., 15 Park Pl.; Richard P. Lydon, treas., 51 Chambers St.

Catholic Protective Society, 137 West 36th St., N.Y.C. (tel. Fitz Roy 2099). To deal with all Catholic offenders against the law, boys and girls, men and women, in Children's Court and all branches of the Criminal Courts. To keep first offenders from being sent to prison. To perform probation and parole work in regard to the courts, state prisons and penal and reformatory institutions.

Rev. Thomas J. Lynch, supervisor.

Catholic Protectory. See NEW YORK CATHOLIC PROTECTORY.

***Catholic Total Abstinence Union, The.** To promote total abstinence, with auxiliary societies in the Catholic parishes in the City. Address all correspondence to Rev. John J. Buckley, C.S.P., Church of St. Paul the Apostle, West 59th St. and Ninth Ave.

Cedar Knolls School (Jewish Protectbry and Aid Society) (org. 1912), Hawthorne, N. Y. An educational undertaking for the moral, mental and physical development of the Jewish delinquent girl committed through the Juvenile Court. Vocational, academic, and industrial training given to suit the individual needs of each girl.

Officers: Mrs. Sidney C. Borg, chrm., Exec. Com.; Miss Viola Eckstein, supt.

Central Branch, Y. W. C. A. See YOUNG WOMEN'S CHRISTIAN ASSOCIATION.

Central Club for Nurses, 132 East 45th St. (tel. Murray Hill 8700). The Club offers to Graduate Nurses, social and religious privileges and all the advantages of a well run club. Accommodates 250 residents—is non-sectarian. Affiliated with the Young Women's Christian Association of the City of New York.

Miss Alice H. MacLellan, gen. secy.

Central Committee for the Relief of Jews Suffering Through the War, 51 Chambers St., N.Y.C.

Leon Kamaiky, chrm.; Harry Fischel, treas.; Stanley Bero, general manager.

Central Committee for Friendly Aid to Jewish Girls, Room 32, 356 Second Ave., N.Y.C. (tel. Gramercy 3253).

Mrs. Sidney C. Borg, chrm.; Mrs. Anthony Slesinger, exec. secy.

DEPARTMENT OF COURT, PROBATION, PAROLE AND AFTER-CARE, in co-operation with the Probation Bureau of the City, provides assistance to Jewish girls arraigned in the Woman's Court, and takes charge of Jewish girls paroled and discharged from Cedar Knolls School, the New York Training School for Girls (q.v.), the Workhouse, Penitentiary and Auburn Prison.

Mrs. Mortimer M. Menken, chrm.

UNMARRIED MOTHERS DEPARTMENT, 28 St. Marks Place (tel. Orchard 7311). Conducts investigations in cases of unmarried mothers; sends eligible ones to the Lakeview Home (q.v.) and cares for others through its field department. It also controls the after-care work of the girls discharged from the Lakeview Home.

Mrs. Joseph Proskauer, chrm.

See also JEWISH BIG SISTERS.

Central Council of Public Health. See HEALTH FEDERATION.

Central Day Nursery. See BROOKLYN BUREAU OF CHARITIES.

***Central Homeopathic Dispensary, The** (incorp. 1883), 15 Columbia

* *Current information not received.*

Pl., Brooklyn. Gives free homeopathic medical and surgical aid to the poor. Treats diseases of the eye, ear, nose, and throat. Supported by voluntary contributions only.

Central Howard Association, Inc., 608 S. Dearborn St., Chicago, Ill. Interstate prison reform, and prisoners' aid association.

Officers: George W. Dixon, pres.; T. C. MacMillan, treas.; F. Emory Lyon, supt.

Central Islip State Hospital (est. and incorp. 1889), Central Islip, Long Island. City Office, Hall of Records Building, cor. of Centre and Chambers Sts., N.Y.C. A State Hospital for the insane of New York, Queens and Suffolk Counties. Capacity 5,000 beds, all free, but those able to pay do so, rate $5.00 a week.

G. A. Smith, M.D., superintendent and medical director; Miss M. E. Dunn, social service worker, Room 703, Hall of Records Building, Chambers St., N.Y.C.

Clinic at Cornell University Medical College, 1st Ave. and 27th St. Thursdays from 2 to 4 P. M. and 6 to 8 P. M. Maintained primarily for patients paroled from Central Islip but free examination and advice given all mental cases. G. W. Mills, M.D., clinical director.

Central Jewish Institute (incorp 1912), 125 East 85th St., N.Y.C. (tel. Lenox 1177–1178). A Community Center, chiefly Jewish, affiliated with Federation for the Support of Jewish Philanthropic Societies.

Officers: Jacob H. Rubin, pres.; Jacob Wener, treas.; A. P. Schoolman, exec. director.

Central New York Institution for Deaf Mutes, The (incorp. 1875), 711–713 North Madison St., Rome, N. Y. A State institution for the free education of children over five years of age too deaf to be properly educated in the public schools and whose parents are residents of the State of New York. The course of instruction covers the branches commonly taught in the public schools and includes manual training, printing, carpentry, cooking, and cane-seating for boys, and sewing, dressmaking, ironing, cooking, and general housework for girls; classes for both sexes in drawing, rug-weaving, basket-making, and plasticine modeling.

Officers: A. C. Kessinger, pres. Board of Trustees; Ezra A. Vary, treas.; James I. Stone, secy.; Otis A. Betts, principal.

Central Park Baptist Church, 235 East 83rd St., N.Y.C. Social center, clubs, concerts, etc., industrial school Saturdays.

Rev. Milton W. Pullen.

Central Presbyterian Church, Madison Ave. and 57th St. Rev. Dwight W. Wylie, Pastor.

PARISH HOUSE, 422 West 57th St. (tel. Columbus 7897). Conducts neighborhood clubs and classes, provides recreational opportunities for all ages. Summer camp at Bear Mountain.

Miss Florence Clendenning, head worker.

Ceres Sewing Circle, meets at 113–115 East 101st St. every Wednesday, 2 P. M. (tel. Lenox 3374). District Boundary: North side of 96th St. to North side of 99th St., East River to Fifth Ave.

Chamberlain, Bureau of the, City of New York, eighth floor, Municipal Bldg. (tel. 4227 Worth).

Chapel Hill Fresh-air Mission (incorp. 1893). Owns the EUNICE HOME at Chapel Hill, near Atlantic Highlands, N. J., which is loaned, fully equipped and furnished, to well-known charitable organizations who maintain it as a Summer Home for the poor. Capacity, about 100.

Chapin Home for the Aged and Infirm, The (incorp. 1869), Jamaica, N. Y. For worthy aged and infirm men and women in reduced circumstances, irrespective of creed. Applicants must be not less than sixty-five years of age. An admission fee of $800 is required. Supported by voluntary contributions and admission fees. Apply to the Committee on Applications, Mrs. E. E. Mapes, chrm., 2211 Broadway, N.Y.C.

Officers: Mrs. Horace E. Fox, pres., 21 West 84th St., N.Y.C.; Mrs. Ernest Bunzel, treas., 758 West End Ave., N.Y.C.; Mrs. Charles L. Stickney, rec. secy., 560 West 149th St.; Mr. Richard Brenton, supt.

Charities, Department of Public, City of New York. See PUBLIC WELFARE, CITY OF NEW YORK, DEPARTMENT OF.

Charity Fund of the Chamber of Commerce (1883), 65 Liberty St. Consists of $60,000 bequeathed by the late John C. Green, and $150,000 by the late Amos R. Eno, the income of which is to be applied to the relief of distressed merchants who shall have been members of the Chamber, in good repute, and whose misfortunes were not the result of, or attended by, any dishonorable transaction on their part.

Charity Organization, National. See AMERICAN ASSOCIATION FOR ORGANIZING FAMILY SOCIAL WORK.

Charity Organization Society of Castleton. See STATEN ISLAND SOCIAL SERVICE.

Charity Organization Society of the City of New York, The (org. January 22, 1882, incorp. May 10, 1882). Central Office, United Charities Bldg., 105 East 22d St. (tel. Gramercy 4066. Cable Address, "Charity," New York). Office hours, 9 A. M.–5 P. M., on Saturdays until 12 M.

The Charity Organization Society of the City of New York was founded by a Committee appointed in a resolution of the State Board of Charities. This action was based on a report, dealing with the non-institutional or out-door relief work conducted in the City, presented by Mrs. Josephine Shaw Lowell on behalf of the New York members of the Board.

The objects of the Society, as stated in its charter, are:

1. To be a center of intercommunication between the various churches and charitable agencies in the city. To foster harmonious co-operation between them, and to check the evils of the overlapping of relief.

2. To investigate thoroughly, and without charge, the cases of all applicants for relief which are referred to the Society for inquiry, and to send the persons having a legitimate interest in such cases full report of the results of investigation. To provide visitors who shall personally attend cases needing counsel and advice.

3. To obtain from the proper charities and charitable individuals adequate relief for suitable cases.

4. To procure work for poor persons who are capable of being wholly or partially self-supporting

5. To repress mendicancy by the above means and by the prosecution of impostors.

6. To promote the general welfare of the poor by social and sanitary reforms, by the inculcation of habits of providence and self-dependence, and by the establishment and maintenance of any activities to these ends.

7. To provide philanthropic education and to promote the training of practical workers in charity.

The work of the Society is carried on in three general divisions: the Department of General Work and affiliated committees, the Department for the Improvement of Social Conditions and the New York School of Social Work.

Department of General Work

Lawson Purdy, general director; Miss V. O. Wilder, acting supt.; Miss Catherine Sanders, acting asst. supt.; Miss E. I. Scott, registrar; Miss Isabel Hoes, acting asst. secy. Investigation Bureau; Miss Sarah F. Burrows, secy. Reception Bureau; Miss A. B. Strickland, cashier; Miss Lina D. Miller, editor Directory of Social Agencies; Walter Archer Frost, secy. Finance Committee; Mrs. G. H. Springer, secy. Bureau of Advice and Information and Social Service Exchange; Mrs. Lina F. Copley, business manager; Miss Clare M. Tousley, secy. Committee on Co-operation and District Work; Miss Emma A. Winslow, secy. Committee on Home Economics; Roy P. Gates, secy. Joint Application Bureau; John J. Murphy, secy. Tenement House Committee; Charles M. Keefer, supt. Woodyard and Laundry.

District Offices

Bronx District, Harlem River to City Line, East of Broadway. Office: 355 East 149th St. Miss Anne S. Hoyt, chrm.; Miss Cornelia Le Roy, district secy. (tel. Melrose 9841).

Chelsea District, 14th St. to 30th St., West of Fifth Ave. Office: 330 West 24th St. Dr. E. H. Lewinski-Corwin, chrm.; Miss Gertrude C. Scott, district secy.; Miss Josephine Buck, assoc. district secy. (tel. Watkins, 6997).

Clinton District, 46th St. to 59th St., West of Fifth Ave. Office: 312 West 54th St. Rev. W. R. Ackert, chrm.; Miss Elizabeth Dutcher, district secy. (tel. Circle 5334).

Corlears District, South of Houston St., East of Broadway. Office: 192 Bowery. B. Ogden Chisolm, chrm.; Miss A. M. Decker, district secy.; Miss Helen P. Story, acting district secy. (tel. Spring 5348).

Gramercy District, Houston to 28th Sts., East of Broadway and Fifth Ave. Office: 105 East 22d St. Walter W. Pettit, chrm.; Miss Helen B. Large, district secy. (tel. Gramercy 4066).

Greenwich District, South of 14th St., West of Broadway. Office: 59 Morton St. Mrs. Barry C. Smith, chrm.; Miss Myra R. Manifold, acting district secy. (tel. Spring 5215).

Harlem District, 116th St. to Harlem River, East of Seventh Ave. Office: 71 East 125th St. Elmer E. Sanborn, chrm.; Miss Mary E. Downs, district secy. (tel. Harlem 793).

Hudson District, 59th to 96th Sts., West of Fifth Ave. Office: 1974 Broadway. Lionel Sutro, chrm.; Miss Helen I. Fisk, district secy. (tel. Columbus 3253).

Jefferson District, 104th to 116th Sts., East of Third Ave. Office: 215 East 116th St. Henry W. Thurston, chrm.; Miss C. N. Townsend, district secy. (tel. Harlem 4731).

Kennedy District, 90th to 104th Sts., between Fifth Ave. and East River; and 104th to 116th Sts., between Seventh and Third Aves. Office: 172 East 95th St. Mrs. J. W. Duff, chrm.; Miss Maud Bozarth, district secy. (tel. Lenox 7767).

Kips Bay District, 28th to 63d St., East of Fifth Ave. Office: 151 East 49th St. Dr. S. F. Hallock, chrm.; Miss Katherine E. Young, district secy. (tel. Plaza 4248).

Lowell District, 30th to 46th Sts., West of Fifth Ave. Office: 224 West 34th St. Mrs. Hugh Minturn, chrm.;

Miss Anna Kempshall, district secy. (tel. Longacre 2787).

Riverside District, 96th St. to City Line, West of Seventh Ave., Harlem River, and Broadway. Office: 118 Lawrence St. Dr. Ira S. Wile, chrm.; Miss A. H. Rankin, district secy. (tel. Morningside 1303).

Yorkville District, 63d to 90th Sts., East of Fifth Ave. Office: 255 East 71st St. Ogden L. Mills, chrm.; Miss Jean M. Lucas, district secy. (tel. Rhinelander 3970).

The district offices are neighborhood centers where committees of residents of the vicinity and representatives of the local social agencies consult, in order to bring to the help of families needing assistance the maximum resources of the neighborhood. These committees also are frequently able to obviate abuses and improve living conditions in their territory. In each of the districts, salaried and volunteer visitors carry out the plans of the Committee for the welfare of the families under their care.

The Society aims to develop self-reliance and self-dependence in the families for which it cares, to help them out of their poverty, by removing obstacles from their paths and by offering them new opportunities for self-support and self-development.

The purpose of the Society is achieved by bringing to the aid of families their natural resources, such as relatives, friends, neighbors, employers, churches, and also by stimulating and encouraging them through personal relationships established with them by members of the staff and by volunteer workers. The Society co-operates with the welfare agencies of the city—dispensaries, settlements, church societies, and the like—so that each organization is able to do its share in carrying out plans adopted by all the agencies which are helping the same family.

Central Office

Central Office, 105 East 22d St. (tel. Gramercy 4066). The work of the Society with families brings great numbers of requests for advice about and from persons in trouble of various kinds and concerning institutions and organizations engaged in welfare work. The Central Office offers this kind of help.

The Reception Bureau, Miss Sarah F. Burrows, secy., receives inquirers needing personal help or seeking assistance for relatives, friends, or others. It gives advice about opportunities for the care of the aged, the sick, the mentally deficient. It supplies information concerning suitable homes for working girls. It is the consulting room of the Society.

Joint Application Bureau, 105 East 22d St. (tel. Gramercy 2081), Roy P. Gates, supt. This Bureau is conducted by the Society and the New York Association for Improving the Condition of the Poor. It is open from 9 A. M. to 12 midnight and is designed to care for homeless men and women. Able-bodied men are given temporary work. Permanent work is secured for many applicants. The sick are placed in hospitals or convalescent homes. Relief is given when necessary, and transportation is secured when possible for applicants having homes in other places.

The Registration Bureau, Miss E. I. Scott, registrar, has charge of the records of families that were under the care of the Society. These records now number about 100,000. Here persons who have a legitimate interest in such families may obtain information about them.

Social Service Exchange, Mrs. Gertrude Springer, secy., 105 East 22d St. (tel. Gramercy 6276). Receives inquiries from social agencies seeking to know what other agencies are in touch with the families or individuals they are trying to serve. Inquiries are recorded in a card index, each card bearing the names of the members of the family, the address, and the names of the organizations which have inquired about them. The Exchange carries no information whatever about the family.

By assisting social agencies to coordinate their services, duplication of work is minimized and a maximum of co-operation is secured. There are more than 400,000 family cards in the index. During the year ending October 1, 1920, the Exchange was used by 405 agencies. Inquiries received numbered 53,820.

THE INVESTIGATION BUREAU, Miss Isabel Hoes, acting secy., supplies individuals and charity organization societies in other cities with information concerning families or individuals in New York City in whom they are interested.

COMMITTEE ON CO-OPERATION AND DISTRICT WORK, Miss Clare M. Tousley, secy. The chief function of the Committee is the stimulation of volunteer service for the Organization, and the raising of standards in this field.

The Secretary has charge of general publicity, through which channels many volunteers are secured, and the work of the Organization more generally understood.

A series of three months' courses are given by her to combine the practical work with theoretical and she also supervises the volunteers' training and progress in the Districts.

The Committee also has the broader function of strengthening friendly relations between the Society and other charitable agencies and securing their co-operation in the work and objects of the Society. Within the Organization it is chiefly interested in the activities of the district committees.

COMMITTEE ON HOME ECONOMICS, Emma A. Winslow, secy., conducts special investigations of living costs, formulates budget standards, aids social workers in advising families concerning better homemaking adjustments, endeavors to promote a closer relationship between home economics and social work, assists in community efforts to improve home conditions.

Conducts the Morningside Nutrition and Homemaking Center, 100 Lawrence St. (tel. Morningside 4604) in co-operation with Teachers College, Columbia University, and the New York County Chapter of the American Red Cross, for experimentation in the organization and conduct of nutrition work for children and homemaking conferences for mothers, and for the provision of supervised field work for qualified students preparing for certain positions in educational and social work.

Also conducts a June Course for Practice in Homemaking Adjustments to provide special field work training for a limited group of home economics students.

THE BUREAU OF ADVICE AND INFORMATION, Mrs. G. H. Springer, secy., offers general information to all inquirers and to members of the Society and of certain affiliated organizations special reports on work done by social agencies soliciting funds in New York City.

TENEMENT HOUSE COMMITTEE, John J. Murphy, secy., exists to improve the housing conditions of the people of New York who live in many-family buildings known legally as tenement houses; to mitigate the evils growing out of a long period of unregulated tenement house construction; to prevent the enactment of amendments which would weaken the present Tenement House Law; to secure from time to time such new housing legislation as public necessity requires or advancing standards demand;

to study and co-operate in the enforcement of existing laws by local authorities and, where necessary, to stimulate them to more efficient administration. Recognizing that in the housing field, work to be effective must be largely preventive, the Committee studies local tendencies, especially in outlying districts, with a view to forestalling the creation of new slum areas. In general it seeks to formulate remedies for existing evils and to encourage all practicable improvements in tenement house conditions.

Through the efforts of this Committee, the appointment of the Tenement House Commission of 1900 was secured, the passage of the present Tenement House Law attained, and the Tenement House Department established. It conducts educational work wherever the opportunity offers; maintains a clearing-house for information on housing matters in the city; prepares and distributes pamphlets and organizes lectures and conferences.

THE DIRECTORY OF SOCIAL AGENCIES, Miss Lina D. Miller, editor, is an encyclopaedia of 2,000 social agencies in Greater New York, including a subject index in which the agencies are classified, a list of the churches of all denominations and a name index of 5,000 persons mentioned in the book in connection with the agencies listed.

The circulation of the Directory is steadily increasing, and this is an encouraging sign of added interest in social work. The Directory was self-sustaining, as it ought to be. It is so no longer because the cost of production has increased almost three times. The price of the book is two dollars.

Two activities of the Society closely allied to the Department of General Work are the Woodyard and the Laundry.

WOODYARD, Charles M. Keefer, supt., 516 West 28th St. (tel. Chelsea 421). Temporary work is offered to men who desire to support themselves while they are seeking permanent employment. The Woodyard is supported by sales of wood and of tickets, and by voluntary contributions.

Kindling	Price
¼ Cord	$8.50
½ Cord	16.00
1 Cord	32.00
Hickory	
¼ Cord	$10.50
½ Cord	19.50
1 Cord	39.00
Pine Knots or Oak	
¼ Cord	$8.50
½ Cord	16.00
1 Cord	32.00

LAUNDRY, Charles M. Keefer, supt., 516 West 28th St. (tel. Chelsea 421), is fully equipped and competent to do first-class work for the public; its object being to teach women all kinds of laundry work, so that they may be able to support themselves and earn higher wages. Novices are not allowed to work on family garments until sufficiently expert to do fine work. Names and addresses of graduated expert laundresses can be obtained at the Laundry.

DEPARTMENT FOR THE IMPROVEMENT OF SOCIAL CONDITIONS

Lawrence Veiller, director, Rooms 615–622, 105 East 22d St. (tel. Gramercy 2860). Under this Department the various activities of the Society for the improvement of social conditions and the removal of the underlying causes of poverty in the community are included. The Department seeks to secure the solution of the city's social problems upon a constructive and permanent basis, having as its chief purpose the accomplishment of definite results rather than the discussion or exploitation of theoretical views of social reform.

COMMITTEE ON CRIMINAL COURTS, Lawrence Veiller, secy.; Mrs. Mary E. Paddon, exec. secy. This Committee was organized with the definite purpose of aiding the administration of justice in the lower criminal courts.

The keynote of the Committee's work is sympathetic co-operation with the judges, with the public, with social workers, with court clerks and city officials, and with the Legislature. It watches all legislation affecting the work of the inferior courts in New York City; it opposes undesirable amendments, and drafts and supports desirable legislative amendments; it serves to bring to the aid of the judges the force of public sentiment in behalf of needed changes; it makes careful surveys of specific problems connected with the work of the courts; it aids in securing necessary appropriations for reforms needed to make the work of these courts effective.

The Committee has been of great assistance in the establishment of a proper probation system with paid Civil Service officers for delinquent children in the Children's Courts and for the less hardened offenders in the Magistrates' Courts. It has secured legislation which does away with double trials and unnecessary imprisonment for minor misdemeanants; it has separated the Children's Courts from Adult Criminal Courts; ahd has established a Municipal Term court for cases in which city and state departments are the complainants. It has helped to get proper buildings for the Children's Courts and other courts. It has standardized records and reports. It supports the judges, officials, and heads of institutions in requests for appropriations of money to better handle the unfortunate and the delinquent brought into the courts. It is active in bringing about a better solution of the desertion and abandonment problem through the Domestic Relations Court. It makes independent investigations on which to base its suggestion. It is constantly interested in every function of these courts which handle nearly a quarter of a million of people yearly and affect indirectly a million lives. There are ten sub-committees, as follows: General administration, domestic relations courts, women's court, probation, law, the legislation, buildings, children's courts, Court of Special Sessions, record system and court records, and institutions.

SCHOOL OF SOCIAL WORK

THE NEW YORK SCHOOL OF SOCIAL WORK (est. 1898, Summer Session; 1903-1904, Winter Session; 1914 Institutes), United Charities Bldg., 105 East 22d St., N.Y.C.

Porter R. Lee, director.

The School is conducted by the Charity Organization Society and affiliated with Columbia University, and is primarily a professional training school for civic and social work. It aims to give fundamental courses of instruction and of field work which will prepare for usefulness in any of the rapidly multiplying kinds of organized social movements and for efficiency in those governmental positions, national, state, and municipal, which have to do directly with the promotion and protection of social welfare.

Curriculum. The course extends throughout the academic year from October to May inclusive, for a period of two years. (The work of the two years is sharply differentiated.) The instruction of the first year includes courses which are believed to be valuable to all who are expecting to engage in any kind of social work on either a professional or a volunteer basis [with opportunity for specialization in field work]. In the second year the work is strictly vocational and specialized.

The Summer School is planned for the following groups of people: Teachers, ministers, nurses, and other professional workers; students in theological schools; volunteers; social workers who may wish to concentrate on technical problems in their own particular field of work, or to ascertain what is being done in other fields of work; college seniors and others who may wish to obtain advanced credit on entering the School as regular students.

The curriculum represents most of the subjects taught in the winter school concentrated into a brief period of time with emphasis on practical work.

Special courses, adapted to the needs of particular groups of social workers in New York City and vicinity, are arranged as opportunities arise. Institutes are conducted for employed social workers in various fields.

Staff (1920-1921): Porter R. Lee, director; Walter W. Pettit, asst. director; Catharine Maltby, registrar; Kate Holladay Claghorn, Henry W. Thurston, John A. Fitch, Ordway Tead, George W. Kirchwey, Margaret Leal, Georgia Ralph, Haven Emerson, M.D., Bernard Glueck, M.D., June Joslyn.

For announcement address The New York School of Social Work, 105 East 22d St., New York City.

Officers of the

CHARITY ORGANIZATION SOCIETY

President

Robert W. de Forest	30 Broad St.

Vice-Presidents

George F. Baker, Jr.	2 Wall St.
George L. Cheney	30 West 86th St.
Cleveland H. Dodge	99 John St.
Charles S. Fairchild	37 Fifth Ave.
Homer Folks	105 East 22d St.
E. M. Grinnell	36 East 50th St.
Lloyd C Griscom	52 William St.
Edward S. Harkness	26 Broadway
E. C. Henderson	58 East 54th St.
Harold Herrick	25 Liberty St
Charles E. Merrill	432 Fourth Ave.
W. J. Matheson	182 Front St.
Robert Grier Monroe	26 Liberty St.
J. P. Morgan	23 Wall St.
Morgan J. O'Brien	120 Broadway
Peter B. Olney	68 William St.
J. R. Roosevelt	319 Fifth Ave.
Mrs. Jas. A. Scrymser	107 East 21st St.
Mrs. Francis Louis Slade	18 West 52d St.
James Speyer	24 Pine St.
Henry L. Stimson	32 Liberty St.
I. N. Phelps Stokes	100 William St.
Felix M. Warburg	52 William St.

Central Council

Robert W. de Forest	President
Otto T. Bannard	Vice-President
Harold T. White	Treasurer
Lawson Purdy	Secy.

(Term expires October, 1921)

Robert S. Brewster	51 Wall St.
Robert W. de Forest	30 Broad St.
Alfonso de Navarro	30 Broad St.
Edward T. Devine	112 East 19th St.
William Greenough	120 Broadway
Silas F. Hallock	36 East 65th St.
Percy Hall Jennings	25 Broad St.
Edwin G. Merrill	80 Broadway
Nathan A. Smyth	61 Broadway

(Term expires October, 1922)

Otto T. Bannard	26 Broad St.
Paul D. Cravath	52 William St.
Mrs. John M. Glenn	136 East 19th St.
Miss A. B. Jennings	48 Park Ave.
Mrs. Frederic S. Lee	125 East 65th St.

Philip J. McCook 15 William St.
James Alexander Miller 379 Park Ave.
Jeremiah Milbank 40 Wall St.
Ogden L. Mills 15 Broad St.
Mrs. H. O Taylor 135 East 66th St.
Bronson Winthrop 32 Liberty St.

(Term expires October, 1923)

Miss Kate Bond 230 West 59th St.
Mrs. Richard S. Childs 8 West 9th St.
Henry P. Davison 23 Wall St.
Johnston de Forest 30 Broad St.
Charles E. Merrill, Jr. 432 Fourth Ave.
Charles D. Norton 2 Wall St.
Jackson E. Reynolds 2 Wall St.
Mrs. Wm. B. Rice 17 West 16th St.
John H. Towne 9 East 40th St.
Harold T. White 14 Wall St.
Harrison Williams 60 Broadway

District-Delegate Members

GREENWICH: Mrs. Ralph Berrisch, 125 Prospect Park, W., Brooklyn.

CORLEARS: Henry Solomon, 58 East 65th St.

CHELSEA: Dr. E. H. Lewinski-Corwin, 17 West 43d St.

GRAMERCY: Lewis M. Isaacs, 52 William St.

CLINTON: Eugene W. Small, 57 West 70th St.

HUDSON: Harold A. Rosenbaum, 74th St. and Columbus Ave.

KENNEDY: Mrs. Giuseppe Previtali, 127 East 57th St.

KIPS BAY: Mrs. Minturn Post Collins, 16 East 75th St.

LOWELL: Mrs. Hugh Minturn, 116 East 22d St.

RIVERSIDE: Dr. Wm. A. McCall, 505 West 122nd St.

YORKVILLE: Ogden L. Mills, 15 Broad St.

HARLEM: George C. Lay, 99 Claremont Ave.

BRONX: David Layton, 669 Dawson St.

JEFFERSON: Mrs. George W. Severn, 235 Ft. Washington Ave.

Ex-Officio Members

The Mayor of the City of New York.
The Police Commissioner.
The Commissioner of Health.
The Commissioner of Correction.
The Commissioner of Public Welfare.
The Tenement House Commissioner.
The United States Commissioner of Immigration.

John A. McKim of the State Charities Aid Association.

Professor Samuel McCune Lindsay of Columbia University.

Cornelius N. Bliss, Jr., of the New York Association for Improving the Condition of the Poor.

The governing body of the Society is the Central Council, which meets monthly. The President appoints the following Standing Committees of the Central Council, viz.:

1. Executive Committee: Robert W de Forest, chrm.; Otto T. Bannard, Johnston de Forest, Mrs. John M. Glenn, William Greenough, Silas F. Hallock, Miss A. B. Jennings, Ogden L. Mills, Charles D. Norton, Mrs. Frederic S. Lee, Jackson E. Reynolds, Mrs. William B. Rice, Harold T. White, Harrison Williams.

2. Committee on Finance and Membership: Harrison Williams, chrm.; Walter Archer Frost, secy.; Edwin G. Merrill, Jeremiah Milbank, Charles D. Norton.

3. Committee on Co-operation and District Work: Mrs. John M. Glenn, chrm.; Miss Clare M. Tousley, secy.; Miss Adelaide Case, Mrs. Richard S. Childs, Miss Joanna C. Colcord, Mrs. J. W. Duff, Miss Sarah Dean, Miss Elizabeth Dutcher, Very Rev. H. E. W. Fosbroke, Miss Helen Gregory, Dr. S. F. Hallock, Miss Anne Hoyt, Mrs. John

Lefferts, Oscar Lowenstein, Miss Jean Lucas, Miss May Mathews, Mrs. Hugh Minturn, Miss Mary E. Richmond, Lawson Purdy, Mrs. Barry C. Smith, Miss M. deG. Trenholm, Miss Myra R. Tutt, Miss V. O. Wilder, Miss E. A. Winslow.

4. Committee on Legal Questions: George Gordon Battle, Addison A. Van Tine.

5. Committee on Home Economics: Benjamin R. Andrews, chrm.; Miss Emma A. Winslow, secy.; Maurice Bigelow, F. G. Bonser, Mrs. Richard S. Childs, Miss Kate Holladay Claghorn, Miss Joanna C. Colcord, Miss Jane F. Culbert, Miss Elizabeth Dutcher, Miss Jane Fales, Miss Helen L. Hollister, Miss Marjorie Kinney, Miss Jessie A. Long, William F. Ogburn, Lawson Purdy, Mrs. Mary Swartz Rose, Henry C. Sherman, Mrs. Amy D. Storer, Miss V. O. Wilder, Miss Cora M. Winchell, Miss Elizabeth A. Woodward.

6. Committee on Industrial Building: Charles W. Ogden, chrm.; Johnston de Forest, treas.; George C. Hollister, Charles E. Merrill, Jr., Henry Solomon.

7. Committee on School of Social Work: Robert W. de Forest, chrm.; Appointive members: John M. Glenn, William Greenough, Dr. S. F. Hallock, Miss A. B. Jennings, Jackson E. Reynolds, George W. Kirchwey, Nathan A. Smyth, Alfred T. White, David H. McAlpin Pyle, Roswell C. McCrea. Ex-officio members: Alfred E. Marling, Cornelius N. Bliss, Jr., Nicholas Murray Butler, Leopold Plaut, Michael J. Scanlan.

8. Tenement House Committee: Lawson Purdy, chrm.; John J. Murphy, secy.; Grosvenor Atterbury, Charles S. Brown, Paul D. Cravath, Robert W. de Forest, Edward T. Devine, Abram I. Elkus, Matthew C. Flemming, Robert W. Higbie, Darwin R. James, Jr., E. A. MacDougall, Alfred E. Marling, Robt. Grier Monroe, Frederic B. Pratt, Allan Robinson, Robt. E. Simon, Walter Stabler, Andrew J. Thomas, Myles Tierney, Alfred T. White.

9. Committee on Bureau of Advice and Information: Jackson E. Reynolds, chrm.; Mrs. G. H. Springer, secy.; William J. Matheson, Nathan A. Smyth.

10. Committee on Criminal Courts: Bronson Winthrop, chrm.; Lawrence Veiller, secy.; Mrs. Mary E. Paddon, exec. secy.; Charles W. Appleton, Otto T. Bannard, Robert W. de Forest, Victor J. Dowling, Homer Folks, John M. Glenn, Frederick Trevor Hill, Ralph K. Jacobs, George W. Kirchwey, Philip J. McCook, Julius M. Mayer, Morgan J. O'Brien, Alfred R. Page, Alton B. Parker, Frank L. Polk, Ezra P. Prentice, George W. Schurman, Nathan A. Smyth, Henry W. Thurston, Lawrence Veiller.

11. Committee on Prevention of Tuberculosis: Lawrence Veiller, chrm.; Edward T. Devine, Johnston de Forest, Lee K. Frankel, Lawson Purdy.

12. Red Cross Emergency Relief Committee: Robert W. de Forest, chrm.; Otto T. Bannard, Mrs. John M. Glenn, Charles D. Norton.

13. Joint Committee of the Charity Organization Society and the Association for Improving the Condition of the Poor: C. C. Burlingham, chrm.; Charles E. Merrill, Jr., Harold T. White, Wm. H. Matthews, Lawson Purdy.

Charlton Industrial Farm School, Ballston Lake, N. Y. A Christian family home to reclaim boys who are drifting toward a life of crime. Legally committed. Capacity 30.

L. H. Sears, supt.

Charlton Street Memorial Church (Interdenominational), 34-40 Charlton St., N.Y.C. A social center for the neighborhood providing clubs, classes, gymnasium, library, swimming, industrial classes, etc.

Theo. R. Brining, general secy.

Chattel Loan Society of New York, Inc. (incorp. and began business 1912), 289 Fourth Ave. Loans of $20 to $200 on household furniture, secured by chattel mortgage at the rate of two per cent. per month. Territory covered, New York, Bronx, Kings, and Queens counties. Capital employed, $200,000.

Officers: Johnston deForest, pres.; Mortimer L. Schiff, vice-pres.; Harold T. White, treas.; George H. Loh, secy. and gen. manager.

Chautauqua Institution, Chautauqua, N. Y. 1. Assembly July and August, including lectures, concerts, etc. 2 Summer Schools, July and August. Languages, science, mathematics, pedagogy, arts and crafts, music, etc. 3. Home Reading Department, a four-years' course of systematized home readings aims to give a general increase of knowledge and of culture.

Chelsea Day Nursery (1912), 346 West 27th St., N.Y.C. (tel. Chelsea 41). To care for children from tubercular families between 7 A. M. and 6 P. M. Accommodates sixty. Maintained by Society for Prevention and Relief of Tuberculosis, Tuberculosis Clinics.

Mrs. Cornelius N. Bliss, Jr., chrm. Nursery Committee, Miss Florence Le Fevre, R.N., supt. of Nursery.

***Chelsea House Association** (incorp. 1909), manages two non-sectarian self-supporting boarding houses for business girls.

CHELSEA HOUSE, 434 West 20th St., accommodates thirty-eight

CHELSEA SECOND, 363 West 34th St., accommodates fifty.

Chelsea Neighborhood Association (org. 1912, incorp. 1917), 111 Fifth Ave. (tel. Stuyvesant 6464). Promotes the social, civic, and economic improvement of the Chelsea neighborhood (14th to 42nd St., Fifth Ave. to Hudson River). Supported by voluntary contributions.

Knowlton Durham, pres.

Chester Crest Home for Intemperate Men, Mt. Vernon, N. Y. (tel. Mt. Vernon 248). Open air, wholesome food, best sanitary conditions, all needed medical treatment. Booklet free on request.

Officers: Rev. D. Stuart Dodge, pres.; A. W. Bertine, treas.; William S. Edgar; secy.; George Sanford Avery, manager.

Child Health Organization of America, Acting with the National Child Labor Committee, Inc., 156 Fifth Ave., N.Y.C. (tel. Watkins 7875–7876).

Co-operating with the United States Bureau of Education, the purpose of the Child Health Organization of America is to raise the standard of health of the American school child.

Officers: Dr. L. Emmett Holt, chrm. Executive Committee; V. Everit Macy, treas.; Owen R. Lovejoy, secy.; Sally Lucas Jean, director; Marie L. Rose, Anne L. Whitney, Anne Raymond and J. Mace Andress, associate directors.

Child Labor Committee. See NATIONAL CHILD LABOR COMMITTEE; also, NEW YORK CHILD LABOR COMMITTEE.

Child Welfare Board. See BOARD OF CHILD WELFARE.

Child Welfare Committee. See NEW YORK CHILD WELFARE COMMITTEE.

Child Welfare Exhibit Association. See NATIONAL CHILD WELFARE ASSOCIATION, INC.

Children's Aid Society (org. 1853 by the late Charles Loring Brace; in-

* *Current information not received.*

corp. 1855). Central office: 105 East 22d St. (tel. Gramercy 2420). Cares for homeless boys and girls in lodging houses; procures family homes for them in rural districts and in the West; maintains, in populous districts where the greatest poverty prevails, Industrial Schools and Kindergartens, designed to co-operate with the Board of Education in reaching and influencing the children of the poor; operates homes for convalescent children in the country throughout the year and at the seashore in summer.

The fundamental principle of the Society is that of teaching children how to help themselves. The work is supported by voluntary contributions and bequests.

Officers: William Church Osborn, pres., 71 Broadway; Edwin G. Merrill, treas., 52 Wall St.; C. Loring Brace, secy.; H. K. Holt, asst. treas.; Robert N. Brace, E. H. Opitz, Miss A. L. Hill, R. L. Neill, Miss Lancaster, Miss Anderson, Miss A. A. Bogardus, Miss C. B. Comstock, Frederick King, and J. W. Swan, agents.

Departments of Work

Home-finding

The Placing-out or Emigration Department, 105 East 22d St., receives boys and girls who are to be provided with homes in the country. The department also aids families with children to find and locate themselves on suitable farms or desirable places where employment is assured.

Educational

Industrial Schools, all of which include night schools, are maintained for children who cannot attend the public schools because of ill-health or other handicaps.

Avenue B, 533 East 16th St.
53d St., 552 West 53d St.
Henrietta, 224 West 63d St.
Italian, Elizabeth and Hester Sts.
Jones Memorial, 407 East 73d St.
Rhinelander, 350 East 88th St.
6th St., 630 East 6th St.
Sullivan St., 219 Sullivan St.
Tompkins Sq., 295 East 8th St.
West Side, 417 West 38th St.

Classes for Crippled Children are maintained at the Rhinelander School, 350 East 88th St. A warm lunch is provided, and a wagonette conveys them to and from their homes daily. Application for admission should be made to the principal in charge.

Clubs and Roof Playgrounds are maintained at 156 Hester St., 552 West 53d St., 417 West 38th St., and 247 East 44th St.

Kips Bay Boys' Club, 825 Second Ave., Arthur Huck, supt.

West Side Club for Boys, 22 West 35th St., George Blum, supt.

Harlem House and Community Center, 136 East 127th St., Raymond L. Anderson, supt.

Brace Farm for Boys, Valhalla, Westchester County, N. Y. Affords probationary farm training for boys, to test their habits, capabilities, and willingness to work, after which provision is made for their future by placing them in permanent homes with farmers. Four hundred and twenty-four boys were received during the past year.

Boarding Houses, Homes, etc.

Brace Memorial, or Newsboys' Lodging House, 14 New Chambers St., William L. Butcher, supt.

Elizabeth Home for Girls, 307 East 12th St., provides board and lodging for working girls at $1.50 to $4.00 a week. Country branch at Chappaqua for girls needing rest, or desiring special training in house-work. Mrs. J. G. Colby, supt.

FORTY-FOURTH STREET HOME FOR BOYS, 247 East 44th St., Arthur Huck, supt.

SHELTER FOR WOMEN WITH CHILDREN, 311 East 12th St. For evicted and homeless women of good character with children. Owing to limited capacity, arrangements should be made by telephone (Orchard 1992). Two hundred and sixty-one received last year.

Mrs. J. G. Colby, supt.

A. LOUISE ERLANGER HOME, formerly known as the New York Home for Destitute Crippled Children, 442 W. 23d St.

Miss C. E. Peterson, supt.

DAY NURSERIES

Avenue B Nursery, 535 East 16th St.

Italian Nursery, 154 Hester St.

Columbus Hill Day Nursery, 224 West 63d St.

MEDICAL BUREAU, 150 East 45th St. (tel. Murray Hill 2936). All children who are applicants for convalescent care or home finding are examined physically and psychologically and advice given by experts as to their needs.

CHILDREN'S CONVALESCENT HOME, Chappaqua, N. Y., ideally situated upon the south side of Chappaqua Mountain, 600 feet above sea level, in a picturesque hill country, accommodates about 200 convalescent children. Open all the year Co-operates with the visitors and nurses of the industrial schools, hospitals, and dispensaries.

"KINDERFOLD," Valhalla, N. Y., for convalescent and anaemic boys, and New Brighton, S. I. for girls. Open all the year.

DENTAL CLINICS are maintained for poor children at

552 West 53d St.

295 East 8th St.

Elizabeth and Hester Sts.

219 Sullivan St.

224 West 63d St.

Summer Charities

CHILDREN'S SUMMER HOME, Bath Beach, L. I., for poor children of the tenement districts, giving them a week's rest and pleasure; also providing day picnics.

HAXTUN COTTAGE, Bath Beach, L. I., for crippled girls under fifteen years of age.

HEALTH HOME, Bath Beach, for mothers with sick babies. Mrs. A C. Gardiner, supt.

MARTHA SUMMER HOME, Ossining, N. Y. (opened 1881 as a memorial to Martha Green Potter, wife of the late Orlando B. Potter). Accommodates thirty children.

GOODHUE HOME, New Brighton, S. I., provides convalescent care for children, a camp for boys, school gardens for poor children, and days' outings for mothers with little children.

Children's Bureau. See FEDERAL CHILDREN'S BUREAU.

Children's Clearing Bureau, Department Public Charities. See PUBLIC WELFARE DEPARTMENT, CITY OF NEW YORK.

Children's Convalescent Home. See CHILDREN'S AID SOCIETY.

Children's Country Home Association, The, Westfield, N. J. (est. 1891, incorp. 1898). To aid convalescents, especially cripples, children from four to twelve years exclusive of tubercular cases; no other limitations. District covers New Jersey, New York City, and vicinity. Capacity, thirty-eight.

Children's Courts. For the hearing and disposition of cases involving the trial or commitment of children under the age of sixteen years. Court is held by Justices of the Children's Court designated from among the Justices of the Court of Special Sessions for various terms by the Mayor of the City of New York.

Children's Courts for the several boroughs as follows:

MANHATTAN, 137 East 22d St. (tel. Gramercy 3611).

THE BRONX, 355 East 137th St. (tel. Melrose 9092).

BROOKLYN, 102 Court St. (tel. Main 8611).

QUEENS, 30 Union Hall St., Jamaica (tel. Jamaica 2624).

RICHMOND, Borough Hall, New Brighton, S. I. (tel. Tompkinsville 2190).

Children's Haven, The (est. 1914), Far Rockaway, N. Y. Cares for Jewish children under seven whose mothers because of illness are unable to do so. Capacity, twenty-nine. Supported by the Federation for Support of Jewish Philanthropic Institutions.

Officers: Florence M. Sommerich, pres.; Bernice M. Rosenbaum, treas.; Mrs. Louise Kramer, secy.

Children's School Farm League. See INTERNATIONAL CHILDREN'S SCHOOL FARM LEAGUE.

Children's Village, The (formerly the New York Juvenile Asylum), Dobbs Ferry, N. Y. (incorp. 1851, opened 1853). Office: 103 Park Ave. at 41st St., N.Y.C. (tel. Murray Hill 1315). For street boys of New York between seven and sixteen years of age who are committed by competent authority. Supported by donations, legacies, and city appropriations. (See Advertisement.)

The Village at Dobbs Ferry accommodates 500 boys in twenty-nine cottages and a reception house. The Village consists of homes and a school which provides for their support and affords them the means of moral, intellectual, and industrial education. Also, a reformatory for truant and disobedient children, committed by the Children's Court, by a magistrate, or surrendered by parents or guardians. Visiting days for children at the village, first Sunday in the month.

The Schools are under the supervision of the Board of Education. Friendless, destitute, and homeless or surrendered children are placed in homes in the country. Entire number in the institution during the past year, 1062.

Officers: Edmund Dwight, pres., 56 Maiden Lane, N.Y.C.; Charles Elliot Warren, treas., 60 East 42d St.; Henry N. Tifft, secy., 15 William St.; Guy Morgan, supt., whom address.

China Medical Board. SEE ROCKEFELLER FOUNDATION.

Chinatown and Bowery Settlement (est. 1905), 10 Mott St., N.Y.C., under the Rescue Society (q. v.). For rescue, preventive, and settlement work among the girls in the neighborhood of Mott, Pell, and Doyer Sts., and the Bowery. The work includes visiting houses of ill fame, furnished room houses, dance halls, rescue homes, and hospitals, keeping in touch with relatives and friends, co-operating with the police, curing drug habits, etc. Maintains a

RECREATION ROOM for girls which is open day and night. Supported by voluntary contributions.

Officers: Miss Annette B. Boardman, pres.; Dr. Alice M. Spence, vice-pres.; James B. Nimmons, treas., 36 West 37th St.; Miss C. L. Boardman, secy., 128 East 34th St.; Miss Florence M, Heberling, missionary in charge; Miss. Lenore Morgan, assistant.

Christ Congregational Church, 91st St., Woodhaven, L. I. A social center for the neighborhood. See also under CONGREGATIONAL CHURCHES (Queens) in the Church List.

Christ Presbyterian Church, 344

West 36th St. Rev. Theodore F. Savage, Pastor. Maintains:

CHRIST CHURCH HOUSE, which provides a kindergarten, sewing-school, cooking-school, industrial classes, gymnasium, boys' and girls' clubs, general and dental clinics.

SUMMER SCHOOL and PLAYGROUND. (See also under PRESBYTERIAN CHURCHES in the Church List.)

Christ P. E. Church, Broadway at 71st St., N.Y.C. Maintains a cafeteria, etc. See also under Protestant Episcopal Churches in the Church List.

Christian Aid Association (est. 1888), 84 Bible House, Fourth Ave. and 9th St. To counsel and help self-supporting gentlewomen in every possible way toward securing the employment for which they are best fitted. Mrs. Alida Stanwood, founder in charge.

Christian Chinese Burial Association (incorp. 1901). The object is to provide a Christian burial place for Chinese and members of the Association who may die in the vicinity. The Association owns a plot in Kensico Cemetery.

Officers: Maj. Edward W. Peet, M.D., pres., 144 West 93d St., N.Y.C.; Rev. Huie Kin, treas., 223 East 31st St.; John H. Woodley, secy., 40 Clendenny Ave., Jersey City, N. J.

Christian Herald Children's Home (org. 1894, incorp. 1898), Mont-Lawn, Nyack-on-Hudson, N. Y. City office: Bible House, Fourth Ave. and 9th St. (tel. Stuyvesant 3900). For girls from six to eleven and boys from six to ten years of age, from tenement houses of New York City, for ten-day vacations. Capacity, 320 at a time. Supported exclusively by voluntary contributions through "The Christian Herald." The Home includes a main building, five dormitories, Children's Temple, dining hall, library, bath house, wading and swimming pool, two pavilions and twenty-eight acres of woodland and lawn. Over 50,000 children have been entertained at the Home for a ten-days' outing. Only the poorest, entirely unable to pay, are admitted. All contributions acknowledged. Applications should be addressed to the office.

Christian Home for Girls. See MAEDCHENHEIM.

Christian Home for Intemperate Men. See CHESTER CREST HOME FOR INTEMPERATE MEN.

Christian and Missionary Alliance, The (incorp. 1897), 692 Eighth Ave., N.Y.C. Maintains:

NYACK SCHOOLS, South Nyack, N. Y., for the preparation of men and women for Missionary work.

Publishes the "Alliance Weekly," Sunday School papers and quarterlies, religious books and tracts.

Christian Waiters' Home (International Christian Waiters' Association), 427 East 51st St., N.Y.C. (tel. Plaza 3822). A home for young men, mostly Germans, Austrians, and Swiss. Conducts meetings and lectures at a time suitable for hotel and restaurant employees, by representatives of the various denominations, in English and German. The sick are visited, the unemployed assisted in securing positions, etc.

R. Menzel, pres. and treas., 61 Dittmars Ave., Astoria, L. I.; P. Kurt Mueller, secy. and manager of the Home.

Christian Workers' Training School. See WOMAN'S BRANCH, NEW YORK CITY MISSION SOCIETY.

Christodora House (org. 1897), 145-147 Avenue B, 603 East 9th St. and Northover Camp, Bound Brook,

N. J. For the physical, social, intellectual, and spiritual development of the people in the crowded portions of the City of New York, and hearty co-operation with the religious, civic, and philanthropic work of the neighborhood. Open from 8 A. M. to 10 P. M. daily. The Settlement maintains Educational classes, forty-two clubs, classes in English for foreigners, citizenship, dramatic expression, interior decorating, a Music School, Boy Scouts, Girl Scouts, and is a Red Cross Health Centre. Open on Sundays for Gospel meetings and Children's Hour.

Officers: Mrs. Arthur Curtiss James, pres.; Mrs. Richard L. Beckwith, vice-pres.; John Sherman Hoyt, treas.; Miss Sallie N. Whitney, secy.; Miss C. I. MacColl, head worker.

Chrystie Street House, The (incorp. 1905), 77 Horatio St. (tel. Chelsea 5758). A temporary home for young men and boys over 16 years of age who are in trouble. They are given shelter, food, and clothing and assisted in procuring employment. Non-sectarian, capacity twenty. Supported by voluntary contributions. Total annual expense about $7,000.

Officers and Members Board of Trustees: Mark W. Maclay, chrm.; Parmly S. Clapp, treas., Produce Exchange Bldg.; George C. Kalle, asst. treas.; Lewis Jackson, secy.; William Prosnitz, asst. secy.; Miss Laura Jay Edwards, Mrs. Samuel C. Van Dusen, Charles Wisner, Frederick C. Boynton, Stephen G. Williams, S. Walter Kaufmann, A. Chalmers Charles, Kenneth McEwen, William M. Carson, William H. Taft, II, Henry Hennefrund, supt. in residence.

***Church Association for the Advancement of the Interests of Labor, The ("C.A.I.L.")** (org. 1887), 416 Lafayette St., N.Y.C. By means of sermons, addresses, lectures, literature, and public meetings, to further measures for the betterment of social and industrial conditions. Supported by voluntary contributions.

Church Charity Foundation of Long Island, The (incorp. 1851). Office: St. John's Hospital, Albany and Atlantic Aves., Brooklyn. A foundation under the auspices of the Protestant Episcopal Church for the purpose of administering and maintaining the institutions listed below.

Officers: Rev. Frederick Burgess, D. D., Bishop of Long Island, pres.; David H. Lanman, treas., Brooklyn Trust Co., Clinton and Montague Sts.; Rev. Bishop Falkner, secy.; Rev. Paul F. Swett, supt.

DEPARTMENTS

ST. JOHN'S HOSPITAL (1870), Atlantic and Albany Aves., Brooklyn. For acute, sub-acute, curable and non-contagious cases.

Training School for Nurses, covering a three years' course. Apply to the Superintendent of the hospital, or to Miss Ida Pratt, supervisor of nurses.

HOME FOR THE AGED (1851), Herkimer St. and Albany Ave. For indigent persons over sixty-five years of age, communicants of the Episcopal Church of Long Island. Capacity, seventy.

ORPHAN HOUSE (1851), Albany Ave., cor. Herkimer St. For indigent orphan and half-orphan children between six and ten years of age.

HOME FOR THE BLIND (1896), Albany Ave. and Herkimer St. Capacity, twenty-four. Deaconess Agnes Hodgkiss in charge.

Church Club of New York, The (incorp. 1893), 53 East 56th St. For the promotion of social intercourse, historical study of the history and

* *Current information not received.*

doctrines of the Church, and to stimulate the efforts of churchmen for her welfare and for the maintenance of the faith, and to maintain a library and reading room.

Officers: Henry L. Hobart, pres.; Edward S. Pegram, treas., 23 Wall St.; Francis S. Marden, secy., 7 Wall St.

Church of God Missionary Home, The (incorp. 1907), 2132–2142 Grand Ave., Bronx (tel. Fordham 1879). A stopping place for foreign missionaries and a home free of charge for evangelists and city workers. Supported by voluntary contributions.

Officers: C. J. Blewitt, pres.; John Snyder, vice-pres.; M. Anna Blewitt, secy. and treas.

Church Institute for Negroes. See AMERICAN CHURCH INSTITUTE FOR NEGROES.

Church Mission to Deaf-Mutes, The (incorp. 1872), 511 West 148th St., N.Y.C. To promote the temporal and spiritual welfare of adult deaf-mutes; to minister to the sick and needy; to get work for the unemployed, and to hold religious services in sign language in various places. Social Center, "The Guild House," at above address. Supported by voluntary contribution.

Officers: H. G. Wisner, treas., 45 Cotton Exchange; Albert L. Willis, secy., 124 West 183d St.; Rev. John Chamberlain, D.D., gen. mgr., 450 West 149th St. Maintains

THE GALLAUDET HOME for worthy aged and infirm deaf-mutes in the State of New York, on a farm by the Hudson River, six miles below Poughkeepsie; P. O., Wappinger's Falls, N. Y. The Domestic Department is entrusted to a Board of Lady Managers; Mrs. D. Crosby Foster, pres.; Miss A. I. Young, treas.; Miss F. E. Thropp, secy. Office at 132 South Hamilton St., Poughkeepsie, N. Y.

Church Mission of Healing (Endorsed by the Bishop of New York), 49 West 20th St., N.Y.C. (tel. 9–10 A. M. Morningside 4595; 2–3 P. M. Chelsea 9848). Provides Christian psychoanalysis for nervous, mental and spiritual sufferers under the direction and diagnosis of psychological physicians.

Rev. Thomas E. Calvert, M.A. (Edin.), Litt.D. director of psychotherapy; Estelle C. Beach, M.D. lecturer and physical examiner for women and children; Caroline Horsler, friendly visitor.

Officers: John F. Scott, pres.; Walter Scott Silver, hon. treas.; Alice O. Kane, fin. secy.; Margaret Kerr, hon. secy.

Church Mission of Help (org. 1911, incorp. 1913), Room 152, 2 East 24th St., N.Y.C. Work both rescue and preventive. Girls and women assisted through shelter and employment. In addition to the general visitors, are white and colored workers in the Women's Day Court and Court of Special Sessions, an institutional visitor, a director of volunteer work, and a secretary for work in Westchester County.

THE NATIONAL COUNCIL of the Church Mission of Help was organized June 1919 for the extension of the work to all dioceses of the Church. Temporary headquarters, Room 152, 2 East 24th St. Mrs. John M. Glenn, pres.; Miss Elsie Morrell, secy. The Church Mission of Help exists in the diocese of Long Island, New Jersey, Pennsylvania, Maine and New York.

Officers: Rev. Wm. T. Manning, D.D., pres.; Haley Fiske, treas.; Mrs. L. Frederick Pease, secy.; Miss A. M. Penrose, asst. secy.

Church Pension Fund, 14 Wall St.

Church Periodical Club (incorp. 1892), 2 West 47th St., Room 1104 (tel. Bryant 4253). To provide good reading matter free for individuals and institutions unable to obtain it otherwise. Institutions are also supplied with pictures, games, cards, etc. Supported by voluntary contributions.

Officers: Mrs. Otto Heinigke, pres., 420 Ovington Ave., Bay Ridge, Brooklyn; Mrs. D. G. Luckett, treas., 44 West 10th St.; Miss Mary E. Thomas, exec. secy., 2 West 47th St.

Church Temperance Society, The (org. 1881, incorp. 1889), 88 St. Nicholas Ave., N.Y.C. (tel. Cathedral 10,008). Promotion of temperance, reformation of the intemperate, removal of causes, and the issue of temperance publications.

Officers: Rev. James V. Chalmers, pres.; William Jay Schieffelin, Ph.D., treas.; Rev. James Empringham, D.D., natl. supt., whom address.

Circle for Negro Relief, Inc., 489 Fifth Ave., N.Y.C. Experimenting in organizing negroes to handle own problems, particularly in connection with public health.

Officers: Charles H. Towne, pres.; Dr. E. P. Roberts, treas.; Belle Davis, exec. secy.

Citizens Union of the City of New York (est. 1897, incorp. 1901), 41 Park Row, N.Y.C. (tel. Cortland 5898-9). A union of citizens of New York City, without regard to party, for the purpose of securing the honest and efficient government of the City.

William J. Schieffelin, chrm.; Walter T. Arndt, secy.

City Clerk and Clerk of the Board of Aldermen, 2d floor, Municipal Bldg. (tel. Worth 4430).

City Club, The (org. and incorp. 1892), 55 West 44th St. (tel. Vanderbilt 1816). A Social Club and a non-partisan civic organization, watching the work of the State Legislature and of the various branches of the municipal government.

Officers: Nelson S. Spencer, pres.; Perley Morse, treas.; Raymond V. Ingersoll, secy.

City Court, 32 Chambers St. (tel. Cortland 122).

City Farm Colony, Staten Island. See PUBLIC WELFARE DEPARTMENT, CITY OF NEW YORK, "Sea View Sanatorium."

City Federation Hotel (incorp. 1907), 462 West 22d St., N.Y.C. A boarding home for working girls of moderate wages. Rates: $5.50-$6.50 a week for board and lodging. Capacity, fifty. No limitations as to race or creed.

City Federation of Women's Clubs. See NEW YORK CITY FEDERATION OF WOMEN'S CLUBS.

City History Club of New York (incorp. 1897), Tilden Building, Room 709, 105 West 40th St., N.Y.C. (tel. Bryant 1073). An organization for training citizens. Gives instruction in civics and local history by means of clubs and classes in schools, settlements and libraries. Maintains a bureau of lectures on historical and civic topics; conducts parties to historic scenes in and around New York City; publishes the "Historical Guide to the City of New York," besides numerous leaflets and pictures relating to local history. Student membership 1919-20 about 800. It is supported by membership dues and voluntary contributions by patriotic citizens and societies.

Officers: Mrs. A. Barton Hepburn, pres., 630 Park Ave.; Benjamin L. Allen, treas., 105 West 40th St.; Mrs. Carr Van Anda, secy., 205 West 57th St.; Frank Bergen Kelley, acting supt.

City Homes for the Aged. See

PUBLIC WELFARE DEPARTMENT, CITY OF NEW YORK.

City Hospitals. See PUBLIC WELFARE DEPARTMENT, CITY OF NEW YORK, also BELLEVUE AND ALLIED HOSPITALS.

City Islands. Persons wishing to visit institutions on the islands should communicate with the respective department maintaining them.

BLACKWELL'S ISLAND, entrance from Queensboro Bridge.

HART'S ISLAND, ferries operated by DEPARTMENT OF CORRECTION, from foot of East 26th St.

HUNTER'S ISLAND, Westchester R. R. to City Island and bus from there.

NORTH BROTHER ISLAND, ferries operated by the DEPARTMENT OF HEALTH, from foot of East 132d St.

RANDALL'S ISLAND, ferries from foot of East 26th St., East 53d St., East 70th St., East 120th St., and East 125th St.

RIKER'S ISLAND, ferries operated by the DEPARTMENT OF CORRECTION, from foot of East 26th St.

STATEN ISLAND, ferry from North 2d St., Brooklyn, and from South St., Manhattan.

The Sea View Farms' Stage runs daily, excepting Sundays.

WARD'S ISLAND, ferry from foot of East 116th St.

City Magistrates' Courts. Office of the Chief City Magistrate and the Chief Clerk, and the Chief Probation Officer, 300 Mulberry St., Manhattan (tel. Spring 9420).

COURTS

Manhattan and the Bronx

First District, 110 White St. (tel. Franklin 1971)

Second District, 125 Sixth Ave. (tel. Chelsea 1051)

Third District, Second Ave. & 2d St. (tel. Forsyth 1204)

Fourth District, 151 East 57th St. (tel. Plaza 2302)

Fifth District, 121st St. & Sylvan Pl. (tel. Harlem 225)

Sixth District, 162d St. & Brook Ave., Bronx (tel. Melrose 3670)

Seventh District, 314 West 54th St. (tel. Circle 605)

Eighth District, 1014 East 181st St., Bronx (tel. Fordham 5744)

Women's Court, 125 Sixth Ave. (tel. Chelsea 1051)

Night Court for Men, 151 East 57th St. (tel. Plaza 2302)

Domestic Relations Court, 151 East 57th St. (tel. Plaza 2302)

Twelfth District, 1130 St. Nicholas Ave. (tel. Wadsworth 5402)

Domestic Relations Court, Bronx, 1014 East 181st St. (tel. Fordham 5808)

Municipal Term, Room 500, Municipal Building (tel. Worth 1800)

Traffic Court, 301 Mott St. (tel. Spring 9884)

Bureau of Domestic Relations, 151 East 59th St. (tel. Plaza 2302)

Brooklyn

Deputy Chief Clerk's Office, 44 Court St. (tel. Main 7411)

First District, 318 Adams St. (tel. Main 216)

Fifth District, Williamsburg Bridge Plaza (tel. Greenpoint 3395)

Sixth District, 495 Gates Ave. (tel. Bedford 14)

Seventh District, 31 Snyder Ave. (tel. Flatbush 741)

Eighth District, West 8th St., Coney Island (tel. Coney Island 13)

Ninth District, Fifth Ave. & 23d St. (tel. South 1453)

Tenth District, 133 New Jersey Ave. (tel. E.N.Y. 2222)

Domestic Relations Court, 402 Myrtle Ave. (moving contemplated) (tel. Prospect 2700)

Municipal Term, Part 2, 2 Butler St. (tel. Main 211)
Women's Night Court, 318 Adams St. (tel. Main 216)
Traffic Court, 182 Clermont Ave. (tel. Prospect 241)
Bureau of Domestic Relations, 327 Schermerhorn St. (tel. Main 2453)

Queens

First District, 115 Fifth St., Long Island City (tel. Hunters Point 4171)
Second District, Town Hall, Flushing, L. I. (tel. Flushing 228)
Third District, Central Ave., Far Rockaway (tel. Far Rockaway 164)
Fourth District, Town Hall, Jamaica, L. I. (tel. Jamaica 517)

Richmond

First District, Lafayette Ave., New Brighton (tel. Tompkinsville 500)
Second District, Village Hall, Stapleton (tel. Tompkinsville 1150)

City Mission Society. See New York City Mission Society; Brooklyn City Mission Society, etc.

City Officials and Departments. See list in Subject Index in the front of the book.

City Prisons. See Correction, Department of.

City Record, The. Official journal of the City of New York. Supervisor's office: 8th floor, Municipal Bldg. Distributing division, 125 Worth St. (tel. Worth 3490).

City Reformatory. See Correction, Department of.

Civic Club, The, 14 West 12th St., N.Y.C. (tel. Watkins 4797).

Civic Forum, The (org. 1907), The Town Hall, 113–123 West 43d St. (tel. Bryant 2636). Evening lectures.

Board of Trustees: Henry Clews, chrm.; Trowbridge Hall, treas.; Robert Erskine Ely, director.

Civil Service Commission. See Municipal Civil Service Commission; also, State, and United States Civil Service Commissions.

Civil-Service Reform Association, The (org. 1877), 8 West 40th St., N.Y.C. (tel. Vanderbilt 2376). To establish a system of appointment, promotion, and removal in the Civil Service. Founded upon the principle that public office is a public trust, admission to which should depend upon proved fitness. Annual dues, $5.

Officers: Samuel H. Ordway, pres., 27 William St.; A. S. Frissell, treas., 530 Fifth Ave.; Harry W. Marsh, secy.

Civitas Club of Brooklyn. Meets at 114 Pierrepont St. Object: To awaken an interest in civic and social welfare and to further all movements that aim to advance human progress.

Officers: Mrs. William P. Earle, Jr., pres.; Mrs. Rudolph Reimer, Jr., treas., 96 Warwick St.; Mrs. Ernest G. Draper, secy., 61 Prospect Park, West.

Clara de Hirsch Home for Immigrant Girls. See Hannah Lavanburg Home.

Clara de Hirsch Home for Working Girls (incorp. 1897), 225 East 63d St., N.Y.C. A non-sectarian home for the benefit of girls between fourteen and eighteen years of age; to improve their mental, moral, and physical condition; to train them for self-support. Rate: $4 to $7 a week for board and lodging. Maintains trade classes in hand sewing, machine operating, dressmaking, and millinery. Supported by endowment.

Officers: Mrs. Oscar S. Straus, pres.; Mrs. J. E. Hoffman, vice-pres.; Walter E. Beer, treas.; Mrs. Walter Liebman, secy.; Miss Rose Sommerfield, resident directress.

Clark Neighborhood House. See ALFRED CORNING CLARK NEIGHBORHOOD HOUSE.

Clear Pool Camp (est. 1902, incorp. 1910), Carmel, N.Y. City Office, 9 East 44th St. (tel. Murray Hill 7810). The object of the camp is to provide working boys between the ages of fourteen and eighteen with an opportunity for a healthy, athletic, open-air vacation, without charge (boys sixteen and over pay own fare). During the past season vacations were given to 220 boys without respect to race, creed or color. It is supported entirely by voluntary contributions, and is able to give these vacations on a small expenditure, owing to the non-moneymaking aim of the owners of the camp.

Board of Directors: Thomas S. McLane, pres.; Richard L. Morris, vice-pres.; E. Coster Wilmerding, secy. and treas.; George B. Hedges, counsel; Ashbel H. Barney, Hamilton Fish Benjamin, Charles D. Dickey, Jr., Charles D. Draper, Seton Henry, Alfred O. Hoyt, James Ford Johnson, Jr., Barent Lefferts, Huntington Lyman, Allan McLane, Jr., E. P. Mellon, Arthur M. Milburn, Wm. Ross Proctor, Jr., Lawrason Riggs, Jr., George E. Roosevelt, Warren Thorpe. Apply to Mrs. H. Perrine, exec. secy.

Clergymen's Retiring Fund Society of the Protestant Episcopal Church in the United States (incorp. 1874), 281 Fourth Ave., N.Y.C. Grants annuities to members sixty years of age. Membership fee, $12 a year. Capital fund, $431,654.88.

Officers: Rt. Rev. Frederick Burgess, D.D., pres.; Rev. Henry Anstice, D.D., fin. secy. and treas.

Clinic for Functional Re-Education of Disabled Soldiers, Sailors and Civilians, 5 Livingston Pl., Stuyvesant Sq., near 15th St., east of Second Ave., N.Y.C. The Clinic is established primarily for the treatment of the mutilated of our Army and Navy, and to afford instruction for medical officers, nurses and attendants in their specialized care. It is, however, intended to make it a permanent institution for those who may become disabled through accident, as in processes of manufacture, or transportation, or through explosions, street accidents, etc.

The buildings of the Clinic have been leased for a term of years from the New York Infirmary for Women and Children and consist of a therapeutic building and hospital. The equipment of the therapeutic building comprises the following departments: 1. Complete hydrotherapy outfit. 2. The novel mechanical apparatus devised by Professor Tait McKenzie, professor of Physical Education in the University of Pennsylvania, and Professor E. A. Bott of Hart House, Toronto. 3. An electrotherapeutic department. 4. A department for special exercises and games, and for local massage. 5. Workshops. 6. An X-ray department. 7. A Social Service and Occupational Therapy Department 8. A rest and reading room with a library for the patients and an extensive out-door garden court where many of the exercises may be given. The buildings face Stuyvesant Park, which secures excellent light and air with an exceptionally attractive outlook.

Hours. The Clinic is open daily, Sundays and holidays excepted, 9 A. M. to 5 P. M. Mondays, Wednesdays and Fridays, 7 to 9 P. M. All treatment is offered free to the poor, but hospital patients, referred by the city authorities or by accident insurance companies, the War Risk Insurance Bureau or similar organizations, will be charged the rates which these organizations are accustomed to pay other hospitals and dispensaries of the city.

Officers: W. Gilman Thompson, M.D., pres.; Miss Gertrude Parsons, secy.; Mrs. Carlos M. De Heredia, treas.; Walter T. Pilgrim, supt.

Clinic for Speech Defects. See EDUCATION, DEPARTMENT OF.

Clothing Bureau, The, 138 East 22d St. Receives discarded clothes, bed, and table linens, blankets, comfortables, and any articles which may be of use to others. These are sold at a nominal price to those in need upon satisfactory recommendation.

Miss Julia Lathers, manager.

College Settlement of Rivington Neighborhood Association, The (org. 1889, incorp. 1908), 84-86 1st St., N.Y.C., and Mt. Ivy, N. Y. (tel. Orchard 6670). Endeavors to cultivate among its neighbors, its resident workers, and its associate workers, broad sympathies and a true insight into existing civic conditions. Special training courses arranged for community workers in connection with Inter-Collegiate Community Service Association. A social center for the neighborhood, carrying on classes, clubs, etc. Supported by annual contributions.

Officers: Mrs. J. E. Johnson, pres., Hartsdale, N. Y.; Harris A. Dunn, treas., 358 Fifth Ave.; Mrs. Eva Whiting White, director of training in connection with the I. C. S. A.; Miss Helen Marburg, head worker.

Collegiate School (org. 1633-1638), 241-243 West 77th St. Maintained by the COLLEGIATE REFORMED CHURCH. A day school with classical, intermediate, and primary departments. (See also under REFORMED CHURCHES in the Church List.)

Colored Mission. See NEW YORK COLORED MISSION.

* *Current information not received.*

Colored Orphan Asylum and Association for the Benefit of Colored Children (est. 1836, incorp. 1838), West 261st St. and Palisade Ave., Riverdale-on-Hudson, N. Y. Receives colored children between two and ten years. Seven cottages, six nurseries. Instruction in home industries. Day school under Board of Education, P. S. 49. Institution accommodates 290 children under the management of a Board of Trustees.

Officers: Mrs. Willard Parker, Jr., 1st directress; Miss Helen Moore, 2d directress; Miss Helena L. Knox, treas.; Mrs. Robert L. MacLaren, secy.; Dr. Mason Pitman, supt.

Colored Working Girls. See ST. JOHN'S HOME FOR WORKING GIRLS.

Columbia House Settlement, 27 Columbia Pl., Brooklyn, N. Y. A center for neighborhood work supported by the Church of the Saviour. Not incorporated. Free kindergarten, social and civic clubs, manual, domestic training, music school, Girl Scouts, dramatics, dancing, indoor playground, thrift fund, library, gymnasium, bowling, baths, lectures, district nurse, fresh-air work.

Mrs. Donald MacLean, headworker.

***Columbia Religious and Industrial School for Jewish Girls,** 133 Eldridge St., N.Y.C. Instruction in sewing, Jewish history, and religion to Jewish girls over seven years of age.

Columbia University Appointments Office, 316 University Hall, 116th St. and Broadway (tel. Morningside 1400, Ext. 131). Receives applications for full or part time student employment and assists Columbia University students in obtaining employment.

Miss Ethel A. Breed, secy.

Columbia University Dental Infirmary, 437 West 59th St., N.Y.C.

***Columbus Hill Day Nursery,** 224 West 63d St., N.Y.C. For colored children of working mothers.

Columbus Hospital. See MISSIONARY SISTERS OF THE SACRED HEART OF JESUS.

Comforter, Chapel of the, 10 Horatio St., N.Y.C. Conducts a school, sewing, and cooking, manual training, athletics, clubs, etc., and does general relief work. Maintains

OPEN DOOR MISSION (est. 1913), 633 Hudson St., N.Y.C. For the rescue of men reduced to destitution through drunkenness and other vices. They are cared for until religion has re-established them. Supported by voluntary contributions.

Officers: Rev. C. C. Clark, Rector; Ernest T. Hargrove, chrm.; J. F. B. Mitchell, treas., 33 Pine St.

See also under PROTESTANT EPISCOPAL CHURCHES in the Church List.

Commission for the Blind. See NEW YORK STATE COMMISSION FOR THE BLIND.

Commission for Mental Defectives. See STATE COMMISSION FOR MENTAL DEFECTIVES.

Commission on Milk Standards. See NATIONAL COMMISSION ON MILK STANDARDS.

Committee for the Care of the Jewish Tuberculous, 356 Second Ave., N.Y.C. (tel. Gramercy 4918). For limited number of families provides medical and nursing care and general relief. Acts as social service agency for Bedford Sanatorium. Information and diagnostic service for Jewish patients. Conducts one workroom for negative sputum patients and another for positive sputum patients. Patients can be referred for workrooms.

Officers: Fred M. Stein, chrm.; Dudley D. Sicher, treas.; Dr. Leon N. Adler, secy.; Edward Hochhauser, exec. secy.

Committee for Christian Relief. See FEDERAL COUNCIL CHURCHES OF CHRIST.

Committee on Criminal Courts of the Charity Organization Society. Rooms 615–622, 105 East 22d St., N.Y.C.

See CHARITY ORGANIZATION SOCIETY, sub-title "Department for the Improvement of Social Conditions."

Committee on Dispensary Development of the United Hospital Fund. Dispensary Service Bureau—executive agent (org. 1920), 15 West 43rd St. (tel. Vanderbilt 9673). Encouragement and assistance to existing dispensaries through (1) demonstration centers (2) advisory and consultative service to dispensaries throughout city (3) training of clinical executives and social workers and dispensary administrators.

Officers: Henry J. Fisher, chrm. of committee; John Sherman Hoyt, treas.; Michael M. Davis, Jr., exec. secy.

Staff of Bureau on full time: Dr. Anna M. Richardson, Raymond H. Greenman.

Committee of Fourteen (org. 1905, incorp. 1907). Office, 27 East 22nd St., N.Y.C. (tel. Gramercy 5489).

The purpose of this Committee is the suppression of commercialized prostitution in New York City. It co-operates with all officials in the investigation of vice conditions and the prosecution of violators.

The Committee follows court procedure in vice cases and when desirable seeks legislative amendments to secure more effective laws.

The Committee welcomes complaints of such conditions, which are carefully investigated and takes immediate action to secure the suppression

* *Current information not received.*

of violations. When conditions found do not constitute violations of law, other means are used to correct them.

Officers: Dr. John P. Peters, hon. chrm.; Percy S. Straus, chrm.; Francis Louis Slade, treas., 115 Broadway; Frederick H. Whitin, gen. secy.

Committee for Men Blinded in Battle, 111 East 59th St., N.Y.C. Cares for and re-educates blinded French soldiers.

Officers: John H. Finley, acting pres.; William Forbes Morgan, treas.; Maud E. Howard, exec. secy.

Committee for the Prevention of Blindness. See NATIONAL COMMITTEE, etc.; also NEW YORK STATE COMMITTEE FOR THE PREVENTION OF BLINDNESS.

Committee for the Reduction of Infant Mortality. See NEW YORK MILK COMMITTEE.

Committee of Reference and Counsel of the Foreign Missions Conference of North America, Inc., 25 Madison Ave., N.Y.C. (tel. Madison Sq. 9890). Dr. P. de Schweinitz, chrm.; Alfred E. Marling, treas.; F. P. Turner and F. W. Bible, secretaries.

Commonwealth Fund, The (incorp. 1918), 1 East 57th St., N.Y.C. (tel. Plaza 5553). The particular objects for which the corporation is formed are the application to charitable purposes of the income or the principal of such property as from time to time the Corporation shall possess; including the giving of income or of principal to any other charitable corporation or corporations.

Officers: Edward S. Harkness, pres.; Otto T. Bannard, treas.; Max Farrand, general director; Samuel C. Fairley, asst. director.

Community Church, The, 61 East 34th St., N.Y.C. (tel. Murray Hill 4138). Rev. John Haynes Holmes, Rev. Harvey Dee Brown and Rev. John Herman Randall, Ministers.

THE SOCIAL SERVICE LEAGUE conducts the Community Forum Sunday evenings and other public meetings on social questions; maintains a Social Service Bureau. The 39th St. Neighborhood Rooms, co-operates with philanthropic societies and reform organizations, furthers legislation, etc.

SOCIAL CENTER activities at Murray School, 32d St. PLAYGROUND.

THE BENEVOLENT COMMITTEE of Messiah Branch Alliance sews for many charitable societies of the city, does war relief work, distributes clothing, magazines, etc.

CHARITY COMMITTEE contributes to the work of the C. O. S., the A. I. C. P., etc., and gives relief.

See also under UNITARIAN CHURCHES.

Community Councils of the City of New York. Headquarters: Room 2240, Municipal Bldg. (tel. Worth 8815).

F. G. Randall, pres.; Charles C. Bauer, 1st vice-pres.; John K. Clark, 2nd vice-pres.; A.W. Richardson, treas.; Mrs. J. Gilmore Drayton, secy.; Eugene C. Gibney, exec. secy.

Community Hospital in the City of New York (formerly New York Medical College and Hospital for Women), 19 West 101st St., N.Y.C. (tel. Riverside 1341). Capacity 100 beds. Dispensary open 2 to 4 P. M.

Officers: William H. Dieffenbach, M.D., pres.; John H. Storer, M.D., treas.; H. B. Vannote, secy.; Ella A. Lawrence, R.N., supt.

Community Motion Picture Bureau, 46 West 24th St., N.Y.C. (tel. Gramercy 162). Warren Dunham Foster, president.

Organized to supply educational and recreational motion picture service for community development. Has a staff of trained editorial reviewers; records covering millions of feet of films; highly developed library data, and is prepared to combine programs for any community purpose, school, church, to meet the needs of any groups or occasion. Its aim is to render service to humanity through the most skilful use possible of this great instrument of the human intelligence—the motion picture—for the entertainment and enlightenment of the race.

Community Service (Inc.), 1 Madison Ave., N.Y.C. Organized in February, 1919, to help people of all communities employ their leisure time to their best advantage for recreation and good citizenship. While Community Service helps in organizing the work in communities, extending an invitation to national headquarters, in planning the program and raising the funds and will, if desired, serve in an advisory capacity, the community itself, through a committee representative of community interests, determines policies and assumes complete control of the local work. Community Service through its national headquarters publishes literature, trains workers for local communities, supplies community organizers and specialists, and acts as a clearing house for information.

H. S. Braucher, secy.

Community Workers, The, of the New York Guild for the Jewish Blind, maintain a community centre for the blind at 240 East 105th St., N.Y.C., where reading rooms, club rooms, recreation, and a work-shop are provided.

Henry K. Heyman, pres., 157 West 79th St., N.Y.C.

Coney Island Hospital, Ocean Parkway and Avenue Z, Coney Island. See PUBLIC WELFARE DEPARTMENT, CITY OF NEW YORK.

Conference on the Education of Backward, Truant, Delinquent, and Dependent Children. See NATIONAL CONFERENCE, etc.

Congregational Church Building Society (incorp. 1853), 287 Fourth Ave. (tel. Gramercy 2240). Aids in building churches and parsonages by grants and loans taking first mortgage as security. Receipts, 1919, $431,748.89.

Officers: R. H. Potter, D.D., pres.; Charles H. Baker, treas.; Charles E. Burton, D.D., James Robert Smith, D.D., and Charles H. Richards, D.D., secretaries.

Congregational Church Extension Society of New York and Brooklyn, The, 287 Fourth Ave., N. Y. Hon. E. M. Bassett, pres.; Rev. Charles W. Shelton, secy. and supt.; Rev. George D. Egbert, rec. secy.

Congregational Home for the Aged, The New York (incorp. 1910), 123 Linden Ave., Brooklyn. A home for aged men and women of the Congregational denomination. Admission fee, $500. Capacity, thirty-six. Mrs. William C. Peckham, chrm., Board of Managers, 132 St. James Place, Brooklyn; Alvah Miller, treas., 52 Vanderbilt Ave., Manhattan.

Congregational Home Missionary Society, The (org. 1826, incorp. 1871), 287 Fourth Ave., N.Y.C. (tel. Gramercy 2240). To assist congregations that are unable to support the Gospel ministry, and to send the Gospel to the destitute within the United States.

Rev. C. E. Burton, D.D., gen. secy.; C. H. Baker, treas.

Congregational Sunday School Extension Society, The (org. 1917, incorp. 1918), 287 Fourth Ave., N.Y.C. (tel. Gramercy 2240). Aids and establishes Sunday Schools on the frontier, in the rural community, in new city communities and among immigrants.

Rev. C. E. Burton, D.D., gen. secy.; Rev. W. K. Bloom, extension secy.; C. H. Baker, treas.

Constantinople College, Arnautkeuy, Constantinople (founded 1871, incorp. 1890 as the American College for Girls at Constantinople in Turkey). Headquarters: 70 Fifth Ave., N.Y.C. (tel. Watkins 4041). Non-sectarian. Provides a liberal education for young women of every nationality. Supported by voluntary contributions. Mary Mills Patrick, Ph.D., LL.D., pres.

Officers of the Corporation: Charles R. Crane, pres.; Susan H. Olmstead, bursar and gen. secy.; Cecil O. Dunaway, exec. secy.

Consuls.—Note: Residents of foreign countries desiring advice or protection may apply to their respective representative or agent having office in New York City as follows:

ARGENTINE REPUBLIC: Ernesto C. Perez, consul general, 17 Battery Place, (tel. Whitehall 1455).

AUSTRIA-HUNGARY: See Sweden.

BELGIUM: Pierre Mali, hon. consul general; Johnston Mali, hon. vice-consul; Leon J. Garcey, consular agent, 25 Madison Ave. (tel. Madison Square 9146).

BOLIVIA: José Manuel Gutierrez, consul general, 233 Broadway (tel. Barclay 2837).

BRAZIL: Helio Lobo, consul general; Joao Carlos Muniz, deputy consul, 17 State St.

BULGARIA:

CHILE: Emilio Edwards Bello, consul general, U. S., 165 Broadway (tel. Cortland 3567).

CHINA: Juming C. Suez, consul; Chain Kwang-Shi, vice-consul, 291 Broadway (tel. Worth 3760).

COLUMBIA: José Maria Arango G., consul general; Rafael del Castillo, vice-consul, 17 Battery Place (tel. Whitehall 1793).

COSTA RICA: 17 Battery Place (tel. Whitehall 1557).

CUBA: Felipe Taboada y Cruz, consul general; José A. Ramos y Aguirre and Francisco Cañellas y Warti, consuls; Pedro E. Desvernine y Zequeira, vice-consul, 44 Whitehall St. (tel. Bowling Green 9588).

CZECHOSLOVAKIA:

DENMARK: George Bech, consul; Mads Henningsen and Aage Carl Heinrich Bull, vice-consuls, 8 Bridge St. (tel. Bowling Green 5797).

DOMINICAN REPUBLIC: Manuel de J. Camacho, consul general for U. S., 17 Battery Place (tel. Whitehall 156).

ECUADOR: Gustavo R. de Ycaza, consul general, 17 Battery Place (tel Whitehall 1482).

FINLAND: Axel Solitander, 443 Broome St. (tel. Canal 3827).

FRANCE: Gaston Ernest Liebert, consul general, 471 Park Ave. (tel. Plaza 9714); Stanislas Henri M. J. d'Halewyn, vice-consul.

GERMAN EMPIRE: In charge of the Swiss consulate. See Switzerland.

GREAT BRITAIN: Henry Gloster Armstrong, consul general; Frederick Watson, consul; Claud Kirkwood Ledger, Gerald Harrington, J. Douglas Scott, Whitson Black Kirkpatrick, Robert John Robinson, Russell Duncan Macrea, Leonard A. H. Parish, Charles Gordon Thomas, François E. Evans, vice-consuls, 44 Whitehall St. (tel. Bowling Green 9638).

GREECE: Constantin Psaroudas, consul general; P. Armyriotis and Theodore Papagianopulo, vice-consuls.

GUATEMALA: Dr. Ramon Bengoecha, consul general, 10 Broadway (tel. Broad 321).

HAITI: André Faubert, consul general; Ernest Bastien, vice-consul, 31 Broadway (tel. Whitehall 246).

HONDURAS: Timoteo Miralda, consul general; Emilo V. Soto, hon. vice-consul, 277 Broadway (tel. Worth 1079).

ITALY: Comm. T. Bernardi, consul general; Chevalier Luigi Mariani, vice-consul, 20 East 22d St. (tel. Gramercy 1057).

JAPAN: Kyo Kumasaki, consul general, 165 Broadway (tel. Cortland 314).

LIBERIA: Edward G. Merrill, consul; E. B. Merrill, vice-consul, 98 Park Place (tel. Barclay 8414).

MEXICO: Bernardino Mena Brito, in charge of consulate general; Guillermo S. Seguin, consul, 154 Nassau St. (tel. Beekman 5565).

MONACO: Paul Fuller, consul general, 2 Rector St. (tel. Rector 580).

MONTENEGRO: William Frederick Dix, hon. consul general:

NETHERLANDS: D. J. Steyn Parve, in charge of consulate general, 90 West St. (tel. Rector 5424).

NICARAGUA: Fernando Elizondo, consul general; Virgilio Lacayo, vice-consul, 80 Wall St. (tel. Hanover 6470).

NORWAY: H. Say, consul general, 27 William St. (tel. Broad 1160).

PANAMA: Belisario Porras, Jr., consul general; Carlos Carbone, Jr., vice-consul, 11 Broadway (tel. Bowling Green 8377).

PARAGUAY: William Wallace White, consul general; Philip De Ronde, vice-consul, 233 Broadway (tel. Barclay 6030).

PERSIA: H. H. Topakyan, consul general, 40 West 57th St. (tel. Circle 1139).

PERU: Eduardo Higginson, consul general, 42 Broadway (tel. Broad 2115).

POLAND: Stefan Grotowski, consul general, 953 Third Ave. (tel. Plaza 9460).

PORTUGAL: Jorge de Silveira Duarte d'Almeida, consul general, 8 Bridge St. (tel. Broad 3530).

ROUMANIA: T. Tileston Wells, consul general; Jean U. Koree, vice-consul, 655 Lexington Ave. (tel. Plaza 3947).

RUSSIA: Michel Oustinow, consul general; Peter A. Routsky, acting consul; Baron O. A. Korff, vice-consul; Dimitri T. Florinsky, acting vice-consul, 55 Broadway (tel. Whitehall 368).

SALVADOR: Trinidad Romero, consul general, 42 Broadway (tel. Broad 4669).

SERBS, CROATS AND SLOVENES, KINGDOM OF THE: Vladimir Savitch, consul general; Vasilje Yovanovitch, consul, 443 West 22d St. (tel. Chelsea 4829).

SIAM: F. Warren Sumner, consul; John C. Harlan, vice-consul, 81 New St. (tel. Broad 317).

SPAIN: Alejandro Berea y Rodrigo, consul general; José Gimeno y Aznar, vice-consul; Manuel de Soler, hon. vice-consul, Pier 8, East River (tel. Bowling Green 6267).

SWEDEN: Olaf Herman Lamm, consul general; Johan Martin Kastengren, vice-consul, 119 Nassau St. (tel. Cortland 3061).

SWITZERLAND: Louis H. Junod, consul; Henri Escher, vice-consul, 104 Fifth Ave. (tel. Chelsea 7935).

TURKEY: See Spain.

URUGUAY: Mario L. Gil, consul general; César C. Guadencio and Henry H. Jennings, vice-consuls, 17 Battery Place (tel. Whitehall 1228).

VENEZUELA: Pedro Rafael Rincones, Sr., consul general; Nicolas Veloz, vice-consul, 80 South St. (tel. John 6142).

Consumers' League of the City of New York, The (org. 1890, incorp. 1898), 289 Fourth Ave., N.Y.C. (tel. Gramercy 2910). The object of the League is to lead consumers to recognize their responsibilities and their power, and in general to educate public opinion and so direct its force to ameliorate the conditions of employees, especially of women.

The Junior Board is an organization of working women, who, by their actual contact with factory and store conditions, aid the League in securing and enforcing the laws.

Officers: Miss Amey Aldrich, pres.; Mrs. Landreth H. King, treas.; Miss Helen Bryan, exec. secy.

Consumers' League. See also NATIONAL, and BROOKLYN, etc.

Cooper Union for the Advancement of Science and Art (incorp. 1857), Third and Fourth Aves., 7th and 8th Sts. (tel. Orchard 6600). An institution devoted to the instruction and improvement of the inhabitants of the United States in practical science and art. Maintains free day and evening classes in science and art for men and women at least sixteen years of age; a free library, reading room, lecture courses, and museum of decorative art. Supported by income from endowments and voluntary contributions.

Last year's receipts, $224,379.10, expenditures, $219,773.57, permanent fund, $4,319,958.70.

Officers: R. Fulton Cutting, pres.; Chas. R. Richards, director; Peter Cooper Bryce, secy.; E. L. Rehm, asst. secy., to whom apply from 9 A. M. to 5 P. M.

Co-operative Committee for the Housing of Jewish Girls and Women. See YOUNG WOMEN'S HEBREW ASSOCIATION.

Co-operative League of America (est. 1916), 2 West 13th St., N.Y.C. (tel. Chelsea 9478). J. P. Warbasse, pres.; M. W. Cheel, treas.; A. Sonnichsen, secy.; A. D. Warbasse, educational secy.

Co-operative Social Settlement Society of the City of New York, The (incorp. 1902). To promote the best interests of the neighborhood and through concrete experience the best interests of the city, to attempt to meet the need of groups and individuals; and to train youth for self-government. Maintains:

GREENWICH HOUSE, 27 Barrow St. (tel. Spring 9833). A community center maintaining the following activities:

Social and Recreational Department, Miss Marion E. Porter in charge. Social Clubs, gymnasium, entertainments, classes for children and adults, country outings, boys camp, working girls vacation house, summer home for mothers and babies.

Henry Street Settlement Nurses Headquarters for Greenwich District.

Maternity Center Association for Greenwich District.

Greenwich House Health Center, Mrs. Wortham James, chrm.

Neighborhood Art School, Victor Salvatore, chrm.

Greenwich House Music School, Mrs. W. L. McFarland, chrm.; Miss Frances Brundage, secy.

Personal Service Bureau.

Nursery School.

Officers: Herbert Parsons, pres.; Mrs. Harry Payne Whitney, vice-pres.; Bernard E. Pollak, treas., 27 Barrow St.; Walter G. Merritt, secy.; Mrs. Mary K. Simkhovitch, director; Mrs. Mabel F. Spinney, associate director.

Cornell University Medical College (org. 1898), First Ave., 27th and 28th Sts. Maintains an OUT-PATIENT DEPARTMENT in the College Building. Furnishes medical and surgical aid and medicine free to the sick poor. Open from 10 A. M. to 3.30 P. M. Departments of Medicine, Surgery, Orthopedics,

Gynecology, Neurology, Psychiatry, Dermatology, Urology, Otology, Ophthalmology, Laryngology, Rhinology, and Radiology.

Corner House, The, for working boys (est. 1915), 21 Charles St., N.Y.C. (tel. Chelsea 6224). Affiliated with the Federation for Support of Jewish Philanthropic Societies. For the benefit of graduates from the Hebrew Orphan Asylum of New York who have no immediate families to go to on discharge. There are a few beds for boys of other institutions. Ages 15 to 20. Capacity 20. Rates $6.00 per week. The boys are assisted in procuring employment; are taught the value of thrift; amusements and outings are organized; religious service is held on Friday nights.

Officers: De Witt P. Rosenheim, pres.; Alfred G. Bernheimer, vice-pres.; Harry M. Lewy, house chrm.; Milton J. Levy, treas.; Charles H. Meyer, secy.; John D. Beller, supt.

Coroners' Offices. See MEDICAL EXAMINERS, CITY OF NEW YORK.

Corporation for the Relief of Widows and Children of Clergymen of the Protestant Episcopal Church in the State of New York, The (incorp. 1769). For the purposes named in title. Benefits are for families of contributors only. Annual contribution from clergymen to secure annuities to widows and minor children, $8.00. Assets (Sept. 1, 1920), $434,564.14. Payments during year previous, $15,165.17 to 100 annuitants, representing seventy-four families. All payments made out of income.

Rev. E. Clowes Chorley, D.D., secy., Garrison-on-Hudson; William Harison, treas., 43 Cedar St.

Correction, Department of, City of New York (est. Chap. 912, Laws of 1895). Office: Room 2400, Municipal Bldg., New York, has general supervision over the following institutions:

DISTRICT PRISONS (Peter A. Mallon, warden), Office Fifth District Prison.

Second District Prison (Jefferson Market), 10th St. and Sixth Ave., Manhattan. Also serves the Ninth District, which is the Night Court for Women.

Third District Prison (Essex Market), 1st St. and Second Ave., Manhattan.

Fourth District Prison (Yorkville), 153 East 57th St., Manhattan. Also serves the Tenth District, which is the Night Court for Men, and the Eleventh District, which is the Domestic Relations Court for Manhattan.

Fifth District Prison (Harlem), 121st St. and Sylvan Pl., Manhattan.

Sixth District Prison (Morrisania), 162d St. and Brook Ave., The Bronx.

Seventh District Prison (West Side), 317 West 53d St., Manhattan.

Eighth District Prison, 1014 East 181st St., The Bronx.

Twelfth District Prison, 1130 St. Nicholas Ave., Manhattan.

Traffic Detention, 301 Mott St. Serves the Traffic Court.

House of Detention for Male Witnesses, 49 Lafayette St., Manhattan.

CITY PRISONS

City Prison, Manhattan (Tombs), 101 Center St., receives persons held on Grand Jury Indictments or for trial by Special Sessions, General Sessions, Supreme and Federal Courts; also serves Magistrates' Courts of the First District. It also serves for the confinement of misdemeanants on short sentences.

City Prison, Brooklyn, 149 Raymond St., receives persons held on indictment or for trial by the Special Sessions, County, Supreme, and Federal Courts. It also serves Magistrates' Courts of

Brooklyn. Persons convicted of misdemeanors on short sentences are also received at this institution.

City Prisons, Queens, Court Sq. and Jackson Ave., Long Island City.

Serves Magistrates' Courts of Queens and receives persons held for trial by Special Sessions, County, Supreme, and Federal Courts. Since April, 1914, all women committed to the Penitentiary serve sentences here.

Workhouse, Blackwell's Island for the reception and employment of prisoners sentenced for definite and indeterminate periods by the Special Sessions and Magistrates' Courts.

The Municipal Farm, Riker's Island, for the reception and employment of excess Workhouse men prisoners, also for self-committed drug cases.

New York County Penitentiary and Reception and Classification Division, Blackwell's Island, for the reception, classification, and employment of prisoners convicted of specified offenses, from the Magistrates' Courts, and prisoners convicted of felonies and misdemeanors from the Special Sessions, General Sessions, County and Supreme Courts. Sentences are for indeterminate periods.

The Reformatory Prison, Hart's Island, for the reception and employment of Penitentiary male prisoners and excess Workhouse prisoners.

New York City Reformatory, New Hampton Farms, Orange County, N.Y., for the reception and employment of male first offenders between the ages of sixteen and thirty, on misdemeanor sentences. The sentences are for an indeterminate period, with a maximum of three years. Inmates may be paroled by, and placed under the supervision of, the Parole Commission.

PAROLE COMMISSION, 25th floor, Municipal Bldg. (tel. Worth 2254).

Council of Jewish Women, The National (est. 1893, incorp. 1906). Purpose: To bring about a union of Jewish women for conference and work; to further united efforts in behalf of Judaism and in the work of social betterment through religion, philanthropy, and education. Its work is done through National Committees on Religion, Religious Schools, Philanthropy, Blind, Deaf, Education, Sex-Hygiene, Purity of the Press, Peace, Legislative, Civic and Communal Affairs, Juniors, and

DEPARTMENT OF IMMIGRANT AID, 146 Henry St., N.Y.C. The special work of this department is the guidance, safeguarding, and Americanization of immigrant girls.

The Program of Work of the Council is issued triennially. Local work is done through its various sections in 144 cities in 36 states and Canada. Supported by dues and contributions.

Officers: Mrs. Nathaniel E. Harris, pres., 114 South Ave., Bradford, Pa.; Miss Rose Brenner, 1st vice-pres., 252 Carroll St., Brooklyn, N. Y.; Mrs. Israel Cowen, 2d vice-pres., 437 East 48th St., Chicago, Ill.; Miss Grace Goldstein, rec. secy., 2409 North Pearl St., Dallas, Tex.; Mrs. Leon Stern, treas., 669 Oak St., Terre Haute, Ind.; Mrs. Leo H. Herz, acting exec. secy., 45 Sheldon Terrace, New Haven, Conn.

Council of Jewish Women, The New York Section of the (org. 1894, incorp. 1909). Secretary's address, 59 West 92d St. Down Town office: 74 St. Marks Pl. To bring about union of Jewish women in work and conference; social betterment, through religion, philanthropy, and education. It works exclusively with and for girls. Supported by dues and voluntary contributions.

Officers: Mrs. A. Kohut, hon. pres.,

Mrs. William D. Sporborg, pres., Port Chester, N. Y.; Mrs. Simon Baruch, Mrs. Julius Beer, Mrs. Isabella Freedman, Mrs. Nathan Glauber, Mrs. Daniel Guggenheim, Mrs. Frederick Nathan, Mrs. Cyrus Sulzberger, Mrs. Oscar Straus, Mrs. Jacob H. Schiff, Mrs. Henry Zuckerman, hon. vice-prests.; Mrs. May V. Fisher, 1st vice-pres.; Mrs. Irving Lehman, 2nd vice-pres.; Mrs. William Singer, Mrs. Robert Weil, Mrs. N. Taylor Phillips, vice-prests.; Mrs. Emil Klein, treas., 974 St. Nicholas Ave.; Miss Sara X. Schottenfels, secy., 59 West 92d St.; Mrs. Samuel H. Bijur, rec. secy.; Mrs. Ira Leo Bamberger, auditor.

ACTIVITIES

A teacher of religion at the Children's Hospital, Randall's Island, and all penal institutions which have amongst their inmates Jewish girls and women.

Co-operates with all organizations doing work for the blind and the deaf.

Maintains an office at 74 St. Mark's Pl. for the proper conduct of Americanization and immigrant aid work. Assists and advises girls and women upon arrival in regard to employment, learning, English, etc. Has five experienced workers for this work with a corps of volunteers.

Co-operates with a number of organizations taking charge of paroled girls.

418 East 50th St. A shelter for Jewish Girls who may be in danger of becoming delinquents.

Council of Jewish Women, Brooklyn Section. Hebrew Educational Bldg., Hopkinson and Sutter Aves., Brooklyn (tel. Glenmore 5724). Aid for female immigrants, probation work in connection with the Children's Court and correctional institutions, visitors for blind and to state institutions. Maintains housekeeping centers and a Council Home for Jewish girls.

Fanny Schulman, supervisor.

County Home for Convalescent Babies (incorp. 1895), Sea Cliff, L. I. (tel. Glen Cove 662). A home for convalescent children under seven years of age. The home contains fifty beds and is kept open from April until November. Children received from all New York and Brooklyn Hospitals.

Officers: Mrs. William D. Guthrie, pres., Locust Valley, L. I.; Mrs. Charles Steele, treas., Westbury, L. I.; Mrs. W. F. Sheehan, secy., Manhasset, L. I.; Miss L. F. G. Ames, R.N., supt.

Courts. See list in SUBJECT INDEX.

Covenant, Church of the (Presby.), 310 East 42d St. (tel. Murray Hill 4686). Maintains evening classes in English for foreigners, five nights a week; also, clubs for boys, girls, and women; summer school. See also in the PRESBYTERIAN CHURCH LIST.

Craig Colony (est. 1894; Chap. 363), Sonyea, Livingston Co., N. Y. A state institution the object of which is to secure the humane, curative, scientific, and economical care and treatment of epileptics, exclusive of insane epileptics. It is modelled after the Colony for Epileptics in Bielefield, Westphalia. Epileptics of all ages who are residents of the state are received. Capacity, 1,400.

Application for admission should be made to the Superintendent of the Poor, or the Commissioner of Charities of the county or city in which the patient resides.

Crawford Shops. See ASSOCIATION FOR THE IMPROVEMENT OF THE CONDITION OF THE POOR.

Crippled Children's East Side Free School, The, 157 Henry St. (tel. Orchard 6474). To provide the crippled children of the lower East Side with facilities for securing an education and learning a trade, so that they may become self-supporting. Academic instruction and school material furnished by Board of Education. Workrooms maintained where older cripples fill orders for all kinds of needlework and hand stitching. Playground on roof of building, to which pupils go after school hours.

MEDICAL AND SURGICAL TREATMENT given at the school. Nourishment, careful supervision of physical needs, and transportation provided.

SOCIAL CLUB, maintained by a committee of ladies for members of the workroom.

BATHS in Infirmary furnish opportunity for bathing twice a week under supervision of trained nurses. Applications for admission received at the school.

COUNTY HOME at Oakhurst, N. J., accommodating 130, where children may remain from three to ten weeks in summer.

Officers: Mrs. Arthur Lehman, pres., 31 West 56th St.; Mrs. Gustav Kaufman, treas., 251 West 95th St.; Mrs. Harry Goldsmith, secy., 333 West 76th St.

Cumberland Street Hospital. See PUBLIC WELFARE DEPARTMENT, CITY OF NEW YORK.

Custodial Asylum. See PUBLIC WELFARE DEPARTMENT, CITY OF NEW YORK.

D

Daily Vacation Bible School Association of New York, Inc., 88 Bible House, N.Y.C. To promote church and college ministry to children during the summer in Daily Vacation Bible Schools, lasting six weeks.

Robert W. Anthony, pres.; Walter W. Howlett, Metropolitan Director.

Daisy Fields Home and Hospital for Crippled Children, The (opened 1893, incorp. 1894), Central Ave., Englewood, N. J. (tel. Englewood 17). For the care and cure of crippled white children, admitted between the ages of four to ten years. Only curable cases taken. Capacity, twenty. No limitations as to sex, nationality, or sect. Supported by voluntary contributions. When possible, a very small sum for board is paid. Application for admission must be made to the President.

Officers: Mrs. Lewis D. Mowry, pres.; Mrs. James H. Coe, vice-pres.; Fred S. Bennett, 149 Dwight Pl., treas.; Mrs. G. L. Miller, secy., Brayton St., Englewood; Dr. Fred Albee, Post Graduate Hospital, N.Y.C., surgeon-in-charge; Mary E. Bennett, R.N., supt.

Danish Aid Society. See DANISH WOMEN'S CIVIC LEAGUE.

***Danish Home for the Aged,** 1051 41st St., Brooklyn. For Danes over sixty-five years of age having been residents of New York and vicinity for ten years previous.

Danish Mission Home (est. 1896), 130 Prospect Ave., Brooklyn (tel. South 486). For mission work among Danish people and chiefly for the protection of young girls. Supported by the Danish Lutheran Church (q. v. in the Church List), and by board of inmates.

Wm. Hellenberg, manager.

Danish Women's Civic League and Aid Society, 193 Ninth St., Brooklyn, N. Y. (tel. 4631 W. South). Mrs. J. de Neergaard, pres., 9447 Ridge Blvd.; Mrs. S. Reimann, treas., 118 72nd St., Brooklyn; Mrs. F. Rambush, secy., 50 Morningside Ave., N.Y.C.

Darrach Home for Crippled Children (incorp. 1903), 118 West 104th St.

* *Current information not received.*

A home for the care of crippled children; to help and, if possible, make them self-supporting. Non-sectarian. Accommodates about eighteen. Supported by voluntary contributions.

Elizabeth G. Baner, secy.

Daughter of Israel Day Nursery, 220 East 5th St., N.Y.C. For the care of children of Jewish working mothers.

Officers: Mrs. Mollie Unger, pres.; Paul Rothman, secy.; Elias D. Saphirstein, supt.

Daughters of Israel, Harlem Home of the (est. 1907, incorp. 1914), 32 East 119th St. (tel. Harlem 3986). For poor Hebrews over sixty-five years of age. Present number accommodated, fifty-four.

Daughters of Jacob, Home of the (incorp. 1897), 167th St. Findlay and Tellar Aves., Bronx. For poor Hebrews of both sexes over sixty years of age. Accommodates 500.

Officers: Mrs. A. J. Dworsky, pres., 53 East 93rd St.; Mrs. H. Sklamberg, treas., 1809 Seventh Ave.; Dr. Wm. G. Wolfert, secy., 973 Simpson St.; Albert Kruger, supt.

Daughters of the King, The (org. 1885), 84 Bible House, N.Y.C. (tel. Stuyvesant 7054). An organization of the Protestant Episcopal Church for women. Publishes "The Royal Cross."

Mrs. A. Denmead, Baltimore, Md., pres.; Mrs. Charles H. Arndt, treas., Germantown, Philadelphia, Pa.; Miss Marietta E. Atwood, national secy.

Deaf-Mutes' Union League (org. 1886, incorp. 1901), 143 West 125th St. Social, recreative and intellectual advancement of male deaf-mutes twenty-one years of age or over. No limitations as to nationality or sect.

Officers: Samuel Frankenheim, pres.; Emil Basch, treas.; Anthony Capelli, secy.

Demilt Dispensary. See CLINIC FOR FUNCTIONAL RE-EDUCATION, etc.

Department of Correction. See CORRECTION, DEPARTMENT OF.

Department of Health. See HEALTH, DEPARTMENT OF.

Department of Parks. See PARKS, DEPARTMENT OF.

Department of Public Charities. See PUBLIC WELFARE DEPARTMENT, CITY OF NEW YORK.

Deportation, Bureau of. See STATE HOSPITAL COMMISSION.

Devin Clare Home for Working Girls. See INSTITUTION OF MERCY.

De Witt Memorial Church. See NEW YORK CITY MISSION SOCIETY.

Diet Kitchen Association. See NEW YORK DIET KITCHEN ASSOCIATION.

Dietz Memorial Italian Baptist Church. See FIRST ITALIAN BAPTIST CHURCH.

Diphtheria Hospital. See LOUISA MINTURN HOSPITAL.

Dispensary and Hospital for Joint Diseases (incorp. 1905). 1913-29 Madison Ave., N.Y.C. (Harlem 6022-6023-3733-2935). For the treatment of all persons, regardless of age, race, creed, or color, suffering with acute and chronic joint diseases or any deformity, congenital or acquired. Free beds to the poor, no charge for splints or apparatus to the indigent. Capacity of 100 beds.

The Dispensary is situated at 41-43 East 123d St., and treats from 500 to 700 patients daily. Twenty-five per cent of these are cases of Infantile Paralysis, who receive massage and electric treatment with muscle education before a mirror. 120 people are required to give treatments in this clinic, including physicians, nurses, masseurs and physical culture teachers.

District Attorneys and Offices, NEW YORK COUNTY, Criminal Courts Bldg. (tel. 2304 Franklin).

KINGS COUNTY, 66 Court St., Brooklyn (tel. 2954 Main).

BRONX COUNTY, Tremont and Arthur Aves. (tel. 1100 Tremont).

QUEENS COUNTY, County Court House, Long Island City (tel. 3871 Hunters Point).

RICHMOND COUNTY, Borough Hall, St. George, S. I. (tel. 50 Tompkinsville).

Divine Paternity, The Church of the (THE FOURTH UNIVERSALIST SOCIETY IN THE CITY OF NEW YORK) (incorp. 1838), Central Park West and 76th St. Joseph Fort Newton, D.D., Pastor. Maintains:

PRESCOTT MEMORIAL, 247 East 53d St., for general club work, gymnasium, classes in household economics.

FRESH-AIR FUND, 4 West 76th St., supports a camp for children. See also under UNIVERSALIST CHURCHES in the Church List.

Divine Providence Home for Old French Ladies. See SISTERS OF DIVINE PROVIDENCE.

Dobbs House. See MASTERS SCHOOL DAY NURSERY.

Docks, Department of, City of New York. Office: Pier A, North River.

Murray Hulbert, commissioner; L. Hitch Harrison, supt. of docks.

Doe Ye Nexte Thynge Society (incorp. 1892). Settlement House, 18 Leroy St., N.Y.C. (tel. Spring 6043). To bring its members into close relationship with the people of the neighborhood. It maintains a coal club, social clubs, boys' and girls' clubs for afternoons and evenings, mothers' meetings, current topics, lectures and talks, etc. Supported by members' dues, subscriptions, proceeds from entertainments, and voluntary contributions.

Officers: Mrs. Ansel Phelps, pres., 125 East 61st St.; Miss Annette Boardman, vice-pres.; Mrs. D. McRae Livingston, treas., 159 East 36th St.; Miss E. L. Norrie, rec. secy., 145 East 35th St.; Mrs. Lowell Lincoln, cor. secy., 166 East 64th St.; Miss Maree R. Blair, resident head worker.

Domestic and Foreign Missionary Society of the Protestant Episcopal Church in the United States of America. See PRESIDING BISHOP AND COUNCIL OF THE PROTESTANT EPISCOPAL CHURCH.

Domestic Relations Courts. See FAMILY COURT OFFICES; also PROBATION BUREAU.

Dominican Convent of Our Lady of the Rosary (incorp. 1880), 329 East 63d St., N.Y.C. For religious charitable, educational, and reformatory purposes.

ST. AGNES' CONVENT, Sparkill, N. Y., is a branch of the above. Cares for and trains destitute children from two to sixteen years of age, committed by Department of Public Welfare and by Magistrates. Capacity, 1,100. Apply to the Superioress.

Dominican Home for Working Girls (Retreat for Ladies and for Homeless Girls) (incorp. 1884), 207 East 71st St., N. Y. Under the direction of the Dominican Sisters. Accommodations for 75. Non-sectarian. Supported by donations and revenues.

Dominican Sisters of the Sick Poor (incorp. 1904), 140 West 61st St. (tel. Columbus 3963). The Sisters visit the sick poor in their homes, nurse and, when necessary, supply medicine, food, and clothing. without remuneration. Their work has no limit as to creed, color. Supported by voluntary contributions.

Door of Hope, The (org. 1890, incorp. 1892). Office: 122 West 14th St. A work founded by Mrs. E. M. Whittemore, and conducted by The Salvation Army for destitute and fallen girls.

Staff Capt. Mrs. E. M. Whittemore, pres. and treas., 773 St. Nicholas Ave., N.Y.C.

Down Town Day Nursery (est. 1903, incorp. 1906), 120-122 Cedar St., N.Y.C. To care for children between three weeks and six years of age of working mothers. Supported by voluntary contributions.

Du Bois Fund (org. 1887). To assist repectable, poor sick persons to obtain the services of trained nurses. The attention of physicians is called to this society as a valuable aid in their work among the poor. Mrs. Talbot Olyphant, treas., 911 Park Ave. (tel. Rhinelander 5728).

Dyker Heights Home for Blind Babies. See INTERNATIONAL SUNSHINE BRANCH FOR BLIND BABIES.

E

East Harlem Presbyterian Church 233 East 116th St. (English, Hungarian, Italian, Swedish and Spanish). Affiliated with the AMERICAN PARISH (q. v.).

East Side Clinic for Children (licensed 1906), 325 East 84th St., N.Y.C. Open daily from 1.30 to 4 P. M.

East Side House Settlement (incorp. 1891), 540 East 76th St., N.Y.C. (tel. Rhinelander 2454). For the people of the neighborhood. Maintains clubs and classes for boys and girls, men and women; music school, literary, social and industrial clubs, lectures, concerts, plays, dancing, etc.; reading room, gymnasium, baths, etc.

WINIFRED WHEELER, a day nursery and a training class for day nursery attendants.

The work of the Settlement is always open for inspection. Visitors are very welcome.

Officers: R. Stuyvesant Pierrepont, pres., Far Hills, N. J.; C. J. Schmidlapp, treas., 57 Broadway; Ansel Phelps, secy., 125 East 61st St.; Miss M. deG. Trenholm, head worker.

East Side Parish. See SETTLEMENT AND CHURCH OF ALL NATIONS.

Eastern District Branch, Y. M. C. A. See BROOKLYN YOUNG MEN'S CHRISTIAN ASSOCIATION.

Eastern Long Island Hospital (incorp. 1905), Greenport, Suffolk Co., Long Island, N. Y. (tel. Greenport 104). For the care, medical and surgical attendance of the indigent sick poor and those of limited means. Capacity, twenty-five beds. Supported by voluntary contributions.

Eastern New York Reformatory, Napanoch, Ulster Co., N. Y. (est., Chap. 684, 1906). To care for the surplus population of the State Reformatory (q. v.) at Elmira. Capacity, 496.

Frank L. Christian, supt.

Economic Club of New York, The Town Hall, 113-123 West 43rd St., N.Y.C. (tel. Bryant 2636). To aid in the creation and expression of an enlightened public opinion on the important economic and social questions of the day.

Officers: George W. Wickersham, pres.; William Church Osborn, Abram I. Elkus, vice-presidents; Joseph French Johnson, treas.; Robert Eskine Ely, secy.

Edgewater Creche, The (org. 1886, incorp. 1889), Broad Ave., Englewood, N. J. (tel. Englewood 775). New York City office: United Charities Bldg., 105 East 22d St.

THE SUMMER WORK consists of day outings for mothers and little children. (Temporarily discontinued.)

The ALL YEAR WORK provides for the accommodation of twenty children under three years of age who require convalescent care. Trained nurses and helpers are in attendance, and work under medical supervision.

The Creche occupies six and one-quarter acres of ground rising to an elevation of 260 feet above sea level. It is reached via Fort Lee ferry, foot of West 130th St.; connect with Englewood cars, to Van Nostrand and Broad Aves. The Gate House is about 100 feet from the corner.

Officers: Mrs. Bend, hon. pres., 563 Park Ave., N.Y.C.; Mrs. Irwin H. Cornell, pres., 201 West 55th St., N.Y.C.; Mrs. C. Tiffany Richardson, treas., 414 Madison Ave., N.Y.C.; Miss Lucy C. Kellogg, secy., Englewood.

Edith Summer Home. See BELLEVUE HOSPITAL.

Education, Board of, 500 Park Ave., southwest corner 59th St., N.Y.C. (tel. Plaza 5580). This Board has supervision over all the Public Schools of the City of New York and such Corporate Schools as participate in the school moneys of the state.

A. Emerson Palmer, secy.

THE COMPULSORY EDUCATION LAW of New York (Chap. 671, Laws of 1894, as amended in 1895, 1896 and 1903) provides as follows:

All children between seven and sixteen years of age in proper physical and mental condition are required to attend upon instructions, as in said law specifically stated, namely:

All children between seven and fourteen years of age must attend school during the entire period the school is in session.

All children between fourteen and sixteen years of age must attend when not lawfully employed. Between fourteen and eighteen years of age employed boys and girls not graduates of a four year high school course must attend a part time or continuation school as follows:

1. Beginning September 1920, employed boys and girls between 15 and 17 years of age, not graduates of elementary schools.

2. Beginning September 1921, employed boys and girls between 17 and 18 years of age not graduates of elementary school, in addition to those between 15 and 17 years of age included in group 1.

3. Beginning September 1922, employed boys and girls between 14 and 15 years of age, graduates of elementary schools in addition to those between 15 and 18 years of age, not graduates of elementary schools included in groups 1 and 2.

4. Beginning September 1923, employed boys and girls, graduates of elementary schools between 15 and 16 years of age, in addition to all employed boys and girls included in groups 1, 2, and 3.

5. Beginning September 1924, employed boys and girls, graduates of elementary schools 16 to 18 years of age in addition to all included under groups 1 to 4.

An accurate record of the attendance of all children between seven and sixteen years of age must be kept by the teacher of every school, showing each day by the year, month, day of the month, and day of the week, of such attendance and the number of hours in each day thereof.

All persons in parental relation to such children are required to cause such children to attend upon instruction as specifically stated in the law, and neglect to do so is a misdemeanor, punishable by fine, or fine and imprisonment.

BUREAU OF ATTENDANCE, 154 East 68th St. The compulsory education law is enforced by the Bureau of Attendance, created by chapter 479-480 of the laws of 1914.

THE TRUANT SCHOOLS to which pupils may be committed by the Board are:

Manhattan Truant School, 215 East 21st St.

Brooklyn Truant School, Jamaica Ave. and Enfield St.

New York Parental School, Jamaica Rd., Flushing.

SPECIAL CLASSES have been provided by the Board for children who are anaemic and predisposed to tuberculosis, for the blind, the deaf, for the crippled and those having speech defects.

CLINIC FOR SPEECH DEFECTS at the College of the City of New York, 138th St. and Amsterdam Ave.

VISITING TEACHERS are employed to interest parents in school work and seek their co-operation.

THE VOCATIONAL OR TRADE SCHOOLS are:

Vocational Schools for Boys, 138th and 139th Sts., west of Fifth Ave.

Manhattan Trade School for Girls, Lexington Ave. and 22d St.

Trade School for the Deaf, P. S. 47-225 East 23rd St.

Murray Hill Vocational School, P. S. 49-37th and 38th Sts., west of Second Ave.

Brooklyn Trade School for Boys, Carey Bldg., Jay and Nassau Sts.

For admission to any of the Trade Schools, apply to the Principal in charge.

Education, State Department of. See STATE DEPARTMENT OF EDUCATION.

Educational Alliance, The (incorp. 1889, re-org. 1893), East Broadway and Jefferson St. (tel. Orchard 1971). Maintains an institution for the purpose of providing opportunities for the thousands of immigrants to America, in order to help them become adapted to the new conditions and readily assimilate American ideas and ideals. The work carried on is divided into the following divisions:

EDUCATIONAL: Lectures in English and Yiddish on American history and civics, naturalization classes. Citizenship "Quiz" classes; art classes; Civil Service classes, reading room, domestic art school, domestic science school, manual training, day and evening classes for adult immigrants, physical culture school, telegraphy class, Red Cross work, Food Conservation classes.

SOCIAL: Auditorium entertainments (concerts, lectures, dramatic performances, moving pictures, etc.); boys' and girls' clubs, scout work; mother's club, social rooms for boys, girls, men, and women; roof garden, boys' summer camp, boys' week-end camp; girls' summer home, parents' meetings, summer outings, inter-settlement activities, indoor playground for girls, indoor and outdoor playgrounds, free baths, etc.

RELIGIOUS: People's Synagogue, Special Services on Holy Days, school of Religious Work, Post Graduate classes, Sabbath morning and afternoon services, lectures on moral topics. Young People's Synagogue.

SOCIAL SERVICE: Home and School Visitor; Desertion Bureau, Legal Aid Bureau, Information Bureau, East Side Day Nursery.

Officers: Samuel Greenbaum, pres., 27 Madison Ave.; Lee Kohns, 1st vice-pres., 42 Warren St.; Benjamin Tuska, 2nd vice-pres., 165 Broadway; Jacques Weinberger, treas., 24 Broad St.; Bernard M. L. Ernst, secy., 31 Liberty St.; Dr. Henry Fleischman, administrator.

Educational Clinic, College of the City of New York. St. Nicholas Terrace and 139th St. Its purpose is to render service to children in the solution of their educational, vocational, and social problems.

Recommendations are made after careful study of the child's social history in conjunction with the results of the psychological, neurological and physical examinations given at the Clinic.

Samuel B. Heckman, Ph.D., director.

Edward Whitney House, 88th St., St. Nicholas Ave., N.Y.C. See ALL SOULS P. E. CHURCH.

Eighth Avenue Mission, The (incorp. 1899), 290 Eighth Ave. (tel. Chelsea 6716). Ministers to the needs of the neighborhood; maintains a trained nurse and friendly visitors who relieve distress, visit the sick in their homes, in prisons and hospitals. Reading room for enlisted men. Supported by voluntary contributions. For religious services see under MISCELLANEOUS CHURCHES AND MISSIONS in the Church List.

George C. Sleeth, pres., 457 Washington Ave., Belleville, N. J.; Frank Mann, vice-pres., 105 East 22d St.; S. Wray, treas., 290 Eighth Ave.; Henry T. Schluenzer, secy., 10 West 64th St.

Men's Bible Class Sunday 9.30 A. M. Bible Study Wednesday, 9 P. M.

Elections, Board of, City of New York. General office and

MANHATTAN BOROUGH OFFICE, 18th floor, Municipal Bldg. (tel. 1307 Worth). Commissioner John R. Voorhis, pres.; Charles E. Heydt, secy.; James Kane and Jacob A. Livingston, commissioners; S. Howard Cohen, chief clerk.

BRONX BOROUGH OFFICE, 442 East 149th St. (tel. 336 Melrose).

BROOKLYN BOROUGH OFFICE, 26 Court St. (tel. 1932 Main).

QUEENS BOROUGH OFFICE, 64 Jackson Ave., Long Island City (tel. 3375 Hunters Point).

RICHMOND BOROUGH OFFICE, Borough Hall, New Brighton, S. I. (tel. 1000 Tompkinsville).

Elizabeth Home for Girls. See CHILDREN'S AID SOCIETY.

Elmendorf Chapel. See HARLEM REFORMED CHURCH.

Elmhurst Baptist Church, Whitney Ave. and Judge St., Elmhurst, N. Y. Maintains a fresh-air farm at Commack, L. I. See also under BAPTIST CHURCHES in the Church List.

Elsinor Camp. See ST. PETER'S LUTHERAN CHURCH, this List.

Emanu-El Brotherhood, The (incorp. 1907), 309–311 East 6th St., N.Y.C. (tel. Orchard 2148). To provide a religious, educational and social center for the Jewish people of the East Side. Its activities include religious services, reading room, clubs and classes, entertainments, lectures, game rooms, kindergarten, etc.

Officers: Rev. Dr. Joseph Silverman, pres., 45 East 75th St.; E. G. Gerstle, 1st vice-pres.; M. H. Winkler, 2d vice-pres.; B. H. Stern, secy., 149 Broadway; Arthur S. Zinn, treas., 210 Eleventh Ave.; Bernhart A. Friedman, supt.

Emanuel Sisterhood of Personal Service, 318–320 East 82d St., N.Y.C. (tel. Lenox 8647). Maintains a kindergarten, day nursery, meals for public school children, a clinic for anaemic children, a visiting nursing station, a summer home for children and boys'

and girls' camps, an employment bureau, a workroom school which sews linen-room supplies for hospitals and teaches unskilled dependent women a trade, a music school, industrial classes, a religious school, cooking classes, a library, citizenship school, besides the various educational and recreational activities ordinarily supplied by a Neighborhood House.

Officers: Mrs. Alexander Kohut, pres.; Mrs. Jacob H. Schiff, 1st vice-pres.; Mrs. Henry Meyers, 2d vice-pres.; Mrs. Daniel Guggenheim, treas.; Miss Carrie Wise, rec. secy.; Mrs. Joseph E. Hoffman, fin. secy.; Mrs. Leopold S. Bache, cor. secy.; Mrs. Celia L. Strakosch, head worker.

Emeline York-Tyndall, The, 58 East 102d St., N.Y.C. See PEOPLE'S TABERNACLE.

Emma L. Hardy Memorial Home for the Blind, Cornwall-on-Hudson, N. Y. See NEW YORK ASSOCIATION FOR THE BLIND.

Emmanuel House, 131 Steuben St. Brooklyn (tel. Prospect 3505). A community house providing athletics, gymnasium, game room, cooking and sewing classes, clubs, etc.

A. E. Parkhause, house secy.

See also EMMANUEL BAPTIST CHURCH in the Church List.

Employment Bureau for the Handicapped, 405 Lexington Ave., N.Y.C.R. 220 (tel. Vanderbilt 5240). Placement of men and women in industries including cardiac and arrested tuberculosis cases.

Officers: Mrs. John S. Sheppard, chrm.; Mrs. Wm. Greer, treas.; Mrs. William Woodward, secy.; Mrs. Ida M. Duggan, director.

Erlanger Home. See CHILDREN'S AID SOCIETY.

Estimate and Apportionment, Board of, City of New York, 13th floor, Municipal Bldg. (tel. 4560 Worth).

Ethical Culture Society. See SOCIETY FOR ETHICAL CULTURE.

Eunice Home. See CHAPEL HILL FRESH-AIR MISSION.

Eurana Schwab Home for Children. See NEW YORK FOUNDLING HOSPITAL.

Eva Home for Young Women. See LADIES CHRISTIAN UNION.

Evangelistic Committee of New York City (est. 1905), 541 Lexington Ave. (tel. Plaza 9515–16). Organized to carry the Gospel to the unevangelized American and foreign-speaking people through meetings and in tents, shops, halls, and on the streets. See also under EVANGELISM in the Church List.

Evening School. See EDUCATION, BOARD OF.

Exempt Firemen's Benevolent Fund of the City of New York, The Trustees of the (incorp. 1798), 10 Greenwich Ave., N.Y.C. (tel. Chelsea 1548). Assists sick and disabled exempt members of the old VOLUNTEER FIRE DEPARTMENT, of the City of New York, and their widows and orphans.

Officers: John Mulligan, pres. Board of Trustees, 341 West 28th St.; James Y. Watkins, treas., 20 Catharine St.; Augustus Collier, secy., 29 Glendenning Ave., Jersey City, N. J.

Eye Clinics. See HEALTH, DEPARTMENT OF, Children's Clinics.

F

Faith Home for Incurables (incorp. 1878), 546 Park Pl., Brooklyn (tel. Prospect 7687). A home for homeless incurable women. Application for admission can be made to the Advisory

Board at the Home the second Friday of each month, in the morning. Accommodates about fifty-six; no cancer or consumption cases admitted.

Faith Presbyterian Church, 359 West 48th St., N.Y.C. Rev. Ray Freeman Jenney, Pastor. Maintains a Neighborhood House at 349 West 48th St. Gymnasium, men's, boys' and girls' clubs. See also under PRESBYTERIAN CHURCHES in the Church List.

Family Court Offices, Manhattan, 151 East 57th St. (tel. Plaza 2302); Brooklyn, 402 Myrtle Ave. (tel. Prospect 2700). All cases of domestic difficulties coming to the Domestic Relations Courts are investigated and supervised from these offices.

Farm Colony, Castleton Corners, S. I. See PUBLIC WELFARE DEPARTMENT, CITY OF NEW YORK. See View Farms.

Farmingdale Preventorium, Farmingdale, N. J. See TUBERCULOSIS PREVENTORIUM FOR CHILDREN.

Farmingdale Trade School, Farmingdale, L. I. See SISTERS OF ST. DOMINIC, Nazareth Trade School.

Federal Board for Vocational Education, Division of Rehabilitation, 1901 D St., Washington, D. C. All disabled soldiers whether in or out of the hospitals, should address the district office of the Federal Board of the district in which they are located as follows:

District No. 1: Maine, Vermont, New Hampshire, Massachusetts, and Rhode Island. Office: 101 Milk St., Boston, Mass.

District No. 2: Connecticut, New York, and New Jersey. Office: 23 West 43rd St., New York, N. Y.

District No. 3: Pennsylvania and Delaware. Office: 140 North Broad St., Philadelphia, Pa.

District No. 4: District of Columbia, Maryland, Virginia, and West Virginia. Office: 450 Lexington Bldg., Baltimore, Md.

District No. 5: North Carolina, South Carolina, Georgia, Florida, and Tennessee. Office: 823 Forsythe Bldg., Atlanta, Ga.

District No. 6: Alabama, Mississippi, and Louisiana. Office: 412-432 Madison Blanche Annex, New Orleans, La.

District No. 7: Ohio, Indiana, and Kentucky. Office: Denton Bldg., Cincinnati, Ohio.

District No. 8: Michigan, Illinois and Wisconsin. Office: 14 East Congress St., Chicago, Ill.

District No. 9: Iowa, Nebraska, Kansas, and Missouri. Office: 6801 Delmar Ave., St. Louis, Mo.

District No. 10: Minnesota, North Dakota, South Dakota and Montana. Office: Room 600 Keith-Plaza Bldg., 1700 Hennepin Ave., Minneapolis, Minn.

District No. 11: Wyoming, Colorado, New Mexico, and Utah. Office: 400 Mercantile Bldg., Denver, Colo.

District No. 12: California, Nevada, and Arizona. Office: 544 Flood Bldg., San Francisco, Cal.

District No. 13: Idaho, Oregon, and Washington. Office: Arcade Bldg., Seattle, Wash.

District No. 14: Arkansas, Oklahoma, and Texas. Office: Dallas Club Bldg., Dallas, Tex.

Federal Children's Bureau, U. S. Department of Labor (est. by Act of Congress, April 9, 1912), Washington, D. C. Authorized to investigate and report upon all matters relating to children and child life among all classes of our people, and shall especially investigate questions of infant mortality, the birth rate, orphanage, juvenile courts, desertion, dangerous occupations, accidents, and diseases of children, employment and legislation affecting children in the several states and territories.

Miss Julia C. Lathrop, chief of Bureau.

Publications available free or at small cost upon application to the Bureau.

Federal Council of the Churches of Christ in America (org. 1908, incorp. 1915). National office: United Charities Bldg., 105 East 22d St., N. Y.C. (tel. Gramercy 3475).

Officers: Rev. Frank Mason North, pres.; Alfred R. Kimball, treas.; Rev. Charles S. Macfarland, gen. secy.; Rev. Samuel C. Cavert, associate secy.; Rev. James I. Vance, chrm. Executive Committee; Rev. Albert G. Lawson, chrm. Administrative Committee.

Washington Committee: 937 Woodward Bldg., Washington, D. C. Bishop William F. McDowell, chrm.; Rev. E. O. Watson, secy.; Chicago Office: 19 S. La Salle St., Rev. H. L. Willett, representative.

The Federal Council is constituted by thirty-one Protestant Evangelical denominations to express their common voice and unite them in co-operative activities. Its range of work is indicated by the following Commissions and Committees:

COMMISSION ON CHURCH AND SOCIAL SERVICE: Shelby M. Harrison, acting chrm.; Rev. Worth M. Tippy, exec. secy.; Rev. F. Ernest Johnson, research secy.

COMMISSION ON EVANGELISM: James M. Speers, chrm.; Rev. Charles L. Goodell, exec. secy.

COMMISSION ON INTERNATIONAL JUSTICE AND GOOD-WILL: President W. H. P. Faunce, chrm.; Rev. Henry A. Atkinson, secy.

COMMISSION ON CHRISTIAN EDUCATION: Dr. John H. Finley, chrm.; Rev. B. S. Winchester, acting secy.

COMMISSION ON TEMPERANCE: Hon. Carl E. Milliken, chrm.

COMMISSION ON CHURCH AND COUNTRY LIFE: Gifford Pinchot, chrm.; Rev. Edmund de S. Brunner, exec. secy.; Rev. Charles O. Gill, field secy.

COMMISSION ON INTERCHURCH FEDERATIONS: Fred B. Smith, chrm.; Rev. Roy B. Guild, exec. secy.

COMMISSION ON RELATIONS WITH THE ORIENT: Rev. William I. Haven, chrm.; Rev. Sidney L. Gulick, secy.

COMMISSION ON RELATIONS WITH FRANCE AND BELGIUM: Rev. Arthur J. Brown, chrm.

COMMISSION ON RELATIONS WITH RELIGIOUS BODIES IN EUROPE: Rev. Nehemiah Boynton, chrm.; William Sloane Coffin, chrm. Executive Committee.

EDITORIAL COUNCIL RELIGIOUS PRESS: Rev. E. C. Waring, chrm.; Rev. Jasper T. Moses, secy.

COMMITTEE ON FOREIGN MISSIONS: Rev. William I. Chamberlain, chrm.

COMMISSION ON HOME MISSIONS: Bishop John M. Moore, chrm.

COMMITTEE ON NEGRO CHURCHES: Bishop William P. Thirkield, chrm.

Federal Employment Service. See UNITED STATES EMPLOYMENT SERVICE.

Federated Boys' Clubs. See BOYS' CLUB FEDERATION.

Federation of Associations for Cripples (org. 1912), 311 Fourth Ave. (tel. Gramercy 1467). For the purpose of uniting all associations dealing with cripples into one central federation, in order to secure the best possible co-operation and efficiency in the work throughout Greater New York. Departments: Bureau of Information for Cripples, Home Visitors, Fresh Air Service, official organ "American Journal of Care for Cripples."

Officers: Douglas C. McMurtrie,

pres.; E. L. McLean, treas.; Elizabeth H. McCleery, exec. secy.

Federation of Bronx Jewish Charities (incorp. 1915), 1685 Topping Ave. (tel. Tremont 2821). Conducts a day and night nursery and temporary shelter. Supported by voluntary contributions.

Mrs. Emanuel Friendlich, pres.; Mrs. Bertha Freid, treas.; Mrs. Tillie Kuher, secy.

Federation for Child Study (org. 1897), 2 West 64th St. N.Y.C. (tel. Columbus 7770). For the purpose of helping parents make their parenthood more intelligent, more efficient and of the highest use to their children.

Officers: Mrs. Howard S. Gans, pres., 260 West 76th St.; Jesse W. Ehrich, treas.; Mrs. Jesse W. Ehrich, secy.

Federation of Churches. See New York Federation of Churches.

Federation Settlement, 236–240 East 105th St., N.Y.C. (tel. Harlem 7482). A community center for social, cultural and moral benefit. Maintains Mothers' club, literary, social, athletic clubs, classes in sewing, embroidery, basketry, knitting, carpentry, toymaking, cooking, gymnastics and dramatics; classes in social, interpretive and aesthetic dancing, kindergarten, story hour, game rooms and open air playground daily; Sunday School, Camp Fire Girls, Girl Scouts, Boy Scouts, Annex to P. S. 109 for evening classes in English and civics to foreigners. Classes in citizenship. Music and Art school, orchestra for juniors and seniors, circulating library and reading room. Headquarters of South Harlem Community Council. Medical and Dental Clinic. Health education, neighborhood visiting and Social Service Department.

The Settlement is the working medium between the people of the community and the various social, medical, cultural and educational agencies.

Mrs. Pauline Markowitz Ferris, headworker.

Federation for the Support of Jewish Philanthropic Societies (est. 1916, incorp. 1917), 114 Fifth Ave. (tel. Chelsea 453). A clearing house for contributions to all Jewish institutions in Manhattan and Bronx. Supported by subscription.

Officers: Felix M. Warburg, pres., 52 William St.; Arthur Lehman, vice-pres.; Mrs. Sidney C. Borg, 2nd vice-pres.; Judge Otto A. Rosalsky, 3rd vice-pres.; Col. H. A. Guinzburg, treas., 725 Broadway; Fred M. Stein, secy., 50 East 41st St.; Mrs. H. B. L. Goldstein, comptroller, 52 William St.; Solomon Lowenstein, executive director.

Federation of Welfare Agencies of Staten Island. See Staten Island Social Service.

Federation of Women's Clubs. See General Federation of Women's Clubs.

Fellowship House, Inc. (est. 1913), 1192 Lexington Ave., N.Y.C. (tel. Lenox 7167). Organized for continuation care of the children discharged from the Hebrew Sheltering Guardian Society, Pleasantville, N. Y. Making connections with homes, jobs, educational and recreational opportunities renewal of old and making of new social ties.

Jacob Kepecs, exec. secy.

Fellowship of Reconciliation, The, 118 East 28th St., N.Y.C. A group of persons who, believing that love is not only the basis of a true human society but the effective power for overcoming evil, find themselves in opposition to war and called, on the contrary, to practise love unswervingly in all relations of personal, social, industrial, national and international life. Information as to membership, methods, literature, etc. may be had from the Secretary.

Female Guardian Society. See AMERICAN FEMALE GUARDIAN SOCIETY.

Ferries to City Islands. See CITY ISLANDS.

Ferry Boats Used for Fresh-air Work:

Manhattan, foot of East 90th St., under the Department of Health.

Rutherford, foot of Broadway, Brooklyn, under the Department of Health.

Fifth Avenue Hospital, The, under construction. Organization headquarters, 294 Madison Ave., N.Y.C. (tel. Murray Hill 5700).

Officers: T. Frank Manville, pres.; Henderson M. Wolfe, secy. treas.; Wiley E. Woodbury, M.D., director.

Fifth Avenue Presbyterian Church, Fifth Ave. and 55th St. Rev. John Kelman, D.D., Minister; Rev. James Palmer, Ph.D., Associate. Maintains the:

JOHN HALL MEMORIAL CHAPEL and ASSOCIATION HOUSE, First Ave., 62d and 63d Sts. Office, 342–344 East 63d St.; Rev. Paul F. Landis, Minister; Rev. Joseph Giardina, Italian Minister; C. B. Thompson, Boys' supt.; Miss Evelyn DuBois, Girls' worker; Mrs. Agnes Phillips, Miss L. F. Martin, visitors; Miss Virginia Laguardia, Italian Missionary; Miss Maria Carpenter, visiting nurse.

The activities include clubs for men, women, boys, and girls, gymnasium, baths, bowling, pool, educational classes, sewing school. Penny Provident Fund, library, summer camp and outings, employment bureau, entertainments, and general relief. Also

SUNBEAM DAY NURSERY AND KINDERGARTEN, 1147 First Ave., for the care of children, two weeks to seven years of age, of poor working mothers unable to care for them during the day. Kindergarten instruction is given to the older children. A charge of eleven cents a day for each child is made.

Mrs. Chauncey Marshall, chrm.; Mrs. Carl Schoen, secy.; Mrs. Frank M. Humphrey, treas.; Miss M. A. Powell, matron.

SEASIDE HOME, Branchport, N. J., for the children and mothers of the Mission Sunday Schools. Capacity, 100; season, 500, no charges.

Hugh Getty, chrm.; Edwin J. Gillies, treas.; Mrs. James H. Schmelzel, chrm. Ladies' Committee.

See also under PRESBYTERIAN CHURCHES in the Church List.

Finance, Department of, City of New York. Comptroller's office: 5th floor, Municipal Bldg. (tel. 1200 Worth); Deputy Comptroller, 7th floor.

Finch School Neighborhood Association (est. 1909), 336 East 69th St., N. Y. C. (tel. Rhinelander 0433). For the purpose of neighborhood betterment. The work includes a day nursery, kindergarten, public school children's lunch, mothers' club, girls' club, music school, needlecraft guild, mothers' mutual benefit society, etc. Unlimited as to age, sex, race, etc.

Finnish Women's Co-operative Home, 241 Lenox Ave. (tel. Morningside 813). The object of this co-operative association is to better the economical and educational condition of the women by means of useful and edifying literature, and to furnish board and room at moderate cost.

Fire Department, City of New York, 11th floor, Municipal Bldg. (tel. Worth 4100). Brooklyn, 365 Jay St. (tel. Main 7600). Thomas J. Drennan, commissioner.

RELIEF FUND, Headquarters, P. J. Quigley, secy.

Firemen's Home of the State of New York (incorp. 1890), Hudson, N. Y. For indigent firemen who have served as Volunteer firemen in the State of New York, or who are now serving as Volunteer firemen and are unable to work. Supported by two per cent. tax on foreign insurance premiums, and also by voluntary contributions from fire companies in the State.

First Aid to the Injured, The Society for Instruction in (incorp. 1883), 105 East 22d St., N.Y.C. (tel. Gramercy 4802). Holds private classes at its rooms for instruction in first aid to the injured in emergency cases. Organizes classes for working men, factory workers, church and settlement clubs, etc. Works in co-operation with the free public lecture centers.

Officers: Rev. John A. Wade, pres., 80 Washington Sq.; A. A. Campbell, treas., 1293 Carroll St., Brooklyn; Louis F. Bishop, M.D., secy., 109 East 61st St.

First Baptist Church. See MARINERS' TEMPLE.

First Baptist Church, Keap St., cor. Lee Ave., Brooklyn. Maintains a Community House at Keap St. and Marcy Ave.

Leon S. McDaniel, director.

***First Chinese Church,** 223–225 East 31st St., N.Y.C. Conducts institutional work with and for Chinese; maintains a reading room, bowling alley, dormitories, etc.

First Hebrew Day Nursery and Kindergarten of Brooklyn, The, 174 Leonard St. Cares for children between the ages of two and eight years, whose relatives are unable to provide for them during the day. A small charge is made; some are free. A temporary night shelter gives aid in case of illness or death, and when children are not immediately admitted to an orphanage.

Mrs. Leo Weil, president.

First Hungarian Baptist Church, 225 East 80th St., N.Y.C. (tel. Lenox 8899). Conducts a sewing school, clubs and classes for boys and girls, women's meetings, English classes and a Home for Hungarian working girls.

Rev. Nicholas Dulity, Pastor; Miss Helena Toth, asst. See also under BAPTIST CHURCHES in the Church List.

First Italian Baptist Church, 16–18 Jackson St., Brooklyn (tel. Greenpoint 2157). Maintains, besides regular religious services, a social hall and lecture room, social service meetings, Americanization classes in English and in Italian, industrial school, light gymnastics, girls' and mothers' clubs, shower baths, dispensary, kindergarten, a debating club for boys, Boy Scouts of America, lodge for men and women, etc.

Rev. V. Coletta, Pastor.

First Presbyterian Church, (Old First, University Place and Madison Square Foundation), Fifth Ave., 11th and 12th Sts., N. Y. C. Maintains clubs for men, boys, women, and girls, mothers' meetings, sewing school, Bible schools, summer home, etc. See also under PRESBYTERIAN CHURCHES in the Church List.

First Universalist Mission Society of the City of New York, The, Prescott Memorial Bldg., 247 East 53d St., N.Y.C. Maintains: Sunday school, sewing school, classes in cooking, millinery, calisthenics, dancing, men's club, mother's club, maternity and child welfare clinic.

Ove C. Sparre, supt.

Fiscal Supervisor of State Charities (created by Sec. 42, Chap. 252, Laws of 1902), The Capitol, Albany,

* *Current information not received.*

N. Y. The duties of the Fiscal Supervisor are to examine into the condition of all buildings, grounds, and other property connected with State, charitable, and reformatory institutions, and into all matters relating to their financial management. There are at the present time eighteen institutions entirely supported by the State in the charitable and reformatory group, which does not include the State hospitals for the insane nor the State prisons.

Frank R. Utter, fiscal supervisor; Henry O'Brien, 1st deputy; Thomas H. Lee, 2d deputy.

Five Points House of Industry, The (founded 1850, incorp. 1854). Office and Reception House, 454 West 23d St., N.Y.C. (tel. Chelsea 355). Provides homes for children between two and sixteen years of age who are orphans or whose parents are unable to provide for them; many also are received from the Department of Public Charities and the Children's Court. The children are first taken to the Reception House, where they are examined by a doctor and given any treatment necessary; then they are kept under observation until it is determined where it is best to place them, for the institution consists of two departments:

The COTTAGE COLONY at Pomona, which is situated on a farm of 300 acres, in an enchanting valley, in the lovely rolling country of Rockland County. The colony includes a school which follows the syllabus of the City schools The children are also taught many useful things on the farm, and in the manual training rooms. The boarding homes are situated in the country and small villages adjacent to New York. From them the children attend the public schools. The capacity is 225. The work is supported by voluntary contributions, donations, and public funds. Since the home was open there have been more than 35,000 inmates.

Officers: T. Tileston Wells, pres.; William H. Wheelock, vice-pres.; A. Leo Everett, secy.; Hugh N. Camp, Jr., treas.; Claude B. Boorom, supt.

Five Points Mission, Old Brewery, New York (incorp. 1856, est. 1853), 69 Madison St., N.Y.C. (tel. Orchard 4721). To better the conditions of the poor living near the "Five Points" and to educate and provide for the comforts and welfare of destitute children of the vicinity. Maintains clubs and classes, both day and evening, for both sexes; also, industrial work such as basket-making, cobbling, chair-caning, carpentry, dressmaking, etc.; a kindergarten and kitchen garden.

Officers: Mrs. R. M. Holsten, pres.; Mrs. Stephen Merritt, Mrs. L. H. Kane, vice-prests.; Mrs. W. H. Rogers, treas.; Mrs. Jesse Howell, rec. secy.; Miss Mary Reid Lavery, cor. secy.; F. J. Belcher, supt.

Flatbush Boys' Club, 2523 Snyder Ave., Brooklyn (tel. Flatbush 2093). Invites the boys and girls of the neighborhood to join in the work and play of the club. Swimming pool, kindergarten, games, industrial classes, employment bureau, shelter for boys and young men, etc.

Flatbush Congregational Church, Dorchester Road and East 18th St., Brooklyn. Maintains a day nursery, gymnasium, etc.

Flatbush Home. See PUBLIC WELFARE DEPARTMENT, City Home, Brooklyn.

Floating Hospital. See ST. JOHN'S GUILD.

Florence Crittenton League, Inc. (1914), Branch of the National Florence Crittenton Mission. To voluntarily assist women in distress; to provide temporary homes and employment for women and young girls who have led immoral lives, until they can be restored to friends or established in honest industry; and to establish and conduct training homes for working girls and industrial enterprises and such other instrumentalities as may be adapted thereto. Maintains the

FLORENCE CRITTENTON HOME, 427 West 21st St. (tel. Chelsea 8040). For the purpose stated above. Capacity, twenty-five adults. Supported by voluntary contributions.

Flower and Fruit Charity. See NATIONAL PLANT, FLOWER, AND FRUIT GUILD.

Flower Hospital. See NEW YORK HOMEOPATHIC MEDICAL COLLEGE AND HOSPITAL.

Flushing Female Association, The (founded 1814, incorp. 1884), Lincoln St., Flushing, L. I. For the education and amelioration of the condition of the poor of Flushing, especially those of African descent.

Officers: Miss Lydia R. Peck, pres., 110 South Parsons Ave., Flushing; Miss H. B. Clement, treas.; Miss Anna Breath, secy., 146 Franklin Pl., Flushing.

Flushing Hospital and Dispensary (incorp. 1882), Parsons and Forest Aves., Flushing, N. Y. (tel. Flushing 2000–2001). For the medical and surgical treatment of persons residing in the Third Ward of the Borough of Queens. Capacity, 140 beds. Supported by voluntary contributions.

TRAINING SCHOOL FOR NURSES.

***Flushing Public Playground Association** (est. and incorp. 1910), Broadway near Main St., Flushing, L. I.

Fordham Hospital, Crotona Ave. and Southern Boulevard, Borough of the Bronx. Maintained by the city; is a Branch of BELLEVUE HOSPITAL. Ambulance district from 169th St. to City Line, Hudson River to Long Island Sound. For the destitute sick and injured of the City and County of New York. Patients are received at all hours. Capacity, 276 beds. Visiting days and hours, Fridays, from 6–8 P. M.; Wednesdays and Sundays, from 2–4 P. M. No contagious diseases are admitted. Has an

OUT-PATIENT DEPARTMENT; surgical cases treated from 10 A. M. to 12 M.; medical cases from 2–4 P. M.; closed on Sundays and holidays. (See also Bellevue and Allied Hospitals, Board of Trustees.)

***Fordham Italian Baptist Mission,** 2409 Lorillard Pl., Bronx, N. Y. Conducts classes in English for foreigners, a naturalization course, vacation school, industrial classes and boys' clubs. See also under BAPTIST CHURCHES in Church List.

Fordham School of Social Service (est. 1916), Woolworth Bldg., 233 Broadway, N.Y.C. To provide a professional training for social and civic work. Such training will occupy two academic years from October to June and will cover the full field of social work. Capacity, 400. Supported by students' fees and donations.

Foreign Consuls. See CONSULS.

Foreign Missions, Conference of North America. See COMMITTEE OF REFERENCE AND RESEARCH.

Forty-fourth St. Home for Boys. See CHILDREN'S AID SOCIETY.

Foundling Hospital. See NEW YORK FOUNDLING HOSPITAL.

Fox Hills Debarkation Hospital. See UNITED STATES PUBLIC HEALTH SERVICE.

** Current information not received*

Franciscan Missionaries of Mary, The (incorp. 1907), 221-225 East 45th St., N.Y.C. Visit and render aid to the poor and the sick in hospitals; maintain an

INDUSTRIAL SCHOOL FOR IMMIGRANT GIRLS and

ST. AGNES' DAY NURSERY at above address.

Free Home for Young Girls (est. 1863, incorp. 1870), 318 East Mosholu Parkway, N.Y.C. (tel. Fordham 7215). For Protestant white girls of any nationality. Supported by voluntary contributions and income from legacies.

Officers: Mrs. Ernest R. Adee, pres.; Mrs. James B. Lowell, treas., 570 Park Ave., N.Y.C.; Miss Elizabeth Nichols, secy., 44 Park Ave., N.Y.C.

Free Kindergarten Association for Colored Children, The (est. 1895), 202 West 63d St. For the free education of colored children under six years of age, and for afternoon club and social work among older children and parents. Supported by voluntary contributions.

Free Loan Association of Brownsville. See HEBREW FREE LOAN SOCIETY.

Free Out-door Maternity Clinic. See JOHN E. BERWIND FREE MATERNITY CLINIC.

Free Synagogue, Carnegie Hall, services Sunday morning at 10.45.

Stephen S. Wise, Rabbi; Sidney E. Goldstein, associate.

Free Synagogue of the Bronx, Community Bldg., 162d St. and Southern Blvd., Rabbi Louis I. Newman; Free Synagogue of Washington Heights, 502 West 163d St., Rabbi J. Max Weis in charge; Free Synagogue of Flushing, Locust and Main Sts., Flushing, L. I., Rabbi Maxwell Silver; Free Synagogue of Newark, Broad and Marshall Sts., Newark, Rabbi Goldstein in charge.

Office of Synagogue: 36 West 68th St. Frederick L. Guggenheimer, exec. secy.

DEPARTMENT OF SOCIAL SERVICE

Office: 36 West 68th St., N.Y.C. (tel. Columbus 3873). Dr. Sidney E. Goldstein, exec. director; Frederick L. Guggenheimer, asst. exec. director.

Medical Social Service: 1. Bellevue Hospital, in which social care is given to all Jewish patients. 2. Lebanon Hospital, in which social care is given to all patients in wards and in dispensary; a special clinic maintained in infants hygiene; a special clinic maintained for infantile paralysis cases; a district service maintained, giving in homes of district instruction in hygiene, nursing care, medical care, social care. 3. Tuberculosis work done in conjunction with the Committee for the care of the Jewish Tuberculous. 4. Mental hygiene, in which border-line and parole cases are taken under care; two clinics are maintained: Monday and Thursday evening at the Synagogue House, 36 West 68th St.

Child Adoption Committee, which places Jewish children for adoption in suitable homes.

Jane Elkus Home at Oakhurst, N. J., for the care of adolescent girls who are in danger of physical, nervous, mental or moral breakdown; and places boys during the summer.

Educational Activities include seminar in Medical Social Service for professional workers; Training Course for volunteers in Social Service, and Social Service Conferences.

Sewing circles and store-room for receiving and distribution of clothing.

DEPARTMENT OF RELIGIOUS EDUCATION

Includes Religious Schools as follows: Central School, High School and Teachers' Institute, 36 West 68th St.,

Sunday morning at 9.45. Bernard Cantor School, 155 Clinton St., Saturday afternoon at 2; Bronx Schools: Community Bldg., 163d St. and Southern Blvd., Saturday and Sunday morning at 9.45; McKinley Square Casino, 169th St. and Boston Rd., Saturday morning at 9.45; Eagle Bldg., 2642 Third Ave., Saturday morning at 9.45. Washington Heights School, 502 West 163d St., Sunday morning at 9.45. Flushing School, Locust and Main Sts., Flushing, L. I., Sunday morning at 9.45; Newark School, Broad and Marshall Sts., Newark, N. J.

Religious Schools free to all. Total enrolment of schools, 1,500. Each school is organized into a City of Justice with the following departments: Health, Education, Justice, Social Service. Address on Religious, Ethical and Social themes are delivered by invited speakers.

French Benevolent Society of New York (org. 1809, incorp. 1819, Societe Francaise de Bienfaisance de New York), 450-458 West 34th St., N.Y.C. (tel. Longacre 2170).

RELIEF BUREAU, gives general relief to the French poor. Assists the needy by furnishing medical advice and medicines, food, clothing, money, and temporary shelter, directs and finds employment for the newcomers and returns to France those remaining a charge upon the Society.

HOSPITAL for the sick poor. Indigent patients are admitted free, but those able to pay are charged according to circumstances. Apply at the Hospital daily, except Sundays and holidays, from 2-4 P. M. Accident cases received at any time. Of 2,437 patients who were admitted last year and given 34,712 days of hospital treatment, 908 were free patients, who received 14,432 days of hospital care entirely without charge. Visitors admitted Tuesdays, Fridays, and Sundays from 2-4 P. M.

DISPENSARY, open daily, except Sundays, from 2-3 P. M., for free advice to sick poor, without regard to nationality, but medicine is given to the indigent only; 5,780 treated, who received 20,894 consultations, and 5,541 prescriptions were dispensed last year.

The Society is supported by voluntary contributions and fees from patients. Last year's receipts, $292,734.00; expenditures, $272, 162.79.

Officers: Lucien Jouvaud, pres.; C. T. Stralem, treas.; Vincent Fulchiron, secy.

French Branch Y. W. C. A. See YOUNG WOMEN'S CHRISTIAN ASSOCIATION, French Branch.

French Evangelical Home for French speaking young women (incorp. 1889), 341 West 30th St., N.Y.C. (tel. Chelsea 2330). Receives unemployed teachers, governesses, maids, and nurses. Capacity, twenty-one. Board $8.00-$8.50 a week. Supported by voluntary contributions and income from board.

Edmond E. Roberts, treas., 3 Maiden Lane; Mrs. J. Eugene Robert, secy.; Miss E. Bolliet, matron, to whom apply.

French Heroes Lafayette Memorial Fund, Inc. (est. 1916), 149 West 49th St., N.Y.C. (tel. Circle 4621). Relief of sufferers from the war, mainly in France and also in the countries of the Allies; at the Chateau Lafayette and in co-operation with French committees, maintaining an orphanage, school, preventorium and memorial museum at the Chateau Lafayette.

M. Clemenceau, pres. Comite d'honneur; Mrs. William Astor Chanler, pres.; James A. Blair, Jr., treas.; E. Lawshè, secy.; Marwick, Mitchell, & Co., auditor.

French Hospital. See French Benevolent Society of New York.

French Maternal School (incorp. 1904), 346 West 28th St. (tel. Chelsea 5656). A day nursery and kindergarten for poor children from three to seven years of age whose mothers are obliged to work away from home. It aims also to promote a knowledge of the French tongue among children. Hours, 7 A. M. to 7 P. M. Supported by voluntary contributions and subscriptions from members.

Mme. Anna Fregosi, principal.

French Restoration Fund, Inc., 15 Park Row, N.Y.C. Raises fund for restoration of homes, churches, public buildings, etc., in France.

Officers: John Erskine, chrm.; Ward E. Pearson, treas.; Alma M. Bullowa, executive.

French Tubercular Children's Fund, 501 Fifth Ave., N.Y.C. Maintains homes and sanatoria and provides general care for tuberculous children.

Officers: Walter E. Maynard, pres.; Charles H. Sabin, treas.; E. Lawshe, secy.

Fresh-air Classes. See Education, Board of.

Friend in Need Day Nursery (est. 1908), 95 Bradford St., Brooklyn, N.Y. Caring for the children of working mothers. Average attendance 40.

Officers: Mrs. John C. Creveling, pres.; Mrs. Charles J. Benisch, treas.; Mrs. John H. Wells, secy.

Friendly Aid Society. See Warren Goddard House.

Friendly House Association, The (org. 1902, incorp. 1914), 141–143 Harrison St., Brooklyn (tel. Hamilton 918). For neighborhood, recreational, and civic work. Non-sectarian. Supported by voluntary contributions.

Board of Directors: Mrs. D. D. Campbell, pres.; Mrs. John S. Roberts, treas.; Mrs. Nelson Merritt, secy.; Miss Alice G. Spink, head worker.

Friends' Adult School (est. 1904), 144 East 20th St., N.Y.C. Object: To become acquainted with and enter into intimate friendship with discouraged, broken, destitute men, and by sympathy and brotherly advice and help restore them to self-reliance and positions of usefulness. Men of all nations, races, and creeds. Supported by voluntary gifts of money, clothing, and time.

Fund for the Relief of Men of Letters and Scientists in Russia, 216 Second Ave., N.Y.C. Aids Russian professional men and women in need.

Officers: C. M. Oberoutcheff, pres.; Dr. S. M. Ingerman, treas.

G

Gabriels Sanatorium. See Sanatorium Gabriels.

Gallaudet Home. See Church Mission to Deaf Mutes.

Gardner Sunshine Day Nursery (incorp. 1911), 562 Herkimer St., Brooklyn. To care for the children of working mothers. Capacity, thirty-five. Supported by voluntary contributions.

***Garnet Fresh-air Home,** Westbury, L. I. Cares for colored children and adults of limited means. Supported by donations.

Gary de Vabre Academy (founded 1905), Lake Ronkonkoma, Long Island, N. Y. (Long distance telephone, 63). For the care, training, education, and social deportment of mentally defective children and adolescents, including cripples and those with defective hearing, speech, or sight. No age limit. Individual instruction. Open all year.

* *Current information not received.*

Baron and Baroness J. Gary de Vabre, principals.

Gemilath Chosodim (Free Loan) Association of Brownsville. See HEBREW FREE LOAN SOCIETY, INC.

General Education Board, The (org. 1902), 61 Broadway, N.Y.C. To promote education within the United States, without distinction of race, sex, or creed. Its immediate purpose is to promote, systematize, and make effective various forms of educational beneficence.

Officers: Wallace Buttrick, pres.; Abraham Flexner and Trevor Arnett, secretaries; E. C. Sage, asst. secy.; L. G. Myers, treas.; L. M. Dashiel, asst. treas.

General Federation of Women's Clubs (org. 1890, incorp. 1904). International. Fine Arts, Public Welfare, American Citizenship, Applied Education, Press and Publicity, Legislation departments.

Officers: Mrs. Thomas G. Winter, pres., 2617 Dean Blvd., Minneapolis, Minn.; Mrs. George W. Plummer, cor. secy., Plaza Hotel, Chicago, Ill.

General Italian Missionary (P. E.), 45 Jewett Ave., Port Richmond, N. Y. Conducts religious and civic services among Italians on Staten Island.

Rev. Carmelo Di Sano, B.D., in charge.

General Memorial Hospital, for the Treatment of Cancer and Allied Diseases. See MEMORIAL HOSPITAL, etc.

General Relief Committee, Inc., Hotel Vanderbilt, N.Y.C. Fund-raising organization for approved charitable organizations of United States, Europe and Asia.

Officers: Jacob C. Klinck, chrm.; Charles H. Sabin, treas.; H. Mindell, secy.

General Society of Mechanics and Tradesmen of the City of New York (incorp. 1792), 16–24 West 44th St.

MECHANICS' INSTITUTE SCHOOL, open October to May. Provides evening classes to furnish free instruction to young men in freehand drawing, elementary and advanced; in mechanical and architectural drawing and mathematics; also classes in physics and industrial electricity.

To encourage young men in acquiring a practical knowledge of some useful trade. Maintains free scholarships in the New York Trade School.

James Hopkins, pres., 119 Franklin St.; Daniel T. Wilson, secy., 20 West 44th St.

General Theological Seminary of the Protestant Episcopal Church in the United States, The (org. 1817, incorp. 1822), Chelsea Sq., N.Y.C. (tel. Chelsea 7184). For the theological education of candidates for the ministry of the Protestant Episcopal Church. Tuition free.

Officers: Rev. Hughell Edgar Woodall Fosbroke, D.D., dean; Rt. Rev. Edwin A. Lines, D.D., chrm. Board of Trustees; Rev. Lawrence T. Cole, D.D., secy. and treas.; Cornelius B. Zabriskie, bursar and registrar; George Dobbin Brown, librarian.

George Junior Republic Association of New York, The (org. 1895), Freeville, N. Y. Maintains a Republic to reclaim delinquent and other youth through the method of self-government and industry, thereby instilling habits of self-support and good citizenship.

Officers: Wm. R. George, founder and social director; John M. Weekes, pres.; Charles W. Major, treas.; Charles H. Blood, secy.

German Evangelical Aid Society of Brooklyn (incorp. 1881), 643 Chauncey St., cor. Bushwick Ave., Brooklyn (tel. East New York 304). To provide a home, food, clothing, and medical treatment for the aged, sixty years or over. Admission fee, $600.

German Home for Recreation of Women and Children (incorp. 1898), Harway Ave. and Bay 46th St. (tel. Bensonhurst 941), Brooklyn. A temporary home for rest, recuperation, and recreation of women and children in need of such.

German Hospital of Brooklyn. See WYCKOFF HEIGHTS HOSPITAL.

German Hospital and Dispensary in the City of New York. See LENOX HILL HOSPITAL.

German Housewives' Association. See HOUSEWIVES' AID SOCIETY, INC.

***German Masonic Home, The** (est. 1888), Tappan, Rockland Co., N. Y. For aged, indigent, and worthy Masons over sixty-five years, their wives, and widows, over sixty years.

German Odd Fellows' Home Association of the State of New York. See UNITED ODD FELLOWS HOME AND ORPHANAGE.

German Poliklinik of the City of New York. See STUYVESANT POLYCLINIC.

German Seamen's Mission, of the SOCIETY FOR THE CARE OF GERMAN SEAMEN IN THE PORT OF NEW YORK. See SEAMEN'S MISSION.

German Society of the City of New York, The (org. 1784, incorp. 1804), Room 113, 147 Fourth Ave., N.Y.C. (tel. Stuyvesant 2148). Assists needy Germans by furnishing medical advice, medicines, money, and general relief. Eight physicians visit German families in need of medical attention. Supported by membership dues, voluntary contributions, and interest on funds.

Officers: Paul Lichtenstein, pres.; Daniel Schnakenberg, treas.; Arend Behrens, secy.; A. Bossert, manager.

Gerry Society. See SOCIETY FOR THE PREVENTION OF CRUELTY TO CHILDREN.

***Gilbert A. Robertson Home** (incorp. 1891), Scarsdale, N. Y. A free SUMMER HOME to give poor families (including men) a fortnight of rest and recreation. Accommodates fifty.

Girl Scouts, Inc. (est. 1912, incorp. 1915), 189 Lexington Ave., N.Y.C. (tel. Madison Square 4355). Supported by memberships and donations. Nonsectarian and non-partisan organization; affiliated with sister organizations in other countries; devoted to developing a recreational and educational program for girls in United States and her territories.

Officers: Mrs. Arthur Osgood Choate, pres., 189 Lexington Ave.; Mrs. Nicholas F. Brady, treas.; Mrs. V. Everit Macy, chrm. Executive Board; Mrs. Jane Deeter Rippin, national director.

Girls' Athletic League. See PUBLIC SCHOOLS ATHLETIC LEAGUE.

Girls' Colony, Staten Island. See ROME STATE CUSTODIAL ASYLUM.

Girls' Friendly Society in America (est. 1877, incorp. 1895), 15 East 40th St., N.Y.C. (tel. Vanderbilt 6470). 1. To band together in one society Churchwomen as Associates, and girls and young women as Members, for mutual help (religious and secular), for sympathy and prayer. 2. To encourage purity of life, dutifulness to parents, faithfulness in work, and thrift. 3. To provide the privilege of the Society for its Members, wherever they may be, by

* *Current information not received.*

giving them an introduction from one Branch to another.

The Society has branches in nearly every country in the world.

Officers: Miss F. W. Sibley, pres., 410 Jefferson Ave., Detroit, Mich.; Miss M. B. Anthony, treas., 72 Manning St., Providence, R. I.; Miss Mary M. McGuire, secy., G.F.S., Central Office, 15 East 40th St., N.Y.C.

Girls' Friendly Society, Diocese of New York. Diocesan Office, 147 East 34th St., N.Y.C. (tel. Murray Hill 7845). 87 branches in as many parishes; leaders are communicants of Protestant Episcopal Church, but membership is unsectarian.

New York Diocesan Organization maintains Lodge, 155 East 54th St. (tel. Plaza 2150). Self supporting boarding house for business girls. Capacity, 44.

Vacation House, Huntington, L. I. Open June to October. Capacity, 50.

Officers: Mrs. J. W. Pfau, pres.; Miss Edith Hadley, secy.; Mrs. E. W. Mason, treas.; Miss Julie Stursburg, asst. treas.; Miss Margaret G. King, exec. secy.

Girls' Friendly Society of the Diocese of Long Island. Consists of thirty-one branches.

Mrs. W. S. Shattuck, pres.; Miss J. A. S. Schapps, secy., 753 Bedford Ave., Brooklyn.

Girls' Protective League. See NEW YORK PROBATION AND PROTECTIVE ASSOCIATION.

God's Providence House. See NEW YORK PROTESTANT EPISCOPAL CITY MISSION SOCIETY.

Good Samaritan Dispensary in the City of New York, The (incorp. 1884, in 1891 assumed the property and work of the Eastern Dispensary, incorp. 1832), 75 Essex St., N.Y.C. (tel. Orchard 636). District: East River, 14th St., First Ave., Allen and Pike Sts. For free medical and surgical advice, treatment, and medicines to all unable to pay for them.

Good Will Center, of the Brooklyn City Mission, York and Gold Sts., Brooklyn. Object: Italian services; clubs for boys, girls, mothers; daily kindergartens, classes in Italian, English, Italian lectures, motion pictures, etc.

Sanford Culver Hearn, director.

Good Will Home Association (est. 1889), Hinckley, Me. New York City office, 90 West Broadway. To provide a home, school, disciplinary and religious training to needy and imperilled boys and girls, under fifteen years of age. Incorrigible or delinquent children not received. Undenominational; Protestant. During 1914, ten States were represented by 196 boys and 32 girls, of whom 129 were free and 99 partially supported.

Walter P. Hinckley, supervisor; E. W. Watkins, representative, at New York office.

Goodhue Home. See CHILDREN'S AID SOCIETY.

Gospel Settlement (White Door), (org. 1897, incorp. 1901), 211 Clinton St., N.Y.C. (tel. Orchard 1146), Teaches patriotism, self-control, obedience, thrift and neighborliness, Boy Scouts, etc. Specializes in English language for foreigners.

Officers: Prentice Sanger, pres.; Mrs. John E. Wilson, treas.; Miss Harriet Irwin, head worker.

Gouverneur Hospital, Branch of Bellevue Hospital, Gouverneur Slip and Front St., N.Y.C. (tel. Orchard 4430). For the destitute sick and injured. All classes of cases, except contagious diseases, regardless of age, race, or sex, are received at all hours. Capacity, 196. Visiting days, Tuesdays and Fridays, 6–8 P. M.; Sundays, 2–4 P. M.

Jessie A. Stowers, supt.

AMBULANCE DISTRICT: East River to Bowery, Houston to Market Sts.

OUT-PATIENT DEPARTMENT for medical cases, 10 A. M. to 12 M.; surgical cases, 2–5 P. M.; closed on Sunday.

TUBERCULOSIS DIVISION, cor. Gouverneur and Front Sts., for all classes of cases, of men, women, and children; includes the camp on the ferryboat "Huddleston" at the foot of Jackson St. and the East River. For admission apply to Tuberculosis Hospital Admission Bureau (q. v.).

Grace Institute (incorp. 1897), 149–155 West 60th St., N.Y.C. To furnish women and girls free instruction in cooking, sewing, dressmaking, millinery, laundry work, stenography and typewriting. In charge of the Sisters of Charity of Mt. St. Vincent. Supported by endowment by William R. Grace. Applicants must apply in person.

Grace M. E. Church, West 104th St., between Columbus and Amsterdam Aves., N.Y.C. Office: 131 West 104th St. (tel. Academy 8). Maintains a complete gymnasium, club room, social service department, motion picture plant, and provides Saturday afternoon entertainments. Deaconesses visit strangers and the sick in the neighborhood; the worthy poor are aided.

Rev. Frederick Brown Harris, Pastor.

See also under METHODIST EPISCOPAL CHURCHES in the Church List.

Grace P. E. Chapel, 410 East 14th St., N.Y.C. See also in the Church List.

GRACE CHURCH SETTLEMENT, 413–415 East 13th St. School rooms, branch of N. Y. Kindergarten Association, industrial school, gymnasium, swimming baths, associations, lectures, industrial school.

THE CLERGY HOUSE, 417 East 13th St., residence of Assistant Clergy.

THE CLUB HOUSE, 411 East 13th St. Rooms for Boys' Club, Men's Club rooms, etc.

ST. LUKE'S ASSOCIATION, ministers to the sick and buries the dead. Employs a physician (Dispensary hours, 2–4 P. M., daily, except Sundays), and a trained nurse, who visits sick in their homes.

MISCELLANEOUS WORKS. Societies, instruction and recreation for men and women, boys and girls.

GRACE CHAPEL MUSIC SCHOOL, 415 East 13th St., classes in piano, violin and vocal orchestra.

Grace P. E. Church, Broadway and 10th St. (tel. Stuyvesant 1115). Rev. Charles Lewis Slattery, D.D., Rector. (For religious notices see under PROTESTANT EPISCOPAL CHURCHES in the Church List.)

The various social activities of the parish include:

GRACE HOUSE, 802 Broadway. Open to all persons connected with Grace Church or Chapel; has a LIBRARY and READING ROOM. Open daily, except Sundays, from 10 A. M. for administration purposes.

THE CHORISTERS' TOWER, adjoining the church; school house for boys of the church choir.

THE CHORISTERS' HOME, 86–88 Fourth Ave.

DAY NURSERY, Grace Memorial House, 94 Fourth Ave.; cares for children, from one month to six years of age, of working women, who pay, when able, ten cents a day. Kindergarten instruction is given. Open daily from 7 A. M. to 6.30 P. M. Capacity, ninety.

GRACE CHURCH NEIGHBORHOOD HOUSE, 98 Fourth Ave. Lunch and

rest rooms for women and girls employed in the vicinity. Hours, 11 A. M. to 2 P. M. daily. Afternoon clubs for boys and girls. Hours 3.30 P. M. to 5.30 P. M. daily.

GRACE NEIGHBORHOOD HOUSE ASSOCIATION. Educational and social work for Italians every evening in the week from 8-10 o'clock; and on Sunday from 5.30-7.30 P. M. Classes in English, American Government, music, and athletics; baths, roof gardens, gymnasium.

FRESH-AIR FUND: Sends children and invalids to different places in the country during summer.

GRACE HOSPITAL, 414 East 14th St., comprising House of Simeon (for old men); House of Anna (for old women); House of Holy Child (for little children).

GRACE HOUSE-IN-THE-FIELDS, New Canaan, Conn.; a summer home for children of the Chapel and Day Nursery.

GRACE MISSION HOUSE, 540 East 13th St.; the residence of the Deaconesses of the Parish. Meetings of women (mothers' meetings, etc.) are held here, and also a kindergarten.

WOMEN'S MISSIONARY SOCIETY: Has Domestic, Foreign, Indian, and Freedmen's committees, etc.

Grace P. E. Church, 46 Grace Court, Brooklyn. Maintains a free, daily kindergarten, employment society, etc. See also PROTESTANT EPISCOPAL CHURCHES in the Church List.

Graham Home for Old Ladies, The (incorp. 1851), 320 Washington Ave., Brooklyn (tel. Prospect 2656). Applicants must be over sixty years of age and residents of Brooklyn not less than five years. Capacity, eighty.

Officers: Miss Frances E. White, 1st directress; Mrs. Guy Du Val, treas.; Miss Lizzie K. Miller, cor. secy.

***Gramercy Neighborhood Association** (org. 1910, incorp. 1917), Room 118, 40 Irving Pl., N.Y.C.

Grand Army of the Republic, Memorial Committee, County of New York, Room 1, City Hall, N.Y.C. (tel. Cortlandt 170). Gives relief to needy members, their widows, and orphans.

Grand Army of the Republic, The Memorial and Executive Committee, Kings Co., New York (incorp. 1885), Room 7, Borough Hall, Brooklyn (tel. Main 95). Extends relief to soldiers and sailors of the War of Rebellion, their widows and orphans.

Greenpoint Branch, Brooklyn Y. M. C. A. See BROOKLYN YOUNG MEN'S CHRISTIAN ASSOCIATION.

Greenpoint Home for the Aged. See LADIES' BENEVOLENT ASSOCIATION, etc.

Greenpoint Hospital. See PUBLIC WELFARE DEPARTMENT, CITY OF NEW YORK.

Greenwich House. See CO-OPERATIVE SOCIAL SETTLEMENT SOCIETY.

Greenwich Presbyterian Church, 143 West 13th St., N.Y.C. A social center for the people of the neighborhood; maintains Scout organizations for boys and girls, gymnasium, industrial school, etc.

Rev. William H. Matthews, Pastor.

Greenwich Village Improvement Society. Consolidated with COMMUNITY COUNCILS.

Greer House, 121-123 East 28th St., N.Y.C. An Episcopalian club house for non-resident women students of art under 30 years of age. Rooms from $7.00 to $11.00 a week, meals optional.

Miss Antoinette Greely, director.

***Gregg Chapel,** 190 Fourth Ave., Brooklyn. Maintains a daily kindergarten and an evening English school.

* *Current information not received.*

See also under PRESBYTERIAN CHURCHES in the Church List.

Grosvenor Neighborhood House, Inc. (est. 1915; incorp. 1916), 411 East 50th St., N.Y.C. (tel. 8473 Plaza). Supported by voluntary contributions.

Officers: Mrs. Charles D. Dickey, Jr., pres.; Miss Cornelia Van A. Chapin, treas.; Mrs. A. C. Charles, Social Service; Miss F. Winifred Anderson, supt.

Guild Civic Union, Headquarters. University Settlement, 184 Eldridge St., N.Y.C. (tel. Orchard 1570). Purpose: To foster and direct the zeal for civic usefulness among the young people of the East Side. Conducts local investigations and meetings with a view to neighborhood improvement.

Guild of the Infant Saviour, The (incorp. 1901), Room 418, 105 East 22d St., N.Y.C. (tel. 5306 Gramercy). Co-operates with maternity and foundling hospitals, obtains temporary shelter for destitute mothers with infants. Supported by voluntary contributions.

H

Haarlem House, 311-313 East 116th St., N.Y.C. (tel. Harlem 3663-3664). A Community House situated in a densely populated Italian district. Maintains gymnasium, clubs for boys and girls, young men and women, mothers and fathers; a summer camp, Camp Dixon, Ridgefield, Conn.; music school; thrift bank; circulating library; motion picture entertainments; one Girl Scout troup and two Boy Scout troups. Afternoon and evening classes in English and citizenship for men and women. Sunday forum. Co-operates with Henry Street Nursing Association, Maternity Center Association and Society for the Aid of Crippled Children.

Officers: Mrs. N. M. Pond, pres.; Miss I. M. Cammann, secy.; Frederick Dwight, treas., 45 Cedar St.; Miss B. M. Gage, director; Miss M. C. Myers, associate director; Edward Corsi, head of educational dept.

Hadley Rescue Hall, 293 Bowery. Meetings every night in the year. A vigorous rescue work. Drunkards and criminals of both sexes are welcome and assistance is given when necessary. Under the auspices of the New York City Society of the Methodist Episcopal Church.

Rev. John Callahan, supt.

Hahnemann Hospital of the City of New York, The, Park Ave., between 67th and 68th Sts., N.Y.C. (tel. Rhinelander 3180). In 1875 the New York Homoeopathic Surgical Hospital of the City of New York (incorp. 1872), and the New York Homoeopathic Hospital for Women and Children (incorp. 1874), were consolidated with and merged into the Hahnemann Hospital. First hospital opened in East 55th St. in 1869; present hospital opened in 1878. A wing for maternity patients was erected in 1894, with wards and private rooms.

No contagious cases are admitted.

Private rooms for pay patients, also ward for charity and part-pay patients. Total capacity of hospital, including maternity wards, 135 beds. Controlled by a board of trustees. Supported by voluntary contributions, endowment of beds, bequests, annual subscriptions, and board of pay patients. All applications for beds and rooms must be made to the director.

TRAINING SCHOOL FOR NURSES

Officers: T. Frank Manville, pres.; William A. Nash, vice-pres.; Henderson M. Wolfe, secy.; Wiley E. Woodbury, M.D., director.

Half Orphan Asylum. See SOCIETY FOR THE RELIEF OF HALF ORPHANS AND DESTITUTE CHILDREN.

Hall Memorial House. See HOLY TRINITY PROTESTANT EPISCOPAL CHURCH.

Halsey Day Nursery. See ST. THOMAS PROTESTANT EPISCOPAL CHAPEL.

Hamilton House. See HENRY STREET SETTLEMENT.

Hampton Association of New York, The, 19 West 44th St., N.Y.C. To stimulate interest in the work of Hampton Institute and in the movement for industrial education of Negroes and Indians.

Hannah Lavanburg Home, The 319 East 17th St., N.Y.C. (tel. Stuyvesant 5329). A temporary home for immigrant girls. Rates $4.50 to $6.00 a week.

Officers: Mrs. Oscar S. Straus, pres.; Fred L. Lavanburg, vice-pres.; Walter Beer, treas.; Miss Carrie Wise, secy., 46 Central Park West; Miss Julia Rosenberg, supt.

WELCOME HOUSE SETTLEMENT, in connection with the Home, conducts literary and athletic clubs, social, and educational work.

Happy Day House. See LITTLE MOTHERS' AID ASSOCIATION.

Harlem Branch, Y. W. C. A. See YOUNG WOMEN'S CHRISTIAN ASSOCIATION, Harlem Branch.

Harlem Council of Women, The (est. 1915), 9 West 124th St., N.Y.C. (tel. Harlem 1823). For the civic and social betterment of Harlem. Through a Council Club opened for adults and children at 232 East 110th Street efforts are made toward Americanization and good citizenship.

Officers: Mrs. Wm. L. Voigt, pres., 317 West 81st St.; Mrs. Chas. S. Crane, treas., 703 West 178th St.; Mrs. Edwin G. Davis, cor. secy., 518 West 143rd St.

Harlem Dispensary, The (incorp. 1869), 108 East 128th St. (tel. Harlem 1011). District from 104th St. to the Harlem River and west to Eighth Ave. For medical and surgical relief to the sick poor at the Dispensary. Open daily, except Sundays and holidays, from 1.30-3.40 P. M. For medicines, a small charge to those able to pay.

Officers: Edwin F. Corey, pres., 30 East 129th St.; George H. Corey, treas., 545 West 111th St.; B. Herschfield, registrar.

Harlem Eye and Ear Hospital, The (incorp. 1882), 2090 Lexington Ave., cor. 127th St., N.Y.C. (tel. Harlem 2882). For gratuitous medical and surgical treatment of the poor for diseases named in title. Capacity, twenty-five beds. Daily except Sunday, 2-3.30 P. M. Hospital always open. Supported by voluntary contributions.

Officers: E. E. Hinkle, pres.; Wm. A. Ten Eick, treas.; C. B. Meding, M.D., surgeon and secy., 115 East 54th St. to whom apply for hospital accommodations.

Harlem Hebrew Day Nursery, 38 West 115th St., N.Y.C.

Harlem Home of the Daughters of Israel. See DAUGHTERS OF ISRAEL, HARLEM HOME.

Harlem Hospital, Lenox Ave., 136th to 137th Sts., N.Y.C. (tel. Harlem 5000). A branch of Bellevue Hospital. For the destitute sick and injured of the City. Patients are received at all hours. No contagious diseases are admitted. Visiting days, Tuesdays and Fridays, 6-8 P. M.; Sundays, 1-4 P. M. Children's visiting days. Tuesdays, Sundays and Fridays, from 2-4 P. M.

AMBULANCE DISTRICT from 96th St. to Third Ave., from 110th St. up Eighth Ave., up Bradhurst Ave., to south side of 145th St.

OUT-PATIENT DEPARTMENT. Surgical cases treated from 10 A. M. to 12 M.; medical cases from 2–4 P. M.

TUBERCULOSIS DIVISION. Men, women, and childre of all ages, and all classes of cases are taken. All beds are free. Cases remain in hospital only until they can be transferred to Metropolitan or other hospitals. Apply to the Tuberculosis Hospital Admission Bureau (q. v.).

MENTAL CLINIC, Wednesday 4 to 5, and 6 to 8 P. M.

CARDIAC CLINIC, Thursdays 8 P. M.

TUBERCULOSIS CLINIC, every day 2 to 4 P. M. Thursday, 8 to 10 P. M.

C. D. O'Neil, supt.

Harlem House and Community Center. See CHILDREN'S AID SOCIETY.

Harlem Reformed Church, Lenox Ave. and 123d St., N.Y.C.

Rev. Edgar Tilton, Jr., D.D., minister; Miss Elizabeth Kemlo, minister's assistant.

Women's Missionary and Aid Societies, Young People's Organizations, Gymnasium.

ELMENDORF CHAPEL, 171 E. 121st St. Maintains industrial classes, men's, boys' and girls' clubs, and has a gymnasium.

A FREE DISPENSARY, 180 East 122d.

Harlem Relief Society of the City of New York, The (incorp. 1893), 71 East 125th St. Affiliated with the Charity Organization Society to provide immediate assistance in urgent cases of distress among the deserving poor in upper Manhattan. Supported and conducted by voluntary contributions and services.

Harriett Judson Boarding Home for Women. See YOUNG WOMEN'S CHRISTIAN ASSOCIATION OF BROOKLYN.

Hartley House (org. 1897, incorp. 1903), 409–413 West 46th St. and 412–414 West 47th St., N.Y.C. (tel. Bryant 367). A neighborhood center; conducts clubs and classes for social and educational purposes; gymnasium for boys and girls; pre-natal clinic, branch of Maternity Center Association. Maintains: Hartley Farm, Towaco, N. J.

Officers: J. G. Phelps Stokes, pres., 100 William St.; George Bingham, treas., 233 Broadway; Miss May Mathews, head worker.

Haven Day Nursery, Inc., The (est. 1912), 443–445 West 24th St., N.Y.C. To care for children of working mothers. Capacity one hundred. Special features of the Haven: Mothers' Club, Montessori Class, Roof Garden for babies, Playground with sand-box and small swimming pool, for runabouts. Luncheon and afternoon care given to school-children of nursery families.

Officers: Mrs. George L. Beer, pres., 329 West 71st St.; Mrs. A. M. Bing, vice-pres., 1155 Park Ave.; Mrs. J. J. Benjamin, treas., 215 West 98th St.; Mrs. M. J. Kaufmann, secy., 44 West 77th St.

Hawthorne School. See JEWISH PROTECTORY.

Haxton Cottage. See CHILDREN'S AID SOCIETY.

Hayden Housekeeping Center. See ALL SOULS' UNITARIAN CHURCH, this List.

Health, Department of, City of New York. Headquarters, 505 Pearl St., N.Y.C. (tel. Worth 9400). Branch offices:

Bronx, 3731 Third Ave.; Brooklyn, Willoughby St. and Flatbush Ave.; Queens, 372–374 Fulton St., Jamaica, L. I.; Richmond, 514 Bay St., Stapleton, S. I.

The work of the Department is organized in nine bureaus as follows: General Administration, Records, Sanitation,

Preventable Diseases, Hospitals, Laboratories, Child Hygiene, Food Inspection, Public Health Education.

Royal S. Copeland, M.D., commissioner.

THE BUREAU OF GENERAL ADMINISTRATION is concerned chiefly in keeping and authenticating the acts, records, papers, and proceedings of the Department; preserving the books and papers of the Department, and conducting its correspondence.

THE BUREAU OF RECORDS issues burial permits, keeps on file all certificates of births, deaths, marriages, etc., makes searches and issues transcripts thereof, and prepares statistical tables based upon the certificates received.

THE SANITARY BUREAU is called upon to abate nuisances and correct unsanitary conditions due to violations of the Sanitary Code.

This Bureau enforces the regulations of the Board of Health relative to the maintenance (under permit) of lodging houses, stables, bathing establishments, bathing beaches, camps, and houseboats.

It maintains a supervision over and enforces the Board regulations in regard to the transportation of refuse materials by private citizens, removal of dead animals and offal, loading of manure on scows and railroad cars, maintenance of inland dumps, maintenance of leaching cesspools, use of well water, keeping of live chickens and pigeons.

In addition, this Bureau has supervision over all mosquito extermination work and gives special attention to the correction of all conditions which cause the breeding of flies.

THE BUREAU OF PREVENTABLE DISEASES has supervision and control of all communicable infectious diseases; the establishment and maintenance of proper quarantine in cases of certain infectious diseases; the administration of immunizing sera and vaccines; the registration of cases of tuberculosis; the maintenance of tuberculosis clinics (see ASSOCIATION OF TUBERCULOSIS CLINICS), and the home supervision of cases of tuberculosis; the admission of tuberculous cases to sanatoria and hospitals; anti-rabies clinic for determination of rabies and prevention of this disease, by the administration of Pasteur treatment, 493 St. Paul's Pl., Bronx; Flatbush Ave. and Willoughby St., Brooklyn; and 505 Pearl St., Manhattan—the disinfection of infected premises and infected material; the maintenance of clinics for the diagnosis of venereal diseases.

It conducts the

Occupational Clinic, 128 Prince St., (tel. Spring 9586). Branches at 493 East 139th St., Bronx, and Willoughby and Fleet Sts. and Flatbush Ave., Brooklyn. Open from 9 A. M. to 12 M. for examination of workers as to occupational diseases; gives advice and general aid and seeks to encourage workers to submit to periodic medical examinations for disease prevention.

THE BUREAU OF HOSPITALS maintains three hospitals for contagious diseases and a sanatorium for tuberculosis as follows:

HOSPITALS

Willard Parker and Reception Hospital, foot of East 16th St., Manhattan, for children and adults sick with contagious diseases and for temporary care of patients awaiting transfer to other hospitals of the Department.

Kingston Avenue Hospital, Fenimore St. and Kingston Ave., Brooklyn, for the treatment of contagious diseases.

Queensboro Hospital, Flushing Ave. and New Lots Rd., Jamaica, L. I. For the care of contagious diseases occurring in the borough of Queens.

Riverside Hospital, North Brother

Island, East River, for the care of contagious diseases and for advanced cases of tuberculosis and venereal diseases. (Boats leave East 132d St. dock every hour, and foot East 26th St. about noon, daily.) Application for admission of tubercular patients to be made to the Tuberculosis Hospital Admission Bureau (q. v.).

Otisville Sanatorium (New York City Municipal Sanatorium), Otisville, N. Y. (Erie R. R. seventy-five miles from New York. Round trip fare, $4.92), for early cases of tuberculosis. An important point in connection with the administration of the Sanatorium consists in requiring patients to render such services as their physical condition allows, as it has been found that carefully regulated work is of decided benefit in improving the physical condition of the patient.

The Bureau of Laboratories works along various lines including: 1. The manufacture of biologic products for the diagnosis, prevention, and treatment of disease. 2. The Clinical Department advises physicians in the use of the above products, and, when requested, administers the treatment to patients in their homes. 3. Chemical and bacteriologic examinations of water, milk, and food (including shellfish). 4. Bacteriologic and epidemiologic investigations of local epidemics of various infectious diseases. 5. Serologic diagnosis of syphilis, gonorrhoea and glanders. 6. Diagnosis of cultures from cases of suspected diphtheria; of specimens of sputum from cases of suspected pulmonary tuberculosis; of specimens of blood for typhoid (Widal test), and malaria; of smears for gonococci; and dark-field condenser examination for treponema pallida. 7. Experimental work on infectious and other diseases.

Bureau of Food and Drugs is charged with the inspection and supervision of the production, manufacture, and sale of all kinds of food and of drugs; chemical examination of adulterated or suspected foods and drugs.

Bureau of Public Health Education was created in 1914 to extend and to co-ordinate work being carried on by the Department of Health. The activities of this Bureau include:

1. Publications—Regular: Weekly Bulletin, Monthly Bulletin, Food and Drug Bulletin, School Health News, Staff News. Irregular: Reprints and Monographs. Occasional: Health Leaflets, Posters, Placards, etc.
2. Lectures—Before schools, colleges, clubs, churches, in factories and before associations and settlements.
3. Exhibits—In addition to the permanent exhibit at headquarters, various travelling exhibits are prepared from time to time for use in various institutions of the city.
4. Motion Pictures—Open air shows are occasionally given. Films are rented and exhibited in regular theatres. Films are furnished free to schools and educational associations and special feature scenarios are occasionally prepared, as well as news feature films.
5. Information Bureau—Persons and organizations desiring information are aided in every possible way and out of town and foreign inquiries are handled in large numbers.
6. Industrial Hygiene — Visits are made to places of employment and to homes of workmen and everything possible is done to further education in personal hygiene and sanitation, as well

as matters regarding first aid and accident prevention.

7. Lunch Room—The Bureau operates a lunch room for Department employees, which also serves as an exhibit in instructing how clean eating places should be operated.
8. Miscellaneous—The Bureau, in addition to its files of health literature, contains a very considerable collection of photographs and other data, which is loaned free to responsible persons.

THE BUREAU OF CHILD HYGIENE (org. 1908) deals exclusively with health problems concerning children from birth to legal age. Its activities are as follows:

Control and supervision of the practice of midwives; investigation of cases of ophthalmia neonatorum, puerperal septicæmia; work directed against infant mortality through Baby Health Stations (see below); supervision of foundlings boarded out in private homes; inspection of institutions caring for dependent children; inspection of day nurseries; medical inspection and examination of school children, securing the correcting of remedial defects; performance of vaccinations; issuance of employment certificates; investigations of still-births and of cases of puerperal septicæmia; special investigation of congenital deaths for research purposes; special work in checking up registry of births, etc.

The field work, including that of Baby Health Stations and Clinics for school children, consists of visits, physical examinations, lectures, consultations, investigations of applicants for permits. A staff of medical inspectors and nurses visit all babies whose births have been reported by midwives, and instruct the mothers in the proper care of babies. They canvass tenements and instruct all mothers of babies less than a year old. Educational centers are established throughout the city where clinics are conducted by physicians and nurses to demonstrate proper feeding, clothing, preparation of milk, etc. Little Mothers' Leagues, consisting of girls over twelve years of age, are formed during the summer for educational purposes. Tickets for free ice, modified or pasteurized milk, outings, etc., are distributed.

At the stations listed below, pure milk for infant feeding can be obtained. At a majority of the stations a doctor and nurse are in attendance to instruct mothers in the proper care of the baby. Mothers should not wait until their babies are sick, but should take them to the nearest Baby Health station at once. If mothers are nursing their babies they should go to the station to obtain milk for themselves, and also for advice as to how they may care for themselves, so as to continue nursing the baby.

BABY HEALTH STATIONS

Manhattan

1. 306 Avenue A.
2. 73 Cannon St.
3. 108 Cherry St.
4. 172 East 3rd St.
5. 326 East 11th St.
6. 513 East 11th St.
7. 241 East 40th St.
8. 348 East 74th St.
9. 205 East 96th St.
10. 225 East 107th St.
11. 315 East 112th St.
12. 343 Pleasant Ave.
13. 174 Eldridge St.
14. 2155 Fifth Ave.
15. 48 Henry St.
16. 95 Forsyth St.
17. 197 Hester St.
18. 206 Madison St.

19. 214 Monroe St.
20. 244 Mulberry St.
21. 78 Ninth Ave.
22. 209 Stanton St.
23. 27 Suffolk St.
24. 2842 8th Ave.
25. 289 Tenth Ave.
26. 114 Thompson St.
27. 224 West 63d St.
28. 506-508 West 47th St.
29. 322 East 59th St.
30. 348 East 32d St.
31. 402 West 37th St.
32. Mt. Morris Park.
33. Tompkins Square Park.

Bronx

1. 511 East 149th St.
2. 1354 Webster Ave.
3. 2380 Hughes Ave.
4. 428 East 133d St.

Brooklyn

1. 49 Amboy St.
2. 179 Bedford Ave.
3. 296 Bushwick Ave.
4. 49 Carroll St.
5. 107 Dupont St.
6. 994 Flushing Ave.
7. 184 Fourth Ave.
8. 621 Fourth Ave.
9. 165 Ten Eyck St.
10. 698 Henry St.
11. 167 Hopkins St.
12. 208 Hoyt St.
13. 76 Johnson Ave.
14. 359 Manhattan Ave.
15. 604 Manhattan Ave.
16. 176 Nassau St.
17. 144 Navy St.
18. 129 Osborn St.
19. 323 Osborn St.
20. 2346 Pacific St.
21. 592 Park Ave.
22. 268 South 2d St.
23. 594 Sutter Ave.
24. 233 Suydam St.

Queens

1. 114 Fulton Ave., Astoria, L. I.
2. 22 Maspeth Ave., Maspeth, L. I.
3. 753 Onderdonk Ave., Ridgewood, L. I.

Richmond

1. 689 Bay St., Stapleton, S. I.

School Clinics

Nurses or registrars are on duty from 9 A. M. to 5 P. M., daily. Saturdays from 9 A. M. to 12 M.

Dentists on duty from 9 A. M. to 12.30 P. M., daily and on Saturdays from 9 A. M. to 12 M.

Oculists are on duty from 1 P. M. to 4.30 P. M., and Saturdays from 9 A. M. to 12 M.

CONTAGIOUS EYE CLINICS

Manhattan

P. S. 21, 222 Mott St. (tel. Spring 9065), 1 to 4.30 Tuesday and Thursday.

REFRACTION AND CONTAGIOUS EYE CLINICS

P. S. 30, 230 East 88th St. (tel. Lenox 8391), 1 to 4.30 daily, 9 to 12 Saturday.

P. S. 64, 609 East 9th St. (tel. Orchard 474), 9 to 12 daily.

P. S. 65, 55 Eldridge St. (tel. Orchard 567), 1 to 4.30 Monday, Wednesday, and Friday, 9 to 12 Saturday.

343 Pleasant Ave. (tel. Harlem 3230), 1 to 4.30 daily, 9 to 12 Saturday. Refractions: Tuesday, Thursday, Saturday. Contagious: Monday, Wednesday, Friday.

Bronx

P. S. 9, 481 East 138th St. (tel. Melrose 1108), 1 to 4.30 daily, 9 to 12 Saturday.

Brooklyn

P. S. 132, Manhattan and Conselyea Sts. (tel. Greenpoint 2921), 1 to 4.30 daily, 9 to 12 Saturday.

P. S. 28, Herkimer and Ralph Ave. (tel. Decatur 6592), 1 to 4.30 Tuesday and Thursday, 9 to 12 Saturday.

Queens

P. S. 81, Cypress and Ralph Ave., Evergreen (tel. Evergreen 291), 1 to 4.30 daily, 9 to 12 Saturday.

BLIND AND SIGHT CONSERVATION CLINICS

P. S. 30, 230 East 88th St. (tel. Lenox 8391).

DENTAL CLINICS

Manhattan

P. S. 21, 222 Mott St. (tel. Spring 9065). 343 Pleasant Ave. (tel. Harlem 3230), 9 to 12.30 daily, 9 to 12 Saturday.

Bronx

P. S. 27, St. Ann's Ave. and 148th St. (tel. Melrose 1042), 9 to 12.30 daily, 9 to 12 Saturday.

Brooklyn

P. S. 8, Hicks and Poplar Sts. (tel. Main 8154), 9 to 12.30 daily, 9 to 12 Saturday.

P. S. 126, Meserole and Lorimer Sts. (tel. Greenpoint 4094), 9 to 12.30 daily, 9 to 12 Saturday.

P. S. 168, Throop and Bartlett Sts. (tel. Williamsburgh 5466), 9 to 12.30 daily, 9 to 12 Saturday.

P. S. 175, Blake and Hopkinson Aves. (tel. East New York 6015), 9 to 12.30 daily, 9 to 12 Saturday.

Queens

372 Fulton St., Jamaica (tel. Jamaica 1200), 1 to 4.30 daily, 9 to 12 Saturday.

Health Department, State. See STATE DEPARTMENT OF HEALTH.

Health Federation, 17 West 43d St. (tel. Vanderbilt 2094). Purpose: To act as a clearing house for the public health work in the city.

Central Council of Public Health is the administrative body of the Health Federation and consists of:

Charles Loomis Dana, M.D., chrm.; Bailey B. Burritt, Lee K. Frankel, Mrs. Thomas R. French, Miss Pauline Goldmark, Homer Folks, Edward L. Keyes, Jr., M.D., Miss Ruth Morgan, Thomas A. Storey, M.D., Philip Van Ingen, M.D., Miss Lillian D. Wald, C. E. A. Winslow and E. H. Lewinski-Corwin, Ph.D., exec. secy.

Health Officer of the Port of New York, Department of the (est. 1758 under the Colonial Government in New York; transferred to the Federal Government on January 1st, 1921, and operated under the Rules and Regulations of the U. S. Public Health Service, Washington, D. C., on the same basis as other U. S. Quarantine Stations throughout the United States).

QUARANTINE BOARDING STATION, Rosebank, Staten Island, N. Y. (tel. Tompkinsville 1400). Branch office: City Island, Long Island Sound.

Dr. Leland E. Cofer, U. S. P. H. S., is Health Officer of the Port of New York.

Jurisdiction extends over the port of New York and throughout the State of New York and that portion of New Jersey bordering on the upper Bay and Hudson River.

The purpose of the establishment is to prevent the importation through maritime commerce into the port of New York of diseases of a highly contagious or infectious nature.

The scope of the work comprises the examination of all vessels and all passengers from foreign ports, or from ports under the jurisdiction of the United States where epidemic diseases are known to exist; and the detention at the two quarantine islands, Hoffman and Swinburne, in the lower bay, of persons who have been exposed thereto until the period of incubation of the disease in question has expired.

Heartsease Work, The (org. 1899, incorp. 1920), 413 East 51st St., N.Y.C. (tel. Plaza 5746). A preventive and rescue work for women and babies; the adoption of babies; a boarding-out department for babies and the publication of religious literature. Maintains a home and reading room. Instruction given in the Bible, English, stenography, typewriting, sewing, and domestic science. Supported by voluntary contributions. Evangelical, but undenominational.

Anne Richardson Kennedy, pres.; Louise B. Scofield, secy.

Heavenly Rest P. E. Church, 551 Fifth Ave., N.Y.C. Fresh Air work at Copake Falls, N. Y.

***Hebrew Benevolent Society of Staten Island,** 202 Madison Ave., Tompkinsville.

Hebrew Burial Society (1898), 101 Varet St., Brooklyn (tel. Stagg 4754). To give proper burial to poor and indigent Jews.

Officers: Dr. S. A. Gluck, pres., 840 Eastern Parkway, Brooklyn; Alexander Krawitz, treas., 256 Floyd St., Brooklyn; L. Meyer, secy., 78 Throop Ave., Brooklyn; S. Blecher, supt.

***Hebrew Charitable Society of Staten Island** (incorp. 1901), 74 Pennsylvania Ave., Rosebank, S. I.

Hebrew Day Nursery of New York (incorp. 1909), 262 Henry St., N.Y.C. (tel. Orchard 5262). Day Nursery and kindergarten for poor children of the East Side.

HARLEM BRANCH, 61 East 107th St. (tel. Harlem 611).

* *Current information not received.*

Officers: Dora Silberblatt, pres.; Wolf Metchik, secy.

Hebrew Educational Society of Brooklyn (incorp. 1899). Hopkinson and Sutter Aves., Brooklyn. College of music, Hebrew school, Sabbath school, public holiday services, physical education, dancing classes, lectures and forums, English classes for foreigners, Americanization and preparation for citizenship, art studio, free legal aid society, dramatics, entertainments and concerts. Club department; seventy different organizations for educational, literary and social purposes meet weekly. Boy Scouts and Girl Scouts, vocational classes, community social events.

Officers: Dr. Oswald Schlockow, pres., 1162 Pacific St., Brooklyn; Herman Brickman, supt.; Sybil H. Hartman, asst. supt.

Hebrew Free Burial Association. See AGUDATH ACHIM CHESSED SHEL EMETH.

Hebrew Free Loan Association. See BROOKLYN HEBREW FREE LOAN ASSOCIATION.

Hebrew Free Loan Society, Inc. (est. 1892), 108 Second Ave., N.Y.C. (tel. Orchard 8516). Branches: 69 East 116th St., 1321 Boston Rd., 1878 Pitkin Ave., Brooklyn. This Society loans money from $5 to $500 to applicants without distinction of nationality, religion, or race, on notes endorsed by responsible persons, without charge of interest or expense. The aim of the Society is to help the needy and to make them self-supporting without humiliation. The expenses of the office and losses are covered by members' dues and donations.

The Society during the fiscal year 1919 made 17,395 loans aggregating $913,855.00 and $849,830.92 were returned in weekly installments. Since its organization the Society has made 367,920 loans amounting to $10,410,-104.00. The Society is affiliated with the Federation for the Support of Jewish Philanthropic Societies.

Officers: Julius J. Dukas, pres.; Morris Jacoby, 1st vice-pres.; Meyer Goldberg, 2d vice-pres.; Hirsh Rabinowich, treas.; Simon Landres, hon. fin. secy.; Abraham Bakst, hon. rec. secy.; Jacob M. Marcuson and A. Henry Brill, counsel to the Society; and Samuel Seinfel, manager.

Hebrew Infant Asylum of the City of New York, The. See HOME FOR HEBREW INFANTS.

Hebrew Kindergarten and Day and Night Nursery (est. 1905, incorp. 1909), 35–37 Montgomery St., N.Y.C. To feed, clothe, nurse children from four weeks to six years, whose mothers are compelled to work (widows, ill or deserted mothers), also to provide meals for orphans (school children) between the ages of six to ten years.

Officers: Jacob Rabinowitz, pres.; M. Abramowitz, treas.; S. Zuckerman, secy.; J. Deutsch, supt.

Hebrew National Orphan House (est. 1914, incorp. 1912), Tuckahoe Road, Yonkers, N. Y. City office: 52 St. Marks Place, N.Y.C. (tel. Orchard 4197). Maintains Jewish orphan boys. Capacity 500. Supported by voluntary contributions.

Officers: Leo. Lerner, pres., 550 West 146th St.; Aaron Branower, treas., 24 West 20th St.; H. B. Rosen, treas. of Building Fund, 20 West 33d St.; Solomon Diamant, supt., 208 East 10th St.

Hebrew Orphan Asylum of the City of New York, The (incorp. 1832 as Hebrew Benevolent Society of the City of New York, re-incorp. 1860), Amsterdam Ave., between 136th and 138th Sts. (tel. Audubon 910). For the support, education, and industrial training of Hebrew orphans and half-orphans of both sexes. Capacity, 1,250; present number, 1,150. Also gives Out-Door Relief and conducts a Boarding Department. Supported by voluntary contributions and city funds. Guardians must apply for admission to Executive Committee at the Asylum.

Officers: Hon. Joseph E. Newberger, pres.; Martin Beckhard, treas.; William I. Spiegelberg, hon. secy.; Aaron Schiff, secy.; Lionel J. Simmonds, supt.; Feist M. Strauss, asst. supt.

Hebrew Sheltering Guardian Society of New York Orphan Asylum (founded 1879). Since July 1, 1912, Pleasantville, Westchester Co., N. Y. Has seventeen cottages with individual kitchens, dining rooms, social rooms, two dormitories and shower baths, thirty children in each cottage; has also three school buildings, reception house for new children, general hospital, contagious hospital, power house, and laundry. Present number of children in Pleasantville about 600.

The school is organized as a Junior High School under the supervision of the Board of Education of the City of New York.

Cottage Mothers must have requisite educational, cultural, and executive qualifications. The children do all housework and cooking. They maintain seventeen miniature republics in their cottages, and one larger republic, known as the Lewisohn Democracy.

The after-care work of the institution is done by a separate organization called Fellowship House (q. v.), at 1192 Lexington Ave. In addition, the institution maintains a Boarding Bureau for 250 children in New York City, office 470 West 145th St. The institution is supported partly by public funds, partly by private contributions.

Officers: Adolph Lewisohn, pres.;

Judge Samuel D. Levy, 1st vice-pres.; Louis Seligsberg, 2d vice-pres.; Julius H. Sussman, treas.; John G. Greenburgh, asst. treas.; Joseph H. Wise, hon. secy.; Herman W. Block, chrm. Administration Council; Dr. Leon W. Goldrich, exec. dir.; Max Carton, administrator; Frank I. Frishberg, business manager.

Hebrew Sheltering and Immigrant Aid Society of America. National headquarters, 229-231 East Broadway, N.Y.C. (tel. Orchard 9680). Branch Offices in the U. S.: Ellis Island, N. Y., Philadelphia, Boston, Baltimore, Chicago, San Francisco, Seattle and Washington, D. C. Office in Warsaw, Poland. Opened by special commission of the Society to help American citizens and residents to locate their families in Europe. Object: To facilitate the lawful entry of Jewish immigrants at the various ports of the United States; to provide them with temporary shelter and other aid, preventing their becoming public charges; to prevent the ineligible from emigrating to the United States; to teach American ideals, history, and patriotism; to spread a knowledge of the advantages of desirable immigration. No charge is made for the services and no distinction of race or creed. Maintains the

HOME FOR IMMIGRANT AND NEEDY WAYFARERS at 229 East Broadway, N.Y.C., where departments of Education, Employment, Distribution, Social Service, Statistics, and Foreign Relations are conducted, and the

"Jewish Immigration Bulletin" is published monthly.

Supported by voluntary contributions, and aid from the Rose N. Lesser Auxiliary (Mrs. Leon Kamaiky, pres.); and the Hebrew Sheltering House League (Abraham M. Fisch, pres.).

Officers: John L. Bernstein, pres.; Leon S. Moiseiff, hon. secy.; Harry Fischel, treas.; Jacob R. Fain, general manager.

Hebrew Technical Institute (incorp. 1884), 36 Stuyvesant St. A nonsectarian free technical and trade school for boys over thirteen. Instruction covers three years and comprises preparation for trades and the English branches.

Officers: Eugene E. Sperry, pres.; Edward S. Steinman, treas.; Moise L. Erstein, secy.; Edgar S. Barney, principal.

Hebrew Technical School for Girls (est. 1880, incorp. 1884, and 1887), Second Ave. and 15th St., N.Y.C. A non-sectarian school for girls having completed the public grammar school. The course covers eighteen months and aims to educate the students to be self-supporting.

Those admitted are selected after examination on the basis of the best comparative mental equipment and greatest financial need, and on the assumption that commercial pupils must become self-supporting in 24 months and manual pupils in 18 months. The terms commence on the first Monday in March and September. Two departments—Commercial and Manual, 610 pupils. Free instruction is given in stenography, typewriting, bookkeeping, penmanship, commercial arithmetic, and geography to commercial students, who are preparing to become stenographers, bookkeepers, and office assistants. Manual students, who are to become assistants in dressmaking or millinery establishments, are given free instruction in sewing, dressmaking, millinery, embroidery, drawing and costume designing. All the students are taught rhetoric, history, literature, physiology, choral music, social ethics, cooking, laundering, swimming and gymnastics.

The school has a library, an auditorium seating 432, a roof garden, gymnasium, and swimming pool. Milk and cocoa are served at 10.15 o'clock in the forenoon and again at noon. The school maintains also an employment Bureau. In January, 1920, 3329 graduates were earning an aggregate of $3,386,240 per annum—an average of $84.75 per month each. It is managed by a Board of Directors. Its annual budget is about $90,000.00 supplied by voluntary subscriptions.

Mrs. J. N. Bloom, secretary.

Hedding House, a Home for Working Girls, 335 East 17th St. Is designed for the self-respecting working girl, whose income does not exceed $12 a week, regardless of religion or nationality. Under the auspices of the New York City Society of the Methodist Episcopal Church.

Helping Hand Association. See LADIES' HELPING HAND ASSOCIATION.

Henrietta Industrial School. See CHILDREN'S AID SOCIETY.

Henry Meinhard Memorial. See MEINHARD MEMORIAL.

Henry Street Settlement (est. 1893 as the Nurses Settlement, incorp. as Henry Street Settlement, 1903). Main office: 265 Henry St. (tel. Orchard 8200). Maintains a visiting nurse service with a staff of trained nurses to give professional care under the physicians' direction to the sick who cannot or should not go to the hospitals.

During the year 1919, 272,100 visits were paid by the nurses to 35,433 patients. First aid was given 12,469 cases.

The nurses care for general cases of illness, maternity cases, and communicable diseases. Fees are charged according to the circumstances of the individual patient and at the discretion of the nurse. Patients are not carried except under the direction of physicians, but calls are accepted from all sources.

The service actively co-operates with all organizations and city departments. There is an increasing demand for the nurses' attendance at clinics with the consequent follow-up work.

Through the 79th street office in zone 7 (extending from 55th to 100th street and from Central Park West to the East River) in co-operation with the Manhattan Maternity Hospital, there is a continuous day and night maternity service, the nurses working on an eight-hour schedule.

Pre-natal, baby welfare, nutritional and diagnostic clinics are held in various parts of the city.

A SOCIAL SERVICE DEPARTMENT is conducted at 258 Henry St. (tel. Orchard 8825).

Officers: Lillian D. Wald, pres.; L. Emmett Holt, M.D., vice-pres.; V. Everit Macy, treas.; Viola Percy Conklin, secy.; Anne W. Goodrich, director of nurses, Felix M. Warburg, chrm. finance committee.

Directors: John G. Agar, Leo Arnstein, Henry Bruere, Charles C. Burlingham, Paul D. Cravath, L. Emmett Holt, M.D., Herbert Lehman, Alice Lewisohn, V. Everit Macy, treas.; Mrs. Max Morgenthau, Jr.; Lillian D. Wald, Felix M. Warburg.

HEADQUARTERS

265 Henry St. (Henry Street Settlement) (tel. Orchard 8200).

OTHER NURSING CENTERS

Hamilton House, 72 Market St. (tel. Orchard 8898).

Stuyvesant, 435 East 17th St. (tel. Stuyvesant 6523).

Kips Bay Neighborhood Assn., 829 Second Ave. (tel. Vanderbilt 9523).

79th Street, 232 East 79th St. (tel. Rhinelander 6174).

Union, 237 East 104th St. (tel. Harlem 1690).

Harlem, 311 East 116th St. (tel. Harlem 3663).

Greenwich & Richmond, 27 Barrow St. (tel. Spring 9067).

Chelsea, 441 West 28th St. (tel. Chelsea 7220).

Longacre, 525 West 47th St. (tel. Longacre 1899).

Columbia, 509 West 121st St. (tel. Morningside 7800).

Morningside, 500 West 126th St. (tel. Morningside 8788).

Kingsbridge, 5222 Broadway (tel. Marble 707).

Urban League, 2303 Seventh Ave. (tel. Morningside 781).

Red Cross Health Center, 677 Morris Ave. (tel. Melrose 8878).

Tremont, 505 East Tremont Ave. (tel. Tremont 5638).

Melrose, 916 Brooke Ave. (tel. Melrose 6056).

Staten Islander Bldg., Bay Street & Central Ave. (tel. Tompkinsville 2646).

The Visiting Nurse Service co-operates with the Department of Nursing and Health of Teachers' College, Columbia University, by providing supervised field work required in certain special courses. Application for these courses should be made to the Department of Nursing and Health, Teachers' College, Columbia University, N.Y.C., or Miss Anne W. Goodrich, 265 Henry St.

NEIGHBORHOOD CENTERS: In addition to the district nursing service, the Settlement maintains educational, civic, social, and philanthropic activities. The main houses (265 and 301 Henry St.) and branches at 232–234 East 79th St., 202 West 63d St., 466 Grand St. (the Neighborhood Playhouse), and 72 Market St., are neighborhood centers and are used for a variety of organized and informal work. The residents, men and women, and the non-residents and lecturers and instructors conduct these activities. Playground is open morning, afternoon, and evening under the direction of trained supervisors.

KINDERGARTENS: Four kindergartens are maintained, two under the supervision of the New York Kindergarten Association, two under the Department of Education. The Settlement gives the rooms, milk and country outings, and provides social opportunities for the children and families.

CONVALESCENT HOUSES: In addition to its activities in the city, the Settlement maintains a convalescent house:

At "The Rest," Grand-View-on-Hudson, N. Y., a convalescent home for women in charge of a nurse, and open all the year; a summer home for children under 6 years of age at Riverholm in charge of a nurse; for girls at Echo Hill Farm, Yorktown Heights, N. Y.; and for boys and young men at "Camp Henry," Mahopac Falls, N. Y. Regular schedule of charges for the recreational summer homes, which are open to members of the Settlement clubs.

SEVENTY-NINTH STREET NEIGHBORHOOD HOUSE (Branch of Henry Street Settlement), 232–234 East 79th St. For general settlement work for the neighborhood and a nursing center for the staff of the Henry St. Settlement. Mrs. Jean Gordon Hanson, head worker.

LINCOLN HOUSE BRANCH, Henry St. Settlement, 202 West 63d St., for social and educational work among the colored people, through a free kindergarten, clubs, and classes for vocational and industrial training. Has gymnasium and carpentry shop; also facilities for domestic science work. Supported by voluntary contributions.

Miss B. H. Haynes, head worker.

HAMILTON HOUSE, 72 Market St. Formerly an independent settlement, is now affiliated with Henry Street Settlement. Nursing center; branch of Maternity Center Association; general settlement and Americanization work.

Mrs. Joseph Girsdansky, head worker.

THE NEIGHBORHOOD PLAYHOUSE, 466 Grand St. Well-equipped theater, performances daily. Selected moving pictures with special features. Festivals, dramatics, concerts, and entertainments of artistic merit by the Settlement groups or distinguished visitors in drama, dance, and music. Rooms and roof used for classes, social dancing, exhibits, lectures, etc.

Address Miss Alice or Miss Irene Lewisohn.

Hephzibah House Bible School and Home of Rest (est. and incorp. 1893), 263 West 25th St., N.Y.C. A Bible school and home of rest for Christian Workers. Headquarters for the extension work of Hephzibah House. Supported by private fund.

Miss L. E. Gayley, supt.

Herman Knapp Memorial Eye Hospital (founded 1869 as the "New York Ophthalmic and Aural Institute"), 500 West 57th St., N.Y.C. Maintains a dispensary and hospital with fifty-two beds for the study and treatment of eye diseases.

Arnold Knapp, exec. surgeon; Rowena H. Raymond, R.N., supt.

Herriman Farm School. See BROOKLYN CHILDREN'S AID SOCIETY.

High School of Commerce Employment Bureau, 155 West 65th St. (tel. Columbus 2932). For boys. No fees. Summer afternoon and regular employment for graduates and for boys who leave school before graduation. Stenography, bookkeeping, and general office help.

G. P. Fallon, director.

Highways Protective Society. See NATIONAL HIGHWAYS PROTECTIVE SOCIETY.

Hill Crest and Uplands. See WORKING GIRLS' VACATION SOCIETY.

Hiram Deats Memorial Home for Children. See MEMORIAL BAPTIST CHURCH.

Historic Preservation Society. See AMERICAN SCENIC AND HISTORIC PRESERVATION SOCIETY.

Holiday Farm Home (est. 1902), Rhinebeck, N. Y. (tel. Rhinebeck 14). For convalescent children not able to pay their way into the country. They are taken from the hospitals of New York City. If coming from their homes, a doctor's certificate must be sent that the child is free from contagious disease and that there is not any in their family or house. Board, railway fare, and clothing are supplied free. The children must be brought to the Grand Central depot and met on their return. Feeble-minded children and heart cases are not taken. Ages for boys: Six to nine; girls, six to fifteen. Supported by voluntary contributions.

Officers: Vincent Astor, pres.; Miss Ruth Morgan, vice-pres.; Mrs. Tracy Dows, treas.; Mrs. R. P. Huntington, secy.; Miss A. C. Lynch, R.N., supt.

Holy Communion P. E. Church, 20th St. and Sixth Ave., N.Y.C. Rev. Henry Mottet, D.D., Rector.

PARISH HOUSE, 49 West 20th St.

SISTERHOOD OF THE HOLY COMMUNION, 328 Sixth Ave. The Sisters and their Associates look after the poor and sick of the Parish, do parish nursing and visiting, take charge of the Home for the Aged, Free Clothing Department, the altar, the clergy and choir vestments.

GUARDIANS OF THE SISTERHOOD OF THE HOLY COMMUNION hold in trust THE SISTERS' HOUSE, at 328 Sixth Ave., and its funds, and administer such trust.

HOME FOR AGED WOMEN, St. Johnland. Provides a home for aged women. Parishioners of the Holy Communion over sixty years of age are received, if necessary, free of cost; all others pay at the rate of $7.00 per week.

WOMAN'S AUXILIARY, Holy Communion Branch. Invites requests of missionaries on the outposts, and supplies such requests.

JUNIOR AUXILIARY.

GUILD OF ST. MONICA (MOTHERS MEETING AND CHILDREN'S GUILD). For Christian culture and the development of an active interest in the general work of missions. Meets at the SISTER'S HOUSE, every Tuesday at 8 P. M. during the winter.

COMMUNICANTS' CLUB, SR. Girls' Club. Works for Babies' Shelter. Meets every Friday from 8–9.30 P. M., Parish House, 49 West 20th St.

COMMUNICANTS' CLUB, JR. Girls' Club. Meets every Thursday from 8–9.30 P. M., in the Parish House.

CHOIR CLUB, composed of boy choristers, meets with the Rector weekly for religious instruction.

JUNIOR WORKING MEN'S CLUB, composed of lads from fourteen to eighteen. Meets in Parish House each Monday night for instruction and social pastime.

JUNIOR MEN'S PARISH CLUB, composed of boys from ten to fourteen. Meets in Parish House every Thursday night for instruction and social pastime.

ST. CECILIA'S CHOIR CLUB. An organization of women members of the regular choir who volunteer for choir service for all occasions not provided for by regular choir. They meet weekly for practice, and they give two concerts yearly.

EMPLOYMENT SOCIETY, Church of the Holy Communion. Provides the poor of the parish with sewing weekly during the winter.

CHURCH PERIODICAL CLUB, Holy Communion Branch. Distributes books, periodicals, etc., yearly, where good literature is appreciated but means are not available.

BOARD OF EDITORS OF "Brotherly Words."

WORKINGMEN'S CLUB. A social and beneficiary society for workingmen.

MEN'S PARISH CLUB, for social recreation. All well-recommended young men eighteen years of age or over are eligible. Club Rooms in Parish House.

BABIES' SHELTER, THE (incorp. 1881), St. Johnland, King's Park, L. I. For homeless children not over five years old, and those whose parents are too poor, sick, or overworked to care for them.

SUMMER HOME CHURCH, OF THE HOLY COMMUNION, Ashford Hill Retreat, Ardsley P. O., Westchester Co., N. Y. Under the direct management of the "Tribune Fresh-air Fund" of this City. Present accommodation, 200 per week. Cares for all worthy women and children, whether attached to the Parish or not.

THE CONFERENCE, an organization of men and women. Meets every Monday, 2.30 P. M., at 49 West 20th St., to discuss plans of parish efficiency. Public invited.

THE MUHLENBERG CLUB, composed of older boys. Purposes: Work for the church and social pastime.

THE CADET CORPS, a military organization of boys, drilling twice each week.

THE GIRLS' FRIENDLY SOCIETY, Miss Charlotte Knecht, leader, meets in the Parish House Wednesday 8 P. M.

Holy Cross House. See SISTERHOOD OF ST. JOHN BAPTIST.

Holy Family Day Nursery (est. 1889), 250–254 East 112th St., N.Y.C. (tel. Harlem 3465). To care for children of working mothers during the day. Kindergarten instruction and first-year work; sewing class for older girls on Saturdays. Supported by voluntary contributions.

Mother M. Matilda, Superior.

Holy Family Hospital (incorp. 1909), 155 Dean St., near Hoyt St., Brooklyn. A general hospital for the aid and support of indigent sick. Maintains also a

TRAINING SCHOOL FOR NURSES.

Under the care of the R. C. Sisters of Charity.

Holy Family House for Incurables. See SISTERS OF DIVINE COMPASSION.

Holy Name of Jesus, Congregation of the, Mt. Kisco, N. Y. An Episcopal sisterhood which maintains

ST. CLARE'S SCHOOL FOR GIRLS, 38 Hope St., Stamford, Conn. (boarding and day), all grades from kindergarten through college preparatory; also ecclesiastical embroidery taught.

Summer outings for children at Mt. Kisco, N. Y.

***Holy Name Mission for the Bowery District, Inc., The** (1906), 319 Bowery.

Holy Nativity P. E. Church, 204th St. and Bainbridge Ave., Bronx. A neighborhood church conducting clubs and classes, guilds, etc. See also under PROTESTANT EPISCOPAL CHURCHES in the Church List.

Holy Redeemer Italian Church. See GENERAL ITALIAN MISSIONARY.

Holy Trinity Lutheran Church, 65th St. and Central Park West. Rev. Paul E. Scherer. Maintains clubs for boys and girls; relief societies for the poor and sick; also, a summer home for poor children. See also under LUTHERAN CHURCHES in the Church List.

Holy Trinity P. E. Church (The Church of the Holy Trinity in the Parish of St. James), 312–332 East 88th St., N.Y.C.

ST. CHRISTOPHER HOUSE, 316 East 88th St., societies, gymnasium classes, sewing school, etc. Louis Cope, director of boys' work.

CHURCH WORKERS' HOUSE, 341 East 87th St. Miss Mary Rogers, Miss Alice W. Budlong, Miss Mildred Howell, parish visitors.

See also under P. E. CHURCHES in Church List.

Holy Trinity P. E. Church, Lenox Ave. and 122d St., N.Y.C. Rev. Harry P. Nichols, D.D. Maintains clubs, athletic association, dancing assembly, Boy Scouts, Woodcraft, industrial school, etc. See also under PROTESTANT EPISCOPAL CHURCHES in the Church List.

Holy Trinity P. E. Church, Clinton and Montague Sts., Brooklyn. Maintains

HALL MEMORIAL HOUSE (1904), 157 Montague St. The Parish House and club for young men, governed in large part by the members themselves. Boys' clubs, gymnasium, social diversions, etc. Room for seven resident workers.

TRINITY HOUSE (1911), 124 Pierrepont St. A house for professional women, governed by the women residents and self-supporting.

SOCIAL SERVICE LEAGUE, maintains a public playground at York Street.

HOLY TRINITY GUILD HOUSE (1905), 122 Pierrepont St. A center for social work for women, girls, and children. A corps of volunteers together with the residents of the house conducts the work. Maintains a Dorcas Society, a

* *Current information not received.*

Mothers' Meeting, and Employment Society for women; a Girls' Friendly Society for young working women; a Junior Club, a Candidates' Club and a Sewing School for children.

HOLY TRINITY HOLIDAY HOUSE, Brookhaven, L. I. Kept open from June throughout September for the rest and recreation of women and children. A nominal charge made for board.

Home. NOTE: Titles beginning with this word other than those following will be found listed under the next important word or the subject of such titles.

Home for Aged and Infirm Hebrews of New York, The (org. 1870, incorp. 1872), West 105th and 106th Sts., between Columbus and Amsterdam Aves., N.Y.C. (tel. Academy 2124). For aged and infirm Hebrews of both sexes, over sixty years of age, and resident of the Boroughs of Manhattan and the Bronx, for over three years; of good moral character, sound mind, and without any means of support. Applications must be made to the Executive Board. Accommodates 350. Supported by voluntary contributions, bequests, and members' dues. Controlled by a board of twenty-five trustees. Visiting days, Thursdays, Saturdays, and Sundays, from 1–4 P. M.

Officers: Julius Ballin, pres.; Mrs. L. Zeckendorf, 1st vice-pres.; Sol Kohn, 2d vice-pres.; Sol Friedman, treas.; Arthur J. Cohn, secy.; Mr. and Mrs. M. Pollatchek, supts.; S. N. Leo, M.D., physician in charge.

Home Bureau, the Medical Supply House. National Headquarters for every necessity of the sick room, hospital, and nursery (org. 1890, incorp.), 36 West 39th St. (tel. Fitz Roy 2803–2809). Graduate and undergraduate nurses, male and female, can be procured at all hours, day and night. Foods for invalids, diabetics, and children; medical and surgical supplies; obstetrical outfits, sterilized and sealed for immediate shipment.

Officers: Mrs. Mary Hatch Willard, pres.; B. J. Parke, secy.

Home for Colored Working Girls. See ST. JOHN'S HOME FOR WORKING GIRLS.

Home and Foreign Missionary Department, African Methodist Episcopal Church (est. 1844, reincorp. 1914), 62 Bible House (tel. Stuyvesant 5067). For the purpose of operating foreign missionary work in West Africa, South Africa, the West Indies, South America, including Haiti. Supported by missionary collections, etc.

Home for the Friendless. See AMERICAN FEMALE GUARDIAN SOCIETY.

Home for Friendless Girls. See WASHINGTON SQUARE HOME FOR FRIENDLESS GIRLS.

Home Garden of New York City. See HAARLEM HOUSE.

Home for Hebrew Infants of the City of New York (incorp. 1895), Kingsbridge Road and University Ave. (tel. Fordham 29). For the care of orphan children of Jewish birth from infancy to five years of age; for those left without proper guardianship, or with a parent unable to care for them.

Aaron E. Nusbaum, pres.

Home for Incurables (incorp. 1866), Third Ave., 181st to 184th Sts., Fordham. For incurables of the better class, irrespective of religious belief. Consumptives are received in single rooms. Insane and contagious cases are not admitted. Capacity for and average number of inmates, 300. Unsectarian. Ordinary charge in the wards, $14 per week, to be paid four weeks in advance. Private rooms from $18 and upwards. One-third of the beds are free. Laundry work is done on the premises free of charge to patients. Supported by voluntary contributions and endowments. Visitors are welcome daily from 11 A. M to 5 P. M.

Fiscal year from January 1, 1919, December 31, 1919. Receipts, $188,-276.92, expenditures, $212,869.41; number under care during the year, 398.

Officers: Ogden Mills, pres.; Cortlandt F. Bishop and Newbold Morris, vice-prests.; Grenville T. Emmet, treas., 52 Wall St.; John Lloyd Thomas, secy. 161 West 36th St.; J. Vernon Smith, M.D., med. supt., 183d St. and Third Ave., to whom apply for admission on forms to be had on request.

Home for Industrious Boys. See MISSION OF THE IMMACULATE VIRGIN.

Hope Day Nursery, 33 West 133d St., N.Y.C. Care of colored children of working mothers, from 7 A. M. to 7 P. M. Capacity, thirty-five. Supported by voluntary contributions.

Hope Farm, Verbank, Dutchess County, N. Y. Office: Hope Farm City House, 437 East 58th St., N.Y.C.

A Community for Protestant children, between the ages of two and sixteen, who are committed to the Farm by competent authority. Private charges also received. The children are well cared for, are given a substantial school education, including industrial and agricultural training. This is not a sectarian work and is supported principally by voluntary contributions.

Officers: Dr. Russell A. Hibbs, pres.; Mrs. James M. Varnum, vice-pres.; William A. Greer, treas., 209 East 42d St.; Miss Florence Rapallo, secy., to whom apply for all information and particulars at city office.

Hope Hall. See VOLUNTEERS OF AMERICA.

Hospital Admission Bureau. See BELLEVUE HOSPITAL.

Hospital Book and Newspaper Society, Rooms 420–421, United Charities Bldg., 105 East 22d St. Receives donations of reading matter for gratuitous distribution to public institutions and individuals. About 50,000 books, magazines, and papers are distributed annually.

Officers: Mrs. J. W. Miller, pres.; James C. Green, treas.; Miss Alice Weekes, secy.

Hospital for Deformities and Joint Diseases. See DISPENSARY AND HOSPITALS, etc.

Hospital and House of Rest for Consumptives, The (incorp. 1869), Bolton Road, Inwood, N.Y.C. Office: 927 Madison Ave. Object: The care of indigent persons suffering from pulmonary tuberculosis, in all stages of the disease. The hospital is reached by the Broadway branch of the Subway to Dyckman St. station. Capacity, seventy-five. Men, women, and children. Supported chiefly by voluntary contributions, partly by endowment. Visiting days and hours: Daily, 2–5 P. M. Apply to Superintendent at hospital.

Officers: Maitland F. Griggs, pres.; Wm. M. Cruikshank, treas.; Benjamin Welles, secy.

Hospital and Institutional Bureau of Consultation, 289 Fourth Ave., N.Y.C. Gives advice with regard to the plans and construction of hospitals and institutions through qualified consultants. It also investigates going hospitals and institutions and conducts social surveys.

Henry C. Wright, director.

Hospital for Ruptured and Crippled. See NEW YORK SOCIETY FOR THE RELIEF OF RUPTURED AND CRIPPLED.

Hospital Saturday and Sunday Association of New York City. See UNITED HOSPITAL FUND OF NEW YORK.

Hospital Saturday and Sunday Association of Brooklyn, Inc. To interest the general public in Hospital charity. Appeal days are the last Saturday and Sunday in the year.

Officers: William G. Low, pres., 58 Remsen St., Brooklyn; Edward Barr, treas., 109 State St., Brooklyn; Arthur T. Hewlett, secy., 68 Remsen St., Brooklyn.

Hospital for Scarlet Fever and Diphtheria Patients, foot of East 16th St., N.Y.C. See LOUISA MINTON HOSPITAL.

Hospital Social Service Association (est. 1912), 405 Lexington Ave., N.Y.C. (tel. Murray Hill 2942). Hours 9 to 5. To stimulate the growth of social work in hospitals, dispensaries, etc., and to standardize such work. To organize experimental social service work and to collect and correlate information in regard thereto. To hold public meetings and to disseminate information through publications and otherwise in regard to Hospital Social Service. Supported by voluntary contributions.

Officers: Dr. Henry Dwight Chapin, pres., 51 West 51st St., N.Y.C.; Mrs. Armitage Whitman, treas.; Miss Louise Iselin, secy.

House of the Annunciation for Crippled and Incurable Children (incorp. 1893), cor. 155th St. and Broadway, N.Y.C. Controlled by and under the care of the Sisters of the Annunciation of the Blessed Virgin Mary, who receive into the House, free of charge, destitute incurable and crippled girls, from four to sixteen years of age. Thirty-nine cases cared for last year. Consumptive and infectious cases are not received. It maintains:

ST. ELIZABETH'S HOUSE as a Summer Home at Wilton, Conn.

Application should be made to Mother Francesca, Mother Superior, at the House.

Officers: Rev. L. T. Cole, D.D., warden; Rev. H. A. Dows, chaplain; W. S. McMurdy, M.D., and W. W. Bostwick, M.D., physicians; T. Halsted Myers, M.D., orthopædic surgeon; S. H. Huntington, M.D., physician at Wilton; A. B. Ely, D.D.S., dentist.

House of Calvary (incorp. 1900), Featherbed Lane, Bronx. For the care and maintenance of men and women suffering from cancer, lupus, etc., who are incurable and unable to pay for treatment. Capacity, 100. Supported by voluntary contributions.

House of the Good Shepherd, Mount Florence, Peekskill, N. Y. See ST. GERMAIN'S HOME.

House of the Good Shepherd (Roman Catholic) (incorp. 1858, amended 1882), foot of 90th St. and East River (tel. Lenox 180 or 181). For the reformation of inebriates and fallen women (except confirmed invalids) who wish to reform their lives for the care of those who may be in danger of falling, and of the girls committed by City Magistrates. Young women from any part of the country are received without regard to creed or nationality, and no one is detained against her own will, except those committed by the City Magistrates. Capacity for 530. Supported by the county and by the Sisters and inmates. Controlled by and under the charge of the SISTERS OF THE GOOD SHEPHERD.

Sister Mother of the Good Shepherd, Provincial.

House of the Good Shepherd (incorp. 1868), Hopkinson Ave. and Pacific St., Brooklyn. For the reformation of erring females. In charge of the Roman Catholic Sisters of the Good Shepherd.

House of the Holy Comforter, Free Church Home for Incurables, The (Prot. Epis.) (incorp. 1880), 196th St. and Grand Concourse, Bronx, N.Y.C. A free home for incurables among Protestant women and female children of the better class, who are without means or friends who can support and care for them, and who can not be received into hospitals and homes for the young or aged. All patients come on a trial of three months. Visiting days are Tuesday, Thursday, and Saturday, between 1.30 and 4. Number of inmates in the home last year, sixty-four. Controlled by a board of Trustees and a Board of Managers composed of ladies. Supported by voluntary contributions and bequests.

Officers: Beverly Chew, pres.; J. Sanford Barnes, secy. and treas., 52 Vanderbilt Ave.; Rev. Milo Hudson Gates, chaplain; Miss M. R. Swarr, supt. Applications should be made to Mrs. H. W. Munroe, Tuxedo Park, N. Y.

House of the Holy Family, 136 Second Ave., N.Y.C. See SISTERS OF DIVINE COMPASSION.

House of Mercy, Valhalla, N. Y. Temporary. Accommodates 30 girls.

House of Our Lady for Business Girls. See SISTERS OF DIVINE COMPASSION.

House of Refuge, Randall's Island, ferry foot of East 125th St., at Harlem River, N.Y.C. (tel. Harlem 1425). A reformatory for boys under sixteen years of age, when convicted of juvenile delinquency; between sixteen and eighteen years of age when convicted of a misdemeanor. Boys are held under supervision during minority. Release on parole may be earned in minimum period of fifteen and one-half months. Receives boys from all courts of competent jurisdiction in the first three and ninth judicial districts of the State for juvenile delinquency and from all judicial districts of the State for misdemeanor. Under control of the MANAGERS OF THE SOCIETY FOR THE REFORMATION OF JUVENILE DELINQUENTS in the City of New York.

House of Relief. See SOCIETY OF THE NEW YORK HOSPITAL.

House of St. Giles the Cripple, The (incorp. 1891) (Protestant Episcopal). Office: 1346 President St., Brooklyn; Home at Garden City, L. I. A Home and Hospital for Destitute Crippled Children of either sex, from New York State, irrespective of creed, color, and nationality.

Miss Anne F. Hasbrouck, supt., to whom all applications for entrance must be made in person or by letter.

House by the Sea. See UNION SETTLEMENT.

House and School of Industry. See NEW YORK HOUSE AND SCHOOL OF INDUSTRY.

Housewives Aid Society, Inc., 121 East 59th St. (incorp. 1897). A woman's society for the assistance of all women who require work. To supply servants with positions free of charge, to improve the conditions and abilities of domestics, and to counteract the evils of ordinary intelligence offices. A premium is given to each servant who has retained her position for two years. They are assisted in case of need. Servants are procured for members of the society only. For membership and other information apply at the rooms of the society.

Officers: Mrs. J. J. Kittel, hon. pres.; Mrs. Paul Lichtenstein, pres.; Mrs. M. Schreitmiller, treas.; Mrs. R. Erbsloh, secy.

Housewives' League. See NATIONAL HOUSEWIVES' LEAGUE.

Hudson Guild. See SOCIETY FOR ETHICAL CULTURE.

Hudson River State Hospital (est. 1871), Poughkeepsie, N. Y. For the treatment, particularly, of the poor and indigent insane of Albany, Columbia, Dutchess, Green, Putnam, Rensselaer, Washington and Westchester counties. Capacity, 2,850. The hospital receives committed patients and suitable cases who come voluntarily. Clinics in Poughkeepsie, Yonkers, Mt. Vernon and Peekskill.

Walter G. Ryon, M.D., medical supt.

Hudson St. Hospital. See UNITED STATES PUBLIC HEALTH SERVICE.

Huguenot Home (est. 1900), 237 West 24th St. For French-speaking girls recently arrived or out of employment. Terms, $7.00 a week. Capacity, forty. Apply to M. Schmit, matron.

Humane Society of New York, The (incorp. 1904), 102 Fulton St., N.Y.C. (tel. Beekman 8644). For the prevention of cruelty to animals.

Officers: David Belais, pres.; Hon. Daniel M. Bedell, treas., 51 Chambers St.; Francis Colgate Dale, secy., Cold Spring, Putnam Co., N. Y.

Humanitarian League, The, 148 West 74th St., N.Y.C. A non-sectarian educational organization for developing modern thought on art, music, economics, prison reform, child labor, etc,

Misha Appelbaum, pres.

Hungarian-American Club. See LENOX HILL SETTLEMENT.

Hungarian Relief Society, 32 Pearl St., N.Y.C. Immigrant home now used by the Government for War Relief Work.

I

Immaculate Conception. Day Nursery, 117 Sands St., Brooklyn.

Immanual Evangelical Lutheran Church (German and English), 88th St. and Lexington Ave. Maintains a kindergarten and other institutional activities. Rev. George F. Schmidt, pastor, 1376 Lexington Ave., N.Y.C. See also under LUTHERAN CHURCHES in the Church List.

Immigrant Girls' Home. See METHODIST EPISCOPAL IMMIGRANT GIRLS' HOME.

Immigrant Mission. See NORWEGIAN EVANGELICAL LUTHERAN EMIGRANT MISSION.

Immigrant and Port Mission. See NEW YORK CITY SOCIETY OF THE METHODIST EPISCOPAL CHURCH.

Immigration Station. See UNITED STATES IMMIGRATION STATION.

Incarnation P. E. Church, Madison Ave. and 35th St., N.Y.C., Rev. H. Percy Silver. Maintains

BETHLEHEM DAY NURSERY, 249 East 30th St. For children, from one week to seven years of age, of working women, who pay five cents a day for each child. Open daily from 7 A. M. to 7 P. M., except Sundays and holidays.

Also varied forms of social service as nutritional lunches for school children, dental and medical clinics.

Community Music School, Men's Neighborhood Club, 243 East 34th St.

Incarnation Chapel, 240 East 31st St. (tel. Murray Hill 1094). Rev. George Ferrand Taylor, Vicar. Parish House, 240 East 31st St.

INDUSTRIAL CLASSES FOR CHILDREN. Sewing, dressmaking and cooking for girls, cobbling and carpentry for boys, Saturdays, 10 A M.

SUMMER HOME, Lake Mohegan,

Westchester Co., for mothers, children and working girls. July-September.

FRESH-AIR AND CONVALESCENT HOME, Lake Mohegan, N. Y.

LIBRARY, Girls' Friendly Society, clubs for men, women, boys, and girls.

GYMNASIUM, daily, except Sunday.

Independent Order of B'nai B'rith, Home for the Aged and Infirm. Office: 2307 Broadway, N.Y.C. (tel. Schuyler 9062). Home, Yonkers, N. Y. For aged and infirm members and their wives over sixty-five years of age, unable to maintain themselves.

William Goldschmidt, pres.; Max Levy, secy.

Indians. All Indians residing in New York are under State control. Indians who have strayed from their reservations should be referred to the Public Welfare Department, City of New York (q. v.).

There are several Indian Associations and missionary boards of the various church bodies which are active in promoting the political, educational, moral and spiritual improvement of the Indians and can supply information thereof. See American Missionary Assn., 287 Fourth Ave., Boards of Home and Foreign Missions of the Presbyterian Church, 156 Fifth Ave.; Domestic and Foreign Missionary Society of the P. E. Church, 281 Fourth Ave.; Baptist Home Mission Society, 23 East 26th St.; Home Mission Board of the M. E. Church, 150 Fifth Ave.; and the National Indian Association, 156 Fifth Ave.; Marquette League, 105 East 22d St., etc. See also Thomas Indian School.

Industrial Building, Charity Organization Society, 516 West 28th St., N.Y.C. See CHARITY ORGANIZATION SOCIETY, "Woodyard and Laundry."

Industrial Christian Alliance, The (incorp. 1891), 243 West 11th St., N.Y.C. (tel. Chelsea 1565). Helps the homeless and unemployed man who is able and willing to work, by giving temporary employment, which provides food and lodging while he is seeking work. Maintains:

An Employment Bureau for men, women and juveniles where service is free to all unable to pay; relieves distress where found; Thanksgiving and Christmas baskets are given to the worthy poor of the neighborhood.

Workshop and Shelter, 35 Perry St. Nearby lodging houses also used. The work is supported by membership dues and contributions and the work of the inmates. There are no salaried officers.

Application should be made to Miss Lucy L. Smedley, head worker at 243 West 11th St.

Officers: George T. Brokaw, pres.; Hamilton Fish, Jr., 1st vice-pres.; John A. Offord, 2nd vice-pres.; Benjamin H. Doane, secy.; Charles W. Knight, asst. secy.; Bruce M. Falconer, treas.; William W. Hoppin, counsel; Edwin Zimmerman, M.D., medical supervisor; Charles W. Knight, general manager.

Trustees: George T. Brokaw, Charles Suydam Cutting, Benjamin H. Doane, Bruce M. Falconer, Hamilton Fish, Jr., Barent Lefferts, John A. Offord, James R. McAfee, Herbert C. Pell, Howard P. Homans, E. Maurice B. Roche, Theodore Roosevelt, William Rhinelander Stewart, Theodosius Stevens, Edwin Zimmerman, M.D.

Industrial Home for the Blind, The (est. 1893, incorp. 1895), 512-524 Gates Ave., Brooklyn. To provide workshops and a home for blind mechanics.

Officers: W. C. Humstone, pres.; Herbert W. Heyer, treas.; Fenwick B. Small, secy.; E. P. Morford, supt.

Industrial Removal Office, The (est. 1900), 174 Second Ave., N.Y.C. (tel. Stuyvesant 5720). A philanthropic society designed to relieve the congestion in the Jewish quarters of New York City. Distributes able-bodied Jews in those sections of the country offering superior social and industrial opportunities. In the past eighteen years has sent over 80,000 persons to over 1,781 cities and towns in the United States. Thereby nuclei have been formed attracting dependent relatives and friends who would otherwise have remained in New York.

Isidore Frank, acting manager.

Industrial School Association of Brooklyn, E. D. (incorp. 1860), 141 South 3d St., Brooklyn, N. Y. (tel. Greenpoint 1242). Maintains a nonsectarian home for destitute children, two to sixteen years of age.

Kindergarten Annex, 482 Humboldt St.; Summer home, Hauppauge, L. I.

Col. A. D. Baird, pres.; Miss Anita J. Fernandez, supt.

Inebriety, Board of, City of New York. Abolished May, 1920. Work now carried on by the Department of Corrections. See CORRECTIONS, DEPT. OF., ETC.

Infantorium, The (est. 1918, incorp. 1919), 509 East 77th St., N.Y.C. (tel. Rhinelander 6755). (Admitting Office: tel. Columbus 702–703, office hours 11.00 A. M. to 1.00 P. M.) Purpose: Feeding cases and faulty metabolism. Capacity: twenty beds. Age limit under one year. Supported by private voluntary contributions.

Officers: Joseph A. Judd, pres.; Hon. Herman A. Metz, treas.; Anthony Gould, secy.; Louis Fischer, M.D., medical director.

Inner Mission Society of the Evangelical Lutheran Church, The, 70 East 128th St., N.Y.C. (tel. Harlem 2105). To relieve the needy; care for the sick, the fallen, prisoners, ex-convicts and their families, etc. Society maintains a Summer Home for needy children.

Rev. M. Luther Canup, pres., above address; Rev. F. F. Buermeyer, D.D., missionary, 21 West 126th St.

Institute for Crippled and Disabled Men, The (org. by Red Cross 1917, incorp. 1920), 101 East 23d St. (tel. Gramercy 1567). To discover and provide suitable means to enable men, and boys of work age, with a physical disability impairing the use of their limbs, to earn their living; to promote general interest in the problem of the rehabilitation of the disabled; to offer counsel and advice to individuals and organizations seeking help for crippled and disabled men.

Maintains a free employment agency for the placement of crippled and disabled men and boys. Makes surveys of industrial processes suitable for handicapped persons. Gives training in the following occupations: mechanical drafting, oxy-acetylene welding, monotype operating, jewelry making, motion picture projecting, typewriter repair, nickel plating, enameling, telephone switchboard operating. Manufactures and provides artificial limbs and appliances at cost and on easy terms to deserving persons. Maintains a special library on work for the disabled. Publishes and disseminates literature on the subject. Co-operates with social and industrial agencies in formulating plans for the training and placement of men crippled and disabled by accident or disease. Supported by voluntary contributions.

Officers: Samuel M. Greer, pres.; Jeremiah Milbank, treas.; Douglas C. McMurtrie, secy.; John Culbert Faries, director.

Institute for Government Research, Inc., 818 Connecticut Ave., N. W., Washington. Studies problems of public administration; makes known scientific principles and procedure in methods of government.

Officers: Robert S. Brookings, chrm.; Frederick Strauss, treas.; W. F. Willoughby, director.

Institute of Our Lady of Christian Doctrine. See SISTERS OF OUR LADY OF CHRISTIAN DOCTRINE.

Institute for Public Service (est. 1915), 423 West 120th St. Training school for Public Service with training in actual service.

Institution for the Improved Instruction of Deaf-Mutes (org. 1867, incorp. 1869), 904–922 Lexington Ave., cor. 67th St., N.Y.C. To educate children who, on account of deafness, cannot receive instruction in the public schools. It provides an education in the common school branches. Speech and lip-reading are taught to all, the Oral Method of Instruction being used exclusively. Maintains also Kindergarten and Industrial Departments. A trade is given to each pupil; a gymnasium is provided, and systematic physical culture exercises are required.

Children between five and twelve years are admitted upon certificates from the Commissioner of Charities; over twelve, upon appointment by the Commissioner of Education. Mentally deficient children are not accepted. Accommodates 278. Children not residing in the State are charged $450 a year for tuition and maintenance, or $275 for tuition alone. Support by State and County funds, membership dues, and voluntary contributions. Controlled by a Board of Trustees.

Officers: Felix H. Levy, pres.; Clarence J. Housman, treas.; Samuel M. Newburger, secy.; Harris Taylor, principal, to whom apply for admission.

Institution for the Instruction of the Deaf and Dumb. See NEW YORK INSTITUTION, etc.

Institution of Mercy (org. 1848, incorp. 1854), N. E. cor. 81st St. and Madison Ave., N.Y.C. (tel. Lenox 865). A work with, and a home for destitute girls committed by city, or referred by other agencies. Maintains also two homes for working girls:

THE REGINA ANGELORUM, 112 East 106th St.

THE DEVIN CLARE, 415 West 120th St.

Mother Mary Rose, Superioress.

Institutional Synagogue, The (created and org. 1917), 1893 Seventh Ave., N.Y.C. A traditional Synagogue in modern Jewish life; its activities are religious and civic, social service, educational, employment bureau, relief, athletic.

Officers: Hon. Isaac Siegel, pres., 51 Chambers St.; Rabbi Herbert S. Goldstein, organizer and director.

Intercession Chapel of Trinity Parish, 155th St. and Broadway, N. Y. C. Rev. Milo H. Gates, D.D., S.T.D., Vicar. Maintains:

CLUBS AND CLASSES for men, women, and children.

FREE EMPLOYMENT BUREAU, 10 A. M. to 12 M.

INDUSTRIAL CLASSES in cooking, sewing and embroidery, tooled leather, brass work, and basketry.

CLOTHING BUREAU.

CHILDREN'S FARM GARDEN.

KINDERGARTEN.

See also under PROTESTANT EPISCOPAL CHURCHES in the Church List.

Interchurch Committee on Unemployment. See NEW YORK FEDERATION OF CHURCHES.

Interchurch World Movement, 45 West 18th St., N.Y.C.

International Association of Daily Vacation Bible Schools, 90 Bible House, N. Y. (tel. Stuyvesant 5161). To bring together in every community and in every communion, idle children, idle churches, idle students, idle vacationists in unsectarian Daily Vacation Bible Schools, combining worship, work, play, and patriotism.

International Children's School Farm League, The Mansion, N. Y. Botanical Garden, Bronx Park, N.Y.C. (tel. Williamsbridge 215). An organization to spread the use of gardens in the education of children and headquarters for expert advice and information.

International Christian Police Association, New York Branch (1892), 226 East 58th St. (tel. Plaza 3723). To promote the welfare of policemen and their families. Unsectarian.

S. R. Kendall, pres.; Rev. J. L. Spicer, secy. and chaplain.

International Church Film Corporation, 920 Broadway, N.Y.C. Works for the production of films illustrating scriptural and others subjects for use in Churches and Sunday schools.

International Committee of Young Men's Christian Associations, The (org. 1854, incorp. 1883), 347 Madison Ave., N.Y.C. (tel. Vanderbilt 1200). Is composed of nearly 200 representative business men scattered throughout North America. Employs 217 supervisory secretaries in America and 203 abroad.

Officers: A. E. Marling, chrm.; B. H. Fancher, treas.; J. R. Mott, gen. secy.

THE NATIONAL WAR WORK COUNCIL has striven in a comprehensive and united way to promote the spiritual, mental, physical and social welfare of men in the military and naval force of the United States, both in America and over-seas; and has also extended its helpful ministry to the men of the Allied Armies, and to the Prisoners-of-War in Europe.

Officers: William Sloane, chrm.; Cleveland H. Dodge, treas.; J. R. Mott, gen. secy.

International Health Board. See ROCKEFELLER FOUNDATION, THE.

International Institute for Young Women, Y. W. C. A. Headquarters, 121 East 21st St., N.Y.C. (tel. Gramercy 2434). To educate, protect, and advise foreign-born women of any nationality, living in New York City; it employs visitors who speak the principal European languages; conducts free classes in English and other useful subjects; co-operates with all social agencies in the interest of foreign-born people; provides recreation and arranges outings and vacations; maintains a boarding home for foreign-born girls earning small wages.

Officers: Mrs. Francis McNeil Bacon, chrm.; Mrs. Dunlevy Milbank, vice-chrm.; Mrs. Wm. E. Baker, secy.; Mrs. E. M. Cravath, treas.; Edith L. Jardine, gen. secy.

BRONX INTERNATIONAL INSTITUTE, Y. W. C. A. (est. 1918), 245 East 152d St., N.Y.C. A service bureau for foreign-speaking people of all nationalities in the Bronx.

Officers: Mrs. E. Jean Nelson Penfield, chrm.; Mrs. J. M. Hodson, treas.; Miss Anna Gardner, secy.; Mrs. James R. Harrison, exec. secy.

International Medical Missionary Society (org. 1881, incorp. 1886), 156 Fifth Ave., N.Y.C. Aids young men and women who are preparing to become Medical Missionaries, and maintains a summer home for missionaries at Goshen, Mass. Supported by voluntary contributions. Receipts for the year ending Sept. 30, 1920, $6,696,-98; expenditures, $6,645.87 incomplete.

International Order of The King's Daughters and Sons, The (founded 1886, incorp. 1888). Headquarters: 280 Madison Ave., N.Y.C. (tel. Vanderbilt 2632). An interdenominational society, whose objects are to develop spiritual life and to stimulate Christian activities. The order works in circles of few or many members, each circle choosing and directing its own work. All relief work is done by the individual members or by branches of the order. Reports of the work are printed in a monthly magazine, "The Silver Cross."

Officers: Mrs. Robert J. Reed, Wheeling, W. Va., pres.; Mrs. Charles A. Menet, gen. secy.; Mrs. Anthony H. Evans, editor.

International Peace Forum. See WORLD'S COURT LEAGUE, INC.

International Reform Bureau (incorp. 1896), 206 Pennsylvania Ave. S. E., Washington, D. C. To promote by legislation, lectures, literature, and correspôndence those moral reforms on which churches are generally agreed, especially those related to intoxicants, sex abuses, gambling, and Sabbath observance; moral legislation in Congress, completion of crusade against race gambling, federal censorship of films, restoration and improvement of daily Bible reading in schools and homes, and civic evangelism. This Bureau owns two unencumbered office buildings, one in Washington, the other in Peking. The former has adjacent land on which a reform literature endowment building is to be erected.

Officers: Rev. Robert Watson, D.D., pres.; Rev. Lucius C. Clark, secy.; Rev. Wilbur F. Crafts, supt. and treas.; Rev. Henry N. Pringle, asst. supt.; Prof. John A. Nicholls, Foreign Field secy.; Rev. John F. Brant, Boston Branch Office, secy.; Mrs. W. F. Crafts, missionary secy.; Mrs. Rosa E. Pennell, office secy. and cashier; B. B. Bassette, auditor.

International Serbian Educational Institute, 701 Madison Ave., N.Y.C. Offers training in American technical schools or colleges to limited number of Serbian students.

Officers: Dr. Rosalie S. Morton, chrm.; Paul F. Cooley, treas.; K. S. Ward, exec. secy.

International Sunshine Branch for Blind Babies, Room 32, 96 Fifth Ave., N.Y.C. (tel. Chelsea 4315). Maintains the

SUNSHINE HOME FOR BLIND BABIES, 84th St. and Thirteenth Ave., Brooklyn. City and private children admitted, $547.50 a year.

Officers: Mrs. John Alden, pres.; Mrs. Mary D. Beattie, treas.; Mrs. Nellie E. C. Furman, secy.

***International Union of Gospel Missions** (incorp.). New York District, 126 Bible House, N.Y.C. To establish fellowship and co-operation with all engaged or interested in Gospel Missions and other rescue work.

Interstate Park Commission. See PALISADES INTERSTATE PARK, COMMISSIONERS OF THE.

Investigation Bureau of the Charity Organization Society, 105 East 22d St., N.Y.C., supplies individuals and charity organization societies in other cities with information concerning families or individuals in New York City in whom they are interested.

Miss Isabel Hoes, acting secy.

Inwood House. Temporarily closed.

Irish Emigrant Society (org. 1841, incorp. 1844), 51 Chambers St. and 29 Reade St., N.Y.C. Affords advice, information, aid, and protection to immi-

* *Current information not received.*

grants from Ireland, and endeavors generally to promote their welfare. Apply from 9 A. M. to 3 P. M.

These works are supported by the sale of drafts, money orders, and passage tickets.

Officers: Michael F. McDermott, pres.; Thos. V. Brady, treas.; John J. Foley, secy.

Isaac T. Hopper Home. See WOMEN'S PRISON ASSOCIATION.

Isabella Home, formerly The Isabella Home Society of Astoria (org. 1875, incorp. 1889), Amsterdam Ave., cor. of 190th St., N.Y.C. For the gratuitous care of aged persons, chronic invalids, and convalescents. Can accommodate 172. A home for the care and maintenance of aged persons, without distinction of sex, creed, or nationality, males over sixty-five years of age, and females over sixty years of age, of fair average health, unable to support themselves. Applications and admission will be denied to: (a) Those having children, who are legally or morally bound to support their parents. (b) Those suffering from infectious diseases, cancer or urinary incontinency. (c) Consumptives, epileptics, idiots, blind persons, paralytics, helpless cripples. (d) All those requiring constant personal attendance. The privilege of sending convalescents has also been granted to most large hospitals. Any qualified person deemed worthy is taken free of charge.

Application for admission to the Home Department must be made personally to the Committee on Admission, at the Home, on Thursdays from 2–4 P. M. Application to the Convalescent Wards can be made to a member of the Consulting Board of Physicians during their office hours. August Caille, M.D., 753 Madison Ave.; A. G. Gerster, M.D., 34 East 75th St.; Curt Nicolai, M.D., 81 West 119th St.

Officers: Mrs. Anna Woerishoffer, pres.; Adolph Kuttroff, vice-pres.; August Zinsser, treas.; C. A. Schwab, rec. secy.; W. Wettengel, M.D., attending physician; Mr. and Mrs. C. von Boetticher, supt. and matron.

Island Mission, The (org. 1887, incorp. 1891) (tel. Stuyvesant 2750). To cheer the lives of the destitute and sick in the public institutions, by giving various comforts and amusements beyond those provided from public funds. Supported by voluntary contributions.

Officers: Mrs. Cadwalader Jones, pres.; Mrs. Max Farrand, treas., 285 Prospect St., New Haven, Conn.; Miss Adah Marks, secy., 45 East 82d St., N.Y.C., to any of whom apply.

Israel Hospital of Brooklyn. See UNITED ISRAEL ZION HOSPITAL AND DISPENSARY.

Israel Orphan Asylum (incorp. 1917), 274 East 2d St., N.Y.C. (tel. Orchard 3254–7617). A home for Jewish orphan children; also furnishes temporary shelter to needy children, one to five years of age.

Officers: Judge Gustave Hartman, pres.; David Friedman, supt.; David Baum, secy.

Italian Benevolent Institute and Italian Hospital of the Borough of Manhattan (incorp. 1905), 83d St. and East River, N.Y.C. (tel. Lenox 7990–7992). For the relief of sick and needy Italians. Capacity, 100 beds, seventy-five per cent free. Chronic or contagious cases not admitted. No other discrimination made. Maintains also a Dispensary.

Executive Committee: John W. Perilli, M.D., pres.; Ruffino Conti, treas.; Amedeo Riggio, secy.

Italian Benevolent Society of the Sons of Columbus Legion, The (org. 1897, incorp. 1900), 450 East 117th St., N.Y.C. Branch for Mutual Aid.

Italian Educational League, Inc. (est. 1909; incorp. 1910). P. S. 21, 222 Mott St., N.Y.C. The League proposes to study the natural, healthy interests of Italian children, and provide for their encouragement and growth.

Italian Hospital. See ITALIAN BENEVOLENT INSTITUTE AND HOSPITAL.

Italian Day Nursery. See CHILDREN'S AID SOCIETY.

Italian War Relief Fund of America, Inc., 347 Madison Ave., N.Y.C. Varied relief work in Italy; care of war orphans.

Officers: Robert Underwood Johnson, pres.; S. Reading Bertron, treas.; Mrs. William Vanamee, secy.

Italian Welfare League (est. 1920), 315 East 28th St., N.Y.C. (tel. Mad. Sq. 2344). Supported by contributions and membership.

Officers: Mrs. Lionello Perera, pres.; Mrs. Stefano Berizzi, treas.; Mrs. Felice Bava, secy.

Italica Gens. Temporarily closed.

J

Jacob A. Riis Neighborhood Settlement, The, including the Jacob A. Riis House and The King's Daughters' House (org. 1890, incorp. 1894), 48-50 Henry St., N.Y.C. (tel. Orchard 34). To work for better neighborhood conditions. Clubs and classes for men, women, children. Two kindergartens, playground and gymnasium, two summer camps. Under the direction of a Board of Managers.

Officers: Mrs. Jacob A. Riis, pres.; Mrs. Ezra Todd, treas.; Mrs. Chas. D. Sinclair, asst. treas.; Miss Nellie Twyeffort, secy.; Miss Helen H. Jessup, head worker; Theodora Bates, community worker; Edna W. Storm, girls' director; Wm. J. de Forest, boys' director; Mabel S. Briggs, fin. secy.; Louis Di Lorenzo, director of gymnasium; Drusilla Matthews, club worker; Irene O'Neil, club worker.

Jacobi Hospital. See A. JACOBI HOSPITAL.

Jamaica Hospital, The (incorp. 1892), New York Ave., Jamaica, N. Y. (tel. Jamaica 87-279). A general hospital. Capacity 63 beds. Supported by voluntary contributions. Managed by a board of fourteen trustees, representing the Protestant Churches of Jamaica.

Officers: W. C. Reid, pres.; W. C. Witherstine, treas.; Mrs. E. R. Carman, secy.; Miss R. A. Saffeir, R.N., supt.

Jan Hus Bohemian Presbyterian Church and Neighborhood House, 347-351 East 74th St., N.Y.C. Under the Board of Home Missions of the Presbyterian Church. Maintains classes and other social activities for the people of the neighborhood.

See also under PRESBYTERIAN CHURCHES in the Church List.

Jane Elkus Home. See FREE SYNAGOGUE.

Japanese Christian Association, Shiudo Kwai (est. 1908), 102 West 123d St., N.Y.C. Center for Japanese, chiefly young men. A dormitory accommodates twenty residents.

Officers: Dr. T. Takami, pres., 176 Washington Park, Brooklyn; Saburo Bito, secy. and treas.; Rev. Tamezo Harada, missionary.

Japanese Christian Institute, Inc., 328-330 East 57th St., N.Y.C.

An institutional mission for Japanese people. Free employment, aid to sick and poor. Free night-school to teach English. Religious, social, educational meetings during week. Home Department accommodates twenty young men.

Rev. Sojiro Shimizu, pastor; Geo. Z. Shigeta, secy.

Jeanes Foundation, Anna T. See NEGRO RURAL SCHOOL FUND.

Jeanne D'Arc Home for French Girls. See SISTERS OF DIVINE PROVIDENCE.

Jennie Clarkson Home for Children, The (incorp. 1892), Valhalla, Westchester County, N. Y. A Protestant unsectarian home, free for destitute orphans of both sexes and half orphans in cases where the surviving parent is unable to support the child. Children received from five to ten years of age. Capacity, sixty. Visiting days for relatives and friends are the first Sunday and the third Saturday of each month.

School instruction to the eighth grade is given, and in addition, girls receive instruction in cooking, dressmaking, sewing, laundry, and all household work. Boys receive regular household instructions, also in gardening and care of stock. Controlled by a board of directors and supported by invested funds, subscriptions, and donations.

Officers: Edward McK. Whiting, pres., 48 Wall St., N. Y.; Leonard D. White, treas., 60 Broadway, N. Y.; Joseph M. Lesser, secy., 126 Liberty St., N. Y.; Martin K. Sherwin, supt.

Jewell Day Nursery, The (incorp.), 20 Macdougal St., N.Y.C. (tel. Spring 3080). For children, from six weeks to six years old, of poor mothers working away from home, who pay, when able, ten cents a day for each child. Capacity for fifty. Open from 7 A. M. to 7 P. M. daily, except Sundays and legal holidays. Has a kindergarten.

Officers: Mrs. Arthur M. Dodge, pres.; Mrs. August Hecksher and Mrs. J. B. Erhardt, vice-prests.; Miss C. W. Stewart, treas., Glen Ridge, N. J.; Mrs. Marshall J. Dodge, secy.; Miss M. V. Miles, superintendent.

Jewett Training School for Nurses. See BUSHWICK HOSPITAL.

Jewish Agricultural and Industrial Aid Society, The (org. 1900), 174 Second Ave., N.Y.C. Assists and encourages agriculture among Jewish immigrants in the United States.

The Society's activities extend to every State in the Union.

Officers: Cyrus L. Sulzberger, pres.; Morris D. Waldman, treas.; Eugene S. Benjamin, secy.; Gabriel Davidson, general manager.

Jewish Big Brother Association. See JEWISH PROTECTORY AND AID SOCIETY.

Jewish Big Sisters (est. 1912). Main office, 356 Second Ave., N.Y.C. Branches, 137 East 22d St. and 355 East 137th St. (tel. Gramercy 4985–3253). An organization which stresses on the preventive aspects of work with girls who are referred by their parents, visiting teachers, truant officers, settlements and other organizations. Co-operates with the Society for Prevention of Cruelty to Children, Children's Court, Domestic Relations Court, Truancy Court. The activities are personal, educational, and recreational. Also conducts a psychiatric and dental clinic.

THE ANCHORAGE, the vacation home of the Jewish Big Sisters, for working girls at Arverne, Long Island. The girls are permitted to remain for two weeks, paying one-third of their salary, weekly. Mrs. Sidney C. Borg, chrm.; Mrs. A. Slesinger, exec. secy.

THE BLUE BIRD CAMP, for children of school age, at Spring Valley, N. Y. The children are permitted to remain at the camp for two weeks, and board is only charged to those who can afford to pay.

Jewish Community (Kehillah) (org. 1909, incorp. 1914), 114 Fifth Ave., N.Y.C. Purpose: To further the cause of Judaism in New York City, and to represent the Jews of this city in all local matters of Jewish interest. Reorganized (1918) on district plan. Greater City divided into 18 districts, in which 540 organizations are represented: 160 synagogues, 30 educational institutions, 14 recreation centers, 139 mutual aid societies, 107 lodges, 19 economic agencies, 60 philanthropic institutions, and 21 Zionist societies. Each district administered by local board, of which chairman is ex-officio member of Kehillah Executive Committee.

Officers: J. L. Magnes, chrm.; Cyrus L. Sulzberger and Bernard Semel, vice-chrm.; William Fischman, treas.; S. Benderly, chrm. Administrative Council.

Jewish Consumptives' Relief Society (Denver Sanatorium), (org. and incorp. 1904). New York office, 31 Union Square, West; Sanatorium Edgewater, Colorado. A national institution open to all indigent patients of the United States for the cure of tuberculosis, admitting all stages of the disease. Maintained by voluntary contributions. Total number of cases treated up to Jan. 1, 1920, 3,514. Capacity, 180. All free beds.

H. Rosen, manager; C. Miller, secy., N. Y. office.

Jewish Deaf, Society for the Welfare of, 40 West 115th St., N.Y.C. (tel. Harlem 7637). To furnish industrial education and secure work for the unemployed Jewish deaf-mutes of New York; to promote their social and intellectual welfare; to give them religious instruction and opportunities for public worship.

The following activities are maintained: Communal Center for the Jewish Deaf, Employment Bureau, Bureau of Advice, Relief and Information, Social Service Department, Evening Classes for Immigrant Deaf and partly educated deaf, publishes monthly magazine, "The Jewish Deaf," supplies Rabbi to Hebrew Congregation of the Deaf; religious services held regularly; religious classes at the New York Institution for the Deaf, 163d St. and Ft. Washington Ave., and P. S. 47 for the Deaf; lectures on current topics, socials and entertainments, organizes clubs of the deaf.

Officers: Abraham Erlanger, pres., 350 Broadway; Louis J. Robertson, vice-pres., 41 Spruce St.; Norman M. Cohen, vice-pres., 694 Broadway; Sydney B. Erlanger, treas., 354 Fourth Ave.; Mark G. Holstein, hon. secy., 35 Nassau St.; Rabbi Albert J. Amateau, exec. director.

Jewish Home for Aged and Infirm, The (org. 1912), 107 West 4th St., Mt. Vernon, N. Y. City Office: 44 7th St., N. Y. (tel. Orchard 2313). Cares for homeless, aged and infirm Jews free of charge; also receives convalescents. Present number accommodated is forty.

Officers: Dr. P. A. Siegelstein, pres.; A. L. Kalman, vice-pres., 220 East 12th St.; Dr. J. E. Braunstein, secy., South 9th St. and Marcy Ave., Brooklyn.

***Jewish Hospital of Brooklyn** (incorp. 1901), Classon and St. Mark's Aves. and Prospect Place.

***Jewish Ladies' Day Nursery, The** (est. 1916), 1668 Bathgate Ave., N. Y. C.

Jewish Maternity Hospital (incorp. 1906), 270–272 East Broadway, N.Y.C. (tel. Orchard 4015). To provide medical and surgical care and treatment

* *Current information not received.*

to patients during confinement. Capacity, fifty beds. Supported by voluntary contributions.

Officers: Sam Finkelstein, pres.; Mark L. Abraham, treas.; A. Bakst, secy; Helen Rosenberger, supt.

Jewish Memorial Hospital (formerly Philanthropin Hospital) (1905), Fifth Ave. and 128th St., N.Y.C. (tel. Harlem 6131–6132). Free to the poor; others able to pay are charged from $12 per week and upward.

Officers: Edmund Schwartz, pres.; Isidor S. Schweitzer, treas.; Joseph Feinberg, secy.; Dr. A. N. Schiller, supt.

Jewish People's Relief Committee, 175 East Broadway, N.Y.C. Collects funds in America for the Jewish war sufferers in Europe. Branch of Joint Distribution Committee.

Officers: Alexander Kahn, chrm.; Shepard J. Goldberg, treas.; B. Zuckerman, mgr.; Isador Garelick, secy.

Jewish Protectory and Aid Society, Inc., 356 Second Ave., N.Y.C. (tel. Gramercy 3253). Maintains the following:

HAWTHORNE SCHOOL, Hawthorne, N.Y. (tel. Pleasantville 391). Capacity, 375. John Klein, supt.

CEDAR KNOLLS SCHOOL (for girls), Hawthorne, N. Y., Mrs. Sidney C. Borg, chrm.

COMMITTEE ON OUTSIDE ACTIVITIES, 356 Second Ave., N.Y.C. Lawrence H. Marks, executive director; Benjamin D. Kaplan, exec. secy.; Departments: (a) Jewish Big Brother Association, Lawrence H. Marks, chrm.; (b) Department of Prevention and After-care; (c) Department of Parole.

Officers: Mortimer L. Schiff, pres.; Edgar J. Kohler, secy.

Jewish Sabbath Alliance of America, Inc., 110 Fifth Ave., N.Y.C. (tel. Watkins 6268). Branch office: 433 Grand St. Object: To promote the observance of the Seventh Day Sabbath in every possible way and manner. Maintains an Employment Bureau for Sabbath Observers, free to both employer and employee.

William Rosenberg, exec. secy.

Jewish Theological Seminary of America (founded 1886, reorg. 1902), 513–535 West 123d St., N.Y.C. Gives to Jewish men free education and training for the Jewish ministry. Teachers' Institute for men and women established 1909 in connection with its work at 36 Stuyvesant St., N.Y.C.

Officers: Dr. Cyrus Adler, pres.; Joseph B. Abrahams, secy.; Louis Marshall, chrm. Board of Directors.

Jewish Welfare Board, 149 Fifth Ave., N.Y.C. (tel. Ashland 7770). This Board conducts welfare activities for soldiers, sailors and marines in camps and communities. Work being extended to include promotion and supervision of Jewish community centers throughout the country.

Officers: Dr. Cyrus Adler, acting chrm. of Executive Committee, Philadelphia, Pa.; Walter E. Sachs, treas.; Joseph Rosenzweig, secy.; Harry L. Glucksman, exec. director.

Jewish Working-Girls' Vacation Society (est. 1890, incorp. 1892), Bellport, L. I., Big Indian, N. Y., and Arverne, L. I. Provides vacation homes for working girls. Bellport Home, capacity, 102. Big Indian Home, capacity, sixty-eight, and Arverne, week-ends for working girls, mid-week for mothers.

Any working girl, sixteen years or over, of good character, is accepted, if her condition is such as to be no menace to others. There is no limitation as to nationality, race, or sect. District limited to Greater New York. Application Bureau during summer months at Educational Alliance, 197 East Broadway, by courtesy of the Educational Alliance. The three branches named (No. 3) constitute the work of the organization controlled by a managing board of directors.

The working girls are expected to pay $7 a week for board; but a free fund, specially collected by directors for the purpose, provides board payment for girls who are in need of the rest and country life, and are unable to pay the nominal sum asked. The vacations are of one week or a fortnight's duration. In exceptional cases or upon physician's request, a longer period is granted.

John E. Berwind Maternity Clinic, 125–129 East 103d St., N.Y.C., formerly Free Out-door Maternity Clinic at 216 East 76th St. (org. 1902). For only such cases as are unable to pay.

Advice and information of maternity cases and examination and guidance of pregnant women, Wednesdays and Saturdays, 2–4 P. M. Care and supervision both at home and clinic by prenatal nurses during entire pregnancy.

Attendance by doctors and nurses at the home during confinement.

Supervision, care and treatment of the infants for a year; medical supervision and instruction in infant feeding, at the clinic every week-day afternoon, 2–4 P. M.

A gynecological clinic, open only to women already under the care of the maternity clinic, Tuesdays, 10 A. M. to 1 P. M.

Emergency cases attended in the homes of patients by doctors and nurses from the clinic, at any time.

A social investigator is employed for the re-enforcement of the clinic's work.

Training in obstetrical cases is offered for nurses and medical students.

Officers: Clinic conducted by Mr. John E. Berwind and Dr. I. L. Hill. Chief of Obstetrical Department, Dr. I. L. Hill; chief of Pediatric Department, Dr. Herman Schwarz; head resident physician, Dr. Edward J. Goodbody.

John F. Slater Fund (Trustees of the John F. Slater Fund; incorp. 1881), 61 Broadway, N.Y.C. (tel. Bowling Green 7100). To promote education among the negroes of the South, special attention being paid to industrial training and education for the work of teaching.

Dr. James H. Dillard, pres. and director, Charlottesville, Virginia.

John Hall Memorial Chapel and Association House. See FIFTH AVENUE PRESBYTERIAN CHURCH, this List.

John Hus Bohemian Church. See JAN HUS, etc.

Joint Application Bureau, 105 East 22d St., N.Y.C. Roy P. Gates, superintendent. Maintained jointly by the Charity Organization Society (q. v.) and the N. Y. Association for Improving the Condition of the Poor (q. v.).

Open from 9 A. M. to midnight every day in the year. All homeless applicants to both societies are under the treatment of this Bureau. Relief is given when necessary; able-bodied men are given work; permanent work is secured for many applicants; the sick are placed in hospitals or convalescent homes. Transportation is secured when possible for applicants having homes in other places.

Joint Distribution Committee of the American Funds for Jewish War Sufferers, 20 Exchange Pl. (tel. Hanover 915). Represents the American Jewish Relief Committee (q. v.), the Central Relief Committee (q. v.), and the Jewish People's Relief Committee (q. v.).

Officers: Felix M. Warburg, chrm.; Paul Baerwald, treas.; Albert Lucas, secy. Address the Secretary.

Joint Committee on Tuberculosis. See COMMITTEE FOR THE CARE OF THE JEWISH TUBERCULOUS.

Joralemon Street Boys' Club. See YOUNG MEN AND BOYS' CLUB.

Judson Memorial Baptist Church, Washington Square South, N.Y.C. Rev. A. Ray Petty, Pastor. Maintains various features of institutional church work for all ages, including clubs, classes, gymnasium, kindergarten, nursery, community meetings and district visitation and relief.

See also under BAPTIST CHURCHES in the Church List.

Julia Richman High School Placement Bureau, 60 West 13th St. (tel. Chelsea 4478). For girls, students or graduates of the school only, stenographers, bookkeepers, clerical workers, etc. No fees.

Junior Employment Service. See VOCATIONAL GUIDANCE AND EMPLOYMENT SERVICE FOR JUNIORS.

Junior House, Inc., 90 State St., Brooklyn, N. Y. To aid young boys to become self-supporting and to surround them with home influence. Supported by voluntary contributions.

Miss M. L. Proudfoot, resident mgr.

Junior League of the City of New York, Inc. (org. 1900), 6 East 45th St., N.Y.C. (tel. Vanderbilt 3009–3008). To foster among its members interest in the social, economic, and educational conditions in New York and by volunteer service to bring them in touch with what is done along these lines.

Officers: Mrs. Vanderbilt Webb, pres.; Miss Sarah T. Bulkley, treas.; Mrs. J. T. Johnston Mali, secy.

Junior League of Brooklyn (org. 1910), 93 Court St., Brooklyn (tel. Main 9248). To promote active interest in social and industrial problems. Supported by contributions.

Officers: Miss Elizabeth G. Haight, pres.; Miss Helen L. Babbott, treas.; Miss Mary O. Polak, secy.

Juvenile Courts. See CHILDREN'S COURTS.

K

Kallman Scandinavian Orphanage, The (incorp. 1898), Eighteenth Ave., between 67th and 69th Sts. Brooklyn (tel. Bath Beach 1451). Number of inmates, eighty. Annual expenditure, approximately $10,000. Supported by voluntary contributions.

Officers: Charles A. Ogren, pres., 1344 Pacific St.; David Woodworth, treas.; William C. Johnson, secy.; John Lindblom, manager.

Katherine, The. See LADIES' CHRISTIAN UNION.

Keating Day Nursery (est. 1898), 431 East 12th St. Capacity, 177. Children received from the ages of three months to six years.

Sister Annunciata in charge.

Kennedy House, 423 West 43d St., N.Y.C. (tel. Longacre 1335). A small settlement in New York's middle West Side. In addition to clubs and classes, it takes an active interest in civic and social affairs of the district.

William Demarest, director.

Keswick Colony of Mercy. Discontinued.

Kindergarten Association. See NEW YORK KINDERGARTEN ASSOCIATION; also NATIONAL KINDERGARTEN ASSOCIATION.

Kings County Hospital. See PUBLIC WELFARE DEPARTMENT.

King's Daughters' House in Harlem. See MARGARET BOTTOME MEMORIAL.

King's Daughters' League of Needlewomen, The (org. 1897). Sales of new garments are held twice a year, for which tickets are given to worthy working women, whereby they may purchase garments at a nominal price. Miss Elizabeth Merrell, secy., 131 South Ave., Mariners' Harbor, Staten Island.

Kings Park State Hospital (est. 1885), Kings Park, L. I. (tel. Kings Park 11) New York City Office, Hall of Records, 51 Chambers St., N.Y.C. (tel. Worth 4424), Wednesday, 9.30 A. M. A State hospital for the insane of Borough of Kings and Counties of Nassau and Suffolk, situated forty-five miles from New York City. Accessible by trains on the Long Island Railroad. Visiting days, Sundays, Wednesdays and holidays. Free for insane poor and indigent persons. Capacity, 4800.

Wm. C. Garvin, M.D., supt.

Kingston Ave. Hospital. See HEALTH, DEPARTMENT OF.

Kips Bay Boys' Club, (org. 1915), 825 Second Ave., N.Y.C. (tel. Vanderbilt 9522). Co-operatively maintained by the Children's Aid Society and the Kips Bay Neighborhood Association. Educational, athletic and social activities for boys and young men. Gymnasium, vocational classes, employment bureau, auditorium, clinic, Boys' Camp, etc. Club House open afternoons and evenings throughout the year.

Arthur Huck, supt.

Kips Bay Day Nursery, The (org. 1902, incorp. 1903), 402 East 50th St., N.Y.C. For the care, during the day, of children not over six whose mothers are the breadwinners of the family. Open 7 A. M. to 6.30 P. M.

Agnes L. Gifford, supt.

Kips Bay Neighborhood Association (org. 1913, incorp. 1917). Composed of those who live or have business or social interests between 28th and 59th St., Fifth Ave. and East River. It aims to bring individuals and welfare agencies together, to encourage co-operation; to aid in governmental activities and to act as a community clearing house for the district.

Officers: George Debevoise, pres.; Charles C. Burlingham, Mrs. Samuel Sloan, vice-presidents; Samuel Sloane, treas.; Miss Sara Cleveland Clapp, secy., 829 Second Ave.

Knapp Memorial Eye Hospital. See HERMAN KNAPP, etc.

Knickerbocker Hospital (incorp. 1862, 1895, 1913, opened 1884), Amsterdam Ave. and 131st St., N.Y.C. (tel. Morningside 63). Free medical and surgical treatment to the worthy poor. Incurable, contagious, alcoholic, maternity, or insane patients not admitted. Capacity, 55. Supported by voluntary contributions. Visiting days, Tuesday, Friday, and Sunday from 2–4 P. M.

Ambulance Service for the district. Dispensary free to the poor only.

Lucy M. Moore, supt.

L

Labor Bureau. See STATE INDUSTRIAL COMMISSION.

Labor, State Department of. See STATE INDUSTRIAL COMMISSION.

Labor Temple (est. 1910), 239 East 14th St., at Second Ave., N.Y.C. (tel. Stuyvesant 3368). An institutional church under the Presbytery of New York. Provides employment, clubs, and classes for foreigners, general relief, children's playground, motion pictures. Supported by voluntary contributions and private subscriptions.

Jonathan Day, director; Edmund B. Chaffee, associate.

Ladies' Benevolent Association of the Seventeenth Ward of Brooklyn (org. 1872). Meets first Friday in the month. Maintains

GREENPOINT HOME FOR THE AGED (incorp. 1882), Oak and Guernsey Sts., (tel. Greenpoint 1520), for the aged of the 17th Ward of Brooklyn.

Ladies of Charity of the Catholic Charities of New York (formerly Association of Catholic Charities) (org. 1902, incorp. 1912), 667 Lexington Ave., N.Y.C. (tel. Plaza 8047). To promote cordial co-operation between all workers in the line of Catholic philanthropy, social welfare and civic work, and by unity to strengthen and enlarge their sphere of usefulness. The membership of 3,500 is engaged in the various fields of charitable endeavor under an Executive Committee composed of the following chairmen: Harlem Parish Centers, Mrs. E. D. Farrell; Manhattan Parish Centers, Mrs. Edward Mandel; Bronx Parish Centers, Miss Louise J. Madden; Association of Catholic Day Nurseries of New York, Mrs. John A. Jackson; French Charities, Countess de Laugier-Villars; Catholic Big Sisters, Mrs. H. Gloster Armstrong; Hospital Visiting, Blackwell's Island, Mrs. Nicholas F. Brady; Bellevue, Miss Yvonne Gourd; Incurables, Mrs. H. Knickerbocker Viele; Fresh Air Work, Mrs. Thomas Shanley; Settlements, Mrs. William Arnold; Auxiliaries to Catholic Institutions, Mrs. Charles Murray; Clubs and Homes for Working Girls, Mrs. DeLancey A. Kane; Work Among the Blind, Mrs. J. Walter Wood; Co-operative Work, Miss Gertrude O'Connor; Tuberculosis Committee, Mrs. Pierre Hoguet; Queen's Daughters, Mrs. Warren E. Mosher; League of Catholic Women, Miss Teresa R. O'Donohue.

Officers: Miss Georgine Iselin, pres.; Mrs. Joseph Slevin, Jr., Countess de Laugier-Villars, Mrs. Nicholas F. Brady, Mrs. H. Gloster Armstrong, vice-prests.; Mrs. Cornelius Tiers, treas.; Miss Teresa R. O'Donohue, secy.; Rev. Bryan J. McEntegart, moderator; Miss Adele Le Barbier, exec. secy.

Ladies' Christian Union of the City of New York (org. 1858, incorp. 1866), 49 West 9th St., N.Y.C. Aims to promote the temporal, moral and religious welfare of self-supporting young women, by providing boarding houses with home-like appointments. Maintains the Young Women's Home, 49 West 9th St.; Branch Home, 308 Second Ave.; The Eva, 153 East 62d St., The Rosemary, 24 West 12th St.; The Katharine, 118 West 13th St.; and The Milbank Memorial Home, 11 West 10th St.

Ladies' Helping Hand Association, The (incorp. 1870), 416 West 54th St., N.Y.C. To improve the condition of poor women by teaching them to help themselves; to provide them with employment, instructing them in sewing, etc. Supported by voluntary contributions. Apply, from November to April, 2–5 P. M., Fridays only.

Lakeview Home, The, Arrochar, Staten Island, N. Y. (tel. Tompkinsville 784). Admission office: 356 Second Ave., R. 30, N.Y.C. (tel. Gramercy 3253). A home and school for Jewish unmarried mothers. Capacity 26 mothers with babies. Apply at the home or office.

Officers: Mrs. Louis G. Kaempfer, pres., 333 Central Park West; Miss Laura Popper, treas., 450 West End

Ave.; Mrs. Albert E. Solomon, secy., 46 East 76th St.

Laundry of the Charity Organization Society, 516 West 28th St., N.Y.C. (tel. Chelsea 421). Is now and has been for years serving the most critical laundry customers in New York City; its object is to teach women all kinds of laundry work, so that they may be able to support themselves and earn higher wages. Novices are not allowed to work on family garments until sufficiently expert to do fine work. Names and addresses of graduated expert laundresses can be obtained at the Laundry.

Charles M. Keefer, supt.

Laura Franklin Free Hospital for Children in the City of New York (org. 1886, incorp. 1888), 17-19 East 111th St., N.Y.C. (tel. Harlem 383). Medical and surgical treatment of sick, maimed, and injured children from two to twelve years, suffering from acute or curable chronic diseases. Capacity, fifty beds. Supported by endowment fund and donations.

Registered Training School for Nurses.

Law Department, City of New York, MAIN OFFICE: Sixteenth floor, Municipal Bldg. (tel. 4600 Worth). John P. O'Brien, corporation counsel.

BROOKLYN OFFICE: 153 Pierrepont St. (tel. Main 2948).

Laymen's Missionary Movement of the United States and Canada (org. 1906), 1 Madison Ave., N.Y.C. Religious work, promoting Christian conventions, publishes literature.

Officers: James A. Speers, chrm.; Eben E. Olcott, treas.; Wm. B. Millar. gen. secy.

League to Enforce Peace (est. 1915, incorp. 1916), Cluett Bldg., 22 West 19th St., N.Y.C. (tel. Chelsea 8998). Advocates a League of Nations to maintain peace by their united economic and military power. Supported by voluntary contributions and membership fees.

Officers: William H. Taft, pres.; Herbert S. Houston, treas.; William H. Short, secy.; Irwin Smith, asst. secy.

League of Foreign Born Citizens (incorp. 1913, est. 1914), 303 Fifth Ave. (tel. Longacre 4361). Branches: 95 Second Ave. and 407 East 73d St., N.Y.C. To interest immigrants in the ideals of American citizenship; to help those who are not yet citizens to become citizens and to bring about active public interest in the Americanization of immigrants. Classes in citizenship and English, clubs, reading rooms, public meetings, co-operates with public officials. Present membership about 5,000.

Officers: Nathaniel Phillips, 261 Broadway, pres.; Charles L. Bernheimer, treas. Finance Committee; Harold Fields, exec. director.

League of Free Nations Association, 3 West 29th St., N.Y.C. Working for a liberal and constructive American foreign policy.

Officers: James G. McDonald, chrm.; Robert H. Gardiner, treas.; Christina Merriman, exec. secy.

League of Nations Union. See WORLD'S COURT LEAGUE.

League for Political Education, Inc., The (org. 1894), Town Hall, 113-123 West 43d St., N.Y.C. (tel. Bryant 2636). Morning and evening lectures. Program on application.

Robert Erskine Ely, director; Mary B. Cleveland, exec. secy.

Board of Trustees: Henry W. Taft, chrm.; Robert G. Mead, treas.; Miss Laura V. Day, secy.

Leake and Watts Orphan House in the City of New York, The Trustees of the (incorp. 1831). New York office: 262 Green St. Home at Hawthorne Ave. and City Line, Yonkers, N. Y. (reached via N.Y.C.R.R. to Ludlow Station; Putnam Division, N.Y.C.R.R. or Lowerre Station, or West Side subway to Van Cortlandt Park and trolley to Valentine's Lane). Non-sectarian. For orphan children of any nationality between three and twelve years of age. Capacity, 250. The aim is to give normal, wholesome, and happy home life. Instruction in general English, manual, and industrial branches. Supported by private contributions, income from invested funds, and payment for individual children. Visitors are always welcome. A. S. McClain, supt.

Lebanon Hospital Association (incorp. 1890), Westchester, Cauldwell and Trinity Aves., Bronx, N.Y.C. A general hospital for the medical and surgical care of patients irrespective of race or creed. Chronic or contagious cases not admitted. Capacity, 180 beds.

Dispensary open daily, 2–4 P. M. Supported by voluntary contributions, membership, and paying patients.

Legal Aid Society, The (incorp. 1876). Attorney's principal office, 239 Broadway (tel. Barclay 6120). Branch offices: Seamen's Branch, 121 Broad St.; West Side Branch, 253 West 58th St.; Harlem Branch, 51 East 125th St.; Brooklyn Branch, Eagle Bldg., 305 Washington St., Brooklyn.

Attorney in chief, Leonard McGee.

The purpose of this society is to render legal aid, gratuitously, if necessary, to all who may appear worthy thereof, and who are unable to procure assistance elsewhere, and to promote measures for their protection. In cases where the applicant is able to pay it, a retainer fee of ten cents is charged and in some cases a legal fee of fifteen cents; in cases of money collections exceeding $5, the society retains ten per cent. as a commission. This legal charitable society co-operates with all the charitable organizations and societies in this city. Supported by voluntary contributions. It publishes "The Legal Aid Review," a quarterly containing a statistical report and interesting information about the Society's work.

The annual report for 1919 shows that during the year 34,355 persons were aided at the several offices of the society, and collections for clients amount to $130,859.06. From the time of its inception up to January 1, 1920, the society has taken care of the claims of 702,212 applicants, and by its efforts $2,817,098.09 have been obtained in their behalf and paid over to them.

Board of Directors: Hon. Charles E. Hughes, pres., 100 Broadway; Carl L. Schurz, vice-pres., 15 Park Row, N.Y.C.; Allen Wardwell, treas., 15 Broad St.; Cornelius P. Kitchel, secy., 43 Cedar St.; John G. Milburn, Jr., Philip J. McCook, Louis Stoiber, Nathan A. Smyth, Geo. S. Hornblower, Robert G. Monroe, Clarence C. Chapman, Dave H. Morris, John T. Pratt, Samuel Thorne, Jr., Chas. F. Wiebusch, Thos. D. Thacher, Wm. M. Calder, Mrs. Richard Aldrich, Chas. W. Ogden, Rev. John A. Wade, Manfred W. Ehrich, hon. vice-prests.; Hon. Woodrow Wilson, Hon. Wm. H. Taft, Francis L. Stetson, Robert W. de Forest, and others.

Lenox Hill Hospital (incorp. 1861), East 76th and 77th Sts., Park and Lexington Aves. (tel. Rhinelander 3600). For the free medical and surgical treatment of the sick poor, regardless of creed or nationality. If able, ward patients pay $21 a week; for private rooms, according to size and location. Emergency cases received at any hour; others apply between 10 and 11 A. M.

Capacity, 310. Visiting days, Wednesdays and Sundays, 2–4 P. M. Supported by voluntary contributions and endowments.

DISPENSARY, 76th St. and Park Ave. Patients treated during 1919, 22,706.

TRAINING SCHOOL FOR NURSES, East 77th St. and Lexington Ave., Miss E. Lindheimer, supt.

Officers: Fritz Achelis, pres.; Wm. J. Amend, treas.; Carl Heye, secy.; George F. Sauer, supt.

Lenox Hill Settlement Association (founded 1894 by Associate Alumnae of Hunter College) (incorp. 1911), 511 East 69th St., N.Y.C. Purpose: To hold all real and personal property, and to offer co-operative and executive supervision to any agency within its districts interested in neighborhood welfare. It maintains, or supervises:

LENOX HILL HOUSE: 511 East 69th St., where social, literary, dramatic and athletic clubs are conducted.

Furnishes living quarters for the workers, rooms for clubs, kindergartens, cardiac children's classes, children's lunches, a library, gymnasium, theatre, showers and playground.

Under the Americanization Department, the foreign born are taught English and qualified to fulfil the requirements for citizenship; special attention being given to prospective citizens in the matter of the preparation of their naturalization papers.

The Arts and Crafts Department provides foreign-born women who are skilled needle workers with the practical means of earning money without leaving their homes and families.

It provides: A clearing house for sending children into the country, through outside agencies; children's lunches to the children suffering from cardiac trouble, which class meets regularly—district nursing in the neighbor hood, by one nurse connected with Lenox Hill House.

UNITED COMMUNITY HOUSE, 316 East 63d St. Provides in this section the same facilities as Lenox Hill House, furnishes rooms for clubs and classes, and acts as the central meeting house for all the civic work in this section.

THE BOYS' CLUBS occupy rooms at 404 East 64th St. and 321 East 71st St. which were formerly saloons. There is also a fully equipped workshop at 326 East 71st St. These serve as meeting places for scores of clubs devoted to the special interests of their members.

THE HUNGARIAN-AMERICAN CLUB, 95 East End Ave., is not limited to Hungarians, but functions as a neighborhood club. The building it occupies was formerly a saloon which has been converted into comfortable reading rooms, a restaurant, and a bowling alley. This Club carries on citizenship classes with the help of the Board of Education.

THE VETERANS' CLUB, 336 East 69th St., was organized in 1920. The Club occupies a four-story building which is equipped for all sorts of recreational purposes, and is a center of civic and educational work among the young men of the district.

Officers: (Lenox Hill House) Thomas S. McLane, pres.; Mrs. Harry Arnold Day, 1st vice-pres.; Mrs. R. Penn Smith, Jr., 2d vice-pres.; Mrs. Paul Dougherty, 3d vice-pres.; Mrs. Oliver Iselin, corresponding secy.; Miss Clara Byrnes, recording secy.; Dr. S. M. Milliken, treas.; Miss Rosalie Manning, head worker.

Officers: (United Community House) Mrs. Snowden A. Fahnestock, pres.; Mrs. James Lloyd Derby, 1st vice-pres.; Mrs. Joseph S. Auerbach, 2d vice-pres.; Mrs. R. Penn Smith, Jr., treas.; Mrs. Allan McLane, Jr., secy.

Letchworth Village (est. by Chap. 331, Laws of 1907, org. by Chap. 446, Laws of 1909), Thiells, Rockland Co., New York. New York office, 7 Wall St. For the custodial care of feebleminded persons, including such as are in state charitable institutions or are supported at public expense and require custodial care. The Village will have an ultimate capacity of 3,000 patients. It now has 610 beds for patients. Eight dormitories, containing in all 560 additional beds, will be completed in 1920.

Officers: Chas. S. Little, M.D., supt., Thiells, Rockland Co., N. Y.; Frank A. Vanderlip, pres.; Franklin B. Kirkbride, secy., 7 Wall St.; Oscar E. Reynolds, treas.

Library for the Blind, a branch of the circulation department of the NEW YORK PUBLIC LIBRARY, Room 116, 476 Fifth Ave., at 42d St. (tel. Vanderbilt 3600). The collection contains over 18,000 volumes printed in the various types; 5,800 music scores; all available embossed magazines and all magazines in ink print relating to work of the blind.

Reading matter from this collection is lent to blind residents of New York City and also to blind persons residing in the states of New York, New Jersey, and Connecticut. Books may be called for at the library or may be sent free through the mails to the nearest postoffice or postal station, although the free postage law does not require their delivery by letter carriers.

In addition to reading matter, the Library circulates a limited number of desk and pocket tablets for writing Braille and New York point types, being lent only to those residing in New York City. Alphabet sheets in any type and printed catalogues of books in the collection are available for distribution.

A TEACHER is employed who gives instruction in reading to adult blind residents of Greater New York. These lessons may be given at their homes or at the Library, as desired.

AN EXHIBIT consisting of books in the various types, music scores, magazines, games, writing appliances, and maps, is on view at the Library for the Blind for information of visitors. The room is open on week-days from 9 A. M. to 5 P. M.

Library for the Blind (1905) BROOKLYN PUBLIC LIBRARY. Pacific Branch, Fourth Ave. and Pacific St. It has about 1,948 volumes in "American Braille," "Boston Line," "English Braille," "Moon," and "New York Point" types, including 350 volumes of sheet music. The Library provides a teacher, who gives a regular course of instruction in the home, free of charge.

Licenses, Department of, City of New York. Main office, 57 Center St. (tel. Worth 9600).

BROOKLYN, 381–387 Fulton St. (tel. Main 1497).

RICHMOND, Borough Hall, New Brighton (tel. Tompkinsville 1000).

DIVISION OF LICENSED VEHICLES, 517–519 West 57th St. (tel. 6387 Columbus).

Life's Fresh Air Fund (incorp.), 17 West 31st St., N.Y.C. To give fortnight's outings in the country free to poor children from New York. Maintains a farm at Branchville, Conn. Entertained 703 children during 1920.

Apply to the Superintendent at the farm, from June 1 to October 1; at the office from October 1 to June 1.

***Life Saving Benevolent Association of New York, The** (est. and incorp. 1849), 51 Wall St., N.Y.C., P. O. Box 402. To encourage meritorious conduct, make awards, donations

* *Current information not received.*

and premiums in recognition of such conduct in saving life.

No one is authorized by this Association to solicit money in its behalf.

Light House for the Blind. See NEW YORK ASSOCIATION FOR THE BLIND.

Lincoln Agricultural School. See NEW YORK CATHOLIC PROTECTORY.

Lincoln Hospital and Home of the City of New York (formerly the Colored Home and Hospital; org. 1839, incorp. 1845; title changed 1902), East 141st St. and Concord Ave., west of Southern Boulevard (tel. Melrose 4100).

A GENERAL HOSPITAL for the medical and surgical treatment of pay and free patients without distinction of race, creed or color, having separate building for maternity patients and gynecological cases, and a detached pavillion for infectious diseases. Maternity Department receives lying-in cases also from the Department of Public Welfare which partly pays for their support.

DISPENSARY, open daily, except Sundays and holidays, from 9.30–11.30 A. M., for medical and surgical cases, and on Mondays, Tuesdays, Thursdays, and Fridays from 2–3 P. M. for gynecological and maternity cases. Dental department, daily 9.30 to 11.30 A. M.

A TRAINING SCHOOL FOR COLORED NURSES, established 1898.

AMBULANCE SERVICE, covering a district bounded by the East River to Harlem River, 132d St. to 170th St. and Sedgwick Ave.

A HOME for the support and comfort of aged, infirm, and destitute colored persons of both sexes.

The buildings are thoroughly fireproof, and have a capacity of 450 beds, including rooms for private patients. Supported by voluntary subscriptions, donations, bequests, endowed beds, municipal grant, and receipts from paying patients. Ward patients able to pay are charged $22.75 per week; those in private rooms from $38 to $50 per week; in semi-private rooms $30 to $35, payable in advance; those unable to pay are treated free. Visiting days: Tuesdays and Fridays, 2–4 P. M., and 7–8 P. M.; Sundays, 2–4 P. M. Visiting hours for children are Mondays and Thursdays 2–4 P. M., Sundays, 10–11 A. M.

Officers: Mrs. Henry L. Stimson, acting pres., Huntington, L. I.; Mrs. D. H. McAlpin Pyle, treas., Morristown, N. J.; Farmers Loan and Trust Co., asst. treas., 22 William St.; Mrs. Samuel Adams Lynde, secy.; Frederick Gwyer, M.D., supt.

Lincoln House. See HENRY STREET SETTLEMENT.

Lincoln Settlement Association (incorp. 1914), 105 Fleet Pl., Brooklyn (tel. Main 2044). A settlement for colored people. Maintains a free kindergarten, day nursery, clubs and classes for boys, girls, men, and women.

William H. Baldwin, pres.

Lisa Day Nursery, The (1894), 458 West 20th St., N.Y.C. For the care and instruction of infants and children under seven years of age, whose mothers are workingwomen. Open from 7 A. M. to 6 P. M.

Lithuanian Central War Relief Committee, Inc., 294 Eighth Ave., N.Y.C.

P. Buksnaitis, secy.

Little Italy Neighborhood Association, The (org. 1904), 146 Union St., Brooklyn (tel. Henry 754). A settlement organized for social work among the Italians of Brooklyn. Maintains a visiting nurse, kindergarten, clubs, and classes. Supported by voluntary contributions.

Officers: Otis S. Carroll, pres.; Mrs. T. W. Reynolds, treas., 61 Pierrepont St.; Miss Helen Van Voorhis, head worker.

***Little Missionary's Day Nursery** org. 1896, incorp. 1901), 93 St. Mark's Pl., N.Y.C. (tel. Orchard 2251). Maintains also the

NETHERWOOD FRESH-AIR HOME, Netherwood, N. J.

Little Mothers' Aid Association, The. Gives to little girls, obliged to care for younger children while their mothers are at work, lessons in sewing, mending, dressmaking, cooking, laundering, and hygienic care of the baby and home.

Day Nurseries have been established at all branches to allow the Little Mothers to attend school and their lessons.

Home Making Circles are maintained the year around at 236 Second Ave., 66 Greenwich St., 746 Eleventh Ave., Manhattan, and 41 Rush St., Brooklyn. Instruction in cooking is also given in tenement homes.

Mothers' Clubs and Working Girls' Clubs meet at the various branches for class instruction and recreation. Christmas and Easter festivals are given with suitable gifts and refreshments. Summer day and week outings, from May to October are given.

The aid given by this Association has enabled mothers to keep their children with them in the home, instead of placing them in institutions. About five thousand children are cared for each year. There are no salaried officers. Non-sectarian and entirely dependent upon contributions for its support.

Mrs. Clarence Burns, pres., 236 Second Ave.; Frank F. Hazard, treas., Union Dime Bank, 701 Sixth Ave.

* *Current information not received.*

Little Mothers' Leagues. See HEALTH DEPARTMENT, Bureau of Child Hygiene.

Little Sisters of the Assumption (a French Sisterhood; branch established in America 1891 and incorp. 1892), 246 East 15th St., N.Y.C., Sister Marie Louise, superior; and 340 Convent Ave., Sister Marie Elizabeth, superior. They nurse the sick poor of every creed, color, or nation, in their own homes, without charge.

Little Sisters of the Poor of the City of New York, The, maintains homes for the aged over sixty years and of good moral character, at the following addresses: 213 East 70th St.; 135 West 106th St., N.Y.C.; Belmont Ave. and 183d St., Bronx; and at 16th St. and Eighth Ave., Brooklyn; and Bushwick and DeKalb Aves., Brooklyn.

Loeb Memorial Home for Convalescents. See SOLOMON AND BETTY LOEB MEMORIAL HOME.

Long Island Church Mission of Help, 170 Remsen St., Brooklyn (tel. Main 1414). Work with young girls: preventive, unmarried mothers, and court cases. Visits made to hospitals, homes and courts. Girls assisted with advice, shelter, employment and friendship.

Officers: Rt. Rev. Frederick Burgess, D.D., hon. pres.; Rev. J. Clarence Jones, Ph.D., pres.; Miss Emma B. Lewis, chrm.; Mrs. Edwin B. Babcock, treas.; Miss Frank L. Clawson, exec. secy.

Long Island College Hospital, The (incorp. 1858), Henry, Pacific, and Amity Sts., Brooklyn. Maintains also a dispensary and a training school for nurses.

John M. Cratty, supt.; Miss Mary E. Robinson, R.N., supt. of nurses.

***Long Island I. O. O. F. Home Association, The** (incorp. 1891), Hollis, L. I., N. Y. A home for aged and indigent Odd Fellows, Rebekahs, wives and widows. Capacity, seventy-five. Supported by per capita tax.

Long Island State Hospital. See BROOKLYN STATE HOSPITAL.

Loomis Sanatorium, Liberty, Sullivan Co., N. Y. For the treatment of tuberculosis. Acute, advanced, and febrile cases are admitted to the Reception Hospital (rate $45 per week). Ambulant cases, after an initial stay in the Hospital, are admitted to the various cottages, where the rates range from $30 to $50 per week. Incipient and early stage, non-febrile cases are admitted to the Annex (rate $15 per week).

Dr. Bertram H. Waters, physician in chief, to whom apply.

Lord's Day Alliance of the United States, The (incorp. 1890), 156 Fifth Ave., N.Y.C. (tel. Watkins 739). Interdenominational, national, Christian, officially represents sixteen of the strongest Christian denominations. Object: To defend and preserve the Christian Sabbath and secure the weekly rest day for all laborers.

Officers: James Yereance, pres.; George M. Thomson, treas.; Rev. H. L. Bowlby, D.D., gen. secy. whom address. Correspondence invited.

Loretto Nativity Mission House. See NATIVITY, CHURCH OF THE.

Louisa Minturn Hospital, The, foot of East 16th St., N.Y.C. (tel. 1600 Stuyvesant). Under the Health Dept. For scarlet fever and diphtheria patients. Separate pavillions for each disease.

Dr. E. Giddings, Resident Physician.

Louise Erlanger Home. See CHILDREN'S AID SOCIETY.

* *Current information not received.*

Loving Arms Day Nursery (est. 1912), 746 Eleventh Ave., N.Y.C. Taking care of children from one to five years of age for widows and deserted mothers while they are at their daily work.

Louise Middlecamp, supt.

Low Maternity. See BROOKLYN HOSPITAL.

Lula Thorley Lyons Home for Crippled and Delicate Children, The. See WILLIAM H. DAVIS FREE INDUSTRIAL SCHOOL.

Lutheran Bureau of the National Lutheran Council, 437 Fifth Ave., N.Y.C. (tel. Murray Hill 9406). A national medium for information and service to Lutheran Churches and church organizations and to set forth the relationship between Lutherism and current intellectual, political, religious and social movements.

O. H. Pannkoke, secy.

***Lutheran Day Nursery, The** (est. 1915), 513–46th St., Brooklyn, N. Y. Care of infants, care of older children after school.

Lutheran Emigrants' House Association, The (incorp. 1871), 147 West 23d St. (tel. Farragut 9368). Maintains the Lutheran Emigrant Mission at above address. Emigrants of any nationality, especially Germans, are met at their arrival, directed, cared for, protected and placed in suitable positions. No charges for any services.

Officers: Martin Wulff, pres.; Rev. G. C. F. Haas, D.D., vice-pres.; Cora H. Schroeder, treas.

Lutheran Hospital Association of the City of New York and Vicinity (incorp. 1881), East New York, L. I. (tel. Glenmore 5500). Capacity, seventy beds. Board, $17.50 to $35 per week to those able to pay; others free. Supported by Lutheran congregations.

DISPENSARY (1908), East New York Ave. and Powell St. Treats diseases of the throat, nose, ear, and eye A charge of ten cents is made for each treatment, and $3 to $5 for the more important operations.

Officers: D. Tietjen, pres., Forest Ave., Englewood, N. J.; W. F. Weber, treas., 141 West 103d St., N.Y.C.; A. H. Legenhausen, fin. secy., 10 Schenck Ct., Brooklyn; Rev. H. Pottberg, secy., 501 East 142d St., N.Y.C.; Miss A. Abel, supt.

Lutheran Hospital of Manhattan (est. 1909, incorp. 1911), Convent Ave. and 144th St. (tel. Audubon 600). For care and relief of ill and indigent poor of the Borough of Manhattan, without regard to race, creed, or color. Accommodates about forty daily.

Lutheran Immigrant Society OF THE EVANGELICAL LUTHERAN SYNOD OF MISSOURI, OHIO, AND OTHER STATES (org. 1869, incorp. 1889, reincorp. 1911), 234 East 62d St. N.Y.C. (tel. Plaza 9758). The Society cares for the spiritual and secular welfare of Lutheran immigrants at their arrival, protects them from imposition and renders them general aid as may be necessary.

H. F. Ressmeyer, pres.; Rev. O. H. Restin, missionary and supt.

Lutheran Publicity Bureau. See AMERICAN LUTHERAN PUBLICITY BUREAU.

Lying-in Hospital. See SOCIETY OF THE LYING-IN HOSPITAL, etc.

M

Madison Avenue Exchange for Woman's Work, The, 749 Madison Ave., between 64th and 65th Sts., N.Y.C. (tel. Plaza 3683). Depositors pay three dollars annually; and fifteen per cent. is charged on all sales.

Officers: Mrs. Ira Barrows, pres.; Mrs. P. B. Jennings, treas.; Mrs. Chauncey Kerr, secy.; Mrs. Helen Hudson, supt.

Madison Ave. Methodist Episcopal Church, Madison Ave. and 60th St. Rev. Ralph W. Sockman, Ph.D., Pastor, 480 Park Ave.; Rev. Leland P. Cary, Associate, 685 Madison Ave. Social work carried on at WESLEY HOUSE, 59th St. and Avenue A, sewing school, mothers' clubs, Boys' Scouts. See also under METHODIST EPISCOPAL CHURCHES in the Church List.

Madison House, 216 Madison St., N.Y.C. (tel. Orchard 4507). Residence, 257 East Broadway, (tel. Orchard 7112). A neighborhood house that offers opportunities for the development of ethical conduct through experience in self-government as a working practice and belief in the power of public opinion to make it work. For these reasons there are developed and encouraged clubs, dramatics, debates, classes, games, athletics, and camps, as a definite means to a definite end—the proper adjustment of human relations.

Camp Rossbach, Tompkins Corner, Peekskill, N. Y. A summer colony for members of both sexes, all ages. Housed in separate units which form a community.

Officers: Moritz Kirchberger, pres.; Board of Trustees, 333 Central Park, West; Emanuel Moses, vice-pres.; Max Meyer, treas.; Herman H. Wolff, hon. secy.; Israel Ben Scheiber, cor. secy.; Ruth Larned, head worker.

Madison Square Boys' Club, 312-316 East 30th St. (tel. Vanderbilt 9352). Clubs, classes, gymnasium, summer camp, etc., for boys.

Officers: Leeds Johnson, pres., 20

Fifth Ave.; George Bodman, treas., 15 Wall St.; C. C. Curran, secy., 39 West 69th St.; Albert B. Hines, director.

Madison Square Church House, 432–436 Third Ave., at 30th St., N.Y.C. (tel. Madison Sq. 3558). Conducts Bible classes; clubs for men, boys, and girls; industrial classes; mothers' meetings; information bureau; gymnasium; fresh-air work; milk station; employment, etc.

Rev. Lee W. Beattie, D.D., supt.

Madonna Day Nursery. See SISTERS OF OUR LADY OF CHRISTIAN DOCTRINE.

Maedchenheim (est. 1895, incorp. 1900), 217 East 62nd St., N.Y.C. (tel. Rhinelander 7907). A home for domestic service girls and a place for social intercourse in a Christian spirit; permanent or temporary lodgings; also assists girls in acquiring greater fitness for their calling, and gives advice and protection.

Miss H. E. Altherr, matron.

Magdalen Home. See INWOOD HOUSE.

Magistrates Courts. See CITY MAGISTRATES COURTS.

Managers of the Society for the Reformation of Juvenile Delinquents in the City of New York, The (incorp. 1824). Maintain the HOUSE OF REFUGE, Randall's Island (which see).

Manhattan Congregational Church, Broadway and 76th St., N.Y.C. Office 213 West 76th St. A social center for young people, provides gymnasium, etc.; clothing bureau, etc. See also under METHODIST EPISCOPAL CHURCHES in the Church List.

Manhattan Eye, Ear, and Throat Hospital (special incorp. 1896, Chap. 584), 210 East 64th St., N.Y.C. (tel. Plaza 5391). For the free treatment of indigent persons only, suffering from diseases of the eye, ear, nose, and throat, who are too poor to pay for medical advice. Patients who are able are expected to pay board; if unable, they are admitted free. No limitations as to sex, nationality, race, or sect, merely the inability to pay a physician. Capacity, 200 beds. Controlled by a Board of Directors, and supported by voluntary contributions.

The Dispensary is open daily from 1.30–3 P. M., except Sundays and legal holidays.

Officers: J. Amory Haskell, pres., 1764 Broadway; William B. Potts, treas., 111 Broadway; Henry J. Fisher, secy., 22 William St.; Reuben O'Brien, supt.

Manhattan Maternity and Dispensary (incorp. 1901, est. 1905), 327 East 60th St. (tel. Plaza 6986–6987). A hospital for treatment of woman during pregnancy and the puerperium, both in the hospital and in the homes of the very poor. Capacity of hospital, 30 adults; 34 babies. Supported by private donations.

Nancy E. Cadmus, supt.

Manhattan State Hospital (incorp. 1905), Ward's Island (tel. Harlem 1869). Accessible from the foot of East 116th St. New York City Office: Room 703, Hall of Records Bldg., corner Center and Chambers Sts. (tel. 4424 Worth). For the care and treatment of the insane. No limitations as to age, sex, nationality, race, or sect. Patients received from the Borough of Manhattan, the Bronx, and Richmond. Regular visiting days, Sundays, Mondays, and Saturdays, from 1–3 P. M.

Manhattan Trade School for Girls. See EDUCATION, BOARD OF.

Manhattanville Nursery Association (org. 1909, incorp. 1913), 71 Old Broadway, N.Y.C. To preserve families by giving daily care to children whose mothers are of necessity breadwinners. Capacity, 75. Has day and night baby department for temporary care of very young children who are deprived of parents' protection in times of dire distress, caused by illness, fire, accident, or any calamity.

Marcy Avenue Baptist Church, Marcy Ave. and Putnam, Brooklyn. Rev. John M. Moore, Pastor. Provides recreation for young people, a Community Forum, etc. See also under BAPTIST CHURCHES in the Church List.

Margaret Bottome Memorial, The King's Daughters' House in Harlem (incorp. 1907) 222 East 123d St., N.Y.C. Maintains a sewing school, clubs and classes.

Officers: Mrs. Edmund B. Rose, pres., 274 Fulton Ave., Jersey City; Mrs. E. J. Brookins, treas., Ridgefield Park, N. J.; Miss M. E. Coburn, resident worker.

Margaret Fahnestock Training School for Nurses. See NEW YORK POST-GRADUATE MEDICAL SCHOOL AND HOSPITAL.

Margaret Louisa, The. See YOUNG WOMEN'S CHRISTIAN ASSOCIATION, Central Branch.

Margaret and Sarah Switzer Institute and Home (for girls) (incorp. 1909), Christopher St. and Waverly Place (tel. Spring 8543). For the advancement and uplifting of girls and young women, to house those coming to New York to look for work and to give lodging and board at low rates to respectable girls and young women, earning less than $15 per week. Non-sectarian. Sunnysidè Farm, at Manasquan, N. J., is open throughout the year, with a matron in attendance, to accommodate girls and young women requiring rest after operations and for those run down in health.

For admittance, ages 16 to 30 years, single, respectable, a small rate is charged for those having no dependents. For further particulars apply to Head Matron, 27 Christopher St.

Margaret Strachan Home for Women (incorp. 1887), 103–105 West 27th St., N.Y.C. A Christian Home under management of the Salvation Army, for the temporary shelter and instruction of erring girls.

Marien-Heim of Brooklyn, The (founded 1895, incorp. 1898), Eighteenth Ave. and 64th St., Brooklyn (tel. Bath 1367). A home for aged Germans of both sexes. Applicants must be over sixty.

Officers: Miss M. Behr, pres.; Mrs. G. Heubach, treas.; Mrs. Johanna Overbeck, secy., 429 5th St., Brooklyn.

Marine Hospital. See UNITED STATES PUBLIC HEALTH SERVICE.

Mariners' Family Asylum, Port of New York, The (incorp. 1843 as The Mariners' Family Industrial Society; re-org. and re-incorp. 1851; present institution opened 1853, known as the Old Ladies' Home), 119 Tompkins Ave., Stapleton, S. I. (tel. Tompkinsville 412). An asylum for aged and destitute widows, wives, mothers, sisters, and daughters of seamen, sixty years of age or over, of the port of New York. This being the only institution of its kind in the United States, the management reserves the right, in exceptional cases, to receive applicants from other ports.

Applicants are received on probation for one year. Capacity, fifty. Admission fee, $200. Committee on Admission meets the last Thursday in each month, when application is to be made by mail or in person. Supported entirely by voluntary contributions.

Officers: Elmer W. Durkin, treas., 142 Manor Rd., West New Brighton, S. I.; Mrs. Henry Cattermole, cor. secy., 18 Pommer Ave., Tompkinsville, S. I.; Mrs. G. D. Pine, rec. secy., 25 South Elliott Pl., Brooklyn.

Mariners' Harbor Mission. See NATIONAL BIBLE INSTITUTE.

Mariners' Temple, Henry St., cor. of Oliver St. (tel. Orchard 1213). Conducts religious, athletic, social; and industrial clubs.

Rev. Wm. N. Hubbell, Pastor, 55 West 12th St. G. M. Childs, social director; Miss Cora M. Beath, Missionary.

See also under BAPTIST CHURCHES.

Marquette League (1904), Room 423, United Charities Bldg., 105 East 22d St., N.Y.C. To uplift the Indians in the United States, spiritually, educationally, and industrially. To bring them to Christianity and to develop in them the spirit of self-help.

Officers: W. Bourke Cockran, pres.; John T. Brennan, treas.; William Quinn, secy.

Martha Summer Home, Ossining, N. Y. See CHILDREN'S AID SOCIETY.

Mary Fisher Home, The. See SEABURY MEMORIAL HOME.

Mary Immaculate Hospital Association, The (incorp. 1902). Maintains St. Mary's Hospital, Shelton Ave. and Ray St., Jamaica, N. Y., for the medical and surgical care of the sick and injured. Also a Training School for Nurses. Supported by voluntary contributions and paying patients.

Officers: M. Augustine Fleck, O.S.D., pres.; Sister M. Thomas, supt.

Mary Louise Heins Memorial Home for the Aged and Infirm, Mt. Vernon, N. Y. Entrance fee, $1,000.

Rev. G. C. Berkemier, director.

Mary Zinn Home for Convalescent Children, Inc. (est. and incorp. 1919), Mamaroneck Road, White Plains, N. Y. (tel. White Plains 2631). Takes compensated ambulatory cardiac cases. Boys, 6 to 10, girls, 6 to 16.

Officers: Mrs. Benedict Erstein, pres., 50 West 75th St.; Mrs. Arthur Zinn, vice-pres.; Mrs. G. M. Thurnauer, treas., Hotel Hamilton, N. Y.; Mrs. Richard Lewisohn, secy., 1155 Park Ave., N.Y.C.

Masonic Board of Relief of the City of New York, The (org. 1880, incorp. 1899), 71 West 23d St. N.Y.C. Aids distressed members and the widows and orphans of deceased members. Supported by voluntary contributions. Board meets 7 P. M., on Tuesday and Saturday.

Officers: Wm. J. Matthews, pres.; George B. Knickerbocker, treas.; Robert S. Wardle, secy.

Masonic Free Employment Bureau of Brooklyn and Long Island, Clermont and Lafayette Aves., Brooklyn (tel. Prospect 3594). Places members of the fraternity only and their dependents (except in rare cases), both male and female. All kinds of work, professional and skilled and unskilled labor.

Jacob H. Erb, Manager.

Masonic Hall and Asylum Fund. Trustees of the (incorp. 1864), 46 West 24th St., N.Y.C. Maintains the MASONIC HOME (est. 1893), Utica, N. Y. For the free education of orphan children of Masons, and the relief support, and care of worthy and indigent Masons, their wives, widows, and orphans. Capacity, 500.

***Masters School Day Nursery,** 519 East 86th St., N.Y.C. (tel. Lenox 4431). Capacity for ninety children. Two large open air porches, trained nurse in residence; also

Dobbs House, 512 East 87th St., N.Y.C. Includes Girl Scouts Troupe, Evening Boys' Club, Child Welfare Station (clinic), Polly Platt Library and playground open all the year for after school children.

Officers: Miss F. G. Benjamin, pres.; Mrs. W. J. Worcester, treas.; Miss L. Talmadge, secy., Netherwood, N. J.

Maternity Aid Society. A charitable organization composed of Jewish women, for the purpose of assisting the poor. Provides layettes for expectant babies. A bed is maintained at Suydenham Hospital for an expectant mother or she may be cared for at home, if she prefers. From $5 to $10 is given for immediate needs. During the Passover Holidays groceries are distributed to needy cases, not necessarily maternity cases. The Society meets on the second and fourth Tuesdays of each month at the Y. W. H. A. Bldg., 31 West 110th St.

Mrs. C. Kleinman, secy., 636 West 172d St. (tel. Wadsworth 4323).

Maternity Center Association (est. 1918, incorp. 1919), 18 West 34th St., N.Y.C. (tel. Knickerbocker 365). It aims to promote maternity care in order to reduce deaths and ill-health incident to child bearing. It maintains Centers throughout Manhattan to secure, by co-ordination of the work of all existing agencies, adequate medical and nursing supervision for every pregnant mother.

The Association is supported entirely by voluntary contributions.

It maintains a Central Record Office and a clearing house for all maternity care in Manhattan. Patients may be reported by telephone to the main office and a nurse will call.

Officers: Miss Mabel Choate, pres.; Miss Mary L. Davison, vice-pres.; Mrs. Arthur Scott Burden, treas.; Stephen G. Williams, asst. treas.; Anne A. Stevens, general director.

Matilda Ziegler Publishing Company for the Blind, Inc., The (incorp. 1907), 250 West 54th St., N.Y.C. Publishes a monthly magazine printed in raised type (one edition in "New York Point" and one in "American Braille"), distributed free to any blind person in the United States and Canada who can read. Supported entirely by an individual gift.

Matteawan State Hospital (est. 1855, Chap. 456, at Auburn, removed 1892, to Matteawan), P. O. Beacon, N. Y. (tel. Beacon 236). For the custody and treatment of insane criminals. Insane patients, pending trial or acquitted on grounds of insanity are committed to its custody by the courts. Similar patients, also former inmates of the hospital, and those who have served sentences in penal institutions (Chap. 525, Laws 1904), are transferred here from other State hospitals by the State Hospital Commission. Inmates of various penal institutions who become insane while undergoing sentence (except males convicted of a felony) are transferred by order of the court to this hospital. Capacity for about 507 men, and 110 women.

Mayor's Office, City of New York. City Hall (tel. Cortlandt 1000).

McAuley Cremorne Mission. See NATIONAL BIBLE INSTITUTE.

McAuley Water Street Mission (org. 1872, incorp. 1876), 316 Water St., N.Y.C. (tel. Beekman 4038). A rescue mission for degraded and profligate criminals and drunkards, both men and women. Open from 7 A. M. to 10 P. M. daily. Religious services every night and Sundays. Relief given when necessary. Supported by voluntary contributions.

John H. Wyburn, supt.; Mrs. John H. Wyburn, missionary.

Trustees: F. Murray Olyphant, pres.; B. DeF. Curtiss, secy., 983 Park Ave.; R. Fulton Cutting, treas., 32 Nassau St.; Rev. J. Frederick Talcott, chaplain; Allen Wardwell, Everett L. Crawford, Thomas Savage Clay, James H. Flaconer, Fleming H. Revell, William Halls, Jr., Alexander M. Hadden, Jordan L. Mott, Henry Fletcher, J. Nelson Borland, Le Roy E. Kimball, Gilbert S. Mott.

Mediator, P. E., Church of the, 260 West 231st St., N.Y.C. Rev. John Campbell, Pastor. A social center providing gymnasium, dancing classes, Boy Scouts, etc. See also under PROTESTANT EPISCOPAL CHURCHES in the Church List.

Mechanics' Institute School. See GENERAL SOCIETY OF MECHANICS AND TRADESMEN.

Medford Tuberculosis Sanatorium for Working Men and Women (est. 1913, incorp. 1909), Medford, L. I. Office: 69 Schermerhorn St., Brooklyn (tel. Main 8200). For the care of tuberculosis patients, men, women, and children, regardless of nationality, race, or creed. Capacity, 55. Supported by voluntary contributions, labor unions, and the Committee on the Prevention of Tuberculosis, Brooklyn.

Mediation and Arbitration, Bureau of. See STATE INDUSTRIAL COMMISSION.

Medical Examiners (Coroners) in the Greater City of New York.

MANHATTAN, Municipal Bldg., 2d floor (tel. Worth 3711).

BRONX, Arthur and Tremont Aves. (tel. Tremont 1250).

BROOKLYN, Willoughby and Fleet Sts. (tel. Main 4004).

QUEENS, Town Hall, Jamaica, L. I. (tel. Jamaica 1330).

RICHMOND, New Court House, St. George, S. I. (tel. Tompkinsville 7).

Medical Men's Widows and Orphans. See NEW YORK SOCIETY FOR THE RELIEF OF WIDOWS AND ORPHANS OF MEDICAL MEN.

Medical Missionary Society. See INTERNATIONAL MEDICAL MISSIONARY SOCIETY.

Medico-Psychological Association. See AMERICAN MEDICO-PSYCHOLOGICAL ASSOCIATION.

Meinhard Memorial Neighborhood House, Henry, 102 East 101st St., N.Y.C. (tel. Lenox 217) (founded 1914 by Morton H. Meinhard). A neighborhood house and community center which conducts clubs and classes and other activities for children, young people, and adults, and co-operates with the Board of Education in the maintenance of a kindergarten. The house is open daily throughout the year.

Miss Grace H. Gosselin, head worker; Miss Frieda Lustgarten, associate.

Board of Directors: Dr. David Beck, Prof. Clara Byrnes, George L. Cohen, Mrs. George L. Cohen, Mrs. Helena Katz, Morton H. Meinhard, Mrs. Morton H. Meinhard, Daniel M. Murphy.

Memorial Baptist Church. See JUDSON MEMORIAL.

Memorial Day Nursery (est. 1910), 196 Bleecker St., N.Y.C. (tel. Spring 1752). Day Nursery for children whose parents are working away from home through the day. Ages from two to six years. No babies. Non-sectarian. Supported by voluntary contributions. Capacity, forty.

Memorial Dispensary for Women and Children (incorp. 1894), 827 Sterling Pl., Brooklyn (tel. Lafayette

98). Medical and surgical advice and treatment to women and children by women physicians.

Officers: Dr. Lottie A. Cort, pres.; Dr. Jennie V. H. Baker, treas.; Dr. Mary F. Fleckles, secy.; Dr. M. Elizabeth Ellis, resident physician.

Memorial Hospital for the Treatment of Cancer and Allied Diseases, formerly the New York Cancer Hospital (incorp. 1884, title changed 1899), Central Park West and 106th St. (tel. Academy 2420). For study and treatment of cases of cancer whose condition admits of cure or relief.

Supported by charitable subscriptions.

Terms $14–$21 a week in the wards. Private rooms at $6–$7 a day. Those unable to pay are treated free. Capacity, 100 beds. Apply in person daily, except Thursdays and Sundays, from 10 A. M. to 12 M., or by letter with certificate from a physician.

Officers: Herbert Parsons, pres., 52 William St.; Paul Armitage, treas., 233 Broadway.

George F. Holmes, supt.

Messiah Home for Children, Spring Valley, Rockland County, New York (tel. Spring Valley 404). New York City Office, 501 Fifth Ave., Room 2008 (tel. Vanderbilt 4370). Capacity, 60. Object: To provide a home for minor children, orphans or half-orphan girls, or for those in need of temporary care on account of sickness of their parents or other exigencies. They are educated and trained as if in a private home. When old enough, they are assisted to obtain situations and become useful members of a community. Ages of admission from 6 to 12 years. Supported by voluntary contributions.

Officers: Mrs. George F. Shrady, pres., 929 Park Ave.; Dave Hennen Morris, treas., 19 East 70th St.; Mrs. L. C. French, secy.

Messiah Unitarian Church. See COMMUNITY CHURCH.

Methodist Child Welfare Society, The (1911), 150 Fifth Ave. N.Y.C. (tel. Watkin 7520). Supported by memberships and voluntary contributions. Home finding and supervision, specialized health care, training of the juvenile delinquent, information in Mental Hygiene, visualization, adequacy of the program for neglected children.

Reuben P. Brewer, treas.; Burdette B. Brown, secy.

Methodist Deaconess Home. See NEW YORK DEACONESSES ASSOCIATION.

Methodist Episcopal Church Home in the City of New York (incorp. 1851), Amsterdam Ave. and 92d St., N.Y.C. (tel. Riverside 7193). A home for poor, aged, and infirm persons who have been members of the Methodist Episcopal Church ten years and of a city church for five years. No admission fee. Apply through the church to which candidate belongs. Supported by subscriptions and bequests.

Officers: Mrs. M. K. Robinson, president emeritus; Mrs. G. Waldo Smith, pres., Bayside, L. I.; Mrs. J. G. Judd, treas., 685 West End Ave., N.Y.C.; Mrs. Alexander Carmichel, cor. secy., 311 West 76th St.; Mrs. J. Edgar Leaycraft, secy., 31 West 76th St.

Methodist Episcopal Foreign Missions Board (Board of Foreign Missions of the Methodist Episcopal Church; org. 1819, incorp. 1839; Charter amended April 6, 1906), 150 Fifth Ave., N.Y.C. For foreign work only. Controlled by the General Conference.

Officers: Bishop L. B. Wilson, LL.D.,

pres.; Rev. Frank Mason North, D.D., S. Earl Taylor, LL.D., cor. secys.; Rev. George M. Fowles, D.D., treas.

Methodist Episcopal Hospital, The (incorp. 1881), 6th and 7th Sts., and Seventh and Eighth Aves., Brooklyn (tel. South 123). Cares for the sick, without reference to religious belief, race, or ability to pay. Capacity 295 patients. Supported by voluntary contributions, by payment from patients, etc. Apply at the hospital, from 9 A. M. to 5 P. M. Maintains a TRAINING SCHOOL FOR NURSES and a DISPENSARY.

Officers: Alfred P. Sloan, pres.; Wm. Halls, Jr., vice-pres.; John F. Bouker, treas.; Frank A. Horne, secy.; Rev. J. E. Holmes, D.D., supt.

Methodist Episcopal Immigrant Girls' Home, 273 West 11th St., N.Y.C. (tel. Chelsea 2523). A temporary home for immigrant girls and women. Under the auspices of the Women's Home Missionary Society of the M. E. Church.

Officers: Mrs. Wilbur Thirkield, pres.; Mrs. H. C. Jennings, treas.; Mrs. May L. Woodruff, secy.; Mrs. A. R. Alberti, supt.

Metropolitan Hospital, Blackwell's Island. See PUBLIC WELFARE DEPARTMENT, CITY OF NEW YORK.

Metropolitan League, Y. M. H. A's., R. 1807, 114 Fifth Ave., N.Y.C. An organizing center of information in social service, relief work, educational and institutional activities.

Metropolitan Museum of Art, The (incorp. 1870), Central Park at Fifth Ave. and 82d St., N.Y.C. (tel. Lenox 723). Purposes:

To establish and maintain in the City of New York a Museum and Library of Art. To encourage and develop the study of fine arts, and the application of the arts to manufactures and practical life. To advance the general knowledge of kindred subjects, and, to that end, to furnish popular instruction.

It is a private corporation governed by a Board of Trustees, and derives its income from the following sources: A yearly grant from the City of New York, contributions from its various grades of members, and the income from its endowment funds.

The Museum's collections cover all periods in the history of art. The Library contains upwards of 38,000 volumes and 49,000 photographs illustrative of the art of all periods. They are housed in buildings owned by the City and leased to the corporation. The Museum is open daily from 10 A. M. to 5 P. M., from 1 to 6 P. M. on Sundays, and is free to the public except on Monday and Friday, when an admission fee of twenty-five cents is charged. Sketching and snapshot photography are permitted in the galleries. Permits to copy are issued upon request and every facility afforded to students and classes visiting the Museum for purposes of study.

Officers: R. W. de Forest, pres.; Edward Robinson, director; H. W. Kent, secy.

Metropolitan Throat Hospital (incorp. 1874), 351 West 34th St. (tel. Greeley 4327). For the treatment of the poor only. Unsectarian. Accommodates ten patients. Its dispensary for outdoor patients is open daily from 2–4 P. M. Supported by voluntary contributions.

Officers: Edward H. Floyd-Jones, pres.; F. D. Denton, treas.; G. B. Hope, M.D., secy. and med. supt., to whom apply.

Middletown State Homeopathic Hospital (est. 1874, chap. 446) Middletown, Orange Co., N. Y. For the treatment and care of insane persons, indigent and otherwise. Indigents are supported by the State. Private patients charged from $6 up per week. The income is derived from the State and from the board of private patients.

Mills Hotels Trust, The, 161 West 36th St. (tel. Greeley 403). John L. Thomas, manager. Maintains

MILLS HOTEL No. 1 (1897) Bleecker, Sullivan and Thompson Sts. (tel. Spring 347). A fireproof hotel, with all modern conveniences, for respectable men of small means. Steam heat, electric lighting, shower baths, reading and writing rooms, and laundry. One thousand five hundred fifty-four rooms at thirty to forty cents per night; meals in restaurant at low prices.

MILLS HOTEL No. 2 (1898), N. W. corner Rivington and Chrystie Sts. (tel. Orchard 737). A fireproof hotel for respectable men of small means. Similar in all conveniences and advantages to Hotel No. 1; but with 600 rooms at thirty to forty cents per night; meals in restaurant at low prices.

MILLS HOTEL No. 3 (1907), Seventh Ave. and 36th St. (tel. Fitz Roy 403). A new fireproof hotel for respectable men of small means. One thousand eight hundred seventy-five bedrooms, electric lighting, shower baths, forty to fifty cents per night; elevator service, library; meals a la carte.

Mineola Home. See PUBLIC EDUCATION ASSOCIATION.

Ministers' and Missionaries' Benefit Board of the Northern Baptist Convention, 276 Fifth Ave., N.Y.C. Provides for aged and infirm Baptist ministers and missionaries, their wives, widows and orphans.

Minturn Hospital. See LOUISA MINTURN HOSPITAL.

Miriam Osborn Memorial Home Association of the State of New York (incorp. 1892), Boston Post Rd., Rye, N. Y. (tel. Rye 247). Office: 55 Wall St., N.Y.C. (tel. Hanover 8116). For respectable gentlewomen over sixty-five years of age, in needy circumstances. Applicants must have been residents of New York, Bronx, or Westchester Counties for ten years preceding application.

An admission fee of $500, in addition to burial fees, must be prepaid.

Land sufficient for additional buildings as necessity arises and as endowments permit, has been acquired. Form of bequest and devise as follows: "I hereby give, devise and bequeath to the Miriam Osborn Memorial Home Association of the State of New York (here insert amount of money or description of property), the same to be used for the general uses and purposes of the said Association." See ADVERTISEMENT.

H. C. Adams, secy.

Misericordia Hospital (formerly New York Mothers' Home; incorp. 1888; title changed 1904), 531 East 86th St., N.Y.C. (tel. Rhinelander 7787–7788). A general and maternity hospital including the care of children. Capacity, 135 maternity beds, 61 for medical and surgical cases, and 125 for children. Under the management of the Sisters of Misericordia.

Officers: Sister of the Holy Heart of Mary, pres.; Sister St. Damase, treas.; Sister Mary of the Guardian Angel, secy.

Mission of the Immaculate Virgin for the Protection of Homeless and Destitute Children (incorp. 1870). Office: 381 Lafayette St., N.Y.C. Rev. Mallick J. Fitzpatrick, in charge. The Mission maintains the

MOUNT LORETTO, Pleasant Plains, Staten Island, where trade schools provide training for senior boys. Capacity for 1,800 children.

ST. ELIZABETH'S HOME FOR GIRLS, Princess Bay, S. I. Capacity for 400 orphan girls.

DUVAL COTTAGE FOR INFANT GIRLS (branch of above). Capacity, 100.

ST. JOSEPH'S ASYLUM FOR BLIND GIRLS, Pleasant Plains, S. I. Has a capacity for 100.

ST. BENEDICT'S HOME FOR DESTITUTE COLORED CHILDREN, Rye, N. Y. Cares for 160. Rev. Mallick J. Fitzpatrick, supt. Address all communications to the office.

Missionary Education Movement of the United States and Canada, The, 160 Fifth Ave., N.Y.C. (tel. Chelsea 9660). Is an organization for missionary education, and is the clearing house for the educational departments of the Home and Foreign Mission Boards of the United States and Canada.

Missionary Sisters of the Sacred Heart, Fort Washington Ave., and 190th St., N.Y.C. A boarding school for girls.

SACRED HEART SCHOOL, 141 Broadway. Dobbs Ferry, N. Y.

SACRED HEART ORPHAN ASYLUM, West-Park-on-the-Hudson. Receives, cares for and educates orphans and half-orphans and destitute children, especially from New York City and vicinity. Helped by voluntary contributions. Reception House, 226 East 20th St., N.Y.C.

COLUMBUS HOSPITAL (incorp. 1895), 226 East 20th St., N.Y.C. For the free treatment of the sick poor, and injured. Capacity, 100 beds. Pay patients received and cared for in private pavilions. Apply to the Mother Superior.

Missionary Sisters, Third Order of St. Francis (org. 1879), 250 South St., Peekskill, N. Y. Maintain the ST. JOSEPH'S HOME for destitute and orphan children under sixteen years of age of both sexes, from New York City and adjacent counties. Supported chiefly from public funds.

Mother M. Joseph, Superior.

Mizpah Chapel and Parish House. See CENTRAL PRESBYTERIAN CHURCH.

Monday Club. An organization of social workers and those interested in social and civic affairs. Its objects are to promote acquaintanceship among social workers and to promote the discussion of professional subjects. Regular monthly meetings are held, and informal tramps and out-door exercise are arranged for interested members from time to time. The dues are $1.00 a year. No club house or club rooms are maintained and the officers change annually.

Officers: Miss J. C. Colcord, pres.; Edwin J. Cooley and Miss Frances Taussig, vice-pres.; LeRoy Bowman, secy. and treas. Communications should be addressed to the secy.-treas., in care of New York County Chapter, American Red Cross, 119 West 40th St.

Montclair Fresh Air and Convalescent Home (est. 1902, incorp. 1905), 86 Lakeside Ave., Verona, N. J. (tel. Verona 5364). For convalescent children and young people. Capacity, forty. Time of stay, one to three months.

Officers: Mrs. Walter L. Conwell, pres., 429 Park St.; Mrs. Frank E. Bliss, secy., 29 Northview Ave.; Mrs. Frank E. Pendleton, treas., 37 Erwin Park Road; Mrs. F. W. Wilcox, chrm. on applications, 193 Inwood Ave., Upper Montclair, N. J.

Montefiore Home and Hospital for Chronic Diseases (incorp. 1884), Gun Hill Road near Jerome Ave., N. Y. (tel. Olinville 800). Reached by subway, Lexington Ave. division and 6th Ave. elevated. Also N. Y. C. R. R. (Harlem Division) to Williamsbridge. An unsectarian charity hospital to afford medical treatment, food and shelter to those unfortunates, who, by reason of the apparent incurability or protracted course of their diseases are refused admission to general hospitals. Capacity 482. Controlled by a board of thirty directors. Supported by voluntary contributions, bequests and public funds. Also maintain

THE MONTEFIORE HOME, COUNTRY SANATORIUM FOR THE TUBERCULOUS (opened 1897), Bedford Hills, N. Y. Reached from New York by the Harlem Division of the N. Y. C. R. R. For incipient cases of phthisis. Dr. B. Stivelman, supt.

Officers: S. G. Rosenbaum, pres.; Henry Solomon, Samuel Kridel and William Goldman, vice-pres.; Dr. S. Wachsmann, medical director; M. D. Goodman, supt.

Ladies' Auxiliary Society, Mrs. Sidney C. Borg, pres.

Morningside Nutrition Center. See CHARITY ORGANIZATION SOCIETY, Committee on Home Economics.

Morningstar Chinese Mission, 13 Doyers St., N.Y.C. A center for Chinese; Boy Scouts, English school, sewing classes, etc.

Rev. Lee To, Pastor.

***Morristown Summer Shelter, The,** Morristown, New Jersey (org. 1890, incorp. 1892). A fresh-air home for poor little girls over three years of age from New York City. Open from June 1 to September 15. Non-sectarian. Guests remain two weeks or longer, and are clothed meanwhile. Supported by annual subscriptions and donations.

***Mother's Aid Day Nursery** (est. 1910), 97 Lawrence St., Brooklyn. Care of children under six years of age. Capacity, twenty-five.

Annetta G. Paine, matron.

Mothers' Co-operative Home Club (boarding home for working women and children) 60 West 92 St., N.Y.C.

Mt. Carmel Settlement and Kindergarten, 307 East 112th St. (tel. Harlem 3521). Supported by the Roman Catholic parish of Our Lady of Mt. Carmel, 447 East 115th St.

Rev. G. Dallo, Pastor; Miss M. Mancini, head worker.

Mount Loretto. See MISSION OF THE IMMACULATE VIRGIN.

Mt. Sinai Hospital (incorp. 1852, amended 1857 and 1866), 99th to 101st St., between Madison and Fifth Aves., N.Y.C. (tel. Lenox 4010). A general hospital for the medical and surgical care of the sick of all creeds and classes, except those suffering from contagious diseases. Free to the worthy indigent sick; board from $7 per week and upwards for those able to pay. Cases of accident are admitted gratuitously at any hour. Capacity for 511 beds. Average number of patients, 424; 9,913 cases were treated last year. Controlled by a board of thirty trustees. Supported by voluntary contributions, pay of patients, municipal grant, and interest on invested funds.

Hours for examination by the Admitting Physician from 9 A. M. to 5 P. M.; Sundays, from 9 A. M. to 12 M.

THE DISPENSARY, at Madison Ave. and 100th St., is for the free treatment of out-patients, irrespective of creed or nationality, who are unable to pay for either physician or medicine. Open daily, except Sundays and holidays, from 9 A. M. to 3 P. M. Consultations in 1916, 243,161.

THE OUT-DOOR RELIEF AND DISTRICT CORPS OF PHYSICIANS care temporarily for cases outside of the Hos-

* *Current information not received.*

pital for which beds cannot immediately be provided, and furnish nurses at the homes of the sick poor.

THE MT. SINAI TRAINING SCHOOL FOR NURSES, at Madison Ave. and 101st St., works in connection with Mt. Sinai Hospital. Hugo Blumenthal, pres.; Miss Elizabeth A. Greener, supt.

SOCIAL SERVICE DEPARTMENT does medico-social work in hospital and dispensary. Mrs. Alfred A. Cook, pres., Social Service Auxiliary; Mrs. Mabel A. Boorum, head worker.

Officers: Geo. Blumenthal, pres.; Leo Arnstein, and S. Herbert Wolfe, vice-prests.; S. S. Prince, treas.; S. Herbert Wolfe, secy.; Dr. S. S. Goldwater, director.

Mulberry Community Center. See ASSOCIATION FOR IMPROVING THE CONDITION OF THE POOR.

Municipal Civil Service Commission, Municipal Bldg., 14th floor (tel. Worth 1580). Examinations for all classes of employment in the City Service, from laborer to high scientific and executive positions. Competitive examinations advertised in "City Record" and daily papers. Applications for competitive examinations received only as examinations are scheduled. Applications for labor positions received at any time.

Charles I. Stengle, secy.

Municipal Lodging House. See PUBLIC WELFARE DEPARTMENT, CITY OF NEW YORK.

Municipal Reference Library, 5th floor, Municipal Bldg., N.Y.C. (tel. Worth 1072). Maintains a general information and reference service for city officials and the public. Publishes a weekly bulletin, "The Municipal Reference Library Notes." One library has two branches: A Public Health Division located in the Health Department building, 505 Pearl St., and a Civic Art Division in the Offices of the Art Commission, City Hall Building.

Rebecca B. Rankin, librarian.

Municipal Sanatorium, Otisville, N. Y. See HEALTH, DEPARTMENT OF.

Municipal Sanatorium. See Sea View Farms under PUBLIC WELFARE DEPARTMENT, CITY OF NEW YORK.

Murray Hill Vocational School. See EDUCATION, BOARD OF.

Museum of Art. See METROPOLITAN MUSEUM OF ART.

Museum of Natural History. See AMERICAN MUSEUM OF NATURAL HISTORY.

Museum of Safety. See SAFETY INSTITUTE OF AMERICA.

Music School Settlement, The Society of the (est. 1893, incorp. 1903), 51–53 East 3d St., N.Y.C. (tel. Orchard 3103). Provides a good musical education for those who otherwise could not afford it; a social center for the neighborhood. Three string orchestras and one symphony orchestra. Large musical library. Public concerts first Sunday afternoon each month, November to May.

Officers: Mrs. Frank Baily Rowell, pres.; Chester Holmes Aldrich, secy.; Frank H. Simmons, treas.; Melzar Chaffee, musical director; Mary Birnie, head resident.

Musician's Foundation, The (est. 1912, incorp. 1904). For the financial assistance of musicians in the United States who may be in temporary need. Supported through donations and public concerts. Only the income of the fund is employed.

Officers: Franz Kneisel, pres., 329 West 84th St.; Sigmund Herzog, secy., 520 West 114th St.

N

Nassau Cottage Association, Inc. See WAYSIDE HOME.

Nassau Hospital Association (incorp. 1896), Mineola, L. I., N. Y. (tel. Garden City 1037). A hospital and dispensary for the care, maintenance, medical and surgical advice, aid, and treatment of indigents and others, ill or injured. Capacity, seventy-six. Supported by paying patients, subscriptions, donations, voluntary contributions, and income from invested funds.

TRAINING SCHOOL FOR NURSES (org. 1900), provides a three-years' course.

Officers: William M. Baldwin, pres., Garden City; George S. Emory, treas., Mineola; James S. Cooley, M.D., secy.; Ada F. Adams, R.N., supt.

Nathan Straus Laboratories. See HEALTH DEPARTMENT, Baby Health Stations.

National Academy of Design, West 109th St. and Amsterdam Ave. Maintains Art Schools; alike free to both men and women students. Open from October to May.

Officers: Edwin N. Blashfield, pres.; Francis C. Jones, treas.; Charles C. Curran, secy.

National Allied Relief Committee (incorp. under the laws of the State of New York; est. 1915, incorp. 1918), 149 West 49th St., N.Y.C. (tel. Vanderbilt 4980). Relief of war sufferers in America and counties of the Allies.

Mrs. William Astor Chanler, pres.; I. E Morton, secy.; James A. Blair, Jr., treas.; James Marwick, auditor.

National American Woman Suffrage Association, 171 Madison Ave., N.Y.C. Works for the enfranchisement of women.

Officers: Mrs. Carrie Chapman Catt, pres.; Mrs. Henry Wade Rogers, treas.; Mrs. Frank J. Shuler, cor. secy.; Mrs. Halsey W. Wilson, rec. secy.

National Association for the Advancement of Colored People (org. 1909, incorp. 1911), 70 Fifth Ave., N.Y.C. (tel. Chelsea 9386-7). Official organ, "The Crisis"; circulation, 1920, 80,000 monthly; has 350 local branches and 85,000 members; supported by membership fees and voluntary contributions.

Objects: To make 12,000,000 Americans physically free from peonage, politically free from disfranchisement, mentally free from ignorance and socially free from insult, and generally to promote equality of opportunity for, and insure equal protection of the laws to, colored people.

Through its national office and branches in 43 states, the District of Columbia, Canada, the Canal Zone and the Philippine Islands, it carries on educational and protective work and seeks to establish better race relations on the basis of justice and fair play.

Maintains an Anti-Lynching Fund for the investigation and publication of the facts concerning lynching and race riots and for educational work and legal action to stamp out lynching and mob violence.

Officers: Moorfield Storey, pres., Boston; Mary White Ovington, chrm. of the Board of Directors, New York; J. E. Spingarn, treas., New York; Dr. W. E. B. DuBois, director of publications and research and editor of "The Crisis," New York; James Weldon Johnson, acting secy.; Walter F. White, asst. secy., New York.

National Association of Audubon Societies for the Protection of Wild Birds and Animals, Inc. Home office: 1974 Broadway, N.Y.C. (tel. Columbus 7327). Educational and legislative work for protection of wild birds and animals. Publishes much material; employs large force of bird wardens. Supported by membership fees and interest from endowment.

T. Gilbert Pearson, exec. secy.

National Association of the Deaf (org. 1880, incorp. 1900). Endeavors to safeguard the interests of the deaf. It advocates the "Combined System" in the education of deaf children, and aims to educate the public that the deaf do not beg; impostors should be promptly arrested.

Officers: Dr. J. H. Cloud, pres., St. Louis, Mo.; A. L. Roberts, secy.-treas.; Kendall Green, Washington, D. C.

National Association of Junior Republics, The (est. 1908), Freeville, N. Y. To organize Junior Republics in the various states and to see that they and all existing Junior Republics in the Association are carried on according to Junior Republic ideas and principles.

W. R. George, National Director.

National Association for the Study of Epilepsy. Camden, N. Y. Objects: To promote the pathologic, therapeutic, social and medico-legal aspects of the epilepsies. To disseminate knowledge concerning the cause, care and treatment of the various epilepsies.

Officers: Dr. G. Kirby Collier, pres., Lake Ave., Rochester, N. Y.; Dr. Arthur L. Shaw, secy. and treas., Camden, N. Y.

National Association of Traveler's Aid Societies (est. 1917, incorp. 1920), 25 West 43d St., N.Y.C. (tel. Murray Hill 5381). Composed of non-commercial social agencies which protect and assist travelers and help them become assimilated in the community. Co-ordinates, standardizes and establishes Traveler's Aid work and methods. Publishes a directory annually and a bulletin bi-monthly. Non-sectarian in scope.

Virgil V. Johnson, general secretary.

National Bible Institute, The (est. 1906, incorp. 1908). Headquarters Bldg., 214 West 35th St., N.Y.C. Don O. Shelton, pres.; Hugh R. Monro, treas.

Maintains Out-door Evangelistic Campaign, April to November; Schools for training Christian workers, for resident students and for day and evening students. Three Gospel Halls (see below); publishes monthly, "The Bible Today;" has branches in Yonkers, N. Y., Philadelphia, San Francisco and New Haven, Conn.

BEACON LIGHT GOSPEL HALL, 2350 Third Ave., N.Y.C. Albert E. Blaise, supt.

MCAULEY CREMORNE MISSION, THE (incorp. 1882), 216 West 35th St., William McQuere, supt.

BRONX GOSPEL HALL, 499 East 153d St. Hendry W. Gault, supt.

National Board of Review of Motion Pictures, 70 Fifth Ave., N.Y.C. (est. 1909 by People's Institute). An extra-legal volunteer organization reflecting public sentiment and co-operating nationally with producers and city officials in the review and regulation of motion pictures on the basis of minimum standards, and with numerous organizations, individuals, groups, etc., in the extension of the use of worthwhile motion pictures both inside the theatres and without.

COMPOSITION: Review Committee, 125 members; General Committee (board of directors and court of appeals) 29; National Advisory Committee, 93; Religious Advisory Committee, 25; advisory committee from Authors' League, 29. The office staff alone receive compensation, but possess no vote on pictures policy or personnel. Al new members are elected by General Committee after thorough investigation of qualifications and eligibility. Any connection with motion pictures debars from membership.

Everett Dean Martin, chrm.; Sam A. Lewisohn, treas.; staff: W. D. McGuire, exec. secy.; Orrin G. Cocks, advisory secy.; Warren M. Covill, membership secy.; Wilton A. Barrett, review secy.; Alice B. Evans, cor. secy.

PUBLICATIONS: annual reports; literature on censorship question, in promotion of "better films," and the use of motion pictures for special purposes; monthly "Bulletin of Affiliated Committees for Better Films;" monthly lists of selected entertainment pictures; catalogues of these and of educational films; special lists of interest to school, libraries, churches, community centers; weekly bulletin for city officials of action on all films reviewed (practically the entire entertainment output).

NATIONAL COMMITTEE FOR BETTER FILMS (a department of Board): to recommend and further the use of high grade pictures especially those suitable for family and young people's entertainment. Clarence A. Perry, chrm.; Orrin G. Cocks, secy.

National Board of the Young Women's Christian Associations of the United States of America, 600 Lexington Ave., N.Y.C. (tel. Plaza 4700). Object: To participate in the work of the World's Young Women's Christian Associations; to establish, develop, and unify Young Women's Christian Associations in the United States; to advance Christian social service by advancing the physical, social, intellectual, moral and spiritual interests of young women.

TOTAL MEMBERSHIP: Total membership in the national organization now numbers 559,315, of whom 100,000 are girls between the ages of 12 and 18 enrolled in the Girl Reserve Corps of the Association.

HEADQUARTERS, FIELDS AND LOCAL ASSOCIATIONS: The headquarters of the National Board are in New York City; there are branch offices in eleven cities, namely: New York, Philadelphia, San Francisco, Richmond, Chicago, St. Louis, Denver, Dallas, Minneapolis, Seattle and Cincinnati. These cities are headquarters for field committees which the National Board has appointed to represent it in various sections of the country. Each field committee employs a staff of secretaries to do the direct work of organizing local association and to aid in developing the activities for girls and women which form the general Association program. One hundred and eighty-five field secretaries are now working. Local associations in the eleven fields may be enumerated as follows: 347 city associations in 234 cities, 78 town associations, 27 county associations, 711 student associations all of which are members of the National Association.

GENERAL ASSOCIATION PROGRAM: The general Association program includes many activities. Bible study and mission study classes are always conducted. All other activities are not included in the program of any one association; those undertaken being determined by the character of the community. Each is a part of a united effort to develop Christian leadership among women and to raise standards of women's health, women's work, and women's thought. The general Association program includes: Classes in Bible and Mission Study, Physical Training, Commercial Subjects, Language Study (French, Italian, Spanish, English), Domestic Arts and Sciences, Vocational Training, Elocution and Dramatics, Trained Attendance, Business Law, Parliamentary Law, Current Topics.

CLUBS: Recreational, Musical, Social.

MANAGEMENT of Cafeterias, Boarding Residences, Housekeeping Apartments, Room Registries, Residential and Transient Hotels, Summer Camps, Vacation Homes, Employment Bureau, Health Centers, Homes Investigation Bureaus.

SPECIAL ASSOCIATION PROGRAM: Special 'Association work include general Association activities augmented or adapted to the special needs of Industrial Workers, Colored Women, Indian Women, Business and Professional Women, Women of Foreign Birth, Students.

In 1920 the National Board conducted forty 10-day summer conferences for girls, with a total attendance of 10,840. It maintains a national training system to prepare young women for executive positions.

Part of this course must be taken in residence at the National Training School, 135 East 52d St., N.Y.C.

FOREIGN: The National Board has extended its work into the foreign field; in October 1920 it had 59 centers in Europe and the Near East with 118 secretaries; and in the Orient and South America 32 centers with 118 secretaries.

OFFICIAL ORGAN of the National Board: The official organ of the National Board is the "Association Monthly."

Officers: Mrs. Robert E. Speer, pres.; Mrs. John French, chrm. exec. committee; Mrs. Samuel A. Broadwell, treas.; Mrs. Lewis H. Lapham, secy.; Miss Mabel Cratty, gen. secy.

National Bureau of Economic Research, Inc., 175 Ninth Ave., N.Y.C. Engaged in determining facts bearing upon economic, social and industrial problems.

Officers: Edwin F. Gay, pres.; George E. Roberts, treas.; Oswald W. Knauth, secy.

National Child Labor Committee (org. 1904, incorp. 1907). Offices: Room 415, United Charities Bldg., 105 East 22d St., N.Y.C. (tel. Gramercy 5320), Greensboro, N. C. Objects: 1. To investigate conditions affecting children, especially in the fields of labor, education, vocational guidance, delinquency, relief, and health. 2. To publish reports and arouse public sentiment in favor of the improvement of conditions. 3. To co-operate in promoting administration and development of children's codes and in the drafting and enactment of legislative measures. Supported by voluntary contributions. Estimated expenses per annum, $100,-000.

Officers: Felix Adler, chrm., 33 Central Park West; Homer Folks and Samuel McCune Lindsay, vice-chrm.; V. Everit Macy, treas., 128 Broadway; Owen R. Lovejoy, gen. secy.

National Child Welfare Association, Inc. (est. 1912, incorp. 1914), 70 Fifth Ave., N.Y.C. Originates and publishes exhibit material visualizing condition affecting the physical, mental and moral development of children. Also lantern slides and literature. Cooperates with communities, educators, and organizations through exhibits, child welfare campaigns, etc. Supported by voluntary contributions.

Officers: Judge William H. Wadhams, pres.; Amos L. Prescott, treas.; Charles F. Powlison, gen. secy.

National Civic Federation, The, Woman's Department, Room 503, 105 West 40th St., N.Y.C. An educational movement for the advancement of industrial and social progress, to aid in the crystallization of the most enlightened public opinion, and to promote legislation in accordance therewith.

Miss Maude Wetmore, chrm.; Mrs. Coffin Van Rensselaer, exec. secy.

National Civic Federation, Woman's Department, NEW YORK AND NEW JERSEY SECTION (est. 1908), 105 West 40th St., N.Y.C. The Woman's Department concerns itself with problems dealing with industrial, social and economic life; through survey and construction experimentation arriving at a basis for remedial legislation. Co-operates in the general work of the Civic Federation.

Mrs. Francis McNiel Bacon, chrm.; Miss Olive Wade, exec. secy.

National Civil Service Reform League, 8 West 40th St., N.Y.C. (tel. Vanderbilt 2376). Richard Henry Dana, pres.; A. S. Frissell, treas., 530 Fifth Ave.; H. W. Marsh, secy.

National Commission on Milk Standards, 30 Church St., N.Y.C. Organized in 1911 by the New York Milk Committee for the purpose of securing an agreement among the leading authorities as to what proper standards should be for the control over milk supplies in the interest of public health. Results of the Commission's work have been unanimous agreement among the members favoring pasteurization, establishment of bacterial standards, establishment of grades of milk, and standards for butter, ice cream and other milk products.

Charles E. North, M.D., secy.

National Committee for Better Films. See NATIONAL BOARD OF REVIEW, etc.

National Committee for Constructive Immigration Legislation, 105 East 22d St., N.Y.C. Purposes to secure Congressional action on immigration problems, and to raise naturalization standards.

Officers: Henry W. Jessup, chrm.; Central Union Trust Co., New York, treas.; Sidney L. Gulick, secy.

National Committee for Mental Hygiene, The (founded 1909, incorp. 1916), 50 Union Square, N.Y.C. (tel. Stuyvesant 5965). The general purposes of the National Committee for Mental Hygiene and its affiliated state societies and committees are organized to work for the conservation of mental health; to help prevent nervous and mental disorders and mental defect; to help raise the standards of care and treatment to those suffering from any of these disorders and mental defect; to secure and disseminate reliable information on these subjects and also on mental factors involved in problems related to industry, education, delinquency, dependency and the like; to aid ex-service men disabled in the war; to co-operate with federal, state, and local agencies and with officials and with public and private agencies whose work is in any way related to that of a society or committee for mental hygiene. Though methods vary, these organizations seek to accomplish their purposes by means of education, encouraging psychiatric social service, conducting surveys, promoting legislation, and through co-operation with the many agencies whose work touches at one point or another the field of mental hygiene.

In addition, agencies for mental hygiene have been organized in more than twenty states and the District of Columbia. A movement toward organizing them in many other states is now being made. Information regarding the work of the state societies and committees for mental hygiene, and copies of pamphlets may be had for the asking. The National Committee for Mental Hygiene publishes a quarterly magazine, "Mental Hygiene," subscription $2.00 per year.

Officers: Dr. Walter B. James, pres.; Dr. Thomas W. Salmon, medical director; Dr. Frankwood E. Williams, Dr. V. V. Anderson, associate medical directors; Dr. Clarence J. D'Alton, exec. asst.; Clifford W. Beers, secy.

National Committee for the Prevention of Blindness, Inc., National headquarters and office, 130 East 22d St., N.Y.C. (tel. Gramercy 231). A volunteer association. Objects: To ascertain the causes of preventable blindness and impairment of vision, and to advocate such measures, in co-operation with the medical profession, as may eliminate such causes and promote in every way the conservation of vision throughout the United States. Acting as a bureau of information, with headquarters in New York City, the National Committee collects and imparts information, and endeavors, through cooperation with official and volunteer agencies, through legislative measures, by the preparation and distribution of publications, lectures, lantern slides, exhibits, etc. to create and arouse an active public interest in support of its objects. Every state in the Union is represented in the membership of the National Committee. Its Field Agent visits annually many parts of the country. Supported entirely by voluntary contributions.

Officers: William H. Taft, hon. pres.; William Fellowes Morgan, pres.; F. Park Lewis, M.D., Miss Louisa Lee Schuyler, vice-pres.; George Blagden, treas.; Edward M. Van Cleve, managing director; Mrs. Winifred Hathaway, secy.; George D. Easton, field secy.

See also NEW YORK STATE COMMITTEE, etc.

National Committee on Prison and Prison Labor, General office, Broadway and 116th St., N.Y.C. (tel. Morningside 1400). Washington office, Union Trust Bldg., Washington (tel. Main 9313). The primary object of this organization is to study the whole problem of labor in prisons and correctional institutions, with a view to securing legislation among the States of the Union, to the end that all prisoners may be employed so as to promote their welfare and at the same time reimburse the institutions for expense of maintenance, while preventing unfair competition between prison-made goods and the product of free labor, and securing to their dependent families a fair proportion of the rightful earnings of prisoners.

On April 14, 1917, the National Committee on Prisons and Prison Labor was officially recognized to serve as a relief society to accomplish the humane purposes with respect to prisoners of war, provided for in Article 15 of Section 1 of the Convention (IV) at The Hague, October 18, 1917, ratified by the United States, November 27, 1909.

Officers: Adolph Lewisohn, pres., 61 Broadway; Perley Morse, treas.; E. Stagg Whitin, chrm. Executive Committee.

National Committee for Teaching Citizenship, 3421 Lowell St., N. W., Washington. Established to teach boys and girls the responsibilities of citizenship.

Officers: Thomas M. Balliet, chrm.; Harry H. Moore, secy.-treas.; L. C. Staples, exec. secy.

National Conference of Catholic Charities (incorp. 1910). Meets biennially. Rev. John O'Grady, Ph.D., Catholic University, Washington, D.C., secy.

National Conference of Charities and Correction, The. See NATIONAL CONFERENCE OF SOCIAL WORK.

National Conference on City Planning (est. 1909), 60 State St., Boston, Mass. An annual conference presenting city planning problems and proposed solutions.

National Conference on the Education of Dependent, Truant, Backward, and Delinquent Children (1903). For the mutual benefit of those interested in the classes of children mentioned in the title, which ultimately must result in the benefit of the children themselves.

Officers: Joseph M. Frost, pres., Lansing, Mich.; Hobart H. Todd, secy.-treas., Industry, N. Y.

National Conference of Jewish Social Service (1899), 114 Fifth Ave. N.Y.C. (tel. Watkins 6998). Two hundred and fifteen constituent organizations in ninety-eight cities, and 1,500 sustaining, contributing and subscribing members.

Officers: Louis H. Levin, pres., Baltimore; Sidney E. Pritz, treas., Cincinnati; Boris D. Bogen, secy.; Frances L. Goldsmith, associate secy.

National Conference of Social Work (est. 1874). Headquarters: 23-25 East Ninth St., Cincinnati, Ohio. General professional association of persons engaged in all branches of humanitarian endeavor. Permanent Divisions on: children, delinquents and correction, health, public agencies and institutions, the family, industrial and economic problems, the local community.

Members receive proceedings of annual meetings and quarterly bulletin.

Dues: Regular, $3.00; Sustaining, $10.00; Institutional, $25.00 a year.

Meeting at Milwaukee, Wis., June 22-29, 1921.

Allen T. Burns, pres., New York; Wm. Hammond Parker, gen. secy., Cincinnati.

National Congress of Mothers and Parent-Teacher Associations (incorp. 1897), 1201 Sixteenth St., N. W., Washington, D. C. For Child Welfare in home, school, church, and state. To raise the standards of home life; to develop wiser, better trained parenthood; to bring into closer relations the home and the school; to secure proper care for erring and orphan children.

National Conservation Association, Woodward Bldg., Washington, D. C. Object: The conservation of our natural resources.

Gifford Pinchot, pres.; Harry A. Slattery, secy.

National Consumers' League (est. 1899), Room 1102, 44 East 23d St., N.Y.C. (tel. Gramercy 5923). To awaken responsibility for conditions under which goods are made and distributed and through investigation, education and legislation, to mobilize public opinion in behalf of enlightened standards for workers and honest products for all.

Officers: Newton D. Baker, pres., Washington, D. C.; G. H. Kinnicutt, treas.; Mrs. Florence Kelley, gen. secy.; J. R. Shillady, exec. director.

National Desertion Bureau (incorp. 1914, est. 1911), 356 Second Ave., N.Y.C. (tel. Gramercy 5218). To locate family deserters; induce them to reunite with or support their families; or failing this, to prosecute them according to law.

Officers: Walter H. Liebmann, pres.; Joseph M. Proskauer, treas.; Monroe M. Goldstein, secy. and chief counsel-in-charge.

National Education Association of the United States (est. 1857, incorp. 1907), 1201 Sixteenth St., N. W., Washington, D. C. To elevate the character and advance the interests of the profession of teaching, and to promote the cause of popular education in the United States.

Fred M. Hunter, Supt. of Schools, Oakland, Cal., pres.

National Employment Exchange (incorp. under the laws of the State of New York, 1909). Office and general mercantile branch, Hudson Terminal Bldg., 30 Church St., New York City. Organized following investigations made during the winter 1908–1909 by Edward T. Devine into state, philanthropic and commercial employment exchanges throughout the country, and the need for systematic distribution of labor. While this Association has been formed for philanthropic purposes, its underlying principle is that it shall be conducted not as a charity but as a business; and to that end it will seek to serve employers by furnishing to them employees suitable for the work to be done. Departments for executives, engineers and other technical men, salesmen, banking men, accountants, bookkeepers, stenographers, clerical men and clerical women.

George S. Anthony, gen. manager.

National Federation of Day Nurseries (org. 1898), 289 Fourth Ave., N.Y.C. (tel. Gramercy 5258). Office hours, 10–4; Saturdays, 10–1. To unite in one central body all day nurseries; to endeavor to secure the highest attained standard; to act as a central bureau for information in regard to existing day nurseries, and for the publication and distribution of literature that may prove helpful in the organization of new day nurseries; a directory of day nurseries and pamphlets on the methods of this work are published.

Officers: Mrs. Arthur M. Dodge, 563 Park Ave., pres.; Miss H. M. Sears, office secy.

National Federation of Religious Liberals (org. 1908). To promote the religious life by united testimony for sincerity, freedom, and progress in religion, by social service and a fellowship of spirit beyond the lines of sect and creed.

Frank H. Burt, secy., 813 Barristers' Hall, Boston, Mass.

National Federation of Remedial Loan Associations (est. 1909), 346 Fourth Ave., N.Y.C. To advance the remedial loan movement by encouraging the formation of local remedial loan societies; by aiding and directing persons interested in the work; by giving information and advice concerning problems of organization and management; and by assisting in drafting and securing the passage of constructive legislation for the regulation of the small loan business. Membership in the Federation has been limited to societies which have formed primarily for the purpose of improving loaning conditions and have given satisfactory evidence of the motives and purposes of their organizers in the form of a definite and reasonable limitation of dividend.

Officers: Arthur H. Ham, chrm., New York City; D. S. Coffey, vice-chrm., St. Paul, Minn.; J. E. Ryan, secy.-treas., Detroit, Mich.

National Federation of Settlements (1911). To reinforce all phases of federated action among neighborhood agencies; to bring together the results of settlement experience throughout the country; to secure capable recruits; to urge measures of State and National legislation suggested by settlement experience; to promote the better organization of neighborhood life generally.

John L. Elliott, pres., 436 West 27th St., N.Y.C.; Robert A. Woods, secy., 20 Union Park, Boston, Mass.

National First Aid Association of America, The (incorp. D. of C.).

Executive office: 637 Massachusetts Ave., Arlington, Mass. Clara Barton, ounder and pres. (in Memoriam); Roscoe G. Wells, acting pres. and treas.; Dr. Frederick H. Morse, medical dir.; Mary Kensel Wells, secy.

National Highways Protective Society (incorp. 1909), 80 Maiden Lane, N.Y.C. (tel. John 1900). Object: Safe streets and highways; enforcement and judicious amendment of speed laws; suppression of "joy-riding," smoke nuisance, and criminal, unauthorized, dangerous, or obnoxious use of motors, motorcycles, and other vehicles; better methods and practice in street paving, repairing, and cleaning; good roads and honesty, economy, and efficiency in their making and maintenance; enforcement of the law in regard to posting of advertising signs on trees, poles, etc., on highways; sane automobile and highway legislation; reciprocity laws between States, whereby a single, adequate, and uniform motor license may safely be recognized in all States.

Officers: Joseph A. Herron, treas.; Edward S. Cornell, secy.

National Home for Disabled Volunteer Soldiers (est. 1866). National headquarters: National Military Home, Dayton, Ohio.

The Branch Homes are as follows:

Central Branch, Dayton, Ohio.

Northwestern Branch, Milwaukee, Wis.

Eastern Branch, Togus, Me.

Southern Branch, Hampton, Va.

Western Branch, Leavenworth, Kan.

Pacific Branch, Santa Monica, Cal.

Marion National Sanatorium, Marion, Ind.

Danville Branch, Danville, Ill.

Johnson City National Sanatorium, Johnson City, Tenn.

Battle Mountain Sanitarium, Hot Springs, S. D.

Open to all honorably discharged officers, soldiers and sailors who were in the service of the United States during any war in which the country was engaged (including Mexican border service), and in any campaigns with hostile Indians, and who by reason of wounds received, disease, or old age, are unable to earn a living, and have no adequate means of support.

Managers: The President, the Chief Justice, the Secretary of War, ex-officios; Gen. Geo. H. Wood, pres. Board of Managers; Capt. John C. Nelson, 1st vice-pres., Logansport, Ind.; Major James W. Wadsworth, 2d vice-pres., Geneseo, N. Y.; Hon. James S. Catherwood, secy., Hoopeston, Ill.; Col. H. H. Markham, Pasadena, Cal.; Hon. M. Dennett, Lewiston, Me.

Officers: Col. C. W. Wadsworth, gen. treas.; Col. James A. Mattison, inspector general and chief surgeon; Col. Chas. M. Pearsall, asst. gen. treas. and asst. insp. gen.; Col. O. K. Marshall, asst. insp. gen.

National Housing Association (est. 1910), Room 617, 105 East 22d St., N.Y.C. To improve housing conditions, both urban and suburban, in every practicable way. Local associations or committees are organized, aid given in campaigns of education, in drafting, enacting, and enforcing legislation, in organizing improved housing companies, and in carrying on the continued work after good standards have been established. Acts as a clearing house of information, publishes literature dealing with housing, holds housing institutes in different sections of the country, and an annual housing conference.

Lawrence Veiller, secy. and director.

National Indian Association, The (org. 1879, incorp. 1887), Room 1013, 156 Fifth Ave., N.Y.C. To aid in civilization, teach industry, and give religious instruction to the Indians of our country.

Officers: Mrs. Otto Heinigke, pres.; Mrs. Anna B. Clark, treas.; John W. Clark, cor. and exec. secy.

National Information Bureau, Inc. (est. Oct. 1918, formerly National Investigation Bureau). 140 Metropolitan Tower, 1 Madison Ave., N.Y.C. (tel. Gramercy 2487). To investigate national, social, civic and philanthropic activities soliciting funds.

Officers: Gustavus D. Pope, pres., Detroit; Paul L. Feiss, 1st vice-pres. and treas., Cleveland; Lawson Purdy, 2d vice-pres., New York; Allen T. Burns, secy., New York; Barry C. Smith, director.

National Jewish Hospital for Consumptives, The (incorp. 1900), 3800 East Colfax Ave., Denver, Col. For the treatment and cure of tuberculosis and research work. Capacity, 175 beds. All free. No limitations as to sex, nationality, sect, or age. Supported by voluntary contributions, subscriptions, donations, and bequests.

Officers: Mrs. S. Pisko, natl. secy.; Dr. Samuel Swezey, supt.; Dr. Harry J. Corper, director of research laboratories.

National Jewish Immigration Council (org. 1911), 80 Maiden Lane, N.Y.C. The purpose of this council is general supervision of all work for Jewish immigrants at the seaports of the United States. Agencies at New York, Boston, Philadelphia, and Baltimore.

National Kindergarten Association (est. and incorp. 1909), 8 West 40th St., N.Y.C. (tel. Murray Hill 2030). To promote kindergarten education throughout the United States. Supported by voluntary gifts.

Officers: Major Bradley Martin, pres.; Julian M. Gerard, treas.; Miss Bessie Locke, cor. secy.

National League of Girls' Clubs (formerly National League of Women Workers, est. 1897). Headquarters: 130 East 59th St., N.Y.C. (tel. Plaza 798). Organized in the interest of working girls and women, through clubs which offer social and educational opportunities. All clubs are self-governing, non-sectarian, and either partially or wholly self-supporting.

The League numbers 150 clubs with an approximate membership of 30,000 girls. Individual clubs are federated into Sectional Leagues which in turn are members of the National League.

The League employs secretaries to strengthen clubs already within the organization and also to establish new clubs upon the call of a community or of an interested group of girls. It publishes a magazine called the "Club Worker" and also issues pamphlets on methods of organizing and on club ideals. A national convention is held every alternate spring at the larger women's colleges, which large numbers of club delegates attend. Bryn Mawr, 1920; Vassar, 1922.

The National League conducts a training course for leaders in girls' recreational work.

Officers: Mrs. Bernard E. Pollak, pres.; Mrs. Charles Sabin, treas.; Miss Jean Hamilton, gen. secy.

For New York State and City activities, see NEW YORK LEAGUE OF GIRLS CLUBS.

National League on Urban Conditions Among Negroes. See NATIONAL URBAN LEAGUE.

National Lend-A-Hand Society Inc., Room 212, 106 Park Row, N.Y.C Object: To "lend a hand" to discharged prisoners and help them temporally. morally, and spiritually, irrespective of race or creed; also receives prisoners paroled to the care of the society. Supported by voluntary contributions.

Directors: Charles Hamilton Sabin, pres.; Hon. Charles C. Nott, Jr., vice-pres.; Arthur B. Hatcher, treas.; Hon. Myer Nussbaum, William A. Brady, Charles C. Auchincloss, Charles M. Lang, Ellwood Hendrick, George Sanderson, exec. secy.

National Liberal Immigration League (est. 1906), 108 East 31st St., N.Y.C. (tel. Madison Square 7427). Aims to preserve for our country the benefits of immigration while keeping out undesirables. Distributes pamphlets. Spreads Americanization and patriotism.

Officers: Joseph G. Cannon, pres., Danville, Ill.; Antonio Zucca, treas.; B. A. Sekely, field representative; N. Behar, managing director.

National Motion Picture League (est. March, 1918), 381 Fourth Ave., N.Y.C. (tel. Madison Sq. 860). To work for better motion pictures for children and families.

National Municipal League (est. 1894), 261 Broadway, N.Y.C. Publishes monthly the "National Municipal Review," devoted to current government topics. Supported by voluntary contributions and the dues of members.

Officers: Charles E. Hughes, pres.; Frank A. Vanderlip, treas.; H. W. Dodds, secy.

National Organization for Public Health Nursing, The (est. 1912), 156 Fifth Ave., N.Y.C. (tel. Watkins 793). Scope of work: Public health nursing activities. Supported by membership subscriptions and guarantors.

Officers: Miss Edna L. Foley, pres., Chicago; Miss Elizabeth G. Fox, 1st vice-pres., Washington, D. C.

National Plant, Flower, and Fruit Guild (org. 1896, incorp. 1906), 70 Fifth Ave., N.Y.C. (tel. Chelsea 5293). To give to the sick poor in hospitals and tenements, sympathy and cheer through the distribution of plants, cut flowers, fruit, and jelly. To establish garden clubs, children's community gardens in cities and towns, and supply flowering window boxes for congested tenement districts. Supported by subscription and donations.

St. Quentin Committee, Mrs. Bernard Didisheim, chrm., assists in reconstruction work in St. Quentin, France, by providing funds for the purchase of fruit trees, distributed to refugee families as they return to build up their broken homes.

National officers: Mrs. John Wood Stewart, founder and pres.; John Burroughs, hon. pres.; Virginia D. H. Furman, treas.; Ellen Eddy Shaw, secy.; Mrs. Frank V. Anderson, exec. secy.

New York City Branch maintains an office at the same address. Officers: Mrs. George Stewart Brown, pres.; Mrs. John Wood Stewart, vice-pres.; Mrs. Frank V. Anderson, secy.

National Popular Government League, Munsey Bldg., Washington. Promotes constitutional and legislative measures to increase efficiency of representative government.

Officers: Robert L. Owen, pres.; Judson King, exec. secy. and treas.

National Red Cross. See American Red Cross.

National Security League, Inc., 17 East 49th St., N.Y.C. Propagandist organization, interested in promoting national defense and Americanism, and in combating radicalism in all its forms.

Officers: Charles D. Orth, pres.; Alexander H. Hemphill, treas.; E. L Harvey, exec. secy.

National Short Ballot Organization, The (est. 1910), 8 West 9th St., N.Y.C. (tel. Stuyvesant 3822). Object is to explain the principle of the short ballot and to secure its adoption wherever applicable. Headquarters for information on city charters, commission government, county government, the "city manager" plan, etc.

Woodrow Wilson, pres.; Richard S. Childs, secy.

National Social Unit Organization, The (est. 1916, incorp. 1919), 117 West 46th St., N.Y.C. (tel. Bryant 248). The National Social Unit Organization is a body formed to promote a plan of community organization and to test the principles upon which the plan is based by actual experimentation in a community or communities.

William C. Phillips, executive.

National Social Workers' Exchange, 130 East 22d St., N.Y.C. (tel. Gramercy 4916). A membership organization of men and women in social work for the purpose of developing professional standards in social work, encouraging adequate training, recruiting new workers and developing a better adjustment between workers and positions in social work. To this end an employment service is maintained.

Mrs. Edith Shatto King, manager.

National Society for the Friendless, Massachusetts Bldg., Kansas City, Mo. Operates as general directing organization for state Societies for the friendless, engaged in prisoners' aid work and prison reform.

Officers: T. F. Carver, pres.; W. H. Barnard, treas.; Rev. James Parsons, national supt.

National Society for Vocational Education, 140 West 42d St., N.Y.C. (tel. Bryant 3840).

William J. Bogan, pres.; John Clyde Oswald, treas.

National Temperance Society and Commission on Temperance of the Federal Council of the Churches of Christ in America (est. 1865, incorp. 1866, united in 1917), Room 51, 289 Fourth Ave., N.Y.C. (tel. Gramercy 3475). Objects: General temperance movements, including publication of three temperance papers, the publication and distribution of temperance literature.

Officers: Rev. D. Stuart Dodge, National Temperance Society, pres.; Alfred R. Kimball, treas.; Rev. Charles Scanlon, acting exec. secy.; Gov. Carl E. Milliken, chrm. Commission on Temperance.

National Tuberculosis Association (org. 1904), Room 501, 381 Fourth Ave., N.Y.C. Officers: Gerald B. Webb, M.D., pres., Colorado Springs, Colo.; Col. George E. Bushnell, hon. vice-pres.; James A. Miller, M.D., and Philip K. Brown, M.D., vice-prests.; George M. Kober, M.D., secy.; Henry B. Platt, treas.; Charles J. Hatfield, M.D., managing director.

National Urban League (for social service among Negroes) (est. 1911), 127 East 23d St., N.Y.C. (tel. Gramercy 3967, 3978). Purpose: To bring about co-ordination and co-operation of social agencies working with Negroes and to develop such agencies and organizations where necessary; to secure and train Negro social workers; to investigate conditions of city life as a basis for practical work. Supported by voluntary contributions.

Officers: L. Hollingsworth Wood, chrm.; A. S. Frissell, treas.; William H. Baldwin, secy.; Eugene Kinckle Jones, exec. secy.

See also New York Urban League.

National War Work Council of the Y. M. C. A. See International Committee Young Men's Christian As-

SOCIATION, 347 Madison Ave., New York City.

National Women's Trade Union League of America (founded 1903). Headquarters: 64 West Randolph St., Chicago, Ill. Stands for self-government in the workshop through organization, and also for the enactment of protective legislation. Official organ, "Life and Labor."

Mrs. Raymond Robins, pres.; Miss Emma Steghagen, secy.-treas.

Nativity, Church of the, 44 Second Ave., N.Y.C. Attached to the Church are the following works which depend for support entirely on voluntary contributions:

BARAT SETTLEMENT HOUSE, 223 Chrystie St., near Houston St. For the betterment of the Italian children of the neighborhood, by religious and social training and by kindergarten work.

BARAT DAY NURSERY, 221 Chrystie St. For Italian children of the neighborhood.

Natural History Museum. See AMERICAN MUSEUM OF NATURAL HISTORY.

Naturalization Aid League (org. 1908), Forward Bldg., 175 East Broadway, N.Y.C. (tel. Orchard 6364). An organization to assist aliens to become American citizens. Supported by trade unions, fraternal organizations and societies.

Officers: Reubin Guskin, pres.; L. Ginsburg, treas.; Ephim H. Jeshurin, manager.

Naturalization Bureau, Supreme Court, First Department: New York County Court House, Chambers St.; Second Department: Brooklyn Hall of Records; Queens County Court House, L. I. C.

Naval Hospital. See UNITED STATES NAVAL HOSPITAL.

Navy Legal Aid Association, Inc., 25 West 43d St., N.Y.C. Provides competent defense for enlisted men of United States Navy in court-martial cases.

Officers: William McAdoo, pres.; Fred. L. Eldridge, treas.; Emery C. Weller, exec. chrm.

Nazareth Hospital. See SETON HOSPITAL.

Nazareth Industrial School. See SOCIETY OF ST. JOSEPH.

Nazareth Nursery (incorp. 1902), 214 West 15th St., N.Y.C. (tel. Chelsea 1881). Cares for infants and children while their mothers are employed. Capacity, forty. Supported by voluntary contributions.

Sister M. Liguori, in charge.

Nazareth Trade School. See SISTERS OF ST. DOMINIC.

Near East Relief (est. 1915, incorp. by Act of Congress), 1 Madison Ave., N.Y.C. (tel. Gramercy 1024). For the relief and repatriation of the Armenians, Syrians, Greeks and other destitute people in Persia, Russia, Caucasus, Syria and Turkey. Supported by private subscriptions and contributions.

Officers: James L. Barton, chrm.; Cleveland H. Dodge, treas.; C. V. Vickrey, secy.

Needlework Guild of America, The (founded 1885, incorp. 1896). National office: 505 Franklin Bldg., Philadelphia. The object is to collect and distribute in hospitals, homes, etc., new plain clothing. Non-sectarian. There are about 540 branches in thirty-six states; 815,843 garments collected and distributed in 1919.

Rosamond K. Bender, exec. secy.

Needlework Guild of America, NEW YORK CITY BRANCH (org. 1891). Office: Room 312, 42 West 39th St.,

N.Y.C. Office hours: Tuesday and Friday, 10 to 1 (tel. Greeley 2884). To furnish new, plain, suitable garments to meet the great need of our hospitals, homes, and other charities, and to supply a channel through which all persons may work in unity for this object. Men, women, and children of all classes may become members. Un-sectarian. The annual meeting is held in November for the reception and distribution of garments. Apply at office for further information.

Officers: Miss Grace Bigelow, pres.; Mrs. Harold G. Henderson, treas., 82 Irving Pl.; Mrs. Hermann M. Biggs, secy.; Miss H. E. Howson, exec. secy.

Needlework Guild of America, BROOKLYN BRANCH.

Officers: Mrs. J. Elliot Langstaff, pres., 19 Seventh Ave.

Negro Fresh-air Committee, The (est. 1906), 131 East 66th St., N.Y.C. (tel. Rhinelander 140). An agency for securing fresh-air opportunities for colored people of New York. It manages a small home in July and August and depends upon voluntary contributions.

Rev. William H. Hubbell, 55 West 12th St., chrm.; Miss H. T. Emerson, secy. and treas.

Negro Rural School Fund, Anna T. Jeanes Foundation, 61 Broadway, N.Y.C. (tel. Bowling Green 7100). For the improvement of the rural public schools for Negroes in the Southern States.

Officers: James H. Dillard, Box 418, Charlottesville, Va., pres. and director; George Foster Peabody, 25 Broad St., N. Y., treas., whom address.

Neighborhood Club, The, 104 Clark St., Brooklyn, N. Y. Under the auspices of the Brooklyn Society of the New Church (Swedenborgian).

Robert Alfred Shaw, pres.

* *Current information not received.*

Neighborhood House. See AMERICAN PARISH.

***Neighbors League of America, Inc., The** (est. 1917, incorp. 1919). Room 526, 156 Fifth Ave., N.Y.C. To promote neighborly relations between native and foreign-born residents of the U. S.

Neponsit Beach Hospital for Children (1915), Neponsit, Rockaway Beach, N. Y. (tel. Belle Harbor 2117). Under Board of Trustees, Bellevue, and Allied Hospitals. For the care of and treatment of bone, joint, and glandular tuberculosis. Boys under twelve, girls under fourteen years of age.

Officers: Josephine T. W. Brass, supt. Examining physicians at 419 East 26th St., Monday, Wednesday, and Friday afternoons.

Netherland Benevolent Society of New York, The (incorp. 1908), under the patronage of H. M. the Queen of the Netherlands, 217 East 19th St., N.Y.C. Relieves and generally assists those of Dutch birth or extraction.

Officers: E. Bunge, vice-pres.; J. G. Kreijenbroek, treas.; James Penninck, exec. secy., whom address.

Netherwood Fresh-air Home. See LITTLE MISSIONARY'S DAY NURSERY.

Neurological Institute of New York (incorp. 1909), 149–151 East 67th St. (tel. Rhinelander 4120). A hospital and laboratory for the study and treatment of nervous and metabolic diseases. Besides private rooms and private wards, there are wards for both men and women, where the patients are received at very moderate charges, less than the cost of maintenance. Hours of admission, 9 A. M. to 6 P. M., daily, except Sundays and holidays. Maintains also a

DISPENSARY, 1–3 P. M. daily, except Sundays and holidays, fully equipped with hydrotherapy, mechanotherapy, electropathy, hot air, etc.

Officers: R. P. Perkins, pres., 25 Madison Ave.; Harrison Williams, treas., 60 Broadway; Sherman Day, secy., 120 Broadway; Miss E. F. Rivington, R.N., supt.; Miss G. M. Dwyer, R.N., supervisor of nurses.

Neustadter Home, cor. MacLean and Central Aves., Yonkers, N. Y. (tel. Yonkers 6648). A convalescent home for women and children. No boys over thirteen and no children over eight, unaccompanied by an adult are taken.

Officers: William I. Walter, pres.; Walter E. Beer, treas.; Samuel A. Sicher, secy.; Helen Butler, R.N. supt.

***New Brighton Day Nursery** (est. 1895), 5th St. near Jersey St., New Brighton, Staten Island.

New Church Board of Publication, The (incorp. 1883), 3 West 29th St., N.Y.C. (tel. Longacre 4047). Publishing house of the General Convention of the New Jerusalem (Swedenborgian); issues liturgies, hymnals, and works explanatory of Swedenborg's teachings. Supported by invested funds and sales.

Robert Alfred Shaw, pres.; John F. Seekamp, treas.

THE NEW CHURCH PRESS (incorp. 1913) is selling agent.

New England Society in the City of New York (est. 1805, incorp. 1833), 43 Cedar St., N.Y.C. (tel. 6022 John). For the aid of needy New Englanders. Supported by dues and income from investments.

Officers: Darwin P. Kingsley, pres., 346 Broadway; George W. Hodges, treas., 14 Wall St.; Harry A. Cushing, secy.

New Era Club (org. 1900, incorp. 1901), 274 East Broadway, N.Y.C. (tel. Orchard 2777). To provide, in its commodious building, a wholesome social atmosphere for the Jewish young men of the East Side. The social welfare of the members is promoted through the stimulation of their moral, mental, and physical facilities.

Louis S. Posner, pres.; Samuel J. Krangel, treas.; Irving Klausner, secy.

New Fifth Avenue Hospital. See FIFTH AVENUE HOSPITAL.

New Hampton Farms, New Hampton, Orange Co., N. Y. See CORRECTION, DEPARTMENT OF.

***New Windsor Fresh-air Society** (org. 1894), New Windsor, N. Y.

New York Academy of Medicine, The (est. 1847, incorp. 1851), 17 West 43d St., N.Y.C. (tel. Vanderbilt 974). Purpose: The advancement of the science and art of medicine, the maintenance of a Public Medical Library and the promotion of the Public Health.

Officers: George David Stewart, M.D., pres.; Seth M. Milliken, treas.; Royal S. Haynes, M.D., rec. secy.; John S. Brownne, librarian.

New York Academy of Medicine. Public Health Committee. See PUBLIC HEALTH COMMITTEE OF THE NEW YORK ACADEMY OF MEDICINE.

New York Annual Conference of the Methodist Episcopal Church, Trustees of the (incorp. 1843). Hold real estate and invested funds for the sole benefit of needy, disabled ministers and needy families of deceased ministers of the M. E. Church.

New York Anti-vivisection Society, "THE OPEN DOOR" (incorp. 1908), Room 901, 456 Fourth Ave., N.Y.C. (tel. Madison Sq. 8513). For information and particulars address the office of the Society.

Officers: Mrs. Diana Belais, pres.; Mrs. Anna N. Polhemus, treas.; Mrs. Janette L. Boynton, secy.

* *Current information not received.*

New York Association for the Blind, The (incorp. 1906). The Lighthouse, headquarters and salesroom, 111 East 59th St., N.Y.C. (tel. 3370 Plaza). Objects: To prevent unnecessary blindness, to help the blind to help themselves, to relieve and cheer the aged and infirm blind, and to provide summer outings. Supported by voluntary contributions. (See advertisement.) The work of the Association includes:

INFORMATION BUREAU. Information concerning the blind sought and given.

REGISTRATION BUREAU.

TICKET BUREAU for distributing tickets for musical and dramatic performances.

WORKSHOP FOR BLIND MEN, at 338 East 35th St.

CLASSES FOR BLIND WOMEN, at 111 East 59th St.

CLASSES FOR BLIND MEN: Individual instruction when required.

MUSIC SCHOOL FOR THE BLIND.

SUMMER SCHOOL FOR BLIND CHILDREN, six weeks' session.

HOME TEACHING. The Association gives out raw material to and through blind and sighted home teachers, instructs in the making of marketable articles and sells the finished products.

VACATION HOUSE. The Emma L. Hardy Memorial Home at Cornwall-on-the-Hudson maintained during the summer for parties of blind men, women and children.

CLUBS: Men's Club, Tuners' Guild, Women's Club, Bowling Club for Men, Dancing and Physical Culture for Women, Lighthouse Boy Scouts, Lighthouse Camp Fire Girls, etc.

SOCIAL SERVICE. Advice and relief where needed are given to the blind.

SALESROOM. For the sale of articles made by the blind and the exhibition of reading and writing appliances, games, etc., for their use.

"The Searchlight Magazine" for children, printed in improved Braille.

Officers: Dr. John H. Finley, pres.; Hon. William Howard Taft, Hon. Charles Evans Hughes, Miss Helen Keller, Dr. F. Park Lewis, vice-prests.; Robert W. de Forest, vice-pres.; Frederick L. Eldridge, Esq., treas.; Miss Winifred Holt, secy., to whom all communications should be sent.

New York Association for Improving the Condition of the Poor. See ASSOCIATION FOR IMPROVING THE CONDITION OF THE POOR.

New York Association of Women Workers. See N. Y. LEAGUE OF WOMEN WORKERS.

New York Bible and Common Prayer-book Society (org. 1809), 214 East 23d St., N.Y.C. For gratuitous distribution of the Bible and the Book of Common Prayer, in English and various languages, to the parishes and mission stations of the Protestant Episcopal Church in the United States and colonies. Upwards of 80,000 volumes distributed during past year. The board meets quarterly at Church Missions House, 281 Fourth Ave.

Officers: Frank T. Warburton, treas., 46 Cedar St.; Edwin S. Gorham, secy., 11 West 45th St.; R. M. Pott, agent, 214 East 23d St.

New York Bible Society (original Society, 1809, incorp. 1866), 5 East 48th St. (at Fifth Ave.), N.Y.C. The only Society having for its sole work Bible distribution in the City and Harbor of New York. Issues only Bibles and portions of the Bible in all languages and styles of binding. Supplies the Scriptures at cost and by gift. Unsectarian, interdenominational, the work being conducted without regard to creed, class, or color. Co-operates with missionaries and missionary societies of all denominations. Employs missionaries among the immigrants and sailors. Hotels, hospitals, prisons, and needy homes supplied. Makes large distribution among United States soldiers and sailors. Total distribution during the past year, 232,610 volumes in fifty-three languages and in raised type for the blind. Instituted Universal Bible Sunday, second Sunday in Advent. Supported by Church collections, donations, and legacies.

Officers: John C. West, pres.; James H. Schmelzel, treas.; Rev. George William Carter, Ph.D., gen. secy., to whom apply.

New York Botanical Garden, Bronx Park. See BOTANICAL GARDEN.

New York Branch, Division of Information, United States Immigration Service. See U. S. DEPT. OF LABOR, DISTRIBUTION BRANCH, etc.

New York Catholic Protectory, The (incorp. 1862), Westchester, N. Y.

City office and reception house, 415 Broome St., N.Y.C. (tel. Spring 175).

Branches: Lincoln Agricultural School, Lincolndale, N. Y.

The Boys' Protectory is in charge of the Brothers of the Christian Schools. The Girls' Protectory is in charge of the Sisters of Charity of Mount Saint Vincent.

ST. PHILIP'S HOME FOR INDUSTRIOUS BOYS, 417 Broome St., N.Y.C.

New York Chapter American Red Cross. See AMERICAN RED CROSS IN GREATER NEW YORK.

New York Child Labor Committee (org. 1902, incorp. 1907), Room 410, 105 East 22d St., N.Y.C. (tel. Gramercy 496). To increase the efficiency of existing child labor laws by securing needed amendments. To assist the authorities in enforcing compulsory education and child labor laws. To educate public sentiment concerning the prevention of child labor. Supported by voluntary contributions.

Officers: George W. Alger, chrm.; James G. Blaine, Jr., treas.; George A. Hall, secy., to whom send communications.

New York Child Welfare Committee (est. 1909, incorp. 1910), 70 Fifth Ave., N.Y.C. (tel. Watkins 6270). Activities: 1. Conducts a Bureau of Child Welfare Information. 2. Conducts classes for instruction of young women in proper methods of baby care. 3. Conducts educational campaigns to reach the parents living in the congested section of the city. Through child welfare exhibits, motion pictures, illustrated lectures, classroom instruction, etc., in more than six hundred centers the principles of proper child care have been presented to more than 2,474,000 individuals. 4. Assists local child helping agencies in neighborhoods in which the child problems are found to be particularly pressing. In some instances the assistance is financial in character. 5. Promotes public policies and public measures designed to safeguard our city children and seeks to obstruct those policies and measures which are likely to have a contrary effect. Supported by voluntary contributions.

Officers: Robert Van Iderstine, chrm.; Raymond B. Fosdick, vice-pres.; Amos L. Prescott, treas.; Frank Clayton Myers, exec. secy.

New York Christian Home for Intemperate Men, Mt. Vernon, N. Y. See CHESTER CREST.

New York City Association of Congregational Churches, The, meets second Thursday of May and November. The official body in which the Congregational ministers of New York City and nearby suburbs hold their official ministerial standing.

Rev. George D. Egbert, pres.; Rev.

Charles J. Allen, secy-treas., 1776 45th St., Brooklyn.

New York City Baptist Mission Society, 276 Fifth Ave., N.Y.C. To promote Churches, Missions, Sunday-schools, Vacation Schools, Settlements and other missionary and charitable work. Supported by voluntary contributions and church offerings.

English Speaking Churches. Missions and Churches for Foreign Population; Chinese, Finnish, Hungarian, Italian, Lettish, Polish, Russian, Slovak-Bohemian, Swedish-Finnish.

Vacation Bible Schools.

New York City Branch, National Plant, Flower, and Fruit Guild. See NATIONAL PLANT, FLOWER, AND FRUIT GUILD.

New York City Children's Hospitals and Schools. See PUBLIC WELFARE DEPARTMENT, CITY OF NEW YORK.

New York City Conference of Charities and Correction (org. 1910), 287 Fourth Ave., N.Y.C. (tel. Gramercy 5957). All who are officially connected with public or private charitable or correctional work in New York City, or who take an active interest therein, are invited to enroll themselves as members of the Conference and to attend its sessions. There are no other tests of membership and no membership fee is charged, the expenses of the Conference being met by voluntary contributions.

The Twelfth Conference will be held May 18, 19, 1921, in Brooklyn, Manhattan, and at the Sea View Hospital, Staten Island. Address all communications to the secretary.

Officers: George J. Gillespie, pres., 22 Vesey St.; Charles Loring Brace, treas., 105 East 22d St.; Julius Brown, secy., 287 Fourth Ave., Room 502.

New York City Federation of Women's Clubs (incorp. 1905), Hotel Astor, N.Y.C.

Mrs. Harry Lilly, pres.

New York City Home for the Aged and Infirm, Blackwell's Island, N.Y.C. See PUBLIC WELFARE DEPARTMENT, CITY OF NEW YORK.

New York City Mission Society (org. 1827, incorp, 1866), United Charities Bldg., 105 East 22d St., N.Y.C. (tel. Gramercy 6070). Office hours, 9 A. M. to 5 P. M.

The objects of the Society are to promote morality and religion among the poor and destitute of the City of New York, by the employment of missionaries, the diffusion of evangelical truth, and the establishment of Mission Churches and Chapels, Mission Sunday-schools, etc. Protestant, otherwise undenominational. Supported by voluntary contributions. Owns $900,000 real estate in churches.

Officers: William Sloane Coffin, pres.; Stephen Baker, treas.; Luther H. Lewis, secy.; Rev. A. H. McKinney, D.D., supt., to whom address all correspondence. (See advertisement.)

THE CHURCHES FOR THE PEOPLE of the Society, doing institutional work, are listed below; for religious notices, see under NON-SECTARIAN in the Church List.

DEWITT MEMORIAL, 280 Rivington St., near Cannon St., N.Y.C. Rev. William T. Elsing, D.D., 286 Rivington St.; Rev. A. Roeandt, German Pastor, 59 2d St.; Rev. L. H. Ordile, Italian Pastor, 59 2d St. English, German, and Italian services and meetings, meetings for Hebrew Christians, free circulating library, King's Daughters' Circle, sewing classes, mothers' meeting, Christian Endeavor and gymnasium.

OLIVET MEMORIAL CHURCH, 59–63 2d St., N.Y.C. Rev. Harry L. Oldfield,

Pastor; Rev. A. Roeandt, German Pastor; Rev. L. H. Ordile, Italian Pastor. Maintains: English, German, and Italian services and classes, free public library, reading room, children's hours, Young People's Association, societies and clubs, King's Daughters' Circle, Kindergarten, mothers' meetings, gymnasium, and baths. Out-door preaching in summer.

Olivet Missionary Association helps various missionary objects at home and abroad.

Emergency Association: To provide for the burial of any deceased member.

BROOME STREET MEMORIAL CHURCH, 395 Broome St., N.Y.C. Rev. Joseph Brunn, Pastor, and missionaries visit the sick, and when necessary send them to hospitals. They help the needy poor, find work for the unemployed, and find home shelter for friendless Italian children. Maintains gymnasium, clubs, baths, etc. Services and preaching in Italian and English.

CHARLTON STREET MEMORIAL CHURCH, 30-40 Charlton St., N.Y.C. Rev. P. Griglio, Pastor. The pastor and missionaries work for the physical, moral, and spiritual welfare of the multitudes of Italians in the neighborhood. Maintains a gymnasium, bowling alley, clubs, classes of various kinds, reading room, library, etc. Services and preaching in Italian and English.

SPANISH EVANGELICAL CHURCH in the United Charities Bldg., 109 East 22d St.

See also WOMAN'S BRANCH OF THE NEW YORK CITY MISSION SOCIETY.

New York City Municipal Sanatorium. See HEALTH, DEPARTMENT OF.

New York City Penitentiary. See CORRECTION, DEPARTMENT OF.

New York City Society of the Methodist Episcopal Church, The (est. 1838, incorp. 1866), 150 Fifth Ave. (tel. Chelsea 3656). To promote churches, missions, and Sunday-schools in the Boroughs of Manhattan and Bronx and vicinity. Maintains, wholly or in part, forty-five churches, chapels, missions, and other agencies in this city. Supported in co-operation with the Board of Home Missions and Church Extension of the Methodist Episcopal Church by voluntary contributions and church collections.

Officers: Watson S. Moore, pres.; Charles R. Saul, treas.; Rev. Millard L. Robinson, exec. secy.; Frederick Buckley Newell, asst. exec. secy.; Carl F. Price, rec. secy.

The following churches, with names and addresses of the pastors, may also be found under the list of METHODIST EPISCOPAL CHURCHES in the Church List:

ENGLISH-SPEAKING CHURCHES AND CHAPELS.

Below 18th St.:

CHURCH OF ALL NATIONS, formerly EAST SIDE PARISH, 9 Second Ave.

PEOPLE'S HOME CHURCH AND SETTLEMENT, 545 East 11th St.

West Side:

WEST SIDE CHURCH, 461 West 44th St.

UNION CHURCH, 231 West 48th St.

SALEM MEMORIAL (colored), Lenox Ave. and 133d St.

East Side:

BEEKMAN HILL, 321 East 50th St.

CORNELL MEMORIAL, 231 East 76th St.

CHURCH OF THE SAVIOUR, 111th St. and Lexington Ave.

Beyond the Harlem River:

BOSTON ROAD (West Farms), Boston Rd. and 172d St.

BUTLER MEMORIAL (colored), East 223d St. near White Plains Rd.

VAN NEST, Morris Park and Cruger Aves.

St. Stephen's, 228th St. and Marble Hill Ave., Kingsbridge.

Morris Heights, 1788 Sedgwick Ave., Morris Heights.

Mott Avenue, cor. 150th St.

Epworth (colored), 162d St. and Grant Ave.

Tremont Church, Washington Ave. and 176th St.

Woodlawn Heights, 241st St. and Katonah Ave., Woodlawn.

Missions Among Foreign Populations.

Swedish:

Battery Church, 127–131 West 89th St.

Bethel Church, 177th St. and Grand Concourse.

Chinese Missions:

Union (with Baptist), 11–13 Doyers St., Rev. Lee Towe.

Church of all Nations, 9 Second Ave., Miss Mary E. Banta.

Italian Missions:

(1) Cor. Catherine and Madison Sts. (Five Points). Rev. Wm. G. Nesi.

(2) Jefferson Park Parish, Jefferson Park Church, 407 East 114th St. and Casa del Popolo, 317–21 East 118th St., Rev. A. M. D. Riggio.

(3) 545 East 11th St., Rev. Eduardo Mascellaro.

(4) Church of All Nations, 9 Second Ave., Rev. Eduardo Mascellaro.

Japanese Church, 131 West 104th St., between Columbus and Amsterdam Aves., Rev. A. Kato.

Norwegian Mission, Park Ave. and 86th St., Rev. A. M. Trelstad.

Russian Church, 9 Second Ave.

Immigrant and Port Mission, 25 Pearl St. To guide and assist English-speaking and Scandinavian immigrants. Rev. Charles Samuelson in charge.

Special Agencies

Hadley Rescue Hall, 293 Bowery. Meetings every night in the year. A vigorous rescue work. Drunkards and criminals of both sexes are welcome and assistance is given when necessary.

Rev. John Callahan, supt.

Hedding House, a Home for Working Girls, 335 East 17th St. Is designed for the self-respecting working girl, whose income does not exceed $12 a week, regardless of religion or nationality.

New York City Sunday School Association, The (org. 1816, incorp. 1874; re-org. and re-incorp. 1910), Room 257, 25th floor, Metropolitan Tower (tel. Gramercy 3810). An incorporated interdenominational association composed of the church schools of Manhattan, the Bronx and Richmond, the purpose of which is to increase the efficiency of the church schools, foster week-day religious instruction, promote Daily Vacation Bible Schools, train leaders and in general to promote co-operation in community religious education. It is supported by voluntary contributions of individuals, churches and Sunday Schools. Contributions should be sent to the office of the association and made payable to the treasurer.

The Association is managed through a Board of Directors composed of educators, ministers and business men and women, representing the various denominations. The active direction is in the hands of a general secretary, assisted by a staff of specialists.

Officers: William J. Thompson, pres.; Charles T. Terry, vice-pres.; A. W. Stephens, treas.; James C. Egbert, chrm. Board of Directors; Harry Wade Hicks, gen. secy.; Wilhelmina Stooker, children's work; C. C. Miles, business supt.

The work is carried on through the following divisions: General Administration, Children's, Young People's and

Adults' Work, Week Day Religious Schools, Superintendents' Union; Officers' Union (for colored workers), Union of Secretaries and Treasurers, Graded Union, District Conferences, Community Conventions, Institutes and Classes. A Bureau of Information is maintained in the office. The Association serves each religious school in Manhattan, the Bronx and Richmond in any way possible, by counsel or help in its work.

The Training Department conducts two community Training Schools on Monday and Wednesday evenings respectively for twenty weeks during the winter, where instruction is given for workers in every department of the church school. It promotes the establishment of Teacher Training Classes in individual schools or groups of schools, and trains and furnishes teachers for such purposes when desired.

The Department of Week Day Religious Schools federating the Protestant Teachers' Association and Protestant denominations with the City Sunday School Association promotes the organization of Week Day Religious Schools of both local church and community types by counsel, supervision, securing and training teachers, choosing curriculum and where necessary by helping to secure funds for maintenance.

The Superintendents' Union is composed of church school superintendents. It holds four meetings a year, at which topics of special interest to superintendents are presented by experts, after which there is general discussion.

Officers: Chester H. Stevens, pres.; Ben A. Matthews, vice-pres.; George A. Molleson, treas.; Elsa Lotz, secy.

Officers' Union (for colored workers) composed of general and departmental officers of church schools in colored churches. It holds four meetings a year, with program especially suited to the needs of workers in colored schools of religion.

Officers: A. A. Rives, pres.; W. J. Walker, treas.; Edward Frye, secy.

Union of Secretaries and Treasurers composed of general and departmental officers as indicated by title. Holds four meetings a year for discussion of subjects dealing with the work of these officers.

Officers: W. D. Boyle; pres.; A. H. Fechtenburg, secy.; M. K. Barrett, treas.

Graded Union conducts a training class in Story Telling the first Tuesday afternoon of each month from 3 to 5 o'clock at 7 Gramercy Park, West.

Officers: Miss Sara R. Stoutenburgh, pres.; Mrs. W. D. Boyle, treas.; Miss Constance C. Pesatura, rec. secy.

New York Civic League, 452 Broadway, Albany, N. Y. Devoted to the interest of all moral reforms in the State of New York.

Rev. O. R. Miller, State supt.; George H. West, supt. Law and Order Dept.

New York Clinic for Speech Defects (inc. 1917), 143 East 37th St., N.Y.C. (tel. Murray Hill 3686). The first free medical clinic devoted solely to the cure of defective voice and speech conditions. The clinic has been organized with certain definite objects in view:

To cure all forms of speech and voice disorders, such as stuttering (stammering), lisping, nasality, cleft palate speech, etc.

To take care of defective teeth, mouth, or jaw conditions when such conditions are the causative factors of defective speech.

To take care of nervous and mental conditions when such conditions are causative or associated with defective speech.

To re-educate patients to overcome their faulty voice or speech habits.

To educate or re-educate patients who are deaf or hard-of-hearing.

To maintain a central information bureau and clearing house for speech and voice disorders.

Clinical hours: Every afternoon, 4 to 6 P. M.; Monday, Wednesday, and Friday evenings, 8 to 10 P. M. The clinic is open all year round.

The work is non-sectarian and offered free to all, irrespective of race or color.

Officers: Willard S. Morse, pres.; Mrs. Gilbert H. Montague, vice-pres.; B. S. Moss, secy.; Albert Bigelow Paine, treas.; Dr. James Sonnett Greene, medical director.

New York Colored Mission (org. 1865, incorp. 1871), 8 West 131st St., N.Y.C. For the religious, moral, and social elevation of the colored people. It maintains:

An Employment Office open daily from 9 A. M. to 5 P. M.; Saturdays, 9 A. M. to 11 P. M., for furnishing respectable colored persons with situations.

A Day Nursery, Children's Happy Hour every week-day afternoon.

A Missionary visits the sick and poor, and gives relief in food and clothing in cases of necessity. Sunday school every Sunday at 3 P. M.

Sewing Classes are held during the winter. Religious services Friday evenings, from 8–9 P. M.

New York Committee on After-Care of Infantile Paralysis Cases (est. 1916). Object: To facilitate the after-care of patients recovering from poliomyelitis in co-operation with orthopedic hospitals and dispensaries, physicians, and existing institutions or agencies.

Robert Stuart, director, 69 Schermerhorn St., Brooklyn (tel. Main 8000).

New York Committee on Feeble-mindedness. See State Charities Aid Association, Committee on Mental Hygiene.

New York Community Chorus, Circle Studio Building, 5 Columbus Circle, N.Y.C.

Mrs. William Shannon, pres.; W. Kirkpatrick Brice, treas.; Harry Barnhart, director.

New York Community Service, 15 East 40th St., N.Y.C. (tel. Murray Hill 8210). Victor Manning, acting director.

Soldiers and Sailors Service Club at 320 West 46th St., entertainment organized.

Information: All kinds of community information furnished the general public through public booths.

Recreation: Central clearing agency for information on and promotion of all forms of recreation, through City Recreation Committee, representing thirty city-wide agencies concerned with recreation.

Music: Community singing conducted, volunteer song leaders and accompanists trained, choruses and operas directed.

Drama: Assistance in selection and production of plays and pageants; coaches trained; costumes rented at cost.

New York Conference on Hospital Social Service. See Hospital Social Service Association.

New York Congregational Conference, Inc. (1914), 287 Fourth Ave., N.Y.C. Its object, the establishment of new churches, assistance of weak churches, and maintenance of religious life within the city and state.

Officers: Warner James, Esq., pres., Brooklyn, N. Y.; Rev. A. M. Wight, vice-pres., Syracuse, N. Y.; Rev Charles W. Shelton, D.D., supt. and treas.

New York Congregational Home for the Aged, The. See CONGREGATIONAL HOME.

New York Cooking School (incorp. 1898), 158 East 61st St., N.Y.C. (tel. Plaza 4815). Mission cooks, demonstration and private classes. Evening classes for business women.

Mrs. C. B. Mitchell, secy., Far Hill, N. J.

New York County Chapter American Red Cross. See AMERICAN RED CROSS IN GREATER NEW YORK.

New York Deaconess Association of the Methodist Episcopal Church, The, 1175 Madison Ave. (tel. Lenox 0833). Maintains a home for deaconesses who are engaged in parish and settlement work. Conducts fresh-air work for women, children, and working girls.

Miss Margaret L. Eckley, supt.

New York Diet Kitchen Association, The (incorp. 1873), Central office: 33 West 42d St., N.Y.C. (tel. Vanderbilt 2580).

Officers: Mrs. Henry Villard, pres.; Mrs. Wm. Curtis Demorest, 1st vice-pres.; Mrs. Henry P. Davison, 2d vice-pres.; Mrs. Jos. W. Tilton, treas.; Mrs. Geo. Reese Satterlee, secy.; Miss M. L. Daniels, director.

The Association supports eight milk and health stations in crowded sections of the city, and maintains a staff of doctors, nurses, assistants and dietitians by whom the work is carried on both at the centers and in the homes of the stations' districts which have definitely assigned boundaries.

The Association activities include prenatal, baby welfare and family health work and cover dispensing of milk at cost, baby conferences, pre-school age activities, instruction and demonstration for mothers at stations and in their homes, and general welfare work.

The organization is supported mainly by contributions and subscriptions.

Stations

Wickham Station, 169–171 Mott St.
Raymond Station, 437 West 41st St.
Anne Barbara Station, 1254 Second Ave.
Riverside Station, 126 West 100th St.
Gibbons Station, 453 East 121st St.
Villard Station, 500 West 126th St.
Tuck Station, 35 West 139th St.
Demorest Station, 583 Courtlandt Ave.

New York Dispensary, The (org. 1790, incorp. 1795), 34–36 Spring St., N.Y.C. (tel. Canal 5270). District bounded by North River, Spring St., Broadway, 14th St., First Ave. to Allen and Pike Sts., to East River. Furnishes free medical aid to the sick poor, and visits those living in the district at their homes. No limits as to age, sex, nationality, or sect. Open week-days, except holidays, from 9 A. M. to 3 P. M. for medical attendance; from 9 A. M. to 5 P. M. for medicines and social service. Supported by voluntary contributions.

Officers: William Foulke, pres.; W. Emlen Roosevelt, treas.; G. Beekman Hoppin, secy.; T. W. Cleaveland, M.D., physician-in-chief; Mary Crohan, social service secy.

New York Exchange for Woman's Work, The (incorp. 1878), 541 Madison Ave. bet. 54th and 55th Streets., N.Y.C. (tel. Plaza 2330). Receives the work of gentlewomen, for sale, charging them 15%. Annual subscriptions of $5.00 admits work of three persons in one family. Single tickets admitting work, $2.00. It maintains a

VOCATIONAL BUREAU OF SKILLED WORKERS, through which positions are secured in any line of service a woman can give.

Officers: Mrs. John Seely Ward,

pres.; Mrs. William V. Lawrence, Mrs. John T. Terry, vice-prests.; Miss V. D. H. Furman, treas.; Miss K. Lambert, asst. treas.; Mrs. Samuel H. Ordway, rec. secy.; Mrs. Ida Jane Dutton, business manager.

New York Eye and Ear Infirmary (org. 1820, incorp. as the New York Eye Infirmary, 1822, re-incorp. as above 1874), 218 Second Ave., cor. 13th St., N.Y.C. (tel. Stuyvesant 851). For the free treatment and care of indigent persons suffering from diseases of the eye and ear. In-patients are admitted to the hospital on recommendation of a surgeon, and are charged board, unless satisfactorily certified as unable to pay, Emergency cases are received at any hour. Capacity, 175 beds. Number of house-patients for the year ending Dec. 31, 1919, 6,348 who received 52,427 days of care. Supported by subscriptions, legacies, and permanent fund. (See advertisement.)

DISPENSARY open daily, except Sundays and legal holidays, from 1 to 3 P. M.; 53,252 new patients and total of 167,700 visits were made to the infirmary during the year.

SCHOOL OF INSTRUCTION in diseases of the eye and ear, and clinics are held week-days, except holidays. Apply to the Superintendent for information.

POST-GRADUATE COURSE FOR NURSES. Regular instruction in the special departments of the eye and ear. Maintains a Training School for Nurses, special course, six months. Diplomas awarded.

A hospital wing was opened in 1857, and the old building was rebuilt and opened in 1893. In 1901 a pavilion for treatment of contagious ophthalmia, the gift of Mrs. Justin A. Bliss and daughters, was added to the infirmary. In 1903 the Schermerhorn Pavilion, the gift of the late William C. Schermerhorn, was added. This building is devoted exclusively to the care and treatment of diseases of the ear.

Officers: John J. Riker, pres.; Lewis Iselin, treas.; John M. Wheeler, M.D., secy.; Thomas K. Robertson, supt., to whom apply for admission; Miss Elizabeth N. Meek, supt. of nurses.

New York Federation of Churches, The (org. 1895, incorp. 1901), Room 258, 200 Fifth Ave., N.Y.C. (tel. Gramercy 2298). Informs, associates and assists the churches of Greater New York for co-operative work.

Interchurch Fellowship Division: (1) Clerical Conference. (2) Laity League.

Research and Recommendation Division: (1) Population Research Bureau. (2) Church Distribution Council. (3) Church Efficiency Bureau.

Neighborhood Federation Division: (1) Responsibility District Bureau. (2) Clergy and Laity League Department.

Interborough Federation Division: (1) Community Commissions. (2) Welfare Committees.

Legislation Division: (1) Law Enactment and Law Enforcement Bureau.

Clearing House and Institute: (1) Interchurch Clearing House. (2) Interchurch Institute.

Rev. Anson P. Atterbury, D.D., pres.; L. Roy Curtiss, treas.; Rev. Clarence E. Krumbholz, rec. secy.; Rev. Walter Laidlaw, Ph.D., exec. secy.

New York Female Bible Society, The (org. 1816, incorp. 1877). Committee Room, Bible House, N.Y.C. An auxiliary to the American Bible Society, for the distribution of the Bible and the employment of Bible readers who strive to improve the temporal and spiritual conditions of the poor throughout the city, including all nationalities.

New York Fire Department, Relief Fund. See FIRE DEPARTMENT.

New York Flower and Fruit Mission. See ALL SOULS' UNITARIAN CHURCH, this list.

New York Foundation (incorp. 1909). Administers funds for the encouragement of charitable and other philanthropic efforts.

Trustees: Alfred M. Heinsheimer, pres.; Mortimer L. Schiff, Felix M. Warburg, Lee K. Frankel, Herbert H. Lehman, Sam A. Lewisohn, David M. Heyman, treas.; William F. Fuerst, secy., 87 Nassau St.

New York Foundling Hospital, The (incorp. 1869; title changed by special order from Supreme Court, 1891), 175 East 68th St., near Lexington Ave., N.Y.C. (tel. Plaza 1187). Receives foundling and deserted children of New York City. Mothers who are willing to act as nurses are received with the infants; also needy and homeless mothers. From 600 to 700 children are provided for in the Asylums. Supported by voluntary contributions and per capita allowance from the city.

THE OUT-DOOR DEPARTMENT ministers to and cares for cases in their homes. The nurses of this department are respectable poor women with families, who use the money paid them principally for rent.

Controlled by and under the charge of the Sisters of Charity. Sister Anna Michella, directress and treas. Apply at the Hospital at any hour of the day. Visitors are welcome at any time. The sisters also maintain

ST. ANN'S MATERNITY HOSPITAL, 130 East 69th St. Destitute and married women are received; unmarried women, pregnant for the first time, are sheltered, and strangers, who can afford to pay, but do not wish to remain at a hotel or boarding house during confinement, may be cared for.

THE EURANA SCHWAB, St. Joseph's by the Sea, near Huguenot, Staten Island, a country home for the children of the New York Foundling Hospital.

New York Home for Homeless Boys (incorp. 1916), 441 East 123d St., N.Y.C.

Officers: Lawrence B. Elliman, pres.; Wm. R. K. Taylor, treas.; Mrs. P. A. S. Franklin, chrm. Women's Auxiliary; H. C. Eva, supt.

New York Home Missionary Society. See NEW YORK CONGREGATIONAL CONFERENCE.

New York Homoeopathic Medical College and Flower Hospital (incorp. 1860), 63d, 64th Sts. and Ave. A, N.Y.C. (tel. Plaza 5506). A general hospital for men, women and children without regard to creed, race, nationality or color, desirous of receiving treatment in medicine and surgery. Capacity, 200 beds.

Medical College, maternity wards, medical and surgical wards, private pavilion, training school for nurses, ambulance service and active dispensary or out-patient department. Does a large amount of emergency surgical, medical and obstetrical work and is supported by voluntary contributions and endowments.

Officers: Howard C. Smith, 1st vice-pres.; Wm. H. Baldwin, 2d vice-pres.; Edward R. Tinker, treas.; Leeds Johnson, secy.; Dr. W. W. Blackman, president of college; Dr. Rudolph F. Rabe, dean of the college; Dr. F. Montgomery Smith, executive officers of the hospital; David R. Reynolds, supt. of hospital.

New York Hospital, 8 West 16th St., N.Y.C. See SOCIETY OF THE NEW YORK HOSPITAL.

New York House and School of Industry (org. 1850, incorp. 1851), 120 West 16th St., N.Y.C. (tel. Chelsea 377). Assists destitute women by employment at needlework. Supported by contributions and sale of work in the store on the premises. Material for institutions made up at ten per cent. of the cost of sewing; cutting and furnishings extra.

THE ORDERED WORK DEPARTMENT fills orders for fine underwear and embroidery by skilled workwomen.

Officers: Mrs. Nathan W. Green, pres., 152 West 57th St.; Miss H. L. Knox, treas., 129 East 76th St.; Miss G. W. Sargent, secy., 28 East 35th St.

New York Infirmary for Women and Children (incorp. 1853), 321 East 15th St. (tel. Stuyvesant 1290). Capacity, 115. Supported by endowment, voluntary contributions and city aid.

Officers: John L. Wilkie, pres.; Earle Dailey, treas.; Mrs. Nelson Holland, secy.

New York Institute for the Education of the Blind, The (opened 1832, incorp. 1831), 412 Ninth Ave. N.Y.C. (tel. Longacre 2360). For the physical, mental, and moral education of the young blind, of suitable age and capacity, in such ways as will qualify them for citizenship and for the duties of life. Instruction is given in usual elementary and high school subjects, in music, manual training, and physical culture. Capacity for 180. Visiting day, Wednesday from 9 A. M. to 12 M. and 1.30 to 4 P. M. Supported by income derived from invested legacy fund, legacies and receipts for tuition.

Officers: Paul Tuckerman, pres.; William W. Appleton, vice-pres.; Frederic de P. Foster, treas.; Linzee Blagden, secy.; Robert G. Hone, cor. secy.; Edward M. Van Cleve, principal, to whom application should be made.

New York Institution for the Instruction of the Deaf and Dumb (incorp. 1817), 99 Fort Washington Ave., cor. West 163d St., N.Y.C. (tel. Wadsworth 6010). A free school for all deaf children of the State over five years, without regard to parents' circumstances. Apply to Isaac B. Gardner, M.A., principal of the institution.

The only military school for the deaf in the world. Accommodates 500. Children not residing in the State are charged $500 per annum. Every known instrument and aid which is of value in their education is used. Lip-reading and articulation are taught to all; and education of the ear, where there is a remnant of hearing. The course of study is equivalent to that of common school and academies.

A Mechanical Trade is given to each pupil and classes in cooking are held for both boys and girls. Thorough instruction in all departments of Art is a special feature. A completely equipped gymnasium, under the supervision of physical directors has also been provided. Supported by the State, counties, and by voluntary contributions. Controlled by a Board of Directors.

Officers: Francis V. Greene, pres.; Bronson Winthrop, treas.; F. Ashton de Peyster, secy.

New York Juvenile Asylum. See CHILDREN'S VILLAGE.

New York Kindergarten Association (est. 1889, incorp. 1892), 524 West 42d St. (tel. Bryant 1752). To promote the establishment and maintenance of free kindergartens in this city, for the purpose of furnishing physical, moral, and intellectual training. It is unsectarian. Children from four to six years old are received. It is dependent on voluntary gifts to carry on the kindergartens already established and to open new kindergartens.

Officers: George McAneny, pres.; Samuel Sloan, treas.; Elizabeth J. Frazier, gen. secy.

New York League of Girls' Clubs, Inc. (org. 1885, incorp. 1918 as New York League of Women Workers; incorp. under the present name in 1920), 6 East 45th St., N.Y.C. (tel. Vanderbilt 1160). To organize and develop clubs for wage earning girls and women, which offer social and educational opportunities. A club must be nonsectarian, self-governing, and either self-supporting or striving towards self-support. The League numbers 32 clubs, 29 of them in or near New York City. It employs secretaries to strengthen the clubs already members of the organization and to establish new clubs in communities which have few educational and recreational opportunities for wage earning girls and women.

Officers: Mrs. Courtlandt D. Barnes, pres., 67 Park Ave.; Miss M. Louise Dixon, treas., 52 West 49th St.; Mrs. A. S. Hobart, state secy.

Clubs

Acorn Club, 209 Concord St., Brooklyn, N. Y.

Bronx Girls' Community Club, 434 East 154th St., N.Y.C.

Brooklyn Girls' City Club, 169 Livingston St., Brooklyn, N. Y.

Community Service Club of Floral Park, Tyson Ave., Floral Park, L. I.

Community Service Girls' Club of Freeport, N. Main St., Freeport, L. I.

Community Service Girls' Club of Manhasset, Manhasset, L. I.

Community Service Girls' Club of Roslyn, Roslyn, L. I.

Domestic Circle, 501 West 50th St., N.Y.C.

Fern Club, 659 Harrison Place, West New York, N. J.

Friendly Club, 318 East 82d St., N.Y.C.

Friendship Club, 458 Broadway, Astoria, L. I.

Gamma Kappa Club, 110 Main St., Flushing, L. I.

Girls' Community Club of College Point, College Point, N. Y.

Girls' Community Club of New Rochelle, 585 Main St., New Rochelle, N. Y.

Girls' Community Club of Oyster Bay, Oyster Bay, L. I.

Girls' Community Club of Port Washington, Port Washington, L. I.

Girls' Community Club of Walden, 27 Main St., Walden, N. Y.

Girls' Community Service Club of Hempstead, 13 Main St., Hempstead, L. I.

Good Will Club of Amsterdam, 24 Grove St., Amsterdam, N. Y.

Good Will Club of Brooklyn, 41 Tompkins Place, Brooklyn, N. Y.

Great Neck Girls' Club, Great Neck, L. I.

Holly Club, 580 Clinton Ave., West Hoboken, N. J.

Huntington Club, 476 South Warren St., Syracuse, N. Y.

Industrial Society, 220 Willow Ave., Hoboken, N. J.

Irene Club, 501 West 50th St., N.Y.C.

Ivy Club, New York City.

Jersey City Circle, 110 Hutton St., Jersey City, N. J.

Myrtle Club, Woodcliffe, N. J.

Prospect Hill Club, 411 East 50th St., N.Y.C.

United Club, 226 East 16th St., N.Y.C.

Westbury Community Service Girls' Club, Westbury, L. I.

Women's Institute, 38 Palisade Ave., Yonkers, N. Y.

Vacation Houses: Holiday House, Holiday Harbor, and Holiday Cottage, Miller's Place, L. I. Accommodates 90 girls in three houses, situated in 18 acres of ground with beach front. Board reasonable to club members.

Camp Sunshine, Staten Island. A week-end camp, accommodates 50 girls, from Saturday to Monday.

Camp Matasac, three and one-half miles back of Peekskill, accommodates 48 girls. Boating, bathing, out-of-door sports.

Mutual Benefit Association. An inexpensive sick and death benefit society. Miss Gertrude Whiting, pres.

New York League for the Hard of Hearing, Inc., The, 126th East 59th St., N.Y.C. (tel. Plaza 2490). Clearing House and Information Bureau on all subjects connected with the deafened.

Annex to P. S. 32 (lip-reading classes). Meeting room for religious meetings and lectures equipped with hearing devices.

Educational Department. Gives free and part scholarships in lip-reading. Conducts free practise department, also clubs, lectures, etc., for lip-readers.

Employment Department. Free Junior and Adult Placement and Vocational Direction Bureau. Does not place deaf-mutes. Business and Professional Women's Club.

Welfare Department. Case and follow-up work. Recreation and physical training clubs for young people, men and women.

Handwork Shop. Sells work of hard of hearing men and women. Conducts mending department.

Officers: W. J. Curtis, hon. pres., 233 Broadway; Harold Hays, M.D., pres., 2178 Broadway; Mrs. John Peyton Clark, chrm. Board of Directors, 411 West 114th St.; Wendell C. Phillips, M.D., 40 West 47th St.; George P. Putnam, treas.; Miss Annetta W. Peck, exec. secy.

New York League on Urban Conditions Among Negroes. See URBAN LEAGUE OF NEW YORK.

New York League of Women Workers. See NEW YORK LEAGUE OF GIRLS' CLUBS.

New York Medical College and Hospital for Women. See COMMUNITY HOSPITAL IN THE CITY OF NEW YORK.

New York Milk Committee. See NATIONAL COMMISSION ON MILK STANDARDS.

New York Neurological Institute. See NEUROLOGICAL INSTITUTE OF NEW YORK.

New York Nursery and Child's Hospital, 161 West 61st St. (tel. Columbus 8816). (Formed March 2, 1910, by consolidation of the Nursery and Child's Hospital, incorp. 1854, and the New York Infant Asylum, incorp. 1865; also includes the Old Marion St. Maternity Hospital, incorp. 1827; work transferred to present location, 1900.)

Receives dependent and sick children and has the power to procure adoption through the State Charities Aid Association, by suitable foster parents. A Boarding-out Department is maintained and a large number of children are temporarily boarded-out in private homes.

Needy women are received for confinement or are attended in their homes in the vicinity of the Hospital. Follow-up work is done by an efficient Social Service Department.

A number of private rooms and wards are provided for women and children patients who are able to pay.

Supported by public funds, voluntary donations, and board of paying patients. Capacity, 283 beds.

Officers: Dr. Edward L. Partridge, pres., 19 Fifth Ave., N.Y.C.; Charles Boucher, treas., 52 William St., N.Y.C.; Moses Ely, secy., 52 Wall St., N.Y.C.; Daniel C. Adams, chrm. Executive Committee, 71 Broadway, N.Y.C.

New York Nutrition Council (org. 1920). Holds bi-weekly conferences for the exchange of information concerning the organization and conduct of nutrition work. Membership limited to representatives of agencies which carry on nutritional activities as part of their program.

Officers: Mrs. Mary S. Rose, chrm. Teachers College, Columbia University; Emma A. Winslow, secy.

New York Ophthalmic Hospital, The (incorp. 1852), 201 East 23d St., N.Y.C. (tel. Gramercy 783). A homeopathic institution for the free treatment of diseases of the eye, ear, and throat. Capacity, seventy-four beds.

Connected with the institution is the COLLEGE offering a course of instruction in diseases of the eye, ear, nose and throat.

New York Orphan Asylum. See ORPHAN ASYLUM SOCIETY IN THE CITY OF NEW YORK.

New York Orthopaedic Dispensary and Hospital (org. 1866, incorp. 1868), 420 East 59th St. (tel. Plaza 1416). For treatment of poor with diseases and deformities of bones and joints. Capacity, 100 beds. Admission through Dispensary, daily, except Sundays and holidays, from 1 to 3.30 P. M. Supported by voluntary contributions.

Country Branch (opened 1905), White Plains, N. Y. For long-term convalescent care of children with tubercular joints. Capacity, 134 beds. Admission through Dispensary. Supported by endowment.

Officers: Robert S. Brewster, pres.; John Sloane, vice-pres.; F. A. Juillard, treas.; Chas. R. Munn, secy.; Russell A. Hibbs, M.D., surgeon-in-chief; Miss Theodora S. Root, supt. city hospital; Mrs. Statira M. Bridgman, supt. country branch.

New York Osteopathic Clinic (incorp. and est. 1914), 35 East 32d St., N.Y.C. (tel. Murray Hill 0309). Registrar's office open 2-5 P. M., Monday, Tuesday, Thursday, and Friday. Open to patients four evenings and two afternoons in week. To give osteopathic treatment to those who cannot otherwise obtain it. Supported by voluntary contributions and fees.

Officers: W. Strother Jones, pres., 25 Broad St.; Marcus Goodbody, treas., 115 Broadway; Hamilton Fish Benjamin, secy., 61 Broadway; Miss Jeannette Pidgeon, registrar.

New York Peace Society, The (org. 1815, re-org. 1906, incorp. 1910), 70 Fifth Ave., N.Y.C. (tel. Chelsea 9569). For international justice and friendship.

Officers: Oscar S. Straus, pres.; Central Trust Co., 42d St. and Madison Ave., treas.; John Bates Clark, chrm. exec. comm.; Charles H. Levermore, secy.

New York Polyclinic Medical School and Hospital. See U. S. PUBLIC HEALTH SERVICE.

New York Port Society. See SOCIETY FOR PROMOTING THE GOSPEL AMONG SEAMEN.

New York Post-Graduate Medical School and Hospital, University of the State of New York (org. 1882, incorp. 1884; founded by members of the Post-Graduate Faculty of the University of New York, to offer systematic courses of clinical instruction to graduates in medicine), cor. Second Ave. and 20th St., N.Y.C. (tel. Gramercy 7080).

Officers: James F. McKernon, M.D., pres.; John F. Erdmann, M.D., 1st vice-pres.; William V. Griffin, 2d vice-pres.; William Fahnestock, treas.; Arthur F. Chace, M.D., secy. of the Corporation.

A general hospital for the care of

medical and surgical cases admitted to its wards, irrespective of creeds and nationalities. It contains wards for men, women, and children, with two floors in the southwest wing of the building for the care of children under five years of age. Contagious and chronic cases are not admitted. Capacity, 419 beds. Those who are destitute are treated free of charge. Private rooms from $35 to $60 per week. Supported by tuition fees, paying patients, private donations, and municipal grant.

Alexander H. Candlish, superintendent.

DISPENSARY for free treatment of the poor.

THE MARGARET FAHNESTOCK TRAINING SCHOOL FOR NURSES, 304 East 20th St., is an integral part of the institution. Miss Jessie M. Murdoch, directress of nurses.

New York Preachers' Meeting of the Methodist Episcopal Church, The, 150 Fifth Ave., N.Y.C. Mondays, 11 A. M.

J. A. Cole, pres., Madison, N. J.; Walter Kinsey, secy., Harrison, N. J.

New York Probation and Protective Association (org. 1908, incorp. 1909), 130 East 22d St., N.Y.C. (tel. Gramercy 4818). To improve the probation system in courts, aid in reformation of offenders and prevention of crime. Maintains

WAVERLEY HOUSE, 38 West 10th St., for temporary care of delinquent girls over sixteen years of age, referred by courts, probation officers, or individuals. Complete understanding of the individual girl is made the basis of treatment. Industrial classes and after-care work.

MENTAL CLINIC, 38 West 10th St., for psychiatric and psychological examinations for difficult girls. Monday, Wednesday and Friday afternoons.

HILLCREST FARM, Taconic, Conn. Provides training in farm and household work. Girls remain voluntarily for several months.

GIRLS' PROTECTIVE LEAGUE, 130 East 22d St. Protective officers and district visitors do personal, constructive work with girls in moral danger, many of whom are runaways from home. Also investigates complaints about immoral conditions and seeks to remedy them.

EMPLOYMENT EXCHANGE, 130 East 22d St. Gives vocational guidance and secures positions for young women under the care of the Association and referred by co-operating agencies.

GIRLS' SERVICE LEAGUE, 138 East 19th St. An organization of girls banded together for the purpose of protecting other girls. Has two club houses with clubs, classes, recreation, and opportunities for service work. Girls' Service Club, 138 East 19th St. and Yorkville Service Club for Girls, 331 East 68th St.

Officers of the Association: George W. Alger, pres.; Mrs. Ruth Standish Baldwin, 1st vice-pres.; Frederic Kernochan, 2d vice-pres.; Milton I. D. Einstein, treas.; Maude E. Miner, secy.

Girls' Protective League Committee: Mrs. Charles Cary Rumsey, chrm.; Stella A. Miner, secy.

New York Protestant Episcopal City Mission Society (org. 1831, incorp. 1833), 38 Bleecker St., N.Y.C. (tel. Spring 898). The objects of the Society are to provide by building, purchase, hiring, or otherwise, at different points in the City of New York, churches in which the seats shall be free, and mission-houses for the poor and afflicted; and also to provide suitable clergymen and other persons to act as missionaries and assistants in and about the said churches and mission-houses. Conducts various activit'es for the elevation of the poor and the reformation of the degraded aside from the religious work. Daily visits are made to prisoners in their cells, and at the bedside of the sick in the hospitals. Supported by voluntary contributions.

Harry Pelham Robbins, secy., 52 Vanderbilt Ave.; Lincoln Cromwell, treas.; Rev. L. Ernest Sunderland, supt.

Its Mission Houses and Chapels are located as follows (see also under PROTESTANT EPISCOPAL CHURCHES in the Church List):

ST. BARNABAS'S HOUSE, CHAPEL, and A DISPENSARY, 304–306 Mulberry St. A temporary resting-place for destitute and homeless women and children, and friendless convalescent women discharged from hospitals, all of whom are admitted, without regard to creed, race, or color. Children old enough to learn are taught in Sunday-school and kindergarten while inmates of the House and the women are aided in their efforts to find work. Capacity, fifty beds for adults, fifty for children.

Miss E. R. Hopkins, headworker.

THE DISPENSARY, 306 Mulberry St., open week-days from 11 A. M. to 12 M., for free medical advice, attendance, and medicine to the temporary lodgers as well as to the outside poor.

FRESH-AIR FUND. Excursions are made during the summer under the direction of the chaplain and matron of St. Barnabas's House for poor, deserving women and children, who are also sent for a week or more to the country.

ST. BARNABAS'S CHAPEL, 306 Mulberry St. (See Church List.)

CHAPEL OF CHRIST THE CONSOLER, Bellevue Hospital.

CHAPEL OF THE GOOD SHEPHERD, adjoining City Home for the Aged and Infirm, Blackwell's Island.

CHURCH OF SAN SALVATORE (Italian Mission), 359–361 Broome St.; Rev. H. J. Chiera, Vicar; Ladies' Aid Association; Men's Club; Sunday-school; sewing-school; cooking-school; kindergarten; mothers' meetings; choral society.

ST. CYPRIAN'S CHAPEL (Mission to colored people), 177 West 63d St., Rev. John W. Johnson, Vicar. Sunday-school; Industrial School; soup kitchen; cooking-school; sewing-school; gymnasium.

GOD'S PROVIDENCE HOUSE, 330 Broome St.; day nursery and kindergarten. For children whose parents are obliged to work away from home during the day. The first day nursery in New York. Established in St. Barnabas's House, and moved to God's Providence House in 1892.

Miss E. R. Hopkins, head worker.

SARAH SCHERMERHORN HOUSE, Milford, Conn. Fresh-air home. Accommodates 120 girls and women of any age.

CAMP BLEECKER, Milford Haven, Milford, Conn. For boys of the N. Y. P. E. City Mission Society.

RETHMORE HOME (incorp. 1893), Tenafly, N. J. A fresh-air home for children of New York in summer.

Mrs. J. Hull Browning, manager.

New York Red Cross Hospital, 100th St. and Central Park West, N.Y.C. See PARK HOSPITAL.

New York Sabbath Committee, The (org. 1857, incorp. 1884), 31 Bible House, Fourth Ave. and 8th St., N.Y.C. (tel. Stuyvesant 4121). To protect and promote Sunday rest and observance. It aims to awaken public sentiment by the press, the pulpit, and the platform; to secure the prudent enforcement of existing laws and new legislation whenever necessary, and vigilantly to guard against unfavorable legislation; to prevent, by remonstrance and otherwise, unnecessary public work on Sunday;

and to enlist the help of all good citizens, of whatever creed or party, in the promotion of its ends.

The committee is prosecuting with University Assistance a Comprehensive Scientific Research into the Influence of the Sabbath upon Human Welfare. It maintains a valuable reference library; publishes bi-monthly the "Bulletin of the New York Sabbath Committee" (twenty-five cents per year), and also books and documents for general circulation; is a bureau of information on the Sunday question in this country and abroad; holds public meetings when expedient; is the ally of the pulpit, philanthropic agencies, the working classes and whoever seeks the good of the community in maintaining Sunday rest. Supported by voluntary contributions.

Officers and members: Theodore Gilman, chrm.; E. Francis Hyde, treas., 80 Broadway; W. S. Hubbell, rec. secy.; Duncan J. McMillan, gen. secy., 31 Bible House; Powell Crichton, Esq., atty.; Cornelius R. Agnew, George W. Brush, Charles F. Darlington, James Gear, William J. Gies, R. Granville Green, Arthur L. Lesher, Robert L. Maitland, James B. Murray, Eben E. Olcott, Joseph H. Fargis, Edward C. Parish, Eugene A. Philbin, George H. Richards, Samuel Thorne, Jr.

New York School of Social Work. See CHARITY ORGANIZATION SOCIETY.

New York School for Stammering (est. 1888), 69 West 49th St. To correct speech disorders, by educational methods.

Frank A. Bryant, M.D., principal.

New York Skin and Cancer Hospital (incorp. 1882), N. E. cor. 19th St. and Second Ave. (tel. Gramercy 1526). For free treatment of skin diseases and cancer. Capacity, 100 beds. Supported by voluntary contributions.

THE OUT-PATIENT DEPARTMENT cares for the far greater number of patients. Many cases, although incapacitating the patient from work, can be effectively treated at home.

Officers: E. J. Murphy, pres.; Alfred R. Kimball, treas.; Frederick Haas, secy.; Miss Sara Burns, supt., to whom apply between 9 to 11 A. M. and 2 to 4 P. M.

New York Social Hygiene Society, The. See AMERICAN SOCIAL HYGIENE ASSOCIATION.

New York Society for the Prevention of Cruelty to Children. See SOCIETY FOR THE PREVENTION OF CRUELTY TO CHILDREN.

New York Society for the Relief of the Ruptured and Crippled, The (incorp. 1863), 321 East 42nd St., N.Y.C. (tel. Murray Hill 1253).

HOSPITAL for curable children from four to fourteen years of age who are received as in-patients. Appliances and bandages are furnished free to indigent children. Capacity, 200 beds.

Joseph D. Flick, supt.

DISPENSARY for out-door patients. Open daily, except Sundays and holidays, from 1 to 3 P. M.

SOCIAL SERVICE DEPARTMENT, Jessie H. Prest, in charge.

New York Society for the Relief of Widows and Orphans of Medical Men (incorp. 1843), 17 West 43d St., N.Y.C. Aids the classes indicated in the title when thus related to any one having been a member of the Society for the two years previous to his death. In special cases, relieves an aged parent, or sister, who had been dependent upon the deceased member.

Andrew F. Currier, M.D., secy.

New York Society for the Suppression of Vice, The (incorp. 1873), 215 West 22d St., N.Y.C. (tel. Watkins

2454). For the enforcement of laws to suppress the trade in and circulation of obscene literature, illustrations, advertisements and articles of indecent and immoral use, including lotteries and gambling. Controlled by a Board of Managers and an Executive Committee. Supported by voluntary contributions.

Thus far the Society has made 4,511 arrests and seized 15,372,480 articles of unlawful and contraband matter. Annual report and monthly letter mailed free on application. Lovers of children and youth are invited to call at the Society's office and learn more of its work. All information is kept strictly confidential when so desired.

Officers: Rev. Anson P. Atterbury, D.D., pres.; Landreth H. King, Fred E. Tasker, vice-prests.; William H. Parsons, treas., 299 Broadway; John S. Sumner, secy., to whom address communications.

Executive Committee: Rev. Anson P. Atterbury, chrm.; Landreth H. King, Seth Sprague Terry, William H. Parsons, John Whalen.

New York State Colonization Society (1885). To colonize, with their own consent, people of color from the United States to the coast of Africa, and through them to civilize and Christianize the African tribes. Dr. Eben C. Sage, pres., 61 Broadway; L. G. Myers, treas., 26 Broadway, N.Y.C.; Dr. Newell W. Wells, secy., 155 South 3d St., Brooklyn.

New York State Commission for the Blind (est. 1913), Hall of Records, Chambers St., N.Y.C. (tel. Worth 3249). The Commission maintains:

A central office in New York City where applications for assistance are received on behalf of any blind person living within the state. Address Grace S. Harper, secretary.

A staff of blind home teachers who give instruction in reading and writing of varied types to individuals in their homes, also training in home industries; knitting, crocheting, basketry, art weaving, machine stitching, rug-making and chair caning.

A workshop for training and employment in broom making in co-operation with the Rochester Association for the Blind at 155 St. Paul St., Rochester, N. Y. Arthur Male, Superintendent. Applications should be sent to the secretary at the central office, New York City.

Through its own efforts and in close co-operation with local Associations for the Blind, the work of the Commission includes:

Encouragement of occupation in the home for such blind persons as are unable to undertake industrial or professional work outside.

Supervision of home work and sale of the finished product.

Placement of blind persons in industrial and commercial positions throughout the State.

Establishment of blind men in small business.

Officers: M. C. Migel, chrm., 1 Madison Ave., N.Y.C.; Mary V. Hun, vice-chrm., 31 Elk St., Albany, N. Y.; Hon. Charles H. Himmelsbach, commissioner, 124 Fordham Drive, Buffalo, N. Y.; Hon. C. Schuyler Davis, commissioner, Wilder Bldg., Rochester, N. Y.; Dr. William H. Mehl, 417 Franklin St., Buffalo, N. Y.

New York State Committee for the Prevention of Blindness (est. 1908; consolidated with the National Committee for the Prevention of Blindness as a Standing Committee, 1915), 130 East 22d St., N.Y.C. (tel. Gramercy 231). The objects of this Committee are the same as those of the National Committee and its methods of work are the same. It has the same secretary, the same office and is maintained from the same treasury. It differs from the National Committee in that the scope of its work is specifically confined to the State of New York, with freedom to organize and conduct this work, as it may deem best. The membership of the Committee is composed solely of residents of the State of New York, and it publishes a separate annual report.

Officers: Mrs. William Adams Brown, chrm.; Mrs. Winifred Hathaway, secy.

See also NATIONAL COMMITTEE, etc.

New York State Conference of Charities and Correction (1900). To afford an opportunity for those engaged in charitable and reform work to confer respecting their methods, principles of administration and results accomplished, to diffuse information respecting charitable and correctional work, and encourage co-operation in humanitarian efforts, with the aim of further improving the system of charity and correction in the State of New York.

The Conference holds an annual meeting in the State of New York, at a place agreed upon at the preceding annual session. The twenty-second session will be held in Utica, Nov. 15-17, 1921.

All who have an active interest in the charitable or correctional work in New York State are invited to enroll themselves as members of the Conference. No other tests of membership are applied. There is no membership fee, but the publication of proceedings and other necessary expenses amount to about $2 per year for each member.

Officers: Dr. Orlando F. Lewis, pres., 135 East 15th St., N.Y.C.; Rt. Rev. Mgr. Francis H. O'Hara, Brooklyn, Mrs. Sidney C. Borg, Irvington-on-Hudson, Mrs. William E. Warner, Rochester, vice-presidents; George J. Gillespie, treas., 20 Vesey St., N.Y.C.; Richard W. Wallace, secy., Room 431, The Capitol, Albany.

New York State Federation of Women's Clubs. See STATE FEDERATION OF WOMEN'S CLUBS.

New York State Federation of Workers for the Blind, Inc., 104 Livingston St., Brooklyn, N. Y.

Officers: Frank L. Frost, pres.; W. I. Scandlin, vice-pres.; Aaron Lopez, treas.; Chester A. Gothard, secy.; L. J. Oswald, A. W. LaRose, J. E. Wyant, directors.

New York State Hospital for the Care of Crippled and Deformed Children. See STATE HOSPITAL, etc.

New York State Hospital for the Treatment of Incipient Pulmonary Tuberculosis. See STATE HOSPITAL, etc.

New York State Prison Council. See WELFARE LEAGUE ASSOCIATION.

New York State Reconstruction Commission. See RECONSTRUCTION COMMISSION OF NEW YORK.

New York State Reformatory (est. Chap. 408, Laws of 1869; opened 1876), Elmira, Chemung Co., N. Y. For the reformation and educational, industrial, and moral instruction and training of males between the ages of sixteen and thirty, convicted of a felony, who have not been previously convicted of a crime punishable by imprisonment in a state prison or convicted of a misdemeanor having been formerly convicted of a misdemeanor. Capacity, 1,440.

Walter N. Thayer, M.D., supt.

EASTERN NEW YORK REFORMATORY, Napanoch, Ulster County, N. Y. The work of this institution is similar to that of the above and receives all its inmates from that institution, by transfer. George Deyo, asst. supt.

New York State Reformatory for Women. See STATE REFORMATORY, etc.

New York State School for Training Nurses. See PROSPECT HEIGHTS HOSPITAL.

New York State Soldiers' and Sailors' Home. See STATE SOLDIERS' AND SAILORS' HOME.

New York State Training School for Boys. See STATE TRAINING SCHOOL FOR BOYS.

New York State Training School for Girls. See STATE TRAINING SCHOOL FOR GIRLS.

New York State Women's Relief Corps Home (est. Chap. 468, Laws of 1894, as the New York State Home for the Aged, Dependent Veteran and his Wife, Veterans' Mothers, Widows, and Army Nurses; name changed by Chap. 47, Laws of 1897; opened 1897), Oxford, Chenango Co., N. Y. A home for aged dependent veterans and their wives, veterans' mothers, widows, and army nurses, residents of the State of New York. Capacity, 230.

Officers: Mrs. Georgianna Griffith, pres., 616 Madison Ave., N.Y.C.; Hon. Charles W. Brown, treas., Oxford, N. Y.; Mrs. Ella B. Scott, secy., 308 West 137th St., N.Y.C.; Col. James S. Graham, supt.

New York Sunday School Commission, Inc. (est. 1898, incorp. 1914), 73 Fifth Ave., N.Y.C. (tel. Stuyvesant 3635). Exhibit (free) of supplies for religious education. Interdenominational.

Officers: Rev. Pascal Harrower, pres.; A. C. Thadwald, treas.; Rev. William Walter Smith, A.B., A.M., M.D., secy.

New York Tax Reform Association, 29 Broadway, N.Y.C. (tel. Whitehall 446).

New York Throat, Nose, and Lung Hospital, The (incorp. 1893), 229–233 East 57th St., N.Y.C. (tel. Plaza 5246). For the free treatment of diseases of the throat, nose, eye, ear, lungs, and teeth. Maintains fifty beds. Clinics in all departments at 10 A. M. and 2 P. M. daily.

Also two social service societies which provide for the visitation of the homes of all patients and the providing of food and clothing where necessary. Supported entirely by voluntary contributions.

New York Trade School (org. 1881, incorp. 1892), First Ave., 67th St. and 68th Sts., N.Y.C. (tel. Rhinelander 4213). Founded by the late Col. R. T. Auchmuty, to afford young men, between seventeen and twenty-five years of age, practical instruction in plumbing, bricklaying, plastering, sheet metal work, steam and hot-water fitting, printing, house and sign painting, plain decorating, electrical work, patternmaking, auto vehicles and drawing. Non-sectarian. Evening classes are held from September to April. Supported by students' tuition fees (which are nominal only), and by endowment fund. Attendance last season, 400 students. Catalogue of particulars will be mailed on application. Visitors are always welcome.

Trustees: R. Fulton Cutting, pres.; Lewis Iselin, treas.; Walter L. Suydam, secy.; J. Pierpont Morgan, J. Roosevelt Roosevelt, Richard L. Morris, Fulton Cutting.

New York Training School for Deaconesses (incorp. 1891), Cathedral Close, Amsterdam Ave. and 110th St., N.Y.C. (tel. Cathedral 6249). For the training of women for parish and missionary work under the canons of the Protestant Episcopal Church. Supported by voluntary contributions.

Rev. Francis Branch Blodgett, B.A., S.T.B., warden; Miss Marian H. Fuller, acting treas.

New York Tuberculosis Association, Inc. (incorp. and est. 1919), 10 East 39th St., N.Y.C. (tel. Murray Hill 7772). For the study of tuberculosis and of the means of preventing it; the dissemination of knowledge as to the nature of the disease, its causes and the methods of its prevention and of its treatment; the promotion of adequate facilities for the prevention of tuberculosis and for the care, treatment and economic rehabilitation of persons afflicted therewith, and the co-ordination of the work of public and private agencies engaged in any of the foregoing activities. Supported by voluntary contributions and the sale of Christmas Seals.

Officers: James Alex. Miller, M.D., pres., 379 Park Ave.; Homer Folks, vice-pres., 105 East 22d St.; Thos. W. Lamont, treas., c/o J. P. Morgan & Co., 23 Wall St.; Nathan E. Brill, M.D., secy., 48 West 76th St.; John S. Billings, M.D., director, 10 East 39th St.

New York University, The University and Bellevue Hospital Medical College, First Ave. and 26th St., N.Y.C. (tel. Madison Square 4020). Maintains a

Dispensary in the Medical College Bldg. to provide medical and surgical aid and medicines to the sick poor. A nominal charge of 10 cents is made for medicine. Open from 10 A. M. to 4 P. M. Has departments for the following: skin, eye, ear, nose and throat, orthopedics, genito-urinary, X-Ray, general medicine, general surgery, gynecology, nervous diseases, diseases of the rectum and children's diseases.

Officers: Elmer E. Brown, LL.D., chancellor, Washington Sq.; Samuel A. Brown, M.D., dean of Medical Faculty, 338 East 26th St.; Frank A. Fall, bursar, Washington Sq.; William J. Pulley, M.D., chrm. Dispensary Committee, 338 East 26th St.

New York University Bureau of Community Service and Research, 32 Waverly Pl., N.Y.C. (tel. Spring 9300). For boys and young men.

H. P. Fairchild, director; C. M. Panunzio, fellow.

New York University Bureau of Employment (est. 1913), 32 Waverly Pl., 8th floor, N.Y.C. (tel. Spring 9300). Places accountants, bookkeepers, secretaries, stenographers, correspondents, sales and factory managers, engineers, advertising men, journalists, credit men, bank employees, etc.

Clay C. Duggan, director.

New York Urban League. See URBAN LEAGUE OF NEW YORK.

New York Women's League for Animals (incorp. 1910), 350 Lafayette St., N.Y.C. For maintaining a free hospital and dispensary for animals at above address. Capacity, seventy. Supported by voluntary contributions.

Officers: Mrs. James Speyer, pres., 1058 Fifth Ave.; H. C. Holt, treas., Central Union Trust Co.

New York Zoological Society (incorp. 1895), 111 Broadway, N.Y.C. (tel. Rector 2710). To establish and maintain a Zoological Park (q. v.) and also Aquarium (q. v.) for the City of New York in South Bronx Park and Battery Park respectively, and to promote the study of zoology.

Officers: Henry Fairfield Osborn, pres.; Madison Grant, vice-pres. and chrm. Executive Committee; Percy R. Pyne, treas.

Newark State School for Mental Defectives (est. 1878 as a branch of the Syracuse State Institution; incorp. by Chap. 281, Laws 1885), Newark, Wayne Co., N. Y. For the custody and maintenance of indigent, mentally defective who are residents of the state. It aims to improve their mental, moral, and physical condition. Capacity, 1,000.

Application for admission should be made to the Superintendent of the Poor of the county of which the patient is a resident, or the Commissioner of Charities of the City of New York, who will make the same on a blank furnished by the institution.

Ethan A. Nevin, M.D., supt.

Newsboys' Lodging House. See Brace Memorial, under CHILDREN'S AID SOCIETY.

Night Courts. See CITY MAGISTRATES COURTS.

Nitchie Service League, Inc. See NEW YORK LEAGUE FOR THE HARD OF HEARING.

Nonsmokers' Protective League of America (est. 1910, incorp. 1911), 101 West 72d St., N.Y.C. Object: Abolition of tobacco-smoking in public and semi-public places.

Officers: Dr. Charles G. Pease, pres.; Eugenie di Pirani, secy. Board of Directors: Drs. Burt G. Wilder, David Starr Jordan, Harvey W. Wiley, William A. McKeever, Jenkin Lloyd Jones and others.

North American Civic League for Immigrants (est. 1908). A Patriotic Society. National headquarters, 173 State St., Boston, Mass. New York City Office, 289 Fourth Ave., Room 45. Purpose: The complete assimilation and regulation of the immigrant and resident foreigner through his protection, education, etc. Protection at ports of entry; relief by employment; legal aid and advice; distributes "Messages for New Comers," published in English and foreign languages; also special messages written by great Americans; illustrated lectures in schools, etc. Branches in New York, Philadelphia, and other cities.

The League co-operated with the Departments of War and Justice during the War, and with Government co-operation organized the "Order and Liberty Alliance."

North Shore Holiday House (est. 1914), Huntington, L. I. Takes girls 6 to 12 years for two weeks in the country. Open for 10 weeks in summer. No fee. Capacity, 60. Supported by voluntary contributions.

Officers: Mrs. George S. Franklin, pres.; Mrs. George A. Crocher, treas.; Mrs. Arthur W. Page, secy.

Northeastern Dispensary in the City of New York, The (incorp. 1862), 222 East 59th St., N.Y.C. (tel. Plaza 4174). District bounded by 40th St. and 90th St. East of Sixth Ave. to East River. Furnishes free medical and surgical advice and medicines, also vaccination, dentistry, and medical attendance to the sick, afflicted, and injured persons unable to procure the same.

Northern Dispensary of the City of New York, The Trustees of the (incorp. 1828), 165 Waverly Place, N.Y.C. (tel. Spring 5549). Affords medical, surgical, and dental relief to sick poor at the dispensary and in their homes. District west of Broadway from Spring St. to West 23d. Open week-days 8 A. M. to 4.30 P. M.

Officers: Robert L. Harrison, 59 Wall St.; Wm. C. Smith, treas., 99 Varick St.; W. D. Luks, supt.

Northminster Presbyterian Church, 141 West 115th St., at St. Nicholas Ave., N.Y.C. (tel. University 6749). Maintains clubs and all usual church activities, including Red Cross work. See also under PRESBYTERIAN CHURCHES in the Church List.

Northover Camp, Bound Brook, N. J. See CHRISTODORA HOUSE.

Northwestern Dispensary in the City of New York, The (incorp. 1852), N. W. cor. 36th St. and Ninth Ave., N.Y.C. (tel. Longacre 564). District bounded by 23d St., Fifth Ave., 59th St. and Hudson River. Clinic hours, 1–3 P. M. Supported by voluntary contributions.

Officers: Samuel W. Fairchild, pres.; M. M. Kittel, secy. and treas.; H. C. Hanscom, M.D., physician in charge.

Norwegian Children's Home Association, The, 43 Gubner St., Brooklyn (tel. Bath Beach 1362). Orphanage houses seventy-seven children. Supported by private contributions.

***Norwegian Christian Home for the Aged** (re-incorp. 1911), 1250 67th St., Brooklyn. A non-denominational home for dependent men and women over sixty years of age.

Norwegian Evangelical Lutheran Emigrant Mission and Emigrant Home, belonging to the Norwegian Church of America, 45 Whitehall St. N.Y.C. (tel. Bowling Green 8892). Providing a temporary first home for immigrants, especially Norwegians, protecting and assisting them.

Rt. Rev. H. G. Stub, D.D., pres., 806 Sheldon Ave., St. Paul, Minn.; Rev. Iver Tharaldsen, missionary.

Norwegian Lutheran Deaconesses' Home and Hospital, The (founded in 1883, re-incorp. under present title 1892), Fourth Ave. and 46th St., Brooklyn.

A HOME FOR DEACONESSES, and a HOSPITAL to administer to the wants of the sick and needy. Capacity, 190 beds. Supported by voluntary contributions, and board of patients. Visiting days, Tuesdays, Thursdays, and Sundays, 2 to 4 P. M.

Rev. C. O. Pedersen, supt.

Norwegian Lutheran Inner Mission, 4611 Fourth Ave., Brooklyn (tel. Sunset 5259). Religious and institutional work. Supported by voluntary contributions.

Norwegian Seamen's Mission Church, 111 Pioneer St., Brooklyn (tel. Henry 557). Rev. Christen Bruun. Maintains reading and writing rooms, library, etc., for sailors; also ministers to seamen aboard vessels, in boarding houses and hospitals. See also under LUTHERAN CHURCHES in the Church List.

Noyes Memorial Home. See ST. MARY'S FREE HOSPITAL FOR CHILDREN.

Nuns of the Order of St. Dominic. See SISTERS OF ST. DOMINIC.

Nurses' Settlement. See HENRY STREET SETTLEMENT.

Nursing Sisters of the Sick Poor (est. 1911), 439 Henry St., Brooklyn (tel. Hamilton 450). Roman Catholic Sisters care for the sick poor in their homes, without charge. Supported by voluntary contributions and by a committee of Catholic women.

O

Occupational Clinic. See HEALTH, DEPARTMENT OF.

Ocean Hill Memorial Dispensary and Hospital, 343–345 Ralph Ave., Brooklyn (tel. Decatur 6466). Provides medicines and medical and surgical aid and attendance at low prices or free to those unable to pay.

Officers: Frank G. Seymour, pres.; Louis Wedel, treas.; Charles Rippier, secy.

* *Current information not received.*

Ocean Parkway M. E. Church, Ocean Parkway at Foster Ave., Brooklyn. Rev. William Benjamin West, D.D. A social center providing athletic clubs, Girl Scouts, Boy Scouts, entertainments, lectures; also medical and osteopathic clinic.

Old Ladies' Home. See ASSOCIATION FOR THE RELIEF OF RESPECTABLE AGED AND INDIGENT FEMALES.

Old Marion Street Maternity Hospital. See NEW YORK NURSERY AND CHILD'S HOSPITAL.

Old McAuley Mission. See MCAULEY WATER STREET MISSION.

Old Men and Aged Couples, Home for (incorp. 1872), N. W. cor. Amsterdam Ave. and 112th St., N.Y.C. (tel. Morningside 272). For the temporal and spiritual welfare of those especially named in title who, having been accustomed to the comforts of life, through loss of property or other causes find themselves in their old age without means of support; all religious teachings and exercises shall be in accordance with the doctrine, discipline, and worship of the Protestant Episcopal Church, controlled by a board of trustees consisting of twenty-one clergymen and laymen, residents of New York and vicinity.

An admission fee of $400 is required for each man, and $700 for a couple. Capacity for sixty. Supported by voluntary contributions and interest on permanent fund.

Edward B. Sexton, pres.; Anson B. Moran, vice-pres.; John G. Jackson, treas., 30 Pine St.; Richard P. Kent, secy., 184 Montague St., Brooklyn. Apply to the Committee on Admission, 1060 Amsterdam Ave.

Old South Brooklyn Civic League (est. 1913, incorp. 1916), 139 Harrison St., Brooklyn (tel. Henry 283). Hours 9 A. M. to 5 P. M. daily, Saturdays 9–12, Tuesday and Thursday evenings 7.30–9.30. Does Civic Welfare Work of the community. Americanization work in charge of Miss Edna A. Holden. Dental dispensary for all kinds of dental work except orthodontia. Supported by voluntary subscriptions.

Officers: Mrs. Cornelius Zabriskie, acting pres.; Wm. Creamer, treas.; Mrs. Natalie Holden Lander, exec. secy.

Olive Tree Inn. See CALVARY P. E. CHURCH, this list.

Olivet Memorial Church. See NEW YORK CITY MISSION SOCIETY.

Open Door, The, 17 Beekman Pl., N.Y.C. A temporary shelter for homeless women, chiefly court cases, irrespective of race or creed. Capacity, 25 adults; 6 babies.

Deaconess Young, in charge.

Open Door Mission, 633 Hudson St., N.Y.C. See COMFORTER, CHAPEL.

Ophthalmic and Aural Institute. See HERMANN KNAPP MEMORIAL EYE HOSPITAL.

Order and Liberty Alliance. See NORTH AMERICAN CIVIC LEAGUE FOR IMMIGRANTS.

Orphan Asylum of the German Odd Fellows' Home Association. See UNITED ODD FELLOWS' HOME ASSOCIATION.

Orphan Asylum Society of the City of Brooklyn, 1435 Atlantic Ave., Brooklyn (tel. Decatur 711–712). For the protection, care, and instruction of orphans and half-orphans.

Orphan Asylum Society in the City of New York (incorp. 1807). Executive Committee meets Thursdays 10.30–12 M., Room 516, United Charities Bldg., 105 East 22d St., N.Y.C. Maintains an

ORPHANAGE at Hastings-on-Hudson, N. Y. For destitute orphans of Protestant parentage, two to ten years of age, and for half-orphans when the surviving parent is destitute or disqualified mentally or physically to support the child. Conducted on the cottage plan. Capacity, 240. The children are subject to physicians' examination before being admitted. Besides the regular academic school instruction, girls are taught cooking, sewing, dressmaking, and laundry, dining room and chambermaid service. Boys are instructed in manual training, gardening, care of poultry and stock and all of the ordinary home-making industries.

Controlled by a board of trustees. Supported by subscriptions, donations, and invested funds. Visiting days for the relatives and friends of the children are all legal holidays and the last Saturday of each month. For admission of children apply to the Executive Committee, at the office, or by letter to the Superintendent, Hastings-on-Hudson, N. Y.

Officers: Mrs. Benj. Perkins, first directress; Mrs. John S. Sheppard, Jr., treas.; Mrs. Samuel B. Hawley, secy.

Orphans' Home and Asylum of the Protestant Episcopal Church in New York, The (org. 1851, incorp. 1859), Convent Ave. and 135th St., N.Y.C. (tel. Morningside 979). Receives American Protestant orphans and half-orphans from three to eight years of age, keeping them, ordinarily, until graduation from school, when they are returned to friends or relatives or a home and work is found for them. Children with incurable diseases or who are physically imperfect, not received. Supported by voluntary contributions and legacies.

SUMMER HOME, Beacon, N. Y.

Officers of board: Mrs. Byam K. Stevens, 1st directress; Mrs. James J. Goodwin, 2d directress; Mrs. William E. Iselin, treas, 745 Fifth Ave.; Mrs. Robert Ellis Jones, secy., 611 West 112th St.; Dr. Fred. E. Bauer, attending physician, 400 West 145th St.

Rev. James Sheerin, supt., 168 Convent Ave., to whom apply.

Orthopaedic Dispensary and Hospital. See NEW YORK ORTHOPAEDIC DISPENSARY AND HOSPITAL.

Otisville Sanatorium. See under HEALTH DEPARTMENT

Ottilie Orphan Asylum Society of New York (incorp. 1892), Asylum: Kaplan and Degraw Aves., Jamaica, L. I. (tel. Jamaica 1679). For the care, maintenance, and disposal of orphans, half-orphans, and destitute children. Supported by voluntary contributions and membership fees.

Our Lady of Loretto Mission. See NATIVITY, CHURCH OF THE.

Our Lady of the Rosary, Mission of (incorp. 1883), 7 State St., N.Y.C. (tel. Bowling Green 6866). For the care and relief of Irish immigrant girls, Scotch, English and others, discharged to the Mission by the immigration authorities, until they are met by friends, proceed to their destination or find suitable employment. Supported by the parish, voluntary contributions and the Rosary Society.

Rev. M. J. Henry, director; P. McDonough, agent.

See also under ROMAN CATHOLIC CHURCHES in the Church List.

Our Lady of the Rosary Villa, High and Spring Sts., West Hoboken, N. J. (tel. Union 1376) under the Pallotine Sisters of Charity. Maintains a home for working girls.

Ozanam Association of the City of New York, The. Central office: 312 West 16th St., N.Y.C. (tel. Watkins 597). For the physical, mental and moral training of Catholic boys of

New York City. It maintains club houses with gymnasia, reading rooms, classes, lectures, games, entertainments, etc.

Joseph R. Buckley, supervisor.

Ozanam Home for Friendless Women of Brooklyn, New York City, The (1901), 40–48 Concord St., Brooklyn (tel. Main 48). Object: To care for, encourage, reclaim and provide employment for friendless women. Personal applications received at Home, hours 7 A. M. to 9 P. M., from women to be admitted as inmates. Capacity, 100 beds. Average stay, three weeks. About 1,000 assisted annually.

Officers: Very Rev. Mgr. Francis J. O'Hara, pres.; Wm. D. S. Kelly, secy.; Miss S. Gough, supt.

P

Palisades Interstate Park, Commissioners of the. An interstate body created by the legislatures of New York and New Jersey. Commissioners are appointed by the Governors of the respective states for the administration of a large public park.

General Office of Commission: 90 Wall St., N.Y.C. (tel. John 4326). Applications for the occupancy of camp plants may be made by addressing Edward F. Brown.

The personnel of the Commission follows:

New York Commissioners: Franklin W. Hopkins, pres.; J. Du Pratt White, secy.; Edward L. Partridge, treas., Richard V. Lindabury, William H. Porter, W. Averell Harriman, Frederick C. Sutro, Charles W. Baker, John J. Voorhees.

New Jersey Commissioners: Richard V. Lindabury, pres.; Edward L. Partridge, vice-pres.; J. Du Pratt White, secy.; Frederick C. Sutro, treas.; Charles W. Baker, Myron W. Robinson, John J. Voorhees, William H. Porter, W. Averell Harriman.

William A. Welch, general manager of Park; Elbert W. King, asst. secy.-treas.

Roughly outlined, the Park begins at a point north of Fort Lee, N. J. (opposite 129th St., N.Y.C.,) and takes in 12 miles of Palisades on the west bank ot the Hudson River, going north. The second major section of the Park commences at Bear Mountain, N. Y., 5 miles south of West Point, running westward for approximately 15 miles into the Ramapo Hills. The Commission also holds the State Rifle Range at Blauvelt, N. Y., a large tract of land at Hook Mountain and some land at Rockland Lake, N. Y. The Park embraces upwards of 36,000 acres of land.

The recreation features of the Park in the Palisades section include:

(a) Spacious pavilions, jutting out into the Hudson river, for picnic parties and storm shelter.

(b) Bath houses and beaches, accommodating thousands.

(c) A beach for canoe camping, with facilities for winter storage of canoes.

(d) Motor boat basin for small pleasure craft.

(e) Week-end camps for working boys maintained north of Alpine, N. J., by the Jacob A. Riis Social Centre, Educational Alliance, Emanuel Settlement, Y. M. H. A.

(f) Hundreds of individual camps are established north of Alpine, N. J., under the permit, the charge being $1.00 to $1.50 per week for the permit.

In the Harriman Park and Bear Mountain sections of the Palisades Park system there are:

(a) Bear Mountain Inn, a large restaurant built with private funds and operated by the Commissioners for the sale of food at reasonable prices.

(b) Sightseeing omnibuses are operated by the Commissioners to give the Park visitors an opportunity to visit the interior of the Park lying between Bear Mountain and Tuxedo.

(c) A large open dance pavilion with music, maintained by the Commissioners, under supervision, is free for public use.

(d) Nearly 300 row boats are available for limited periods for the free use of visitors.

(e) Over 150 miles of mountain trails open to hikers.

(f) Swings and rest pavilions are open for free use.

(g) Mothers' rest stations, where children are cared for, without cost, in the absence of parents, while on the day's outing.

(h) The Commission offers to social and civic organizations opportunities to use standard camp plants at cost. These plants consist of rustic pavilions with fire-places, accommodating groups from 30 to 200.

The following social organizations conduct camps in the Palisades Park:

Association for Improving the Condition of the Poor.
American Guard.
Brooklyn Children's Aid Society.
Brooklyn Industrial School Association and Home for Destitute Orphans.
Big Brother Movement.
Boy Scouts of America maintain camps for groups from Manhattan, Bronx, Brooklyn, Queens, Westchester counties, as well as a number of Jersey Scout Organizations.
Camp Fire Girls of Emerson, N. J.
Chelsea Church.
Children's Aid Society.
Church of the Divine Paternity.
Church of the Holy Trinity.
Church of Our Lady of Lourdes.
First Presbyterian Church of Nyack.
Friendly House of Brooklyn.
Girls' League of Yonkers.
Girls' Patriotic League of Bergen County, N. J.
Grace Church Chapel.
Greenwich House.
Harlem and Heights Business Girls' Athletic League.
Hebrew Orphan Asylum.
Holy Cross Church of Jersey City.
Jacob A. Riis Social Settlement.
Jewish Big Sisters.
Jewish Protectory and Aid Society.
Kennedy House.
Manhattan Council of Girl Scouts.
Negro Fresh Air Committee.
New York Community Center.
New York City Mission Society.
New York Edison Troop Boy Scouts.
New York Deaconess Association.
New York State Military Training Commission.
Plymouth Church of Brooklyn.
St. Raphael's R. C. Church.
Seward Park Rehabilitation Station (for wounded soldiers).
Striker's Lane Community Center.
Union Settlement.
Warren Goddard House.
Women's Benevolent Society of the Central Presbyterian Church.
Yorkville Social Centre.
York Street Goodwill Centre.
Y. M. C. A. (Colored Branch).
Y. M. C. A. of Orange County.
Y. W. C. A. (Senior Branch).
Y. W. C. A. (Junior Branch).
Y. W. C. A. of Brooklyn.

The Park maintains the largest civil encampment in the world, last year having had 52,350 individuals, averaging 8 consecutive days' vacation each.

No concessions of any kind are granted in the Park.

***Panhellenic Union in America** (incorp. 1909), 56 West 30th St., N.Y.C. Objects: Mutual aid among Greeks; affection for the laws and institutions of

* *Current information not received.*

the United States; to encourage the study of English; assistance to obtain American citizenship.

Paralytic Hospital. See PUBLIC WELFARE DEPARTMENT, CITY OF NEW YORK, Hospital for Incurables.

Parish of All Strangers (org. 1902). Headquarters, 108 West 77th St., N.Y.C. Serves strangers in hotels and others without church affiliations.

Other ministries of the Parish are The Hospital Guild and the Save-a-Life-League (q. v.). See also under Miscellaneous in the Church List.

Rev. H. M. Warren, D.D., pres. and general director; Mrs. Adelaide B. Warren, missionary; Ruel W. Poor, treas., 200 Fifth Ave.

Park Avenue Branch Tompkins Avenue Congregational Church. See PURITAN CHAPEL.

Park Hospital (formerly NEW YORK RED CROSS HOSPITAL; incorp. 1902), 100th St. and Central Park West (tel. Riverside 8000). Sixty-four beds. Conducts also a training school for nurses.

Allen Wardwell, pres.; Dean C. Molleson, treas.; C. K. B. Wade, secy.; Mrs. Maud H. Metcalf, supt. of hospital and Training School.

Parks, Department of, City of New York.

MANHATTAN OFFICE: 10th floor, Municipal Bldg. (tel. Worth 4850). Francis D. Gallatin, pres. Park Board and commissioner for Manhattan and Richmond; Willis Holly, secy. Park Board; Julius Burgevin, landscape architect; Edward A. Miller, chief engineer; William J. Lee, supervisor of recreation; John J. Ryan, secy.

BRONX OFFICE: Zbrowski Mansion, Claremont Park (tel. Tremont 2640). Joseph P. Hennessy, commissioner; William T. Wagner, secy.; Henry Geiger, supt.

BROOKLYN OFFICE: Litchfield Mansion, Prospect Park (tel. South 2300). John N. Harman, commissioner; Wm. H. Muldoon, secy.; George A. Colgan, supt.; John J. Dowling, supervisor of recreation.

QUEENS OFFICE: Forest Park (tel. Richmond Hill 2300). Albert C. Benninger, commissioner; Bernard M. Patten, secy.

The Park Department has supervision over the public squares, parks, and playgrounds of the City and issues permits to responsible persons or organizations for the use of athletic fields, for baseball, croquet, camping, cricket, cross-country runs, football, golf, lacrosse, picnics, tennis, etc.

RECREATION PARKS

Manhattan

ABINGTON SQUARE, Hudson St. and Eighth Ave.—playground.

BATTERY, Battery Pl. and State St., athletic field and playground.

CARL SCHURZ, 86th St. and East River, playground.

CARMANSVILLE, 151st St. and Amsterdam Ave., playground.

CENTRAL:

North Meadow, 100th St. off Eighth Ave., May parties and picnics.

South Meadow, 96th St., entrance Eighth Ave., Clay Tennis Courts.

Children's Playground, 99th St. off Fifth Ave.

East Meadow, 99th St., off Fifth Ave., baseball and football field.

Sheep Meadow, 66th St. and West Drive, tennis, baseball, and football field, May parties.

Playground Lawn, 65th St. below Sheep Meadow, May parties, picnics, football field.

CHELSEA, 28th St. and Tenth Ave., playground, baseball, football, and athletic field.

CHERRY AND MARKET, Cherry and

Market Sts., athletic and ball field, boys' playground.

CLARK, 174th St. and Ft. Washington Ave., playground.

COLONIAL, 150th St. and Bradhurst Ave., playground.

COLUMBUS, Baxter and Worth Sts., athletic and ball field, boys' playground.

CORLEARS HOOK, Jackson St. and Corlears Hook, playground, athletic and ball field.

DE WITT CLINTON, 53d St. and Eleventh Ave., playground, athletic and ball field.

EAST 12TH ST., between Ave. A and First Ave., playground, athletic and ball field.

EAST 17TH ST., East 17th St. and East River, playground.

FIVE POINTS, Baxter and Worth Sts., playground.

GRACE, 104th St. between Columbus and Amsterdam Aves., playground.

HAMILTON FISH, Houston and Pitt Sts., playground, athletic, and ball field.

HIGHBRIDGE, 170th St. and Amsterdam Ave., playground.

HUDSON, Hudson and Clarkson Sts., playground.

JACKSON SQUARE, Horatio St. and Eighth Ave., playground.

JASPER OVAL, 137th St. and Convent Ave., athletic and ball field.

JOHN JAY, 77th St. and East River, playground, athletic, and ball field.

QUEENSBORO, foot of East 59th St., playground, athletic, and ball field.

MT. MORRIS, 120th St. off Madison Ave., playground.

RESERVOIR, 174th St. and Amsterdam Ave., ball field.

RIVERSIDE, 96th St. and Riverside Drive, playground.

RIVERSIDE OVAL, 77th to 83d Sts. and Riverside Drive, ball field.

RYAN, 42d St. and Pleasant Pl., playground.

ST. GABRIEL'S, 35th St. and Second Ave., playground, athletic, and ball field.

ST. NICHOLAS, 133d St. and St. Nicholas Ave., playground

SEWARD, Canal and Jefferson Sts., playground, athletic, and ball field.

THOMAS JEFFERSON, 112th St. and Pleasant Ave., playground, athletic and ball field.

TOMPKINS SQUARE, 10th St. and Avenue A, playground, athletic, and ball field.

WATERGATE, 134th St. and Amsterdam Ave., playground.

WEST 59TH ST., between Tenth and Eleventh Aves., boys' playground, ball, and athletic field.

YORKVILLE, 101st St., between Second and Third Aves., playground.

18TH ST. and Tenth Ave., playground.

44TH ST., Twelfth Ave., ball field.

67TH ST. and First Ave., playground.

ASTOR FIELD, playground, ball, and athletic field.

FT. WASHINGTON, 177th St. and Riverside Drive, playground.

ESPLANADE, Williamsburgh Bridge, playground.

EAST 19TH ST. and First Ave., playground.

Richmond

ST. PETER'S, Richmond Terr., New Brighton, S. I., playground.

WESTERLEIGH, Maine and Jewett Aves., Westerleigh, S. I., playground.

RECREATION PIERS

WEST 129TH ST., North River, playground.

WEST 50TH ST., North River.

BARROW ST., North River.

ALBANY ST., North River.

EAST THIRD ST., East River.

MARKET ST., East River.

EAST 24TH ST., East River.

EAST 112TH ST., East River.

INDOOR GYMNASIA

CHERRY AND OLIVER STS., gymnastics, athletics, calisthenics, basketball, folk dancing, swimming.

RUTGER PLACE.

EAST 54TH ST.

WEST 28TH ST.

CARMINE ST.

HAMILTON FISH PARK

WEST 59TH ST.

Bronx

BRONX, East 180th St. to Burke Ave. Southern Boulevard to tracks of N. Y. C. & H. R. R. (Harlem Division) and Bronx Park East, boating, band concerts, croquet, tennis, picnics, school garden, skating, Zoological Park (twenty-five cents on Mondays and Thursdays), Botanical Garden, Park Department Greenhouses, Bronx Society of Arts and Science Museum; outside of the Park Greenhouses the Botanical and Zoological Gardens are under the Jurisdiction of the respective Societies.

CROTONA, Third Ave., Crotona Park East, Tremont Ave. and Crotona Park South, baseball, boating, band concerts, croquet, football, playgrounds, tennis, picnics, skating, athletic field, Victory Garden.

CLAREMONT, Teller Ave. Clay Ave. 170th St. Mt. Eden Ave. East, band concerts, croquet, tennis, picnics, playground.

FRANZ SIEGEL, Mott Ave. Walton Ave. 152nd St. & 158th St., baseball, band concerts, croquet, football, tennis, picnics, playgrounds.

POE, East 192nd St. Kingsbridge Road, Valentine Ave. & Concourse, historical Museum, special concerts.

ST. JAMES', Jerome Ave. East 191st St. East 193d St. Crescent Ave., band concerts, tennis.

ST. MARY'S, St. Ann's Ave., 149th St. St. Mary's St. Jackson Ave., band concerts, football, baseball, tennis. school gardens, playgrounds, croquet.

MCCOMB'S DAM PARK, Jerome Ave. 161st St. Harlem River, athletic field, baseball, band concerts, croquet, football, tennis, playgrounds, picnics, rowing clubs.

PELHAM BAY, N. E. end of City on Long Island Sound, athletic field, showers, lockers, dressing rooms, baseball, boating, croquet, camping, cricket, football, golf, lacrosse, tennis, picnics, band concerts, bathing with dressing rooms, fishing, skating.

VAN CORTLANDT, City line, Broadway & 240th St. Jerome Ave. Mt. Vernon Ave. & Van Cortlandt Park South, baseball, boating, croquet, cross country runs, football, golf, bridle paths, lacrosse, tennis, picnics, polo, skating, band concerts, bowling green, curling, hockey, Colonial garden and historical museum.

WILLIS AVE. & SOUTHERN BOULEVARD, playgrounds and picnics.

Brooklyn

AMERSFORT, Avenue J, East 38th St., Avenue I and East 29th St., tennis courts.

BEDFORD, Kingston and Brooklyn Aves., Prospect and Park Places.

BENSONHURST, Bay Parkway, Gravesend Bay, Twenty-first and Cropsey Aves., beach bathing, band concerts.

BETSEY HEAD MEMORIAL, Livonia, Dumont, Hopkinson Aves., and Douglass St. and Dumont Blake, Hopkinson Aves., and Bristol St., playground, athletic field, bath, swimming pool and children's farm gardens.

BOROUGH HALL, Joralemon, Court, and Fulton Sts.

BROOKLYN BOTANIC GARDEN AND ARBORETUM, Eastern Parkway, Washington and Flatbush Aves. and Malbone St.

BROOKLYN BRIDGE PLAYGROUND, York St. near Fulton St.

BROOKLYN HEIGHTS, Columbia Heights, fronting on Furman St.

BUSHWICK PLAYGROUND, Knickerbocker and Putnam Aves., playground.

BUSHWICK PARK, Knickerbocker Ave. and Suydam St., band concerts.

CANARSIE, Skidmore, Sea View, and Denton Aves., East 88th and East 93d Sts., Byrne Pl. and Jamaica Bay, athletic field, baseball, gymnasium.

CARROLL, President, Court, Carroll, and Smith Sts., band concerts, motion pictures.

CITY PARK, St. Edwards and Navy Sts., Park and Flushing Aves., band concerts, playground.

CONEY ISLAND CONCOURSE LANDS (exclusive of Seaside Park), West 5th St., Sea Breeze Ave. and Atlantic Ocean.

COOPER, Maspeth and Morgan Aves., Sharon and Olive Sts., tennis courts, band concerts, playgrounds.

COOPER GORE, junction of Metropolitan and Orient Aves.

CUYLER GORE, Cumberland and Fulton Sts. and Greene Ave.

DREAMLAND, West 5th St., West 8th St., Surf Ave. and Atlantic Ocean, beach bathing, children's day camp.

DYKER BEACH, Seventh Ave., Bay 8th St., Cropsey and Fourteenth Aves., and Gravesend Bay, beach bathing, cross-country runs, golf, picnics.

FORT GREENE, DeKalb Ave., Washington Park, Willoughby, and St. Edwards Sts., and Myrtle Ave., band concerts, children's playground, farm gardens, motion pictures.

FORT HAMILTON, Fourth Ave., 101st St., Ft. Hamilton Ave. and Shore Rd.

FULTON, Chauncey and Fulton Sts. and Stuyvesant Ave.

HIGHLAND, Jamaica Ave., U. S. Nat. Cemetery, Borough Line and Warwick St. Extension, baseball, band concerts, croquet, cross-country runs, picnics, tennis courts, children's farm gardens, motion pictures.

IRVING SQUARE, Hamburg and Knickerbocker Aves., Weirfield and Halsey Sts., band concerts.

LINCOLN TERRACE, Eastern Parkway, Buffalo and Rochester Aves., and President St., band concerts.

LINTON, Bradford St., Blake, Dumont and Miller Aves.

MCCARREN, Berry, Lorimer, Leonard, Bayard, and North 12th Sts., Nassau, Driggs, Manhattan and Union Aves., playground, athletic field, tennis courts, baseball diamonds, children's farm gardens.

MCKIBBIN, Seigel, White and McKibbin Sts., playground.

MCKINLEY, Ft. Hamilton and Seventh Aves. and 73d St., picnics, baseball, football.

MCLAUGHLIN, Bridge, Tillary and Jay Sts., athletic field, playground, gymnasium.

MANHATTAN BRIDGE PLAYGROUND, York and Pearl Sts.

NEW LOTS, Sackman St., Riverdale, Newport and Christopher Aves., playground.

PARADE GROUND, Coney Island, Parkside and Caton Aves., football, baseball, cricket, bowling on Green Lawn.

PROSPECT, Prospect Park West, Flatbush, Ocean, Parkside, Coney Island Aves., and 15th St., boating, band concerts, croquet, tennis, picnics, skating, hockey, coasting, horseback, Zoological Garden.

RED HOOK, Richards, Verona, Dwight and Pioneer Sts., band concerts, playground.

SARATOGA SQUARE, Saratoga and Howard Aves., Halsey and Macon Sts. band concerts.

SEASIDE, Ocean Parkway, Concourse,

West 5th St. and Sea Breeze Ave. beach bathing, and camping.

STUYVESANT GORE, Stuyvesant and Vernon Aves., and Broadway.

SUNSET, 41st and 44th Sts., Fifth and Seventh Aves., band concerts, picnics, tennis courts.

TOMPKINS, Tompkins, Greene, Marcy and Lafayette Aves., band concerts.

UNDERHILL GORE, Underhill and Washington Aves., and Pacific St.

VANDEVEER, East New York and Pitkin Aves., Barrett and Grafton Sts.

WILLIAMSBURGH BRIDGE, Bedford and Kent Aves., South 5th and 6th Sts., playground, gymnasium.

WINTHROP, Nassau and Driggs Aves., Russell and Monitor Sts., band concerts.

WOODPOINT GORE, Bushwick, Metropolitan, and Maspeth Aves.

UNNAMED PARK, Eastern Parkway, Washington and Classon Aves.

UNNAMED PARK, Roebling St., Division and Lee Aves.

UNNAMED PARK, Fourth Ave. and 9th St.

UNNAMED PARK, Myrtle and Bushwick Aves.

UNNAMED PARK, Fulton St. and Lewis Ave.

RECREATION PIER, foot of Metropolitan Ave., band concerts.

Queens

ASHMEAD, Canal and South Sts. playground.

ASTORIA, Ditmars Ave., Barclay St., Hoyt Ave. and East River, playground, baseball picnics, band concerts.

BAISELEY'S POND, Locust Ave. and Rockaway Rd., skating.

COLLEGE POINT, Fifth Ave., 15th St., Louisa and 14th Sts., band concerts.

FLUSHING, Broadway and Main St.

FOREST, Cypress Hills Cemetery, Myrtle Ave., Union Turnpike, Park Lane and Ashland St., golf, baseball, tennis, playground, picnics, band concerts.

HIGHLAND, Vermont Ave., Cypress Ave., Ridgewood Reservoirs, Borough Line, and Highland Boulevard, picnics, band concerts.

JACOB RIIS Land of U. S. Government, Jamaica Bay, Land of Neponsit Realty Co., and Atlantic Ocean, playground, camping, beach bathing.

KING, Alsop St., Shelton Ave., Ray and Fulton Sts., tennis, field hockey, band concerts.

KISSENA LAKE, Rose St., Oak Ave., Renwick Ave. and Old Stewart Railroad, playground, tennis, picnics, skating, wading pool, band concerts.

LEAVITT, Congress Ave., Myrtle Ave., and Leavitt St., athletic fields, baseball, running track, tennis.

LINDEN, Lake St., Sycamore Ave., Park and Linden Sts., skating, band concerts.

OLD NEWTON CEMETERY, Toledo Ave. and Court St.

ONE MILE POND, Merrick Rd.

RAINEY, Vernon Ave., Sanford St., and East River, playground, baseball, tennis, band concerts.

ROCKAWAY, Triton Ave. and Atlantic Ocean, beach bathing.

UPLAND, Highland Ave., skating.

WAYANDA, Hollis Ave.

SIX UNNAMED Street Gores.

Parks and Playground Association of the City of New York (org. 1905, incorp. 1908), Room 606, 1123 Broadway (tel. Watkins 9177). Purpose: To secure and preserve parks and playgrounds for the City, especially in the congested districts; to establish and conduct a system of recreation, play and playgrounds wherever the City does not make adequate provision; to foster in children a spirit of fair play and instill in them principles of honor and good citizenship.

Field of Activity: Establishes and maintains play centers—such as vacant lot playgrounds, backyards and roofs, wherever available; co-operates with the City authorities through the use of its properties; organizes and directs street play in districts where all other play facilities are lacking. Supported by voluntary contributions through membership.

Officers: Geo. Gordon Battle, pres.; Miss Lillian D. Wald, vice-pres.; Wm. H. Williams, treas.; Miss L. Morton, secy.

Passover Relief Association (org. 1877, incorp. 1882). To aid poor, deserving Israelites, not assisted by other societies, in the observance of the Passover. Supported by donations and annual dues. Over 800 families aided last year.

Officers: M. Silberstein, pres.; L. J. Saruya, treas.; Adolph Schwarzbaum, secy., 2677 Creston Ave., to whom apply ten days before the Passover.

***Patrick Henry Community Center Association** (org. 1917). For the purpose of conducting a social and community center at the Patrick Henry School, P. S. 171, 19 East 103d St. With the exception of one paid worker from the Board of Education, the center is managed and supervised entirely by volunteer workers.

Peabody Home for Aged and Indigent Women, The (incorp. 1874), 2064 Boston Rd., West Farms, N.Y.C. A free home for Protestant women in reduced circumstances, over sixty-five years of age, residents of Greater New York. Domestic servants and colored women excepted. Capacity, thirty-two. Supported by voluntary contributions.

* *Current information not received.*

Officers: H. R. Kunhardt, pres., 17 Battery Pl.; Robert Y. Hebden, 64 Wall St., secy. and treas. Apply to Mrs. W. Tonnele, 550 Park Ave., chrm. Committee on Admissions.

Pelham Summer Home for Children, The (est. 1894, incorp. 1898), Pelham Manor, N. Y. (tel. Pelham 1389). Cares for convalescing cardiac children from five to thirteen years of age. Open all the year. No limitations as to race or sect. Apply to the president.

Officers: Mrs. R. E. Rogers, pres.; Mrs. Clifford Black, treas.; Mrs. C. E. Scott, secy.; Miss Adele Smeath, supt.

Penitentiary, Blackwell's Island. See CORRECTION, DEPARTMENT OF.

People's Choral Union and People's Singing Classes (org. 1894. incorp. 1898), 1556 Broadway, N.Y.C. To promote the love and culture of music by means of sight-singing and choral singing and to give an opportunity to all who desire to learn to read music from notes. A charge of ten cents per lesson is made, to cover incidental expenses. Classes in every borough.

Dr. Frank Damrosch, director and founder; Ed. G. Marquard, conductor.

People's Home Church and Settlement, 543 East 11th St., New York City. Rev. Leslie G. Davis.

Maintains a kindergarten, class and club work for young people and children, religious, social and educational services for families of the community.

People's Hospital, Inc. (incorp. 1908), 203 Second Ave. (tel. Stuyvesant 5761). A general hospital. Supported by voluntary contributions. Maintains also a registered

TRAINING SCHOOL FOR NURSES.

Wm. I. Sirovich, M.D., supt.

People's Institute, The (incorp. 1897), 70 Fifth Ave., N.Y.C. (tel. Chelsea 7565). The institute works with the people for better educational, cultural and recreational opportunities.

THE PEOPLE'S FORUM: Tuesday nights at Cooper Union; gives full discussion to all matters of public concern and all shades of opinion honestly put forward for bettering human conditions. Lectures by the ablest speakers available.

EDUCATIONAL FORUM: Friday nights at Cooper Union. Lectures by Everett D. Martin.

SCHOOL OF PHILOSOPHY: Meets five nights a week at the Manhattan Trade School.

MUSIC LEAGUE: Aims to give good music to people of New York City at popular prices and assists artists. Gives each year a series of concerts in public schools and eight weeks of Open Air Concerts in the Lewisohn Stadium.

THE UKRAINIAN NEEDLECRAFT GUILD is developing and marketing the needlecraft of the Ukrainians.

NATIONAL BOARD OF REVIEW OF MOTION PICTURES. Inspired by the People's Institute and connected with it.

People's Institute, United Neighborhood Guild, 176 Nassau St. Brooklyn (tel. Main 7871). To maintain neighborhood centers for the people and to promote educational, social, and civic improvement. It maintains also

GUILD FARM, New City, N. Y.

Mrs. H. Edward Drier, pres.

People's Synagogue. See EDUCATIONAL ALLIANCE.

People's Tabernacle of New York City, The (incorp. 1898). To found churches of free seats and to do missionary and benevolent work among the poor and neglected. Supported by voluntary contributions.

Rev. Henry M. Tyndall, mgr., 56 East 102d St., N.Y.C.

People's University Extension Society of Greater New York, The (incorp. 1898), Suite 21, Room B, 1425 Broadway, N.Y.C. (tel. Bryant 3997). Dr. Rossiter Johnson, pres. and executive officer; Miss Florence K. Johnson, secy. and treas.

Maintains free classes in manual and domestic training and other practical subjects for the poor of all races and creeds of Greater New York. Special Free Classes for the Handicapped form most important branches of its work as follows:

Crippled children are taught corrective physical exercises for the relief of their bodily defects, and are also given free lessons in Manual and Domestic Training, fitting them for self-support.

Blind persons are trained in simple forms of hand-work to give interesting occupations and to fit them to support themselves as far as possible.

Mentally defective children are taught attractive forms of handwork that stimulate and develop the brain. Many of them soon become fit to enter regular classes in the Public Schools.

Children with speech defects are cured in special classes for stammering and other defects that seriously interfere with the progress of those otherwise bright and capable.

Girls in Reformatories are instructed in practical housekeeping, cooking, dressmaking, millinery, etc., thus fitting them to earn an honorable living when they are released from those institutions.

Saving the Babies. The appalling infant mortality is due to the ignorance and carelessness of mothers. To prevent children's diseases this Society furnishes simple, practical lectures by experienced physicians, nurses, and teachers. Printed Health Hints in English, Italian, and Yiddish languages have been distributed without charge by this Society, to the number of more than 500,000.

The keynote of its work is hearty co-operation with local societies, thus benefitting the largest possible number of people with every dollar received.

More than 1,400 societies and schools in the crowded tenement districts of Manhattan and Brooklyn have been helped by us with free classes in industrial training and domestic economy since its work began in 1898.

It gives classes for women and girls in economic cooking, sewing, dressmaking, millinery, embroidery, crochet, basketry, housekeeping, hygiene, physical training, industrial art, knitting, etc.

It gives classes for boys in carpentry, chair caning, basketry, cobbling, hammock making, brush making, sloyd, industrial art, mechanical drawing, etc

Need of funds: This important free education, which is for those beyond the reach of our public school system, is supported by voluntary contributions. Money is urgently needed to continue free classes and start new ones. The number of its free classes is limited only by donations received to pay its teachers. Twenty-five dollars gives lessons to a class for three months. Checks to aid the work should be made payable to the order of this Society and mailed to the Treasurer.

Permanent Blind Relief War Fund for Soldiers and Sailors of the Allies, Inc., 590 Fifth Ave., N.Y.C. (tel. Bryant 1613). Permanent reconstruction work for soldiers and sailors blinded in the war. The scope of work includes social and industrial education, maintenance of workshops and schools, purchasing raw materials, marketing handiwork, providing pensions for those both blind and mutilated, etc.

Board of Directors: James M. Beck, Wm. Nelson Cromwell, John Foster Dulles, Samuel W. Fairchild, James W. Gerard, Otto H. Kahn, Miss Helen Keller, Mrs. Cora Parsons Kessler, Alvin W. Krech, Rev. Charles S. Macfarland, Julius M. Mayer, Morgan J. O'Brien, Sir Arthur Pearson, Bt., Samuel Robert, L. Livingston Seaman, Rev. Ernest M. Stires.

Philanthropic Committee, Twentieth Century Club, Richmond Hill, L. I. (tel. Richmond Hill 960J). Organized for work along charity organization lines.

Philanthropin Hospital. See JEWISH MEMORIAL HOSPITAL.

Pilgrims Congregational Church, Remsen and Henry Sts., Brooklyn. Rev. Richard Roberts.

Maintains clubs for men, women and children, gymnasium, children's story hour, civic work and other social activities. (See also under CONGREGATIONAL CHURCHES in the Church List.)

Plant and Structures, Department of, City of New York, 18th floor, Municipal Bldg. (tel. Worth 380). Grover A. Whalen, commissioner.

Playground and Recreation Association of America (org. 1906), 1 Madison Ave., N.Y.C. To aid communities through the services of field secretaries, correspondence, conferences and the publishing of literature, to establish year-round municipal recreation systems. Conducts the National Physical Education Service.

Polhemus Memorial Clinic (incorp. 1897), 350–352 Henry St., Brooklyn (tel. Henry 1113). For the medical and surgical care of the poor.

Police Courts. See CITY MAGISTRATES' COURTS.

Police Department, The. Headquarters, 240 Center St., N.Y.C. (tel.

Spring 3100). Richard E. Enright, commissioner.

The functions of this Department are to preserve the public peace, prevent crime, detect and arrest offenders, suppress riots, mobs and insurrections, disperse unlawful or dangerous assemblages, and such as obstruct the free passage of public streets, sidewalks, parks and places; protect the rights of persons and property, guard the public health, preserve order at elections and all public assemblages; regulate, direct, control, restrict, and order the movement of teams, horses, carts, wagons, automobiles, and other vehicles in streets, bridges, squares, parks and public places, for the facilitation of traffic and the convenience and protection of the public.

It is the duty of the Police Department to remove all nuisances in the public streets, parks, and highways; arrest all street mendicants and beggars; provide proper police attendance at fires; assist, advice, and protect emigrants, strangers, and travelers in public streets, at steamboat and ship landings, and at railroad stations; observe and inspect all places of public amusement, all places of business having excise or other licenses to carry on any business; all houses of ill-fame or prostitution, and houses where common prostitutes resort or reside; all ottery offices, policy shops, and all places where lottery tickets or lottery policies are sold or offered for sale; all gambling-houses, cockpits, ratpits, and public common dance houses, and to repress and restrain all unlawful and disorderly conduct or practices therein.

It is the duty of the Police Department to enforce and prevent the violation of all laws and ordinances in force in said city. Its members may arrest all persons guilty of violating any law or ordinance for the suppression or punishment of crimes or offenses. They are required to call ambulances for sick or injured; care for detained witnesses; co-operate with humane Societies, and in general aid and assist other departments of the government in performing functions. The Police Commissioner has authority to maintain and operate telegraph and telephone lines and use same in assisting the Department of Health. The Police Department has general supervision over steam boilers, their inspection, licensing of engineers, runners, and masquerade balls, issuing of parade and pistol permits and permits to hold religious meetings on public thoroughfares, and to lead cattle through the street.

Polish Children's Relief Fund, 44 Morningside Drive. (tel. Cathedral 7669), Mrs. Herbert L. Satterlee, treas.; Miss Zofia Naimska, secy.

Polish National Alliance Immigrant Home (incorp. 1904, est. 1910), 180 Second Ave., N.Y.C. (tel. Stuyvesant 5844). A home for Polish, Lithuanians, and Ruthenians who may not be in a position promptly to locate their relatives or friends; aids and assists them against abuse or oppression; furnishes information and employment; investigates cases of abuse against immigrants and aids them in their complaints or grievances against unlawful treatment.

S. Swierczyuski, manager.

Polyclinic Hospital. See UNITED STATES PUBLIC HEALTH SERVICE.

Poppenhusen Institute (incorp. 1868), Second Ave. and 5th St., College Point, L. I. A free institution for the advancement of science and art. Departments: Drawing and design, mechanical and architectural drawing, mathematics, cabinet making, civil service, commercial branches, gymnastics, dressmaking, embroidery, clubs, etc. Both sexes. Endowed by Conrad Poppenhusen.

John G. Embree, principal.

Port Jefferson Home for Blind, Crippled and Defective Children. See BROOKLYN HOME FOR BLIND, CRIPPLED, etc.

Port Richmond Day Nursery and Central Relief Society (est. 1892), 93 Park Ave., Port Richmond, S. I., N. Y. Cares for children whose mothers have to work by the day. Provides help for really destitute families.

Post-Graduate Hospital. See NEW YORK POST-GRADUATE MEDICAL SCHOOL AND HOSPITAL.

Postal Savings System. See UNITED STATES POSTAL SAVINGS SYSTEM.

Practical Housekeeping Centers. See ASSOCIATION OF PRACTICAL HOUSEKEEPING CENTERS.

Pratt Institute (est. 1887, incorp. 1887), 215 Ryerson St., Brooklyn (tel. Prospect 220). For technical education. Day and evening classes. Has four schools: Fine and Applied Arts, Science and Technology, Household Science and Arts and Library Science.

Frederic B. Pratt, secy.

Presbyterian Board of Foreign Missions (The Board of Foreign Missions of the Presbyterian Church in the U. S. A.; incorp. 1862), 156 Fifth Ave., N.Y.C. (tel. Chelsea 9950). To promote missionary work in foreign lands.

Officers: Rev. George Alexander, D.D., pres.; Robert E. Speer, D.D., Rev. Arthur J. Brown, D.D., Rev A. Woodruff Halsey, D.D., and Rev. Stanley White, D.D., secys.; Dwight H. Day, treas.

Presbyterian Board of Home Missions (Board of Home Missions of the Presbyterian Church in the U.S.A.; incorp. 1872), 156 Fifth Ave., N.Y.C. (tel. Chelsea 9930). To make America Christian for the friendly service of the world.

Officers: Wilton Merle-Smith, D.D., pres.; Fleming H. Revell, vice-pres.; John A. Marquis, D.D., gen. secy.; Baxter P. Fullerton, D.D., secy. in Western Office (St. Louis); John McDowell, secy.; William Robert King, secy.; Varian Banks, asst. treas.; Warren H. Wilson, Ph.D., director Church and Country Life Work; William P. Shriver, D.D., director City and Immigrant Work; H. N. Morse, Director Publicity and Editorial Work; E. Fred Eastman, director of Educational Work.

Presbyterian Church Erection Fund (The Board of the Church Erection Fund of the General Assembly of the Presbyterian Church in the U. S. A., incorp. 1855), 156 Fifth Ave., N.Y.C. Assists feeble congregations to erect houses of worship, chapels, and manses; also aids in the establishment of schools and chapels among the exceptional populations of Mormons, Indians, and foreign speaking people of the United States. A condition of the benefit is the completion of the edifice without debt.

The annual payments in the form of gifts and loans aggregate between $500,000 and $1,000,000. Supported by annual contributions from churches, individuals, legacies and interest of permanent fund.

Officers: Rev. Ford C. Ottman, D.D., pres.; Mr. Wm. H. Parsons, vice-pres.; Rev. David G. Wylie, D.D., LL.D., secy.; Rev. Jesse C. Bruce, D.D., field secy.; Rev. George R. Brauer, treas.

Presbyterian Headquarters for Brooklyn, 32 Court St., Brooklyn.

R. W. Anthony, secy.

Presbyterian Home for Aged Women in the City of New York, The (incorp. 1866), 49 East 73d St., N.Y.C. (tel. Rhinelander 9419).

Officers: Mrs. James E. Ware, pres., 1173 Broadway; Francis B. Griffin, treas., 71 Murray St.; Miss Euphemia M. Olcott, secy., 111 West 13th St.

Presbyterian Hospital in the City of New York, 41 East 70th St., N.Y.C. (tel. Rhinelander 7300). For acute medical and surgical diseases only. Communicable diseases, tuberculosis and chronic cases not admitted. Out-Patient Department. Training School and Registry for Nurses.

Officers: William Sloane, pres.; William M. Kingsley, vice-pres.; Cornelius R. Agnew, treas., 16 William St.; Matthew C. Fleming, secy.; Charles H. Young, M.D., supt.

Presbyterian Union of Brooklyn and Vicinity. Organized to promote sociability among members of Presbyterian churches and to emphasize and support Christian leadership in civic, business, and social affairs.

W. F. Atkinson, pres., 44 Court St., Brooklyn.

Prescott Memorial. See FIRST UNIVERSALIST MISSION SOCIETY.

Presentation Day Nursery and Settlement of Blessed Virgin Mary (incorp. 1904), 230 East 32d St., N.Y.C. (tel. Murray Hill 5581). To care for children of working and widowed mothers; also, temporary night shelter.

Presiding Bishop and Council, The (adopted 1919) of the Protestant Episcopal Church, 281 Fourth Ave., N.Y.C. (tel. Gramercy 3012). Exercises all the powers of the Domestic and Foreign Missionary Society, has charge of the unification, development and prosecution of the work of missions, church extension, religious education and Christian social service.

Right Rev. T. F. Gailor, D.D., president of the Council; Lewis B. Franklin, treas.; Rev. F. J. Clark, secy.

Presser Foundation, The, Johnson and Jefferson Sts., Germantown, Philadelphia, Pa. An endowed institution for the relief and care of distressed or aged musicians and music teachers, and the education, through scholarships, of deserving students of music.

James Francis Cooke, pres.

Preventorium, The. See TUBERCULOSIS PREVENTORIUM FOR CHILDREN.

***Pringle Memorial Home** (incorp. 1899), 153 Academy St., Poughkeepsie, N. Y. A home for respectable, aged, indigent men, especially educated or literary men. Non-sectarian.

Prison Association of New York (founded 1844, incorp. 1846), 135 East 15th St., N.Y.C. (tel. Stuyvesant 1470). A charitable organization devoted to the study, treatment and prevention of crime, and the rehabilitation of offenders. The Association receives no public money, but is supported entirely by voluntary contributions. It has an unbroken record of activity since 1844.

The following bureaus of activity are maintained: Probation, Parole, Relief, Employment, Inspection of Institutions, Advice and Information, Prevention of Juvenile Delinquency. The chief objects of the Association are the following: 1. The protection of society against crime; 2. The reformation of the criminal; 3. Protection for those unjustly accused; 4. Probation when advisable for first offenders; 5. Proper use of parole; 6. Improvement in prisons and prison administration; 7. Employment and other assistance to released prisoners; 8. Necessary aid to prisoners' families; 9. Needed legislation; 10. Maintaining of a clearing-

* *Current information not received.*

house on penological and criminological matters; 11. Publicity and educational campaigns in the field of prison reform; 12. Furthering of co-operative community movement for the reduction and prevention of delinquency. The Prison Association may be called upon for advice, information and assistance in all matters relative to the treatment of crime and criminals.

Particularly in the cases of application of alleged ex-prisoners for assistance should the Prison Association be consulted by those thus approached, because great injustice may be done to the one applied to, or perhaps to the one applying, in case the full facts are not known. The Prison Association is ready at all times to verify statements, obtain additional facts, and in general to advise in matters of employment of men who have been in prison.

Officers: Eugene Smith, pres.; Robert W. De Forest, Thomas Mott Osborne, George W. Kirchwey, George W. Wickersham, vice-prests.; C. C. Auchincloss, treas., 135 East 15th St.; Decatur M. Sawyer, secy.; O. F. Lewis, gen. secy.; E. R. Cass, asst. gen. secy.

Executive Committee: Ira Barrows, B. Ogden Chisolm, J. Fenimore Cooper, Mrs. James F. Curtis, Fulton Cutting, J. E. Davis, William H. Gratwick, Henry G. Gray, Henry E. Gregory, Alexander M. Hadden, E. Trowbridge Hall, Edwin O. Holter, Richard M. Hurd, Frank D. Pavey, Wilson M. Powell, Mrs. George T. Rice, Dean Sage, John Seely Ward, Mornay Williams.

Probation Bureau, City Magistrates' Courts, City of New York. Edwin J. Cooley, Chief Probation Officer. General administrative charge of all the probation work of the Magistrates' Courts of the five boroughs, 300 Mulberry Street, Manhattan (tel. Spring 9420, after 4.30 P. M. Spring 5529).

Central Office, Manhattan, 300 Mulberry St. (tel. Spring 9420). George J. Lavender, Deputy Chief Probation Officer. General supervision over the probation work in Manhattan and Bronx. Investigates and receives on probation all cases from the District Courts, Manhattan. This office carries a central index file covering the work of all the boroughs.

Central Office, Brooklyn, 44 Court St. (tel. Main 7411). John T. Coffey, Deputy Chief Probation Officer. General supervision over the probation work in Brooklyn, Queens and Richmond. Investigates and receives on probation cases from the District Courts of Brooklyn. This office carries a central index file covering the work of the three boroughs.

FAMILY COURT OFFICE, MANHATTAN, 151 East 57th St. (tel. Plaza 2302). Joseph J. Mackey, Probation Officer in charge. Investigates and supervises all cases of domestic difficulties coming to the Domestic Relations Court.

BRONX DISTRICT PROBATION OFFICE, 1014 East 181st St. (tel. Fordham 2787-8429). Maurice E. Stafford, Probation Officer in charge. Investigates and supervises all cases from the Domestic Relations Court and the District Courts of the Borough.

WOMEN'S COURT, MANHATTAN, 125 Sixth Ave. (tel. Chelsea 1051). Miss Alice C. Smith, Probation Officer in charge. Investigates and receives on probation all cases of women arising in the Women's Court and the District Courts in the Boroughs of Manhattan and Bronx.

FAMILY COURT OFFICE, BROOKLYN, 402 Myrtle Ave. (tel. Prospect 2700). Frank L. Graves, Probation Officer in charge. Investigates and supervises all cases of domestic difficulties coming to the Domestic Relations Court.

QUEENS DISTRICT PROBATION OFFICE, Fourth District Magistrates' Court, Town Hall, Fulton St., Jamaica (tel. Jamaica 517). Investigates and receives on probation all cases arising in the four District Courts. Includes also cases of non-support.

RICHMOND DISTRICT PROBATION OFFICER, Second District City Magistrates' Court, Village Hall, Stapleton, S. I. (tel. Tompkinsville 1150). Investigates and receives on probation all cases arising in the two District Courts. Includes also cases of non-support.

Probation Officers are provided for by Article 6, chapter 659, Laws of New York, 1910. They are in the competitive class of the Civil Service. Examinations are held by the Municipal Civil Service Commission. The Probation Law provides that no police officer shall be designated as a probation officer. The probation officers conduct, at the direction of the Magistrates, preliminary investigations of defendants prior to sentence. They receive on probation and exercise supervision over cases of delinquents convicted of nonsupport of families, disorderly conduct, public intoxication, vagrancy, soliciting and kindred offenses.

Professional Children's School. See REHEARSAL CLUB.

Prospect Heights Hospital and Brooklyn Maternity and New York State School for Training Nurses (incorp. 1871), cor. Washington Ave. and St. Johns Pl., Brooklyn (tel. Prospect 152). Physicians of either school of medicine in good standing may enter patients.

TRAINING SCHOOL FOR NURSES.

Prospect Hill Day Nursery (est. 1915), 2 Prospect Pl., N.Y.C. (tel. Murray Hill 8984). For children under five years of age. Capacity, twenty-four.

Protestant Episcopal City Missions. See DOMESTIC AND FOREIGN MISSIONARY SOCIETY OF THE PROTESTANT EPISCOPAL CHURCH.

Protestant Episcopal City Mission Society. See NEW YORK PROTESTANT EPISCOPAL CITY MISSION SOCIETY.

Protestant Episcopal Social Service Commission. See SOCIAL SERVICE COMMISSION, DIOCESE OF NEW YORK, PROTESTANT EPISCOPAL.

Protestant Episcopal Society for Promoting Religion and Learning in the State of New York, The (incorp. 1839). For purposes indicated in its title.

Officers: Wm. Harison, treas., 43 Cedar St.; Rev. Lawrence T. Cole, D.D., supt. and secy., 147 West 91st St.

Provident Loan Society of New York, The (incorp. by special act of Legislature, 1894). Executive Office: Fourth Ave. at 25th St., N.Y.C. (tel. Madison Sq. 6830). (See advertisement.)

Fourth Ave. Office, 346 Fourth Ave., N.Y.C.

Eldridge St. Office, 186 Eldridge St., N.Y.C.

Times Sq. Office, 736 Seventh Ave., N.Y.C.

Mt. Morris Office, 124th St. and Lexington Ave., N.Y.C.

Grand St. Office, 409 Grand St., N.Y.C.

East 72d St. Office, 180 East 72d St., N.Y.C.

East Houston St. Office, East Houston and Essex Sts.

Eighth Ave. Office, cor. 127th St. and Eighth Ave., N.Y.C.

City Hall Office, 55 Chambers St.

Bronx Office, 148th St. and Courtlandt Ave., N.Y.C.

Brooklyn Office, Smith and Livingston Aves., Brooklyn.

Williamsburg Office, 24 Graham Ave., Brooklyn.

Brownsville Office, Pitkin and Rockaway Aves., Brooklyn.

The Provident Loan Society was organized as the result of efforts initiated by the Charity Organization Society of the City of New York, to do a general pawnbroking business. Loans on pledges of personal property at the rate of 1 per cent. a month. Loans repaid within two weeks, one-half per cent.

Officers of Board of Trustees: Otto T. Bannard, pres.; Mortimer L. Schiff, treas.; George S. Brewster, secy.

Executive Officers: Frank Tucker, Arthur H. Ham, Frederick L. Leining, vice-presidents; Harald A. Lange, asst. treas.; Charles Schimko, asst. secy.; Ernest Bing, cashier.

Public Buildings and Offices, Bureau of, BOROUGH OF MANHATTAN, Municipal Bldg. (tel. Worth 4227). Has charge of public buildings and offices, interior free public bath buildings, public comfort stations and free floating baths.

The interior baths are open from 6 A. M. to 10 P. M. from June 1 to November 1; 7 A. M. to 10 P. M. from November 15 to June 1. White or gray bathing suits only are permitted.

Those marked with a dagger (†) have swimming pools.

INTERIOR BATHS

†The Dr. Simon Baruch Bath, 326 Rivington St.
133 Allen St.
538 East 11th St
†23d St. and Avenue A.
347 West 41st St.
†232 West 60th St.
†407 West 28th St.
523 East 76th St.
243 East 109th St.
83 Carmine St.
Cor. Cherry and Oliver Sts.
†5–7 Rutgers Pl.
†342 East 54th St.

They are allotted for the use of men and women on alternate days as follows:

23d Street Bath.—Women: Mondays, Thursdays, and Saturdays. Men: Tuesdays, Wednesdays, and Fridays.

28th Street Bath.—Women: Mondays, Thursdays and Saturdays. Men: Tuesdays, Wednesdays, and Fridays.

60th Street Bath.—Women: Tuesdays, Wednesdays, and Fridays. Men: Mondays, Thursdays, and Saturdays.

Rutgers Place Bath.—Women: Tuesdays, Thursdays, and Saturdays. Men: Mondays, Wednesdays, and Fridays.

Rivington Street Bath.—Women: Mondays, Wednesdays, and Fridays. Men: Tuesdays, Thursdays, and Saturdays.

East 54th Street Bath.—Men: Daily except Sundays. Women: Daily, except Sundays.

PUBLIC COMFORT STATIONS

Battery Park.
Hanover Square.
City Hall Park, Mail St.
Chatham Square.
Sheriff and Delancey Sts.
Greeley Square.
Longacre Square.
125th St. and Park Ave.
125th St. and First Ave.
Abingdon Square.
129th St. and Third Ave.
Queensboro Bridge.

FREE FLOATING BATHS

North River at the Battery, two baths; West 99th St., one bath; West 130th St., one bath.

East River, Pike St., East 10th St.,

East 90th St. and East 120th St., one bath each.

At the Battery one bath is open daily for men and the other for women. At all the other points the baths are open for men on Tuesday, Thursday, Saturday and Sunday mornings, and for women on Monday, Wednesday, Friday and Sunday afternoons. The floating baths are open during the months of July, August, and to October from 5 A. M. to 9 P. M. Boys and girls under the age of fifteen are admitted only between 7 A. M. and 6 P. M. Admission is free, but may be refused for sanitary, police, or disciplinary reason. White or gray bathing suits only are permitted.

Public Buildings and Offices, Bureau of, BOROUGH OF BROOKLYN, Terminal Bldg. (tel. Main 9100). Has in charge seven interior baths, seven public comfort stations. Assignments are made by the Superintendent of Public Buildings and Offices for Brooklyn.

INTERIOR BATHS

Hicks St., near Degraw St.
Pitkin Ave., near Watkins St.
Montrose Ave., near Union Ave.
Huron St., near Manhattan Ave.
Concord St., near Duffield St.
Nostrand and Myrtle Aves.
Fourth Ave. and President St.
Hamburg and Willoughby Aves.

Coney Island Bath has accommodation for almost 6,000 bathers.

PUBLIC COMFORT STATIONS

Fulton and Joralemon Sts.
Hamilton Ave. and Richards St.
East New York and Liberty Aves.
Pulaski St. and Reid Ave.
Lorimer St. and Broadway.
Manhattan and Greenpoint Aves.
Williamsburg Bridge Plaza.

Public Buildings and Offices, Bureau of, BOROUGH OF QUEENS, Queens Subway Bldg., Long Island City (tel. Hunters Point 5400).

Interior Bath for Men and Women, 8th St. between Vernon and East Aves., Long Island City. Open daily, between 7 A. M. and 11 P. M.

Public Charities. See PUBLIC WELFARE DEPARTMENT, CITY OF NEW YORK.

Public Education Association of the City of New York (founded 1895, incorp. 1899), 8 West 40th St. (tel. Vanderbilt 4485-6). To organize and represent sound public opinion in regard to public education, and to seek the better adaptation of the public school system to the needs of the community. The work is carried out through a trained staff and volunteer standing committees. The results are presented to the public through reports, bulletins, leaflets, public conferences and discussion in the daily press. It maintains among other activities a Psychologist, at work on the grading problem in P. S. 64, Manhattan; a staff of visiting teachers, who are assigned to public schools in Manhattan and the Bronx; and the

TOMBS SCHOOL, The Tombs, Center St., between White and Leonard Sts., which offers general, non-religious instruction to inmates of the Boys' Department. Visitors must obtain a pass from the Department of Correction.

Officers: Charles P. Howland, pres., 37 Wall St.; Mrs. Miriam Sutro Price, chrm. Exec. Com., 307 West 93d St.; W. K. Brice, treas., 60 Wall St.; Howard W. Nudd, director, 8 West 40th St.; George Marvin, principal Tombs School; Jane F. Culbert, executive of the Visiting Teacher Staff.

Public Forum. See FORUMS, in the Subject Index.

Public Health Committee of the New York Academy of Medicine, The (org. 1911), 17 West 43d St., N.Y.C. (tel. Vanderbilt 2094). Objects: 1. To study the city budget as it relates to the medical needs of the community. 2. To promote efficiency in hospital administration. 3. To stimulate interest and co-operation in the public health movement in all its aspects. The Committee aims to act as a clearing house for public health activities, advising the medical profession of current activities in public health conditions, and to give an authoritative medical opinion on public health matters.

Executive Committee: Chas. L. Dana, M.D., chrm.; James Alex. Miller, M.D., secy.; John S. Billings, M.D., Nathan E. Brill, M.D., Lewis F. Frissell, M.D., John A. Hartwell, M.D., Frederick E. Sondern, M.D., W. Gilman Thompson, M.D., Philip Van Ingen, M.D., Herbert B. Wilcox, M.D., E. H. Lewinski-Corwin, Ph.D., exec. secy.

Public Improvement Bureau. See BOARD OF ESTIMATE AND APPORTIONMENT, CITY OF NEW YORK.

Public Kitchen Committee. See ASSOCIATION FOR IMPROVING THE CONDITION OF THE POOR, Bureau of Welfare of School Children.

Public Schools Athletic League of the City of New York (incorp. 1903), 157 East 67th St., N.Y.C. Aims to provide suitable athletics for every school boy in the City, believing that this will result in increased general health, suitable recreation, proper neuro-muscular education and training in practical civics. To this end it has organized class athletics, the athletic badge test, and conducts seasons in track and field athletics, baseball, basketball, soccer, foot ball, swimming, cross-country, marksmanship and tennis. Supported wholly by voluntary contributions.

Officers: Gen. Geo. W. Wingate, pres.; S. R. Guggenheim, treas.; C. L. Myers, asst. treas., 120 Broadway; A. K. Aldinger, M.D., secy.

GIRLS' BRANCH, PUBLIC SCHOOLS ATHLETIC LEAGUE (est. 1905), 157 East 67th St. Aims to provide wholesome after-school recreative exercise for all public school girls and secure facilities and supervision for the same. To this end, it conducts free instruction classes in folk dancing and girls' athletics, for all public school teachers, who will organize and conduct girls' athletic clubs after school hours. It promotes such activities as hockey, tennis, basketball and swimming, by securing suitable places to carry on these activities, and by training and arranging for coaches for this work. Supported by voluntary contributions.

Officers: Miss Catherine S. Leverich, pres.; Mrs. John Garrett Underhill, treas.; Mrs. Gustavus T. Kirby, secy.; Miss Emily A. O'Keefe, exec. secy.

Public Service Commission of the First District, 49 Lafayette St., N.Y.C. (tel. Franklin 5820). Lewis Nixon, commissioner; James B. Walker, secy.

Public Welfare Department, City of New York (est. Chap. 912, Laws of 1895; powers outlined Chap. XIII, 1900). Principal office: tenth floor, Municipal Bldg., N.Y.C. (tel. Worth 4440).

Bird S. Coler, commissioner; Stephen A. Nugent, 1st deputy; Patrick J. Carlin, 2d deputy; Christopher J. Dunn, 3d deputy; Dr. John F. Fitzgerald, gen. medical supt.; Mary C. Tinney, gen. inspector; J. McKee Borden, secy.; Edgar Pitske, private secy.

BOROUGH OFFICES

Manhattan, 124 East 59th St. (tel. Plaza 8731). Frederick E. Bauer.

Bronx, Bergen Bldg., 177th St. and Tremont Ave., Bronx (tel. Tremont 798). Mrs. Mary O'Connor.

Brooklyn, 327 Schermerhorn St., (tel. Sterling 1677). Wm. Heaton.

Queens, Town Hall, Flushing, L. I., Queens (tel. Flushing 1081). Miss Mary E. Davies.

Richmond, Borough Hall, St. George, S. I., Richmond (tel. Tompkinsville 1000). Miss E. McGowan.

The department of Public Welfare has charge of all the charitable institutions of the City Government except Bellevue and Allied Hospitals, the Otisville Sanitarium, and the hospitals for contagious diseases of the Department of Health. The Commissioner of Public Welfare is overseer of the poor of the City of New York.

The STATE POOR LAW provides:

Art. 1, Sec. 2.

A "poor person" is one unable to maintain himself and such a person shall be maintained by the town, city, county, or State............ The Town Poor are such persons as are required by law to be maintained or supported at the expense of the town or city; and the State Poor are such persons as are required by law to be relieved or supported at the expense of the State.

Art. 4, Sec. 40.

Every person of full age who shall be a resident and inhabitant of any town or city over one year and the members of his family who shall not have gained a separate settlement shall be deemed settled in such town or city and shall so remain until he shall have gained a like settlement in some other town or city in this State or shall remove from this State and remain therefrom one year. A minor may be emancipated from his father and mother and gain a separate settlement (under certain specified conditions).

Art. 4, Sec. 42.

...............every poor person, except the State poor, shall be supported in the town or county where they may be.............

Art. 7, Sec. 90.

Any Poor Person who shall not have resided sixty (60) days in any county in this state within one year preceding the time of an application by him for aid to any superintendent or overseer of the poor or other officer charged with the support and relief of poor persons, shall be deemed to be a State poor person........ The State Board of Charities shall ....contract........with the authorities of not more than fifteen counties or cities of this State for the reception and support in the alms houses of such counties or cities respectively, of such (State) poor persons who shall be committed thereto.

The STATE CHARITIES LAW provides as follows:

The State Board of Charities...... may cause to be removed to the state or county from which he came any non-resident or alien poor found in any institution (subject to its supervision).

BUREAU OF INVESTIGATION, BOARDING OUT AND INSPECTIONS

DIRECTOR'S OFFICE: 10th floor, Municipal Bldg., N.Y.C. (tel. Worth 4440). Victor S. Dodworth, director.

All cases of destitution in need of public relief may be referred to the nearest office. Provision will there be made for temporary or permanent care or relief. The bureau places in private homes, both boarding and free, children up to seven years of age, who are committed to the Department of Public Welfare for support. It inspects public charitable institutions and those maintained by private organizations receiving money from the City of New York for the care and support of public charges.

Poor Adult Blind citizens of good character who have lived in New York

City continuously for two years preceding application for aid, and who are not inmates of any city institution may receive annually a share of a special appropriation made for their support. This amount averages about $50.00 a year for each person.

The Tuberculosis Hospital Admission Bureau (q. v.) conducted by the Department of Public Welfare makes all admissions to tuberculosis hospitals, sanatoria, and preventoria.

Institutions

Municipal Lodging House, 432 East 25th St., Manhattan (tel. Madison Sq. 977). For the temporary accommodation of homeless men and women.

Dispossessed families, mothers with babies, the sick, and the aged are given special care.

Edward E. McMahon, supt.

The City Mortuary, at 29th St. and First Ave., is a central receiving Mortuary for all of the dead of Greater New York.

Michael J. Rickard, supt.

Blackwell's Island

New York City Home for Aged and Infirm, Blackwell's Island (tel. Plaza 8150). For destitute persons unable to earn a livelihood and whose relatives, within the required degree, are unable to support them.

Advisory Committee: Rev. C. P. Tinker, pres.; Rev. Sydney N. Ussher, vice-pres.; S. Jane Manahan, secy. and treas. (tels. Spring 989 or Plaza 8150, Ex. 38).

Central and Neurological Hospital. A department of the Home (Manhattan Division) receives indigent adults suffering from nervous diseases.

Cornelius B. Cosgrove, supt.

City Hospital, Blackwell's Island. For the care of dependent sick and injured, except those having contagious diseases. The hospital operates on alternate days, in connection with the Metropolitan Hospital, first-aid and emergency ambulance service at the Reception Hospital, Blackwell's Island, entrance from Queensboro Bridge (tel. Plaza 8150, 7160).

Dr. Charles B. Bacon, medical supt.; Mrs. Katherine D. Ermold, head worker of Social Service Department.

The City Hospital School of Nursing (registered by the University of the State of New York). Course, two years and six months, including three months' preparatory term. Minimum requirements, one year of High School or equivalent. Allowance, $28.66 per month. first year; $31.66 per month, remainder of course.

Theodora H. Le Febvra, principal.

Metropolitan Hospital, Blackwell's Island. Medical, surgical, gynecological, maternity, skin, eye, ear, throat, nose, genito-urinary, erysipelas, and leprosy wards. Admission through Reception Hospital, Blackwell's Island, entrance from Queensboro Bridge (tel. Plaza 7500).

Dr. Walter H. Conley, medical supt.

Children's Division, provides for all diseases including whooping cough and vaginitis. Admission through Reception Hospital, Blackwell's Island, entrance from Queensboro Bridge (tel. Plaza 7500).

Tuberculosis Division, receives all classes, ages, and conditions of patients suffering from tuberculosis. Admission is made through the Tuberculosis Hospital Admission Bureau (q. v.).

Metropolitan Hospital Training School for Nurses (registered by the University of the State of New York). Provides a course of two years and six months including two months' probationary term.

Sabra H. Datesman, supt.

Social Service Bureau, headquarters, Metropolitan Hospital (est. 1911). To look after the social needs of the patients in the hospitals of the Department of Public Welfare. The work includes convalescent relief, child welfare, maternity work.

Jessy C. Palmer, Chief of Bureau.

RANDALL'S ISLAND

THE NEW YORK CITY CHILDREN'S HOSPITAL AND SCHOOL, Randall's Island, reached by ferry from East 125th St. (tel. Harlem 6754). Admits for observation cases of children over two years who are mentally defective or epileptic and offers recommendation, treatment and training. Receives applications for and transfers to Craig Colony (epileptics) and Rome State School for Mental Defectives, Letchworth Village, Syracuse State School for Mental Defectives, Newark State School for Mental Defectives. Applicants for these may be admitted pending transfer.

THE MENTAL CLINIC, at Post-graduate Medical School and Hospital, 303 East 20th St., is an integral part of the institution. It is also the admission bureau and the out-patient department of the institution. Open mornings, except Wednesday and Sunday, 9 to 11. It is held at the Cumberland Street Hospital, Brooklyn, on Tuesdays and Wednesdays, 9 to 11.

Dr. John S. Richards, medical director

BROOKLYN

NEW YORK CITY HOME FOR THE AGED AND INFIRM, Brooklyn Division, Clarkson Ave., Flatbush, Brooklyn (tel. Flatbush 4000). Non-resident poor who have no settlement in any other county of the state are also admitted to this home.

Dr. Mortimer D. Jones, medical supt.

KINGS COUNTY HOSPITAL, Clarkson Ave., Brooklyn (tel. Flatbush 4000). For all cases of destitute sick, except contagious diseases. Dispensary for medical and surgical treatment of outdoor poor, open from 8-10 A. M.

Dr. Mortimer D. Jones, supt.; Lucy A. Connelly, head worker Social Service Dept.

BRADFORD STREET HOSPITAL, 113 Bradford St., East New York (tel. East New York 240). A branch of the Kings County Hospital for emergency cases of the destitute sick, excepting contagious diseases. Dispensary, open from 8-10 A. M.

CONEY ISLAND HOSPITAL, Ocean Parkway and Avenue Z, Brooklyn (tel. Coney Island 1141). For all cases except contagious diseases.

Dr. Adam Eberle, deputy medical and acting supt.

CUMBERLAND STREET HOSPITAL (Homeopathic), 109 Cumberland Street near Myrtle Ave., Brooklyn (tel. Prospect 1300). For all cases of destitute sick except contagious diseases. Visiting days, Tuesdays, Thursdays, and Saturdays, 2-4 P. M.; Sundays and holidays, 12 M.-4 P. M. Dispensary daily, except Sundays and holidays, from 2-4 P. M.

Wm. F. Jacobs, M.D., deputy med. and acting supt;. Bessie A. Vojik, head worker Social Service Dept.

GREENPOINT HOSPITAL, Kingsland Ave. and Jackson St., Brooklyn (tel. Greenpoint 4431). For treatment of acute cases, except contagious diseases. Medical, Surgical, and Gynecological-Obstetrical services. Maintains an Isolation Hospital for temporary detention of contagious diseases. General dispensary from 9 A. M.-4 P. M., Monday, Wednesday, and Friday of each week. Visiting days: Thursday, Sunday and holidays, from 2-3 P. M.; no children under fourteen years of age admitted as visitors to any ward. No visitors admitted to children's service except in serious cases.

Raymond G. Loub, M.D., deputy med. and acting supt.; Ethel B. MacQueen, head worker Social Service Dept.

STATEN ISLAND

SEA VIEW HOSPITAL AND SANATORIUM, Castleton Corners, West New Brighton, S. I. (tel. New Dorp 360). Cover a tract of 367 acres. Maintain ambulance service to all parts of Staten Island. Comprise the following divisions:

THE SANATORIUM for the care of tubercular patients; capacity, 750. For admission to this division, apply to the Tuberculosis Hospital Admission Bureau (q. v.)

New York City Farm Colony for semi-able-bodied men in destitute circumstances. Employs its beneficiaries in farming, gardening, building, road-making, in broom-making and printing, and in the general work of the institution.

The Cottages for aged and infirm couples, widows, and single women. The residents in these cottages are cared for in individual sleeping rooms, each cottage having its own sitting room, dining room and kitchen. For admission to this division, apply to the Bureau of Social Investigations, Municipal Bldg., New York, or to one of the district offices.

The Psychopathic Service for the reception of alleged insane of the Borough of Richmond.

G. Kremer, M.D., director.

HART'S ISLAND

CITY CEMETERY, Hart's Island, for the burial of the destitute poor, friendless, or unclaimed dead of the city.

Puritan Chapel Branch of Tompkins Ave. Congregational Church, Marcy and Lafayette Aves., Brooklyn. Rev. Ernest E. Youtz, Pastor. Maintains kindergarten, clubs, lectures, entertainments, etc., and does relief work and fresh air work.

Q

Queens County Chapter American Red Cross. See AMERICAN RED CROSS IN GREATER NEW YORK.

Queens County Prison, Jackson Ave. and Court Sq., L. I. C. See CORRECTION, DEPARTMENT OF.

Queensboro Society for the Prevention of Cruelty to Children, Inc. (est. and incorp. 1920), Butler Bldg., Fulton St. and Twombly Place, Jamaica, L. I. (tel. Jamaica 614).

Officers: H. P. Williams, pres., Bridge Plaza, North, Long Island City; C. G. M. Thomas, treas., 130 East 15th St., N.Y.C.; Alexander Dienst, secy., Front and Pidgeon Sts., Long Island City.

R

Rainbow House. See VOLUNTEERS OF AMERICA.

Ray Brook Sanitarium for Tuberculosis. See STATE HOSPITAL FOR TREATMENT OF INCIPIENT PULMONARY TUBERCULOSIS.

Reception Bureau of the Charity Organization Society, 105 East 22d St., N.Y.C. Miss S. F. Burrows, agent. See CHARITY ORGANIZATION SOCIETY.

Reception Hospital, Department of Health, foot of East 16th St., N.Y.C. See HEALTH, DEPARTMENT OF.

Reception Hospital, Department of Public Welfare, Queensboro Bridge, foot of East 70th St. See PUBLIC WELFARE DEPARTMENT, City Hospital.

Reconstruction Commission, State of New York (est. 1919), Room

302, Hall of Records, N.Y.C. (tel. Worth 5067). Appointed by Governor Alfred E. Smith to consider after-war problems.

Officers: John G. Agar, chrm. Executive Committee; Charles H. Sabin treas.; Mrs. Henry Moskowitz, secy.

Reconstruction Educational Alliance, Inc. (est. 1918), 21 East 40th St., N.Y.C. (tel. Vanderbilt 3626). A non-partisan, non-profit making organization for the collection and dissemination of constructive knowledge for meeting the needs of new world conditions. It works in co-operation with other movements for mental and material reconstruction.

E. F. Bailey, secy.

Recreation Piers. See PUBLIC BUILDINGS AND OFFICES, BUREAU OF.

Recreation Rooms and Settlement (1898), 186–188 Chrystie St., N.Y.C. (tel. Orchard 4415). General settlement and neighborhood work, gymnasium, roof garden, visiting nurse and maternity center. Maintains summer vacation house Central Valley, New York.

Officers: Mrs. Cyrus L. Sulzberger, pres., 516 West End Ave.; Mrs. Emil Frenkel, treas., 8 East 81st St.; Mrs. H. A. Guinzburg, secy., 115 West 86th St.; Josephine Schain, head worker.

Red Cross. See AMERICAN RED CROSS, NATIONAL; also AMERICAN RED CROSS IN GREATER NEW YORK.

Red Cross Emergency Relief Committee of the Charity Organization Society (created in 1909), 105 East 22d St., N.Y.C. See CHARITY ORGANIZATION SOCIETY.

Red Cross Hospital. See PARK HOSPITAL.

Reformatory of Misdemeanants. See CORRECTION, DEPARTMENT OF.

Reformed Church Board of Direction (Board of Direction of the General Synod of the Reformed Church in America), 25 East 22d St., N.Y.C.

Reformed Church Board of Domestic Missions (The Board of Domestic Missions of the Reformed Church in America; org. 1830, incorp. 1866), 25 East 22d St., N.Y.C. To aid weak, and found new churches of the denomination. Controlled by the General Synod. Supported by contributions.

Reformed Church Foreign Missions Board (The Board of Foreign Missions of the Reformed Church in America; org. 1832, incorp. 1860), 25 East 22d St., N.Y.C. For maintenance of the foreign missions of the Reformed Church in Arabia, China, India, and Japan. Supported by voluntary contributions. Last year's receipts, $461,-105.07; expenditures, $502,837.32; permanent funds, $397,056.18.

Officers: Rev. Henry E. Cobb, D.D., pres.; Rev. W. I. Chamberlain, Ph.D., foreign secy.; F. M. Potter, associate secy. and treas.

Reformed Church Publication and Bible-school Work (Board of Publication and Bible-school Work of the Reformed Church in America; org. 1854, incorp. 1856), 25 East 22d St., N.Y.C. Publishes "The Intelligencer," Church and Sunday-school literature for sale and for distribution to poor churches, Sunday-schools, missions, missionaries, and seminaries.

Officers: Rev. Ferdinand S. Wilson, pres.; John F. Chambers, treas.; Rev. I. W. Gowen, D.D., secy.; Rev. Abram Duryee, ed. secy.; Lucius W. Hine, business agent.

Regina Angelorum Working Girls' Home. See INSTITUTION OF MERCY.

Registration Bureau of the Charity Organization Society, 105 East 22d St., N.Y.C. See CHARITY ORGANIZATION SOCIETY.

Rehearsal Club (est. 1913, incorp. 1914), 335 West 45th St., N.Y.C. Maintains a club, bedrooms, and a cafeteria lunch for the women and children of the stage. Also maintains

THE PROFESSIONAL CHILDREN'S SCHOOL, 227 West 48th St., approved by the Board of Education.

Officers: Mrs. Franklin W. Robinson, pres.; William A. Greer, treas.; Mrs. Monroe D. Robinson, secy.

***Reinsdorf Maternity Society** (est. and incorp. 1915). 9th St. Branch Public Library, 9th St. and Sixth Ave., Brooklyn. To give material, financial and medical aid to all needy maternity cases. Supported by membership dues.

Relief Committee for Greeks in Asia Minor. See NEAR EAST RELIEF.

Religious Education Association, The (org. and incorp. 1903). Headquarters, 1440 East 57th St., Chicago, Ill. Purpose: The improvement of religious education, through existing agencies, by conventions, conferences, investigations, publications, exhibits, bureau of information, and individual and institutional counsel. Aids churches, schools, church boards, and individuals. All service free. Nonsectarian; international. Fee $4 annually. Members receive all publications.

Henry F. Cope, gen. secy.

Religious Society of Friends, East 15th St. and Rutherford Pl., N.Y.C. (tel. Stuyvesant 1005), and 110 Schermerhorn St., Brooklyn (tel. Main 4228). Office hours: New York, 9 A. M. to 12 M., Monday and Wednesday; 1.30-5 P. M., Friday; Brooklyn office hours 9 A. M. to 12 M., Tuesdays and Thursdays. Anna L. Curtis, secy. Maintains the

FRIENDS' EMPLOYMENT SOCIETY OF NEW YORK (org. 1862, incorp. 1902), which gives sewing to poor women. Mrs. E. E. Bennett, asst. supt., 139 East 16th St., N.Y.C.

YOUNG FRIENDS' AID ASSOCIATION (org. 1873, incorp. 1890), which gives unsectarian, temporary aid to poor families. Miss Jennie C. Kitchin, pres.; J. Hibberd Taylor, treas., 104 West 42d St., N.Y.C.

FRIENDLY HAND ASSOCIATION, which gives unsectarian, temporary relief to poor families. Daniel T. Merritt, pres., 418 Grand Ave., Brooklyn; Caroline J. Titus, secy., 56 Fort Greene Pl.; Robert Underhill, treas., 1099 East 18th St., Brooklyn.

FREE KINDERGARTEN AND VACATION SCHOOL, July and August, 16th St. and Rutherford Pl.

FREE PLAYGROUND AND VACATION SCHOOL during July and August, 110 Schermerhorn St., Brooklyn.

FRIENDS' REFERENCE LIBRARY, at each meeting-house. Open to visitors.

Rescue Society, Inc., The (est. 1893, incorp. 1912), 5-7 Doyers St., N.Y.C. Office: 126 Bible House (tel. Stuyvesant 4340). Combines mission and settlement work. Maintains The Chinatown and Bowery Settlement for Girls, 10 Mott St., also clubs and classes for boys, girls, and mothers. Has a kindergarten, gives vacations and outings in summer; furnishes legal assistance and medical help when necessary. Does personal work among unfortunate girls and drug addicts. Conducts religious services nightly at 10 P. M. for the reclaiming of destitute and homeless men and women; also hospital and prison work. Undenominational. Supported by voluntary contributions.

* *Current information not received.*

Officers: Dr. Thomas H. Spence, pres.; Edward M. Waring, vice-pres.; James B. Nimmons, treas., 36 West 37th St.; T. J. Noonan, secy, and supt.

Rest for Convalescents, The (incorp. 1893), 69 N. Broadway, White Plains, Westchester Co. To provide temporary shelter and care for worthy Protestant women who are discharged from hospitals, or who need rest and are properly recommended. Capacity, seventy. The time of sojourn will be two weeks, unless otherwise ordered by the Board of Managers. Each applicant for admission must be a Protestant over fifteen years of age, and must furnish satisfactory evidence of good character, and a certificate signed by a physician if she is a convalescent.

Officers: Mrs. John P. Duncan, pres., Hotel Plaza, N.Y.C.; Mrs. Charles F. MacLean, 130th St. and Fifth Ave., N.Y.C.; Mrs. A. F. Schauffler, 400 Park Ave., vice-prests.; Mrs. Alexander MacLean, treas., Hotel Gramatan, Bronxville, N. Y.; Mrs. Howard Duffield, secy., 20 Fifth Ave., N.Y.C. Apply by letter to the Committee on Admissions or any of the officers.

Rethmore Home. See New York Protestant Episcopal City Mission Society.

Retired Music Teachers' Home. See Presser Foundation.

Rhinelander School for Crippled Children. See Children's Aid Society.

Richmond County Society for the Prevention of Cruelty to Children, Castleton Ave., Tompkinsville, N. Y. (tel. Tompkinsville 997). Investigates and prosecutes all cases of cruelty or neglect of children under sixteen years of age. Also shelters children remanded by the Children's Court; brought by the police or agents of the Society. Shelter open day and night. Society supported by subscriptions and contributions.

Mrs. S. McKee Smith, supt., 111 Far View Ave., New Brighton, S. I.

Richmond Hill Baptist Church, 114th St. and 91st Ave., Richmond Hill, N.Y. Rev. Rolla E. Hunt, Pastor. A social center providing clubs for men, women, boys and girls.

Richmond Hill House (reorganized from the West Side Branch of the University Settlement, September 1, 1903, incorp. November, 1903), 28 Macdougal St., N.Y.C. (tel. Spring 976). A social settlement for general neighborhood service and community work among the Italians.

Officers: Donald Scott, pres.; Erastus T. Tefft, treas.; Holcombe Ward, secy.; Constance Hook, head worker.

***Ridgewood Day Nursery** (incorp. 1906), 227 Knickerbocker Ave., Brooklyn.

***Riverside Day Nursery,** 149 West 63d St., N.Y.C.

Riverside Sanatorium. See Health, Department of.

Robins' Nest, The (opened 1891, incorp. 1901), Tarrytown-on-Hudson, N. Y. Provides a temporary home in the country, during the summer months, for convalescent children, between the ages of two and twelve years, from a New York hospital. Capacity, 35.

Officers: Mrs. Howard Carroll, pres.; Mrs. J. B. Calvert, treas.; Miss M. V. Lewis, secy.

Rockaway Beach Hospital and Dispensary (incorp. 1903), cor. Hammels Ave. and Bayside Pl., Rockaway Beach, N. Y. (tel. Belle Harbor 70). A general hospital to afford medical and surgical aid and nursing to sick or disabled persons of every creed, nationality

* *Current information not received.*

and color. Capacity, thirty-five beds. Supported by voluntary contributions.

Officers: George Bennett, pres.; Wm. Brunner, treas.; S. I. Goldberg, secy.; Eugenia H. Frost, supt.

Rockaway Hospital. See NEPONSIT BEACH HOSPITAL FOR CHILDREN.

Rockefeller Foundation, The (chartered 1913), 61 Broadway (tel. Bowling Green 7100). To promote the well-being of mankind throughout the world; to provide an agency which shall deal with the problems of human welfare in accordance with the principles and methods most approved in each generation. The Foundation has received from Mr. John D. Rockefeller funds aggregating about $131,500,000. A part of the principal as well as the income from this fund has been expended by the Trustees.

The Foundation has devoted its attention and its funds for the most part to large, comprehensive programs whose aims are: (a) To eradicate certain causes of human ill and to build up positive programs for bettering conditions; and (b) to make demonstrations in various fields and to inaugurate helpful work, responsibility for which may later be assumed by that portion of the public most intimately concerned.

The Foundation has undertaken particularly work in public health and in medical education. Specific divisions of work are carried out by the following departmental organizations:

(1) The International Health Board, Dr. Wickliffe Rose, general director; for the establishment of agencies for promotion of public sanitation and the spread of the knowledge of scientific medicine.

(2) The China Medical Board, Dr. George E. Vincent, general director; for the development of medical education and hygiene in China.

(3) Division of Medical Education, Dr. Richard M. Pearce, director; for aid in the development of important medical centers throughout the world.

Officers: John D. Rockefeller, Jr., chrm. Board of Trustees; George E. Vincent, pres.; Edwin Rogers Embree, secy.; L. G. Myers, treas.

Rockefeller Institute for Medical Research (incorp. 1901), 66th St. and Avenue A, N.Y.C. (tel. Rhinelander 900). To advance the science of medicine through laboratory investigations and clinical observations and study in the Hospital of the Institute. A Department of Animal Pathology is established at Princeton, N. J.

The capacity of the Hospital Department is seventy beds. Only such patients are admitted as are suffering from certain specified diseases, which are from time to time selected for observation and treatment. Patients are admitted only after conference with the resident physician.

Rodeph Sholom Sisterhood, 157 East 94th St. Works as an auxiliary to United Hebrew Charities. Business meetings quarterly. Sewing for poor all day Thursdays. Sewing school, Wednesday afternoons. Religious school, Friday afternoons. Americanization classes, Tuesday and Thursday afternoons.

Roman Catholic Orphan Asylum in the City of New York, The (incorp. 1852). Office: 24 East 52d St., cor. Madison Ave., N.Y.C. (tel. Plaza 1440). Office hours from 9 A. M. to 5 P. M. Maintains two asylums under one management. Boys' Orphan Asylum, and the Girls' Orphan Asylum, Sedgwick Ave. and Kingsbridge Rd., Kingsbridge, N. Y., in which orphan and half-orphan children between three and ten years of age are received. Present number of inmates in the Asylums, 1,000.

Application for admission should be made in writing to the Committee on Admission and Binding, by the clergy of the different parishes, on or before the Saturdays previous to the last Wednesdays of each month, at the Asylum office. Supported by voluntary contributions and bequests.

Eugene J. Quin, general agent.

Roman Catholic Orphan Asylum Society, The (incorp. 1834). Office: 4 Court Sq., Brooklyn (tel. Main 2645), where all applicants for admission and discharge are received. Cares for orphan and half-orphan children, from 4 to 16 years. Supported by voluntary contributions and city appropriation for children committed by the City.

Officers: Rt. Rev. Chas. E. McDonnell, D.D., pres.; John J. Walsh, treas.; John J. Gartland, secy.; George F. Shiebler, general agent.

Maintains the following branches:

St. John's Home for Boys, St. Mark's and Albany Aves., Brooklyn.

St. John's Home, Hicksville, L. I. A country home where delicate boys are sent from St. John's Home to build up.

St. John's Coney Island Summer Home, Surf Ave. and West 28th St., Coney Island. To give each of the inmates of St. John's Home for Boys a two weeks' outing during the summer.

St. Joseph's Female Asylum, Sumner and Willoughby Aves., Brooklyn.

St. Paul's Industrial School (org. 1866), Congress and Clinton Sts., Brooklyn. Girls from St. Joseph's Asylum are transferred to St. Paul's where they receive a training fitting them to be self-supporting when discharged from the institution.

Rome State School (est. Chap. 348, Laws of 1893 as Oneida State Custodial Asylum; Name changed by Chap. 382, Laws of 1894; again changed Chap. 633, Laws of 1919), Rome, N. Y. For the support, maintenance and training of feeble-minded persons.

Nine farm colonies for agricultural purposes for boys are maintained, and nine girls' colonies for inmates at domestic and mill work, distributed generally about the State.

Charles Bernstein, M.D., supt.

Roosevelt Hospital, The (est. by will of James H. Roosevelt, incorp. 1864, opened 1871), 58th to 59th Sts., and Ninth to Tenth Aves. (tel. Columbus 2340). Provides accommodations for about 285 bed patients, besides maintaining an active dispensary and emergency department service, in which are treated about 30,000 patients annually.

The ward service is free to those who are unable to pay, but from those who can afford it, a moderate charge for board is expected. Contagious or chronic cases, also cases that are objectionable or a menace to other patients, are not admitted. In 1916 nearly eighty-one per cent. of the ward day's care were free.

The Private Patients' Pavilion, the rooms of which have private baths and other hotel comforts and conveniences, is maintained, with a private operating room, for the accommodation of people of means who appreciate the advantages of hospital service in time of illness.

The attending staff is ably assisted in their professional work by a resident staff of sixteen physicians, by the staff of the Harriman Diagnostic Laboratory, the X-Ray Department, and the Nurses' Training School, with its staff of three principals, fifteen head nurses, and about 150 pupils.

To erect, furnish, and maintain the buildings, according to the plans adopted, will require additional money beyond the funds provided by the Roosevelt will, and the Trustees solicit contributions for this purpose, and for the endowment of free beds.

Form of General Devise: I give and bequeath to "The Roosevelt Hospital" in the City of New York, incorporated in 1864, under the Laws of the State of New York, the sum of........Dollars, in further support of or addition to said Hospital, and I authorize the Trustees thereof to invest the same in real estate in fee or in such securities as they may deem proper.

Form of Endowment of Bed in Perpetuity: I give and bequeath the sum of Five Thousand Dollars to "The Roosevelt Hospital," in the City of New York, and incorporated in 1864, under the Laws of the State of New York, and request the Trustees thereof to apply the same for the endowment of a free bed in said Hospital in perpetuity (in memory of...........) or (to be called The...........Endowed Bed).

Information relative to any special feature of the work will be gladly furnished by the Superintendent.

Officers: W. Emlen Roosevelt, pres.; W. Irving Clark, vice-pres.; George Emlen Roosevelt, secy.; Chas. B. Grimshaw, supt.

Roosevelt Memorial Association, 1 Madison Ave., N.Y.C. Organized to establish a memorial park at Oyster Bay, to erect a memorial in Washington and to establish a Roosevelt Society.

Officers: Wm. Boyce Thompson, pres.; Albert H. Wiggin, treas.; Harry M. Blair, secy.

See also Woman's Roosevelt Memorial Association.

Rosary Hill Home. See SERVANTS OF RELIEF FOR INCURABLE CANCER.

Rosemary, The. See LADIES' CHRISTIAN UNION.

Russell Sage Foundation, 130 East 22d St., N.Y.C. (tel. Gramercy 7060). The Foundation was established in 1907 by Mrs. Russell Sage in memory of her husband. It was incorporated by an act of the Legislature of New York in April, 1907. Mrs. Sage gave to the Foundation an endowment of $10,000,000. By her will she bequeathed it an additional sum of about $5,000,000. The income only may be spent.

The purpose of the Foundation, as stated in its charter, is "the improvement of social and living conditions in the United States of America." The charter further says: "It shall be within the purpose of said corporation to use any means which from time to time shall seem expedient to its members or trustees, including research, publication, education, the establishment and maintenance of charitable and benevolent activities, agencies and institutions, and the aid of any such activities, agencies, or institutions already established." It does not relieve individual need. The management of the Foundation vests in a board of nine trustees, which is self-perpetuating. The present trustees are:

Robert W. de Forest, pres.; Mrs. William B. Rice, vice-pres.; Charles D. Norton, treas.; Cleveland H. Dodge, John H. Finley, Louisa Lee Schuyler, Mrs. Finley J. Shepard, Alfred T. White, John M. Glenn, secretary and general director.

The Foundation acts through a number of departments of its own and through a few other agencies which are especially equipped to carry on campaigns against certain evils, such as tuberculosis and bad housing. Its departments are as follows:

CHARITY ORGANIZATION DEPARTMENT. Mary E. Richmond, director. The aim of this department is to study, teach and publish in the field of charity organization, bounding that field broadly to include the better co-ordination of all social work. Its studies and efforts have been confined chiefly to social case work, to the co-operation of social agencies and to their administrative details.

Department of Child Helping. Hastings H. Hart, director. The aim of this department is to promote improved methods of dealing with dependent, neglected, delinquent and defective children throughout the United States; to conduct inquiries concerning the condition, needs and care of such children; on request to make intensive studies of particular organizations and institutions, and to give information and advice to those who are founding or re-organizing child-caring agencies, or who are interested in legislation relating to the classes of children named above.

Department of Education. Leonard P. Ayres, director. The aim of this department is to study methods of public elementary education and promote measures designed to increase their efficiency. It studies factors affecting the progress of school children through the grades; devised methods for the development in school systems of exact measuring, careful recording, and judgment on the basis of observed fact; it advises concerning investigation and surveys of school methods and legislation affecting schools.

Department of Industrial Studies. Mary Van Kleeck, director. The aim of this department is to study industrial conditions and to discover facts which may be a guide for public opinion and a basis for constructive action for improving conditions of work and industrial relations.

Department of Recreation. Lee F. Hanmer, director. The aim of this department is to aid in constructive social organization of leisure time. The department studies the best methods of providing and administering facilities for public recreation and encourages their adoption by public and private agencies. Some of the subjects dealt with are recreation, legislation, athletics and games for school children, community use of school plants, holiday celebrations, municipal administration of recreation facilities, and rural recreation.

Division of Remedial Loan. Caro D. Coombs, secy. The aim of this division is to conduct a campaign of education regarding the evils of the small loan business and to urge the passage and enforcement of adequate small loan laws.

Department of Statistics. Leonard P. Ayres, director. The aim of this department is to prepare statistical reports relating to social conditions, to advise the members of the staff of the Foundation and others as to the planning of statistical inquiries, the preparation of schedule forms and tables, and the presentation of statistical results. It revises all statistical material intended for publication by the Foundation.

Department of Surveys and Exhibits. Shelby M. Harrison, director. The aim of this department is to study and develop the social survey and social exhibit as important aids in community improvement, and to give advice about, make plans for, and help in organizing local surveys and exhibits.

Library. Frederick Warren Jenkins, librarian. The library is free to the public and is open week-days from 8.45 A. M. to 6 P. M. It contains about 20,000 books and 60,000 pamphlets on sociology and social work. Its files of reports of public and private agencies, institutions and conferences, national and foreign, are unusually complete. It receives regularly 250 periodicals.

Russian Missionary and Educational Society, Inc., The, 1820 Spring Garden Street, Philadelphia, Pa. To train missionaries for work in Russia. Appeals for prayer. Sample copy of "Friend of Russia" free. Interdenominational.

William Fetler, general director; G. Percy Fox, treas.; W. S. Hottel, secy.

***Russian Orthodox Christian Immigration Society of North America** (est. 1908, incorp. 1909), 347 East 14th St., N.Y.C. For the care and assistance of Russian immigrants.

Russian St. Nicholas Cathedral, 15 East 97th St., N.Y.C. Dean, Rev. Leonid J. Turkevich, Archpriest; Rev. Peter Popoff, Archpriest and Rev. Alexander Kukulevsky, Archpriest, assistants. Maintains social service work for Russians and conducts the Clothing Department of the American Central Committee for Russian Relief, Inc.

Rutgers Presbyterian Church, Broadway, cor. West 73d St., N.Y.C. (tel. Columbus 3887). Maintains clubs and classes for mothers, boys, and girls. Conducts day excursions during summer.

Rev. Daniel Russell, D.D., minister; Miss Elsie Jetter, visitor; Miss Ruth V. Lord, secy.

S

Sacred Heart Orphan Asylum. See MISSIONARY SISTERS OF THE SACRED HEART.

Safety Institute of America (maintaining The American Museum of Safety, chartered 1911), 261 Madison Ave., N.Y.C. (tel. Murray Hill 4230). Devoted to the safety, health, and welfare of industrial workers and the science and technique of industry.

Officers: Arthur Williams, pres.; James Speyer, treas.; William J. Moran, secy.; Riley M. Little, director.

Sage Foundation. See RUSSELL SAGE FOUNDATION.

Sailors' Home and Institute. See AMERICAN SEAMAN'S FRIEND SOCIETY.

Sailors' Snug Harbor (founded 1801, incorp. 1806), New Brighton, Staten Island. City office: 262 Green St., N.Y.C. A home for aged, decrepit, and wornout sailors.

Officers: George E. Beckwith, governor; Darwin P. Kingsley, pres.; James Henry, comptroller; W. A. Guenther, deputy comptroller; Edward H. Cole, application agent, to whom apply.

Salvation Army, The (founded by General William Booth). National headquarters, 120–130 West 14th St. (tel. Watkins 8030). The center for directing the spiritual, social, financial, industrial, slum, prison, rescue, training, and publishing work of the Army in the United States. The Salvation Army is a religious and charitable organization incorporated under the Laws of the State of New York and carrying on its work on a military basis.

Object: To preach the Gospel to the masses and to help the needy, without distinction as to color, age, nationality, or creed. In New York City Gospel services are held every night on the streets and also in several halls, mostly in or near the tenement districts.

Evangeline Booth, commander-in-chief; Thomas Estill, territorial commissioner; Col. R. E. Golz, chief secy.

The social work of the Army in Greater New York embraces: Brooklyn Nursery and Infants Hospital, 396 Herkimer St. Day Nursery for Children, 94 Cherry St., N.Y.C. Employment Bureau, 122 West 14th St., Immigration & Steamship Bookings,

* *Current information not received.*

122 West 14th St. Fresh Air Camp for Mothers and Children, North Long Branch, N. J. Ice and coal distribution, wagons visit the very poorest districts, delivering blocks of ice in hot weather, and coal in pailfuls in winter for a few cents.

INDUSTRIAL HOMES FOR MEN, 508 West 48th St., 229 East 120th St., N.Y.C.; Keap and Hope Sts., Brooklyn; 111 Front St., Hempstead, L. I.; 1-3 Grove St., Mt. Vernon, N. Y.; 248 Erie St., Jersey City, N. J.

INQUIRY AND IMMIGRATION DEPARTMENT for missing relatives, etc., with branches in every part of the world, 120 West 14th St.

INTERSTATE EMPLOYMENT BUREAU, 120 West 14th St., to secure positions for those applying at the various stations, with branches in every large city in the U. S.

LAUNDRY, 316 East 15th St., operated in connection with the RESCUE HOME for fallen women.

MATERNITY HOSPITAL, 316 East 15th St.

POOR MAN'S LAWYER, 122 West 14th St.

PRISON WORK, 120 West 14th St. To aid prisoners, their families, also discharged prisoners. Work in Police Courts regularly carried on.

RELIEF DEPARTMENT renders aid of all kinds to the poor after due investigation. Relief work in slum districts.

WOMEN'S HOME AND HOSPITAL, 318 East 15th St., N.Y.C.

HOTEL FOR MEN, Memorial Hotel, 225 Bowery.

SHELTER FOR HOMELESS WOMEN, 243 Bowery, N.Y.C.

TRAINING COLLEGE FOR OFFICER'S, University Ave. and W. Tremont, Morris Heights.

HEADQUARTERS, Naval and Military, 122 West 14th St.

CANTEENS AND CLUBS for U. S. Soldiers, Sailors and Marines, 13-15 East 41st St., N.Y.C.

FARM FOR DRUG ADDICTS, Tappan, N. Y.

Samaritan Home for the Aged, The (incorp. 1867), 414 West 22d St., N.Y.C.(tel. Chelsea 2875). A Protestant home for aged, indigent men and women, over sixty-five years. Supported by voluntary contributions and entrance fees.

Samaritan Hospital of Brooklyn (incorp. 1904), 608 Fourth Ave., cor. 17th St., Brooklyn (tel. South 2710-2711). For acute, sub-acute, curable and non-contagious diseases. No distinction of race or creed. Capacity, 46. The charges are: Ward, $15, private ward, $16-$18, private rooms, $20-$40. Supported by voluntary contributions.

Maintains Training School for Nurses and a Dispensary.

Eloise Kirby, R.N., supt.

Sanatorium Gabriels (1897), Gabriels, N. Y. For incipient and moderately advanced cases of tuberculosis. No distinction made as to creed or nationality. Capacity, seventy. For further particulars, address: Sisters of Mercy, Gabriels, N. Y.

H. J. Blankemeyer, resident physician.

Sands Fund of the Protestant Episcopal Church, the interest of which is to be used by the Bishop of New York at his discretion in behalf of clergymen of the Diocese of New York. Address the Bishop of New York, Cathedral Close, N.Y.C.

Sanitarium for Hebrew Children of the City of New York (incorp. 1879), Rockaway Park, L. I.

Sanitary Bureau. See HEALTH, DEPARTMENT OF.

Sarah J. Bird Memorial Farm. See BOWERY MISSION.

Sarah Schermerhorn House. See NEW YORK PROTESTANT EPISCOPAL CITY MISSION SOCIETY.

Save-a-Home Fund. The Evening Mail, 25 City Hall Pl., N.Y.C. (tel. Worth 3200). Provides immediate relief and aid of rent in cases of dispossess.

Bertha Pohlman, manager.

Save-a-Life League, The (org. 1916), 108 West 77th St., N.Y.C. (tel. Schuyler 75). For the prevention of suicide. The League gives practical sympathy and advice, personally or by correspondence; aids hospital patients who have attempted suicide; extends consolation to homes that have thus been grief stricken and humiliated. All work is regarded as private and strictly confidential. Cases needing medical treatment are referred to Dr. Gregory of the Psychopathic Department of Bellevue Hospital.

The work requires visits to private homes, hotels, hospitals, courts, and undertakers, where various humane and religious services are performed. It is supported by membership dues and voluntary contributions, and is controlled by an advisory council.

Officers: Harry Marsh Warren, Ph. D., D.D., pres.; Ruel W. Poor, treas.

***Saviour M. E. Church,** Lexington Ave. and 111th St., N.Y.C. Maintains a kindergarten, night school, gymnasium, clubs for boys and girls, men and women. See also under METHODIST EPISCOPAL CHURCHES in the Church List.

Scandinavian Sailors' Temperance Home, The (incorp. 1889), 172 Carroll St., Brooklyn (tel. Henry 730). To promote the welfare of Norwegian, Swedish, or Danish seamen. Supported by donations and board of sailors.

** Current information not received.*

Scandinavian Young Women's Home, 149 South Portland Ave., Brooklyn, of the Swedish Evangelical Pilgrim Church.

Scarlet Fever and Diphtheria Hospital. See LOUISA MINTURN HOSPITAL.

Scenic and Historic Preservation Society. See AMERICAN SCENIC AND HISTORIC PRESERVATION SOCIETY.

School Garden Association of New York (org. 1908), 124 West 30th St. (tel. Farragut 5160). Organized to conduct propaganda for school gardens in New York City, by means of meetings, reports, correspondence, exhibits, and investigations. The Association is non-sectarian and has no branches.

Dr. Gustave Straubenmuller, pres., 500 Park Ave.; Van Evrie Kilpatrick, vice-pres.

School for Midwives, 223 East 26th St., N.Y.C. See BELLEVUE HOSPITAL.

School for Mothers, Hartsdale, N. Y. See ASSOCIATION FOR IMPROVING THE CONDITION OF THE POOR, Caroline Rest.

School of Social Work, 105 East 22d St., N.Y.C. See New York School of Social Work, under CHARITY ORGANIZATION SOCIETY.

School Settlement Association, The (org. 1901, incorp. 1906), 120 Jackson St., Brooklyn (tel. Greenpoint 1817). Maintains clubs and classes in sewing, millinery, cooking, basketry, dramatics, music, dancing, Americanization, kindergarten, etc., and also gymnasium, summer playground, and outings. Eastern District Auxiliary of the Red Cross.

Helen Louise Moss, head worker.

Scientific Temperance Federation, The (est. and incorp. 1906), 73 Tremont St., Boston, Mass. Popular educational work in scientific fact about alcohol. Original posters. Started anti-alcohol exhibit work in United States. Original slides for stereopticon and stereomotorgraph. Pamphlets, popular and technical literature. A large indexed reference library on alcohol question. Lectures. Edits quarterly magazine, "The Scientific Temperance Journal."

Officers: Ernest H. Cherrington, pres.; Ernest L. Miller, treas.; Cora Frances Stoddard, exec. secy.

Sea Breeze Convalescent Home, now **New Sea Breeze.** See ASSOCIATION FOR IMPROVING THE CONDITION OF THE POOR.

Sea Breeze Hospital, West Coney Island, N. Y. SEE NEPONSIT BEACH HOSPITAL.

Sea Cliff Summer Cottage, Sea Cliff, L. I. Entirely a private home maintained by Mrs. Robert Hoe, to afford summer rest to mothers with their children, convalescents from hospitals, or anyone in whom Mrs. Hoe is interested. Capacity for twenty.

Sea and Land Church, 61 Henry St., N.Y.C. (tel. Orchard 978). Rev. Alfred D. Moore, Rev. Joseph A. Villelli, Rev. Warren D. Hall, ministers; Miss Christine Wilson, Miss Helen P. Bonsall, Miss Margaret Winchester, church and club workers; Miss Margaret Winchester, church organist; Miss Lillian E. Bodamer, church secy.

SOCIAL SERVICE WORK: kindergarten, mothers' meetings, sewing-school, industrial and literary clubs and classes, gymnasium, library and reading room, children's meetings, etc.

FIRST AID ROOM, open daily.

FRESH-AIR WORK: Summer Home for women and children on Staten Island. See also under PRESBYTERIAN CHURCHES in the Church List.

Sea View Farms. See PUBLIC WELFARE DEPARTMENT.

Seabury Memorial Home, Inc., The (incorp. 1888), 325 Highland Ave., Mt. Vernon, N. Y. (tel. Mt. Vernon 2767). For the aged who have labored in some one of the various professions, art, music, science, literature, education, etc. Non-sectarian. Capacity 28. Supported by voluntary contributions and interest from admission fees.

Officers: Alexander Wilson, pres.; Alexander T. Sweet, treas.; Albert Hill Seabury, secy., 139 West 72d St., N.Y.C.; Miss Mary L. Pease, supt.

Seamen's Christian Association of the City of New York, The (org. 1888, incorp. 1893). Mission House: 399 West St., N.Y.C. (tel. Chelsea 470). Open daily from 8 A. M. to 10 P. M. Maintains a

FREE SHIPPING BUREAU; also library, reading and correspondence room. Gospel services are held Sundays, Tuesday and Thursday evenings. Mission building open daily from 8 A. M. to 10 P. M. Testaments, tracts and packages of reading matter are distributed. Temperance pledges are also offered and signed. Lodgings in a strictly temperance house; also meals at the Mission House are provided for destitute seamen only. Non-sectarian.

Supported wholly by voluntary donations. Conducted upon strictly cash basis. Aggregate attendance, 85,192; attendance of the seamen, 80,617; visitors, 4,573. Receipts, $16,072; expenses, $15,155. Building Fund, $64,917.56.

Officers: Mr. H. Prescott Beach, pres., Upper Montclair, N. J.; Mr. Donald H. Cowl, treas., Great Neck, L. I.; Miss Emma M. Bangs, secy., 161 East 78th St., N.Y.C.; Stafford Wright, supt. and missionary; H. C. Crosier, Alfred K. Reed, asst. supts.;

E. T. Roney, chaplain; Arthur J. Phillips in charge of Free Shipping Bureau.

The Women's Auxiliary of this Association, supplements its efforts by giving sympathy and aid to worthy seamen.

Miss Emma M. Bangs, cor. secy., 399 West St., N.Y.C.

Seamen's Church Institute of New York (formerly Protestant Episcopal Church Missionary Society for Seamen in the city and port of New York; incorp. 1844), 25 South St., N.Y.C. (tel. Broad 297). For the religious and temporal welfare of seamen and boatmen. Supported by income from small endowment but largely by voluntary contributions.

Officers: Edmund L. Baylies, pres., 54 Wall St.; Frank T. Warburton, secy. and treas., 46 Cedar St.; Rev. Archibald R. Mansfield, D.D., supt. Maintains the following:

THE INSTITUTE at 25 South St. is equipped to care for 244,185 lodgings annually. It is a thirteen-story building. It is many things combined: a chapel, a hotel, reading, writing, and game rooms, a savings department, an employment bureau, a lyceum for entertainment and public lectures, navigation and marine engineering and radio schools, first aid to the injured, a relief society.

THE TENDER, "J. Hooker Hamersley," makes daily trips about the harbor. With the new building and its complete equipment it is now possible to take a crew from an incoming ship, transport it to the Institute, feed it, lodge it, entertain and instruct the men, give relief to the sick and disabled, visit them in the hospitals, secure them fresh employment, outfit them properly and place them on outgoing vessels, having in the meanwhile taken charge of their dunnage, their mail and their money, and having transmitted the latter, free of charge, to their dependents anywhere in the world.

THE CHAPEL OF OUR SAVIOUR, 25 South St., regular Sunday and weekday services in several languages.

THE NORTH RIVER STATION, Church of the Holy Comforter for Seamen, 341 West St., foot of Houston St., and free library, reading, writing, game rooms, and concert hall.

Seamen's Mission, of the SOCIETY FOR THE CARE OF GERMAN SEAMEN IN THE PORT OF NEW YORK, formerly German Seamen's Mission (incorp. 1907), 60–64 Hudson St., Hoboken, N. J. (tel. Hoboken 1079). Maintains a library, reading and correspondence rooms; provides reading matter for German crews; a lodging house, capacity 100 beds, and help for the sick and destitute; Gospel services in the Home and aboard ships; special research work for missing relatives.

Officers: Rev. Dr. J. W. Loch, pres.; George Gravenhorst, treas., 96 Wall St., N.Y.C.; Rev. H. C. Wasmund, secy.; Rev. H. Bruckner, Pastor.

Seamen's Service Center. See UNITED STATES PUBLIC HEALTH SERVICE.

Seaside Home for Crippled Children (incorp. 1912), 4 Summerfield Ave., Arverne, L. I. To care for poor, crippled children during the spring and summer; the home provides excellent food, ocean baths, and healthful recreation. Supported by voluntary contributions and City Funds.

Sea-side Hospital, Cedar Grove, New Dorp, S. I. See ST. JOHN'S GUILD.

Sea View Hospital, Grymes Hill, S. I. See PUBLIC WELFARE DEPARTMENT, CITY OF NEW YORK; Sea View Farms.

Second Avenue Baptist Church, 164 Second Ave., between 10th and 11th Sts., N.Y.C. Rev. Wm. N. Hubbell, Pastor: Italian, Polish, Chinese, and Esthonian departments; kindergartens, industrial and cooking classes, gymnasium, English classes for foreigners, Bible classes, Chinese Sunday-school. See also under BAPTIST CHURCHES in the Church List.

***Second Ave. Boys' and Girls' Club,** 324 East 51st St., N.Y.C.

Serbian Aid Fund, Room 241, 1 Madison Ave., N.Y.C. Administers general relief in Serbia as needed, and special help in sickness and other emergency. Pays to mothers of 5,000 destitute orphans of officers and government officials allowances of $6.00 per month per child. Assists young students and blind and crippled soldiers.

Madame Slavko Grouitch, director; Otto T. Bannard, treas.; Mrs. Mabel R. Greene, secy.

Serbian Child Welfare Association (est. under auspices Serbian Government 1915; formerly Serbian Relief Committee), 7 West 8th St., N.Y.C. (tel. Stuyvesant 8170). Oldest organization for Serbian Relief in America. Operating health centers and American Institute for children. Vocational training, demonstration farm 250 acres under cultivation in 1920 at Chachak, Serbia. Regional health centers maintained in six centers of population and traveling railway dispensary and health car. Divisions of investigation, placing out, boarding out, infant welfare and after care headed by American experts. Serbian public health nurses and visitors trained. American personnel Serbia, 62 including representative in Paris and transport agent in Salonica. $1,000,000 needed to July, 1921.

Officers: Wm. Jay Schieffelin, pres.; A. Barton Hepburn, treas.; John A. Kingsbury, chrm. Executive Committee; R. R. Reeder, commissioner for Serbia.

Serbian War Prisoners Repatriation Fund, 19 Nassau St. N.Y.C. Raising fund to return Austrian and Hungarian prisoners to their homeland.

Officers: Felix M. Warburg, chrm.; Samuel Welldon, treas.; Emil Fischl, secy.

Servants of Relief for Incurable Cancer, The (org. 1896, incorp. 1901), 71 Jackson St. (tel. Orchard 2933), Corlears Park, N.Y.C. A Dominican Sisterhood who join for life and serve without pay, for the relief of incurable cases of cancer among the poor. Supported by charitable donation. No distinctions made as to creed, sex, or nationality. Capacity for 100; average, 80. Mother M. Rose Huber, O.S.D.

ROSARY HILL HOME, Hawthorne, Westchester Co., N. Y. (tel. Pleasantville 19-J). Mother-house, capacity, seventy-five beds; also the novitiate for new members of the community. Mother M. Alphonsa Lathrop, O.S.D.

Service Club for Soldiers and Sailors. See NEW YORK COMMUNITY SERVICE.

Service Home for Wounded Men. See STAGE WOMEN'S WAR RELIEF.

Seton Hospital for Men, Spuyten Duyvil Parkway, N.Y.C. (tel. Kingsbridge 56). For the treatment of all classes of tuberculosis. Nearly all beds are subsidized by the Department of Public Welfare. Applications through the Tuberculosis Hospital Admission Bureau (q. v.).

NAZARETH BRANCH, for women and children, including boys under thirteen years.

Settlement and Church of All Nations, 9 Second Ave., N.Y.C. (tel. Orchard 3388). (English, Yiddish,

* *Current information not received.*

Italian, Chinese, Russian.) Maintains educational classes, gymnastics, sewing school, kindergarten, Fresh-air Home, Russian Forum, Russian Monthly Magazine, etc.

Rev. John R. Henry, supt.

Seventy-ninth St. Neighborhood House, 232-4 East 79th St., N.Y.C. (tel. Lenox 9438). Branch of HENRY STREET SETTLEMENT. For self, neighborhood, and city betterment. Nursing service, manual training classes, Scout work, playground, and bank. Americanization classes. Clubs for men, women, young people, and children. Public meetings. Activities carried on chiefly by volunteers.

J. G. Hanson, head worker.

Sevilla Home for Children, The (incorp. 1889), Lafayette Ave. and Manida St., Hunt's Point, Bronx. For destitute girls between five and ten years of age, who are mentally and physically capable of receiving training for self-support. Non-sectarian. Endowed by will of Jose Seville, Lima, Peru.

Officers: Samuel Sloan, pres.; Harris D. Colt., secy., 30 Broad St.; Miss J. Frances M. Cobban, supt.

Shelter for Respectable Girls. See SISTER CATHERINE'S HOME.

Shelter for Women with Children. See CHILDREN'S AID SOCIETY.

Sheltering Arms, The (incorp. 1864), Amsterdam Ave. and 129th St., N.Y.C. For children from six to twelve years of age, in need of a home and for whom no other institution provides. Children are received temporarily, and parents are expected to pay board when able to do so. Infants are not received. Children are held subject to the order of parents or relatives, and are not surrendered to the institution. They attend P. S. No. 43, and are trained to household and other work. Accommodates 190. Visiting days second and fourth Sundays and first and third Thursdays. Supported by voluntary contributions, income of endowment, and board of children. Apply in person or by letter any week day. Receipts and expenditures about $45,000 a year. (See ADVERTISEMENT.)

Officers: Wm. R. Peters, pres., 55 John St.; Charles B. Meyer, secy., 42 West 44th St.; Alfred A. Whitman, treas.; Mrs. Augusta S. Page, supt.

Shut-in Society, The (org. 1877, incorp. 1885). Headquarters: 129 East 34th St., N.Y.C. A society for the encouragement and comfort of invalids, and the printing and distribution of publications adapted to such work. It is not an almsgiving society but designed for social cheer and spiritual comfort. Unsectarian. Publishes a monthly periodical, "The Open Window." Circulation, 4,800. Has a library, and loans wheel-chairs to members. Numbers 3,000 invalids and 1,200 associates. Supported by subscriptions to "The Open Window" and by the gifts of friends.

National Officers: Mrs. Charles E. Merrill, pres.; Miss Mary Hamilton Hadley, secy. and treas., 355 Willow St., New Haven, Conn. Miss Anna Breath, editor.

NEW YORK STATE BRANCH: 129 East 34th St., N.Y.C. Maintains an exchange for the work of shut-ins. Articles which are approved are accepted for sale on consignment, a charge of 15 per cent. commission being made and a registration fee of twenty-five cents. Loans wheel-chairs, furnishes correspondents, visitors and literature to shut-ins.

Miss Elizabeth Peters, pres.

Silver Cross Day Nursery (org. 1890, incorp. 1892), 249 East 117th St.,

N.Y.C. (tel. Harlem 989). Receives children from two weeks to eight years old. Open daily from 7 A. M. to 7 P. M., holidays excepted. Supported by contributions.

Officers: Mrs. William W. Clendinning, pres.; Mrs. E. Stewart Manee, treas.; Mrs. Edward Goldsmith, secy.; Mrs. F. Baxter, supt.

Sing Sing Prison (1825), Ossining, N. Y. For the reformation of male felons. Men are committed to this institution by indeterminate and definite sentence, the maximum and minimum of which are fixed by the court, or by definite sentence. Capacity, 1,200. It is supported by State appropriations and is under the management and control of the Superintendent of State Prisons.

SOCIAL SERVICE BUREAU, 135 East 15th St., N.Y.C.

Sister Catherine's Home (formerly the Shelter for Respectable Girls, org. 1872, incorp. 1880), 212 East 46th St., N.Y.C. (tel. Murray Hill 1909). A home for young women temporarily out of employment; 412 cared for last year; 20 admitted free; 41 free meals were given; 1,233 outsiders advised and aided. Supported by voluntary contributions. Capacity for twenty-two.

Officers: Rev. Henry M. Barbour, D.D., pres., Baldwin Harbor, L. I.; Miss Margaret R. Baker, treas., 212 East 46th St.; Rev. Floyd S. Leach, Ph.D., secy., 1 West 53d St.; Miss Katherine Gillmore, resident deaconess, to whom apply.

Sisterhood of the Holy Communion. See HOLY COMMUNION P. E. CHURCH, this list.

Sisterhood of St. John Baptist (1881), Central Business Office of the Community, 300 East 4th St., N.Y.C. The Sisters have in charge the following institutions:

ST. MARGUERITE'S, Ralston, N. J. A home for orphans and other children (girls).

ST. JOHN BAPTIST SCHOOL, Ralston, N. J. A boarding and day school for young ladies.

ST. ANDREW'S CONVALESCENT HOSPITAL (q. v.).

ST. ANDREW'S REST, Woodcliff Lake, Bergen Co., N. J.

ST. ANNE'S, Ralston, Morris Co., N. J. A home for wayward girls, sixteen years old and upward.

HOLY CROSS HOUSE, 300 East 4th St., N.Y.C. Boarding house for working girls. Capacity, thirty-four; rates $6 a week.

HOLY CROSS MISSION, 300 East 4th St. Headquarters for the mission work of the Sisters of St. John Baptist among the poor of that locality, in connection with the Protestant Episcopal Mission of the Holy Cross.

ST. MICHAEL'S HOME, Mamaroneck, N. Y. A reformatory for girls. Supported by voluntary contributions.

Stuyvesant F. Morris, M.D., pres., 16 East 30th St.; Francis Parkman, secy. and treas.

ST. MICHAEL'S LADIES' ASSOCIATION, Room 47, 289 Fourth Ave. Mrs. Stuyvesant F. Morris, pres., 16 East 30th St.; Mrs. Charles R. Henderson, vice-pres.; Mrs. Charles S. Brown, secy. For information on admissions apply to Miss Stevens.

Sisterhood of St. John the Evangelist (1872), Sisters' House, 492 Herkimer St., Brooklyn. Has charge of Houses and Departments of the Church Charity Foundation of Long Island (q. v.). No limitations as to age, sex, or religious beliefs. Supported by endowment fund and voluntary contributions.

Sisterhood of St. Mary (P. E.) (founded 1865), Peekskill, N. Y. Has charge of the following institutions:

St. Mary's Free Hospital for Children (q. v.), 405–411 West 34th St., N.Y.C.

Summer Branch, Norwalk, Conn.

St. Mary's Training School for Nurses, 405 West 34th St.

The Noyes Memorial Home, Peekskill, N. Y.

Wilkes Dispensary, 435–437 Ninth Ave., N.Y.C.

House of Mercy, Valhalla, N. Y.

Sisterhood of the Spanish and Portuguese Synagogue (incorp.1909), Neighborhood House, 133 Eldridge St., N.Y.C. (tel. Orchard 9729). For philanthropic and educational work by personal service. Supported by the Federation of Jewish Philanthropic Societies.

Sisters of the Annunciation of the Blessed Virgin Mary. See House of the Annunciation.

Sisters of Bon Secours, The (incorp. 1883), 1195 Lexington Ave., N.Y.C. (tel. Lenox 3720). Trained nurses devote themselves to the care of the sick in their own homes. Families are expected to assist toward supporting the Sisters, the poor being attended free of charge.

Sister Winifred, Superior.

Sisters of Charity of Saint Vincent de Paul, Mother house, Mt.-St.-Vincent-on-Hudson, N. Y. Direct the following institutions, which see under their respective titles:

Holy Family Hospital, 155 Dean St., near Hoyt St., Brooklyn.

New York Catholic Protectory, Westchester, N. Y.

New York Foundling Hospital, 175 East 68th St., N.Y.C.

Roman Catholic Orphan Asylum, Kingsbridge; office, 470 Madison Ave., N.Y.C.

St. Agatha's Home for Children, Nanuet, N. Y.

St. Ann's Maternity Hospital, 130 East 69th St., N.Y.C.

St. Eleanora's Home for Convalescents, Tuckahoe, N. Y.

St. Ignatius' Day Nursery, 240 East 84th St., N.Y.C.

St. Joseph's Home for Aged, 209 West 15th St., N.Y.C.

St. Laurence Hospital, 163d St. and Edgecombe Ave., N.Y.C.

St. Mary's General Hospital, St. Mark's Ave., between Rochester and Buffalo Aves., Brooklyn.

St. Vincent's Hospital, 11th and 12th Sts. and Seventh Ave., N.Y.C.

St. Vincent's Hospital, Richmond, Staten Island.

St. Vincent's Retreat, for nervous and mental diseases, Harrison, N. Y.

Seton Hospital, Spuyten Duyvil, N.Y.C.

Sisters of Divine Compassion, White Plains, N. Y. Maintains the

Good Counsel Training School for Young Girls, White Plains, New York.

Association for Befriending Children and Young Girls (incorp. 1870), 136 Second Ave., N.Y.C.

House of the Holy Family, 136 Second Ave., N.Y.C.

House of Our Lady for Business Girls, 52–54 East 126th St., N.Y.C.

Vacation House for Working Girls.

Sisters of Divine Providence, 255 West 24th St., N.Y.C. Maintain

Jeanne D'Arc Home for French Girls, 251–255 West 24th St., N.Y.C.

Home of Divine Providence, Grassmere, S. I., for aged French ladies.

Sisters of the Good Shepherd. See House of the Good Shepherd.

Sisters of the Holy Nativity, 123 West 46th St., N.Y.C. Conduct the work of the Church of St. Mary the Virgin consisting of guilds and classes for women and girls, visiting the sick, etc.

Sister Mary Kathleen, in charge.

Sisters of Mercy, Saranac Lake, N. Y. See ST. MARY'S OF THE LAKE.

Sisters of Mercy in Brooklyn (incorp. 1865), 273 Willoughby Ave. Visit the sick poor and maintain

ST. MARY OF THE ANGELS home for boys between five and twelve years of age, Syosset, Nassau Co., N. Y.

ANGEL GUARDIAN HOME, Twelfth Ave. and 64th St., Brooklyn, for little children between two and seven years.

Sisters of Notre Dame. See ST. JOSEPH'S ASYLUM.

Sisters of Our Lady of Christian Doctrine. Maintain the

INSTITUTE OF CHRISTIAN DOCTRINE, 171–175 Cherry St., N.Y.C., which conducts religious and industrial classes for R. C. children and adults; visits the sick poor and provides relief, especially for the unemployed. Also

MADONNA DAY NURSERY for children of working mothers.

Sisters of the Poor of St. Francis. See ST. FRANCIS' HOME FOR THE AGED.

Sisters of St. Dominic, 153 Graham Ave., Brooklyn (tel. Stagg 3812). Maintain

ST. DOMINIC ORPHAN HOME (1868), 153 Graham Ave., Brooklyn.

NAZARETH TRADE SCHOOL (1900), Farmingdale, L. I. An orphan home for 420 boys.

ST. DOMINIC'S HOME, New Hyde Park, L. I. A home for girls. Capacity seventy-six.

ST. ROSE INDUSTRIAL SCHOOL, Melville, L. I. Capacity, 110 girls.

SORROWFUL MOTHER, Harrison Pl., near Morgan Ave., Brooklyn. Capacity, 196—139 girls and 57 boys.

ST. JOSEPH'S SANITARIUM (est. 1896), St. Joseph's Station, Sullivan Co., N. Y. For the care of convalescents and those in poor health.

All applications to be made at the office in Brooklyn.

Officers: Mother Augustine Fleck, O.S.D., pres., 157 Graham Ave.; M. Margaret Hammer, O.S.D., treas.; Mother Albertina, secy.; Sr. Perpetual, manager.

Sisters of St. Joseph, Bronxville, N. Y. See SOCIETY OF ST. JOSEPH OF NAZARETH.

Sixty-first Street M. E. Church, 223 East 61st St., N.Y.C. Rev. Benjamin F. Saxon, Pastor; W. W. Blanchard, boys' work; Miss Elva Mackey, social work; Miss Ella Nash, deaconess. Clubs for men, boys, women and girls, summer camp at Lake Hopatcong. See also under METHODIST EPISCOPAL CHURCHES in the Church List.

Skin and Cancer Hospital, 19th St. and Second Ave., N.Y.C. See NEW YORK SKIN AND CANCER HOSPITAL.

Slavonic Immigrant Society (incorp. 1907), 436 West 23d St., N.Y.C. (tel. Chelsea 6094). To give advice, information, aid, and protection to Slavonic immigrants. Supported by membership dues and donations; also a nominal charge for board and lodging to those who can afford to pay. Capacity, thirty.

Officers: M. I. Pupin, pres.; Helen Hartley Jenkins, treas.; A. B. Koukol, secy. and manager of Home.

Sloane Hospital for Women, Columbia University (incorp. 1888), 447 West 59th St., N.Y.C. (tel. Columbus 9150). The wards furnish 94 obstetrical and 24 gynecological beds. Emergency cases received at any hour. Supported by income from endowment and private rooms.

Officers: Dr. W. E. Studdiford, director; Malcolm D. Sloane, treas.; Dr. J. W. Jobling, secy.; Dr. R. N. Pierson, resident physician; A. I. Byrne, supt.

Social Service and Brotherhood of the American Baptist Publication Society, Department of. See BROTHERHOOD AND SOCIAL SERVICE, etc.

Social Service Commission, Diocese of New York, The (1911), (Protestant Episcopal), 416 Lafayette St., N.Y.C. (tel. Spring 9970). Authorized and established by the Convention of the Diocese for the purpose of organizing and enlisting the various parishes of the diocese of New York for more effective effort in behalf of social betterment. It seeks to bring the churches into closer co-operation with secular agencies devoted to human welfare, and to acquaint church people with social needs.

Officers: Very Rev. H. E. W. Fosbroke, D.D., chrm., 1 Chelsea Square, N.Y.C.; Wm. W. Peake, treas., 7 Wall St.; Arthur A. Michell, Esq., rec. secy., 32 Nassau St.; Hon. John A. Kingsbury, 7 West 8th St.; Orlando P. Metcalf, Esq., 115 Broadway; Rev. Chas. Lewis Slattery, D.D., 804 Broadway; Rev. E. Clowes Chorley, D.D., Garrison, N. Y.; Rev. Wm. H. Owen, Jr., Mt. Vernon, N. Y.; Mrs. V. G. Simkhovitch, 27 Barrow St.; Mrs. S. C. Capp, 16 East 87th St.; Mrs. R. M. Hurd, 12 East 68th St.; Deaconess Virginia C. Young, 17 Beekman Place; Rev. Chas. K. Gilbert, 416 Lafayette St., exec. secy.

***Social Service Committee of the Federation of Welfare Agencies of Staten Island** (org. 1913), 105 Stuyvesant Pl., St. George, S. I. Maintains a confidential exchange. Works for family rehabilitation.

Social Service Exchange of the Charity Organization Society, 105 East 22d St., N.Y.C. (tel. Gramercy 6276). Receives inquiries from social agencies seeking to know what other agencies are in touch with the families or individuals they are trying to serve. Inquiries are recorded in a card index, each card bearing the names of the members of the family, the address and the names of the organizations.

By assisting social agencies to co-ordinate their services, duplication of work is minimized and a maximum of co-operation is secured. There are more than 400,000 family cards in the index. During the year ending October, 1920, the Exchange was used by 405 agencies. Inquiries received numbered 53,820.

Gertrude Hill Springer, secy.

Society for the Aid of Friendless Women and Children (incorp. 1870), 20 Concord St., Brooklyn (tel. Main 2664). Maintains a children's home and temporary shelter for women and children.

Officers: Mrs. F. W. Hopkins, pres., Alpine, N. J.; Mrs. A. H. Stein, treas., Hotel Margaret, Brooklyn; Miss Helen Stutzer, secy., 815 St. Mark's Ave., Brooklyn; Mrs. C. Boyer, supt.

Society for the Care of German Seamen. See SEAMEN'S MISSION.

Society for the Employment and Relief of Poor Women, 146 East 16th St., N.Y.C. See ALL SOULS' UNITARIAN CHURCH, this list.

Society for Ethical Culture of New York, The (est. 1876, incorp. 1877), Central Park West and 64th St., N.Y.C. (tel. Columbus 7770). For the furtherance of a new ideal of life, based on the supremacy of the ethical aim above all other human aims whatsoever.

* *Current information not received.*

Dr. Felix Adler, senior leader; John Lovejoy Elliott, Dr. David Saville Muzzey, and Alfred W. Martin, leaders; Prof. E. R. A. Seligman, pres., 324 West 86th St.; Joseph Plaut, treas., 635 Greenwich St.; Robert D. Kohn, secy.; Mrs. R. G. Stone, exec. secy. Affiliated local groups in the Bronx; affiliated Ethical Society in Brooklyn with Sunday meetings at the Academy of Music, Lafayette Ave., Dr. Henry Neumann, leader.

The New York Society has sixteen sub-organizations devoted to religious, educational, philanthropic, and social activities, and maintains

THE ETHICAL CULTURE SCHOOL, 33 Central Park West, "intended to contribute to the solution of the great social problems by means of a profound reformation of the system of education," consists of Kindergarten, Elementary School, High School, and Kindergarten Normal Department. About one-half the pupils in this school are admitted under a system of free scholarships, the funds for which are obtained by public donations through the agency of the United Relief Works (see below). The Society promotes ethical education by a Sunday-school at 2 West 64th St., with classes for the young Sunday mornings, and classes for older persons Sunday evenings. Franklin C. Lewis, supt.

THE HUDSON GUILD (org. 1896), 436-438 West 27th St. A self-governing settlement to teach practically and theoretically the ethics of organization among the wage-earners, and to improve the moral, mental and physical condition of its members. Class instructions free. Club and classes for young children and adults. Public meetings for the discussion of social questions.

Alexander M. Bing, pres.; Chas. J. Liebmann, vice-pres.; Herbert A. Wolff, secy.; Wilfred A. Openhym, treas.; J. L. Elliott, head worker.

MADISON HOUSE, 216 Madison St. A neighborhood house that offers opportunities for the development of ethical conduct through experience in self-government as a working practice and belief in the power of public opinion to make it work. For these reasons there are developed and encouraged clubs, dramatics, debates, classes, games, athletics, and camp life, as a definite means to a definite end—the proper adjustment of human relations.

Ruth Larned, head worker.

THE UNITED RELIEF WORKS (incorp. 1879), 2 West 64th St., supply free scholarships in the Ethical Culture School and maintain district nursing among the sick poor and provides other preventive and remedial charity. Supported by voluntary contributions, etc.

The District Nursing Department sends trained nurses into the homes of the sick poor, to nurse the sick, to teach mothers to take proper care of their children in health and sickness. Such nurses are provided for the Good Samaritan, Northwestern and other dispensaries, to any one of which application should be made.

Leo G. Rose, pres., 34 Pine St.; M. Beckhard, treas., 102 West 87th St.; Mrs. Felix Adler, chrm., of District Nursing Committee, 33 Central Park West.

THE SEWING SOCIETY employs sewing women in making garments which it distributes to dispensaries, hospitals, and to individuals through its district nurses.

Mrs. Adolph Wurzburger, pres.

THE FRESH-AIR FUND COMMITTEE, of the Society for Ethical Culture, maintains a summer home, "Felicia," at Mountainville, Orange Co., N. Y., where children are sent for summer outings. Unsectarian. Children taken from Hudson Guild, Madison House; also independent groups.

Milton M. Klein, 361 Fifth Ave., chrm.

Society for the Friendless. See NATIONAL SOCIETY FOR THE FRIENDLESS.

Society of the Helpers of the Holy Souls of the City of New York, The (incorp. 1894), 112–118 East 86th St., N.Y.C. A Roman Catholic community the members of which devote their lives to nursing the sick poor gratuitously in their own homes, and to other works of mercy, particularly settlement work, including a club for young girls.

Mother Mary of St. Catherine, Superior.

Society of the Infant Jesus. See NURSING SISTERS OF THE SICK POOR.

Society of Inner Mission and Rescue Work, 564 Second St., Brooklyn, N. Y.

Officers: Rev. V. A. M. Mortensen, pres. and general supt.; Rev. J. F. W. Kitzmeyer, rec. secy.; Jens Riis, treas.

Society for Instruction in First Aid to the Injured, The. See FIRST AID, SOCIETY FOR, etc.

Society for Italian Immigrants, (incorp. 1901), 6 Water St., N.Y.C. (tel. Bowling Green 8838). Conducts a lodging house for Italian immigrants temporarily in New York. Establishes and maintains schools for Italians in labor camps. Affords protection of all kinds to Italian immigrants, and meets them at Ellis Island and guides them to their destination or to a place of shelter. Maintains an employment office for Italians, and agents on the steamship docks to assist returning Italians. Supported by subsidy and voluntary contributions.

Officers: Ernesto G. Fabbri, pres.; Alessandro Fabbri, treas.; J. K. Paulding, secy.; August V. Fozzi, manager.

Society of Jewish Social Workers of Greater New York, 114 Fifth Ave., N.Y.C. Object: To read papers, and discuss subjects relating to the work of the members and to promote the social interests of the Jewish community.

Society of the Lying-in Hospital of the City of New York (org. 1798, incorp. 1799). Maintains a hospital at Second Ave., 17th and 18th Sts., N.Y.C. (tel. Stuyvesant 2329). Sub-station, 314 Broome St. For the relief and care, free of charge, at their homes or in the hospital, of women unable to procure necessary medical attendance and nursing during the period of their confinement. Supported by voluntary subscriptions, contributions from patients, and a small endowment.

The service of this hospital offers a practical course of instruction to graduates and students of medicine in normal and abnormal obstetrics.

Board of thirteen Governors.

Officers: Lewis Cass Ledyard, pres., 14 Wall St.; J. Pierpont Morgan, vice-pres., 23 Wall St.; James Gore King, secy., 80 Broadway; William Pierson Hamilton, treas., 23 Wall St.; Stephen Merselis, asst. treas., 23 Wall St.; A. B. Davis, M.D., chief surgeon; W. H. Spiller, medical supt., to whom apply.

Society of the New York Hospital, The (incorp. 1771), 8 West 16th St., N.Y.C. (tel. Chelsea 8700). Maintains the

NEW YORK HOSPITAL (founded 1771), West 15th and 16th Sts., near Fifth Ave., N.Y.C. Office: 8 West 16th St. A general hospital for medical and surgical treatment of pay and free patients. Ward patients able to pay are charged $3.00 a day; private patients from $4.00 to $12.00 per day. Number of patients in hospital last year, 12,478.

Its Ambulance Service responded to 6,218 calls in 1919.

Thomas Howell, M.D., supt.

Out-Patient Department, in the basement of the Administration Bldg., 8 West 16th St., N.Y.C., open daily, except Sundays and legal holidays, from 10.30–11.30 A. M. and 1.30–3 P. M. Number of new cases treated last year, 12,536.

Training School for Nurses, 6 West 16th St.

BLOOMINGDALE HOSPITAL, White Plains, N. Y., for the treatment of nervous and mental disorders. Terms by arrangement. Accommodates 350; cared for 622 patients in 1919. Apply to the Bloomingdale Committee, at 8 West 16th St., or to

William L. Russell, M.D., medical supt.

CONVALESCENT COTTAGES, the Campbell Cottages, at White Plains, N. Y. Cared for 941 women and children during 1919. For admission, apply to the Superintendent of the New York Hospital.

Society for the Prevention of Crime (incorp. 1878), Guardian Life Insurance Bldg., 50 Union Sq., N.Y.C. (tel. Stuyvesant 1887). Aims to remove the sources and causes of crime; assist in the prosecution of lawbreakers; disseminate information by means of the press, and influence correct legislation in favor of measures needed for the honest enforcement of law. Supported by voluntary contributions.

Officers: S. Edward Young, pres.; William Sheafe Chase, vice-pres.; Thaddeus D. Kenneson, secy.; Howard Clark Barber, supt.; Samuel Marcus, counsel. Hon. vice-prests.: Thomas Snell, Frank Mason North, Lucien Knapp and Alfred B. Cruikshank.

Board of Directors: Thaddeus D. Kenneson, Charles H. Parkhurst, Charles E. Bruce, Frank Lugar, Samuel Marcus, Charles R. Saul, Matthew A. Beattie, Maurice H. Harris, Michael J. Horan, William Sheafe Chase, Ernest Spencer Roche, James G. Blaine, Merton L. Cushman and S. Edward Young.

Society for the Prevention of Cruelty to Animals, The American (incorp. 1866), Madison Ave., cor. 26th St. For the purpose indicated in title. Open day and night, also Sundays. Has ambulances for the removal of disabled animals and maintains free dispensaries and hospitals for animals, and shelters for dogs and cats. Supported by voluntary contributions. Applications and complaints should be made at the above address.

Officers: Alfred Wagstaff, pres.; Henry Bergh, treas.; Richard Welling, secy.; W. K. Horton, gen. manager.

Society for the Prevention of Cruelty to Children, The New York (incorp. 1875), 51 Irving Place, N.Y.C. (tel. Stuyvesant 8370). Investigates and prosecutes all cases of neglect or cruelty to children under sixteen years of age; also receives and cares for, pending trial or examination, all children under the age of sixteen held for crime or as witnesses in criminal cases. Supported by voluntary contributions and subscriptions.

Ernest K. Coulter, general manager, to whom apply at any hour, or to the police or judiciary.

Officers: M. Linn Bruce, pres.; Adrian Iselin, Vernon M. Davis, Peter G. Gerry, John G. Agar, Dallas B. Pratt, Morgan J. O'Brien, George G. Haven, Mortimer L. Schiff, George F. Baker, Charles A. Peabody, vice-presidents; Nathan Straus, Sidney C. Borg, William Woodward, Alonzo Potter, W. Averell Harriman, Alvin W. Krech, Alexander J. Hemphill, Edwin Thorne, Louis Wiley, De Lancey Nicoll,

Johnston L. Redmond, Arthur M. Crane, Robert D. McCarter, Corwin Black, directors; Alvin W. Krech, treas.; Arthur M. Crane, secy.; Elbridge T. Gerry, counsel.

Society for the Prevention of Cruelty to Children, Brooklyn. See BROOKLYN S. P. C. C.; also QUEENSBORO S. P. C. C.

Society for Prevention and Relief of Tuberculosis, Inc. Affiliated with the New York Department of Health. To supplement medical care and extension of relief by preventive work. To raise and receive donations by bequests for carrying on such undertakings.

Officers: Mrs. Hermann M. Biggs, 39 West 56th St., pres.

Society for Promoting the Gospel Among Seamen in the Port of New York (known as New York Port Society) (est. 1818, incorp. 1819), 166–168 Eleventh Ave., near 23d St., opp. Ferries, N.Y.C. (tel. Chelsea 2520). Maintains there its

MARINERS' CHURCH for sailors of various nationalities. (See Miscellaneous Churches in the Church List.) Its missionaries visit the seamen's boarding-houses, vessels, steamships, etc. Supported by voluntary contributions. Maintains also a

LIBRARY AND READING ROOM FOR SEAMEN; open daily from 10 A. M. to 10 P. M., where large facilities are furnished for correspondence between sailors and their friends.

Religious services for seamen conducted every Tuesday, Friday, and Sunday evenings at 7.30.

Officers: Wm. B. Isham, pres., 27 William St.; Rev. K. Palmer Miller, M.A. gen. secy. and pastor; George M. Thomson, treas.; Charles S. Yates, missionary in charge of Reading Room, known as New York Port Society.

Society for the Propagation of the Faith, The (1904), 462 Madison Ave. (tel. Plaza 4470). To support Catholic Missions at home and in foreign lands. Very Rev. John J. Dunn, diocesan director.

Society for the Relief of the Destitute Blind of the City of New York and its Vicinity, The (incorp. 1869), Grand Concourse and 193d St., N.Y.C. (tel. Fordham 4319). Home for indigent adult blind persons of both sexes of good moral character, irrespective of creed, free from infectious or incurable diseases, where they may enjoy reasonable comforts and have facilities for work.

Officers: Lewis Spencer Morris, pres., 32 Liberty St.; Frederick F. de Rham, treas., 315 Fourth Ave.; Chas. C. Bull, secy., 27 William St.

Society for the Relief of Destitute Children of Seamen, The (org. 1846, incorp. 1851), Castleton Ave., West New Brighton, Staten Island (tel. West Brighton 184).

The object of the Society is to care for and make a Home for destitute children of seamen, irrespective of creed and nationality. Children are admitted between the ages of two and ten; and receive public school education. If they are not claimed by relatives when they reach a suitable age, homes are found for them. Board $10 a month is required for those able to pay. No child admitted for less than a year. Capacity, 100. The Society is primarily dependent upon voluntary subscriptions, and has no connection with Sailor's Snug Harbor.

Officers: Miss Mary T. Marsh, 1st directress; Mrs. Gugy Æ. Irving, 2d directress; Mrs. Ralph L. Pritchard, rec. secy.; Mrs. C. H. Gostenhofer, cor. secy.; Miss M. Adelaide Irving, treas., 102 Henderson Ave., New Brighton,

S. I.; Miss Grace V. Sloat, supt., to whom application for admittance should be made.

Society for the Relief of Half Orphan and Destitute Children in the City of New York (org. 1835, incorp. 1837), Manhattan Ave., between 104th and 105th Sts., N.Y.C. (tel. Academy 2433). For Protestant children between four and ten years of age, of both sexes, of classes indicated in title. Board, $12 per month, must be paid in advance. No child is received for less than one year. Capacity for 164. All the children except those under six years of age are sent to the public schools. Others receive kindergarten instruction at the Institution. All the girls are given sewing lessons. Visiting days for parents and guardians, first and third Saturdays of each month, from 2–4 P. M. Applications for admission must be made to the Executive Committee at the Home on Wednesday mornings between 11 and 12 o'clock.

The Institution is supported by an inadequate endowment fund supplemented by the pupils board and voluntary contributions.

Officers: Miss Emily O. Butler, 1st directress; Mrs. F. S. Colt, treas., 148 East 61st St.; Mrs. James R. Wheeler, secy., 333 West 117th St.

Society for the Relief of Poor Widows and Small Children (org. 1798, incorp. 1802). Aids any industrious poor widow of good character, with two children under fourteen, who is not assisted by the authorities. Districted from Beekman to 110th St. Suspends work during the summer, except special cases.

Officers: Miss S. Grace Fraser, 1st directress; Mayhew W. Bronson, treas.; Miss Margaret A. Jackson, secy., 556 Madison Ave.

Society of St. Johnland (incorp. 1870), Kings Park, Long Island, N. Y. New York City office: 49 West 20th St. (tel. Chelsea 9836). To maintain homes for aged men and couples in destitute circumstances; to care for friendless children and youth, providing home, schooling, Christian training, and occupation fitting them for self-support; and generally to do such work as shall be required and is practicable with the benevolent designs of the Society.

As far as possible beneficiaries are supported free of expense; free work being limited only by the amount received for the purpose. Supported by voluntary contributions, income from endowments, and payments from relatives and friends of beneficiaries. When necessary, the following payments are required:

Two hundred and seventy-six dollars per year for the support of an aged man.

Five hundred and fifty-two dollars per year for the support of an aged couple.

One hundred and ninety-two dollars per year for the support of a boy or girl.

Children are admitted between the ages of two and ten years. Unruly children are not received. Boys are not retained after fourteen years of age, but girls may be kept until eighteen years old, to be trained for domestic services after completing the school course.

The Society maintains the CHURCH COMMUNITY OF SAINT JOHNLAND, a village of over twenty buildings and a population of about 200. Among the buildings are:

ST. JOHN'S INN, a Home for forty aged men.

MUHLENBERG HOME (a Home for aged women of the Church of the Holy Communion, New York), for twenty-four aged women.

SUNSET HOUSE, a Home for twelve aged couples.

SUNBEAM COTTAGE, a Home for twenty-four girls.

SPENCER AND WOLFE COTTAGE, a Home for twenty boys.

JOHN ROGERS CHISHOLM MEMORIAL, a Home for thirty boys.

THE BABIES' SHELTER (of the Church of the Holy Communion, New York), for twenty-four little children of both sexes.

A KINDERGARTEN AND GRADED SCHOOL under teachers trained in the best methods of instruction.

ROBERT LEWIS HARRISON INFIRMARY.

ADMINISTRATION BUILDING.

***Society of St. Joseph of Nazareth** (SISTERS OF ST. JOSEPH), (incorp. 1892), Bronxville, N. Y. The Sisterhood has charge of

ST. MARTHA'S INDUSTRIAL SCHOOL FOR GIRLS AND NAZARETH SCHOOL, both at Bronxville. Address the Rev. Mother, Bronxville, N. Y.

Society of St. Vincent de Paul in the City of New York (org. 1846), 375 Lafayette St., N.Y.C. A Roman Catholic Society, the objects of which are: (1) the practice of a Christian life; (2) to visit the poor in their dwellings and to carry them succor in kind; (3) to promote the elementary and religious instruction of poor children; (4) to distribute moral and religious books; (5) to undertake any other charitable work to which its resources are adequate.

Conference: Nearly all the Roman Catholic Churches in New York City have conferences of the Society. The name of the conference is usually the same as that of the church with which it is connected; its work is confined to the parish in which it is located, and the parish priest is, in most cases, its Spiritual Director. Applications may be made to the Director or to the President. (See list of Conferences.)

Particular Councils: The officers of the conferences of all or part of a city are united in one organization for the general supervision of the Society and this organization is known as a Particular Council. There are six such councils in the City of New York, as follows:

Particular Council of New York. Territory: 14th St. South, East and West to Battery; 14th St. North to 100th St., Fifth Ave. to North River; 14th St. North to 100th St., Fifth Ave. to East River and the Borough of Richmond.

Particular Council of Upper Manhattan. Territory: Borough of Manhattan north of 100th St.

Particular Council of the Bronx. Territory: Borough of the Bronx.

Particular Council of Brooklyn. Territory: Boroughs of Brooklyn and Queens.

Special Works: In addition to the Conference there are a number of special works, maintained by the Particular Councils and directed by committees made up of members of the Particular Councils and Conferences.

The several Committees above referred to visit regularly every Sunday the Hospitals, prisons, and other city institutions; furnishing reading matter, giving religious instructions to those of their faith, and supplying such material aid and advice as is needed by the sick and convalescent.

METROPOLITAN CENTRAL COUNCIL OF NEW YORK, THE. Office: 215 West 15th St. (temporary), N.Y.C. This council has general jurisdiction of the Society in the province of New York (states of New York and New Jersey), with the exception of the diocese of Brooklyn.

Most Rev. Patrick J. Hayes, D.D., Arch Bishop of N. Y., Spiritual Di-

* *Current information not received.*

rector; James F. Boyle, pres.; Michael J. Scanlan, treas.; James F. McNaboe, secy.

PARTICULAR COUNCIL OF NEW YORK, THE (org. 1857, incorp. 1872; re-organized Oct. 1920, Particular Council of East Manhattan). Office: 216 West 15th St. (temporary). It meets in St. Stephen's Hall, 134 East 29th St., on the second Monday of each month at 8 P. M. Most Rev. Patrick J. Hayes, D.D., Arch Bishop of N. Y., Spiritual Director; James F. Boyle, pres. and treas.; Patrick H. Bird, secy.

Special Works: Catholic Home Bureau (q. v.), 105 East 22d St.; Ozanam Association (q. v.), 5 Beekman St.; St. Vincent de Paul Summer Home (q. v.); St. Elizabeth's Home for Convalescent Women (q. v.); Blackwell's Island, Bellevue, and Allied Hospitals, Randall's Island and Tombs Committees.

There are 20 conferences which meet as follows:

Epiphany, 239 East 21st St., Tuesday, 7.30 P.M. John J. O' Connell, 335 Ave. A.

Immaculate Conception, Tuesday, 8 P. M., Vestry. Thos. J. Walsh, pres., 225 West 15th St.

Our Lady of Good Counsel, Very Rev. Mgr. J. N. Connolly, 230 East 90th St.

Our Lady of Perpetual Help, 323 East 61st St., Monday, 8 P. M. Edward Colligan, Sr., 421 East 65th St.

Sacred Heart of Jesus and Mary, 317 East 33d St., Friday, 9 P. M. D. Patrione, 158 East 26th St.

St. Agnes, 156 East 44th St., Tuesday, 8 P. M. Leo J. Kearney, 353 Mosholu Parkway North.

St. Anthony (in St. Boniface), 340 East 47th St., Tuesday, 8 P. M. N. Picciano, 307 East 48th St.

St. Boniface, 312 East 47th St., Wednesday, 8 P. M. Valentine Stockman, 325 East 79th St.

St. Francis de Sales, Rev. John F. Brady, D.D., 135 East 96th St.

St. Gabriel, 308 East 37th St., Tuesday, 8 P. M. John J. Killian, pres., 316 East 37th St.

St. Ignatius, School Hall, 87th St., Tuesday, 8 P. M. Valentine Maickel, 540 East 87th St.

St. Jean Baptiste, 184 East 76th St., Thursday, 8 P. M. Jeremiah Maher, 185 East 76th St.

St. John Baptist de la Salle, Stapleton, S. I., Monday, 8 P. M., Rectory. Martin J. Walsh, 16 Murray Place.

St. John the Evangelist, Rev. P. F. O'Connor, 351 East 55th St.

St. Lawrence, 74 East 83d St., Tuesday, 8 P. M. Jos. H. Fargis, pres., 131 East 91st St.

St. Monica, 413 East 79th St., Tuesday, 8 P. M. William Slattery, 57 East 86th St.

St. Patrick's Cathedral, Wm. J. Bowe, 59 West 53d St.

St. Stephen, 134 East 29th St., Tuesday, 8 P. M. John McDonald, pres., 515 Second Ave.

St. Vincent Ferrer, 869 Lexington Ave., Tuesday, 8 P. M. Dr. A. V. Freeman, 967 Lexington Ave.

St. Wenceslaus, 323 East 61st St., Tuesday, 8 P. M. Joseph Komarek, 432 East 66th St.

PARTICULAR COUNCIL OF WEST MANHATTAN

14th to 100th Streets, Fifth Ave. to North River (org. October, 1920). Thomas F. Farrell, pres., 6 Church St. (tel. Rector 9100). There are 17 conferences which meet as follows:

Holy Cross, 329 West 42d St., Tuesday, 8 P. M. James J. O'Connell, pres., 424 West 43d St.

Holy Innocents, 126 West 37th St., Tuesday, 7.30 P. M., School. Michael Connolly, pres., 309 West 55th St.

Holy Name, 207 West 96th St., Tuesday, 7.30 P. M. Jeremiah J. Lynch, pres., 175 West 95th St.

Holy Trinity, 216 West 83d St., Tuesday, 8 P. M. Maurice A. O'Connell, pres., 115 West 84th St.

Our Lady of Guadaloupe, 229 West 14th St., Wednesday, 6 P. M. G. B. Puga, pres., 83 Hamilton Place.

Sacred Heart, 457 West 51st St. Rev. Wm. C. Ryder.

St. Ambrose, 513 West 54th St., Monday, 7.30, St. Ambrose Hall. William Moran, pres., 498 West 55th St.

St. Benedict the Moor, 342 West 53d St., Sunday, 12.30. Dr. York Russell, pres , 244 West 131st St.

St. Bernard, 246 West 14th St., Tuesday, 8 P. M. Patrick J. Ward, pres., 246 West 14th St.

St. Columba, 345 West 25th St., Thursday, 8 P. M. Thos. E. Anderson, pres., 66 West 88th St.

St. Francis Xavier, 30 West 16th St., Tuesday, 8 P. M. Robert J. Doherty, pres., 30 West 16th St.

St. Gregory the Great, 138 West 90th St., Thursday, 8 P. M. Dr. Charles F. McKenna, pres., 155 West 91st St.

St. John the Baptist, 210 West 31st St., Friday, 8.15 P. M. Bernard Lawrence, pres., 352 West 41st St.

St. Malachy, 239 West 49th St., Tuesday, 8 P. M. William J. Kelly, pres., 446 West 51st St.

St. Matthew, 216 West 68th St., Tuesday, 7.30 P. M. Henry P. Fall, pres., 161 West 63d St.

St. Paul the Apostle, 415 West 59th St., Tuesday, 8 P. M. Thomas F. Farrell, pres., 6 Church St.

St. Raphael, 502 West 41st St., Rev. M. J. Duffy.

PARTICULAR COUNCIL OF LOWER MANHATTAN

South of Fourteenth Street, East and West, to Battery (org. October, 1920). Office: 216 West 15th St. Meets at office on second Monday of each month at 8 P. M. Thomas A. Wolfe, president.

There are fifteen Conferences which meet as follows:

Most Holy Redeemer, 165 Third St., Wednesday, 8 P. M., 208 East 4th St. Chas. Werckle, pres., 237 East 12th St.

Nativity, 44 Second Ave. Rev. D. J. Quinn, S. J.

Our Lady of Sorrow, 107 Pitt St., Monday, 8.15 P. M. Joseph Sperzel, pres., 247 East 3d St.

St. Alphonsus, 4–6 Thompson St., Monday, 8 P. M. Patrick J. O'Connell, 285 W. Houston St.

St. Anns, 118 East 12th St., Sunday at noon, School East 11th St. John Donat, pres., 214 East 12th St.

St. Anthony, 149–153 Sullivan St., Sunday, 10 A. M., 151 Thompson St. John O'Connor, pres., 560 West 180th St.

St. Brigid, 119 Ave. B., Rectory. Wm. F. McGuirk, pres., 298 East 7th St.

St. Joachim, 26 Roosevelt St., Wednesday, 8 P. M. Ettore De Stafano, pres., 4 Mulberry St.

St. Joseph, Sixth Ave., 109 Washington Place, Tuesday, 8 P. M. John J. Doris, pres., 288 West 12th St.

St. Nicholas, 121 Second St., Friday, 8 P. M. Joseph Schiff, pres., 151 Ave. A.

St. Patrick's (Mott St.), 263 Mulberry St., Tuesday, 8 P. M. Stephen J. Hannigan, pres., 665 McDonough St., Brooklyn.

St. Peter's, 31 Barclay St. Rt. Rev. Jas. H. McGean.

St. Rose, 42 Cannon St., Sunday, 11 A. M., Basement. Lawrence Rooney, pres., 1 Cannon St.

St. Veronica, 657 Washington St., Tuesday, 8 P. M. Thomas A. Wolfe, pres., 275 West 11th St.

Transfiguration, 29 Mott St., Wednesday, 8 P. M. Rocco G. Lalla, 21 Mott St.

PARTICULAR COUNCIL OF THE BRONX (org. 1911, incorp. 1916). Office: 509 Willis Ave. (tel. Melrose 7248). It meets in St. Augustine's School Hall, 1180 Franklin Ave., on the second Monday of each month, at 8.15 P. M.

Rev. William A. Courtney, Spiritual Director, 3223 Perry Ave.; James J. Reid, pres., 1903 Davidson Ave., Peter J. Montague, 2976 Valentine Ave., Edmond J. Butler, 232 East 176th St., and Stephen L. Murphy, 3188 Perry Ave., vice-prests.; James E. Dougherty, secy., 764 East 176th St.; James J. O'Brien, treas., 2241 Valentine Ave.

Special Works: The Hospital Committees visit weekly the following hospitals: Lincoln, Lebanon, Fordham, Riverside, Montefiore Home, Home for Incurables, House of Calvary, Institution for the Blind and Seton Hospital.

The conferences are as follows:

Holy Family, 1071 Castle Hill Ave.

Holy Spirit, 1940 University Ave.

Immaculate Conception, 739 Gun Hill Rd.

Our Lady of Mercy, Fordham, 2496 Marion Ave.

Our Lady of Mt. Carmel, 627 East 187th St.

Our Lady of Pity, 274 East 151st St.

St. Anselm's, 673 Tinton Ave.

St. Anthony, 1495 Commonwealth Ave.

St. Anthony of Padua, 832 East 166th St.

St. Augustine's, 1183 Franklin Ave.

St. Barnabas', 409 East 241st St.

St. Brendan's, 3223 Perry Ave.

St. Clement Hofbauer, Immaculate Conception Church.

St. Jerome's, 230 Alexander Ave.

St. Joseph's, 1949 Bathgate Ave.

St. John Chrysostom, 985 East 167th St.

St. John's (Kingsbridge), 2953 Kingsbridge Ave.

St. Luke's, 623 East 138th St.

St. Mary's, 3649 White Plains Ave.

St. Philip Neri, Rectory, 3025 Concourse.

St. Raymonds, East Tremont and Castle Hill Aves.

St. Rita's, 448 College Ave.

St. Thomas Aquinas', 1913 Daly Ave.

St. Angela Merici, 921 Morris Ave.

St. Pius, 418 East 145th St.

St. Athanasius, 878 Tiffany St.

SS. Peter and Paul, 833 St. Anns Ave.

St. Nicholas of Tolentine, 2342 Andrews Ave.

St. Roch, 734 East 150th St.

PARTICULAR COUNCIL OF BROOKLYN (org. 1857). Office, 4 Court Sq., Room 38 (tel. Main 7756–7757). Has supervision of the Conferences in the Boroughs of Brooklyn and Queens. It meets on the second Thursday of each month at St. James Pro-Cathedral School Hall, Jay St., at 8 P. M.

Rt. Rev. Mgr. Francis J. O'Hara, Spiritual Director, Cathedral Pl.; Thomas W. Hynes, pres., 1332 Pacific St.; vice-prests., Thomas P. Mulligan, William J. Grinden, Thomas M. James, Hugh D. McGrane, Ludwig Merkelin, Thomas J. O'Hare; P. O'Connor, 4 Court Sq., treas.; Joseph Kunkel, secy.

Special Works: Woodcleft Fresh-air Home for Children and Convalescent Women (q. v.).

CONFERENCES

ST. AGNES, 417 Sackett St. Meets Monday, 7.30 P. M., in St. Agnes Chapel. Thomas J. Kavanagh, pres., 361 Degraw St.

ST. AMBROSE, 222 Tompkins Ave. Meets Sunday, 8 P. M., in the Vestry of the Church. William Dooling, 17 Van Buren St., pres.

ST. ANN, 251 Front St. Meets Wednesday, 8 P. M., in St. Ann's School, basement of Church. Thomas F. Tully, pres., 164 High St.

St. Anthony of Padua, 862 Manhattan Ave. Meets Monday, 8 p. m., in Library Church. M. H. Kavanagh, 141 Kent St.

Assumption, 64 Middagh St. Meets Tuesday, 7.30 p. m., in the Vestry of the Church. Francis McPartland, pres., 48 Columbia Heights.

St. Augustine, 116 Sixth Ave. Meets Tuesday, 8 p. m., at 448 Dean St. W. H. Bennett, pres., 448 Dean St.

St. Barbara, 307 Central Ave. William Drennan, pres., 965 Bushwick Ave.

St. Benedict, 927 Herkimer St. Meets Wednesday, 8 p. m., in the School Hall. Sebastian Hass, pres., 966 Herkimer St.

Blessed Sacrament, 200 Euclid Ave. Meets Friday, 8 p. m., in the Rectory. Lawrence J. Mulligan, pres., 387 Arlington Ave.

St. Brigid, 419 Linden St. Meets Tuesday, 8 p. m., in the Rectory. Ed. Collins, 1721 Gates Ave.

St. Catherine of Alexandria, 1119–41st St. Meets Monday, 8.15 p. m., in the School. Charles D. Sanderson, pres., 4619 Fort Hamilton Parkway.

St. Charles Borromeo, 21 Sydney Pl. Meets Monday, 8 p. m., in the School Hall. Augustus Ranch, 67 Atlantic Ave.

St. Edward, 108 St. Edwards St. Meets Monday, 8 p. m., in the basement of the Church. Joseph Bailey, 32 Auburn Pl.

The Epiphany, 96 South 9th St. Meets Monday, 8.30 p. m., at Rectory. Thomas M. James, pres., 132 Clymer St.

St. Finbar, 8720 Bay 20th St. Meets Monday, 8 p. m., in the Rectory. E. J. Huott, pres., 46 Bay 17th St.

St. Francis Xavier, 225 Sixth Ave. Meets Monday, 8 p. m., in the School Hall. William J. O'Brien, 439–6th St.

Gate of Heaven, Broadway and McCormick Ave., Ozone Park, L. I. Meets Tuesday, 8 p. m., in the School Hall. F. D. Orbessan, M.D., pres., 1259 McCormick Ave., Ozone Park, L. I.

St. Gregory, 997 St. John's Pl. Meets Monday, 8 p. m., in the Rectory. J. J. Cunningham, 225 Brooklyn Ave., pres.

St. Gabriel, 749 Linwood St. Meets Wednesday, 8 p. m., in the Rectory. Edward O'Rourke, pres., 299 Arlington Ave.

Holy Family, 205–14th St. Meets Wednesday, 8 p. m., in the St. Vincent de Paul Room. John J. Gallagher, pres., 415–10th St.

Holy Innocents, 1718 Beverly Rd. Meets Sunday at 11 a. m., in School Hall. Joseph F. Ackerman, pres., 360 East 19th St.

Holy Name, 245 Prospect Park, West. Meets Monday, 8 p. m. Thomas Hogan, pres., 29 Fuller Pl.

Holy Rosary, 141 Chauncey St. Meets Wednesday, 8 p. m., in the basement of the Church. J. F. Mallon, pres., 724 Herkimer St.

Holy Trinity, 138 Montrose Ave. Meets Monday, 8 p. m., at the Rectory. George J. Peters, pres., 191 Graham Ave.

Immaculate Heart of Mary, 119 East 4th St. Meets Monday, 8 p. m., at the Rectory. James F. Decker, pres., 2721 Fort Hamilton Ave

Immaculate Conception of the B. V. M., 72 Maujer St. Meets Sunday, 11 a. m., in the School Room. Felix Kelly, pres., 240 Rutland Rd.

St. Ignatius, 1125 Carroll St. Meets Tuesday, 8 p. m., in Loyola Hall, Rogers Ave. and Carroll St. Frederick Kerr, 698 Sterling Pl.

St. James Pro-Cathedral, Cathedral Pl. Meets Wednesday, 8 p. m., in the basement of Church. James Larmour, pres., 226 Clermont Ave.

ST. JOHN THE BAPTIST, St. John's College, Lewis Ave. Meets Wednesday, 8 P. M., in the College Hall. L. W. Malone, vice-pres., 817 Willoughby Ave.

ST. JOHN THE EVANGELIST, 250-21st St. Meets Monday, 7.30 P. M., at 225-22d St. Michael J. Rush, pres., 163-23d St.

ST. JOSEPH, 856 Pacific St. Meets Wednesday, 8 P. M. Wm. J. Tormey, pres., 1010 Fulton St.

ST. LUCY, 802 Kent Ave. Meets on Monday evening in basement of Church. Andrea Basile, pres., 812 Kent Ave.

ST. MARY STAR OF THE SEA, 467 Court St. Meets Monday, 7.30 P. M., in the Chapel. Joseph Medlar, 71 2d St., pres.

ST. MARY STAR OF THE SEA (Far Rockaway), Clarke Ave., Far Rockaway. Meets every Friday, 8 P. M., in the Chapel. Edmund J. Healy, pres., Bay View Ave., Far Rockaway.

ST. MATTHEW, 254 Utica Ave. Meets Friday, 8 P. M., in the School Room. W. T. Matthews, pres., 1282 Prospect Pl.

ST. MICHAEL, 42d St. and Fourth Ave. Meets Monday, 8 P. M., in the School Hall, James Cain, pres., 530-44th St.

ST. MICHAEL (E. N. Y.), 225 Jerome St. Meets Tuesday, 8.30 P. M., in the School. Charles Rudershausen, 2747 Fulton St.

ST. MICHAEL (Flushing), Flushing, L. I. Meets Sunday, 7 P. M., in St. Michael's School. David Barry, pres., 59 Madison Ave., Flushing, L. I.

THE NATIVITY, 495 Classon Ave. Meets Monday, 8 P. M., in the Chapel Hall. J. A. Creighton, pres., 163 Putnam Ave.

OUR LADY OF ANGELS, Fourth Ave. and 74th St. Meets Monday, 8 P. M., in the Rectory. Ludwig Merkelein, pres., 428 Ovington Ave.

OUR LADY OF GOOD COUNSEL, 915 Putnam Ave. Meets Tuesday, 8 P. M., in the Rectory, 915 Putnam Ave. H. D. McGrane, pres., 533 Madison St.

OUR LADY OF MERCY, 284 Schermerhorn St. Meets Monday, 8 P. M., in the Rectory. James Hogart, pres., 464 Pacific St.

OUR LADY OF PERPETUAL HELP, 59th St. and Fifth Ave. Meets Tuesday, 8 P. M., in the Sacristy of the Church. William S. Bartley, 450 59th St.

OUR LADY OF VICTORY, Throop Ave. and Macon St. Meets Tuesday, 8 P. M., in the Sacristy of the Church. Charles Partridge, pres., 288 McDonough St.

OUR LADY OF LOURDES, De Sales Pl. and Broadway. Meets Monday, 8 P. M., in the Rectory. Joseph D. Coffey, pres., 41 Aberdeen St.

ST. PATRICK, 285 Willoughby Ave. Meets Monday, 7.30 P. M., in the School Hall. John A. McCarthy, pres., 239 Emerson Pl.

ST. PATRICK (L. I. C.), 123 Academy St. (L. I. City). Meets Thursday, 8 P. M., in the Vestry of the Church. Robert Flood, pres., 171 Bee Bee Ave., L. I. City.

ST. PATRICK (Fort Hamilton), Fort Hamilton. Meets Tuesday, 8.30 P. M., in the Church Hall. Hugh A. Napier, 259-93d St.

ST. PAUL, 223 Congress St. Meets Tuesday, 8 P. M., in the Church basement. Daniel J. Printy, pres., 296 Warren St.

ST. PETER, 117 Warren St. Meets Monday, 8 P. M., 112 Warren St. James Armstrong, pres., 179 Baltic St.

SS. PETER AND PAUL, 71 South 3d St. Meets every Tuesday, 8 P. M. Joseph Gallagher, 112 Clymer St.

QUEEN OF ALL SAINTS, 101 Greene Ave. Meets every second and fourth Wednesday, at 8.30 P. M., in the School, Richard H. Farley, 284 DeKalb Ave.

ST. RITA, 466 Blvd., L. I. City. Meets Tuesday, 8.30 P. M., in the Rectory. James McConnell, pres., 67 Sherman St., L. I. City.

SACRED HEART, 41 Adelphi St. Meets Wednesday, 8 P. M., in the Rectory, John Long, pres., 116 Clermont Ave.

ST. STEPHEN, 108 Carroll St. Meets Monday, 8 P. M., in the School Hall. P. D. Bradshaw, pres., 426 Clinton St.

ST. TERESA, 563 Sterling Pl. Meets Tuesday, 8 P. M., in the School Hall. Thomas Monahan, pres., Manhattan Beach, N. Y.

ST. THOMAS AQUINAS, 249 9th St. Meets Monday, 8.15 P. M., in the basement of the Church. Wm. H. Peters, 301 7th St.

TRANSFIGURATION, 263 Marcy Ave., Meets Monday, 8 P. M., in the Hall. John O'Rourke, pres., 271 Division Ave.

ST. VINCENT DE PAUL, 167 North 6th St. Meets Wednesday, 8 P. M., in the Chapel. Patrick Mallon, pres., 4–5 Court Sq.

THE VISITATION, 98 Richards St. Meets Monday, 7.50 P. M., in the School Room. Joseph Twiggs, 61 Sullivan St.

Society of Sanitary and Moral Prophylaxis. See AMERICAN SOCIAL HYGIENE ASSOCIATION.

Society for the Suppression of Unnecessary Noise (est. 1906). The purposes of this society are: 1. Nationalization of movement for sane Fourth. 2. Suppression of needless noises, particularly in the vicinity of hospitals, schools, etc.

Mrs. Isaac L. Rice, pres.; Miss Muriel Rice, secy., 12 East 87th St., New York City.

Society for the Welfare of Jewish Deaf, Inc. See JEWISH DEAF, SOCIETY FOR.

Sojourner Truth House (Home for Colored Girls), 15 West 131st St., N.Y.C. (tel. Harlem 7047). Capacity, fourteen.

Officers: Mrs. George W. Seligman, pres., Irvington-on-Hudson; Mrs. Bertha T. Ufford, treas.; James H. Hubert, secy., 2303 Seventh Ave., N.Y.C.

Soldiers and Sailors Service Club. See NEW YORK COMMUNITY SERVICE.

Solomon and Betty Loeb Memorial Home for Convalescents (incorp. 1906), East View, Westchester County, N. Y. Admission office, 356 Second Ave., N.Y.C. (tel. Gramercy 2598). Examining hours: 9 to 12 A. M., Monday, Tuesday, Thursday and Friday. Object: to provide a suitable home for persons who are recovering from severe sickness or are in infirm health, and who would probably be benefited by a temporary sojourn in the country. Capacity, 108 beds, 100 beds for women and children over five years old, regardless of faith or nationality; 8 beds set aside for social workers and nurses. Supported by contributions from members of the family.

Officers: J. J. Hanauer, pres., 52 William St.; Leopold Stern, vice-pres., 68 Nassau St.; Paul Baerwald, treas., 19 Nassau St.; A. A. Cook, secy., 111 Broadway; Miss Kate V. Slevin, registrar, 356 Second Ave.; Mrs. Rachel M. Israel, supt., East View, N. Y.

Sons and Daughters of Israel, The Home of the (est. 1909, incorp. 1912), 230–232 East 10th St., N.Y.C. (tel. Orchard 5713). An institution which aims to cheer and brighten the remaining years of poor, old, and indigent co-religionists. The house is a modern structure, equipped with all improvements. Capacity, 100. Supported by voluntary contributions.

Officers: Judge Aaron J. Levy, pres.; A. Reitman, treas.; Anna Schwartz, secy.

Sophia Fund, The (incorp. 1900), Room 901, 253 Broadway, N.Y.C. Founded by Richard P. Rothwell. To remove friendless girls between one and six years of age from dangerous and demoralizing surroundings, to place them in private families, and to have them legally adopted.

Officers: James N. Taylor, pres.; F. J. Pratt, treas.; Mrs. Etta Hudgins Schick, secy.; Mrs. Margaret Hudgins Boyd, supt.

Sorrowful Mother Orphanage. See SISTERS OF ST. DOMINIC.

***South Side Dispensary of East New York** (incorp. 1910), 238 Wyona St., Brooklyn, N. Y.

***Southern New York Baptist Association, The** (incorp. 1871). For the cultivation of fraternal sympathy, the promotion of each other's spiritual welfare, and the establishing and strengthening of Baptist Churches.

Rev. Enos J. Bosworth, pres., 461 Fort Washington Ave.

Spanish and Portuguese Synagogue. See SISTERHOOD OF THE SPANISH AND PORTUGUESE.

Spanish Home for Immigrants, of the Spanish Protective Society (incorp. 1907), 41 Cherry St., N.Y.C. Aids Spanish immigrants on arrival. Non-sectarian.

Spanish Settlement. See CASA MARIA.

Spanish Society, The (Union Benefica Espanola), 24 West 16th St., N.Y.C. (tel. Watkins 7873). To provide medical and hospital assistance to members. Supported by fees.

Officers: Jose Camprubi, pres., 111 Broadway; Jose Mundet, treas., 24 Stone St.; Delfin Gonzalez, secy., 250 Sherman Ave., N.Y.C.

Speedwell Country Homes Society for Convalescent and Abandoned Children (incorp. 1902), 32½ Sussex Ave., Morristown, N. J. Provides homes in the country for convalescent or abandoned children under 12 years of age, from hospitals, social service bureaus and tenement districts of New York City. The homes have been selected with greatest care, with a view to assuring the benefits of family life for each child, and avoiding the expense and efforts of institutional care. They are under the personal supervision of the managers and the matron, who reside in Morristown. Children are received at any time. Winter is usually the busiest season for the Society's work.

Officers: Mrs. H. A. Alexander, pres.; Mrs. Brayton Ives, secy.; Mrs. Arthur F. Mabon, treas., 518 West 142d St., N.Y.C.; Henry Dwight Chapin, M.D., medical director; Samuel Haven, M.D., attending physician, 14 Elm St., Morristown, N. J.; Miss Mabel Warne, supt., 32½ Sussex Ave., Morristown, N. J.; Mrs. Keeler, attending nurse.

Spence Alumnae Society, The (est. 1899, incorp. 1911), 232 East 62d St., N.Y.C. (tel. 7164 Plaza). Conducts a Home for the care of orphaned babies and places them for adoption. Children obtained through public and private agencies, such as child-caring institutions, hospitals, day nurseries, settlements, the State Charities Aid Association, physicians, and individuals.

Officers: Miss Mary P. Wells, pres., 115 East 81st St.; Miss Janet Gregory, treas., 123 East 53d St.; Mrs. Wm. Demorest, secy., 118 West 76th St.

Springler Summer Home. See ST. MARKS IN THE BOUWERIE, this list.

Spring St. Presbyterian Church, 246 Spring St., N.Y.C. Rev. John W. Darr, Minister. Maintains the

SPRING ST. NEIGHBORHOOD HOUSE, 244 Spring St. (tel. Canal 483). Theodore F. Lentz, resident-in-charge. A

* *Current information not received.*

neighborhood center for men, women, boys, and girls, young women, and mothers. Conducts clubs and classes, kindergarten, cooking school, day nursery, gymnasium, fresh-air work, summer school, etc.

VARICK HOUSE, 11 Dominic St. (tel. Spring 9761). A boarding house for working girls.

William Sloane Coffin, pres.

See also under PRESBYTERIAN CHURCHES in the Church List.

Spurgeon Memorial Sermon Society, 14–16 Tillary St., Brooklyn. Founded July, 1892, for the Free Loan Distribution of Charles Haddon Spurgeon's Sermons as a "Living" and "Literary" monument to his memory. Strictly undenominational. Rev. T. C. Roberts-Horsfield, secy., to whom communications should be addressed.

S. R. Smith Infirmary. See STATEN ISLAND HOSPITAL.

Stage Women's War Relief, 366 Fifth Ave., N.Y.C. (tel. Fitz Roy 2985). Departments of Work:

Supplying entertainment at hospitals. Mrs. Eula Garrison in charge.

Weekly outings for wounded men. Miss Felicia Morris in charge.

Service House, 251 Lexington Ave. Home for permanently wounded men. (Management New York City Board.)

Service House, 38–40 West 48th St. Home for permanently wounded men. (Management New York City Board).

Officers: Rachel Crothers, pres.; Mrs. Shelley Hull, treas.; Mary H. Kirkpatrick, secy.

Stapleton Day Nursery (incorp. 1910), 96 Wright St., Stapleton, S. I.

State Agricultural and Industrial School (est. 1846 as Western House of Refuge for Juvenile Delinquents; name and location changed, 1902), Industry, Monroe Co., N. Y. (tel. Rush 45). Receives boys from twelve to sixteen years of age from all counties in New York State except New York and Kings, boys over twelve years of age from the first, second, third, or ninth judicial district, who have committed a crime amounting to a felony will not be received. Capacity of institution, 755.

The boys are given such scholastic, industrial, and agricultural training as is best adapted to their reformation and will enable them on their discharge to become self-supporting, self-respecting members of society.

Hobart H. Todd, supt.

State Board of Charities, The (est. 1867; created a constitutional body, 1895). State office: The Capitol, Albany, N. Y. New York City office: Room 502, 287 Fourth Ave., N.Y.C. (tel. Gramercy 5957).

The State Board of Charities is composed of twelve commissioners, appointed by the Governor with the consent of the Senate for terms of eight years. One commissioner is appointed for each Judicial District, and three additional commissioners for New York City. Each commissioner is entitled to per diem compensation, for attendance at meetings of the Board and its committees, not exceeding $500 for any one year. No commissioner can be trustee, manager, director, or other administrative officer of any of the institutions subject to the supervision of the Board.

Officers: William R. Stewart, pres.; William H. Gratwick, vice-pres.; Chas. H. Johnson, secy.; Robert W. Hill, supt. of State and Alien Poor; Richard W. Wallace, supt. of Inspection; James H. Foster, supt. Division of Children; Clarence E. Ford, supt. Division of Medical Charities; John B. Prest, supt. New York City office.

Commissioners residing in New York

City: William R. Stewart, 31 Nassau St.; Lee K. Frankel, 1 Madison Ave.; Victor F. Ridder, 182 William St.; J. Richard Kevin, M.D., 252 Gates Ave., Brooklyn.

The Board is required by law to visit, inspect, and maintain a general supervision of all institutions, societies, or associations which are of a charitable, eleemosynary, correctional, or reformatory character, whether State or municipal, incorporated or not incorporated, excepting prisons and reformatories in which adult males convicted of felony are confined, and hospitals and asylums for the insane, and to make an annual report to the Legislature.

The powers and duties are specially enumerated in Articles 2, 15 and 16 of the State Charities Law, the Poor Law, Sec. 482 of the Penal Law, and Arts. 3 and 7 of Membership Corporations Law.

State Bureau of Municipal Information, New York. Municipal information for officials of all cities in the State. Conference of Mayors, 25 Washington Ave., Albany, N. Y.

Officers: Mayor William J. Wallin, Yonkers, N. Y., pres.; Mayor James R. Watt, Albany, treas.; William P. Capes, director.

State Charities Aid Association (org. 1872, incorp. 1880), Rooms 710-714, 105 East 22d St., N.Y.C. (tel. Gramercy 1454). To visit state, county, city, and town charitable institutions, and secure improvements in their administration by legislation or other means; to promote efforts to improve public health, prevent disease, and provide better care for the sick; to help conserve mental health through the prevention of mental diseases and defects and provision for earlier care and treatment; to aid in the care of destitute children by placing them in families and by visiting children who have been so placed, and by such other methods as may prove wise. It is the only unofficial organization devoting itself to this important field of public charity. It has local visiting committees in forty-five counties, with a total of more than 1,000 volunteer visitors to county, city, and town almshouses, state hospitals for the insane, county homes for children, city hospitals, state charitable institutions, and other public charities, with a total of more than 50,000 inmates. It is supported by voluntary contributions; expenses about $280,000 annually.

Officers: George F. Canfield, pres.; Mrs. William B. Rice and Miss Louisa Lee Schuyler, vice-prests.; M. N. Buckner, treas.; Homer Folks, secy.; George A. Hastings, George J. Nelbach, asst. secys.

The Central Association has Standing and Special Committees: (a) on the care, training, and disposition of children who are public charges, and their supervision when placed in free family homes; (b) on hospitals, for improving the construction, organization, and administration of public charitable institutions; (c) on mental hygiene for promoting adequate and proper care of the insane and feeble-minded and for the prevention of mental diseases and defects, throughout the State and City of New York; (d) on the prevention of tuberculosis and the promotion of public health work generally in the State of New York outside New York City.

The Association publishes the "S. C. A. A. News" monthly for the information of its members.

CHILDREN'S DEPARTMENT

COUNTY AGENCIES FOR DEPENDENT CHILDREN, Room 710. Object: To promote co-operation between the County Committees of the Association and public officials in the counties in employing trained agents to investigate the circumstances of all dependent or needy children, and to assist in making wise provision for their care. Organized in one-third of the counties of the state.

Miss H. Ida Curry, supt.; Miss Mary S. Labaree, Miss Margaret C. Carey and Mrs. Jane S. Learn, asst. supts.

CHILD PLACING AGENCY, Room 710. The agency places children who have no known relatives or whose relatives are unable to provide proper homes for them, in permanent free foster homes and maintains supervision over the children so placed. Supported by voluntary contributions.

Miss Sophie van S. Theis, supt.; Miss Constance Goodrich, Miss Anna C. Hoskins, and Miss Viola M. Jones, asst. supts.

EMPLOYMENT FOR MOTHERS WITH INFANTS, Room 702. An agency for advising, assisting, and providing situations in the country for destitute mothers with infants or young children. Arranges for prenatal and convalescent care. Co-operates with charitable agencies, especially with maternity hospitals, infant asylums, foundling hospitals, Department of Public Welfare, Charity Organization Society, and relief societies. The character and standing of employers are thoroughly investigated and correspondence is maintained with women sent to situations. Supported by voluntary contributions.

Miss M. R. Mason, supt.; Miss Jean Loomis, asst. supt.; Marion E. Manter, M.D., examining physician.

COMMITTEES

NEW YORK CITY VISITING COMMITTEE, Room 710. Object: To visit systematically all the wards and public buildings of Bellevue and Allied Hospitals, and of the New York City Department of Public Welfare and Health, and secure such improvements as will contribute to the mental, moral, and physical well-being of the inmates. Submits frequent letters to the Commissioners of these departments; also special reports to the Trustees of Bellevue and Allied Hospitals upon necessary improvements, and to the Board of Estimate and Apportionment upon appropriations needed for hospitals, etc. Supported by voluntary contributions.

Officers: Homer Folks, pres.; Mrs. Frederick L. Cranford, and Mrs. Thomas M. Rianhard, vice-prests.; M. N. Buckner, treas.; Miss Marion R. Taber, secy.

COMMITTEE ON HOSPITALS, Room 710. Object: To keep informed of the conditions of the inmates of public charitable institutions and to urge the adoption of such methods as are best fitted to restore their health, alleviate their sufferings, and secure their humane care; to help in securing additional facilities, hospitals, dispensaries, visiting nurses, and other agencies, by co-operating with the local authorities; to study the conditions of public hospitals and charitable institutions in New York City, and to assist in the establishment of hospitals and industrial colonies for inebriates in New York City and elsewhere, as well as in securing improvements, by legislation and otherwise, in connection with the county hospitals and almshouses of the state.

Theodore L. Frothingham, chrm.; Homer Folks, secy.

COMMITTEE ON TUBERCULOSIS AND PUBLIC HEALTH (org. 1907), Room 710. Conducts in New York State outside of New York City the campaign against tuberculosis in co-operation with the State Health Department. Promotes state and local measures for the administrative control of tuberculosis and related health problems. Supports the enactment and enforcement of tuberculosis and public health legislation. Conducts propaganda work for the information of the people on tuberculosis prevention. Organizes local committees to secure the adoption and enforcement of preventive measures. Conducts investigations, exhibitions, motion picture demonstrations, mass meetings, a press service for the newspapers; distributes literature and posters; carries on a system of follow-up correspondence and extension work; supports and sustains the efforts of local committees; acts as agents for the sale of Christmas Seals in New York State outside of Greater New York; inspects hospitals, dispensaries, and other institutions for the care and treatment of tuberculosis, and assists in securing appropriations for their maintenance, extension, and improvement.

Officers: George F. Canfield, chrm.; Homer Folks, secy.; George J. Nelbach, exec. secy.; Harvey Dee Brown, Dr. Stanley L. Wang. Miss Frances H. Meyer, R.N., Miss Mildred P. Stewart and Mrs. Ruth B. Harter, field agents.

COMMITTEE ON MENTAL HYGIENE, Room 710, 105 East 22d St. Carries on educational work throughout New York State for the prevention of mental and nervous diseases. Promotes adequate provision for the feebleminded. Conducts lectures, popular meetings, exhibits on mental hygiene; publishes and distributes literature on the causes and means for prevention of insanity. Promotes the establishment of psychopathic clinics and observation wards. Assists individuals, threatened with mental disease, to obtain immediate and competent medical and social treatment. Organizes local committees to further educational work, discover incipient cases, and assist persons discharged, recovered, from State Hospitals for the Insane. Supported by voluntary contributions. The New York Committee on Feeblemindedness was merged with this committee.

Officers: Miss Florence M. Rhett, chrm.; Dr. William L. Russell, vice-chrm.; Homer Folks, secy.; George A. Hastings, exec. secy.; Stanley P. Davis, assoc. secy.; Mrs. Margaret J. Powers, social service director.

State Civil Service Commission (Chap. 15, Laws of 1909, as amended), Albany, N. Y. The State Civil Service Commission consists of three Commissioners appointed by the Governor, by and with the advice and consent of the Senate, and not more than two of whom shall be adherents of the same political party. They shall hold no other political place under the State government. The term of office of the Commissioners is fixed by statute at six years.

Commissioners: William Gorham Rice, pres., Albany; John C. Clark, New York; Mrs. Charles Bennett Smith, Buffalo; John C. Birdseye, secy., Albany, N. Y.

The general powers and duties of the Commission are to prescribe, amend, and enforce suitable rules, subject to the approval of the Governor, for carrying into effect the provisions of the Civil Service Law, and Section 9 of Article V of the Constitution; to make investigations concerning and report upon all matters touching the enforcement and effect of the provisions of the Civil Service Law, rules and regulations; to appoint municipal civil service commissioners in case the mayor for any reason fails to make the appointments; to remove municipal civil service commissioners, for incompetency, inefficiency, neglect of duty, or violation of the provisions of the Civil Service Law, rules, or regulations; to approve municipal civil service rules and regulations, or amendments thereto, when prescribed by a municipal civil service commission and approved by the mayor; to make a report annually to the Governor for transmission to the Legislature. The Commission is authorized to appoint a secretary, a chief examiner, and such other officers, clerks, and examiners as it may deem necessary.

The seal of the office is the Arms of the State, surrounded by the inscription "State of New York—Civil Service Commission."

State Colonization Society. See NEW YORK STATE COLONIZATION SOCIETY.

State Commission for the Blind. See NEW YORK STATE COMMISSION FOR THE BLIND.

State Commission for Mental Defectives (created 1918), 105 East 22d St., N.Y.C. (tel. Gramercy 1831). Ethel Anderson Prince, secy.

Commissioners: Dr. Pearce Bailey, chrm.; Charles H. Johnson and Frank R. Utter.

1. This Commission was created by Chapter 197 of the 1918 for the express purpose of administering the law in relation to the custody, care and training of mental defectives.

2. In addition to its administrative duties, the Commission is required to keep in its office, records of the mental defectives in all state institutions. A census of mental defectives in the State, both in and out of institutions, is being compiled.

3. In co-operation with other state departments, the Commission conducts joint Mental Hygiene Clinics throughout the state for consultation and advice concerning defective and subnormal children.

4. The Commission has the power of transfer of inmates from one state school for mental defectives to another.

5. The Commission reports annually to the Legislature, making such recommendations regarding new construction and matters of general policy as may be deemed necessary.

6. The Commission has four field agents for the purpose of extra-institutional work with defectives who are either excluded or discharged from the ungraded classes.

7. The four state schools for mental defectives under the supervision of this Commission are

The Newark State School, Newark, N. Y. (Dr. Ethan A. Nevin, supt.)

The Syracuse State School, Syracuse, N. Y. (Dr. O. H. Cobb, supt.)

The Rome State School, Rome, N. Y. (Dr. Charles Bernstein, supt.)

Letchworth Village, Thiells, N. Y. (Dr. Charles S. Little, supt.)

All letters should be addressed to the Commission in New York.

State Commission in Lunacy. See STATE COMMISSION ON MENTAL DEFECTIVES.

State Commission of Prisons (est. 1895, Chap. 1026; cont. 1907, Chap. 381; re-enacted, Chap. 47, Laws of 1909), Albany, N. Y. The State Commission of Prisons consists of seven members, appointed by the Governor for a term of four years each. Officers: President, vice-president, and secretary, chosen by the Commission. Compensation, $10 per diem while engaged in the performance of their duties, and expenses. Monthly meetings.

Commissioners: John S. Kennedy, pres.; Leon C. Weinstock, vice-pres.; Sarah L. Davenport, Henry Solomon, Mial H. Pierce, Charles S. Rogers, Cecilia D. Patten; John F. Tremain, secy.

The powers and duties of the Commission shall be to visit and inspect all institutions used for the detention of sane adults charged with or convicted of crime, or detained as witnesses or debtors; aid in securing their just, humane, and economic administration; the erection of suitable buildings, and approve or reject plans for their construction or improvement; investigate their management and the conduct and efficiency of the officers or persons in charge; secure the best sanitary conditions of buildings and grounds, and protect and preserve the health of the inmates; collect statistical information in respect to the property, receipts, and expenditures, and the number and condition of the inmates of said institutions; exercise the powers conferred upon it by Chapter 47 of the Laws of 1909, relating to the assignment of labor and industries to penal institutions; close any city jail or police station, town or village jail or lockup which is unsanitary or inadequate to provide for the separation and classification of prisoners required by law.

The rights and powers conferred upon the Commission may be enforced by an order of the Supreme Court, or by indictment.

State Conference on Charities and Corrections. See NEW YORK STATE CONFERENCE, etc.

State Custodial Asylum for Feeble-minded Women. See NEWARK STATE SCHOOL FOR MENTAL DEFECTIVES.

State Department of Education, The, Albany, N. Y. John Huston Finley, commissioner. The Board of Regents was established and incorporated by act of the Legislature in 1784 and continued in the Constitution of 1894. It consists of twelve Regents who are elected, one each year to serve for twelve years, by the Legislature in joint session, as provided for by the Constitution of the State. The Regents are authorized to exercise legislative functions concerning the educational system of the state; to determine its educational policies, and make rules for carrying into effect the laws relating to education and the powers of the University. They have exclusive power to incorporate educational institutions and organizations; they may confer degrees and regulate their issuance within the state: they have the power to visit and inspect educational institutions of the state, conduct examinations therein and require reports therefrom; they register domestic and foreign educational institutions and fix the value of degrees, diplomas, and certificates from all parts of the world, when presented for entrance to schools, colleges, universities, and the professions; they may establish and stimulate educational extension work and conduct examinations and grant credentials therein, and they supervise the entrance requirements to the professions of law, medicine, dentistry, veterinary medicine, pharmacy, optometry, the certification of nurses, public accountants, chiropodists, certified shorthand reporters, and the registration of architects. The Board constitutes and governs as a corporate body:

THE UNIVERSITY OF THE STATE OF NEW YORK. It includes in its constituent membership and has under its supervision all public schools of the state, and also, in the terms of the law, includes, as institutions of the University, all secondary and higher educational institutions which are now or may hereafter be incorporated in this state, and such other schools, libraries, museums, institutions, organizations, and agencies for education as may be admitted to or incorporated by the University.

The chief officers of the University are the Chancellor, Pliny T. Sexton, of Palmyra; and the President of the University, John H. Finley, of Albany.

State Department of Health, Albany, N. Y. Chap. 559. Laws of 1913, amended the Public Health Law generally and effected many changes in the organization and powers of the State Department of Health and created the public Health Council. The Council consists of six members appointed by the Governor in addition to the Commissioner. It is authorized to enact a Sanitary Code dealing with any matters affecting life and health and their improvement and preservation, including regulation of midwifery and promotion of health on Indian reservations. The Sanitary Code has force and effects of law and violation is declared a misdemeanor.

Commissioner, Hermann M. Biggs, M.D.; deputy commissioner, Matthias Nicoll, Jr., M.D.; secy., John A. Smith, M.D.; exec. clerk, Fenimore D. Beagle.

State Department of Labor. See State Industrial Commission.

State Employment Bureau. See State Industrial Commission.

State Federation of Women's Clubs. Mrs. Walter S. Comley, pres., Comley Ave., Port Chester, N. Y. (tel. Port Chester 231).

State Health Officer Department of the Port of New York. See Health Officer.

State Hospital for the Care of Crippled and Deformed Children (est. Chap. 369, Laws of 1900), West Haverstraw, N. Y. For the care and treatment of any indigent children who may have resided in the State of New York for a period of not less than one year, who are crippled or deformed or are suffering from disease from which they are likely to become crippled or deformed. Capacity, 152.

John J. Nutt, M.D., supt. and surgeon-in-chief.

State Hospital Commission (est. 1889, Chap. 283; made a constitutional body, 1894), Capitol, Albany, N. Y. Branch office: Hall of Records Bldg., cor. Chambers and Center Sts., N.Y.C. (tel. Worth 4424). The Commission comprises three members, Dr. Charles W. Pilgrim, chrm., Andrew D. Morgan, Frederick A. Higgins.

All letters to the Commission should be addressed, Everett S. Elwood, secy., Albany.

Social Workers: Miss A. J. Massopust and Mrs. Elizabeth Pierce, Manhattan State Hospital, Ward's Island, N.Y.C.; Miss M. E. Dunn, Central Islip State Hospital, Central Islip; Mrs. Francis C. Tanner and Mrs. Mildred V. Renwick, Brooklyn State Hospital, Brooklyn; Miss Margaret Doherty, Miss Adeline E. Dartt, and Miss Gladys Wellington, Kings Park State Hospital.

The Commission is charged with the execution of the laws relating to the care, custody and treatment of the insane, with the securing of legislation regarding alien and non-resident insane, has the general oversight of the State hospitals and the control of all property thereof, and approves or revises estimates for supplies and improvement submitted quarterly by the superintendents and stewards of the several State hospitals, is authorized to license private institutions for the care of the insane, and to supervise the administrations of such institutions and the care and treatment of patients therein. It maintains a

Bureau of Deportation at the New York office to return alien and non-resident insane to their native countries.

Clinics

Mental Clinics are conducted by the Metropolitan State Hospital as follows:

Eastern District Hospital, 108 South

Third St., Brooklyn. Friday evenings from 7 to 9 and Saturday mornings from 9.30 to 12 noon.

Nassau Hospital, Mineola, N. Y. Monday from 1.30 to 3.30 P. M.

Manhattan State Hospital, Tuesdays, 2 to 3 P. M., 7 to 8 P. M.

St. Mark's Hospital, 177 Second Ave., Fridays, 2 to 3 P. M. and 7 to 8 P. M.

Harlem Hospital, Wednesday, 4 P. M. and 7 P. M.

Brooklyn State Hospital Clinics.

Brooklyn State Hospital, Saturdays, 2 to 4 P. M.

Long Island College Hospital, Fridays, 2 to 4 P. M.

Central Islip State Hospital Clinics.

Cornell Medical College, 1st Ave. and 27th St., Thursdays, 2 to 4 P. M. and 6 to P. M.

Patchogue Clinic at Patchogue, Long Island. Monthly as announced.

State Hospital for the Treatment of Incipient Pulmonary Tuberculosis (opened 1904), Raybrook, Essex Co., N. Y. The requirements are (1) that patient shall have incipient pulmonary tuberculosis, and (2) that he shall be without funds.

The sanatorium makes no collections from patients and pay-patients are not received; the expense of maintenance of the patients is paid by the localities of which they are residents ($5 per week), and the balance by the state. Capacity, 320.

Application for patients living in New York City should be made through the Tuberculosis Hospital Admission Bureau (q. v.), 124 East 59th St.

Harry A. Bray, M.D., supt.

State Industrial Commission (est. June 1, 1915, succeeding former officers of Commission of Labor, Workmen's Compensation Commission and Industrial Board), Capitol, Albany; New York City office, 124 East 28th St.

Commissioners: Edward F. Boyle, chrm.; Frances Perkins, James M. Lynch, Henry D. Sayer. Commissioners are appointed by the Governor. Secretary to the Commission, Edward W. Buckley.

BUREAU OF INSPECTION, 124 East 28th St., N.Y.C. Under immediate charge of First Deputy Commissioner. Inspects and enforces the provisions of the Labor Law.

James L. Gernon, first deputy commissioner; Nelle Swartz, chief Bureau of Women in Industry.

BUREAU OF STATISTICS AND INFORMATION, Albany, N. Y. Under immediate charge of a chief statistician. Collects, prepares and publishes information, statistical or otherwise, in relation to labor and industries in the State.

Eugene B. Patton, chief statistician.

BUREAU OF EMPLOYMENT, 124 East 28th St., N.Y.C. Under immediate charge of a director. To establish and maintain throughout the state a system of public employment offices.

Dr. David S. Flynn, Director.

BUREAU OF MEDIATION AND ARBITRATION, Albany, N. Y. Under immediate charge of the Third Deputy Commissioner. Endeavors by mediation or arbitration to effect amicable settlement of labor disputes; may also make public investigation of the cause of disputes. Third Deputy Commissioner (chief mediator), Edward D. Jackson.

BUREAU OF INDUSTRIES AND IMMIGRATION: 124 East 28th St., N.Y.C.; under immediate charge of a chief investigator. To investigate the condition of aliens in the State, and to administer the law relating to registration of employment agencies with the Department of Labor and licensing of immigrant lodging-places. Marian K. Clark, chief investigator.

Bureau of Workmen's Compensation. Maintains offices in Albany; 124 East 28th St., N.Y.C.; 310 Jay St., Brooklyn; Cahill Bldg., Syracuse; 158 Main St., East Rochester; Iroquois Bldg., Buffalo.

Under immediate charge of Second Deputy Commissioner, to administer the Workmen's Compensation law and examine papers filed in claims of compensation; make investigations and hold hearings upon the same; make medical examinations of injured workmen to ascertain causes of disability and probable duration of same, and to administer the State Insurance Fund for the benefit of injured workmen of employers insured in such fund.

William C. Archer, second deputy commissioner; Dr. Raphael Lewy, chief medical examiner; Leonard W. Hatch, manager, State Insurance Fund.

Legal Bureau, 124 East 28th St., N.Y.C. Advises the Commission with regard to matters coming before it; prepares findings of facts and records on appeal in compensation cases; takes charge of and prosecutes violations of the Labor Law and brings actions for the collection of awards in cases where employers are not insured.

Bernard L. Shientag, chief counsel.

Bureau of Boilers and Explosives, Albany, N. Y. Inspects and tests boilers and issues certificates thereon and issues certificates of compliance for magazines for the storage of explosives.

Chief engineer, George A. O'Rourke.

State Industrial Farm Colony. Project abandoned.

State Prison Department, Albany, N. Y. Has supervision of Auburn, Clinton, Sing Sing, Great Meadow and Wingdale prisons and the State Prison for Women, Matteawan State Hospital, Dannemora State Hospital and the Bureau of Identification.

Charles F. Rattigan, supt.; James L. Long, deputy supt.

Parole Board: Charles F. Rattigan, George W. Benham, E. E. Larkin, M.D.

State Probation Commission, The (created by Chap. 430, Laws of 1907; now Consolidated Laws, Chap. 54, Secs. 30–31), Albany, N. Y. The Commission consists of seven members, four appointed by the Governor for terms of four years each, one appointed by the State Board of Charities from among its members, one appointed by the State Commission of Prisons from among its members, and the State Commissioner of Education, member ex-officio. The Commissioners serve without compensation, except traveling expenses. The Commission appoints a secretary who is the chief executive officer of the Commission and other employers within the sums allowed by the Legislature, the latter being appointed under the civil service.

Commissioners: Edmond J. Butler (New York), pres.; Alphonso T. Clearwater (Kingston), vice-pres.; Edward C. Blum (Brooklyn), Henry Marquand (Bedford Hills), Mrs. Mary E. Paddon, (New York), Henry Solomon (New York) and John H. Finley (Albany). Charles L. Chute, secy., whom address.

The chief duties of the Commission are to exercise general supervision over the work of probation officers and to keep informed as to the work; to collect and publish statistical and other information as to the operations of the probation system; to inquire into the conduct and efficiency of probation officers, and, when advisable, to conduct a formal investigation of the work of any probation officer; to make recommendations and to secure the effective application of the probation system and the enforcement of the probation law in all parts of the State. The Commission makes an annual report to the Legislature of its proceedings and the results of the probation system as administered in the various localities in the State, make suggestions and recommendations. The Commission in the discharge of its duties has access to all offices and records of probation officers.

State Reconstruction Commission. See RECONSTRUCTION COMMISSION OF THE STATE OF NEW YORK.

State Reformatory, Elmira, N. Y. See NEW YORK STATE REFORMATORY.

State Reformatory for Misdemeanants (est. Chap. 502, Laws of 1912). Not yet located. Object: For the reformation and the educational, industrial, and moral instruction and training of males under conviction and sentence for commission of misdemeanors or other minor offenses.

Hon. John J. Brady, pres. of the Board of Managers, 29 Walter St., Albany.

State Reformatory for Women (est. Chap. 637, Laws of 1892; opened 1901), Bedford Hills, Westchester Co., N. Y. For the commitment of any female between the ages of sixteen and thirty years, convicted by any court or magistrate of petit larceny, vagrancy, habitual drunkenness, being a common prostitute, or frequenting disorderly houses or houses of prostitution, or of a misdemeanor, and who is not insane, nor mentally nor physically incapable of being substantially benefited by the discipline of such an institution.

Mrs. Anna Hedges Talbot Ph.D., supt.

State Soldiers' and Sailors' Home (est. Chap. 223, Laws of 1863, as the Soldiers' Home; name changed, Chap. 48, Laws of 1878; opened 1878), Bath, Steuben Co., N. Y. For the reception, care, and maintenance of any needy or disabled honorably discharged soldier or sailor who served in the army or navy of the United States during the Civil War, Spanish War, or Philippine War, who enlisted from the State of New York, or who shall have been a resident of this State for one year preceding his application. Capacity, 2,000.

Col. John C. F. Tillson, commandant, Bath, N. Y.

State Training School for Girls (est. Chap. 187, Laws of 1881, as the House of Refuge for Women; opened 1887; name changed by Chap. 453, Laws of 1904), Hudson, Columbia Co., N. Y. For the reception of all girls, between the ages of twelve and sixteen years, who shall be legally committed thereto or placed in charge of such institution by any court having authority to make such commitments or to place such girls therein. Capacity, 400.

H. V. Bruce, supt.

State Woman's Relief Corps Home. See NEW YORK STATE WOMAN'S RELIEF CORPS HOME.

Staten Island Diet Kitchen Association, The (incorp. 1882), cor. Grant and Van Duzer Sts., Tompkinsville, S. I.

Staten Island Hospital, The, formerly the S. R. Smith Infirmary (incorp. 1869), Castleton Ave., Tompkinsville, S. I. (tel. Tompkinsville 1160). A general hospital for medical, surgical, obstetrical, and contagious cases. Incurables not received. Maintains:

TRAINING SCHOOL FOR NURSES, fifty pupils.

AUTOMOBILE AMBULANCE SERVICE.

Officers: W. L. DeBost, pres., Board of Trustees; W. Y. Wemple, secy.; F. C. Townsend, treas.; Charles W. Goodwin, M.D., supt.

Staten Island Social Service, Inc. (reorg. and incorp. March, 1919), 105 Stuyvesant Place, St. George, S. I. (tel. Tompkinsville 1500). Family social work. Supported by voluntary contributions.

Officers: Mrs. E. M. Deems, pres.; Thos. M. Rianhard, treas., 17 Battery place; Miss Mildred Field, acting exec. secy., 105 Stuyvesant Place, St. George, S. I.

Staten Island Sub-Committee of the New York Tuberculosis Association, 79-81 Jersey St., New Brighton, S. I. (tel. Tompkinsville 948). To spread the knowledge of preventive work for tuberculosis. Maintains two health centers. Supported by voluntary contributions.

Officers: Mrs. Wm. G. Willcox, chrm.; Miss Mary E. Higgins, exec. secy.

Stony Wold Sanatorium (incorp. 1901, opened 1903), Lake Kushaqua, Franklin Co., N. Y. A sanatorium for self-supporting women and girls in the early stages of tuberculosis.

Officers: Mrs. James Edward Newcomb, pres., Room 43, 1974 Broadway, N.Y.C., where application for admission should be made; Mrs. Hermann M. Biggs, Miss Cora P. Van Wyck, Mrs. Frank J. Sprague, vice-prests.; Mrs. Charles Gilmore Kerley, 10 East 81st St., rec. secy.; Mrs. Arthur Coppell, cor. secy., 123 East 56th St.; Waldron P. Belknap, treas., 501 Fifth Ave.; Mrs. Herbert L. Satterlee, asst. treas., 37 East 36th St., N.Y.C.

Strangers' Welfare Fellowship, The (est. 1910). Office: 51 East 42d St., N.Y.C. (tel. Vanderbilt 5462). The late Bishop Burch recognized the Fellowship as an Episcopal organization on Jan. 1, 1920; but it continues as before to furnish a free non-sectarian service to all, irrespective of race or creed. Its special function is to find and restore to active membership in their respective churches newcomers who fail to establish church relations in the city. It is thus doing missionary work in behalf of all the churches.

Officers: Rev. Dr. James B. Wasson, chaplain; Zelah Van Loan, treas.; Hugh Gordon Miller, counsel, 220 Broadway.

Advisory Board: Hon. F. D. Roosevelt, Robert C. Morris and Frank H. Clement.

Street Cleaning, Department of, City of New York, 12th floor, Municipal Bldg. (tel. Worth 4240). Arnold B. MacStay, commissioner.

Strong Place Baptist Church, Strong Place and Degraw St., Brooklyn, Rev. Floyd H. Adams, Pastor. Maintains a kindergarten, gymnasium, playground, clubs, Boy Scout organizations, etc.

Student Volunteer Movement for Foreign Missions (incorp. 1900), 25 Madison Ave., N.Y.C. (tel. Madison Sq. 9890). To awaken and maintain among all Christian students of the United States and Canada, intelligent and active interest in missions, and to enroll a sufficient number of properly qualified students who purpose to devote their lives to foreign missionary work, to meet the demands of the regular mission boards.

Robert P. Wilder, gen. secy.

Studio Club of New York, The (est. 1908, Branch of the Young Women's Christian Association), 35 East 62d St. (tel. Plaza 7261). Object: To provide a resident and social center for young students and professionals in the various arts.

Applications for information and assistance should be made to the gen. secy., Miss Frances Mitchell.

Stuyvesant Neighborhood House, Hebrew Technical Institute Bldg.,

Stuyvesant and Ninth Sts., bet. Second and Third Aves., N.Y.C. (tel. Dry Dock 2200). A social, educational and civic center which aims to serve the community by interpreting its needs and endeavoring to fulfill them. Equipped with gymnasium, shower baths, auditorium, lecture room, library, social and game rooms, large roof garden. Conducts cultural and educational classes, lectures, clubs, dances, dramatic readings, rallies, concerts, dramatic performances, athletic activities, etc., for adults and children of the district. Maintains a summer play school, daily outing. Co-operates with governmental and other private agencies in the neighborhood. Non-sectarian.

George L. Cohen, executive director; Elizabeth M. Walker, asst. director.

Executive Council: Morton H. Meinhard, chrm.; Edward S. Steinam, treas.; Mrs. Fred Bender, Dr. Edgar S. Barney, Joseph L. Buttenwiesser, Mrs. Moise L. Erstein, Moise L. Erstein, Dr. K. George Falk, Prof. Abraham Goldfarb, Prof. Paul Klapper, Mrs. Morris Loeb, Mrs. Bernard E. Pollak, Mrs. Arthur Rosenthal, Mrs. Hugh Grant Straus, Hugh Grant Straus, Eugène E. Sperry, Mrs. Felix M. Warburg, Mrs. Walter Rothschild, Mrs. Louis Levy.

Stuyvesant Polyclinic of the City of New York, The (incorp. 1883), 137 Second Ave. (tel. Orchard 232). For free medical and surgical treatment of the sick and disabled poor of all creeds and nationalities. Open daily, except Sundays and holidays, 1–5 P. M.

Sulgrave Institution, Inc., Woolworth Bldg., N.Y.C. Organized to foster friendship among English-speaking peoples and between them and other peoples of good will.

Officers: Alton B. Parker, chancellor; Gordon Hammersley, treas.; Andrew B. Humphrey, secy.

Supported by voluntary contributions, prescriptions, and Ladies' Auxiliary Society.

Sunbeam Day Nursery. See FIFTH AVENUE PRESBYTERIAN CHURCH, this list.

Sunday Observance Association of Kings County (org. 1882). To secure a better observance of Sunday as a day of rest and worship.

Henry N. Niles, pres., 373 Tompkins Ave., Brooklyn; Rev. W. W. T. Duncan, cor. secy., 268 Stuyvesant Ave., Brooklyn.

Sunnyside Day Nursery (org. 1882, incorp. 1888), 221 East 104th St., N.Y.C. For the care of children from two weeks to six years of age, of poor working mothers who are unable to care for them during the day. Regular kindergarten instruction is given to the older ones, and a charge of five cents a day is made for each child. Open from 7 A. M. to 6 P. M. Supported by voluntary contributions.

Sunshine Mission. See at COLLEGIATE, under REFORMED CHURCHES in Church List.

Survey Associates, Inc., 112 East 19th St., N.Y.C. An adventure in co-operative journalism, chartered in 1912.

Officers: Robert W. de Forest, pres.; John M. Glenn, vice-pres.; Arthur P. Kellogg, secy. and treas.

Publishers of The Survey, a weekly, $5.00 a year; co-operating subscription and annual membership $10.00.

Staff: Paul U. Kellogg, editor; associate editors: Social Forces, Edward T. Devine; Civics and Foreign Service, Bruno Lasker; Industry, William L. Chenery; Education, Joseph K. Hart; Family Welfare and Child Welfare, Paul L. Benjamin; Health, Michael M.

Davis, Jr.; Managing Editor, S. Adele Shaw.

Susan Fenimore Cooper Foundation, Inc., The (est. 1870), Cooperstown, N. Y. (tel. Cooperstown 388-W). A church vocational school for boys and girls. No limitations as to nationality or sect. Capacity, 125. Supported by private contributions, board of county charges and tuitions, Episcopal Churches, Diocese of Albany, endowment.

Officers: Rt. Rev. Dr. Richard H. Nelson, pres., Albany; Harris L. Cooke, treas., Cooperstown; Lee B. Cruttenden, secy., Cooperstown.

Swedish Augustana Home for the Aged, The (org. 1908, incorp. 1909), 1680, 60th St., Brooklyn. A home for worthy old people of Swedish birth or parentage, over sixty-five years of age. Protestants. Capacity, forty-two. Admission $500, if able to pay.

Officers: Rev. J. D. Danielson, pres., 1070, 59th St., Brooklyn; John P. Johnson, treas.; Vilhelm Berger, secy.; John H. Benson, manager, 1680, 60th St., Brooklyn.

Swedish Home for Aged People Association (incorp. 1910). Office: 135 Maiden Lane, N.Y.C. Home: St. George Heights, Staten Island (tel. West Brighton 1096). To care for persons at least sixty years of age, who speak or understand the Swedish language. Capacity, twenty-five. No restriction as to race, sect, or sex; but applicants must be residents of New York or its immediate vicinity. Address or apply to the corporation at the office.

Emil F. Johnson, pres.

Swedish Hospital in Brooklyn, The (incorp. 1896), Rogers Ave. and Sterling Pl. (tel. Prospect 7561-7562). A general hospital in the city of Brooklyn, where Swedes unacquainted with the English language can receive care and medical assistance by Swedish-speaking doctors and attendants. It is also open to the general public.

Dorothea Gothson, supt.

***Swedish Lutheran Immigrant Home, The** (founded 1895), 5 Water St., N.Y.C. Aids Scandinavian immigrants of all creeds and professions; provides a home at low rates or free to those unable to pay; also helps to secure employment. Under the control of the Evangelical Lutheran Augustana Synod of America.

Swiss Benevolent Society (incorp. 1851), 35-37 West 67th St., N.Y.C. Assists indigent Swiss families and individuals, provides medical attendance, etc., and maintains a home for aged Swiss, over sixty-five years, of both sexes. Supported by voluntary contributions. Capacity, forty beds for permanent inmates; twenty-five for transient inmates.

Officers: Henry Escher, Jr., pres.; A. P. Traber, treas.; Pierre Gougelmann, secy.; Charles A. Challandes, supt.

Switzer Institute and Home, Christopher St. and Waverly Pl., N.Y.C. See MARGARET AND SARAH SWITZER INSTITUTE AND HOME.

Sydenham Post-Graduate Course and Hospital (incorp. 1892), 331-347 East 116th St., N.Y.C. (tel. Harlem 5438). No infectious or contagious cases admitted; nor incurable cases, unless there are urgent symptoms which may be relieved. Maintains also

A DISPENSARY, open daily, except Sundays and holidays, 10-11 A. M. and 2-4 P. M.

TRAINING SCHOOL FOR NURSES.

Loretta A. Murray, supt.

Symphony Orchestra. See YOUNG MEN'S SYMPHONY ORCHESTRA.

* *Current information not received.*

Syracuse State School for Mental Defectives (est. Chap 502, Laws of 1851, as the Asylum for Idiots; opened, 1851), Syracuse, Onondaga Co., N. Y. For the care and education of children between the ages of seven and fourteen, who are so deficient in intelligence as to be incapable of being educated at an ordinary school, and who are not epileptic, insane, or greatly deformed. Capacity, 700.

The school is designed to furnish the means of education to that portion of the youth of the state not provided for in any of its other educational institutions, who are of a proper school age, and for such periods of time as shall, in the estimate of the Board of Managers, suffice to impart all the education practicable in each particular case.

O. Howard Cobb, M.D., supt.

ST.

St. Agatha's Home for Children (incorp. 1885), Nanuet, Rockland Co., N. Y. Reception House, 175 East 68th St., N.Y.C. For orphan and other children, fitting them for some useful trade or business.

St. Agnes' Chapel (Trinity Parish), West 92d St. west of Columbus Ave., N.Y.C. Maintains a kindergarten and primary school; employment society for women of the parish; young men's athletic association, and other clubs of social and religious nature. W. W. Bellinger, Vicar. See also under PROTESTANT EPISCOPAL CHURCHES in the Church List.

St. Agnes' Day Nursery, 7 Charles St., N.Y.C. See ASCENSION P. E. CHURCH, this list.

St. Agnes' Day Nursery, 221–225 East 45th St., N.Y.C. See FRANCISCAN MISSIONARIES OF MARY.

St. Agnes' Day Nursery, 419 Degraw St., Brooklyn. For children of working mothers.

St. Agnes' Hospital (incorp. 1908), White Plains, N. Y. For the care, treatment, education, medical and surgical attention of all children. Maintains a staff of thirteen consulting and six attending physicians and surgeons. Capacity, 250 children, two to sixteen years, white. Supported by public funds and private contributions.

St. Ambrose Italian Mission, 236 East 111th St. Maintains a social center for the neighborhood, clubs and classes for boys and girls, kindergarten, fresh-air work, etc.

See also under PROTESTANT EPISCOPAL CHURCHES in the Church List.

St. Andrew's Convalescent Hospital (org. 1886, incorp. 1902), 237 East 17th St., N.Y.C. (tel. Stuyvesant 1764). For women, girls and children of good character who need care, nursing and rest, or who are recovering from acute illness, but are not ill enough to be admitted to a regular hospital. All suitable cases received promptly, with or without payment. Capacity, thirty-five beds. In charge of the Sisterhood of St. John Baptist (q. v.). Supported by voluntary contributions, donations and subscriptions.

ST. ANDREW'S REST (Country Branch open June to October), Woodcliff Lake, Bergen Co., N. Y. (tel. Park Ridge 152). Capacity, eighteen beds.

Officers: Wm. M. Barnum, pres., 10 Wall St.; Charles L. Kingsley, treas., 55 Liberty St.; Wm. W. Boardman, secy., 120 Broadway.

St. Andrew's P E. Church, Fifth Ave and 127th St., N.Y.C. Rev. Albert E. Ribourg, D.D., Rector. Maintains various clubs and societies. See under PROTESTANT EPISCOPAL CHURCHES in the Church List.

St. Andrew's Rest. See ST. ANDREW'S CONVALESCENT HOSPITAL.

St. Andrew's Society of the State of New York (founded 1756, incorp. 1826), Room 515, 105 East 22d St., N.Y.C. For the relief of natives of Scotland and their descendants who might be in want or distress; also, to promote social intercourse among its members. It is one of the oldest societies in the United States.

Officers: Alexander Walker, pres.; Walter E. Frew, treas.; Henry Moir, secy.; Miss Eliza B. Dalzell, almoner, to whom apply between 9 A. M. and 2 P. M.

St. Anne's Home for Wayward Girls. See SISTERHOOD OF ST. JOHN BAPTIST.

St. Ann's Day Nursery, 240 East 90th St., N.Y.C. For care of children of R. C. working mothers.

St. Ann's Maternity Hospital, 130 East 69th St., N.Y.C. (tel. Rhinelander 1187). Destitute or tempted married women are received; unmarried women, pregnant for the first time, are sheltered; and strangers, who can afford to pay, but do not wish to remain at a hotel or boarding house during confinement, may be cared for.

St. Ann's Morrisania P. E. Church, St. Ann's Ave. and 140th St., Bronx. Rev. Harold G. Willis, Rector. Maintains clubs, guilds, etc. See also under PROTESTANT EPISCOPAL CHURCHES in the Church list.

St. Ann's P. E. Church (incorp. 1787), Clinton and Livingston Sts., Brooklyn (tel. Main 5681). Rev. G. Ashton Oldham, Rector. The Parish Guild maintains clubs and classes for boys, girls, young men and women; clothing bureau, etc. See also under PROTESTANT EPISCOPAL CHURCHES in the Church List.

St. Ann's P. E. Church for Deaf Mutes (incorp. 1898), 511 West 148th St., near Amsterdam Ave., N.Y.C. Maintains religious services, lectures, entertainments, etc., for deaf mutes. The Guild of Silent Workers and Women's Aid Society relieve distress and aid in securing employment. Supported by endowment and voluntary contributions.

Officers: Rev. John Chamberlain, D.D., Vicar; Rev. John H. Kent, Curate; Charles C. McMann, treas. See also under PROTESTANT EPISCOPAL CHURCHES in the Church List.

St. Anthony's Day Nursery, 147 Thompson St., N.Y.C. For children of working mothers.

St. Anthony's Hospital, of the Sisters of the Poor of St. Francis (incorp. 1866, est. 1914), Woodhaven Ave., Woodhaven, N. Y. (tel. Richmond Hill 2100). For the care of tuberculosis patients. Capacity, 380 beds.

Sister Tabitha, supt.

***St. Augustine's Chapel** (Trinity Parish), 105-109 East Houston St., between the Bowery and Second Ave., N.Y.C. A church and social center for the people of the neighborhood. See also under PROTESTANT EPISCOPAL CHURCHES in the Church List.

St. Barnabas' House. See NEW YORK PROTESTANT EPISCOPAL CITY MISSION SOCIETY, this list.

St. Bartholomew's P. E. Church, Park Ave. and 50th St., N.Y.C. Rev. Leighton Parks, D.D., Rector; Rev. Abraham Yonhannan, (Emeritus) Rev. Percy Gordon, and Rev. Paul G. Favor, assistant ministers.

Social Workers: John W Fiske, gen. mgr. Parish House and Hospital; Guy Maine, Chinese supt.; J R. Ferguson, mgr. Loan Assn.; George McVicker, Jr., supt. Men's Club: Raymond C.

* *Current information not received.*

Frank, supt. Boys' Club: Miss Claire Darling, supt. Girls' Club; Miss Isabel D. Houston, kindergartner.

ST. BARTHOLOMEW'S PARISH HOUSE, 205-213 East 42d St.

BENEVOLENT SOCIETY; supplies sewing for the poor and deserving women; meets Tuesdays at 10.30 A M.

APPLICATION BUREAU, 209 East 42d St. Office hours: 10 A. M. to 12.30 P. M., except Saturdays; 10 A. M. to 12 M., Saturdays. Application for relief should be made to John W. Fiske, manager.

ST. BARTHOLOMEW'S CHINESE GUILD (org. 1889), 42 Mott St. Relief for the sick, poor and dying members. Renders free legal aid and advice.

Guy Maine, Supt., to whom apply.

CHURCH PERIODICAL CLUB, St. Bartholomew's Branch.

ST. BARTHOLOMEW'S CLINIC AND HOSPITAL for the diseases of the alimentary canal, 215-17 East 42d St. Clinics: Mondays, Tuesdays, Wednesdays, Thursdays, and Fridays, 2 to 4 P. M.

ST. BARTHOLOMEW'S CLOTHING BUREAU, 209 East 42d St. Open daily from 10 A. M. to 12 M.

ST. BARTHOLOMEW'S CLUBS, Parish House, 209 East 42d St., are

Girls' Club, with club room and baths; Mutual Benefit Fund; Classes in dressmaking, millinery, embroidery, cooking, voice culture, English, French, calisthenics, dancing, literature, drawnwork, typewriting, stenography, etc. Classes for children under fourteen years every afternoon (except Saturday) from 3.30-5.30 P. M.

Men's Club: with Club Room, Reading Room, Library, Billiard Room, Gymnasium, and Baths. Classes in gymnastics, civil service, literature, discussion class, lectures.

Boys' Club: with Club Room, Drill Room, and Baths; classes in gymnastics and debating.

ST. BARTHOLOMEW'S KINDERGARTEN, five mornings in the week from 9 A. M. to 12 M., from September to June.

ST. BARTHOLOMEW'S LOAN ASSOCIATION, 8.30 A. M. to 5.30 P. M., every week-day; Saturdays, 8.30 A.M. to 1 P.M. Lends money in sums ranging from $25 to $200, to residents of New York and Bronx counties, on chattel mortgage on household furniture as security. Payments are made monthly with accrued interest. Its purpose is not to give charity, but credit at a reasonable charge.

Rev. Leighton Parks, D.D., pres.; J. Morgan Wing, vice-pres.; William A. Greer, treas.; Alvin W. Krech, secy.; James R. Ferguson, manager.

ST. BARTHOLOMEW'S PRESS; 9 A. M. to 5 P. M.

FRESH-AIR WORK; for the men, women and children of the Parish House.

St. Benedict's Home for Destitute Colored Children, Rye, Westchester Co., N. Y. A foundation of the Roman Catholic Church of St. Benedict the Moor (q. v. in the Church List).

***St. Brendan's R. C. Church,** 207th St. and Perry Ave., Bronx. Maintains a home for working girls at 603 Walton Ave. See also under ROMAN CATHOLIC CHURCHES in the Church List.

St. Catharine's Hospital Association (incorp. 1893). Maintains

ST. CATHARINE'S HOSPITAL AND DISPENSARY, Bushwick Ave., between Ten Eyck and Maujer Sts., Brooklyn (tel. Stagg 1061). For general hospital work, accepting all cases in need of medical or surgical treatment, exclusive only of contagious diseases. Capacity, 250 beds. Supported by voluntary contributions, city appropriations for city patients and paying patients.

ST. CATHARINE'S INFIRMARY, North Amityville, L. I., is a branch.

** Current information not received.*

Officers: Rt. Rev. C. E. McDonnell, D.D., pres.; Rev. G. A. Letzger, treas.; Mother M. Cornelia, O.S.D., supt.

St. Cecilia's Day Nursery, 221½ East 105th St., N.Y.C. For children of working mothers.

St. Cecilia's R. C. Church, Herbert and North Henry Sts., Brooklyn. Maintains a Day Nursery at 23 Monitor St. See also under R. C. CHURCHES in Church List.

St. Christopher's Home for Children (org. 1881, incorp. 1885), Dobbs Ferry, N. Y. Under the patronage of the Methodist Episcopal Church for the care and education of Protestant destitute and orphan children who are received between the ages of two and ten. They remain in the Home until eighteen years old, or until suitable homes have been provided for them.

The Home is conducted on the cottage plan. School instruction to the eighth grade is provided, beyond which attendance is at the public school. Girls are taught cooking, dressmaking, sewing and regular household work. Boys receive instruction in household work, wood-working and gardening. Instruction is with special reference to wholesome living and self-support. Capacity, 110. Supported mainly by voluntary contributions. Visitors always welcome. Friends of the children received on first Saturday of each month from 2–5 P. M. Mrs. Rastus S. Ransom, pres.; Miss Ellen I. Betty, treas., 1032 Fark Ave., N.Y.C. Applications for admission may be made in writing to Mrs. J. H. Littell, 28 West 50th St., N.Y.C., or to the home.

Miss Ida G. Thompson, supt.

St. Christopher's Hospital for Babies, 277 Hicks St., Brooklyn, N. Y. (tel. Main 1711). Free to needy sick children. Finest premature ward and operating room in the city. Modern X-Ray equipment. Dispensary, 3 to 4 P. M. every day except Saturday and Sunday, cares for children to 12 years of age. Visiting nurse and Social Service Department. Capacity, 90 beds.

St. Christopher's House, 316 East 88th St., N.Y.C. See HOLY TRINITY P. E. CHURCH, this list.

St. Chrysostom's Chapel (Trinity Parish), Seventh Ave. and 39th St., N.Y.C. Parish house, 550 Seventh Ave.

Rev. C. Nelson Moller.

St. Clement's Church, 423 West 46th St., N.Y.C. Rev. Thomas A. Sparks, Rector. Does fresh-air work and conducts other social service activities. See also under PROTESTANT EPISCOPAL CHURCHES in the Church List.

St. Columbkill Day Nursery, 165 Eagle St., Greenpoint, Brooklyn. For children of working mothers.

St. Cyprian's Chapel, 177 West 63d St., N.YC. See NEW YORK PROTESTANT EPISCOPAL CITY MISSION SOCIETY.

***St. David's Fresh-air Home,** Silver Lake Park, White Plains, N. Y. For colored women and children, boys under six, girls of any age.

St. David's Society of the State of New York (org. 1835, incorp. 1846), 289 Fourth Ave., N.Y.C. For the relief of worthy distressed and needy Welsh people; also, for social intercourse.

John Castree Williams, pres., 179 West 87th St.; Alfred H. Williams, treas., 232 East 40th St.; George Morgan Lewis, secy.

St. Dominic, Asylum of the Sisters of (incorp. 1890), Blauvelt, Rockland Co., N. Y. For destitute, homeless, and unprotected children, and such as may be committed to it by a magistrate. Provides a home and

* *Current information not received.*

industrial school for their moral and material welfare. Supported chiefly by city appropriation and voluntary contributions. In charge of the Sisters of St. Dominic (New York).

Mother Mary Marcella, vice-pres. and treas., whom address at the asylum.

St. Dominic's Home for Blind Working Girls. See CATHOLIC CENTER FOR THE BLIND.

St. Dominic's Home, New Hyde Park, L. I. See SISTERS OF ST. DOMINIC.

St. Eleanora's Home for Convalescents, Tuckahoe, N. Y. For the free accommodation of convalescents, male or female, without distinction of color, sex, or creed, discharged from city hospitals or recommended through charitable agencies. Capacity, twenty-four. Supported by a private individual. For admission apply to Sister Antoinette Marie, supt.

THE ST. ELEANOR'S COTTAGE receives convalescent children from three to fourteen years of age, free of charge. Mothers with infants also received. Capacity, twenty-six.

St. Elizabeth's Home for Convalescent Women, St. Vincent de Paul Farm, Spring Valley, N. Y. City office: 216 West 15th St., N.Y.C.

The Home is one of the Special Works of the Society of St. Vincent de Paul (q. v.), Particular Council of New York, and has been established for the physical upbuilding of poor, dependent women and girls, as specified in the following classifications: 1. Respectable mothers who are convalescing after child-birth or any other illness, who may be as yet too weak to again undertake the labor of caring for home and family; 2. Women or girls discharged from hospitals or from the observation of private physicians as cured, but who are still in a weak condition and require building up to enable them to again become breadwinners; 3. Working girls and women who, from overwork, lack of nourishment, or other causes, have reached a condition where, though unable to work, they are not fit subjects for a hospital, but require rest, fresh air, and good food to restore them to a physical condition that will enable them to follow their usual occupation.

The Home is not a hospital to receive women or girls in need of medical treatment, nor is it for the aged, infirm, or incurable. Applications should not be made for the admittance of persons for whom the Home is not intended. During the year 1,287 women were cared for in the home. Applications for admission to the home, or information concerning the same, may be obtained by addressing communications to the office.

St. Elizabeth's Home for Girls, Prince's Bay. S. I. See MISSION OF THE IMMACULATE VIRGIN.

St. Elizabeth's Hospital (incorp. 1870), 415 West 51st St., N.Y.C. (tel. Columbus 2672). A private hospital for medical and surgical aid to the sick and disabled. All classes of cases are admitted except contagious diseases or insanity. Capacity, sixty-five beds. Physicians may send their patients there and retain full supervision and care of them. Under the care of the Sisters of St. Francis.

Mother Felista, supt. and treas.

Attending physicians and surgeons: C. Adams, J. R. Alvarez, J. L. Andrews, D. Bissel, J. H. Bryne, A. P. Coll, J. Coyle, J. F. Coyle, E. R. Crowe, W. T. Dannreuter, W. Doran, Geo. W. Kosmack Edgerton, W. T. Gibb, J. R. Graham, H. Griswold, J. C. Herrity, C. J. Hillis, Hasen F. Hollister, G. L. Kellogg, Wm. A. Kellogg, Boling Lee, Moena A. Lesser, J. J. McGlade, John J.

McGrath, Wm. McMurdy, H. P. MacGregor, J. G. MacKenty, Dr. Morrow, Dr. Miller, Dr. Nicholl, Thos. Morgan, W. Morgan, F. E. Neef, H. S. Pascal, C. J. Proben, Ed. Quinn, James Quinn, J. H. Richards, V. V. Sillo, W. H. Stratford, Wm. S. Thomas, J. N. West, J. A. Wyeth, Gil Wylie, R. Wylie, J. V. D. Young.

St. Elizabeth's House. See HOUSE OF THE ANNUNCIATION FOR CRIPPLED AND INCURABLE CHILDREN.

St. Elizabeth's Industrial School (org. 1885, incorp. 1891), Bathgate Ave. and East 189th St., N.Y.C. Object: Educates female children, teaches them useful trades, supervises their work and play; also teaches older girls useful trades; visits sick poor in their homes and hospitals, providing them with necessaries and at times with money. Capacity, ninety, not boarders. Supported by voluntary contributions only.

Officers: Miss Mary Kennedy, pres.; Miss N. McDonald, vice-pres.; Miss Beatrice Smyth, secy. and treas.

St. Faith's House (incorp. 1901), 53 South Broadway, Tarrytown, N. Y. For the rescue of unfortunate girls, especially young unmarried women about to become mothers for the first time, through the agency of shelter, teaching, and other means, by which they may be brought to a better life.

Officers: Miss Lena McGhee, pres., Tarrytown; Mrs. Wm. Usher Parsons, vice-pres., 137 East 37th St., N.Y.C.; Miss Katharine Mason, treas., Tarrytown; Mrs. H. V. Conrad, secy., 122 East 40th St., N.Y.C. Apply to Miss Lena McGhee.

St. Francis' Home for the Aged (formerly St. Francis' Hospital; est. 1865, incorp. 1868), 609 Fifth St. N.Y.C. (tel. Orchard 175). For the care of destitute aged suffering from chronic ailments. Supported by voluntary contributions and board.

Sister Gonzaga, supt.

St. Francis' Hospital (incorp. 1866), East 142d St., between Brook and St. Ann's Aves., N.Y.C. Capacity, 450 beds. The poor are treated gratis; those able to pay are charged a moderate sum. Private and semi-private rooms at moderate prices.

Sister Antoniana, superioress.

St. George's P. E. Church, Stuyvesant Sq. and East 16th St., N.Y.C. Rev. Karl Reiland, Rector; Rev. J. Gilmer Buskie, exec. secy.; and assistants. Maintains besides the religious activities, for which see the Church List, the following:

CLERGY HOUSE, 207 East 16th St. (tel. Stuyvesant 2177). Residence of assistant ministers. A clergyman constantly on call.

DEACONESS HOUSE, 208–210 East 16th St.; residence of the deaconesses, parish nurse, and women workers. A worker constantly on call.

THE MEMORIAL BUILDING, 203–207 East 16th St. Visitors specially invited to come to view the parish activities. This building is used for the various parish organizations and all business is transacted there.

FOR MEN AND WOMEN: Missionary Society.

FOR MEN: Men's Club, Athletic Club, Gymnasium.

FOR WOMEN: Women's Club, Mothers' Meeting, Married Women's Society, and Happy Hour Club, Women's Branch of the Missionary Society works for Foreign, Domestic, Indian, and special missions.

FOR BOYS: Boys' Club, Boy Scouts, gymnasium classes, and other activities. 204 East 16th St.

FOR BOYS AND GIRLS: Library, Sunday-school.

FOR GIRLS: Girls' Friendly Society, King's Daughters, Sewing School, Kitchen Garden, Model Flat.

PARISH RELIEF WORK: Relief Department Woman's Industrial Society with its work-rooms. (Fresh-air work, see below.)

ST. GEORGE'S CLINIC, 208–210 East 16th St. Nutritional and dental, for children.

FOR MEN AND WOMEN: The Summer Club, outdoor activities.

ST. GEORGE'S COTTAGE, Rockaway Park, L. I.; summer home for poor parishioners. Open from June 15 to September 15.

CAMP RAINFORD, Blackhall, Conn. Summer Camp for boys. Open in July and August.

ST. GEORGE'S LUNCH ROOM, 201 East 16th St. A lunch room for respectable working women. It is open daily (except Sunday), 11.30 A. M. to 2 P. M., for service of simple inexpensive lunches. Accommodates between three and four hundred during hours. A rest room is maintained in the Parish House next door for patrons of the Lunch Room.

ST. GEORGE'S YEAR BOOK; an annual publication concerning the Parish work.

St. George's Society of New York (org. 1770, incorp. 1838), 361 West Broadway, N.Y.C. (tel. Broad 1332). Assists needy English residents of New York by alms, advice, hospital care, etc. Special attention is given to destitute and helpless women and children. Recent immigrants not eligible for relief.

Officers: Dr. Walter Eyre Lambert, pres.; Frank H. Trimble, secy.; George Quirk, chrm.; L. D. Langley, almoner.

St. Germain's Home, House of the Good Shepherd (incorp. 1858, amended 1882), Mt. Florence, Peekskill, N. Y. Reception House, 504 East 90th St., N.Y.C. For the reception, protection and care of girls from twelve to sixteen years of age who are in danger of becoming morally depraved or who may be committed by competent authority. Instruction in common English branches and music, sewing, dressmaking, housework and domestic science. Capacity, 300.

Controlled by the Roman Catholic Sister of the Good Shepherd. Supported by public and private funds.

Mother M. St. Raymond, superior.

St. Ignatius Loyola Day Nursery (est. 1915), 240–242 East 84th St., N.Y.C. (tel. Lenox 6737). Has a permit from the Board of Health for 200. Cares for children from 6 weeks to 6 years.

Sister M. Nonna, superior.

St. James' P. E. Parish, Madison Ave. and 71st St., N.Y.C., including Church of The Holy Trinity, 312–332 East 88th St., N.Y.C Rev. Frank Warfield Crowder, D.D., and Rev. Samuel M. Dorrance, vicar (tel. Rhinelander 9509). Maintains, besides the usual religious activities, for which see the Church List, the following works for social service:

CHURCH WORKERS' HOUSE, 341 East 87th St.

ST. CHRISTOPHER HOUSE, 316 East 88th St. Organizing all manner of work for men, women, boys and girls.

ST. JAMES' SUMMER HOME, East Norwalk, Conn.; for children connected with Sunday-schools of the Parish. Accommodates fifty each week. Supported by Charity Fund of the Parish. Miss M. R. Clifford in charge.

BOYS' CAMP each summer at Bear Mountain, N. Y., accommodating sixty each week.

CONVALESCENT HOME: For women and girls, Norwalk, Conn.

EMPLOYMENT SOCIETY: Gives sewing to poor women.

FIVE PARISH VISITORS: Visit the poor and report needs.

SEWING SCHOOL: Saturday, 10 A. M. from November to April.

St. Joachim R. C. Church, 22-26 Roosevelt St., N.Y.C. Maintains day nursery.

St. John the Baptist R. C. Church, 210 West 31st St., N.Y.C. Maintains a boys' military brigade, young men's lyceum, bowling alley, etc., at 214 West 31st St., N.Y.C. Rev. P. L. Werth, Pastor. See also under ROMAN CATHOLIC CHURCHES in the Church List.

St. John the Divine, Cathedral, Morningside Heights and 113th St., N.Y.C. See CATHEDRAL OF ST. JOHN THE DIVINE.

St. John's Coney Island Summer Home. See ROMAN CATHOLIC ORPHAN ASYLUM SOCIETY.

St. John's Day Nursery, 438 Hart St., Brooklyn. For children of working mothers.

St. John's Guild (org. 1866, incorp. 1877). Office: 103 Park Ave., N.Y.C. (tel. Murray Hill 7027). To afford relief to the sick children of the poor of the city of New York, without regard to creed, color, or nationality. All branches of this charity are conducted on a non-sectarian basis, and are absolutely free to all, limited only by the extent of their various capacities. St. John's Guild works in co-operation with the HEALTH DEPARTMENT and the various charitable societies of New York. Controlled by a board of trustees and supported by voluntary contributions.

Board of Trustees: William H. Burr, William R. Corwine, Seymour L. Cromwell, Henry L. Des Anges, W. W. Flannagan, Rowland G. Freeman, M.D., Mrs. Hamilton Hadden, Ralph W. Horne, John West Horner, Jr., John T. Ijams, Leeds Johnson, Joseph Larocque, Duff G. Maynard, Carleton Montgomery, Dudley Olcott, 2d, William W. Owens, Edward Roesler, Joseph L. Seligman, William Sherer, John C. Travis, Allen Wardwell, Richmond Weed, Mrs. Linzee Blagden, Manuel J. Johnson, Frank W. Hills.

Officers: Duff G. Maynard, pres.; William Sherer, 1st vice-pres.; John T. Ijams, 2d vice-pres.; Dudley Olcott, treas.; John West Hornor, secy.; Lloyd F. Hayden, general agent, whom address as above.

The Guild maintains and operates:

THE FLOATING HOSPITAL which makes trips, during the summer months, every week day, rain or shine, day and night, carrying mothers with sick babies and children for twenty-six miles of sailing in the salt air. The Hospital ministers to the different sections of the city, making landings on alternate days along the east side of Manhattan, west side of Manhattan and Brooklyn.

This Hospital provides: 1. Medical Treatment, with Hospital Care, by physicians and trained nurses in properly equipped wards; 2. Hot and Cold Salt Water Bathing, spray or needle baths for women and children, and tubs for the infants; 3. Milk. For infants as prescribed by physician; for older children during morning and afternoon; 4. A Warm Nutritious Midday Meal for all who are able to sit at a table.

No contagious diseases are allowed on board. Well children over six years are excluded. Special instructions are given to mothers by trained nurses. Total number of beneficiaries during the summer of 1920, 33,589.

SEA-SIDE HOSPITAL FOR CHILDREN, Cedar Grove, New Dorp, S. I., which receives, with their mothers, dangerously sick babies requiring more prolonged treatment than is possible on the Floating Hospital and has a capacity for about 375 patients.

This Hospital fronts the ocean, on a sandy beach affording safe bathing, while acres of lawn shaded by cedar trees furnish a cool retreat for the convalescents. Resident physicians, with a corps of trained nurses, a matron, and complete hospital equipment are provided. No well children over six years are received and no contagious diseases are admitted. During the summer of 1920, 447 patients were admitted; average stay of over ten days for each patient.

This year the Floating Hospital inaugurated a night hospital service for sick babies, keeping them in the wards day and night. Two doctors and 27 nurses in attendance. Statistics for this service: Admitted, 115 babies; discharged, 99, deaths, 16; hospital days' treatment, 2,074. Day service on Floating Hospital: Carried 33,584 patients, served 28,630, served 17,800 quarts of milk and 28,146 baths. Also opened this year at Seaside Hospital a cardiac ward for children. Over 150 of these patients were admitted.

St. John's Home for Boys, Hicksville, L. I., and

St. John's Home, St. Mark's and Albany Aves., Brooklyn. See ROMAN CATHOLIC ORPHAN ASYLUM SOCIETY.

St. John's Home for Working Girls (est. 1909), 132 West 131st St., N.Y.C. A home and social center for worthy poor colored girls. Maintains sewing and choral clubs, neighborhood, social, and educational opportunities. Night's lodging, 25 cents; bed for week, $2.50, including all privileges. Supported by the Cathedral of St. John the Divine (q. v.).

Officers: Mrs. Haley Fisk, chrm., Committee of Control; Mrs. Elizabeth L. Young, matron.

St. John's Hospital, Atlantic and Albany Aves., Brooklyn. See CHURCH CHARITY FOUNDATION OF LONG ISLAND.

St. John's Long Island City Hospital (incorp. 1891), 12th St. and Jackson Ave., Long Island City (tel. Hunters Point 2816). For the medical and surgical care of all classes of people. Contagious and infectious cases excluded. Patients without means treated free.

St. John's Protectory, Hicksville, L. I. Receives delicate boys from St. John's Home, Brooklyn.

St. John's Settlement (org. 1909), 367–369 Pleasant Ave., N.Y.C. For general neighborhood work among the Italians in that section of the city. Maintains a

Day Nursery, open from 6 A. M. to 7 P. M. Those able to pay are charged ten cents a day. In charge of the Sisters of Charity Pallotine.

Mother M. Hyacintha, Superior.

St. Joseph's Asylum for Blind Girls, Pleasant Plains, S. I. See MISSION OF THE IMMACULATE VIRGIN.

St. Joseph's Day Nursery of Brooklyn (est. 1896, incorp. 1905), 873 Pacific St., Brooklyn.

St. Joseph's Day Nursery of the City of New York (incorp. 1890), 473 West 57th St., N.Y.C. (tel. Columbus 6869). Open from 7 A. M. to 6 P. M. for children from two months to seven years of age, of working mothers, irrespective of color or creed. Capacity, eighty-seven daily.

In charge of the Dominican Sisters of the Holy Rosary. Supported by voluntary contributions. In charge of the Sisters of St. Dominic.

Officers: John J. Cunningham, pres., 63 West 89th Sts.; Thomas J. O'Reilly, treas.; Wm. H. Carr, secy., 130 Fifth Ave.

St. Joseph's Female Asylum. See ROMAN CATHOLIC ORPHAN ASYLUM SOCIETY.

St. Joseph's Home for the Aged (org. 1868, incorp. 1870), 209 West 15th St., N.Y.C. For respectable women over sixty years of age. Accommodates 360, who pay an annuity for life, prices according to accommodations.

St. Joseph's Home for Destitute Children, Peekskill, N. Y. See MISSIONARY SISTERS, THIRD ORDER OF ST. FRANCIS.

St. Joseph's Home for Destitute Male Children, Tarrytown, N. Y. See INSTITUTION OF MERCY.

St. Joseph's Hospital (est. and incorp. 1905), Central Ave., Far Rockaway, N. Y. (tel. Far Rockaway 520–521).

Sister M. Febronia, supt.

St. Joseph's Hospital for Consumptives, East 143d St. and Brook Ave., Bronx, N. Y. (tel. Melrose 22). Conducted by the Sisters of the Poor of St. Francis. Capacity, 425 beds. For free beds apply to the Tuberculosis Admission Bureau (q. v.). All ages; no distinction of color, sex, or creed. Visiting days, Thursdays and Sundays, 2 to 4 P. M.

Sister Gaudentia, Superior.

St. Joseph's Industrial Home for Destitute Children, cor. 81st St. and Madison Ave., N.Y.C. See INSTITUTION OF MERCY.

St. Joseph's Infirmary, 82d St. and Park Ave., N.Y.C. See INSTITUTION OF MERCY.

St. Joseph's Institute for the Improved Instruction of Deaf-mutes (org. 1869, incorp. 1875), Ferry Point Rd. and Eastern Blvd., Westchester, N.Y.C. Girls' and Boys' Departments. Branch, 113 Buffalo Ave., Brooklyn. For the care and education of children partially or totally deaf. Controlled by Board of Managers. Supported by public funds, fees for private pupils, and voluntary contributions.

Mary I. Scanlin, pres., 1244 Woodycrest Ave., N.Y.C.; Katherine E. McCormack, secy.-treas.; Annie M. Larkin, supt.

St. Joseph's Patronage, 523 West 142d St. (tel. Audubon 7433). A home for working girls maintained by the Felician Sisters of the Order of St. Francis, Orphanage at Lodi, N. J.

St. Joseph's Sanitarium, St. Joseph's Sta., Sullivan Co., N. Y. See SISTERS OF ST. DOMINIC.

St. Joseph's Settlement, 448–450 East 116th St. (tel. Harlem 5655). A Roman Catholic settlement and kindergarten for Italian children of the neighborhood. Affiliated with Our Lady of Mt. Carmel R. C. Church, which see in the Church List.

Rev. G. Dalia, Pastor; Mrs. A. Barbo, head worker.

St. Joseph's Summer Institute (est. and incorp. 1920), 317 East 33d St., N.Y.C. (tel. Murray Hill 6569). Provides vacations during the summer for poor children, chiefly Italian Catholics.

Rt. Rev. Mgr. Michael J. Lavelle, pres.; Rev. Joseph M. Congedo, secy.-treas.

St. Jude's Day Nursery, 19 West 99th St., N.Y.C. For children of colored working mothers.

St. Laurence Hospital (est. 1906), 457 West 163d St., N.Y.C. (tel. Wadsworth 5065). A hospital for the support and aid of the injured and indigent sick. Capacity, fifty-six beds.

Mother M. Josepha, supt.

St. Luke's Chapel (Trinity Parish), 483 Hudson St., below Christopher St., N.Y.C. (tel. Spring 4435). Rev. Edward H. Schlueter.

Parish House, 487 Hudson St.

Maintains clubs for men, women, boys, and girls. See also under P. E. CHURCHES in the Church List.

St. Luke's Home for Aged Women (org. 1852, incorp. 1854), 2914 Broadway and 114th St., N.Y.C. Provides for gentlewomen in reduced circumstances, over sixty years of age. Must have been for five years a resident of the city and a communicant of a Protestant Episcopal Church in the city and diocese of New York. Entrance fee, $500. Six thousand dollars will endow a room, twelve thousand dollars endows a room in perpetuity.

St. Luke's Hospital (incorp. 1850), Cathedral Heights, 113th St. and Amsterdam Ave., N.Y.C. Affords medical and surgical aid and nursing to the sick and disabled, suffering from acute curable and non-contagious diseases, without distinction of race or creed. Contagious, epileptic, opium, alcoholic, venereal, and incurable or offensive cancer cases are excluded.

Apply at the Hospital any day except Sunday from 10 A. M. to 5 P. M. All applicants for admission, if too sick to apply in person, will be examined by a physician at their homes. Cases of sudden injury, requiring immediate care, are received at any hour. Application for admission of patients from out of the city must be accompanied by a physician's certificate. Board in general wards $17.50 per week for adults, $8.75 per week for children under twelve years of age. Free to those unable to pay. Private rooms for pay patients from $4 to $14 per day, besides attending physicians' and surgeons' fees. Board in all cases payable in advance. Friends of ward patients are admitted on Tuesdays and Fridays from 2–3.30 P. M.

Capacity, 400 beds. Number of patients treated last year, 28,130. Total days of treatment were 117,100, of which 61,785 were free. Supported by voluntary contributions and endowments. Last year's receipts toward current expenses, $666,734.01; last year's current expenditures, $680,032.93.

Seven thousand five hundred dollars endows a bed in the general wards; $5,000 endows a bed in the children's wards; $5,000 endows a bed in the general wards during the life of the donor. Annual charge for the support of an adult's bed, $500; annual charge for the support of a child's bed, $300. Subscriptions to the Century Fund, renewable at pleasure, annually $100.

It maintains a

DISPENSARY, 114th St., near Morningside Drive, and a

TRAINING SCHOOL FOR NURSES. Candidates must be of good moral character, in sound health, and from twenty-three to thirty-three years of age.

Officers: Charles Howland Russell, pres., 15 Broad St.; Walter P. Bliss, treas., 71 Broadway; Roger H. Bacon, secy., 30 Broad St.; Rev. George F. Clover, pastor and supt.

St. Malachy's Home (org. 1876), Van Sicklen and Atlantic Aves., Brooklyn (tel. East New York 253). For Roman Catholic orphans and destitute children from two to sixteen years of age.

Sister M. Edmund, supt.

St. Marguerite's Home for Orphan Girls, Ralston, N. J. See SISTERHOOD OF ST. JOHN BAPTIST.

St. Mark's in the Bouwerie, 10th St. and Second Ave., Rev. William Norman Guthrie, Rector. Maintains

ST. MARK'S HALL, CHURCH HOUSE AND CHAPEL, 10th St. and Avenue A, where social activities are conducted.

SPINGLER SUMMER HOME, Morristown, N. J.

See also under PROTESTANT EPISCOPAL CHURCHES in the Church List.

St. Mark's Hospital of New York City (incorp. 1890), Second Ave. and Eleventh St. (tel. Stuyvesant 5940). Object: To give medical and surgical advice, aid, and treatment to persons afflicted with maladies, physical weaknesses, deformities, or infirmities. Capacity, 150 beds. Supported by voluntary contributions and board from pay patients.

Officers: Benjamin T. Tilton, M.D., pres., 14 East 58th St.; Thos. W. Slocum, treas., 11 Thomas St.; Ernest F. Lohr, supt., to whom apply.

St. Mark's M. E. Church (Col.), 231–237 West 53d St., N.Y.C. A social center for the neighborhood.

Rev. William H. Brooks, Pastor.

St. Mark's Episcopal Church for Deaf-mutes, Adelphi St., near DeKalb Ave., Brooklyn.

St. Martha's Community Center and Men's Club, Van Nest, N.Y.C. Rev. John Forbes Mitchell, chrm.

St. Martha's Industrial School, Bronxville, N. Y. See SOCIETY OF ST. JOSEPH OF NAZARETH.

St. Mary of the Angels, home for boys, Syosset, N. Y. See SISTERS OF MERCY IN BROOKLYN.

St. Mary's Free Hospital for Children (org. 1870, incorp. 1888), 405–411 West 34th St., N.Y.C. (tel. Longacre 2930). For the care and medical and surgical treatment of sick, maimed, and crippled children from two to fourteen years of age, suffering from acute or curable diseases; but no chronic or contagious cases are received. Accommodates 122 patients. Visitors are admitted daily from 3–4 P. M.; 2,331 patients were treated last year.

Sister Catharine, Sister Superior.

WILKES DISPENSARY, 435–437 Ninth Ave. For free medical treatment and advice to children; 13,943 treatments were given last year. Open daily for surgical cases at 10 A. M. and for medical cases at 2 P. M.

THE NOYES MEMORIAL HOME, Peekskill, N. Y. A branch of St. Mary's Free Hospital for Children (org. 1888). Exclusively for patients who have been treated in the Hospital and whose diseases assume an incurable form; and for some of those convalescing from illness. Accommodates twenty.

SUMMER BRANCH HOUSE, at Norwalk, Conn. For convalescent children from the Hospital.

St. Mary's Home for Friendless Women, 143 West 14th St., N.Y.C.

St. Mary's Hospital of the City of Brooklyn, The (incorp. 1882), St. Mark's Ave., between Rochester and Buffalo Aves., Brooklyn (tel. Lafayette 6500). Receives the sick of all creeds and nationalities. Contagious and infectious cases not admitted. Maintains also

TRAINING SCHOOL FOR NURSES.

Officers: Rt. Rev. Charles E. McDonnell, D.D., pres.; Charles Partridge, secy.; Sister Mary Margaret, treas.; J. S. Waterman, M.D., attending physician.

St. Mary's Hospital, Jamaica, L. I. See MARY IMMACULATE HOSPITAL ASSOCIATION.

St. Mary's of the Lake, Saranac Lake, N. Y. (tel. Saranac Lake 747). A hospital for the treatment of patients suffering from tuberculosis. Open all the time. Conducted by the Sisters of Mercy. No distinction is made as to creed or nationality.

St. Mary the Virgin P. E. Church, 139 West 46th St., N.Y.C. Rev. J. G. H. Barry, D.D. Maintains at the

PARISH HOUSE, 145 West 46th St., work with the men and boys of the parish guilds, etc.; at the

MISSION HOUSE, 133 West 46th St., under the Sisters of the Holy Nativity guilds and classes in sewing, etc., also a clothing bureau and grocery store. See also under PROTESTANT EPISCOPAL CHURCHES in the Church List.

St. Matthew's Guild for Deaf, 177 South 9th St., Brooklyn. Aids needy deaf. Rev. Arthur Boll, 192 Hewes St., Brooklyn, N. Y. See also under LUTHERAN CHURCHES in the Church List.

St. Matthew's Lutheran Church (English and German), cor. West 145th St. and Convent Ave. Maintains a Parish School and Kindergarten (English). See also under LUTHERAN CHURCHES in Church List.

St. Michael's Day Nursery (org. 1910), 135 Second St., N.Y.C. Receives young children from two and one-half to six years of age. Average daily attendance 78. Children who have been in the nursery and who go to school are also allowed to attend and receive their dinner. Supported by voluntary contributions. In charge of Sisters of St. Dominic.

St. Michael's Home, Mamaroneck, N. Y. See SISTERHOOD OF ST. JOHN THE BAPTIST.

St. Michael's Home for Destitute Children (incorp. 1884), Green Ridge, S. I. Reception House and Branch Home, 424 West 34th St., N.Y.C. (tel. Longacre 2575). For destitute and homeless children of New York City, free from contagious diseases, living at the time of committal in the City of New York, and to furnish them a common school education. Capacity for 400. Controlled by a board of trustees. Supported partly by St. Michael's R. C. Church parish and by public funds. Apply for admission to any City Magistrate or through The Society for the Prevention of Cruelty to Children (q. v.).

Under the care of the Order of the Presentation Nuns. Rev. Wm. F. Dougherty, pres. Board of Trustees.

St. Michael's P. E. Church, Amsterdam Ave. and 99th St., N.Y.C. Rev. Thomas McCandless, Rector. Maintains at the

PARISH HOUSE, adjoining the Church, organizations as follows:

MEN AND BOYS: Boys' Guilds, Boy Scouts; Men's Guild, for youths and men of the parish.

WOMEN AND GIRLS. St. Faith's, for little girls; St. Cecilia, for choir girls; Girls' Friendly Society, Young Women's Parish Aid, Women's Guild for working women.

AUXILIARY MISSIONARY SOCIETY for all women.

GENERAL: Church Periodical Club; Clothing Bureau; Gymnasium.

BLOOMINGDALE CLINIC, 225 West 99th St. Open daily, 2–4 P. M. Supported largely by voluntary contributions. George R. Lewis, treas.; G. F. Michaels, secy., Astoria, L. I. City office, 225 West 99th St.

St. Nicholas Collegiate Reformed Church, Fifth Ave. and 48th St. See at Collegiate under REFORMED CHURCHES in Church List.

St. Nicholas R. C. Church (German), 135 2d St. Maintains a day nursery, and Camp St. Nicholas at Congers, N. Y.

***St. Pascal's Day Nursery,** 334 East 22d St., N.Y.C.

* *Current information not received.*

St. Patrick's Cathedral (1879). Legal Title: Trustees of St. Patrick's Cathedral in the City of New York, 50th and 51st Sts., Fifth and Madison Aves. Rectory, 460 Madison Ave. The Most Reverend P. J. Hayes, D.D., Archbishop; Rt. Rev. Mgr. Michael J. Lavelle, Rector; Very Rev. Mgr. Gherardo Ferrante, D.D.; Rev. William B. Martin; Rev. Joseph P. Dineen; Rev. Patrick Daly; Rev. Bernard F. McQuade; Rev. Francis Fadden; Rev. John M. J. Quinn; Rev. Henry F. Hammer. Sexton, Joseph A. Boyle, Office, 587 Lexington Ave.

Societies:

Cathedral Holy Name Society, 460 Madison Ave., Rev. Patrick Daly, director.

Cathedral Young Men's Club, 144 East 50th St., Rev. B. F. McQuade, director.

Cathedral Boys' Club, for working boys up to 18 years of age, 462 Madison Ave. Rev. John M. J. Quinn, director.

Cathedral Girls' Club, 641 Lexington Ave. Rt. Rev. Mgr. M. J. Lavelle, director.

League of the Sacred Heart, 123 East 50th St. Rev. Wm. B. Martin, director.

Rosary Society, 460 Madison Ave. Rev. B. F. McQuade, director.

Children of Mary, 111 East 50th St. Rev. H. F. Hammer, director.

Society of St. Vincent de Paul, 462 Madison Ave. Rev. Patrick Daly, director; William J. Bowe, treas., 59 West 53d St.

Bureau of the Census, 460 Madison Ave. Rt. Rev. Mgr. Lavelle, director.

Cathedral School for Boys, 111 East 50th St. Rev. Brother Patrick, director.

Cathedral School for Girls and Cathedral High School for Girls, 113–123 East 50th St. Sister Victoire, principal.

St. Patrick's Church (Old Cathedral). Legal title: Trustees of St. Patrick's Cathedral in the City of New York (est. 1809, incorp. 1817), Mott, Mulberry and Prince Sts., New York City. The congregation is Italian. Address all communications and make all applications for assistance or information to the Rector.

St. Paul the Apostle R. C. Church (Paulist Fathers), Columbus Ave., cor. West 60th St., N.Y.C. Legal Title: The Missionary Society of St. Paul the Apostle in the State of New York. The activities of the church include:

St. Joseph's Day Nursery (q. v.).

Spalding Literary Union.

Paulist Athletic Club.

St. Paul's Chapel (Trinity Parish), Broadway and Fulton St., N.Y.C. Rev. Joseph P. McComas, D.D., 29 Vesey St. (tel. Cortlandt 1980). Miss Katharine B. Donovan, parish visitor.

Woman's Auxiliary, Mothers' Meeting, Young Men's and Boys' Clubs, "G.F.S.," Business Women's Lunch Club.

Employment Bureau: Apply to Miss Katherine L. Kistner.

St. Paul's Church, cor. Clinton and Carroll Sts., Brooklyn. Clothing bureau and grocery store for poor.

St. Paul's R. C. Church, 121 East 117th St., N.Y.C. Rt. Rev. John McQuirk, D.D., LL.D. The activities of the church aside from religious worship are:

St. Paul's League.

St. Paul's Free Circulating Library.

St. Vincent de Paul's Conference.

St. Paul's Parochial School.

St. Paul's Female Academy.

St. Paul's Temperance Society.

Society of the Holy Name.

Sacred Heart Society.

St. Anthony Guild.

St. Peter's Home, 395 Hicks St., Brooklyn. A boarding home for working girls.

St. Peter's Hospital, in charge of the Sisters of the Poor of St. Francis (incorp. 1866), Henry St., between Congress and Warren Sts., Brooklyn (tel. Henry 1900). Negroes are admitted. Visiting days and hours are Thursdays and Sundays, 2–4 P. M. Apply to Sister Superior, hours 9 A. M. to 5 P. M.

St. Peter's Lutheran Church, 631–635 Lexington Ave., cor. 54th St. Rev. A. B. Moldenke, Ph.D. Besides the religious services, for which see under LUTHERAN CHURCHES in the Church List, the Church maintains:

PARISH HOUSE, 134 East 54th St.

LADIES' AID SOCIETY.

YOUNG MEN'S ASSOCIATION, with sick and death benefits.

Y. M. A. JUNIORS.—JUNIOR LEAGUE.

YOUNG LADIES' SOCIETY.—CHOIR.

SCHOOL: Instruction in German, singing, and religion, two hours, three times a week, 4–6 P. M.

FREE SEWING SCHOOL, on Saturdays.

FRESH-AIR CAMP for needy children of the Parish, at Watchung, N. J., called "Elsinore Camp."

St. Philip's Home for Industrious Working Boys, 417 Broome St. (tel. Spring 4964). Gives a model home training to friendless working boys; secures positions for them and, when their deportment justifies, introduces them into respectable families to board.

Brother Bonitus, supt.

St. Philip's P. E. Church (Col.), 215 West 134th St., N.Y.C. Rev. H. C. Bishop, Rector. Maintains social activities for the colored people of the neighborhood, including an employment bureau, a home for aged, athletic clubs, etc.

St. Raphael's Italian Emigrant Society (org. and incorp. 1910), 8–10 Charlton St., N.Y.C. (tel. Spring 5744), and Ellis Island. To assist and comfort Italian immigrants detained at Ellis Island; to help them in finding relatives, friends, or money for railroad tickets; to explain the reasons for their detention or exclusion; to exhort them to love and honor this country by faithful and honest work, to respect its laws, and to be good citizens and good Catholics. It is a duty of the Reverend Father to bless Italian marriages and attend Italians dying in Ellis Island Hospital.

The Society maintains a Home, 8-10 Charlton St., where food and lodging are furnished free of charge, especially to poor families, to mothers with children, and to homeless boys and girls. They are allowed to remain until their relatives call for them or honest employment is procured. The assistance and service are entirely free. Many thousands of Italian immigrants at Ellis Island have been aided by the Society.

Rt. Rev. Mgr. Gh. Ferrante, V. G., secy.; Rev. G. Moretto, representative, to whom apply.

St. Raphael's Society (org. 1883), 330 West 23d St., N.Y.C. The Society maintains the LEO HOUSE, for the reception and protection of German Catholic immigrants on arrival. Accommodates seventy. Supported by voluntary contributions and membership dues in the Society. Jos. Schaefer, vice-pres., 23 Barclay St., to whom apply.

St. Raphael's Spanish Emigrant Society, 229 West 14th St., N.Y.C. Rev. Octavius Caron, Rector. To assist Spanish immigrants on arrival, give them information, help them to find employment, etc.

St. Rose's Industrial School for Girls. See SISTERS OF ST. DOMINIC.

St. Rose's Settlement of the Catholic Social Union (org. 1898, incorp. 1900), 257 East 71st St., N.Y.C.

St. Thomas' P. E. Chapel (of St. Thomas Parish, see below), 230 East 60th St., between Third and Second Aves., N.Y.C. Rev. John S. Haight, Vicar; Deaconess Louise Schodts, asst. Office hours at St. Thomas' House, 229 East 59th St., 10 A. M. to 3 P. M.; 8–10 P. M. The activities of the Chapel aside from the religious services, for which see under PROTESTANT EPISCOPAL CHURCHES in the Church List, are:

ST. THOMAS' HOUSE, 229 East 59th St. (tel. Plaza 3587).

PARISH NURSE, Miss Mary Fraser, R.N. Hours, 1–2 P. M.

DEACONESS, Miss Louise Schodts; Miss Margery H. Ranger, Parish Worker. Hours 9.30–11.30 A. M.

THE GYMNASIUM. Classes afternoon and night except Saturday and Sunday.

THE WOMAN'S AUXILIARY—CHAPEL BRANCH. Meets alternate Tuesday afternoons, at 2–3.

ALTAR GUILD, Chapel. Meets last Sunday in month, mornings at 9:

JUNIOR AUXILIARY, Fridays, 3.30.

THE HELPING HAND ASSOCIATION. Meets first Wednesday in the month at 12 o'clock, at the Halsey Day Nursery, 227 East 59th St. It controls the

HALSEY DAY NURSERY, 227 East 59th St., which cares for and gives kindergarten instruction to children under six years of age, of working mothers, who pay five cents a day for each child when able. The association also maintains a

MATERNITY SERVICE for the worthy poor. Families of children attending the Nursery are visited; assistance is rendered when necessary and imposition guarded against.

THE EMPLOYMENT SOCIETY. Meets Wednesdays, 10 A. M.

THE GIRLS' FRIENDLY SOCIETY. Meets Monday, 8 P. M. Various departments for all ages.

THE INDUSTRIAL SCHOOL. Meets Saturday, 10 A. M.

MOTHERS' MEETING. Friday, 8 P. M.

ATHLETIC CLUB. Alternate Mondays, 8.30 P. M.

THE BOY SCOUTS meet Thursdays, 8 P. M.

GIRL SCOUTS meet Fridays, 8 P. M.

ST. THOMAS'S ATHLETIC ASSOCIATION. Meets Thursday, 8 P. M.

THE MEN'S CLUB OF ST. THOMAS'S CHAPEL. Meets every evening at 8 o'clock, except Saturday.

THE GOOD WILL SOCIETY. Meets Wednesday evening at 8.30 o'clock.

THE BROTHERHOOD OF ST. ANDREW. Meets third Friday of each month at 8.15 o'clock.

SUMMER HOME, East Marion, L. I., N. Y. Takes church boys and girls for two weeks in July and August. Apply to vicar.

St. Thomas's P. E. Church, Fifth Ave. and 53d St., N.Y.C. Rev. Ernest M. Stires, D.D., and Rev. Floyd S. Leach, Ph.D. The activities of the church other than the religious services, for which see under PROTESTANT EPISCOPAL CHURCHES in the Church List, are

CHOIR SCHOOL, 123 West 55th St.

PARISH HOUSE, 1 West 53d St.

THE MEN'S ASSOCIATION COUNCIL. Meets second Monday evening of month.

THE EMPLOYMENT SOCIETY. Meets Thursday and Friday mornings, at 10 o'clock.

THE WOMAN'S AUXILIARY. Meets on the third Tuesday of the month at 10.30 A. M.

NEW WORLD SERVICE CLUB. Meets Monday, 2.30 P. M.

THE CHILDREN'S MISSIONARY CIRCLE. Meets Wednesday afternoons at 3.30 o'clock.

THE ALTAR GUILD. Meets Saturday mornings in the Sacristy at 10.30 o'clock.

St. Vincent Ferrer's Day Nursery (est. 1915, incorp. 1917), 209 East 71st St., N.Y.C. (tel. Rhinelander 3964). To care for children of working mothers; also helps to get employment for mothers, etc.

Officers: Mrs. J. B. Duer, pres., 107 East 64th St.; Mrs. Alfred Chapin, treas., 24 East 56th St.; Mrs. J. Walter Wood, 118 East 65th St.; Mrs. S. F. Cann, Supt. of Nursery.

St. Vincent de Paul Day Nursery, 69 Washington Sq., N.Y.C.

St. Vincent de Paul Day Nursery, 190 North 7th St., Brooklyn.

St. Vincent de Paul R. C. Church (French), 127 West 23d St., N.Y.C. For social service activities, see SISTERS OF DIVINE PROVIDENCE.

St. Vincent de Paul Society. See SOCIETY OF ST. VINCENT DE PAUL.

St. Vincent de Paul Summer Home, Ramapo Mts., Spring Valley, N. Y. Office (temporary address): 216 West 15th St., N.Y.C. Founded and maintained by the Society of St. Vincent de Paul (q. v.). Capacity, 350. It offers to the poor Roman Catholic children, twelve years of age and under, all of the city of New York, a two weeks' vacation during the summer months. During the past season 2,228 children were cared for in the Home.

St. Vincent's Home for Boys, Boerum Pl. and State St., Brooklyn (tel. Main 1353).

St. Vincent's Hospital of the Borough of Richmond (org. 1903, incorp. 1907), West New Brighton, S. I. (tel. Port Richmond 740). A general hospital for the medical and surgical care of the sick and injured. Capacity, seventy-four beds.

DISPENSARY open daily except Sunday, from 2–4 P. M. Has also an ambulance service and

NURSES' TRAINING SCHOOL, twenty-three pupils.

Sister Mary Lewis, supt.

St. Vincent's Hospital of the City of New York (org. 1849, incorp. 1870), 11th and 12th Sts. and Seventh Ave., N.Y.C. (tel. Chelsea 4050). For the medical and surgical treatment of the destitute sick, without distinction of creed or nationality. The hospital is composed of two buildings, one for general ward patients, where those who are able to pay contribute according to their means, and those who are destitute are treated free of charge. The Twelfth Street building is set apart for private patients, who have the comforts and seclusion of a home. Rooms from $28 upwards per week. Capacity of hospital, 370 beds.

OUT-DOOR DEPARTMENT open daily, except Sunday, from 2–4 P. M. Has also an ambulance service, dispensary, training school for nurses, 117 pupils.

Mother M. Josepha, pres.; Sister Clement Maria, treas.

St. Vincent's Retreat for the Insane (incorp. 1879), Harrison, Westchester Co., N. Y. For insane women only; conducted on the home plan. Unsectarian. Receives patients from New York City and adjacent cities. Capacity for 150 patients. Supported by patients' board. For terms apply by letter or personally to the Sister in charge.

St. Zita's Homes for Friendless Women. See ST. MARY'S HOME.

T

Taxes and Assessments, Department of, City of New York, 9th floor, Municipal Bldg. (tel. Worth 1800), Jacob A. Cantor, pres.; C. Rockland Tyng, secy.

Temple Israel Sisterhood (incorp.), 2307 Broadway, N.Y.C. (tel. Riverside 8835). Relief amalgamated with United Hebrew Charities. Works with Harlem District Office. Provides sewing units and industrial classes.

Mrs. Bernard Whitlock, pres., 333 Central Park West; Mrs. Lucian D. Bloch, treas.; Mrs. I. Metzger, secy., 560 West 165th St.

Tenement House Department of the City of New York (est. Chap. XIX A. of the Greater New York Charter; adopted 1901).

MANHATTAN AND RICHMOND office, Municipal Bldg. (tel. Worth 1526). Frank Mann, commissioner; John P. Finnerty, first deputy.

BRONX office: 559-561 East Tremont Ave. (tel. Tremont 6018). Walter C. Martin, supt.

BROOKLYN AND QUEENS office: 503 Fulton St. (tel. Nevins 3070). Thomas R. Farrell, second deputy commissioner.

This department is charged with the enforcement of the Tenement House Law and of certain provisions of the Charter, and with the collecting and recording of information in regard to tenement houses. Plans and specifications for new tenements must be submitted here, and complaints in regard to unsafe, unsanitary, and immoral conditions in existing tenement houses should also be referred to the department. The department keeps on file names and addresses of owners of tenements, descriptions of tenement property, carefully classified records of the tenements inspected, and other sociological data.

NEW BUILDING BUREAU. Files, records, and examines plans and specifications for new or altered tenement houses and for buildings to be reconstructed for use as tenements. It also inspects such houses in the course of alteration or construction, and reports violations of the Tenement House Law.

OLD BUILDING BUREAU. Inspects completed tenement houses and reports violations of the tenement house laws and ordinances.

Thomas Davidson Society, Wage Earners' Institute (founded 1899, incorp. 1907), 307 Henry St., N.Y.C. General activities suspended temporarily. Institute is being reorganized. Aim: To provide a cultural education for wage-earners by means of academic and cultural studies, and through fellowship in club life. The work is carried on in the evenings.

Edward M. Kahn, exec. secy.

Thomas Indian School (incorp. 1855, as Thomas Asylum for Orphan and Destitute Indian Children, re-org. and est. as a State institution, 1875; name changed, 1905), Iroquois, Erie Co., N. Y. For destitute and orphan Indian children from any of the several reservations located within this state, and furnishes them such care, moral training, and education, and such instruction in husbandry and the arts of civilization as are prescribed by their rules and by-laws. Capacity, 200.

Mrs. Emily P. Lincoln, supt.

Thursday Hospital After Care, Inc. (est. 1909, incorp. 1918), Majestic Hotel, N.Y.C. Supplies food, milk, surgical appliances and infants' outfits to the patients of Gouverneur Hos. Braces, orthopedic shoes, services of three masseuses for the children crippled by Infantile Paralysis coming to the New York Post Graduate Hospital for treatments. Weekly sewing meetings are held at the Majestic Hotel, 2 P. M. Thursdays.

Mrs. I. Regensberg, pres., 140 W. 71st St., N.Y.C.

Tombs School, The Tombs, Center, White, and Leonard Sts., N.Y.C. See PUBLIC EDUCATION ASSOCIATION.

Tompkins Avenue Congregational Church, 480 Tompkins Ave., Brooklyn. Rev. J. Percival Huget, D.D., Pastor. Provides social and athletic organizations for young people. See also under CONGREGATIONAL CHURCHES in the Church List.

Toynbee House. See ARNOLD TOYNBEE HOUSE.

Trade School for Cardiac Convalescents. Work taken over by BURKE RELIEF FOUNDATION (q. v.).

Training Institute for Sunday-school Workers. See NEW YORK CITY SUNDAY-SCHOOL ASSOCIATION.

Training School for Christian Workers, 7 Gramercy Park West, N.Y.C. See WOMAN'S BRANCH, NEW YORK CITY MISSION SOCIETY.

Training School for Community Workers. See PEOPLE'S INSTITUTE.

Transfiguration, P. E. Church, 1-11 East 29th St., N.Y.C. (tel. Madison Sq. 1171).

George Clarke Houghton, D.D., 1 East 29th St., Rector. Curates: Rev. W. W. Davis, Rev. Earl C. Cleeland.

The church is open every day in the year from 6 A. M. to 6 P. M. Visitors are always welcome during these hours for private prayer or spiritual ministrations. Ministrations to the sick or the poor, and baptisms and burials will be given at any time of the day or evening on application to the Rectory or Parish House. Emergency calls any hour, night or day.

Travelers' Aid Society, 465 Lexington Ave., N.Y.C. (tel. Murray Hill 323-324). A non-sectarian, non-commercial protective organization to safeguard travelers, particularly women and girls, who by reason of inexperience, ignorance, illness, infirmity, or other disability, are in need of assistance. It provides information, advice, guidance, and protection irrespective of age, race, creed, class, or sex. Women workers of the Society, who speak different languages, are known by their official badge. They are on duty day and night, covering all trans-Atlantic and coast line steamers carrying first and second class passengers, and all stations in Manhattan, Brooklyn, and west of the Hudson and at Ellis Island. There is no charge for the service.

The protection of the Society can be extended throughout the United States and abroad through other Travelers' Aid societies and co-operating organizations.

The Society is supported by voluntary contributions.

Officers: William Fellowes Morgan, pres.; Archbishop Hayes, hon. vice-pres.; Rev. Dr. William A. Courtney, Rev. Dr. Samuel Schulman, Rev. Dr. D. J. Burrell, vice-prests.; Mrs. E. C. Harris, rec. secy.; James McAlpin Pyle, treas.; Rush Taggart, chrm. Exec. Com.; Gerald M. Borden, secy.

Virginia M. Murray, general secy.

Tribune Fresh Air Fund (org. 1877, incorp. 1888 as The Tribune Fresh Air Fund Aid Society; corporate title changed to The Tribune Fresh Air Fund, 1918), 154 Nassau St., N.Y.C. (tel. Beekman 3000).

Provides free country vacations for 9,000 to 10,000 poor children from 5 to 16 years of age annually. No limitations as to sex, nationality or religion.

Children accepted for vacations upon the recommendation of approximately 200 social welfare and religious organizations in Brooklyn, Manhattan and the Bronx.

Vacations are provided at Fresh Air farms having accommodations for approximately 6,000 during the season. Also through Fresh Air Committees organized in a large number of rural communities which place children in good homes in their respective localities.

Active June 1st to September 30th each year. Office open all year.

The work is supported by voluntary contributions and the income from a small endowment. Contributed funds expended directly for the children. Budget, $65,000.00.

Officers: Ogden M. Reid, pres.; Edward L. Rossiter, secy. and treas.; Leslie M. Conly, general manager.

Address all communications to the general manager.

Trinity Chapel Home, 1666 Bussing Ave., cor. East 233d St., N.Y.C. For poor women over sixty years of age and of fair average health, communicants of any Protestant Episcopal parish in Manhattan or the Bronx. Capacity, fifteen. Entrance fee, $250. Apply at the Home or to Rev. J. Wilson Sutton, pres., 18 West 25th St., N.Y.C.

Trinity Church (TRINITY PARISH), Broadway, opposite Wall St. Office, 187 Fulton St. Rev. William T. Manning, D.D., Rector, 4 Washington Sq.

The Junior Clergy reside at 61 Church St.

For religious services see under PROTESTANT EPISCOPAL CHURCHES in the Church List. Social service activities include:

TRINITY MISSION HOUSE, 211 Fulton St., headquarters for most of work in downtown district. Under the charge of the Sisters of St. Margaret.

INDUSTRIAL SCHOOL FOR GIRLS, 211 Fulton St., teaches sewing to young girls. Saturdays, October to June, 10 A. M. to 12 M.

GUILDS FOR MEN, WOMEN, BOYS, AND GIRLS; meetings weekly for recreation and instruction.

EMPLOYMENT SOCIETY, 211 Fulton St.; gives sewing to poor women of the Parish.

TRINITY CHURCH MISSIONARY SOCIETY, 211 Fulton St.; makes garments for the poor of the Parish; also gives assistance to workers in Foreign and Domestic Mission fields.

TRINITY CHURCH ASSOCIATION. A corporation organized by communicants of Trinity Church for charitable work downtown. Much of the social service work of the congregation is done through this Association. This includes the maintenance of Trinity Mission House, 211 Fulton St., and Provident Dispensary at 209 Fulton St. For details, see under name of TRINITY CHURCH ASSOCIATION in this section.

TRINITY CHURCH MEN'S COMMITTEE. Interested in general neighborhood conditions, especially work among men and boys.

Trinity Church Association (org. 1879, incorp. 1887), 209-213 Fulton St. Carries on charitable work downtown. Supported by its members and by voluntary contributions of parishioners of Trinity Church.

Rev. William T. Manning, S.T.D., pres.; A. S. Murray, Jr., treas., 22 William St.; Richard M. Coit, secy., 59 Maiden Lane. Maintains the

TRINITY MISSION HOUSE, 209-213 Fulton St. Headquarters of work among the poor, where they may apply for relief. Here are held entertainments and lectures for the poor, mothers' meetings, guild meetings for young women and young girls, Bible classes, etc. In charge of the Sisters of St. Margaret. Controls the following:

PROVIDENT DISPENSARY, in the basement of Mission House, a small uniform fee being paid by all who regularly apply. Open daily, except Sundays, from 9–11 A. M. Persons needing attendance at their homes must apply to the Sisters. A fee of twenty-five cents is charged for each visit, including the prescription. A nurse is in attendance at the dispensary. Bennett S. Beach, M.D., physician-in-charge.

NUMEROUS GUILDS AND INDUSTRIAL CLASSES meet in the Mission House weekly.

Trinity Hospital (est. 1911), 1835 East New York Ave., Brooklyn (tel. East New York 4156). Surgery. No eye, ear, nose, or throat work. Capacity, thirty-two beds.

Dr. William Francis Campbell, surgeon-in-chief; Miss Gertrude V. McMahon, supt.

Trinity House, 122 Pierrepont St., Brooklyn. See HOLY TRINITY P. E. CHURCH, this list.

Trinity M. E. Church, Elizabeth St. and Delafield Ave., West New Brighton, S. I. Rev. H. Eugene Curts, Pastor. A community center, providing educational and athletic programs for boys.

Trinity Parish, Corporation office, 187 Fulton St., N.Y.C. Rev. William T. Manning, D.D., Rector. Maintains nine Churches and Chapels as follows:

1. TRINITY CHURCH, Broadway, opposite Wall St.
2. ST. PAUL'S CHAPEL, Broadway, between Fulton and Vesey Sts.
3. TRINITY CHAPEL, 25th St., near Broadway.
4. ST. AGNES' CHAPEL, 92d St., near Columbus Ave.
5. ST. LUKE'S CHAPEL, Hudson St., opposite Grove St.
6. CHAPEL OF THE INTERCESSION, 155th St. and Broadway.
7. ST. CHRYSOSTOM'S CHAPEL, Seventh Ave., cor. 39th St.
8. ST. AUGUSTINE'S CHAPEL, Houston St., between Bowery and Second Ave.
9. CHAPEL OF ST. CORNELIUS THE CENTURION, Governor's Island.

For religious services and social service activities of each Church and Chapel, see under name of each in this list, and also under PROTESTANT EPISCOPAL CHURCHES in the Church List. The social service activities of the Parish as a whole include:

SEASIDE HOME AT GREAT RIVER, L. I., for the children of the Parish.

WORK AMONG IMMIGRANTS. Gives support to work among immigrants at Ellis Island, through City Mission Society.

BEDS IN ST. LUKE'S HOSPITAL. Two thousand dollars annually appropriated for five beds for sick poor whom the Rector names.

BEDS IN ST. MARY'S HOSPITAL FOR CHILDREN, two beds for sick children are maintained in this Hospital.

A BED AT THE HOUSE OF THE HOLY COMFORTER, Church Home for Incurables.

BEDS IN PRESBYTERIAN HOSPITAL. By the bequest of Minnie Hackett Trowbridge, the Rector of Trinity Church has the right of nomination to six beds—four for adults and two for children.

BURIAL PLOT FOR THE POOR. The destitute poor of the Parish are given free interment in St. Michael's Cemetery, Newton, L. I.

Trinity Reformed Church of Brooklyn, The (St. Petri German Evangelical, Brooklyn), and Evangelical Reformed, Ave. B and 5th St., New York), Union Ave. and Scholes St., Brooklyn.

Chapel, St. Nicholas Ave., bet. Menahan and Grove Sts., Brooklyn.

Rev. George G. Wacker, Pastor, 144 Penn St., Brooklyn (tel. Williamsburg 5262).

Truant Schools, 215 East 21st St., N.Y.C.; Jamaica Ave. and Enfield St., Brooklyn; Parental School, Jamaica Rd., Flushing. See EDUCATION, BOARD OF.

Trudeau Sanatorium of Essex County, State of New York (opened 1884, incorp. 1889), Trudeau, N. Y. To arrest, and when possible to cure, incipient pulmonary consumption. To enable working men and women, when their health breaks down, to have the benefit of a change of climate, an open air life, the best hygienic influences, and special medical treatment.

The Sanatorium is located in the Adirondack Mountains and is conducted on the cottage plan. There are no private patients or graded prices. Capacity, 125 beds, adults only over 16. Per capita cost of maintenance about $17 a week. Patients are charged, when able to pay, $10 a week for board with gratuitous medical attendance, laundry extra. Free beds vary according to yearly subscriptions. Supported by voluntary contributions and income from patients. An Infirmary is maintained for patients who after entering require the services of a trained nurse, $7.50 a week extra.

Trustees: Dr. Walter B. James, pres.; C. M. Lea, Stephen Baker, Edmund Penfold, Harold Phelps Stokes, James R. Sheffield, Ogden Mills Reid, Dr. E. R. Baldwin, Dr. J. A. Miller, Dr. Lawrason Brown, Samuel Mather, W. A. Harriman, Dr. F. B. Trudeau, and George S. Brewster, treas.

Examining physicians in New York: Dr. James Alex Miller, Dr. F. J. Barrett, Dr. Henry James, Dr. W. G. Lough, Dr. E. R. P. Janvrin, Dr. Frederick H. Heise, resident physician. Apply for admission to Sanatorium, Examining Office, or to one of the examining physicians.

Trustees of the New York Annual Conference of the Methodist Episcopal Church. See NEW YORK ANNUAL CONFERENCE, etc.

Tuberculosis Camps on Ferry Boats. See FERRY BOATS USED FOR FRESH-AIR WORK.

Tuberculosis Hospital Admission Bureau (org. 1901), 124 East 59th St., N.Y.C. (tel. Plaza 1414). Conducted by the Department of Public Welfare.

The following tuberculosis institutions in New York City receive their patients through this Bureau:

(a) General tuberculosis hospitals maintained by the city: Metropolitan and Sea View.

(b) General tuberculosis hospitals maintained indirectly by subsidy from the Department of Public Welfare: Seton, Montefiore Home, St. Joseph's, Brooklyn Home for Consumptives, and St. Anthony's.

(c) Reception hospitals: Bellevue (Manhattan) and Kings County (Brooklyn). These last two institutions are for the reception of patients needing immediate care.

(d) Sanatoria for Incipient Cases only: Bedford, subsidized by the City; Ray Brook, maintained by the City and State.

(e) Preventoria for children who have been exposed to pulmonary tuberculosis in households: Sea View, West Brighton, S. I., Farmingdale, N. J., and Nanuet, N. Y. (St. Agatha's Home).

Applicants should be referred to the Tuberculosis Clinic of the district in which they live, where they will be examined and suitable action taken.

Cases are admitted on personal application at the reception hospitals, or are referred by admission Bureau to the hospital when direct application to the Admission Bureau is made too late for admission to a general hospital on the same day: the Admission Bureau transfers all such cases to other hospitals as soon as possible, excepting those cases which the reception hospital authorities wish to retain or which are too ill to be transferred.

Tuberculosis Clinics. See Association of Tuberculosis Clinics.

Tuberculosis Preventorium for Children, Farmingdale, N. J. (est. July, 1909, incorp. 1910), New York office: 105 East 22d St., R. 409 (tel. Gramercy 4270). For the prevention of tuberculosis in children of tuberculous families. Non-sectarian. Capacity, 190. Boys and girls received between four and fourteen years of age, also infants of tuberculous mothers. Active cases of tuberculosis not received. Homes of children admitted will be under supervision during their stay at the Preventorium in order that home conditions may be improved and their families educated as to best methods of preventing infection. Upon their return to the city such children are kept under observation by clinic nurses.

Open-Air Classes are held, in which the elementary branches are taught. The children sleep in open pavilions all the year round.

Directors: Mrs. Hermann M. Biggs, Dr. Hermann M. Biggs, Dr. Charles F. Bolduan, Mrs. Andrew Carnegie, Mrs. George J. Gould, F. W. Greenfield, Dr. Alfred F. Hess, Mrs. Alfred Hess, Mrs. W. B. James, Adolph Lewisohn, William G. McAdoo, Morgan M. Mann, Marcus M. Marks, Eugene Meyer, Jr., Dr. James Alex. Miller, Mrs. Henry Phipps, M. Theodore Rosenberg, Mrs. Allan A. Ryan, Mrs. James Speyer, Henry L. Stoddard, Mrs. Lewis Thompson, Lawrence Veiller, Felix M. Warburg, Alex. S. Webb, Mrs. Mary Hatch Willard, Edward H. Wise.

Officers: Dr. Alfred F. Hess, pres.; Mrs. Henry Phipps, 1st vice-pres.; Mrs. James Speyer, 2d vice-pres.; Edward H. Wise, 3d vice-pres.; Morgan M. Mann, secy., Room 409, 105 East 22d St., N.Y.C.; Alex. S. Webb, treas., Lincoln Trust Co., 204 Fifth Ave.; Dr. Alfred F. Hess, visiting-physician-in-chief, 16 West 86th St., N.Y.C. Visiting physicians: Dr. Charles F. Bolduan, New York. Dr. Jas. Alex. Miller, admitting physician-in-chief, 379 Park Ave., N.Y.C.; Miss Hortense Bibo, asst. secy., Room 409, 105 East 22d St., N.Y.C. Application for admission should be made through the tuberculosis clinic nearest which applicant resides, or at the Tuberculosis Hospital Admission Bureau (q. v.), N.Y.C.

U

Union Benefica Espanola. See Spanish Society.

Union Hospital of the Bronx (incorp. 1910), 2546 Valentine Ave. cor. 188th St., N.Y.C. A general hospital. No limitations as to age, sex, nationality, race, or sect. Territory covered, portion of the Bronx north of 161st St. and west of Third Ave. Capacity, thirty beds. Supported by dues from members, by entertainments, and voluntary contributions.

Board of Trustees: Joseph Bostwick, pres., 2804 Decatur Ave.; Nathan B. Van Etten, M.D., vice-pres.; Gustave Starke, M.D., treas., 320 East 201st St.; Walter M. Jackson, recording secy.; Bernard J. Isecke, financial secy., 68 Clinton Place; J. B. Turk, corresponding secy., 62 William St.; John F. Holmes, M.D., William H. Kahrs,

M.D., Thomas J. Quinn, Alban E. Munson, M.D., Clarence H. Smith, M.D., John C. Griswold, Robert J. Moorhead, William I. Brown, Charles J. Goeller, M.D., Miss Julia Cravey, supt.

Union M. E. Church, 233 West 48th St., N.Y.C. Rev. John G. Benson, Pastor. A community center providing reading room, dormitories, noon luncheon for women, clubs, social clinic, movies, etc.

Union Missionary Training Institute, The (incorp. 1891), 525 Clinton Ave., Brooklyn. Under the auspices of the National Bible Institute (q. v.). Trains young people of all evangelical denominations for foreign missionary work. Courses include the Bible, music, language, medicine, etc. The graduate students represent, besides the United States and Canada, Cuba, Porto Rico, Denmark, Norway, Germany, Russia, Syria, Philippine Islands, etc.

Don O. Shelton, pres.; Hugh R. Monro, treas.

Union Nationale des Eglises Reformees Evangelique. See FEDERAL COUNCIL, CHURCHES OF CHRIST IN AMERICA, 105 East 22d St., N.Y.C.

Union Settlement Association, The (org. 1894, incorp. 1902), 229–241 East 104th St., N.Y.C. Non-sectarian.

Officers: Arthur C. McGiffert, pres.; Edmund Coffin, vice-pres.; John Sloane, treas.; Gaylord S. White, secy. and head worker.

The object as stated in the Constitution, "The establishment and maintenance of settlements in New York City and vicinity where men and women may make their homes, laboring intelligently in the spirit of Jesus Christ, for the needs of their locality and co-operating in every possible way with the religious, philanthropic, civic, and educational work already being carried on there." Is in close but unofficial relation with the Union Theological Seminary.

The Settlement carries on extensive neighborhood work and maintains clubs and classes for men, women, and children, a library, study room, gymnasium, playground, dramatics, co-operates with many social agencies. It also conducts a summer camp for boys in the Interstate Park, and carries on extensive fresh-air work for women and girls at the House by the Sea, East Moriches, L. I.

The Church of the Son of Man (undenominational) is an outgrowth of informal religious services formerly held at the settlement.

THE WOMEN'S AUXILIARY OF THE UNION SETTLEMENT (org. 1896). Mrs. James R. Sheffield, pres.; Mrs. Reginald Barclay, chrm. Board of Managers; Mrs. David Dows, treas.; Miss Hastings, asst. treas.; Miss Ellen S. Marvin, secy., 876 Park Ave. To promote the work of the settlement, especially those departments which particularly require the services of women.

THE HOUSE-BY-THE-SEA, East Moriches, L. I. A convalescent home for women and girls from October to June 1. Application for rates and terms of admission should be made to Union Settlement.

Union Theological Seminary in the City of New York (org. 1836, incorp. 1839), Broadway, 120th to 122d St., N.Y.C. For the training of persons for the Gospel ministry. Equal privileges of admission and instruction, with all the advantages of the institution, are allowed to students of every denomination of Christians.

Officers: William M. Kingsley, pres. of Board of Directors; Clinton B. Price, recorder and treas.; Rev. Arthur C. McGiffert, Ph.D., D.D., LL.D., pres. of Faculty; Rev. Charles R. Gillett, D.D., LH.D., secy. of the Faculty.

United Charities, The (incorp. 1892), 105 East 22d St., N.Y.C. Object: To establish a well-known charitable center in the City of New York in which benevolent institutions can have their headquarters and to provide for the maintenance of any such societies. To that end has erected a building, the United Charities Bldg., at the above address, for housing the general offices of the Charity Organization Society of the City of New York, the Association for Improving the Condition of the Poor, the Children's Aid Society, the New York City Mission Society, and other charitable and benevolent institutions. (See advertisement.)

Horace S. Ely and Co., agents, 21 Liberty St., or Joseph L. Weinert, Manager on premises (tel. Gramercy 2258).

United Club (New York League of Girls' Clubs), 226 East 16th St., N.Y.C. For girls and women. Open Tuesday evenings, 7.30. Membership 400. The club has classes as a branch of the New York Evening High School. Dues monthly 35 cents. Initiation fee $1.00.

Anna Commick, pres.

United Community House. See LENOX HILL SETTLEMENT.

United Hebrew Charities of the City of New York, The (org. 1874, incorp. 1877), 356 Second Ave., N.Y.C, (tel. Gramercy 7170). Incorporated to relieve distress among the Jewish poor and to prevent pauperism. The Society conducts the following departments: Nursing, dietetics and home economics, vocational guidance, self-support (for the rehabilitation of families and handicapped breadwinners by establishment in business). All offices are open daily from 9 A.M. to 5 P.M. (except Saturday); Sundays from 9 A. M. to 12 M.

DISTRICT OFFICES

District 1, 151 Clinton St. (tel. Dry Dock 1101). Boundaries, South of Broome St., East River to Hudson River.

District 2, 356 Second Ave. (tel. Gramercy 7170). Boundaries, Broome to Stanton St., from East River to 3d Ave., Broome St. to W. Houston St., from 3d Ave. to Hudson River.

District 3, 133 Second Ave. (tel. Orchard 4433). Boundaries, Stanton to 42d St., East River to 3d Ave., West Houston to 42d St., 3d Ave. to Hudson River.

Yorkville District, 147 East 86th St. (tel. Lenox 1225). Boundaries, 42d through 99th Sts., East River to Hudson River.

100th St. Center, 411 East 100th St. (tel. Lenox 4702). Boundaries, 100th and 101st Sts., East River to Hudson River.

Harlem District, 192 East 125th St. (tel. Harlem 8894). Boundaries, 102d to 129th Sts., East River to Hudson River.

Bronx District, 355 East 149th St. (tel. Melrose 6930). Boundaries, 130th St. to City Line, East River to Hudson River.

Industrial and Supply Department, 204 East 23d St.

Officers: Leopold Plaut, pres.; Edgar J. Nathan and Louis Stern, vice-pres.; Samuel Weil, treas.; Mark E. Stroock, secy.; Miss Frances Taussig, exec. director.

United Hospital Fund of New York, formerly the Hospital Saturday and Sunday Association (org. 1879, incorp. 1897), Room 413, United Charities Bldg., 105 East 22d St. Object: 1. To obtain benevolent gifts for the hospitals of New York. 2. To further methods of economy. 3. To co-ordinate and extend the work of the hospitals.

Collections are received from churches and synagogues and from committees of business men and women. Receipts last year, $949,423.70.

The funds are distributed, without regard to race or creed, among the united hospitals on the basis of days of free treatment given by each hospital combined with the per capita cost per day, ascertained through carefully audited reports made directly to the Association by the hospitals upon uniform schedules, which cover in detail work, income, and expenses, and throw much light on the needs and merits of each hospital.

Contributors to the Fund have the privilege of securing free hospital treatment for proper cases referred by them to F. D. Greene, gen. secy.

Fifty-seven of the leading hospitals of Greater New York, which depend on voluntary gifts, are members of the Fund.

To join the Fund, a hospital must have (1) a high standard, (2) be incorporated, (3) have 35 beds in its wards, (4) give not less than 5,000 days of free service yearly.

The United Hospitals treat yearly about 180,000 bed patients and 600,000 out patients. They need $3,000,000 yearly in voluntary gifts.

Officers: Robert Olyphant, pres.; George Blumenthal, vice-pres.; Albert H. Wiggin, treas., 57 Broadway; Frederick D. Greene, gen. secy.

United Israel-Zion Hospital of Brooklyn, Dispensary (incorp. 1919), 1245 42d St., Brooklyn (tel. Sunset 5378).

Neuman Dube, pres.; Nathan Schoenfeld, treas.; Boris Fingerhood, exec. director.

United Jewish Aid Societies (incorp. 1909), 732 Flushing Ave., Brooklyn. To keep intact families deprived of their breadwinners, to rehabilitate impoverished persons by granting financial relief. Assistance given consists of cash, clothing, transportation, fuel, milk, medicine, medical supplies and district nursing.

Samuel Rabinovitch, manager.

United Neighborhood Houses of New York, The (est. 1919), 70 Fifth Ave., N.Y.C. (tel. Watkins 2805). To increase the influence and enlarge the usefulness of neighborhood houses by providing an organized union. Supported by yearly dues of member neighborhood houses and by voluntary contributions.

Officers: Harriet T. Righter, pres.; Geo. L. La Monte, treas.

United Odd Fellows' Home Association of the State of New York. City Office of the secretary, 54 East 4th St., N.Y.C. Supported by an annual membership per capita tax of $1.00 and by proceeds from fairs, etc., held periodically by the various lodges. Maintains a home at Unionport, N. Y. For aged and infirm members, their wives, widows, and orphans.

Officers: Marcus Berliner, pres., 301 West 108th St.; Carl Heim, treas., 336 East 55th St.; Henry Raeuber, secy., 54 East 4th St.; Frank J. Fuchs, fin. secy., 881 Cauldwell Ave., N.Y.C.

United Relief Works of the Society for Ethical Culture. See Society for Ethical Culture.

United States Civil Service Commission, Second Civil Service District Custom House, N.Y.C. Holds competitive examinations for positions in the Federal Service.

United States Employment Service, Department of Labor (est. by Acts of Congress, February 20, 1907; March 4, 1913; October 6, 1917; and July 1, 1918). For the recruitment and distribution of all types of labor in the public interest in the emergency created by the war.

Headquarters for New York State, 124 East 28th St., New York City.

Officers: John B. Densmore, director general, Washington, D. C.; Henry D. Sayer, federal director for the State of New York.

United States Immigration Station (est. under Federal control 1890), Ellis Island, New York Harbor (tel. all departments, Broad 6301).

Frederick A. Wallis, commissioner.

Government immigrant inspectors, surgeons of the Public Health Service, and interpreters board all incoming steamers at quarantine, and examine all alien cabin passengers on board ship and also discharge at the dock all citizens arriving by steerage. Such as are not eligible to land are taken to Ellis Island, and are detained there pending investigations. Alien passengers are subjected to a thorough process of inspection under the Immigration Laws. During the war this inspection takes place on ship-board.

Those debarred from landing by decision of the Boards of Special Inquiry are returned to the countries whence they came, at the expense of the Steamship Co. Those admitted are facilitated in reaching their destinations. Those going to New York and vicinity are, when necessary, accommodated until friends call for them. Provision is made for the maintenance, at the expense of the steamship companies, of those who are detained pending investigation; and for the hospital care of arriving immigrants who are ill or disabled.

Alien immigrants who have become a public charge within five years after landing, from causes existing prior to landing, may be returned in certain specified cases. Superintendents of public almshouses and hospitals in which are alien inmates who have been here less than five years are urged to bring such cases to the attention of the commissioner.

The entire service, with the exception of the office of commissioner, is under the Civil Service Rules and Regulations. Many religious and charitable organizations have representatives at Ellis Island.

United States Naval Hospital, Flushing Ave., ft. of Ryerson St., Brooklyn, N. Y. (est. 1838). Exclusively for officers and enlisted men of the Navy and Marine Corps of the United States. Visiting days: Wednesdays, Saturdays and Sundays, 1-4 P. M. Capacity, 822 beds.

Commanding Officer: Captain Charles H. T. Lowndes, Medical Corps, U. S. Navy.

United States Pensions are granted under certain conditions, to ex-U. S. soldiers and sailors (having been discharged from active service prior to Oct. 6, 1917), their widows and children, under the age of sixteen years, and dependent parents. Applications should be made to the Commissioner of Pensions at Washington, D. C.

For information concerning later provisions of the Government for soldiers, sailors and their dependents, see WAR RISK INSURANCE, BUREAU OF.

United States Postal Savings System (est. Jan. 3, 1911, under authority of act of Congress approved June 25, 1910; increased deposits authorized by acts of May 18, 1916, and July 2, 1918).

The United States receives savings deposits from the public at post offices designated for that purpose, and guarantees to repay them on demand with accrued interest.

DEPOSIT OF MONEY. Postal savings

deposits may be made by any person ten years of age or over. A married woman may deposit in her own name and free from any control or interference by her husband. No person shall have more than one postal savings account at the same time.

A deposit of at least one dollar is required for opening an interest-bearing account. Deposits will be accepted to the credit of the depositor up to $2,500, exclusive of accumulated interest.

Amounts less than one dollar may be saved by purchasing savings stamps at ten cents each. A savings card with ten savings stamps affixed will be accepted as a deposit of one dollar either in opening an account or adding to an existing account, or it will be redeemed in cash.

Accounts may be opened in person or through a representative. A person residing at a post office not authorized to accept postal savings deposits may open an account at a depository office by mail through his local postmaster.

After an account is opened, deposits may be made in person, by a representative, by money order, or by registered mail.

WITHDRAWAL OF MONEY. A depositor may withdraw on demand the whole or any part of the money deposited to his credit, with any interest payable thereon, by applying at the post office where the deposits were made. Withdrawals may also be made through a representative or by mail.

INTEREST. Interest at the rate of two per cent. a year is allowed. Interest begins on the first day of the month following the month in which the deposit is made and becomes due and payable at the expiration of each full year from the day interest begins as long as the principal remains on deposit. Interest is not paid for a part of a year.

POSTAL SAVINGS BONDS. Twice each year a depositor may exchange the whole or any part of his deposits for United States registered or coupon bonds of the denominations of $20, $100, and $500, bearing interest at the rate of two and one-half per cent. per annum. On the application of any holder, these bonds will be purchased by the Board of Trustees of the Postal Savings System at their face value.

Further information concerning the Postal Savings System may be obtained by applying at any post office, or by addressing the Third Assistant Postmaster General, Division of Postal Savings, Washington, D. C.

United States Public Health Service (est. 1798). The activities at the Port of New York are a part of the National and International activities of the Service, carried on under the direction of the Surgeon General, U. S. Public Health Service, Washington, D. C., and include the following:

Marine Hospital, Stapleton, S. I., reached by Staten Island Ferry, capacity, 300 patients. Office: 241–245 Barge Office, N.Y.C. (tel. Broad 4477).

Dispensary at the Barge Office, operated as Out-Patient Service for above hospital. Handles all cases, including examinations of Pilots and Seamen. All Pilots are examined for color blindness. All applicants for enlistment in the U. S. Coast Guard are examined as to their physical fitness. Also all applicants for license as able seamen.

G. B. Young, surgeon in charge.

SEAMEN'S SERVICE CENTER, 21 Coenties Slip, N.Y.C., in co-operation with the American Red Cross and other agencies, assists merchant seamen, and serves as a clearing house for the sick, disabled and needy sailors of the merchant fleets of the world.

E. W. Scott, director.

U. S. Public Health Hospital, 345 West 50th St., N.Y.C. (formerly Polyclinic Hospital) (tel. Circle 7200). Capacity, 340 patients.

H. C. Cody, P. A. surgeon in charge

Debarkation Hospital, Fox Hills, S. I. (tel. Tompkinsville 2700). Capacity, 500. Dr. J. O. Cobb, in charge.

Anti-Venereal Clinic, operated under the supervision of the officer in charge, U. S. Public Health Hospital, 345 West 50th St., N.Y.C.

Dr. D. D. Stetson, in charge.

U. S. Public Health Hospital (Hudson St. Hospital), 67 Hudson St., N.Y.C. Capacity, 100 patients. Not yet in commission.

U. S. Public Health Hospital, Ellis Island, N. Y. Capacity, 700 patients. Handling general service patients and patients received from the immigration service. Inspection of arriving Immigrants and Alien Seamen.

J. W. Kerr, surgeon in charge.

Office of the District Supervisor, Bureau of War Risk Insurance, 280 Broadway, N.Y.C. Has general supervision of War Risk Insurance business, Connecticut, New York and New Jersey.

F. C. Smith, surgeon in charge.

Location Office of the Division for the control of Venereal Diseases. Office: Custom House, N.Y.C.

Dr. Stafford B. Smith, in charge.

Service has an office representing local activities, Division of Industrial Hygiene and Medicine, U. S. Public Health Service, 220 West 42d St., N.Y.C.

R. R. Spencer, P. A. surgeon; F. L. Rector, asst. surgeon.

United States Soldiers' Christian Aid Association, 5 Beekman St., N. Y.C. (org. 1861, incorp. 1890).

Officers: Major S. Ellis Briggs, pres.; Major George Breck, secy. and treas.

United Workers of Flushing, The (est. 1892, incorp. 1907), 30 Monroe St., Flushing, N. Y. Day Nursery; Friendly Visitors; Clothing Sales Committee. Ten cents per day is charged for each child in the Nursery.

University Settlement Society, The (org. 1886 as the Neighborhood Guild, re-org. 1891), 184 Eldridge St., N.Y.C. (tel. Orchard 1570). To bring men and women of education into closer relations with their neighbors of this section, for their mutual benefit. The Society is established in a tenement house district and maintains places of residence for 12 residents, college men and women desirous of aiding in the work. The settlement occupies a six story building with rooms where the people of the neighborhood may meet for social and educational purposes. The work includes a gym, public baths, music and dancing classes, lectures, debates, concerts, street play, etc. There are about 125 self-governing groups located in the Settlement, comprising civic, dramatic, musical, political, literary, social, choral and art clubs for children and adults.

The Guild Journal is published monthly through the Guild, which is the federal organization including the head worker and delegates from the Senior Clubs and Residents.

During the summer two playgrounds are conducted, special fresh air excursions given and three camps operated. See Cedar Grove Camp, Camp Toranda, Senior Camp in Fresh Air directory.

Officers: James Speyer, pres.; Nathan J. Miller, treas.; Hugo Kohlman, secy.; Walter E. Sachs, chrm. of the Council.

Women's Auxiliary: Mrs. John R. MacArthur, pres.; Mrs. Joseph Howland, vice-pres.; Mrs. Henry R. Saunders, treas.; Miss Edith Kendall, secy.

Jacob S. Eisinger, head worker.

University of the State of New York. See STATE DEPARTMENT OF EDUCATION.

Upanin Club, 1 Middagh St., Brooklyn (tel. Main 1910). A temporary home for homeless boys (over sixteen years), from courts, prisons, hospitals, and streets. No distinction made as to creed or color.

M. McDonough, supt.

Urban League of New York (for Social Service among Negroes), 2303 Seventh Ave., N.Y.C. (tel. Morningside 781–782). Investigates conditions of city life and serves as a Clearing House for organizations doing welfare work among Negroes; country convalescence, industrial and employment bureaus, clubs for boys and girls and other activities.

Officers: Miss Elizabeth Walton, chrm.; A. S. Frissell, treas., 530 Fifth Ave.; Mrs. Albert J. Erdmann, secy.; James H. Hubert, exec. secy.

V

Vacation Association, Inc. (est. 1911, incorp. 1915), 218 Madison Ave., N.Y.C. (tel. Vanderbilt 6334). To promote the mutual improvement and social purposes of self-supporting girls and women, their health and recreation. Encourage and promote the procurement of vacations for them at moderate prices, and to assist in their plans and preparations therefor.

Vanderbilt Clinic (1886), cor. 60th St. and Amsterdam Ave., N.Y.C. General medical and surgical treatment, including all specialties, also dentistry. Daily except Sundays and holidays, 9 to 11.30 and 12.30 to 2.30.

Frederick Miller, supt.

DAY CAMP, on the roof, furnishes treatment, food, nursing, etc., to cases of incipient tuberculosis. Daily, except Sunday, all the year.

Vanderbilt Working Girls' Home. See ANTHONY HOME.

Van Nest Presbyterian Church, Parish House: 1736–38 Barnes Ave., Bronx. Men's, boys', women's, girls' clubs; girls' community service club. Miss C. L. Singleton of Columbia University, in charge.

Rev. George M. Elsbree, Pastor; Mrs. Bessie Kirk Knight, assistant.

Varick House. See SPRING STREET PRESBYTERIAN CHURCH, this list.

Vermilye Chapel, Collegiate Reformed Church, 416 West 54th St., maintains an

EMPLOYMENT BUREAU; Penny Provident Fund.

GYMNASIUM, FRESH-AIR FUND, etc.

See also at Collegiate under REFORMED CHURCHES in the Church List.

Veterans' Club. See LENOX HILL SETTLEMENT.

Victoria Home for Aged British Men and Women, The (est. 1915, incorp. 1916), 297 Jewett Ave., West New Brighton, S. I. Object: To care for aged British. Supported by voluntary contributions. Application should be made to Mrs. Henry H. Pike, 420 West End Ave., N.Y.C.

Victory Memorial Hospital (formerly Bay Ridge Hospital), 92d St. and Seventh Ave., Bay Ridge, Brooklyn (tel. Shore Road 1469). To administer to the wants of the sick and needy of all classes, including little children. Family physicians may attend their cases in private rooms. Supported by voluntary contributions.

Officers: Leonard Hull Smith, pres.; Wm. E. Cleary, vice-pres.; Ludwig Mirklein, treas.

Vienna Children's Milk Relief, Inc., 150 Nassau St., N.Y.C. Collects funds for relief of Viennese children. Co-operates with American Relief Administration European Children's Fund.

Officers: Mrs. Fritz Kreisler, pres.; Otto Wahle, treas.; C. V. Kerr, exec. secy.

Virginia, The (incorp. 1910), 228 East 12th St., N.Y.C. (tel. Stuyvesant 5748). A hotel for girls on small salaries. Capacity, 87. Rates, including three meals a day, from $6 to $9 a week.

Mrs. S. A. Chinn, supt.

Virginia Day Nursery, 632 5th St., N.Y.C. See WOMAN'S BRANCH, NEW YORK CITY MISSION SOCIETY.

Visiting Guild for Crippled Children. See BLYTHEDALE HOME.

Visiting Nurse Association of Brooklyn, Inc., The, 80 Schermerhorn St., Brooklyn, N. Y. (tel. Main 314). Branch Offices: 136 Broadway; 732 Flushing Ave.; 1022 Gates Ave.; 105 Fleet Place; 1696 Myrtle Ave.; 6005-14th Ave.; 887 Church Ave.; 133 Baltic St.; Bond and Wykoff Sts.

Object: To give skilled nursing care to the sick in their homes; to teach personal hygiene, cleanliness and the prevention of diseases. The Association maintains a staff of trained nurses to give nursing care under the physician's direction to the sick in their homes. The nursing service covers the Borough of Brooklyn. A separate staff is maintained for home treatment and follow-up work of cases of Infantile Paralysis in Kings County. Fees charged according to the circumstances of the individual patient and at the discretion of the nurse.

Elizabeth M. Stringer, supt.

Vivisection Investigation League (incorp. 1911), Room 411, United Charities Bldg., 105 East 22d St., N.Y.C. (tel. Gramercy 5415). To investigate the practice of vivisection upon human beings and upon animals, and to follow up the mental, moral, and physical results of this practice; to hold public meetings and to have lectures and exhibitions; to publish and to distribute literature bearing upon the subject of vivisection. The league will exert itself in favor of any legislation that will tend to improve existing conditions in regard to the practice of vivisection.

Officers: Mrs. Clinton Pinckney Farrell, pres.; Mrs. Lauterbach, Miss Mary Phelps Robinson, vice-prests.; Mrs. Ellen L. Penrose, rec. secy.; Mrs. Maud R. Ingersoll Probasco, cor-secy.; Arthur L. Leland, treas., 50 Broad St.

Vocational Guidance and Employment Service for Juniors (org. 1920) (formerly the Committee for Vocational Scholarships, Vocational Guidance Bureau of the Henry Street Settlement and Junior Employment Service). Administrative office, 17 Lexington Ave. (tel. Gramercy 1542). Bureaus: 1275 Lexington Ave. (tel. Lenox 5503), 150 Delancey St. (tel. Orchard 405), 36 Greenwich Ave. (P. S. 41, Watkins 5323), Kips Bay Neighborhood Assn., 825 Second Ave. (Vanderbilt 9522). Gives scholarships for vocational training of $150 to $300 to children eligible for working papers between the ages of fourteen and sixteen; maintains Vocational Counselors in ten public schools; also the bureaus which give vocational and educational guidance to boys and girls under eighteen and place them, when deemed advisable, in investigated positions.

Officers: Mrs. E. C. Henderson, chrm.; Mrs. Alice K. Pollitzer, director; Miss Margaret Brown, associated director.

Vocational School for Boys, 138th and 139th Sts., west of Fifth Ave., N.Y.C. See EDUCATION, BOARD OF.

Voluntary Defenders Committee, The (incorp. 1917), 32 Franklin St., N.Y.C. (tel. Franklin 3762). To provide counsel for needy defendants in criminal cases.

William Dean Embree, counsel; Louis Fabricant, associate counsel; Miss Alice Waldo, director of investigations.

Voluntary Parenthood League, 51 East 59th St., N.Y.C. Promoting amendments of federal and state laws on the subject of birth control.

Officers: Mrs. Mary W. Dennett, director; Mrs. Eugene Stone, treas.; Frederick H. Robinson, secy.

Volunteers of America (incorp. 1896). National Office: 34 West 28th St., N.Y.C. (tel. Watkins 661). A philanthropic and evangelistic organization, working in all the principal cities of the United States among the wage-earning classes, and in the degraded and neglected sections, to help men and women to higher and better lives.

Officers: General and Mrs. Ballington Booth, commanders-in-chief; Major-General F. Fielding, vice-pres.; Colonel W. J. Crafts, treas.; Colonel James W. Merrill, secy.

The activities of the Volunteers consist of outdoor and indoor religious services and social work as follows:

VOLUNTEER HOSPITAL AND DISPENSARY (incorp. 1906), cor. Beekman and Water Sts., N.Y.C. A general Hospital for the medical and surgical care of the sick admitted to its ward of all creeds and classes except those suffering from infectious or contagious diseases. Free to the worthy indigent sick; board from $14 per week upward for those able to pay. A public ambulance service is maintained day and night and accident cases are admitted any time. The Medical and Surgical Departments are under the control and supervision of twenty-five physicians and surgeons. During the last year, 11,787 new cases and 20,514 old cases were treated in the Dispensary. There were given 3,000 days' treatment to pay patients; public charges, 3,068, and free patients, 2,434, making the total days' treatment 8,502 in the Hospital wards. Any decrease in the above figures as compared with last year is accounted for by the fact that space was limited during building alterations.

Executive Officers: Gen. Ballington Booth, pres.; Col. W. J. Crafts, treas.; Col. James W. Merrill, secy.

VOLUNTEER PRISON LEAGUE, 34 West 28th St., N.Y.C. An organization for aiding discharged and paroled state prisoners and the families of men confined in state prisons. It guarantees to every discharged prisoner coming direct to its office on the day of liberation, a home and protection until employment has been secured. The League is established in thirty-six state and federal prisons; has over 90,000 men enrolled during the past twenty years, and has sheltered over 12,000 in its homes and office center. It maintains:

HOPE HALLS for discharged and paroled state prisoners until they can be provided for.

VOLUNTEER CHILDREN'S HOME (incorp.), West Brighton, S. I., for children whose homes are temporarily being broken up. Children of both sexes are admitted between the ages of four and twelve years. Parents pay what they are able towards the support of their children. Apply to Mrs. O. Buehler, supt., or Col. J. J. Keppel, 1155 Broadway, N.Y.C.

The attendance of outdoor services throughout the country during the past year was 2,654,558; indoor services, 926,036. Lodgings furnished to 339,732 free; lodgings paid for 919,220; 720,460 free meals were given, and 311,574 meals which were paid for by services and otherwise.

W

Wage Earners' Institute, 307 Henry St., N.Y.C. See THOMAS DAVIDSON SOCIETY.

Waiters' Home, 427 East 51st St., N.Y.C. See CHRISTIAN WAITERS' HOME.

War Camp Community Service. See NEW YORK COMMUNITY SERVICE.

War Risk Insurance, The Bureau of, Washington, D. C. By Act of Congress approved Oct. 6, 1917, as amended, the United States makes certain provisions for the: (a) Insurance of members of the military and naval forces against total permanent disability and death: (b) payment of allotments and allowances to the families and certain specified dependent relatives of enlisted men; (c) payment of compensation to disabled men and their families, or to parents and families of deceased men. This Act, popularly referred to as the Soldiers' and Sailors' Insurance Law, and likewise as the War Risk Insurance Law.

An important part of the Bureau of War Risk Insurance is an Investigation Section responsible for the investigation of claims which, for many varied reasons, cannot be settled on the basis of the information contained in the papers made out by enlisted men.

NEW YORK BRANCH OFFICE of the Bureau of War Risk Insurance, 25 West 43d Street. This is the Second District Office of the Bureau of War Risk Insurance and embraces within its territory the State of New York, northern New Jersey, and Connecticut.

Harry Burlingame, supervisor.

The Second District Office, because of the very small number of paid field examiners on the staff, invites men and women of proved loyalty and ability to volunteer their services in helping to investigate cases coming within the jurisdiction of this office. The work is highly important, offering a splendid opportunity for service worth while, and must appeal to those who have at heart the interest of the Government and the enlisted man and his dependents.

The general provisions of the War Risk Insurance Act are:

1. Allotment and Allowance:

Allotment to wife and children is compulsory and allowance is automatic if allotment is made.

Allotment as to certain other relatives or dependents of enlisted men is voluntary and strictly confined to cases of actual dependency on the soldier before enlistment, unless such dependency has arisen from new causes since enlistment. Allotments can be made only by enlisted men or women in active military or naval service.

2. Compensation.

3. Insurance.

There is a general misunderstanding in regard to the difference between "Compensation" and Government Insurance. "Insurance" is paid for by you. "Compensation" is given by your Government. Insurance is payable only upon the death or total and permanent disability of the insured, however and whenever caused.

Compensation is payable to your widow, children, and dependent parents upon your death due to injuries or diseases incurred in active service in the line of duty; or to you (with additional allowances for wife, children, and dependent parents, if any), after your discharge from active service, for total permanent disability, permanent partial disability, temporary total disability, or temporary partial disability, due to injuries or disease incurred in active service in the line of duty. No compensation is payable where the disability is rated at less than 10 per cent.

Insurance is bought by the service man, and is in effect as the result of his having made application for it and paying the premiums. Compensation is payable in a proper case regardless of whether the service man carried insurance.

In general, compensation is payable only for death or disability incurred while in the service or as a result of your service. Insurance, if in force, is payable for death or total and permanent disability occurring either in or out of the service, from any cause at any time.

War Savings Stamps (Series of 1920), including Treasury Savings Certificates of $1,000 and $100 denominations (maturity value), the War Savings Certificate Stamps of $5.00 denomination (maturity value) and the 25 cent Thrift Stamp.

These Savings Securities are direct obligations of the United States Government, and may be purchased at the Federal Reserve Bank, incorporated Banks, Trust Companies, Post Offices and other authorized agencies.

The cost of these securities January 1, 1920, is as follows:

$1,000 U. S. Treasury Savings Certificate $824.00, rate of monthly increase $2.00; $100 U. S. Treasury Savings Certificate $82.40, rate of monthly increase $0.20; $5 U. S. War Savings Stamp Certificate $4.12, rate of monthly increase $0.01. Thrift Stamp always selling at same price, $0.25.

January 1, 1925, the Government will pay for each Certificate of this issue its maturity value. Maturity value is principal plus interest compound quarterly at four per cent (4%).

New Certificate cards are necessary for 1920 Stamps. In addition to the amount purchased in 1918 and 1919 you may purchase $1,000 (maturity value) of the 1920 Series.

Thrift Stamps are identical with those of 1919. Thrift Stamps bought in 1918 or 1919 may be exchanged for War Savings Stamps of the new issue. No new Thrift card is necessary.

The War Savings Certificates with 20 War Savings Stamps affixed are convertible into Treasury Savings Certificates through your Bank or Post Office.

War Work Council Y. M. C. A. See INTERNATIONAL COMMITTEE, Y. M. C. A.

War Work Council Y. W. C. A. See NATIONAL BOARD, Y. W. C. A.

Warren Goddard House (org. 1892, incorp. 1901 as Friendly Aid Settlement, name changed in 1902 to present title), 246-248 East 34th St., N.Y.C. A settlement maintained by the Friendly Aid Society for the purpose of serving the neighborhood. Its activities include:

Classes in dressmaking, cooking, singing, piano, dancing, drawing, etc.

Lectures, concerts, entertainments, roof garden, gymnasium, etc.

Clubs for boys, girls, young men and women.

Wartburg Home for Aged and Infirm (founded 1875), 2598 Fulton St., Brooklyn, N. Y. A society of members of the Lutheran Church, which receives and cares for aged Germans (Protestants only), sixty-five years of age or over. Accommodates eighty.

Rev. Otto Graesser, 602 East 9th St., N.Y.C., to whom apply.

Wartburg Orphans' Farm School of the EVANGELICAL LUTHERAN CHURCH (incorp. 1866 and 1884), Mt. Vernon, Westchester Co., N. Y. For the care and education of orphans. Full legal surrender required. Half-orphans, for whom payment of $9 per month is charged, also received. Receives gratuitously children of both sexes, between two and ten years of age, without distinction as to nationality or creed, who are given a thorough educational and industrial training. Maintains

A FARM, a PRINTING HOUSE, and a KINDERGARTEN.

Rev. G. C. Berkemeier, D.D., director, Mt. Vernon, N. Y., to whom address all applications, etc.

Washington Heights Day Nursery (est. 1902), 350 West 145th St., N.Y.C. No limitations as to race, sex, nationality, or sect. Supported by dues, donations, etc.

Washington Irving High School, Girls' Employment Bureau, 40 Irving Pl. (tel. Stuyvesant 5524). For girls of the School, stenographers, bookkeepers, clerical workers, librarians, dressmakers, designers.

Miss E. T. Gittoe.

Washington Square Home for Friendless Girls (org. 1865, incorp. 1873), 9 West 8th St., N.Y.C. (tel. Stuyvesant 3919). An unsectarian free home for friendless girls, mothers, and babies, who voluntarily commit themselves and conform to the rules and regulations and are subsequently helped toward useful and well adapted lives.

Officers: Edward L. Partridge, M.D., pres., 19 Fifth Ave.; Gilbert Darlington, treas., 6 Bible House; William A. Greer, secy., 209 East 42d St.; Miss Florence L. Giddings, R.N., supt.

Washington Square M. E. Church, 133 West 4th St., N.Y.C. Rev. J. Sumner Stone, Pastor. Conducts a music school, kindergarten, Americanization classes for men and women, and provides social and athletic clubs. See also under METHODIST EPISCOPAL CHURCHES in the Church List.

Water Supply, Board of, City of New York, 22d floor, Municipal Bldg. (tel. Worth 3150). Commissioners: George J. Gillespie, pres.; Charles N. Chadwick and L. J. O'Reilly; Benj. F. Einbigler, secy.

Water Supply, Gas, and Electricity, Department of, City of New York.

MANHATTAN, 23d, 24th, and 25th floors, Municipal Bldg. (tel. Worth 4320). Nicholas J. Hayes, commissioner.

BRONX: Tremont and Arthur Aves. (tel. Tremont 3400). Albert H. Leitenan, Deputy.

BROOKLYN: 50 Court St. (tel. Main 3980). Cornelius N. Sheehan, Deputy.

QUEENS: Annable and Jackson Aves., Long Island City (tel. Hunters Point 3500). James Butler, Deputy.

RICHMOND: Borough Hall, St. George, S. I. (tel. Tompkinsville 840). James L. Vail, Deputy.

Watts de Peyster Industrial Home and School for Girls (incorp. 1894), Tivoli-on-Hudson, N. Y. Under the auspices of the Women's Home Missionary Society of the Methodist Episcopal Church. For the care, maintenance, and education of dependent, orphan, and half-orphan girls, from five to thirteen years of age, who are received and educated until the age of eighteen, when suitable positions are found for them. Supported by voluntary contributions and products of the Home.

Mrs. Mary Fisk Park, chrm., 27 East 62d St., N.Y.C. I. M. Wharton, supt.

Waverly House, 38 West 10th St., N.Y.C. See NEW YORK PROBATION AND PROTECTIVE ASSOCIATION.

Wayside Day Nursery (org. 1883, incorp. 1887), 216 East 20th St., N.Y.C. (tel. Gramercy 3991). Cares for infants and children of working mothers from

7.30 A. M. to 6 P. M.; 15 cents a day for each child.

Industrial Classes, held after school hours for girls from eight to sixteen years of age. Supported by voluntary contributions.

Wayside Home, The (incorp. 1880), Valley Stream, L. I. Receives Protestant young women from the four counties of Long Island, committed by the courts under 295 of the Laws of 1920. Supported by public money, voluntary contributions and the income from the farm.

Mrs. Hobart Porle, pres.; Miss A. W. Rossiter, treas.; Helen G. Gardner, rec. secy.; Jeanette S. Taylor, cor. secy.; Eloise A. Hafford, supt.

Webb Institute of Naval Architecture (incorp. 1889), Sedgwick Ave. and 188th St., N.Y.C. For aged and indigent shipbuilders or marine engine workers of the U. S. and their wives. Free education in ship and marine engine building.

Officers: Stevenson Taylor, pres., 123 West 85th St.; G. P. Taylor, secy., and treas., 66 Beaver St., N.Y.C.

Weeburn Farm. See HARTLEY HOUSE.

Welcome House Settlement. See HANNAH LAVENBURGH HOME.

Welfare Department, City of New York. See PUBLIC WELFARE DEPARTMENT.

Welfare League Association, 4836 Grand Central Terminal, N.Y.C. (tel. Vanderbilt 4747). The particular object for which this association was formed is the improvement of conditions and methods in the establishment, construction, conduct and control of prisons and reformatories in the State of New York and in New York City.

This Association maintains a clearing house for prisoners' families, also an employment bureau for ex-prisoners. The families are referred to us by the prisoner himself, and after investigation the family is referred to the proper association for relief. Our position is that of adviser and friend to the family in all unusual trials which come to them while the man is in prison. In obtaining employment for the families we use already existing agencies.

The Employment Bureau finds positions for ex-prisoners applying at the office. Also for men from Sing Sing and Auburn who apply through the M. W. L. before they are discharged or paroled, so they have places to go to immediately.

Officers: Thomas Mott Osborne, pres.; Judge W. H. Wadhams, Mrs. H. H. Jenkins, Lewis F. Stanton, vice-prests.; Spencer Miller, Jr., treas.; David M. Osborne, secy.; George H. Hodson, asst. secy.

Wendell Branch of the Boys' Club. See BOYS' CLUB.

Wesley House, Inc. (est. 1908), 442 East 59th St., N.Y.C. (tel. Plaza 1985). A settlement for the physical, social, intellectual, and spiritual development of the people in its neighborhood. Maintains a kindergarten, shower baths, clubs, classes in sewing, cooking, carpentry, etc.; open on Sunday for Children's Hour.

Officers: James D. Merriman, pres.; W. H. Dickerson, secy.; E. R. Otheman, treas., 31 Nassau St.; Nina A. Robertson, head worker.

West End Exchange and Industrial Union (incorp. 1896), 169 West 74th St., N.Y.C. Sells on consignment the work of self-supporting women. In the Domestic Department are to be found home-made bread and cake, candy, delicacies for the sick, and various kinds of dainties for the table. Also a large assortment of articles in the Fancy Work Department. Sewing orders taken.

West New Brighton Day Nursery (est. 1913), Campbell St., West New Brighton, S. I. To maintain a place where working women may leave their children during the day in case of necessity.

Mrs. James A. Clark, chrm.; Mrs. James L. Robertson, treas.; Mrs. George Blake, secy.; Mrs. C. D. Griffith, cor. secy.

West Park Presbyterian Church, 86th St. and Amsterdam Ave., N.Y.C. Rev. Anthony H. Evans, D.D., Pastor. Social guilds, clubs, athletics, etc. See also under PRESBYTERIAN CHURCHES in the Church List.

West Side Aid for Friendless Men. See INDUSTRIAL CHRISTIAN ALLIANCE.

West Side Branch, Y. M. C. A. See YOUNG MEN'S CHRISTIAN ASSOCIATION.

West Side Branch, Y. W. C. A. See under YOUNG WOMEN'S CHRISTIAN ASSOCIATION.

West Side Day Nursery Industrial School and Kindergarten (org. 1883, incorp. 1884), 266 West 40th St., N.Y.C. For the care and teaching of young children while their mothers are at work away from their homes; also for a refuge after school hours for young girls. These are taught household work and sewing.

Mrs. Charles Stewart Smith, pres., 25 West 47th St.; Mrs. E. A. Pratt, supt.

West Side Dispensary and Hospital (incorp. 1872), 328 West 42d St., N.Y.C. (tel. Bryant 1740). For the gratuitous medical and surgical treatment of the sick poor, regardless of creed or nationality. Open daily, except Sundays and holidays, from 9 A. M. to 9 P. M.

Officers: James P. Cahen, pres.; R. J. Wade, chrm.; Morris Schneider, treas.; A. V. Mentz, supt.

West Side Home for Boys. See CHILDREN'S AID SOCIETY.

West Side Mission, 269–271 West 47th St., N.Y.C. (tel. Longacre 3113). Visits homes of the poor and does general relief work. Children's and Mothers' meetings.

Clemme Ellis White, supt.

Western House of Refuge for Women, Albion, Orleans County, N. Y. State reformatory for girls. Commitment by Court. Age 16 to 30. Capacity, 215.

Training: Domestic science, household arts, nursing, agriculture, school, 1st to 8th grades, music and gymnasium.

Mrs. Flora P. Daniels, supt.

White Door Settlement, 211 Clinton St., N.Y.C. See GOSPEL SETTLEMENT.

White Rose Mission and Industrial Association (founded 1897, incorp. 1898), 262 West 136th St., N.Y.C. For protection and betterment of colored working girls.

Capacity, fourteen beds for lodgers.

Wiawaka Holiday House, Lake George, N. Y. Provides board and lodging at cost price or less for girls and young women dependent upon their own exertions for support. Open the entire year.

Officers: Mrs. Spencer Trask, hon. pres.; Miss Fuller, pres.; Mrs. Samuel H. McClellan, treas.; Mrs. Edwin A. King, cor. secy., Troy, N. Y.

Widowed Mothers' Fund Association (incorp. 1909), 192 Bowery, N.Y.C. Purpose: To avoid commitment of children by keeping intact the homes of widowed mothers, whose husbands were aliens, and who are efficient, but poor. Each family in charge is provided for promptly and adequately in accordance with a standard of living that preserves the health, happiness, and self-respect of the family.

Mrs. William Einstein, pres.

Wilkes Dispensary, 435 Ninth Ave. (tel. Longacre 2930). Open daily except Sundays and holidays. Surgical clinic, 9 to 10 A. M.; Medical clinic, 1 to 2 P. M.

Social Service Department of St. Mary's Hospital and Wilkes Dispensary, 435 Ninth Ave. (tel. Longacre 2834). Open daily 9 A. M. to 5 P. M.

Willard Parker Hospital, foot of East 16th St., N.Y.C. See HEALTH, DEPARTMENT OF.

William Carey Camp, Jamesport, L. I. See BOYS' CLUB.

William H. Davis Memorial Free Industrial School for Crippled Children, The, 471 West 57th St. (tel. Columbus 3083). The children are conveyed daily to and from their homes in auto bus, and are taught the English branches, kindergarten, and manual training. The last is made a special feature, to train crippled children to be self-supporting. A hot nourishing dinner is served at noon. These are all children debarred from public schools because of physical disabilities. Supported by dues from members and voluntary contributions.

Summer home, "The Lulu Thorley Lyons Home for Crippled and Delicate Children," at Claverack, N. Y.

Mrs. Arthur Elliot Fish, founder; Walter Scott, pres.; Mrs. Charles Thorley, 1st vice-pres.; Mrs. Frank Jefferson Blodgett, 2d vice-pres.; Mrs. Nichols M. Pond, 3d vice-pres.; Mrs. Edward Davis Jones, treas.; Mrs. Mullin Wayne, cor. secy.; Miss Amelia D. Campbell, rec. secy.; F. Ellwood Briggs, auditor; Mrs. M. Eleanor Bullard, supt.

Williamsburgh Hebrew Hospital. See BIKUR CHOLEM KOSHER HOSPITAL.

Williamsburgh Hospital, The (incorp. 1851, org. 1889), Bedford Ave. and South 3d St., Brooklyn (tel. Greenpoint 2290). Medical and surgical cases admitted. Public and private wards. Capacity, seventy-two beds. Non-sectarian. Ambulance service.

Officers: James J. Post, pres., 129 Front St., N.Y.C.; Daniel T. Wilson, Louis C. Wills, vice-prests.; William S. Irish, treas., 260 Broadway, Brooklyn; George F. Jones, secy., 477 Herkimer St., Brooklyn; Miss Margaret T. Herlihy, supt.

Willis Sanitarium, The, 54 St. Paul's Pl., Brooklyn (tel. Flatbush 3747). For patients suffering from nervous diseases, cancer, paralysis, etc. For rates address the Sanitarium. Capacity, eleven.

Harrison Willis, M.D., mgr.

Willoughby House Settlement (org. 1900, incorp. 1905), 97 Lawrence St., Brooklyn. To promote the best interests of the neighborhood, physically, intellectually, socially, and spiritually, by means of clubs and classes demanded by the community itself and for civic betterment through co-operation with other organizations. Maintains a day nursery. Supported by voluntary contributions.

Board of Directors: Miss May Belle Williams, pres.; Mina A. Clement, treas., 254 Clinton Ave., Brooklyn; Edith Burtis, fin. secy.; Anna B. Van Nort, head worker; Ida Ryerson, asst.

Willow Place Chapel House. See COLUMBIA HOUSE SETTLEMENT.

Wilson Industrial School for Girls, The (incorp. 1854), 239 West 69th St., N.Y.C. (tel. Columbus 6984). Conducts industrial classes, such as plain sewing, dressmaking, cooking, and physical culture for girls and women. Has an "all-day" kindergarten for small children and a day nursery for babies. Physical culture for business girls and women and care of a certain number of school children out of school hours, including food for them. Supported by voluntary contributions.

Officers: Mrs. H. W. Everett, 1st directress, 449 Park Ave.; Mrs. O. K. Dimock, treas., 339 Park Ave.; Mrs. Holcombe Ward, rec. secy., 125 East 72d St.; Miss Mary S. Pavey, cor. secy., 119 East 19th St.; Mary E. Butterworth, M.D., visiting physician; Miss R. N. Parker, supt.

Winifred Masterson Burke Relief Foundation. See BURKE RELIEF FOUNDATION.

Winifred Wheeler Day Nursery. See EAST SIDE HOUSE SETTLEMENT.

Woman's Auxiliary to the Board of Missions (P. E.). See PRESIDING BISHOP AND COUNCIL, etc.

Women's Auxiliary of the New York City Baptist Mission Society. Headquarters, 235 East 18th St., N.Y.C. To co-operate with the New York City Baptist Mission Society (q. v.), prosecuting charitable, benevolent work in the City of New York. Supported by voluntary contributions.

Officers: Mrs. W. P. Miner, pres., 545 West 148th St.; Mrs. Guy Wellman, treas., Chippaqua, N. Y.; Mrs. Herbert Anstie, secy.; Miss Grace Daland, supt.

Woman's Auxiliary, St. Vincent de Paul Society, Borough of Queens (est. 1905). Does settlement and prison work. Rev. James J. Higgins, D.D., pres., 251 Front St., Brooklyn, N. Y.

Woman's Baptist Foreign Missionary Association of Long Island, The (org. 1871). Mrs. Charles L. White, 750 Carroll St., Brooklyn, N. Y.

Women's Board of Domestic Missions of the Reformed Church in America (org. 1882, incorp. 1910), 25 East 22d St., N.Y.C. (tel. Gramercy 1593). To assist Mission churches of the denomination and to do evangelistic, educational, and uplift work among the Japanese of New York City, the Mountain people of the South, and the Indians of six tribes, located in Oklahoma, New Mexico, and Nebraska. Supported by voluntary contributions.

Officers: Mrs. John S. Bussing, pres.; Miss Mary M. Greenwood, treas.; Mrs. John S. Allen, cor. secy.

Woman's Board of Foreign Missions of the Presbyterian Church in the U. S. A., The, Room 818, 156 Fifth Ave., N.Y.C. To promote foreign missions especially among women and children in non-Christian lands. Supported by voluntary contributions.

Officers: Miss Margaret E. Hodge, pres.; Miss Mary R. Tooker, rec. secy.

Woman's Board of Foreign Missions of the Reformed Church in America (est. 1875, incorp. 1892), 25 East 22d St., N.Y.C. (tel. Gramercy 1593). To maintain missionary work for women and children in India, China, Japan and Arabia.

Officers: Mrs. Frederick A. Baldwin, pres.; Miss Katharine van Nest, treas.; Miss Eliza P. Cobb, cor. secy.

Woman's Board of Home Missions of the Presbyterian Church, U.S.A. (org. 1878), 156 Fifth Ave., N.Y.C. (tel. Chelsea 9838). For the equipping and maintaining mission schools and medical missions among the exceptional populations of the United States, Alaska, Porto Rico, and Cuba.

Officers: Mrs. F. S. Bennett, pres.; Miss Lucy H. Dawson, gen. secy.

Woman's Branch, Brooklyn City Mission Society (org. 1886), Room 1217, 44 Court St., Brooklyn. Works among women and children in missions, jails, and hospitals. Maintains a Working Girls' Home, 18 Sydney Pl.

Woman's Branch, New York City Mission Society (org. 1822), Room 401, United Charities Bldg., 105 East 22d St., N.Y.C. Aims by evangelistic efforts to promote the welfare of the poor. Visits and helps the sick below 14th St., in their homes and supplies trained nurses and nourishment. Supported by voluntary contributions. (See advertisement.)

Officers: Mrs. A. F. Schauffler, 1st directress; Miss Cuyler, 2d directress; Mrs. W. S. Edgar, secy.; Mrs. E. Lincoln Smith, treas.; Miss Billings, asst. treas.; Miss Edith H. White, exec. secy. Maintains the following:

CHRISTIAN WORKERS' HOME, 7 Gramercy Park West. Used for the Society's Missionaries, Nurses, and those in training.

TRAINING SCHOOL FOR CHRISTIAN WORKERS, 7 Gramercy Park West. A fee of $200 covers the expense of the course, inclusive of home, from October 1 to June 1. Apply to Miss E. H. White, exec. secy., 105 East 22d St.

FRESH-AIR FUND for special cases. Fresh-air work is also done through the "Tribune Fresh-air Fund" and other agencies.

MOTHERS' AND CHILDREN'S MEETINGS, Christian Endeavor, and industrial, social and physical activities are conducted at each of the Mission Churches of the Society.

VIRGINIA DAY NURSERY, 632 5th St., open from 7 A. M. to 7 P. M. daily, except Sundays and legal holidays, for the care of children, from one week to six years of age, of poor working mothers away from home, who pay, when able, five cents a day for each child. Capacity, seventy. Average attendance, seventy-five.

Woman's Christian Temperance Union, of New York County. Office: Room 503, 156 Fifth Ave., N.Y.C. Promotes total abstinence and prohibition and Christian Americanization.

Mrs. D. Leigh Colvin, pres., 661 West 179th St.; Mrs. Pauline Meeker, cor. secy., 598 West 148th St.; Mrs. Mary B. Thomas, treas., 161 West 36th St.

Woman's Christian Temperance Union of the State of New York, The (incorp. 1876); 42,989 members, 1,000 auxiliary societies. Object: To promote the cause of total abstinence and purity; and to secure the abolition of the liquor traffic by preventive, educational, evangelistic, social, and legal measures.

Officers: Mrs. Ella A. Boole, pres., Brooklyn, N. Y.; Mrs. Frances W. Graham, vice-pres., Lockport, N. Y.; Mrs. Lyversa M. De Silva, cor. secy., 156 Fifth Ave., N.Y.C.; Mrs. Mary B. Wood, rec. secy., Ithaca, N. Y.; Mrs. Ellen L. Tenney, treas., Albany, N. Y.

Official organ, "Woman's Temperance Work;" Mrs. Frances W. Graham, editor, 34 Park Pl., Lockport, N. Y.

Women's City Club of New York, Inc., 22 Park Ave., N.Y.C. (tel. Murray Hill 8641). The purpose of the club is to bring together women interested in the welfare of the City of New York and to promote such welfare by such means as may seem from time to time expedient. Membership, 3,000.

Officers: Miss Mary Garrett Hay, pres.; Mrs. Bernard Pollak, treas.; Miss Ethel Stebbins, secy.; Mrs. John Blair, field secy.

Woman's Health Protective Association of Brooklyn (incorp. 1890). To interest women in matters pertaining to health, law, and order.

Mrs. A. E. Fraser, pres., 226 Quincy

St.; Mrs. H. W. Nichols, secy., 209 Underhill Ave., Brooklyn.

Women's Health Protective Association of New York (incorp. 1884), works to secure the enforcement of existing sanitary laws; and to procure new health legislation when needed.

Officers: Mrs. Ralph Trautmann, pres.; Mrs. Benjamin T. Scudder, cor. secy., 27 East Park St., Newark, N. J.

***Woman's Home and Foreign Missionary Society of the Presbytery of Nassau, The** (org. 1884).

Officers: Mrs. Frank W. Rogers, pres., Huntington, L. I.; Mrs. H. P. Palmer, home secy., Elmhurst, N. Y.

Woman's Home Missionary Union of the State of New York. (Congregational) (incorp. 1887). To promote missionary and evangelistic work in the U. S. and Island possessions, under the Congregational denomination.

Mrs. William Spalding, pres., 405 Comstock Ave., Syracuse, N. Y.; Mrs. John J. Pearsall, exec. secy., 114 Fenimore St., Brooklyn, N. Y. (tel. Flatbush 5394).

Woman's Hospital in the State of New York (incorp. 1857), 141 West 109th St., and 110th St. between Amsterdam and Columbus Aves., N.Y.C. (tel. Academy 800). For Gynecology (the treatment of diseases peculiar to women) and Obstetrics. Has a capacity of 244 beds, 100 free. Supported by the receipts from pay patients and voluntary contributions.

The Out-Patient Department for treatment from 9–12 A. M. and 2–5 P. M. daily, except Sundays and holidays.

Officers: Grenville Lindall Winthrop, pres.; Francis L. Hine, treas., 2 Wall St.; Finley J. Shepard, secy.; James U. Norris, supt.; Dr. George Gray Ward, Jr., surgical director.

* *Current information not received.*

***Woman's Legal Education Society, The** (incorp. 1890), New York University, 32 Waverly Pl., N.Y.C. For general legal instruction to self-supporting and property-owning women for the guidance of their business and personal affairs.

Woman's Municipal League of the City of New York (org. 1897, incorp. 1904), 14 East 46th St., N.Y.C. (tel. Vanderbilt 5694). The purpose of the League is to promote among women an intelligent interest in municipal affairs, and to aid in securing good government for the City of New York without regard to party or sectional lines. Membership, 1,500. The League also works through the following Committees: Education; Health; Civic Art, including city planning; Legislative; Parks and Playgrounds; Courts and Prisons, Public Charities, Foods and Markets; Streets and Transit; Iced Water Fountains Committee. Publishes a weekly bulletin on civic matters, "Women and the City's Work."

Officers: Mrs. Frederick C. Hodgdon, pres.; Mrs. Howard G. Myers, treas.; Mrs. Charles F. Bound, rec. secy.; Mrs. Marion Booth Kelley, field secy.

Woman's National Sabbath Alliance, The (org. 1895), Room 507, 156 Fifth Ave., N.Y.C. (tel. Chelsea 9643). To promote the better observance of the Sabbath. Has twenty-eight auxiliary societies.

Officers: Mrs. S. Y. MacNair, pres.; Mrs. Frank R. Van Nest, treas.; Miss Catherine Murray, cor. secy.; Mrs. Robert B. Hull, field secy.

Woman's Peace Society, the underlying principle of this society is a belief in the sacredness and inviolability of human life under all circumstances.

Mrs. Henry Villard, chrm., 525 Park Ave., N.Y.C. (tel. Plaza 1534); Miss Mary Abbott, treas., 29 East 29th St.

Women's Prison Association and Home, 110 Second Ave., N.Y.C. To improve the condition of women prisoners and to support and encourage them, after their discharge, by aiding them to reform and obtain an honest livelihood. It visits penal and reformatory institutions for women throughout the state. It maintains:

The Isaac T. Hopper Home at above address, where discharged women prisoners and especially inebriates are cared for until they find suitable employment or other arrangements are made for them. Capacity, forty.

The Laundry employs the women, encourages their self-respect, and aids them in forming habits of industry and self-control. Supported by income of the Laundry, annual subscriptions, and interest on permanent fund.

Officers: Dr. Annie S. Daniel, 1st director, 105 East 15th St.; Mrs. E. G. Pinney, treas., Scarsdale, N. Y.; Miss Julia T. Emerson, secy., 131 East 66th St.; Mary Vida Clark, exec. secy. of association; Mrs. H. W. Smith, superintendent of home.

Woman's Relief Corps Home, Oxford, N. Y. See New York State Woman's Relief Corps Home.

Woman's Roosevelt Memorial Association, Inc., 1 East 57th St., N.Y.C. Organized to commemorate the life of Roosevelt by restoring and maintaining his birthplace as a memorial.

Officers: Mrs. John H. Hammond, pres.; Mrs. A. Barton Hepburn, treas.; Mrs. A. M. Sanford, secy.

(See also Roosevelt Memorial Association.)

Women's Trade Union League (org. 1904), 7 East 15th St., N.Y.C. (tel. Stuyvesant 7080). To promote among women wage-earners organization into the trade unions of the American Federation of Labor membership and to obtain legislation for the protection of women workers.

Officers: Rose Schneiderman, pres.; Mrs. Fulton and Jo Coffin, vice-prests.; Maud Swartz, secy.

Woman's Union Missionary Society of America (org. 1860, incorp 1861), 67 Bible House, N.Y.C. For the conversion and education of Far Eastern women. Maintains schools and hospitals in foreign lands. Interdenominational. Supported by voluntary contributions and legacies.

Officers: Mrs. S. J. Broadwell, pres.; Mrs. James H. Prentice, treas.; Mrs. S. T. Dauchy, cor. secy.

Woman's Work Exchange and Decorative Art Society, 130 Montague St., Brooklyn. Consignors fix their own prices on articles brought to the Exchange for sale. No charge for entrance; fifteen per cent. commission is charged when article is sold.

Woodcraft League of America, The. Headquarters, 13 West 29th St., N.Y.C. (tel. Longacre 4138). A recreational movement for character building. The League co-operates with educational, social and religious organizations in furnishing a program which provides for outdoor and indoor activities for all seasons of the year. The program utilizes the play instinct and the desire for knowledge to develop its members in citizenship and in ability to see, comprehend and interpret the things of life. Particular use is made of nature study, handicraft and campercraft. The plan provides for the organization of local groups or tribes which may be composed of either boys or girls, men or women. Groups may also be organized independently.

Officers: Ernest Thompson Seton, chief; Philip D. Fagans, exec. secy.

Woodyard of the Charity Organization Society, 516 West 28th St.,

N.Y.C. See CHARITY ORGANIZATION SOCIETY.

Woodyards, Brooklyn Bureau of Charities, 80 Pacific St., 191 Marcy Ave., 1660 Fulton St. See BROOKLYN BUREAU OF CHARITIES.

Workhouse, Blackwell's Island. See CORRECTION, DEPARTMENT OF.

Working Girls' Vacation Society (org. 1883, incorp. 1885), Room 416, 105 East 22d St., N.Y.C. (tel. Gramercy 5151). For respectable unmarried working girls who have satisfactory recommendations, and certificate of a physician that a vacation is needed. Provides two weeks' vacation in the country with fares and board at $4 a week, or to girls unable to pay full board, at the nominal sum of $1.50 a week; pays fares of working girls to their friends in the country. Maintains

HILL CREST AND UPLANDS (est. 1895), Santa Clara, Franklin Co., N. Y. Summer vacation houses, not sanatoria (the gift of Mr. George E. Dodge). Located in the Adirondacks forty miles northwest of Saranac Lake, at an altitude of 1,800 feet. For working girls and women threatened with tuberculosis, or in incipient stages, and for outings to girls of consumptive tendencies. Capacity, fifty-six. Open from June 1 to October 15. Length of stay at the house determined by the examining physician, Dr. Nancy Jenison; Mrs. Chas. McWilliams, secy.

Other homes at Westport, Conn.; Cobalt, Conn.; Farmington, Conn.; Hadlyme, Conn.; Green's Farms, Conn.; Chester, N. Y.; and North Long Branch, N. J. Supported by voluntary contributions. During the summer of 1916, 1,400 girls were sent to the country and fares were paid.

Officers: Mrs. William Herbert, pres.; Miss Adelaide B. Baylis, treas., 11 East 55th St.; Miss Anna E. Roelker, secy.; Miss E. A. Buchanan, asst. secy.

Working Women's Protective Union (org. 1863, incorp. 1868), 289 Fourth Ave., N.Y.C. (tel. Gramercy 3237). To promote the interests of self-supporting women, and especially to provide them with legal protection from the frauds and impositions of unscrupulous employers. Free employment bureau.

Officers: Dr. Henry Dwight Chapin, pres., 51 West 51st St.; Alexander M. Hudnut, treas., 5 Nassau St.; Miss Elizabeth R. Ogilby, supt.

Workmen's Compensation, Bureau of. See STATE INDUSTRIAL COMMISSION.

World's Court League, Inc. (est. and incorp. 1915) and **League of Nations Union** (incorp. 1919), 70 Fifth Ave., N.Y.C. To advocate the establishment of a World Court and to promote international justice, friendship and co-operation in a League of Nations for the common welfare.

Officers: Hon. Theodore E. Burton, pres.; Charles Lathrop Pack, vice-pres.; Charles H. Levermore, secy.

World Peace Foundation (incorp. 1911), 40 Mt. Vernon St., Boston, Mass. Purpose: To educate the people of all nations to a full knowledge of the waste and destructiveness of war, and by every practical means to promote international justice, peace and good will.

Officers: William H. P. Faunce, pres., Brown University, Providence, R. I.; Arthur W. Allen, treas.; Edward Cummings, gen. secy.; Denys P. Myers, cor. secy. and librarian.

World Prohibition Federation, American Branch. See NATIONAL TEMPERANCE SOCIETY.

World's Student Christian Federation (org. 1895 at Vadstena Castle,

Sweden). Composed of the following Christian Student Movements: Australasia, China, The Netherlands and Switzerland, France and Italy, Germany, Great Britain and Ireland, India and Ceylon, Japan, Denmark, Finland, Norway and Sweden, Russia, South Africa, United States, and Canada, and other lands.

John R. Mott, chrm., 347 Madison Ave., N.Y.C.

Wright Memorial Summer Home, Oceanport, N. J. See AMERICAN FEMALE GUARDIAN SOCIETY.

Wyckoff Heights Hospital of Brooklyn (incorp. 1889, Hospital Society of Brooklyn), St. Nicholas Ave., Stanhope and Stockholm Sts. (tel. Evergreen 3200). A general hospital for all except incurable, contagious, and infectious diseases. Also U. S. Naval Ward for Sailors and Marines (est. August, 1918). Ambulance service. Non-sectarian. Capacity, 175.

Training School for Nurses provides a three years' course, Ludwig Nissen, chrm.

Officers: F. A. Schurman, pres.; George Emener, treas.; Henry Schnessler, secy.; Charles Arras, supt.

X

Xavier Deaf-Mutes Society, 30 West 16th St., N.Y.C. Object: The temporal and spiritual benefit of deaf-mutes. Conducts religious and social work for adult deaf-mutes both in Brooklyn and Manhattan.

Xavier Free Publication Society for the Blind of the City of New York (incorp. 1904), 136 West 97th St., N.Y.C. Publishes for free and general circulation among the blind of the U. S., Catholic literature in four tactile systems, viz., in New York Point, in American and Revised Braille, and in Moon.

Two monthly magazines: "The Catholic Transcript for the Blind," in New York Point (subscription $1 yearly), and "The Catholic Review," in American Braille (sent gratis to all applicants) are also published by the Xavier Free Publication Society for the Blind.

Books are loaned for a month at a time and without any charge to any blind person in the United States.

Rev. Joseph M. Stadelman, S. J., director.

Y

***Yorkville Boys' Welfare Association** (est. 1913), 520 East 85th St.

Yorkville District Dispensary, The, Inc. (incorp. 1918), 540 East 76th St., N.Y.C. (tel. Rhinelander 1257). Organized by members of the Yorkville District Committee of the Charity Organization Society (q. v.) to promote oral hygiene among children. The service is limited to those referred by the following co-operating agencies: East Side House, Madison Ave. Presbyterian Church, Yorkville Neighborhood Association, Maternity Neighborhood Association, St. James Protestant Episcopal Church, Emanuel Sisterhood, Yorkville District C.O.S., Lenox Hill Settlement, Kips Bay C.O.S., Finch School Day Nursery.

Extractions of temporary teeth, restorations and treatments are in the hands of a dentist, Dr. Josephine E. C. Luhan; prophylactic treatment and instruction in oral hygiene are carried on by an oral hygienist, Miss Elfrieda H. Lawrence. The Red Cross has an auxiliary of women who assist. The service is free; open from 10 A. M. until 5 P. M. daily.

Officers: Hon. Ogden L. Mills, hon. pres.; Hon. Lawson Purdy, hon. vice-

* *Current information not received.*

pres.; Mrs. Walter Graeme Eliot, pres., 144 East End Ave.; Mrs. Arthur Scott Burden, vice-pres.; Mrs. C. Trenholm Bellamy, treas.; Mrs. Louis Wolff, secy.; Miss Mary deG. Trenholm, officer in charge.

Executive Board: Dr. Walter P. Anderton, Presbyterian Hospital; Dr. Ralph Waldo Lobenstine, Miss Rosalie Manning.

Young Men and Boys' Club, 62 Joralemon St., Brooklyn. Provides a gymnastic instructor and gymnasium, a library, game room, etc., for the use of boys and young men, free of charge. Open evenings from 7-10 o'clock. Senior and junior brass bands, also violin class. Mr. William G. Low, 58 Remsen St., originator and sustainer.

Young Men's Christian Association of the City of New York (est. 1852, incorp. 1866). General office: Room 1402, 2 West 45th St., N.Y.C. (tel. Murray Hill 717). For the improvement of the spiritual, mental, social, and physical condition of young men, by means of educational classes, lectures, libraries, reading rooms, religious and social gatherings, classes for practical Bible Study, gymnasia, dormitories, etc., at the fourteen Branches. Supported by voluntary contributions ($202,560), members' fees, and rents. Expenses in 1919 about $1,180,000 exclusive of about $437,000 expended in the restaurants. Total attendance at rooms, 6,820,000.

Officers: William M. Kingsley, pres.; Cornelius R. Agnew, vice-pres.; John Sloane, treas.; Ernest W. Davenport, rec. secy.; Walter T. Diack, gen. secy.; Henry M. Orne, comptroller.

Maintains the following branches:

ARMY, Fort Jay, Governor's Island; Fort Wood, Liberty Island; Fort Wadsworth, S. I.; Forts Slocum and Schuyler.

BOWERY BRANCH, 8 East 3d St., near Bowery.

BRONX UNION, 470 East 161st St.

EAST SIDE, 153 East 86th St.

FRENCH, 109 West 54th St.

HARLEM, 5 West 125th St.

INSTITUTE, 222–224 Bowery.

THE INTERCOLLEGIATE or "STUDENTS' CLUB," for work among Colleges in the city, 2929 Broadway and 346 West 57th St. Affiliated with eight college associations.

RAILROAD, New York Central and New Haven Lines, 309 Park Ave.; 179 East 150th St.; West 72d St. and Eleventh Ave., and New Durham, N. J.

RAILROAD, Pennsylvania Railroad Station, Seventh Ave. and 32d St.

TWENTY-THIRD ST., 215 West 23d St.

WASHINGTON HEIGHTS, 531 West 155th St.

WEST SIDE, 318 West 57th St.

WEST 135TH STREET BRANCH (for colored men), 181 West 135th St.

ACTIVITIES

The Association owns two endowed beds in the Presbyterian Hospital, and a plot in Woodlawn Cemetery for the burial of young men. It sends papers to Army posts and Naval stations.

Gymnasia are maintained at twelve Branches; also six Summer Camps:

Libraries and Reading Rooms. The various libraries contain 103,000 volumes. In the Reading Rooms there are 1,000 newspapers and magazines on file. The main Association Library is at West Side Branch, 318 West 57th St. Work for boys, religious, soc'al, and educational, is carried on at the 23d St., West Side, Harlem, East Side, Institute, French, Washington Heights, Bronx Union and West 135th Street branches.

Boarding-house Directory, of suitable boarding-houses, at ten branches. Sleeping rooms in fifteen buildings; 2,230 beds; restaurants in ten buildings.

Employment Bureaus, at 23d St., West Side, Harlem, East Side, Bronx Union, Intercollegiate, French, West 135th Street, and Bowery branches, for men only. At the latter place, homeless young men of good character, in destitute circumstances, are furnished with free lodgings and food while seeking employment. There are 400 beds in dormitory at this branch.

Evening Educational Classes are conducted in most of the branches from October to April, inclusive, in 87 subjects, including Commercial and Business, Social Science, Industrial and Technical, Machine and Building Trades, Language and Academic, attended during the last year by 15,509 men and boys.

Young Men's Christian Association, International Committee. See INTERNATIONAL COMMITTEE OF YOUNG MEN'S CHRISTIAN ASSOCIATION.

Young Men's Hebrew Association, The (incorp. 1874), 92d St. and Lexington Ave., N.Y.C. (tel. Lenox 828). Has a free reference library and reading room, gymnasium, swimming pool, vacation camp, employment bureau. Maintains religious work, divine service, evening preparatory school for regent counts, commercial, and technical subjects, musical and dramatic groups, boy scout troop, boys' and young men's clubs. A separate men's building has lunch room, dormitories, smoking room, etc.

Officers: Judge I. Lehman, pres.; Henry M. Toch, treas.; Eugene H. Paul, rec. secy.; Rabbi Lee J. Levinger, exec. director.

Young Men's Hebrew Association of Bath Beach (est. 1911), Cropsy and Twentieth Aves. (tel. Bensonhurst 6267). Athletic, economic, literary, religious, and social work.

Officers: Herman Neaderland, pres.; Albert Rosenblatt, treas.; Max Klotz, secy.; Edgar J. Drachman, exec. dir.

Young Men's Hebrew Association of Borough Park, Inc. (est. 1914), 50th St. cor. Fourteenth Ave., Brooklyn, N. Y. Physical training, educational classes, religious school, dramatics, music classes, clubs, Americanization, social activities, lectures, concerts, entertainments, etc. (No dormitories.)

Officers: William Sugarman, pres.; H. M. Marks, treas.; S. J. Kasendorf, secy.; William Cohen, executive director.

Young Men's Hebrew Association of the Bronx, 1261 Franklin Ave,, N.Y.C. (incorp. 1909) (tel. Tremont 1337). For moral, mental, and physical development of young men. Literary, social, debating, athletic, dramatic, musical and culture clubs. Classes in all phases of commercial art, modern languages, mathematics, history, English, science, commercial subjects, Hebrew, Jewish history. Lectures on all above topics. Musicales, concerts, dances, and socials.

Officers: Hon. M. M. Fertig, pres.; Jacob Markel, treas.; Louis Weinstein, secy.; Charles Nemser, supt.

Young Men's Hebrew Association of Brooklyn (incorp. 1907), 345 9th St., Brooklyn (tel. South 2365). Objects: Intellectual and spiritual advancement, increased efficiency, and physical growth of the young man, offered in congenial surroundings, inducing companionship and healthy recreation. Has a gymnasium where physical instruction is given under competent instructor, educational classes, singing society, junior and senior dramatic departments, entertainments, literary societies, Bible and Jewish History clubs, lecture courses.

The Association is communal, philanthropic in every detail, supported by the Brooklyn Federation of Jewish Charities (q. v.).

Officers: Grover M. Moscowitz, pres., 862 Kenmore Pl.; Harry G. Anderson, vice-pres., 203 Eighth Ave.; Eugene H. Paul, secy., 423 Sterling Place; Hugo H. Piesen, fin. secy., 160 Marlboro Road; Bernard Lebovitz, treas., 116 Duane St., N.Y.C.; Leo A. Harris, exec. secy.

***Young Men's Hebrew Association of Brownsville,** 461 Rockaway Ave., Brooklyn.

***Young Men's Hebrew Association of Harlem,** 12 East 119th St., N.Y.C.

Young Men's Hebrew Association, West Side, 653 Eighth Ave., N.Y.C. (tel. Bryant 1637).

Louis J. Chamansky, pres., 2173 Broadway; Ralph Rosenthal, secy., 417 Tenth Ave.; Sol Bluhm, exec. director, 2396 Valentine Ave.

***Young Men's Hebrew Association of Washington Heights,** 975 St. Nicholas Ave., N.Y.C.

Young Men's Institute, 222–224 Bowery, N.Y.C. See YOUNG MEN'S CHRISTIAN ASSOCIATION.

Young Men's Symphony Orchestra of New York, The (founded by Alfred L. Seligman, 1905). Rehearsal Rooms, 210 East 86th St., N.Y.C. Gives free orchestral training to young musicians and free orchestral accompaniment to young soloists.

Officers: S. Mallet Prevost, pres.; J. L. Seligman, treas.; Henry Walter, secy., 154 Nassau St.; Paul Henneberg, musical director. Address the Secretary.

* *Current information not received.*

Young Men's and Young Women's Hebrew Association of Williamsburg (est. 1909), Broadway, Rodney and South Ninth Sts., Brooklyn, N. Y. A community center for the Jewish people, young and old of both sexes of Williamsburg.

Herman Bergoffen, executive director

Young People's Association House, 342 East 63d St., N.Y.C. See John Hall Memorial under FIFTH AVENUE PRESBYTERIAN CHURCH, this list.

Young Women's Christian Association of Brooklyn (incorp. 1888).

ADMINISTRATION BUILDING: 376 Schermerhorn St., Brooklyn (tel. Main 7046).

EASTERN DISTRICT BRANCH: Bedford Ave. and Keap St. (tel. Williamsburg 200).

ASHLAND PLACE BRANCH (colored), 45 Ashland Place (tel. Main 9821).

THE HARRIET JUDSON (boarding department), 50 Nevins St. (tel. Main 2500); 220 permanent, 10 transient guests.

BUSH TERMINAL BRANCH, 40th St. and Second Ave. (tel. Sunset 4094).

INTERNATIONAL INSTITUTE (foreign girls and women), 106 Montague St. (tel. Main 899).

Activities: Educational classes, gymnasium, swimming pool, self-governing clubs, employment agency, cafeteria, Bible classes, Sunday meetings, Room Directory, library, dances, and general entertainments, public auditorium.

Officers: Mrs. Henry M. Halsted, pres.; Mrs. Thomas J. Hewitt, secy.; Miss Grace Engraham, treas.

Young Women's Christian Association of the City of New York (org. and incorp. 1873), METROPOLITAN BOARD OF DIRECTORS, 134 East 44th St., N.Y.C. (tel. Vanderbilt 7597).

Branches and Centers, for statements of activities see following under:

CENTRAL, 610 Lexington Ave.

HARLEM, 74 West 124th St.

WEST SIDE, 501 West 50th St.

BRONX, 329 East 176th St.

FRENCH, 124 West 16th St.

COLORED WOMEN'S, 179 West 137th St.

INTERNATIONAL INSTITUTE, 121 East 21st St.

INTERNATIONAL INSTITUTE, Bronx, 245 East 152d St.

CENTRAL CLUB FOR NURSES, 132 East 45th St.

STUDIO CLUB, 35 East 52d St.

THE MARGARET LOUISA, 14 East 16th St.

NEEDLEWORK SHOP, 32 East 48th St.

Residences:

TATHAM HOUSE, 138 East 38th St.

LAURA SPELMAN HALL, 607 Hudson St.

COLORED WOMEN'S RESIDENCE, 200 West 137th St.

Y. W. C. A. APARTMENTS, 159 East 104th St.

588 LEXINGTON AVE. (For Physical Education students).

The aim is to develop the highest conception of Christian womanhood and to aid women in realizing this conception: (1) By bringing to them opportunities for all-round development; (2) by utilizing every available resource of the community for their interests, and (3) by offering itself to be used by the community in cooperative service for women.

Supported by membership fees, income from activities, and voluntary contributions.

Officers: Mrs. William Fellows Morgan, pres.; Mrs. W. W. Rossiter, vice-pres.; Mrs. Henry P. Davison, treas.; Mrs. Edward Perry Townsend, secy.; Miss Helen Clarkson Miller, gen. secy.

BRONX BRANCH Y. W. C. A. (incorp. 1914), 329 East 176th St. and 419 Tremont Ave. (tel. Tremont 93). Maintains: Cafeteria, 419 Tremont Ave., business school, 419 Tremont Ave. offering day and night courses in stenography, typewriting and business English. General Administration Building, 329 East 176th St. Classes in cookery, dressmaking, millinery, languages. Bible and World Fellowship courses, gymnastics (class and corrective), dancing (interpretative, æsthetic, folk and social), tennis, basket ball, outings, clubs for business and industrial women, girls' club, high school, grade school and young employed, entertainments, social and recreation nights, room registry department.

Officers: Mrs. J. M. Hodson, chrm.; Dr. Phoebe Van Voast, treas.; Miss Mary Wray, secy.; Miss Ethel G. Hendee, gen. secy.

CENTRAL BRANCH, Y. W. C. A. (org. and incorp. 1870), 610 Lexington Ave. cor. 53d St., N.Y.C. Maintains the following activities:

Day and evening classes (Ballard School) with moderate fee, in Secretarial training, stenography and typewriting, bookkeeping, filing, arithmetic, penmanship, business English, French, Spanish, Italian, English grammar and literature, commercial law, foreign trade, advertising, dressmaking, designing, cookery, home management, lunch and tea-room supervision, millinery, home nursing, an eleven-week course in trained attendance on the sick, dramatics, public speaking and parliamentary law.

Gymnastics (class, special, remedial and corrective), dancing (folk, character and interpretative), swimming, tennis, riding, basket-ball and baseball.

Free concerts, lectures and readings are given in the hall during the year.

Industrial, Business Women and Girls' Clubs. Recreation nights.

Library reference and reading rooms open daily, except Sunday, from 9 A. M. to 9.30 P. M.

Bible and World Fellowship courses.

Employment Department, hours 9 to 12.30, Tuesday evening 6.30 to 9, registers without charge, women and girls for positions in all grades of work outside of domestic service.

Room Registry Department directs applicants to investigated houses.

Vacation House at Allendale, N. J., open all the year.

Officers: Miss Emily B. Wilson, chrm.; Mrs. Warren A. Ransom, treas.; Mrs. Francis B. Fay, cor. secy.; Mrs. Philip LeBoutillier, recording secy.; Miss Sarah C. Wells, gen. secy.

COLORED BRANCH, Y. W. C. A., Administration Building, 179 West 137th St. Maintains vocational and Bible classes; free employment bureau; cafeteria; swimming pool; gymnasium; clubs for girls and women; forum on public questions. Accommodations, permanent and transient, for 75 girls.

Officers: Mrs. Emma S. Ransom, pres.; Mrs. V. E. Scott, treas.; Mrs. Cecelia Cabaniss Saunders, gen. secy.

FRENCH BRANCH, Y. W. C. A. (est. 1887), 124 West 16th St., N.Y.C. (tel. Chelsea 5573). To promote the spiritual welfare of French-speaking girls and young women living in New York City. Provides a home for about fifteen French-speaking girls. Conducts religious meetings, social activities, etc.

Mlle. Rose Delay, gen. secy.

HARLEM BRANCH, Y. W. C. A. (org. and incorp. 1891), 74 West 124th St., N.Y.C. (tel. Harlem 4992).

Officers: Mrs. Elmer E. Cooley, chrm.; Miss Jane W. Button, gen. secy.

Large modern building opened 1919, hours 9 A. M. to 9.30 P. M., daily. Information bureau, room directory, employment bureau, day and evening business school, dressmaking, millinery, cooking, languages, arts, religious education, gymnasium, swimming pool, girls' and women's clubs, entertainments, social evening, outings, summer camps.

Residence, 13 Mt. Morris Park West (tel. Harlem 7993). Permanent and transient guests.

Gill House, 355 West 122d St.

WEST SIDE BRANCH, Y. W. C. A., 50th St. cor. Tenth Ave., N.Y.C. (tel. Columbus 2479). Swimming, gymnasium, tennis, hikes, outdoor games, stenography, typewriting, English, French, Spanish, cookery, dressmaking, millinery, civics, music, etc. Clubs for older and younger girls. Bible Study classes, Sunday afternoon services. Entertainments. Community singing, Red Cross work, opportunities for volunteer service. Dental Clinic (open Wednesday and Friday evenings). Boarding Home (address 460 West 50th St.). Lunch Room open to men and women daily except Sunday from 11.30 to 8. Something for every girl and woman over twelve years of age.

Officers: Mrs. William Rossiter, chrm.; Mrs. Cleveland E. Dodge, vice-chrm.; Miss Dorothy Andrews, treas.; Miss Margaret Webster, gen. secy.

Young Women's Hebrew Association (incorp. 1903), 31 West 110th St., N.Y.C. (tel. University 5660). To promote the religious, social, mental, moral, and physical welfare of Jewish girls and women. Has an attractive dormitory at nominal rates for young women who have no home. Holds Friday evening and Saturday morning religious services for adults, and Saturday morning service for children.

Some of its activities are: Free Employment Bureau, swimming pool, Information Bureau, lectures, entertainments and dances; day commercial school, afternoon and evening classes in domestic science, dressmaking, physical culture, stenography, bookkeeping and Jewish history and Bible study, French, Spanish, English to foreigners, literature, art, millinery. All-day care center for cardiac and anæmic children in July and August. Clubs and classes for children and Hebrew School in session daily.

Officers: Mrs. Israel Unterberg, pres.; Mrs. Jerome J. Hanauer, Mrs. Irving Lehman and Mrs. Felix M. Warburg, vice-presidents; Mrs. Samuel I. Hyman, hon. secy.; Mrs. Simon Liebovitz, treas.; Mrs. Ray F. Schwartz, exec. dir.

Young Women's Hebrew Association of Brooklyn, 374 7th St., Brooklyn.

Young Women's Hebrew Association of Brownsville, 461 Rockaway Ave., Brooklyn.

Young Women's Hebrew Association, Room Registry of the, 31 West 110th St. To provide suitable homes in Jewish families for Jewish girls and women who cannot be accommodated in the organized homes.

Officers: Mrs. Abraham Bijur, chrm., 330 Park Ave.; Mrs. E. F. Seixas, treas.; Miss Rose Sommerfield, secy.; Mrs. I. M. Kellerman, in charge of bureau, open day and evening (tel. University 5686).

Z

Zionist Organization of America (Social Service Activities), 55 Fifth Ave., N.Y.C. Engaged in relief and reconstruction work in Palestine.

Officers: Julian W. Mack, pres.; Peter J. Schweitzer, treas.; Jacob de Haas, exec. secy.

Zoological Park, South Bronx Park, 185th St. and Southern Blvd., N.Y.C. (tel. Fordham 5560). Under the sole control and management of the New York Zoological Society (q. v.). Finest collection of animals in the world, numbering 5,500 mammals, birds, and reptiles. Free to the public every day except Mondays and Thursdays, when twenty-five cents admission is charged.

CHURCH LIST

In this list the churches are arranged denominationally. Those doing any kind of social service work in connection with the religious organization are listed in the Alphabetical List also.

Baptist Churches

Manhattan

Abyssinian (Colored), 242–244 West 40th St.

Baptist Temple (Colored), 159 West 132d St. Rev. M. B. Hucless, D.D., Pastor.

Broadway. See WADSWORTH AVE.

Calvary, 123 West 57th St., between Sixth and Seventh Aves. Rev. Roach Straton, D.D., Pastor.

Central, 92d St. and Amsterdam Ave. Rev. Frank M. Goodchild, Pastor, 144 West 93d St., N.Y.C.

Central Park, 235 East 83d St. Rev. Milton W. Pullen, Pastor. See also ALPHABETICAL LIST.

Day Star (Colored), 512 West 157th St. Rev. R. J. Brown, Pastor.

Fifth Avenue, 4 West 46th St. Rev. Cornelius Woelfkin, D.D., Pastor; Rev. Eugene C. Carder, Associate.

First, Broadway and 79th St. Rev. I. M. Haldeman, D.D., Pastor.

First German, 334–336 East 14th St. Rev. J. R. Miller, Pastor.

First German of Harlem, 220 East 118th St. Rev. John H. Ansberg, Pastor.

First Hungarian, 225–227 East 80th St. Rev. Nicholas Dulity, Pastor. See also in ALPHABETICAL LIST.

First Italian, 1 Henry St.

First Lettish, Judson Memorial Church, 4th Ave. and Thompson St. Rev. John Kweetin, Pastor.

First Mariners', 3 Henry St. See MARINERS' TEMPLE.

First Swedish, 139–141 East 55th St. Dr. Arvid Gordh, Pastor.

Harlem, 219 East 123d St. Rev. Adam Chambers, Pastor.

Immanuel German, 411–413 East 75th St. Rev. K. Roth, Pastor.

Judson Memorial, 55 Washington Square South, cor. Thompson St. Rev. A. Ray Petty, Pastor. See also in ALPHABETICAL LIST.

Madison Avenue, 30 East 31st St. Rev. George C. Moor, D.D., Pastor.

Mariners' Temple (First Baptist Mariners' Church), Henry St., cor. of Oliver St. Rev. Wm. N. Hubbell, Pastor. See also ALPHABETICAL LIST.

Memorial. See JUDSON MEMORIAL.

Metropolitan, 128th St. and 7th Ave.

Morningstar Chinese Mission, 13 Doyers St. Rev. Lee To, Pastor. See also ALPHABETICAL LIST.

Mount Morris, Fifth Ave., at 126th St. Rev. Carl Wallace Petty, D.D., Pastor.

Mount Olivet, 161 West 53d St.

North, 234 West 11th St.

St. Paul (Colored), 352 West 35th St. Rev. H. Arthur Booker.

Second Ave., 164 Second Ave. Rev. Wm. N. Hubbell, Pastor.

Second German, 407 West 43d St. Rev. W. A. Lipphard, Pastor.

Second Union, 225 East 73d St.

Sixteenth, 225 West 16th St.

Union (Colored), 204 West 63d St.

Unity, 70 West 99th St.

Wadsworth Avenue, Wadsworth Ave. and 180th St. Rev. E. S. Holloway, Pastor, 461 Ft. Washington Ave.

Washington Heights, 420 West 145th St. Rev. Harold Pattison, D.D., Pastor.

Zion, 2148 Fifth Ave., 25 West 131st St.

Bronx

Alexander Avenue, Alexander Ave., cor. East 141st St. Rev. Gordon B. Kierstead, Pastor.

Ascension, 291 East 160th St. Rev. Frederick William Hagar, Pastor.

Creston Avenue, Creston Ave. and 188th St. and Fordham Rd.

Ebenezer (Old School), Intervale Ave. and Home St.

First Union of Bronx, 595 Courtland Ave.

North Bronx, White Plains Ave. and East 216th St. Rev. H. P. Hoskins, Pastor.

St. John the Baptist (First Italian), 2409 Lorillard Place, cor. 187th St.

Tremont, Tremont and Webster Aves.

Trinity, 800 East 224th St.

Brooklyn

Baptist Temple, Third Ave., cor. Schermerhorn St.

Bay Ridge (Swedish), 257 Bay Ridge Ave.

Bedford Heights, Bergen, cor. Rogers Ave.

Berean, Bergen St., near Rochester Ave. Rev. A. C. Matthews, Pastor.

Bergen St., 697 Bergen St.

Bethany (colored), Clermont Ave. and Atlantic.

Bethel, 265 Bergen St.

Borough Park, 48th St. and Thirteenth Ave.

Bushwick Ave., Bushwick, cor. Weirfield St.

Calvary, 4th Ave. and 14th St. Rev. George Rittenhaus, Pastor, 311 Twelfth St., Bklyn.

Chinese Mission, 106 S. Oxford St.

Concord (Colored), 166 Adelphi St.

East End, 263 Van Siclen Ave.

Ebenezer (Swedish), 607 Herkimer St. Rev. W. Kohler, Pastor, 1297 Park Place.

Emmanuel, Lafayette Ave., cor. St. James Pl. Rev. A. A. Shaw, D.D., Pastor. See also ALPHABETICAL LIST.

Euclid Ave., Euclid Ave.

First, Lee Ave. and Keap St. Rev. Rivington D. Lord, D.D., Pastor. See also ALPHABETICAL LIST.

First (colored), 2345 East 15th St.

First, Canarsie, Remsen Ave.

First, East New York, Hendrix, near Arlington Ave.

First German, E. D., Montrose Ave., near Union. Rev. Paul Wengel, Pastor, 95 Halleck St.

First Italian, 16–18 Jackson St. See ALPHABETICAL LIST.

First Norwegian, Fourth Ave., near 32d St. Rev. Otto E. Hansen, Pastor.

First Swedish, 513–517 Dean St.

Friendship (colored), 447 Elton Ave.

Grace, 6th Ave. and 53d St.

Greene Avenue, Greene Ave., above Lewis. Rev. Charles F. McKoy, Pastor.

Greenwood, 8th Ave. and 6th St.

Hanson Place, Hanson Place and S. Portland Ave.

Holy Trinity (colored), 595 Classon Ave.

Kenilworth, Bedford Ave. and Ave. G.

Lefferts Park, 76th St. and Fourteenth Ave. Rev. E. H. Lovett, D.D., Pastor, 146 South Portland Ave.

Lenox Road, Lenox Road and Nostrand Ave. Rev. Harvey W. Chollar, Pastor.

McDonough Street, cor. McDonough St. and Patchen Ave.

Marcy Avenue, Marcy and Putnam Aves. Rev. John M. Moore, Pastor. See also ALPHABETICAL LIST.

Memorial, 8th Ave. and 16th St.

Mt. Calvary (colored), Greene and Tompkins Ave.

Mt. Lebanon, 291-293 Howard Ave.

Prospect Park, Ave. C. and East 4th St.

Redeemer, Cortelyou Rd. and East 18th St.

Salem, Snyder Ave. and Prospect Ave.

St. Nicholas Ave. Greek Bapt. Mission, 89th and St. Nicholas Ave.

Second German, E. D., Evergreen Ave. and Woodbine St. W. J. Zirbes, Pastor, 455 Evergreen St.

Sixth Avenue, Sixth Ave., cor. Lincoln Pl.

Strong Place, Strong Pl., cor. Degraw St. Rev. Floyd H. Adams, Pastor. See also ALPHABETICAL LIST.

Sumner Ave., Sumner Ave., cor Decatur St.

Tabernacle, Clinton St. and 3d Place.

Union, Noble St., near Manhattan Ave. Rev. George M. MacDonald, Ph.D., Pastor, 106 Noble St.

Washington Ave., Washington Ave., cor. Gates Ave.

Queens

Ebenezer (Colored), Flushing, South Prince St.

Elmhurst, Whitney Ave. and Judge St. Rev. C. E. Platner, Pastor. See also ALPHABETICAL LIST.

First, Flushing, Sanford Ave. and Union St. Rev. George Douglas, Pastor.

First, Jamaica, cor. Flushing Ave. and Grove St. Rev. Wilfred H. Sobey.

First Woodside, 5th and Woodside Ave.

Richmond Hill, 114th St. and 91st Ave. Rev. Rolla E. Hunt, Pastor. See also ALPHABETICAL LIST.

Union Course, 1st and Shaw Ave., Union Course.

Wyckoff, Evergreen, Forest Ave. and Summerfield St.

Richmond

First, Hamilton and Westervelt Ave., New Brighton, S.I.

Mariners' Harbor, 74 Union Ave.

New Dorp, Ninth St., New Dorp, S. I. Rev. Leonard G. Lynn, Pastor.

Park, Park Ave. and Vreeland St., Port Richmond.

St. Philip's (colored), Elm St., Port Richmond.

South, Main St., Tottenville.

CHURCH OF CHRIST

Brooklyn

Bethel, 225 Chauncey St.

Vanderveer Park, New York Ave. and Ave. D. Rev. Lindsay F. Johnson, D.D., Pastor, 270 East 32d St., Brooklyn.

Central Mission (United), 1434 DeKalb Ave. Rev. Paul Bender.

Metropolitan (United), Flushing and Metropolitan Aves. Rev. Adam Kloepfel.

Queens

Springfield Docks, Jamaica, L. I.

CHURCH OF CHRIST, SCIENTIST

Manhattan and Bronx

First, Central Park West and 96th St.

Second, Central Park West and 68th St. Charles E. Heitman, First Reader.

Third, 111 East 58th St. George Falkenstein, First Reader.

Fourth Church, 178th St. and Ft. Washington Ave.

Fifth Church, Aeolian C. Hall, 34 W. 43d St.

Sixth Church, 1301 Boston Rd., Bronx.

Seventh Church, 112th St., east of Broadway.

Eighth Church, 103 East 77th St. Robert S. Ross, First Reader, Mrs. Marie J. Adams, Second Reader.

Ninth Church, Park Avenue Hotel, 4th Ave. at 33d St. Leslie H. Allen, First Reader, Miss Rose B. Hosking, Second Reader.

Tenth Church, 163 West 57th St. Elmer B. Sanford, First Reader.

Eleventh Church, 2562 Briggs Ave.

Twelfth Church, Anderson Galleries, Park Ave. and 59th St.

Queens

Christian Science Society, Masonic Temple, Union Ave., Jamaica. Geo. J. Bagley, First Reader.

First Church of Christ, Scientist, Richmond Hill, Greenwood Ave., between Jamaica and Lexington Aves.

Richmond

First Church of Christ, Scientist, West New Brighton, S. I., Castleton and Oakland Aves.

Congregational Churches

Manhattan

Armenian Evangelical. Services held in Adams Memorial Church, 207 East 30th St. Rev. A. A. Bedikian, Pastor.

Bethany, 455 Tenth Ave. Rev. James A. McCague, Pastor. See Alphabetical List.

Broadway Tabernacle, Broadway and 56th St. Rev. Charles E. Jefferson, Pastor. See Alphabetical List.

Camp Memorial, 141 Chrystie St.

Immanuel, 308–310 West 139th St. Rev. Carl Hanson, Pastor.

Manhattan, Broadway, near 76th St. Rev. Charles H. Parkhurst, D.D., Acting Pastor, Hotel Ansonia. See also Alphabetical List.

Welsh, 208 East 11th St. Rev. Joseph Evans, Pastor.

Bronx

Bedford Park, East 201st St. and Bainbridge Ave. Rev. Ralph L. Peterson, Pastor, 309 East 201st St. See also Alphabetical List.

Christ. See PILGRIM.

Claremont Park, Teller Ave. and 167th St.

First, of Morrisania, Forest Ave., cor. East 166th St. Rev. Adam M. Reoch, Pastor, 761 East 166th St.

Forest Avenue. See FIRST, OF MORRISANIA.

North New York, 409 East 143d St.

Pilgrim, formerly Christ, 175th St. and Grand Concourse. Rev. Henry M. Brown, Pastor.

Brooklyn

Borough Park, Fort Hamilton Ave. and 49th St.

Bushwick Avenue, Bushwick Ave., cor. Cornelia St. Rev. John Lewis Clark, Pastor, 47 Linden St.

Central, 64 Jefferson Ave. Rev. S. Parkes Cadman, D.D., Pastor.

Clinton Avenue, Clinton and Lafayette Aves. Rev. Nehemiah Boynton, D.D., Pastor.

Evangel, Church of the, Bedford and Hawthorne.

Flatbush, East 18th St. and Dorchester Rd. Rev. Lewis T. Reed, Pastor. See also Alphabetical List.

Kings Highway, Ave. P., cor. 18th St.

Lewis Avenue, 574 Madison St.

Manhattan Terrace. See OCEAN AVE.

Mapleton Park, 1824 65th St., near Eighteenth Ave. Rev. Edward W. Robinson, Pastor, 6416 Twenty-second Ave.

Mayflower Branch of Plymouth Church, 96–98 Johnson, cor. Lawrence Sts.

Nazarene (colored), Troy Ave. and Herkimer St.

Ocean Avenue, Ocean Ave. at Ave. I. Rev. Ernest Milton Halliday, Pastor.

Park Slope, cor. Eighth Ave. and 2d St.

Parkville, Eighteenth Ave. and East 5th St. Rev. Charles J. Allen, 1776 45th St.

Pilgrims, Church of the (org. 1844), 109 Remsen St. Rev. Richard Roberts, Pastor. See also Alphabetical List.

Pilgrim Swedish Evangel, 413 Atlantic Ave.

Plymouth, Orange St., bet. Hicks and Henry Sts.

Puritan Chapel, Lafayette and Marcy Aves. Rev. Ernest E. Youtz, Pastor. See ALPHABETICAL LIST.

Redeemer (Italian), 158 Carroll St.

Rockaway Avenue, Rockaway Ave., near Blake.

St. Mark's, 461 Decatur St.

St. Paul's, New York Ave. and Sterling Place.

South, cor. Court and President Sts. Rev. Raymond A. McConnell, Pastor. See also Alphabetical List.

South Chapel, 118 Fourth Pl.

Swedish-Finnish Evangelical, 740–742 41st St. Rev. August Willandt, Pastor.

Swedish Tabernacle, 326 55th St. Rev. Roy G. Lundgren, Pastor.

Tompkins Avenue, 480 Tompkins Ave. Rev. J. Percival Huget, Pastor. See also Alphabetical List.

Willoughby Avenue, Willoughby Ave., near Grand. Rev. Owen James.

Queens

Broadway, Flushing, 22d St., near Franconia Ave.

Christ, Woodhaven, 91st St. and 85th Road. Rev. Roy L. Minich, Pastor.

Church in the Gardens, Forest Hills.

First, Rockaway Beach, Boulevard and Academy. Rev. John C. Green, Pastor.

First, Woodhaven, 1111–1133 Walker Ave.

Pilgrim, Ridgewood and Oxford, Richmond Hill.

Union, Richmond Hill, Eighty-sixth Ave. and 115th St.

DISCIPLES OF CHRIST

Manhattan and Bronx

Central, 142 West 81st St. Rev. Finis S. Idleman, Pastor.

Russian, 147 Second Ave.

Second, 595 East 169th St.

Brooklyn

First, Park Pace and Vanderbilt Ave. Rev. Mark Wayne Williams, Pastor.

Flatbush, Dorchester Road and East 14th St.

Ridgewood Heights, Forest Ave. and Linden St.

EVANGELICAL LUTHERAN

Manhattan

Dingeldein Memorial, 429 East 77th St. Rev. Carl Zimmerer, Pastor.

First, 424-426 West 55th St. Rev. Daniel Bast, Pastor.

St. Paul's, 163 East 111th St. Rev. Henry Rexroth, Pastor.

Bronx

St. Paul's, 2136 Newbold Ave. Rev. J. P. Schwab, Pastor.

Brooklyn

Bethlehem Evangelical of Flatbush, Cortelyou Rd. at East 7th St. and Ocean Pkwy. (German and English.)

Emanuel, 400 Melrose St. Rev. G. A. Linder, Pastor.

Friedenskirche, Ridgewood and Nichols Aves. Rev. E. M. Glasow, Pastor.

Norwegian Free Church, 15th St. and Fourth Ave.

Salems, 1200 Jefferson Ave. Rev. August D. Pfost, Pastor.

Queens

Bethany, 8767 109th St., Richmond Hill. Rev. Fred. G. Fischer, Pastor.

Emanuel, Woodhaven, Bigelow Ave., near Jerome Ave.

Glendale, Central Ave. and Hooker St.

Harrison Avenue. See BETHANY.

RELIGIOUS SOCIETY OF FRIENDS (Quakers)

Manhattan

East Fifteenth, East 15th St., cor. of Rutherford Pl. See also Alphabetical List.

Twentieth Street (Orthodox), 144 East 20th St.

Brooklyn

Friends, 110 Schermerhorn St., near Boerum Pl. See also Alphabetical List.

Friends (Orthodox), cor. Lafayette and Washington Aves. Dr. Charles E. Tebbetts.

GREEK CATHOLIC

Manhattan

Holy Virgin Mary, 327 East 14th St.

Resurrection, 121 East 7th St.

St. George, 24 East 7th St. Rev. Nicholas Pidhorecki.

St. Nicholas Russian Cathedral, 15-21 East 97th St. Dean, Rev. Leonid J. Turkevich, Archpriest.

Transfiguration, 233 East 17th St.

HEBREW OR JEWISH

(This list includes only such congregations as have responded to our request for information.)

Manhattan

Central Synagogue, 652 Lexington Ave., near 55th St.

First Society of Jewish New Thought, R. 709, Carnegie Hall.

Free Synagogue, Office: 36 West 68th St. Services, Carnegie Hall, Sunday mornings. Rabbi Stephen S. Wise. See also in Alphabetical List.

Kehilath Jeshurun, 117-121 East 85th St.

Mt. Neboh, 564 West 150th St. Rabbi Aaron Eiseman.

New Synagogue, Broadway and 76th St.

Orach Chaim, 1463 Lexington Ave.

People's Synagogue of the Educational Alliance, 197 East Broadway. Rev. Jacob Tarlau, Rabbi.

Shearith Israel (Spanish-Portuguese Synagogue), Central Park W., cor. 70th St. Rev. Dr. H. Pereira Mendez, Pastor.

Temple Ansche Chessed, Seventh Ave. and 114th St.

Temple Emanu-El, Fifth Ave. and 43rd St. Rev. Joseph Silverman, Rabbi.

Temple Israel of Harlem, 96th St. and Central Park West. Rev. Dr. M. H. Harris, Rabbi.

Temple Rodeph Sholom, Lexington Ave. and 63rd St.

Bronx

Kehilath Israel, 1162 Jackson Ave. Rabbi Louis Finkelstein.

Sinai, Stebbins Ave. and East 163d St. Rev. Dr. Max Reichler, Rabbi.

Brooklyn and Queens

Ahavas Chesed, 742 Jefferson Ave.

Ahawath Israel, 108 Noble St.

Ahawath Scholom Beth Aron, 98 Scholes St.

Baith Israel Anshei Emes, 236 Harrison St. Rabbi Israel Goldfarb, 360 Clinton St.

Derech Emunoh, Vernon and Ocean Aves., Arverne, L. I.

Mt. Sinai, 305 State St. Rev. Morris Silverman, 75 Bond St.

Rockaway Park, 192 Beach 116th St. Rabbi Alexander S. Kleinfeld.

Temple Beth Emeth of Flatbush, Church Ave. cor. Marlborough Rd. Rabbi Samuel J. Levinson.

Temple Sinai, Arlington Ave. and Bradford St. Rev. Maxwell L. Sacks, Rabbi.

Lutheran Churches

Manhattan

Advent, Broadway at 93d St. Rev. A. Steimle, 174 West 93d St.

Atonement, S. E. cor. Edgecombe Ave. and West 140th St. Rev. F. H. Knubel, D.D., Pastor, 48 Hamilton Ter.; Sister Jennie Christ, parish deaconess, 125 Edgecombe Ave.

Christ (German and English), 406 East 19th St. G. U. Wenner, Pastor.

City Mission (formerly Seamen's Welfare), 429 East 77th St. Rev. M. Pinkert, City Missionary.

Deaf, Mission for, 233 West 42d St. Rev. Arthur Boll, Pastor, 147 East 33rd St.

Epiphany, 72 East 128th St. Rev. M. L. Canup, Pastor.

Finnish, 72 East 128th St. Rev. Kalle Makinen, Pastor, 2 West 117th St.

Grace, 123 West 71st St. Rev. J. A. Weyl, Pastor, 107 West 68th St.

Gustavus Adolphus (Swedish), 151–153 East 22d St. Rev. M. Stolpe, Pastor.

Harlem (Swedish), 74 West 126th St. Rev. A. F. Borgendahl, Pastor.

Holy Trinity, 65th St. and Central Park West. Rev. Paul E. Scherer, Pastor, 3 West 65th St. See also Alphabetical List.

Holy Trinity (see SLOVAK), 334 East 29th St.

Immanuel (German and English), 88th St. and Lexington Ave. Rev. Geo. F. Schmidt, Pastor, 1376 Lexington Ave.

Immigrant Mission, 234 East 62d St. Rev. O. H. Restin, Missionary. See also in Alphabetical List.

Italian Mission, Rev. A. Bongarzone, Pastor.

Jewish Mission, 250 East 101st St. Rev. N. Friedmann, 1452 Bryant Ave., Bronx, N. Y.

Lettish Mission, 323 East 6th St.

Lutheran Information Bureau, Hartford Building, 22–26 East 17th St., Rooms 831–2 (tel. Stuyvesant 3015). J. F. E. Nickelsburg, secy.

Messiah, 4870 Broadway, near West 204th St. Rev. W. H. Storm in charge, 419 West 145th St.

Our Saviour (Norwegian), 237 East 123d St. Rev. J. C. Gram, Pastor.

Our Saviour, 179th St. and Audubon Ave. Rev. A. S. Hardy, Pastor.

Polish, 233 West 42d St. Rev. J. Dawidowski, Pastor.

Redeemer, 242–244 West 44th St. Rev. F. C. G. Schumm, Pastor.

St. James, S. W. cor. Madison Ave. and 73d St. Rev. Junius B. Remensnyder, Pastor, 900 Madison Ave.

St. John's (German and English), 81 Christopher St. F. E. Oberlander, Pastor, 79 Christopher St.

St. John's (German and English), 217 East 119th St. Rev. H. C. Steup, Pastor; Rev. Robert B. Steup, Assistant Pastor, 229 East 124th St.

St. Luke's (German and English), 233 West 42d St. Rev. W. Koepchen, Pastor, 431 West 43rd St.

St. Mark's, 323–325 East 6th St. Rev. George C. F. Haas, D.D., 312 Manhattan Ave.

St. Matthew's (English and German), cor. West 145th St. and Convent Ave. Rev. A. Wismar, Rev. W. H. Storm, Associate Pastor, 419 West 145th St. See also in Alphabetical List.

St. Paul's, 313 West 22d St. Rev. L. Koenig, Pastor.

St. Paul's (German and English), 149 West 123d St. Rev. F. Bosch, Pastor; Sister Rosa Dittrich, Deaconess.

St. Peter's (German and English), 631–635 Lexington Ave., cor. 54th St. Rev. A. B. Moldenke, Ph.D., 132 East 54th St. See also in the Alphabetical List.

Seaman's Mission. See CITY MISSION.

Slovak, Holy Trinity, 330 East 20th St. Rev. Louis A. Engler, Pastor, 334 East 20th St.

Trinity (German), 139 Avenue B. Rev. Otto Graesser, Pastor, 602 East 9th St.

Trinity, 164 West 100th St. Rev. E. Brennecke, Pastor.

Washington Heights (German-English), West 153d St., near Broadway. Rev. C. B. Rabbow, Pastor.

Zion, 339 East 84th St. Rev. Wm. Popcke, Ph.D., Pastor, 338 East 84th St.

Bronx

Bethany, 582 Teasdale Pl., near Third Ave. Rev. John Gruver, Pastor.

Concordia (German and English), 142d St. and Brook Ave. Rev. H. Pottberg, 505 East 142d St.

Emmanuel, cor. of Brown Pl. and East 137th St. Rev. Paul M. Young, Pastor, 470 East 137th St.

Fordham, 2430 Walton Ave. Rev. F. H. Meyer, Pastor, 2431 Morris Ave.

Grace, Valentine Ave. and 199th St. Rev. A. Koerber, Pastor, 2924 Valentine Ave.

Holy Comforter, Woodycrest Ave. and 165th St., Highbridge. John H. Dudde, Pastor.

Holy Trinity, 881 East 167th St. Rev. F. H. Lindemann, Pastor.

Immanuel (Scandinavian), 1410 Vyse Ave. Rev. Iver Thorwaldsen, Pastor.

Messiah (Swedish), Brook Ave. and 144th St. Rev. John Johnson, Pastor, 424 East 141st St.

St. John's German Evangelical Lutheran Church of Morrisania (German and English), Fulton Ave., between East 169th and 170th Sts. Rev. Theo. O. Posselt, Pastor, 1343 Fulton Ave.

St. Luke's, 1722–1726 Adams St., Van Nest Park. Rev. Walter Rohde, Pastor.

St. Mark's, Martha Ave. and 242d St., Woodlawn Heights. Rev. O. H. Trinklein, Pastor.

St. Matthew's (German and English), Melrose, 376–378 East 156th St. Rev. William T. Junge, 385 East 155th St.

St. Paul's of Tremont, La Fontaine Ave. and East 178th St. Rev. Karl Kretzman, 585 East 178th St.

St. Paul's (German and English), 796–800 East 156th St. Rev. Gustav H. Tappert, 796 East 156th St.

St. Peter's (German and English), 437–439 East 140th St. Rev. O. C. Mees, Pastor.

St. Petrus (German), 739 East 219th St., between White Plains and Barnes Aves., Williamsbridge. Rev. Friedrich Noeldeke, Pastor, 762 East 219th St.

St. Stephen's (German and English), 1001 Union Ave., near East 165th St. Rev. P. Roesener, Pastor; Prof. H. Rippe, Assistant Pastor.

St. Thomas, East 175th St. and Topping Ave. Rev. A. J. Traver, Pastor.

Saviour's. See FORDHAM.

Swedish-Finnish, Oak Terr. and Crimmins Ave. Rev. John Gullans, Pastor, 1671 60th St., Brooklyn.

Trinity (Danish), 1179 Hoe Ave., near Home St. Rev. A. C. Kildegaard, Pastor, 1179 Hoe Ave.

Trinity, Westchester and Glebe Aves., Westchester. Rev. P. Sander, Pastor, 2260 Ellis Ave.

Brooklyn

Advent, cor. Ave. P and East 12th St. Rev. Adolph F. Walz, Pastor, 1520 East 15th St.

Ascension, 51st St. and Thirteenth Ave., Borough Park. Rev. C. P. Jensen, Pastor, 1341 55th St.

Bethany (Norwegian), 60th St. near Twelfth Ave. Rev. C. O. Pederson, Pastor, 1030 73d St.

Bethesda (Scandinavian), 22 Woodhull St. Rev. J. C. Herre, Pastor.

Bethlehem, 107–109 Marion St. Rev. F. W. Behnke, Pastor, 481 Decatur St.

Bethlehem (Swedish), Third Ave. and Pacific St. Rev. F. Jacobson, Pastor.

Bethlehem, 51st St., near Sixth Ave. Rev. A. W. J. Herbert, Pastor, 654 54th St.

Calvary, Rochester Ave., cor. Herkimer St. Rev. G. C. Blessin, Pastor, 346 McDonough St.

Christ, 1084 Lafayette Ave., near Broadway. Rev. C. B. Schuchard, Pastor.

Deaf, Mission for, Services at 177 South 9th St., Sundays, at 3 P. M. Rev. A. Boll, Pastor.

Emanuel, 415–421 7th St. Rev. Emil Roth, Pastor.

Epiphany, 837 Sterling Pl. Rev. W. H. Stutts, Pastor.

Finnish, 752 44th St. Rev. S. Ilmonen, Pastor.

Finnish Seamen's Mission (Finnish and Swedish), 529 Clinton St. Rev. Kalle Makinen, Pastor.

First Scandinavian, 152 Russell St. Rev. Edward Risty, Pastor, 163 Monitor St.

German (German and English), Schermerhorn St., near Court St. Rev. Jacob W. Loch, Pastor, 188 Stratford Rd.

Good Shepherd, 315 Fenimore St. Rev. Walter Brunn, Pastor.

Good Shepherd, cor. 75th St. and Fourth Ave. Rev. Charles Daniel Trexler, 148 74th St., and Rev. Raymond C. Deitz, 264 78th St., Pastors.

Grace, Bushwick Ave. and Weirfield St. Rev. C. F. Intermann, Pastor.

Holy Trinity, Jefferson St., near Knickerbocker Ave. Rev. C. H. Dort, Pastor, 409 Cornelia St.

Immanuel, South 9th St., between Driggs Ave. and Roebling St. Rev. J. Holthusen, 177 South 9th St.

Immanuel (Swedish), Leonard St. near Driggs Ave. Rev. Joshua E. Nelson, Pastor.

Immanuel (Colored), 1524 Bergen St. Rev. W. O. Hill, Pastor.

Incarnation, Fourth Ave., between 53d and 54th Sts. Rev. Harold S. Miller, Pastor.

Mediator, 68th St. and Bay Parkway.

Messiah, Russell St., near Nassau Ave., Winthrop Park. Rev. J. Howard Worth, 141 Russell St.

Norwegian Seamen's Church, 111 Pioneer St. Rev. Christen Brunn, Pastor.

Our Savior, 21 Covert St., between Broadway and Bushwick Ave. Rev. Arthur R. G. Hanser, 37 Covert St.

Our Saviour (Danish), 193–195 9th St., near Third Ave. Rev. R. Andersen, Pastor.

Our Saviour (Norwegian), 632 Henry St. Rev. S. Turms, Pastor.

Redeemer, Eastern Pkwy., between Troy and Schenectady Aves. Rev. E. J. Flanders, 1345 Sterling Pl.

Redeemer, Lenox Rd., near Flatbush Ave. Rev. S. G. Weiskotten, 200 Fenimore St.

Reformation, Barbey St., north of Arlington Ave. Rev. J. C. Fisher, Pastor.

St. Andrew's, St. Nicholas Ave. and Harmon St.

St. Barnabas. See REDEEMER.

St. Jacobi, Fourth Ave., between 54th and 55th Sts. Rev. H. Meyer, Pastor.

St. Johannes (German), Maujer St., near Humboldt St. Rev. A. J. Beyer, 197 Maujer St.

St. John's, Milton St., near Manhattan Ave. Rev. F. W. Oswald, Pastor.

St. John's, 84th St. and Sixteenth Ave.

St. John's, 283–285 Prospect Ave. Rev. F. B. Clausen, Pastor.

St. John's, 225 New Jersey Ave. C. J. Lucas, Pastor.

St. John's (Lettish), Skillman Ave., near Graham Ave. Rev. Geo. Matzat, 105 Creek St., Maspeth, L. I.

St. John's (Swedish-Finnish), 44th St. and Eighth Ave. Rev. John Gullans, Pastor, 1671 60th St.

St. Luke's, Washington Ave., between Willoughby and DeKalb Aves. William A. Snyder, D.D., Pastor, 127 Willoughby Ave.

St. Mark's, 26 East 5th St. Rev. A. C. Misch, Pastor.

St. Mark's, Bushwick Ave., opp. Jefferson St. Rev. S. J. E. Frey and Rev. P. Woy, Pastors.

St. Matthew's, Sixth Ave. and 2d St. Rev. G. B. Young, D.D., Pastor, 490 3d St.

St. Matthew's, Canarsie, East 92d St., near Flatlands Ave. Rev. T. A. Petersen, Pastor, 1182 East 93d St.

St. Matthew's, North 5th St., near Driggs Ave. Rev. G. Sommer, Pastor.

St. Paul's, Henry St., near Third Pl. Rev. J. Huppenbauer, Pastor.

St. Paul's, Palmetto St., cor. Knickerbocker Ave. Rev. J. P. Riedel, 267 Palmetto St.

St. Paul's, West 5th St., Coney Island. Rev. J. F. Kitzmeyer, Pastor.

St. Paul's (German and English), South 5th St., cor. Rodney St. Rev. H. C. Wasmund, Pastor, 306 Rodney St.

St. Paul's, Ashford St., near Glenmore Ave.

St. Paul's (Swedish), 392 McDonough St. Rev. John Eastlund, Pastor.

St. Peter's (German and English), 94 Hale Ave., Cypress Hills. Rev. Arthur Brunn, 45 Hale Ave.

St. Peter's, Bedford Ave., near De Kalb Ave. Rev. John J. Heischmann, 457 Greene Ave., and Rev. J. Geo. F. Blaesi, 1077 Dean St.

St. Phillip's, 287 McKinley Ave. Rev. A. Wuerstlin, Pastor, 401 Eldert Lane.

St. Stephen's, Newkirk Ave., cor. East 28th St. Rev. Luther D. Gable, 448 East 28th St.

Salem (Danish), 128 Prospect Ave. Rev. J. J. Kildsig, Pastor, 130 Prospect Ave.

Salem (Swedish), 46th St. and Fourth Ave. J. Alfred Anderson, Pastor, 418 46th St.

Saxon (Swedish), Flatbush.

Tabor. See St. Paul's, Ashford St. near Glenmore Ave.

Trinity (Norwegian), Fourth Ave. and 46th St. S. O. Sigmond, Pastor, 411 46th St.

Trinity (German and English), 249 Degraw St., near Clinton. Rev. Hugo Burgdorf, 204 Baltic St.

Trinity Chapel, Coney Island Ave. and Ave. G. Rev. G. C. Koenig, Pastor, 336 Parkville Ave.

Trinity Mission, 185 Conover St. Rev. Hugo Burgdorf, 204 Baltic St.

Wartburg Chapel, 33 Georgia Ave., near Fulton St. Rev. Otto Hanser.

Zion, Henry St., near Clark St. Rev. E. C. J. Kraeling, Pastor, 132 Henry St.

Zion (Swedish), 59th St. and Eleventh Ave. Joseph D. Danielson, Pastor, 1070 59th St.

Zion, Bedford and Church Aves. Rev. P. F. Jubelt, Pastor, 2251 Bedford Ave.

Zion (Norwegian), 63d St. and Fourth Ave. Rev. Lauritz Larsen, Pastor, 450 74th St.

Queens

Bethany, Elmhurst, Parcell St. and Medina Place. Rev. Theo. Peterson, Pastor, 109 Judge St.

Christ, Rosedale. Rev. G. L. Kieffer, Pastor.

Christ, Floral Park. Rev. Ralph M. Durr, Pastor.

Christ, Woodhaven, Jerome Ave., cor. Ferry St. Rev. Dr. H. E. Meyer, Pastor.

Christ, Woodside, Fifth St., near Jackson Ave. Rev. H. F. Bunke, Pastor, 144 Fifth St.

Covenant, Ridgewood, Catalpa and Buckmann Aves. Rev. J. Henry Stelljes, Pastor, 2402 Catalpa Ave.

Emmanuel, Corona (German and English), Darrell Ave., cor. Alburtis Ave. Rev. E. G. Holls, Pastor.

Emmanus, Ridgewood, Anthon Ave. and Cornelia St. Rev. Timothy S. Frey, Pastor.

English Chapel, 20 Bell Ave., Bayside. Rev. F. J. Muhlhauser, 22 Bell Ave., Bayside.

English Chapel, 182 Main St., Port Washington. Rev. F. J. Muhlhauser, 22 Bell Ave., Bayside.

Good Shepherd, South Ozone Park, cor. Ashby and Horan Aves. Rev. C. H. Thomsen, Pastor, 61 Messing Ave.

Grace, Jamaica, Jamaica Ave. and Campion St. Rev. W. C. Schmidt, Pastor.

Grace English Chapel, Jericho Turnpike and N. Wertland Ave. Rev. Louis Wagner, Pastor.

Gustavus Adolphus (Swedish), Richmond Hill.

Immanuel, Whitestone (German and English), 21st St. between Seventh and Eighth Aves. Rev. H. C. Wolk, Pastor, 57 North Eighth Ave.

Port Jefferson Mission. Rev. F. Schwarz.

Redeemer, Glendale, cor. Cooper and Fosdick Aves. Rev. Theodore O. Kuehn, 310 Copeland Ave.

St. Andrew's, Glen Morris, Woodhaven. Rev. Carl Zinssmeister, Pastor.

St. Jacob's, Winfield Junction. Rev. Frederick Tilly, Pastor, 51 Prospect St.

St. John's, College Point, Sixth Ave. and 14th St. Rev. A. H. Halfmann, Pastor, 36 North Fourteenth Ave.

St. John's, Maspeth, 7 Martin St. Rev. Otto Graesser, Jr., Pastor.

St. John's, Flushing, 186 Percy St. Rev. C. G. Kaestner, Pastor.

St. John's, Lindenhurst. Rev. A. H. Schaefer, Pastor.

St. John's, Richmond Hill, Stoothoff Ave., near Jamaica. Rev. A. L. Benner, Pastor, 524 Stoothoff Ave.

St. Luke's, Woodhaven, Yarmouth and Dowing Sts. Rev. E. R. Jaxheimer, Pastor, 166 Syosset St., Woodhaven.

St. Mark's, Jamaica, New York Ave. Rev. J. F. K. Riebesell, Pastor.

St. Paul's, 129th St., near 101st Ave., Richmond Hill. Rev. Karl Toebbe, Pastor.

St. Paul's, Richmond Hill, Stoothoff Ave., near Ridgwood. P. B. Frey, Pastor, 719 Stoothoff Ave.

Salem (Swedish), Long Island City, Eighth Ave. Rev. H. Luther Wilson, Pastor, 569 Eighth Ave.

Trinity, Hollis. Rev. A. L. Dillenbeck, Pastor.

Trinity, Long Island City (German and English), 335–345 Eighth Ave., near Jamaica Ave. Rev. Christopher Merkel, Pastor.

Trinity, Maspeth, cor. Andrews and Pacific Sts. Rev. W. H. Pretzsch, Pastor.

Trinity, Middle Village, 12 Juniper Ave. Rev. D. W. Peterson, Pastor.

Trinity (Swedish), Corona, 49th St., near Shell Rd. Rev. H. Luther Wilson, Pastor, 569 Eighth Ave., L. I. C.

Richmond

Bethlehem, Ft. Wadsworth, Fingerboard Road. Rev. M. T. Holls, Pastor.

St. Matthew's, Dongan Hills, Jefferson St. and Alter Ave. Rev. W. Holls, Pastor.

Scandinavian, New Brighton, Fifth Ave. Rev. N. O. Lee, Pastor.

New Brighton, 767 Beach St., Stapleton. Rev. A. Krause, Pastor.

New Springville, 2024 Richmond Ave. Rev. H. A. Meyer, Pastor.

Our Saviour (Norwegian-English), Port Richmond, Nicholas Ave. Rev. S. R. Christensen, Pastor.

St. John's, Port Richmond. Rev. J. C. Borth, 212 Jewett Ave.

St. Paul's, West New Brighton, Cary Ave. and Caroline St. William Euchler, Pastor.

Stapleton, 191 Beach St. Rev. F. Sutter, Pastor.

Tottenville, 5459 Arthurkill Road. Rev. Walter E. Holls, Pastor.

Wasa (Swedish), Decker Ave., cor. Catherine St., Port Richmond. Rev. L. F. Nordstrom, Pastor.

Zion (Scandinavian), Port Richmond, Ave. B. Rev. R. O. Sigmond, Pastor.

Methodist Episcopal

Manhattan

Battery, Swedish, 127 West 89th St.

Beekman Hill, 319 East 50th St.

Blinn Memorial (German), Lexington Ave., cor. 103d St. Rev. H. Schuckai, Pastor.

Calvary, Seventh Ave., and 129th St.

Centenary, Washington Ave. and 166th St.

Chelsea, Fort Washington Ave. and West 178th St.

Church of all Nations, 9 Second Ave.

Cornell Memorial, 231 East 76th St.

Crawford Memorial, White Plains Ave. and 218th St.

Duane, 294 Hudson St.

Eighteenth Street, 307 West 18th St. Rev. B. C. Warren, D.D., Pastor.

First German, 48 St. Marks Pl. Rev. E. W. Peglow, Pastor.

Five Points Mission, 69 Madison St.

Grace, 131 West 104th St. Rev. Frederick Brown Harris, Pastor. See Alphabetical List.

Hadley Rescue Hall, 293 Bowery. Rev. John Callahan, Pastor.

Immigrant and Port Mission (M. E.), 9 State St.

Jane Street, 11–19 Jane St.

Jefferson Park (Italian), 407 East 114th St.

John Street, 44 John St.

Madison Ave., Madison Ave. and 60th St. Rev. Ralph W. Sockman, Ph.D., Pastor. See Alphabetical List.

Metropolitan Temple, 14th St. and Seventh Ave. Rev. J. W. Chasey, B.D., Pastor.

Park Avenue, Park Ave., cor. 86th St.

People's, 223 East 61st St.

People's Home Church and Settlement, 543 East 11th St. Rev. Leslie G. Davis, Pastor. See also Alphabetical List.

St. Andrew's, 76th St., near Columbus Ave.

St. James's, Madison Ave., cor. 126th St. Rev. George L. Nuckolls' Pastor.

St. Mark's (Colored), 231 West 53d St. Rev. William H. Brooks, D.D., Pastor, 237 West 53d St. See also Alphabetical List.

St. Paul's, West End Ave. and 86th St. Rev. Raymond L. Forman, D.D., Pastor.

Saviour, Church of the, Lexington Ave. and 111th St.

Second German, 246 West 40th St.

Settlement and Church of All Nations, 9 Second Ave. See Alphabetical List.

Sixth. See Eighteenth St.

Sixty-First Street, bet. 2nd and 3rd Aves. Rev. Benjamin F. Saxon, Pastor. See also Alphabetical List.

Swedish, Lexington Ave., cor. 52d St.

Trinity, 318 East 124th St.

Union, 233 West 48th St.

Union A. M. E., 109 West 131st St.

Washington Heights, 1868 Amsterdam Ave. Rev. J. E. Price, Pastor.

Washington Square, 4th St. and Washington Sq. Rev. J. Sumner Stone, M.D., Pastor. See also Alphabetical List.

West Side, 461 West 44th St.

Bronx

Bethel, Grand Concourse and 177th St.

Boston Road, Boston Rd. and Suburban Place. Rev. Hartley J. Hartman, Pastor.

Crawford Memorial, 219th St. and White Plains Ave. Rev. Lincoln H. Caswell, Pastor.

Elton Avenue (German), Elton Ave. and East 158th St.

First Norwegian and Danish, 1078 Kelly St.

Fordham, 2543 Marion Ave., Fordham. Rev. Arthur Thompson, Pastor.

Morris Heights, 1788 Sedgwick Ave.

Mott Avenue, Mott Ave. and 150th St. Rev. A. Hamilton Nesbitt, Pastor.

Mt. Hope, 177th St. and Concourse.

St. Stephen's, 144 West 228th St. Rev. Chas. L. Mackey, Pastor.

Tremont (German), 1841 Bathgate Ave.

Tremont, Washington Ave., cor. 178th St. Rev. Wm. H. Moser, Ph.D., Pastor, 454 East 178th St.

Trinity, City Island Ave. and Bay, City Island.

Wakefield Grace, White Plains Ave. and 241st St.

Westchester, 2547 E. Tremont Ave.

Willis Avenue, Willis Ave. and East 141st St. Rev. John E. Zeiter, Pastor.

Woodlawn, N. E. cor. 241st St. and Katonah Ave., Woodlawn.

Woodycrest, 166th St., cor. Woodycrest Ave.

Brooklyn

Andrews, Richmond near Fulton.

Bethel A. M. E., Schenectady Ave., cor. Dean St.

Bethelship Norwegian, 297 Carroll St., near Hoyt St.

Buffalo Avenue, Buffalo Ave., cor. Bergen St.

Bushwick Avenue-Central, Bushwick Ave., cor. Madison St. Rev George Ellsworth Bishop, Pastor. See also Alphabetical List.

Corner-Stone Temple, Manhattan Ave. and Noble St. Rev. Dudley Oliver Osterheld, Pastor.

Cropsey Avenue, Cropsey Ave. at Bay 35th St.

Ebenezer Wesleyan, 377 Hudson Ave.

Eighteenth Street, Eighteenth St. near Fifth Ave.

Elim, Swedish, Seventh Ave., 48th St.

Embury Memorial, Decatur and Lewis Ave.

Fenimore Street, Fenimore St. and Rogers Ave. Rev. Claude C. Coile, Pastor.

First (Sands St.), Henry, cor. Clark St.

First Primitive, Park Place and Nostrand Ave. Rev. John Proude, 378 New York Ave.

Fourth Avenue, 4th Ave., cor. 47th St.

Flatlands, Flatlands Ave. and East 40th St. Rev. Edward E. Wright, Pastor.

Fleet Street, 43 Fleet St.

Grace, Seventh Ave., cor. St. John's Pl.

Goodsell Memorial, Sheridan Ave. cor. McKinley Ave.

Greene Avenue (German), 1171 Greene Ave.

Hanson Place, Hanson Place, cor. St. Felix St.

Immanuel (Swedish), 426 Dean St.

Janes, Monroe, cor. Reid Ave.

Knickerbocker Avenue, Knickerbocker. cor. Menehan St.

Marcy Avenue, Marcy Ave., cor. Penn Ave.

New York Avenue, New York Ave., Dean to Bergen Sts. Rev. John W. Langdale, Pastor, 1294 Dean St.

Norwegian Bethelship, 297 Carroll St.

Nostrand-De Kalb, Nostrand Ave. cor. Quincy St. Rev. H. D. Munson, Pastor.

Ocean Parkway, Ocean Pkwy. and Foster Ave. Rev. William B. West, Pastor. See also Alphabetical List.

Orchard Primitive, 47-49 Oakland St.

Prospect Avenue, cor. Prospect and Greenwood Aves.

Prospect Place (German), 40-42 Prospect Pl.

St. Paul's (German), 308 East 55th St. H. Houst.

Salem, 102 West 133rd St.

Salem (German), Vanderveer Park, East 38th St. and Ave. D.

Sheepshead Bay, cor. Ocean and Voorhies Aves. Rev. Cyrus W. Severance.

Simpson, Clermont and Willoughby Ave.

Sixth Avenue, 6th Ave, and 8th St.

South Third Street, 411 South 3d St. Rev. James H. Lockwood, Pastor.

Summerfield, Washington and Greene Ave.

Sunset Park, 7th Ave. and 45th St.

Swedish Bethany, 1208 St. Johns Pl., near Albany Ave. Rev. C. F. Edwards, Pastor, 1204 St. Johns Pl.

Swedish Elim, 48th St. and 7th Ave.

St. James, 2021 84th St. Rev. Lester Ward Auman, Minister.

St. Mark's, Ocean Ave. and Beverly Rd. Rev. R. M. Moore, D.D., Pastor.

Union, Leonard and Conselyea Sts.

Vanderveer Park, East 31st St. and Glenwood Rd.

Warren Street, 307 Warren St.

Wesley, 831 Glenmore Ave., Rev. P. St. John Colman, Pastor.

Williams Avenue, 50 Williams Ave.

Windsor Terrace. See PROSPECT AVENUE.

Queens

Bayside, West St., and Palace Blvd. Rev. P. E. Shoemaker, Pastor.

Corona, cor. Kingsland and Alburtis Aves.

Corona Italian Mission, 52 Moore St.

Elmhurst, Medina Place and Gerry Ave.

Epworth, Whitestone, Eighth Ave. and 20th St. Rev. Arthur Y. Holter, Pastor.

First, Elmhurst, Medina Pl. and Gerry Ave. Rev. William D. Beach, D.D., Pastor.

First, Flushing, 136 Amity St. Rev. W. W. W. Wilson, Pastor.

First, Hollis, Minnetonka Ave. Rev. A. C. Flandreau, Pastor.

First, Jamaica, 430 Fulton St. Rev. George C. Fort, D.D., Pastor.

First, Ozone Park, Hatch and Kimball Aves.

First, Richmond Hill, Church St. and Beaufort St. Rev. D. D. Irvine, Pastor.

First, Springfield Gardens.

First, Temple and Crescent Ave., Astoria.

First German, Long Island City, 78 Academy St. and Wilbur Ave.

First Italian, 52 Lincoln St., Astoria, L. I. Rev. A. Sartorio, Pastor.

Glendale, Tesla Place.

Jamaica, 430 Fulton St., Jamaica.

Maspeth, Columbia Place, Maspeth.

Middle Village, Metropolitan Ave. Rev. Charles Bell, Pastor.

Ridgewood Heights (German), Woodward Ave. and Grove St. Rev. Gustav Bobilin, D.D., Pastor.

Shaw Avenue, Union Course.

Springfield Gardens. Rev. Samuel E. Lawson, Pastor.

Trinity, Richmond Hill, 86th Ave., cor. 108th St.

Van Alst Avenue, Long Island City, cor. Van Alst Ave. and 11th St.

Richmond

Asbury, New Springville.

Bethel, Amboy Rd. and Bethel Ave., Tottenville.

Grace, Port Richmond, Heberton and Castleton Aves. Rev. William J. Hampton, Pastor.

Graniteville, Willowbrook Rd., near Richmond Ave., Port Richmond. Rev. George H. Cooley, Pastor.

Kingsley, Stapleton, 184 Cebra Ave. Rev. H. B. Leech, Pastor.

St. Mark's, Pleasant Plains, Prince Bay. Rev. D. H. Gridley, Pastor.

St. Paul's, Tottenville, 7559 Amboy Road. Rev. J. Fred Bindenberger, Pastor.

Summerfield, Mariners' Harbor, 102 Harbor Rd.

Trinity, West New Brighton, Elizabeth St. and Delafield Ave. Rev. H. Eugene Curts, Pastor. See also Alphabetical List.

Wandell Memorial, Concord.

Woodrow-St. John's, Prince Bay, 1109 Woodrow Road. Rev. Samuel O. Rusby, Pastor.

MORAVIAN CHURCHES

Third, 224 West 63d St., N. Y. C.

Fourth (Beth-Tphillah), 124 West 136th St.

Second, Wilkins Ave. and Jennings St., Bronx.

United Brethren, 345 J St., Brooklyn. Rev. F. E. Grunert, Pastor.

Collegiate, Castleton Corners, S. I., Richmond Turnpike and Todt Hill Rd. Rev. Frederick R. Nitzschke, Pastor.

First, Stapleton, S. I., 90 Osgood Ave. Rev. Paul T. Shultz, Pastor, 90 Osgood Ave.

CHURCH OF THE NEW JERUSALEM
(Swedenborgian)

New York Society of the New Church, 114 East 35th St. Rev. Julian K. Smyth, Pastor.

Brooklyn Society of the New Church, cor. Monroe Pl. and Clark St. See also Alphabetical List.

First German New Church of Brooklyn, Jefferson and Knickerbocker Aves.

NEW THOUGHT

First Church of Divine Science, Hotel Waldorf Astoria. Rev. W. John Murray, Pastor.

New Thought (Sears Philosophy), 110 West 34th St. Rev. F. W. Sears, Pastor.

PENTECOSTAL

Pentecostal Church of the Nazarene, 210 West 14th St. Rev. Mrs. I. M. Jump, Pastor.

Utica Avenue Pentecostal Church of the Nazarene, between Dean and Bergen Sts., Brooklyn.

PRESBYTERIAN

Manhattan

Adams Memorial, 207 East 30th St.

Ascension (Italian), 340 East 106th St.

Bethany, 420 East 137th St.

Bethlehem Chapel, 196 Bleecker St.

Bohemian Brethren, 589 East 165th St.

Brick, Fifth Ave., cor. 37th St. Rev. William Pierson Merrill, D.D., and Rev. Theodore Ainsworth Greene, Ministers. See Alphabetical List.

Broadway, 114th St. and B'dway. Rev. Walter Duncan Buchanan, Pastor.

Central, Madison Ave. and 57th St. Rev. Dwight W. Wylie, D.D., Pastor.

Chelsea, 208-214 West 23d St. Rev. William Neely Ross, Pastor.

Chinese Church, 225 East 31st St.

Church of the Gospel (Italian), 196 Bleecker St.

Church House, 432 Third Ave.

Christ, 344 West 36th St. Rev. Theodore F. Savage, Pastor. See also Alphabetical List.

Covenant, Church of the, 310 East 42d St. See also Alphabetical List.

East Harlem. The First Magyar, 233 East 116th St. Affiliated with the American Parish (q. v.) in Alphabetical List.

Emmanuel Chapel, University Pl. Church, 735 East 6th St. Rev. G. E. Sehlbrede, D.D., Minister.

Faith, 359 West 48th St. Rev. Ray Freeman Jenney, Pastor. See also Alphabetical List.

Fifth Avenue, 55th St. and Fifth Ave. Rev. John Kelman, D.D., Pastor. See Alphabetical List.

First, Fifth Ave., 11th and 12th Sts. Rev. George Alexander, D.D., Rev. Harry Emerson Fosdick, D.D., and Rev. Thomas Guthrie Sheers, Ministers. See also Alphabetical List.

Fort George, St. Nicholas Ave. and 186th St. Rev. Lyman R. Hartley, M.A., Pastor.

Fort Washington, Broadway and 174th St. Rev. John McNeill, Pastor.

Fourth, West End Ave. and 91st St. Rev. Edgar W. Work, D.D., Pastor.

French Evangelical (Eglise Evangelique Francaise), 126 West 16th St. Rev. Paul D. Elsesser, Pastor.

Good Shepherd, 152–156 West 66th St. Rev. Daniel E. Lorenz, Pastor.

Greenwich, 145 West 13th St. Rev. William H. Matthews, D.D., Pastor. See also Alphabetical List.

Harlem-New York, Mt. Morris Park, cor. 122d St. Rev. Frederick W. Evans, D.D., Pastor.

Italian Mission, 310 East 42nd St.

Jan Hus Bohemian, 347–351 East 74th St. See also Alphabetical List.

John Hall Memorial, 342 East 63rd St.

Labor Temple, Second Ave. and 14th St.

Madison Avenue, 73rd St. and Madison Ave. Rev. Henry Sloane Coffin, D.D., Pastor.

Morningside, 122d St. and Morningside Ave. Rev. Paul E. Baker, Pastor.

Mt. Washington, S. W. cor. Dyckman St. and Broadway. Rev. Walter David Knight, Pastor, 616 West 207th St.

North, 525 West 155th St. Rev. John R. Mackay, Pastor.

Northminster, 141 West 115th St., at St. Nicholas Ave.

Park Avenue, Park Ave. and East 85th St. Rev. Tertius van Dyke, Pastor.

Puritans, 15 West 130th St. Rev. Robert Bruce Clark, D.D., Pastor.

Rutgers, Broadway, cor. West 73d St. Rev. Daniel Russell, Pastor. See also in Alphabetical List.

St. James' (colored), 59 West 137th St. Rev. F. M. Ryder.

St. Nicholas Avenue, 409 West 141st St. Rev. Elliott W. Brown, D.D., Pastor, 58 Hamilton Terr.

Sea and Land Church, 61 Henry St. See also Alphabetical List.

Second (Scotch), 96th St. and Central Park West. Rev. Robert Watson.

Seventh, 138–140 Broome St. Rev. Johns T. Wilds, Pastor.

Spring Street, 246 Spring St. See also Alphabetical List.

University Heights, University Ave. and 181st St. Rev. Percy B. Wightman, D.D., Pastor.

Welsh, 505 West 155th St. Rev. D. Morgan Richards, Pastor.

West End, 165 West 105th St. and Amsterdam Ave. Rev. A. Edwin Keigwin, D.D., Pastor.

West Park, 86th St. and Amsterdam Ave. Rev. Anthony H. Evans, D.D. See also Alphabetical List.

Bronx

Beck Memorial, 980 East 180th St. Rev. Maitland Bartlett, Pastor.

Bedford Park, 200th St., and Bainbridge Ave. Rev. George Mair, Pastor.

Branch for Italians, 204th St. and Villa Ave. Dr. Charles Fama, Pastor.

First, of Williamsbridge, 730 East 225th St., near White Plains Ave. Rev. Albert Dale Gantz, Pastor.

Holy Trinity (Italian), 253 East 153d St. Rev. J. W. Vavola, Pastor.

Hunts' Point, 700–710 Coster St. Basil Douglas Hall, Pastor.

Morrisania, Washington Ave. and East 168th St. Rev. M. F. Johnston, D.D., Pastor, 1205 Washington Ave.

Olmstead Avenue, Olmstead and Newbold Aves. Rev. Merrill F. Clarke, Pastor.

Riverdale, Riverdale Ave.

Tremont, Grand Concourse and 178th St.

Van Nest, Morris Park and Barnes Aves. Rev. George M. Elsbree, Pastor, 780 Morris Park Ave.

Woodlawn Heights, 240th St. and Martha Ave.

Woodstock, Prospect Ave. and 165th St. Rev. James Cromie, Pastor.

Brooklyn

Ainslee Street, Ainslee St. and Manhattan Ave.

Arlington Avenue, Arlington Ave., cor. Elton St. Rev. John H. Kerr, D.D., Pastor, 268 Arlington Ave.

Bedford, Dean St., cor. Nostrand Ave. Rev. S. Edward Young, D.D., Pastor.

Bethany, McDonough St. and Howard Ave. Rev. L. O. Rotenbach, Pastor.

Borough Park, 46th St. and 15th Ave.

Bushwick Avenue (German), Bushwick Ave. and Menahan St. Rev. Herman E. Schnatz, Pastor, 975 Bushwick Ave.

Central, Marcy Ave., cor. Jefferson Ave. Rev. J. F. Carson, Pastor.

Classon Avenue, Classon Ave. and Monroe St. Rev. Raymond M. Huston, Pastor.

Cuyler, 358 Pacific St. Rev. John R. Campbell, Pastor.

Duryea, Sterling Place and Underhill Ave.

Ebenezer (German), Stockholm St., near St. Nicholas Ave. Rev. Charles C. Jaeger, 371 Stockholm St.

Fifth German. See Halsey Street.

First, of Bensonhurst, 23d Ave. and 83d St.

First, Henry St., near Clark St. Rev. L. Mason Clarke, D.D., 138 Henry St.

City Park Branch, 209 Concord St.

Flatbush, 23d St., near Foster Ave. Rev. Herbert H. Field, Pastor.

Franklin Avenue Italian Mission, 165 Franklin Ave. Rev. Stefano L. Testa, Minister, 940 Bedford Ave.

Friedenskirche. See Willoughby Avenue.

Glenmore Avenue, Glenmore Ave. and Doscher St. Rev. A. G. Penney, Pastor.

Grace, cor. Stuyvesant and Jefferson Aves.

Greene Avenue, Greene Ave. near Reid.

Halsey St., 1155-1159 Halsey St. and Central Ave. Rev. Charles H. Schwarzbach, 1159 Halsey St.

Homecrest, Ave. T and East 15th St.

Irving Square, Wilson Ave. and Weirfield St.

Lafayette Avenue, cor. Lafayette Ave. and South Oxford St. Rev. Charles Carroll Albertson, D.D., Pastor.

Lefferts Park, 15th and 72nd St. Rev. Tracy Griswold, Pastor.

Memorial, 7th Ave. and St. John's Place.

Mt. Olivet, Evergreen Ave. cor. Troutman St.

Noble Street, Noble cor. Lorimer St.

Oliver, Bergen St. cor. 6th Ave.

Prospect Heights, Eighth Ave., cor. 10th St. Rev. Edwin D. Bailey, D.D., Pastor.

Ridgewood (German), Halleck and Forest Aves. Rev. Arthur B. Rhinow, Pastor.

South Third Street, South 3d St. and Driggs Ave. Rev. Newell Woolsey Wells, Pastor.

Spencer Memorial, Clinton and Remsen Sts. Rev. Wm. H. Hendrickson, Pastor.

St. John's Place, Seventh Ave., cor. St. Johns Pl.

Throop Avenue, Throop Ave. and Macon St.

Union, Ridge Blvd., cor. 80th St. Rev. H. H. Leavitt, Jr., Pastor.

Wells Memorial, cor. Argyle and Glenwood Roads. Rev. D. Ernest M. Curry, Pastor.

Westminster, Clinton St., cor. First Place.

Willoughby Ave., 860 Willoughby Ave. Rev. Louis Wolferz, Pastor.

Wyckoff Heights, Harman St., near St. Nicholas Ave. Rev. Leroy L. Daniel, 8566 113th St., Richmond Hill, N. Y.

Queens

Astoria, 954 Blvd., Astoria.

Calvary, Maspeth.

Cedar Manor Chapel, Jamaica, Mathias St., near New York Ave.

First, East Williamsburg (German), 34 Prospect Ave. Rev. John Dietz, Pastor.

First, Flushing, Barclay and Murray Sts.

First, Jamaica, cor. Fulton St. and Clinton Ave. Rev. Andrew Magill, Pastor, 25 Clinton Ave., Jamaica.

First, Richmond Hill, Greenwood Ave., near Atlantic Ave.

First, Springfield, Springfield Ave. and Broadway. Rev. W. J. Macdonald, D.D., Pastor.

First, of Newtown, Queens Blvd., Elmhurst.

French Evangelical, Woodhaven, 4176 Chichester Ave. Rev. G. Baechler, Pastor.

Hillside, Jamaica, Fulton St. and Harvard Ave.

Ravenswood, Blvd., cor. Webster Ave. Rev. Wm. S. Wallace, Pastor.

Ridgewood, Forest and Halleck Aves.

Russell Sage Memorial, Far Rockaway.

Springfield, Springfield Ave. and Broadway.

Whitestone, Seventh Ave., cor. 14th St. Rev. Wm. S. Wallace, Pastor.

Woodhaven First, Jerome and Walker Aves.

Richmond

Calvary, West Brighton, cor. Castleton and Bement Aves. Rev. Mebane Ramsay, Pastor.

First of Edgewater, 32 Brownell St., Stapleton. Rev. James A. Fraser, Ph.D., Pastor.

UNITED PRESBYTERIAN

Manhattan

West Forty-fourth Street, 434 West 44th St. Rev. Homer H. Wallace.

Bronx

East One Hundred Eighty-seventh Street, East 187th St. and Tiebout Ave.

Brooklyn

East Brooklyn. See OPEN CHURCH.

Open Church, The, Eldert's Lane, cor. Etna St.

Second, Bond St. and Atlantic Ave. Rev. Wm. M. Nichol, Pastor, 463 Pacific St.

Protestant Episcopal

Manhattan

All Angels', West End Ave. and 81st St. Rev. S. De Lancey Townsend, Rector. See Alphabetical List.

All Saints', Henry and Scammel Sts. Rev. Kenneth S. Guthrie, Vicar. See Alphabetical List.

All Souls (memorial of the Rev. Henry Anthon, D.D.), St. Nicholas Ave., between 114th and 115th Sts. Rev. Clifton Macon, Rector. St. Nicholas Ave. See also Alphabetical List.

Ascension, Fifth Ave. and 10th St. Dr. Percy Stickney Grant, Rector. See Alphabetical List.

Ascension Memorial, 251 West 43rd St.

Beloved Disciple, 59–67 89th St., east of Madison Ave. Rev. George R. Vande Water, Rector.

Calvary, Fourth Ave. and 21st St. The Rev. Theodore Sedgwick, D.D., Rector. See also Alphabetical List.

Cathedral of St. John the Divine, Amsterdam Ave. and 111th St. See Alphabetical List.

Christ the Consoler, Chapel of, adjoining Bellevue Hospital, foot of East 26th St. Rev. E. V. Collins, M.A., and Rev. David Bowen, Chaplains.

Christ, Broadway at 71st St. The Rev. John R. Atkinson, Rector. See also Alphabetical List.

City Hospital Chapel, Blackwell's Island. Frederick W. Cornell, Chapain.

Comforter Chapel, 10 Horatio St. Rev. C. C. Clark, Rector. See Alphabetical List.

Epiphany, Lexington Ave. and 35th St. Rev. Wm. T. Crocker, Rector.

God's Providence Chapel (N. Y. P. E. City Mission Society), 330 Broome St.

Good Shepherd Chapel (N. Y. P. E. City Mission Society), Blackwell's Island. Rev. Sydney N. Ussher, Chaplain.

Grace, Broadway and 10th St. Rev. Charles Lewis Slattery, D.D., Rector. See Alphabetical List.

Grace Chapel, 410 East 14th St. See Alphabetical List.

Grace Emmanuel (Harlem), 214 East 116th St. Rev. Wm. Knight McGown, Rector, 213 East 115th St.

Heavenly Rest, 551 Fifth Ave., near 45th St. Rev. Herbert Shipman, D.D., Rector. See also Alphabetical List.

Holy Apostles, Church of the, Ninth Ave., cor. 28th St.

Holy Comforter, for Seamen (Church of the Seamen's Church Institute of New York), 343 West Houston St. Office: 25 South St. Rev. Archibald R. Mansfield, supt.

Holy Communion, 20th St. and Sixth Ave. See Alphabetical List.

Holy Cross, Ave. C and East 4th St. Rev. W. K. Damuth, Vicar.

Holy Faith, Church of, East 166th St. and Trinity Ave.

Holy Rood, cor. Fort Washington Ave. and 179th St. Rev. G. A. Carstensen, D.D., Rector.

Holy Trinity, 312–332 East 88th St. (Parish of St. James). Rev. Frank Warfield Crowder, Ph.D., Rector. See Alphabetical List.

Holy Trinity, Lenox Ave., cor. 122d St. Rev. H. P. Nichols, Rector. See also Alphabetical List.

Incarnation, Madison Ave. and 35th St. Rev. H. Percy Silver, Rector.

Incarnation Chapel, 240 East 31st St. Rev. George Ferrand Taylor, Vicar. See also Alphabetical List.

Intercession Chapel, 155th St. and Broadway. See Alphabetical List.

Messiah Chapel, 206 East 95th St.

New York Protestant Episcopal City Mission Society, 38 Bleecker St. See Alphabetical List.

Resurrection, Church of the, 115 East 74th St.

San Salvatore (Italian Mission), 359–361 Broome St. See also New York Protestant Episcopal City Mission Society in the Alphabetical List.

St. Andrew's, Fifth Ave. and 127th St. See Alphabetical List.

St. Ann's for Deaf-Mutes, 511 West 148th St. See Alphabetical List.

St. Augustine's, 105 East Houston St. See Alphabetical List.

St. Barnabas' Chapel (P. E. City Mission Society), 304 Mulberry St.

St. Bartholomew's, Park Ave. and 51st St. Rev. Leighton Parks, D.D., Rector. See Alphabetical List.

St. Chrysostom's, Seventh Ave. and 39th St. See Alphabetical List.

St. Clement's, 423 West 46th St. Rev. Thomas A. Sparks, Pastor.

St. Cornelius. See St. Clement's.

St. Cornelius the Centurion, Governor's Island, New York Harbor. Rev. Edmund Banks Smith, D.D., Chaplain.

St. Cyprian's Chapel, 175 West 63d St.

St. Edward the Martyr, 12 East 109th St. Rev. Percival C. Pyle, D.D., Rector, 14 East 109th St.

St. Elizabeth of Hungary Chapel (Memorial Hospital), 2 West 106th St.

St. George's, Stuyvesant Sq. and East 16th St. Rev. Karl Reiland, Rector, 209 East 16th St. See Alphabetical List.

St. Ignatius', West End Ave. and 87th St. Rev. William Pitt McCune, Rector.

St. James, Madison Ave. and 71st St. Rev. Frank Warfield Crowder, D.D., Rector. See Alphabetical List.

St. John the Evangelist, Church of, 222 West 11th St., cor. Waverley Pl. Rev. John Armstrong Wade, Rector, 224 Waverley Pl.

St. Luke's, Convent Ave. and West 141st St. Rev. William T. Walsh, Rector.

St. Luke's Hospital Chapel, Cathedral Heights, 113th St. and Amsterdam Ave. Rev. George F. Clover, Pastor.

St. Margaret's, 940 East 156th St.

St. Mark's-in-the-Bouwerie, 10th St. and Second Ave. Rev. William Norman Guthrie, Rector. See Alphabetical List.

St. Mark's Memorial Chapel, 288 East 10th St.

St. Mary's, 101 Lawrence St. (127th St. and Amsterdam Ave.). Rev. Charles B. Ackley, Rector.

St. Mary the Virgin, 139 West 46th St. See also Alphabetical List.

St. Matthew's, 28 West 84th St. Rev. Arthur H. Judge, D.D., Rector.

St. Michael's, Amsterdam Ave. and 99th St. See Alphabetical List.

St. Paul's Chapel, Broadway and Fulton St. See Alphabetical List.

St. Stephen's, 122 West 69th St.

St. Thomas', Fifth Ave. and 53d St. Rev. Ernest M. Stires, D.D., Rector, 3 West 53d St. See also in Alphabetical List.

Seamen's Church Institute. See Holy Comforter for Seamen.

Swedish Chapel, 123 East 127th St.

Transfiguration, 1 East 29th St. Rev. Dr. Houghton, Rector. See Alphabetical List.

Trinity, Broadway and Wall St. Rev. William T. Manning, D.D., Rector. See Alphabetical List.

Trinity Chapel (Trinity Parish), 15 West 25th St., N.Y.C. Rev. J. Wilson Sutton, Vicar.

Zion and St. Timothy, 334 West 57th St. Rev. Frederick Burgess, Jr., Rector.

Bronx

Advocate, Church of the, Washington Ave. and 181st St. Rev. George N. Deyo, Rector.

Christ, Riverdale Ave. and 252d St., Riverdale. Rev. Glenn W. White, Rector.

Grace, City Island.

Grace, 1909 Vyse Ave. (West Farms).

Holy Nativity, Church of the, 204th St. and Bainbridge Ave. Rev. Chas. F. Kennedy, Pastor. See also in Alphabetical List.

Holy Trinity, Clinton and Montague Sts. See Alphabetical List.

Mediator, Kingsbridge Ave. and West 231st St. Rev. John Campbell, Ph.D., Rector, 260 West 231st St. See also Alphabetical List.

St. Alban's Church, 163d St., Ogden and Summit Aves., Highbridge. Rev. M. K. Crawford, Rector, 979 Ogden Ave.

St. Ann's Morrisania, St. Ann's Ave. and 140th St. Rev. Harold G. Willis, Rector. See Alphabetical List.

St. David's, 384 East 160th St.

St. Edmund's, Mount Hope, East 177th St. and Morris Ave. Rev. J. C. Smiley, Rector.

St. George's, 661 East 219th St. and Willett Ave., Williamsbridge. Rev. David S. Agnew, Rector.

St. James', Fordham, Jerome Ave. and East 190th St. Rev. DeW. L. Pelton, D.D., Rector.

St. Martha's Chapel, Hunt Ave., Van Nest.

St. Mary's, Alexander Ave. near E. 142d St.

St. Paul's, Washington Ave., cor. St. Pauls Pl. Rev. Homer Francis Taylor, Pastor.

St. Peter's, Westchester Ave., cor. St. Peters Ave. Rev. J. A. Foster, Rector.

St. Simeon's, 165th St. and Sheridan Ave.

St. Stephen's, Verio Ave. and 238th St. Rev. R. W. Cochrane, Rector.

Brooklyn

Advent, Church of the, Seventeenth Ave. and 75th St. Rev. Richard R Upjohn, Pastor.

All Saints, 7th St., cor. Seventh Ave.

Ascension, Kent St., near Manhattan Ave.

Atonement, 17th St. near 5th Ave.

Calvary, E. D., 966 Bushwick Ave., between Greene Ave. and Grove St. Rev. John Williams, 1114 Bushwick Ave.

Christ, cor. Clinton and Harrison Sts.

Christ, Ridge Blvd., 73d and 74th Sts. Rev. John H. Fitzgerald, Rector, 7301 Ridge Blvd.

Christ Chapel, Wolcott St., near Van Brunt St.

Emmanuel, 2635 East 23d St.

Epiphany, Church of the, Ave. R and East 17th St.

Good Shepherd, McDonough St., near Lewis Ave.

Grace, 46 Grace Ct. Rev. C. J. Wrigley, D.D., Rector. See also Alphabetical List.

Grace, E. D., 59–63 Conselyea St., near Lorimer St. Rev. William G. Ivie, Pastor.

Holy Apostles, Church of the, Greenwood Ave., near Prospect Ave. Rev. George F. Bambach, Rector, 201 Sherman St.

Holy Cross, 176 St. Nicholas Ave. Rev. James Williams, Pastor.

Holy Spirit, Bay Parkway.

Holy Trinity, Montague and Clinton Sts. Rev. John Howard Melish, Rector. See also Alphabetical List.

Incarnation, Gates Ave. near Clinton St.

Messiah, cor. Greene and Clermont Aves.

Nativity, Ocean Ave. and Ave. F.

Redeemer, cor. Fourth Ave. and Pacific St. Rev. T. J. Lacey, Ph.D., Rector.

St. Agnes, 2005 60th St.

St. Alban's, Ave. F and East 94th St., Canarsie. Rev. F. C. Stevens, Rector, 1012 East 15th St.

St. Andrew's, 50th St. and Fourth Ave. Rev. John W. Gill, D.D., Rector.

St. Ann's, Clinton and Livingston.

St. Bartholomew's, Pacific near Bedford Ave.

St. Clement's, Pennsylvania cor. Liberty Ave.

St. Gabriel's, Hawthorne St., near Nostrand Ave. Rev. George T. Baker, Rector.

St. George's, cor. Gates and Marcy Aves. Rev. Charles G. Clark, Rector.

St. James', St. James Place and Lafayette Ave.

St. John's, 139 St. Johns Pl., near Seventh Ave. Rev. T. B. Holland, Pastor.

St. John's, 99th St., cor. Fort Hamilton Ave., Fort Hamilton.

St. John's Hospital Chapel, cor. Atlantic and Albany Aves. Rev. George D. Graeff, Chaplain.

St. John the Baptist, Ocean Pkwy. and Webster Ave., Parkville. Rev. John Whiting Crowell, Rector.

St. Jude's, 55th St. and Fourteenth Ave.

St. Luke's, Clinton Ave. near Fulton.

St. Lydia's, Glenmore Ave. and Crystal St. Rev. Howard S. Frazer, Rector.

St. Margaret's Chapel, 1051 42d St.

St. Mark's, Eastern Pkwy. and Brooklyn Ave. Rev. Arthur L. Charles, Rector, 309 Brooklyn Ave.

St. Mark's, 230 Adelphi St., near De Kalb Ave.

St. Martin's, 293 President, near Smith St. Rev. F. W. Davis, Rector.

St. Mary's, cor. Classon and Willoughby Aves. Rev. J. Clarence Jones, Ph.D., Rector, 230 Classon Ave.

St. Mary's Syrian Antiochean, State St. and Boerum Pl.

St. Matthew, Tompkins Ave. and McDonough St. Rev. Frederick W. Norris, D.D., Rector, 180 Macon St.

St. Michael's, 217 High St.

St. Paul's, Church Ave. and St. Paul's Place.

St. Paul's, Clinton, cor. Carroll St.

St. Peter's, State St. near Bond.

St. Philip's (Colored), 1606-1610 Dean St., near Troy Ave. Rev. N. Peterson Boyd, Rector.

St. Simon's, Ave. K and East 12th St.

St. Stephen's, cor. Patchen and Jefferson Aves. Rev. Herbert J. Glover, Rector, 547 Madison St.

St. Thomas', Bushwick Ave., cor. Cooper.

St. Timothy's, Howard Ave. near Atlantic.

Trinity, cor. Arlington and Schenck Aves. Rev. Jacob Probst, Rector.

Queens

All Saints, Bayside. Rev. Charles A. Brown, Rector.

All Saints, Richmond Hill, Lefferts Ave., near Broadway.

Annunciation, Glendale, Cooper and Webster Aves. Rev. Wm. P. S. Lander, Rector.

Epiphany, Ozone Park, Kimball and McCormick Aves.

Grace, 41st St., Corona.

Grace, 315 Fulton St., Jamaica.

Grace, 11th Ave. and 18th St., Whitestone.

Grace Chapel, 89 Merrick Road.

Resurrection, Richmond Hill. Rev. Wm. P. Evans, Rector, 401 Church St.

St. Andre's Mission, 204 17th Ave., Astoria.

St. Andrew's-by-the-Sea, Belle Harbor.

St. Gabriel's, Hollis, Woodhull Ave.

St. George's, Flushing, Main, and Locust Sts. Rev. H. D. Waller, Rector, 45 Locust St.

St. George's, Franklin St., Astoria.

St. James's, Elmhurst, Broadway and Corona Ave. Rev. Edward M. McGuffey, Rector.

St. John's, Far Rockaway, Mott Ave., near Central Ave. Rev. W. A. Sparks, Pastor.

St. John's, Flushing, Sanford, and Wilson Aves.

St. John's, Long Island City, 10th St. and Van Alst Ave.

St. Joseph's, Franklin Ave., Queens.

St. Luke's, Forest Hills.

St. Mary's Chapel, Laurel Hill.

St. Mary's, Van Wyck Ave.

St. Matthew's, Brooklyn Manor, 475 96th St.

St. Paul's Chapel, College Point, First Ave. and 13th St. Rev. B. Mottram, Vicar, 25 South 13th St.

St. Paul's, Striker Ave. and 8th St., Woodside.

St. Peter's, Rosedale.

St. Saviour's, Maspeth.

St. Stephen's, Grand and N. 1st St., Jamaica.

St. Thomas', Vernon Ave., Ravenswood.

Richmond

All Saints, Mariner's Harbor. Rev. Albert Ohse, Pastor.

Ascension, West New Brighton.

Christ, Franklin Ave. and 2d St., New Brighton.

Holy Comforter, Eltingsville, S. I.

Holy Redeemer Italian Church, Port Richmond (Protestant Episcopal Diocese of New York), 45 Jewett Ave. Rev. Carmelo Di Sano, Pastor.

St. Andrew's, Richmond, Richmond Rd.

St. John's, New York Ave., Clifton.

St. Luke's, Shore Road and St. Luke's Ave., Rossville.

St. Mary's, West New Brighton, Castleton and Davis Aves. Rev. Francis L. Frost, Rector.

St. Paul's Memorial, 93 St. Paul's Ave.

St. Simon's Chapel, Concord, 44 Price St. Rev. Wm. Winter Mix, Rector.

Trinity, New Dorp, 3d St.

Zion, Douglaston.

REFORMED CHURCH IN AMERICA

Manhattan

Bethany Memorial, see under COLLEGIATE.

Collegiate (The Minister, Elders and Deacons of the Reformed Protestant Dutch Church of the City of New York; org. 1628, chartered 1696). In ecclesiastical connection with the Reformed Church in America. Office, 113 Fulton St., N.Y.C. Maintains the following places of worship, where the customary Church activities are supported and conducted to meet the varied conditions and needs of the several congregations. Religious, social, and welfare societies, organizations and classes, including Foreign and Domestic Missionary Societies, Bible study, Christian Endeavor Societies, Brotherhood of Andrew and Philip, Sewing Society, Ladies' Employment Society, Industrial School, Red Cross Work, Fresh Air Work, Vocal Union, Gymnasiums, Reading and Social rooms, Luncheon Club, and others.

1. Collegiate (MIDDLE), Second Ave. and 7th St. Rev. Edgar Franklin Romig, Pastor; Miss Georgia Brainard, visitor, 50 7th St. Sunday services: 11 A. M. and 8 P. M.; Sunday-school at 9.30 A. M.; prayer meeting, Wednesday at 8 P. M.

2. Collegiate (MARBLE), Fifth Ave. and 29th St. Rev. David James Burrell, D.D., LL.D., Minister, 1 West 29th St.; Rev. Daniel A. Poling, LL.D., Associate; Rev. Oliver Paul Barnhill, D.D., Assistant, 1 West 29th St.; Harry A. Kinports, Director of Church Activities; Miss Merce E. Boyer, Secretary of Young Peoples' Work. Services: Sunday, 11 A. M. and 8 P. M.; Sunday-school, 9.45 A. M.; Bible Class, 10 A. M. Christian Endeavor, 7 P. M.; prayer meeting Wednesday, 8 P. M.

SUNSHINE MISSION (incorp.), 550 West 40th St. Rev. Harry W. Murphy, Sunday services, 8 P. M.; Sunday-school, 3 P. M.; Christian Endeavor, 7 P. M.; prayer meeting, Friday, 8 P. M.

3. Collegiate (ST. NICHOLAS), Fifth Ave. and 48th St. Rev. Malcolm James MacLeod, D.D., Minister, Cedar Knolls, Bronxville, N. Y.; Rev. Robert W. Courtney, Assistant, 1 West 48th St. Sunday services, 11 A. M. and 8 P. M.; Sunday-school at 9.45 A. M.; Bible Classes, 10 A. M.; prayer meeting, Wednesday, 8.15 P. M. Parish House, 16 West 48th St.

FAITH MISSION, 241 West 60th St. Rev. Thomas H. Johnson, Superintendent; Sunday services, 7.45 P. M.; Sunday-school, 2.30 P. M.; prayer meeting, Thursday, 8 P. M.

4. Collegiate (WEST END), West End Ave. and 77th St. Rev. Henry Everston Cobb, D.D., Minister, 370 West End Ave.; Rev. Thomas McBride Nichols, Assistant, 368 West End Ave. Sunday services: 11 A. M. and 4.30 P. M.; Bible School, 9.45 A. M.; prayer meeting, Wednesday, 8 P. M.

5. Collegiate (FORT WASHINGTON), 181st St. and Fort Washington Ave. Rev. Irving Husted Berg, D.D., Minister, 415 Fort Washington Ave.; Rev. C. Willard Cross, Assistant, 729 West 181st St. Sunday services, 11 A. M. and 8 P. M.; Sunday-school 9.55 A. M.; prayer meeting, Wednesday, 8 P. M.

6. Collegiate (NORTH CHURCH CHAPEL), 113 Fulton St. Prayer meeting, Rev. George H. Dowkontt, supt. (J. C. Lanphier, Founder and Former Leader). Daily noon-day prayer meeting.

The first daily noon prayer meeting. Visitors invited.

7. Collegiate (KNOX MEMORIAL), 405–409 West 41st St. Rev. Edward G. W. Meury, D.D., in charge, 405 W. 41st St.; Miss Anna B. Bisbee, visitor. Sunday service at 11 A. M. and 8 P. M.; Sunday-school, 2.30 P. M., in French at 2.30 P. M.; Knox Memorial Bible Class, 3 P. M.; service in French, 3.45 P. M.; Children's Prayer Meeting, 7.15 P. M.; service in Italian, 3.45 P. M. first Sunday. Prayer meeting, Wednesday, 8 P. M.; Waldensian prayer meeting in Italian and French, Thursday, 8 P. M.; Friday Bible Training School and Kindergarten, 4.30 P. M.

8. Collegiate (VERMILYE CHAPEL), 416 West 54th St. (Helping Hand Bldg.). Rev. Winfred R. Ackert in charge; Miss A. A. Woodburn, visitors; Sunday services, 11 A. M. and 8 P. M.; Sunday-school, 9.30 A. M.; prayer meeting, Wednesday, 8 P. M.

COLLEGIATE SCHOOL (org. 1633–1638), 241–243 West 77th St. Maintained by the Collegiate Reformed Church. Arthur F. Warren, A.B., head master. A day school with classical, intermediate, and primary departments and courses in manual training.

9. Collegiate (BETHANY MEMORIAL), 400 East 67th St. Rev. A. B. Churchman, Pastor.

Elmendorf Chapel, 171 East 121st St., near Third Ave.

Evangelical, 351 East 68th St.

First Magyar (Hungarian), 346 East 69th St.

Fourth (German), 410 West 45th St.

German Evangelical, 351–353 East 68th St.

German Evangelical, Ave. B and 5th St. See TRINITY, of Brooklyn.

Grace, Seventh Ave. and 54th St.

Hamilton Grange, Convent Ave. and West 149th St.

Harlem, Lenox Ave. and 123d St. See also in Alphabetical List.

Manor Church, 348–350 West 26th St.

Second Reformed, 306 West 122d St.

Third, 327 West 33d St. Rev. F. M. Foster, Ph.D., Pastor, 305 West 29th St.

Bronx

Anderson Memorial in Belmont, 673 East 183d St., cor. Cambreling Ave. Rev. John A. de Boer, Pastor.

Church of the Comforter, 279 East 162d St. Rev. R. H. Maccrady, Ph.D., Pastor.

Fordham Manor, Kingsbridge Rd. and University Ave. Rev. J. M. Hodson, Pastor, 2505 Davidson Ave.

Mott Haven, 146th St. near Third Ave. Rev. Oscar M. Voorhees, D.D., Pastor, 350 East 146th St.

Union, of High Bridge, Ogden Ave., near 169th St. Rev. Daniel G. Verwey, Pastor, 1176 Woodycrest Ave., Bronx.

West Farms, 771 Fairmount Pl. Rev. Wm. N. MacNeill, Pastor.

Zion (German and English), 1288 Stebbins Ave. Rev. A. F. Hahn, Pastor.

Brooklyn

Brooklyn, Monroe St., bet. Throop and Sumner Aves.

Church of Jesus, 64-66 Menehan St. Rev. Christian Oswald, 79 Harman St.

Church on the Heights, Pierrepont near Henry St.

Dutch Evangelical, Canarsie, L. I. Conklin Ave. and East 93rd St. Rev. J. Meier, Pastor.

Edgewood (Dutch), cor. 53d St. and Fourteenth Ave.

First (Dutch), Seventh Ave. and Carroll St. Rev. John W. Van Zanten, Pastor.

Flatbush, cor. Flatbush and Church Aves.

Flatlands, Kouwenhoven Pl. and East 40th St.

Grace, Lincoln Road and Bedford Ave.

Gravesend, 145 Neck Road.

Greenwood Heights, 709 45th St. and Seventh Ave.

Kent Street, 149 Kent St., near Manhattan Ave.

New Brooklyn (German), 1062 Herkimer St., and Dewey Place. Rev. Frederick C. Erhardt, Pastor.

New Lots, New Lots Road and Schenk Ave.

New Utrecht, Eighteenth Ave., 83d and 84th Sts.

Ocean Hill, cor. Herkimer St. and Hopkinson Ave. Rev. Andrew Hageman, Minister, 1239 Herkimer St.

Old First on Park Slope. See First.

Second of Flatbush, Church and Bedford Aves. Rev. Henry J. Wahl, Pastor.

South, Fourth Ave., cor. 55th St. Rev. R. A. Watson, Pastor, 461 56th St.

South Bushwick, Bushwick Ave., cor. Himrod St. Rev. Andrew J. Meyer, Minister.

St. Petri. See TRINITY.

Trinity (St. Petri German Evangelical and Ave. B Evangelical, N. Y., combined), Union Ave. and Scholes St. Rev. George G. Wacker, Pastor, 144 Penn St.

Twelfth Street, near Fifth Ave. Rev. Dr. John C. Rauscher, Pastor, 136 Prospect Park West.

Woodlawn, East 9th St., between Aves. M and N. Rev. John G. Addy, Pastor, 1460 East 10th St.

Queens

Astoria, Long Island City, 73 Remsen St. Rev. George S. Bolsterle, Pastor.

East New York, Woodhaven. Rev. Floyd L. Cornish, Pastor.

First, Newtown, Broadway, cor. Corona Ave., Elmhurst, L. I.

First German Evangelical, Far Rockaway.

First, New Hyde Park.

Flushing, Bowne Ave. and Amity, Flushing.

Forest Park, Hillside Ave. and Ferry, Woodhaven.

German Evangelical, Jamaica, 120 Herriman Ave. Rev. Frederick Stoebener, Pastor.

German Evangelical, Ridgewood, 601–603 Onderdonk Ave. Rev. M. J. H. Walenta, Pastor.

Jamaica (Dutch), Fulton and Ray Sts., Jamaica.

Ridgewood (Dutch), Evergreen, Decatur St., near Myrtle Ave. Rev. G. R. Israel, Pastor, 1839 Decatur St.

St. Paul's, Herriman and Hillside Ave., Jamaica.

Second German, Astoria, 526 Second Ave., between Grand and Jamaica Aves. Rev. C. D. F. Steinführer, D.D., Pastor.

Steinway, Long Island City, 770 Eleventh Ave. Rev. Preston F. Strauss, Pastor.

Sunnyside, Long Island City, 310 Buckley St.

Winfield, Winfield Junction, Lee and Woodside Aves. Rev. Wm. Ten Eyck Adams, Pastor, 19 Lenox Ave., Winfield.

Zion, Elmhurst, Horton St. Rev. John G. Bosshart, Pastor.

Richmond

Brighton Heights, Tompkins Ave. and Ft. Place.

Huguenot (Dutch), Huguenot Park, Amboy Rd.

Mariner's Harbor, Lockman Ave. and Richmond Terr.

St. Peter's Evangelical (Dutch), Kreischerville. Rev. Jacob Ganss, Ph.D., Pastor.

Staten Island, Richmond Ave., Port Richmond.

Reformed Church in the U. S.

Manhattan

Fourth (German), 410-12 West 45th St.

Bronx

St. Paul's, 606-612 East 141st St.

Brooklyn

Christ, 54 Wyona St.

Emanuel, 396 Graham Ave. Rev. W. Walenta, Pastor.

St. Luke's, 55 Sutton St. Rev. H. Bram, Pastor, 60 Hausman St.

St. Mark's, 601 Onderdonk Ave. Rev. M. J. H. Walenta, Pastor, 1739 Grove St.

Queens

Woodhaven, Woodhaven Ave., near Ridgewood Aves. Rev. F. W. A. Sawitzky, Pastor.

Reformed Episcopal Churches

First, Y. W. C. A. Building, Lexington Ave. and 53rd St.

Redemption, 602 Leonard St., Brooklyn. Rev. William H. Dongan, Pastor, 99 West Fillmore Ave., Corona, N. Y.

Roman Catholic Churches

Manhattan

All Saints', 129th St. and Madison Ave. Rt. Rev. Mgr. J. W. Power, Rector.

Annunciation, Convent Ave. and 131st St. Rt. Rev. Mgr. Wm. L. Penny, Rector.

Ascension, 215-219 West 107th St. Rt. Rev. Mgr. Edwin M. Sweeny.

Assumption (German), 427 West 49th St. Rev. James Veit, Rector.

Blessed Sacrament, 148-166 West 71st St., cor. Broadway. Rt. Rev. Mgr. Wm. J. Guinan, Rector.

City Hospital Chapel, Blackwell's Island. Attended by Jesuit Fathers.

Corpus Christi, 535 West 121st St. Rev. John H. Dooley, Rector; Rev. B. de Negro, Rev. John J. Mallon, Rev. E. J. Power, Assistants.

Epiphany, 373-375 Second Ave. Rev. P. J. Harold, Rector.

See also Alphabetical List.

Good Shepherd, Broadway and 207th St. Rev. Thomas J. McNichol, Rector.

Guardian Angel, 511–515 West 23d St. Rev. James F. Raywood, Rector.

Holy Cross, 331–337 West 42d St. Rev. Joseph F. Flannelly, Rector.

Holy Innocents, 126 West 37th St. Rev. Thomas J. Lynch, Rector.

Holy Name of Jesus, Amsterdam Ave. and West 96th St. Rev. James B. Curry, Pastor, 207 West 96th St.

Holy Name Mission, 319 Bowery. Rev. Wm. J. Rafter. See Alphabetical List.

Holy Rosary, 440–442 East 119th St. Rev. Thomas F. Kane, Rector.

Holy Trinity, 205–211 West 82d St. Rev. John G. McCormick.

Immaculate Conception, 503–513 East 14th St. Rev. T. W. Tierney, Rector, 503 East 14th St.; Rev. P. S. Masterson, Rev. Bernard J. Rourke.

IMMACULATE CONCEPTION CHAPEL FOR ITALIANS, 511–513 East 14th St. Attended by priests above.

Incarnation, West 175th St., between St. Nicholas and Audubon Aves. Rev. Joseph F. Delany, D.D.

Mary Help of Christians, 429 East 12th St. Rev. Pasqual Beccaria, Rector. Maintains also: Keating Day Nursery, 431 East 12th St. See also in Alphabetical List.

Most Holy and Immaculate Heart of Mary (Mission of the Immaculate Virgin), 381 Lafayette St. Rev. Mallick J. Fitzpatrick, Director.

Most Precious Blood, 113–117 Baxter St. Rev. Pacifico Savastano, Rector.

Nativity, 48 Second Ave. Rev. Daniel J. Quinn.

Notre Dame, 40 Morningside Drive. Rev. A. N. Arcibal, Rector.

Our Lady of Angels, 228 East 113th St. Rev. Fulgentius Brem, Pastor.

Our Lady of Esperanza, 156th St west of Broadway, for the Spanish speaking people in New York. Rev. Adrian Buission, A.A., Rector, 559 West 156th St.; Rev. Francisco Garcia, Assistant.

Our Lady of Good Counsel, 232–238 East 90th St. Rt. Rev. James N. Connolly, Rector.

Our Lady of Grace, 14 Stanton St. Rev. C. Pinnola, Rector.

Our Lady of Guadaloupe, 229 West 14th St. Rev. O. Caron, Pastor.

Our Lady of Loretto, 333 Elizabeth St., between Houston and Bleecker Sts. Rev. Joseph Silipiqui, Rector. Attached to the Mission are the following:

BARAT SETTLEMENT HOUSE, 223 Chrystie St.

BARAT DAY NURSERY, 221 Chrystie St.

SEVEN SPRINGS SUMMER HOME, Monroe, N. Y.

See also in Alphabetical List.

Our Lady of Lourdes, West 142d St., between Amsterdam and Convent Aves. Rev. J. H. McMahon, Rev. David W. Petry, Rev. Martin E. Fahy.

Our Lady of Mt. Carmel (Italian and English), 447 East 115th St., near Pleasant Ave. Rev. Gaspar Dalia, Rector.

ST. JOSEPH'S SETTLEMENT, 448–450 East 116th St. (tel. Harlem 5655).

MT. CARMEL SETTLEMENT, 307 East 112th St. See Alphabetical List.

Our Lady of Perpetual Help (Bohemian and English), 323 East 61st St. Rev. James Hayes, C.SS.R., Pastor.

Our Lady of Pompeii, 210–214 Bleecker St., of the Missionaries of St. Charles Borromeo. Rev. Anthony Demo, Pastor.

Our Lady of the Rosary, Mission, 7 State St. Rev. M. J. Henry.

Our Lady of the Scapular of Mt. Carmel, 29th St., between First and Second Aves. Rev. Denis O'Connor, Prior.

Our Lady of Sorrows, 107 Pitt St., near Stanton. Rev. Venantius Buessing, Rector.

Our Lady of Vilna, 568–570 Broome St. Rev. Jos. Shestokas.

Resurrection, 282 West 151st St. Rev. Thomas F. Murphy.

Sacred Heart of Jesus, 449–455 West 51st St. Rt. Rev. Joseph F. Mooney.

St. Agnes's, 145 East 43d St. Rt. Rev. Henry A. Brann, D.D., 141 East 43d St. See also ST. AGNES'S DAY NURSERY in Alphabetical List.

St. Aloysius', 209–217 West 132d St. Rev. Patrick J. Minogue.

St. Alphonsus', 312 West Broadway. Rev. J. J. Frawley, C.SS.R., Rector.

St. Ambrose's, 539 West 54th St. Rev. Peter F. Guinevan.

St. Andrew's, Duane St. and City Hall Pl. Very Rev. Mgr. Luke J. Evers.

St. Ann's, 112–116 East 12th St. Rev. Dr. Wm. J. Sinnott, Rector.

St. Ann's (Italian), 308–310 East 110th St. Rev. Eucherio Perini, Rector.

St. Anthony of Padua, 153–157 Sullivan St. Rev. A. Silvioni.

St. Benedict the Moor (Colored), 342–344 West 53d St. Rev. Thomas M. O'Keefe, 264 West 53d St. The Church is given over entirely to serve the colored Catholics of New York City. These people are free to attend any Catholic Church they find the most convenient, but St. Benedict's is specially their own. See also ST. BENEDICT'S HOME FOR DESTITUTE COLORED CHILDREN in the Alphabetical List.

St. Bernard's, 332 West 14th St. Rev. Joseph F. Smith, Rector.

St. Boniface (German and English), 882 Second Ave., cor. 47th St. Rev. Francis X. E. Albert, Ph.D., Rector.

ST. ANTHONY'S CHAPEL (Italian), 312 East 47th St. Rev. Daniel De Nonno, Director.

St. Brigid's, 121–123 Ave. B. Rev. Phillip J. Magrath, Rector.

St. Catherine of Genoa, 502–504 West 153d St. Rev. P. E. McCorry.

St. Catherine of Sienna, 420 East 69th St. Very Rev. Ignatius Smith, Pastor.

St. Cecilia's, 118–124 East 106th St. Rt. Rev. Michael J. Phelan.

St. Charles Borromeo, 213–219 West 141st St., near Seventh Ave. Rt. Rev. Francis H. Wall, D.D., 211 West 141st St.

St. Clare's, 436–438 West 36th St. Rev. M. Sergenti, O.F.M., Pastor.

St. Clemens', 408–412 West 40th St. Rev. Joseph Letanche.

St. Columba's, 337–341 West 25th St. Rev. Thomas A. Thornton, Rector.

SS. Cyril and Methodius, 552 West 50th St. Rev. Irenaeus Petricak, Rector, 552 West 50th St.

St. Elizabeth's, 187th St. and Broadway. Rectory, 4381 Broadway. Rev. William J. Stewart, Pastor. Rev. Charles J. Finnegan, Rev. Cornelius V. Hayes, Rev. Charlton J. H. Burns, Assistants.

St. Elizabeth of Hungary, 215 East 83d St. Rev. M. A. Tamassy.

St. Francis of Assisi, 141 West 31st St. Rev. Anselm Kennedy.

St. Francis de Sales, East 96th St. betweeen Lexington and Park Aves. Rev. John F. Brady.

St. Francis Xavier's, 42–48 West 16th St. Rev. Patrick J. Casey, Pastor.

St. Gabriel's, 310–314 East 37th St. Rev. Wm. Livingston.

St. Gregory, 138–144 West 90th St. Rev. Wm. F. Hughes, Pastor.

St. Ignatius Loyola's, Park Ave. and East 84th St. Rev. James M. Kilroy, Pastor.

St. Ignatius Loyola Day Nursery, 240–242 East 84th St. See also in Alphabetical List.

St. James, 28–32 James St. Rev. Vincent de P. McGean.

St. Jean Baptiste (Canadian), cor Lexington Ave. and 76th St. Rev. Arthur Letellier, S.S.S., Rector; Rev. J. Alfred Pauze, S.S.S.; Rev. John Graham, S.S.S. Residence, 184 East 76th St.

St. Joachim (Italian), 22–26 Roosevelt St. Rev. V. Jannuzzi, D.D., I.S.C. B., Rector; Senior Assistant, Rev. V. E. Cangiano, I.S.C.B., Rev. Mastopietre.

Chapel, St. Joseph, 64 Catherine St. See also Alphabetical List.

St. John the Baptist (German), 211 West 30th St. Rev. Ludger Werth, Rector.

St. John the Evangelist, 55th St. and First Ave. Rt. Rev. Mgr. James J. Flood.

St. John the Martyr (Bohemian), 250–254 East 72d St. Rev. John A. Lane.

St. John of Nepomuk (Slovak), 350–354 East 57th St. Rev. Stephen Krasula, Rector.

St. Joseph's, 61–65 Sixth Ave. Rt. Rev. Mgr. John Edwards, V. G., Pastor.

St. Joseph's (German), 404–418 East 87th St. Rt. Rev. Mgr. Gallus Bruder.

St. Joseph's of the Holy Family (German), West 125th St. and Morningside Ave. Rev. Gerard H. Huntman, Pastor.

St. Joseph's, 57 Washington St. Rev. Francis Wakim, Rector.

St. Joseph's Italian Church (formerly St. Rocco's Chapel), 64 Catherine St.

St. Leo's, 11 East 28th St. Attended from St. Stephen's.

St. Lucy's, 336–342 East 104th St. Rev. P. J. Lennon.

St. Malachy's, 239 West 49th St.

St. Mark the Evangelist (Colored), 61–63 West 138th St. Rev. Chris. J. Plunkett.

St. Mary's, cor. Grand and Ridge Sts. Rev. James M. Byrnes.

St. Mary's, 225–227 East 13th St.

St. Mary Magdalene's, 531 East 17th St. Rev. A. L. Strube.

St. Matthew's, 215–217 West 67th St. Rev. William F. Meehan, Rector.

St. Michael's, 424 West 34th St. Rev. Wm. F. Dougherty. See also St. Michael's Home for Destitute Children, in Alphabetical List.

St. Monica's, 405–411 East 79th St. Rev. Arthur J. Kenny.

St. Nicholas' (German), 135 2d St., between First Ave. and Ave. A. Rev. John A. Nageleisen, P.R. See also in Alphabetical List.

St. Patrick's Cathedral, Fifth Ave., between 50th and 51st Sts. Rt. Rev. Mgr. M. J. Lavelle, Rector. See also Alphabetical List.

St. Patrick's Church (Old Cathedral). Legal title: Trustees of St. Patrick's Cathedral in the City of New York (est. 1809, incorp. 1817). Mott, Mulberry, and Prince Sts. The priests working in the parish are: Rt. Rev. John F. Kearney, Rector; Revs. Dominic Epifanio, Jerome Pasquarelli, D.D., John A. Walsh, D.D., residence, 263 Mulberry St. See also Alphabetical List.

St. Paul's, 121 East 117th St. Rt. Rev. John McQuirk, D.D., LL.D., 113 East 117th St. See also in Alphabetical List.

St. Paul the Apostle (Paulist Fathers), Columbus Ave., cor. West 60th St. Very Rev. Thomas F. Burke, C.S.P., 415 West 59th St. Legal title: The Missionary Society of St. Paul the Apostle in the State of New York. For activities see in Alphabetical List.

St. Peter's, 18-22 Barclay St. Rt. Rev. James H. McGean, Rector, 31 Barclay St.

St. Raphael's, 504-510 West 41st St., between Tenth and Eleventh Aves. Rev. Michael J. Duffy, Rector.

St. Rose of Lima's, 502-508 West 165th St. Rev. John R. Mahony, Rector.

St. Rose's, 34-36 Cannon St. Rev. Peter McNamee, Rector.

St. Stanislaus', 103-107 7th St. Rev. Ignatius Bialdyga, 109 7th St.

St. Stephen's, 147-149 East 28th St., 144-150 East 29th St. Rev. Francis P. J. Cummings; Rev. Edwin M. Sinnott, Wm. A. Fogarty, Francis A. Fadden, Robert F. Keegan, Assistant Priests.

St. Stephen of Hungary, 420 East 14th St. Rev. John Froelich.

St. Teresa's, 16-18 Rutgers St. Rev. James T. McEntyre.

St. Thomas the Apostle, 118th St. and St. Nicholas Ave. Rev. John B. McGrath, Pastor, 262 West 118th St.

St. Veronica's, 149-155 Christopher St. Rev. Patrick H. Drain.

St. Vincent de Paul's (French), 127 West 23d St. Rev. Theophilus Wucker.

St. Vincent Ferrer's, Lexington Ave. and 66th St. Very Rev. J. R. Heffernan, O. P.

Transfiguration (Italian and English), Mott and Park Sts. Rev. John Voghera, Rector.

Bronx

Holy Family, Castle Hill Ave., Unionport, Bronx. Rectory, 1071 Castle Hill Ave. Rev. Urban C. Nageleisen, Rector; Rev. Patrick D. McLoughlin, Assistant.

Holy Spirit, Morris Heights, Burnside Ave. Rev. John D. Roach, Rector.

Immaculate Conception (Italian), 210th St. and Holland Ave., Williamsbridge. Rev. R. Tonini, Rector.

Immaculate Conception, B.V.M. (German and English), Melrose, 389 East 150th St., cor. Melrose Ave. Rev. Wm. Tewes, C.S.S.R., Rector.

Our Lady of Mercy, Fordham, 2500 Marion Ave. Rev. Patrick N. Breslin, Rector.

Our Lady of Mt. Carmel, 187th St. and Belmont Ave. Rev. Joseph Caffuzzi.

Our Lady of Pity, East 151st St. Rev. Francis Oppici, O.F.M.

Our Lady of Solace, White Plains Rd. and Van Nest Ave. Rev. D. J. Curley, Pastor; Rev. John J. Stanley, Assistant.

Our Lady of Victory, 171st St. and Webster Ave. Rev. B. F. Galligan.

Our Saviour, 2317 Washington Ave. Rev. Francis P. Duffy, D.D., Pastor; Rev. Francis J. Prunty, Rev. Joseph A. Donohue, Assistants.

Sacred Heart, Shakespeare Ave., High Bridge. Rev. John J. Lennon.

St. Adalbert's, East 156th St., between Elton and Melrose Aves. Rev. Joseph Zaniewicz.

St. Angela Merci's, Morris Ave. and 163d St. Rev. John J. Harrington, Rector.

St. Anselm's, Tinton Ave., between East 152d and 153d Sts. Very Rev. Fr. Bernard, O.S.B.

St. Anthony's, cor. Commonwealth Ave. and Mansion St. Rev. P. Maltese.

St. Anthony of Padua (English and German), East 166th St., cor. Prospect Ave. Rev. Joseph F. Rummel, Rector.

St. Athanasius, 878 Tiffany St. Rev. H. F. Xavier, Rector.

St. Augustine's, 167th St., between Franklin and Fulton Aves. Rev. John J. McCabe, Rector.

St. Barnabas', Woodlawn and McLean Heights, Woodlawn. Rev. M. A. Reilly, Rector.

St. Brendan's, cor. 207th St. and Perry Ave. Rev. Wm. A. Courtney, Rector.

St. Francis of Rome, 88 Richardson Ave., Wakefield. Rev. Francis P. Moore, Rector.

St. Jerome's, Alexander Ave., between 137th and 138th Sts. Rev. George T. Donlin, Rector.

St. John Chrysostom's, East 167th St. and Hoe Ave. Rev. Bernard F. Brady, Rector.

St. John's, Kingsbridge, 230th St. and Kingsbridge Ave. Rev. Francis X. Kelly, Rector.

St. Joseph's, Tremont, Bathgate Ave. and 177th St. Rev. Patrick Morris.

St. Luke's, East 138th St., between St. Ann and Cypress Aves. Very Rev. Mgr. D. J. McMackin.

St. Margaret's, Riverdale. Rev. James N. Aylward, Rector.

St. Martin of Tours, East 182d and Grove Sts. Rev. Edw. J. O'Gorman.

St. Mary, Star of the Sea, 600 City Island Ave., City Island. Rev. A. C. Mearns, Rector.

St. Mary's, 215th St. and White Plains Rd. Rev. Henry P. Tracy, D.D.

St. Nicholas of Tolentine, Andrews Ave. and Fordham Rd. Rev. B. J. Zeiser, O.S.A.

SS. Peter and Paul, St. Ann's Ave. and East 159th St. Rev. Thomas F. Duffy, Rector.

St. Philip Neri, 2031 Grand Concourse. Very Rev. Daniel Burke, D.D.

St. Pius', 416–418 East 145th St. Rev. Francis M. Fagan.

St. Raymond's, 2230 Walker Ave., Westchester. Rt. Rev. Mgr. Edward McKenna.

St. Rita of Cascia, East 145th St. and College Ave. Rev. James P. O'Brien.

St. Roch's, East 150th St., between Jackson and Concord Aves. Rev. Costantino Cassaneti, Rector.

St. Thomas Aquinas', 1903–1913 Daly Ave. Rev. D. F. Coyle, Pastor.

St. Valentine's, Williamsbridge, East 221st St. Rev. Charles Czarkowski.

Brooklyn

All Saints' (German), 115 Throop Ave. Rt. Rev. Geo. Kaupert, V.G.

Annunciation of the Blessed Virgin (German), 259 North 5th St. Rev. N. Petkus.

Assumption of the Blessed Virgin Mary, 64 Middagh St. Rev. Wm. B. Farrell.

Blessed Sacrament, 200 Euclid Ave. Rev. John Kiely.

Epiphany, 96 South 9th St. Rev. E. A. Duffy.

Fourteen Holy Martyrs, Central Ave. and Covert St. Rev. Bernard F. Kurz.

Guardian Angel, 2978 Ocean Pkwy. Rev. Joseph F. Conway.

Holy Cross Church, 2530 Church Ave. Rt. Rev. Mgr. John T. Woods.

Holy Family, 205 14th St. Rev. John S. Gresser.

Holy Family, Conklin and Rockaway Aves. Rev. John Reynolds.

Holy Family, (Slovak), 21 Nassau Ave. Rev. Kazimir Zabrajsek, O.F.M.

Holy Innocents, 1718 Beverly Rd. Rev. Francis J. McMurray.

Holy Name, 245 Prospect Park West. Rev. Charles Vitta.

Holy Rosary, 141 Chauncey St. Rev. John McEnroe.

Holy Trinity (German), 138 Montrose Ave. Rev. George A. Metzger.

Immaculate Conception of the Blessed Virgin Mary, 72 Maujer St. Rev. Thomas F. Horan.

Immaculate Heart of Mary, 119 East 4th St. Rev. Matthew J. Tierney.

Nativity of Our Blessed Lord, 20 Madison Ave. Rev. John L. Belford, D.D.

Our Lady of Angels, Fourth Ave. and 73d St. Rev. Matthew J. Flynn.

Our Lady of Charity (Italian), 1665 Dean St. Rev. Louis Caporaso.

Our Lady of Consolation (Polish), 184 Metropolitan Ave. Rev. Aleius Jarka.

Our Lady of Czestochowa (Polish), 183 25th St. Rev. Boleslaus Puchalski.

Our Lady of Good Counsel, 915 Putnam Ave. Rev. Peter Donohoe.

Our Lady of Guadaloupe, 7201 Fifteenth Ave. Rev. Thomas J. Cloke.

Our Lady of Lebanon (Maronite), 295 Hicks St. Rt. Rev. Mgr. K. Stephen.

Our Lady of Loretto (Italian), 124 Sackman St. Rev. Carmelo A. Russo.

Our Lady of Lourdes, 11 DeSales Pl. Very Rev. James Hanlon, S.P.M.

Our Lady of Mercy, 284 Schermerhorn St. Rev. James McAteer.

Our Lady of the Miraculous Medal, 2453 Ralph St. Rev. John J. Oppel.

Our Lady of Mount Carmel (Italian), 304 North 8th St. Rev. Peter Saponara.

Our Lady of Peace (Italian), Carroll St., near Fourth Ave. Rev. Valerian Pianigiani.

Our Lady of Perpetual Help, 526 59th St. Rev. James Barron, C.S.S.R.

Our Lady of Pilar, 264 Cumberland St. Rev. A. Canas.

Our Lady of the Presentation, 1661 St. Marks Ave. Rev. John I. Whelan, Ph.D.

Our Lady of Refuge, 708 Kenmore Pl. Rev. Robert O'Donovan.

Our Lady of the Rosary of Pompeii, 225 Seigal St. Rev. Ottavio Silvestri.

Our Lady of Solace, 17th St. and Mermaid Ave. Rev. Walter A. Kirwin.

Our Lady of Sorrows, 83 Morgan Ave. Rev. F. X. Wunsch.

Our Lady of Victory, 583 Throop Ave. Rev. James Woods.

Queen of All Saints, 300 Vanderbilt Ave. Rt. Rev. Mons. James J. Coan.

Sacred Heart, 41 Adelphi St. Rev. Thomas J. Leonard.

Sacred Heart of Jesus by the Sea, Manhattan Beach. Rev. Edward A. Wallace.

Sacred Heart (Barren Island) (attended from St. John Cantius), 447 New Jersey Ave. Rev. Theo. Regulski.

Sacred Hearts of Jesus and Mary (Italian), 500 Hicks St. Very Rev. John Vogel, P.S.M.

St. Agatha's, 713 49th St. Rev. Martin Fitzpatrick.

St. Agnes, 417 Sackett St. Rev. James Flynn.

St. Aloysius (German), Onderdonk Ave. and Stanhope St. Rev. John W. Hauptmann.

St. Alphonsus (German), 177 Kent St. Rev. Herman J. Pfeifer, D.D.

St. Ambrose, 222 Tompkins Ave. Rev. Louis M. O. Blaber.

St. Anne's, 251 Front St. Rev. John J. Patterson.

St. Athanasius, 2148 62d St. Rev. Eugene J. Donnelly.

St. Anthony of Padua, 862 Manhattan Ave. Rt. Rev. Mgr. Patrick F. O'Hare, LL.D.

St. Augustine's, 116 Sixth Ave. Rt. Rev. Mgr. Ed. W. McCarty, LL.D.

St. Barbara's, 307 Central Ave. Rev. James J. Kuntz.

St. Benedict's (German), 927 Herkimer St. Rev. Joseph Traenkle.

St. Bernard's, 651 Hicks St. Rev. Charles W. Hamma.

St. Blaise (Italian), 375 Hawthorne St. Rev. Vincent Di Giovanni.

St. Boniface's (German), 109 Willoughby St. Rev. Martin Lang.

St. Brenden's, 1525 East 12th St. Rev. Timothy A. Hickey.

St. Brigid's, 409 Linden St. Rev. John B. C. York.

St. Casimir's (Polish), 392 Adelphi St. Rev. Gervase Kubec.

St. Catherine of Alexandria, 1119 41st St. Rev. John J. O'Neill.

St. Catherine of Genoa, 520 Linden Ave. Rev. Frederick J. Hentz.

St. Cecilia's, 84 Herbert St. Rt. Rev. Mgr. Edward J. McGoldrick.

St. Charles Borromeo's, 21 Sydney Pl. Rev. Thomas J. O'Brien.

St. Columbkille's, 146 Dupont St. Theodore J. King.

SS. Cyril and Methodius (Polish), 123 Eagle St. Very Rev. Mgr. Emil F. Strenski.

St. Edward's, 108 St. Edward St. Rev. James F. Mealia.

St. Elias (Ruthenian), 624 Leonard St. Rev. Peter P. Keshelak.

St. Finbarr's, 8730 Bay 20th St. Rev. Wm. A. Gardner.

St. Francis De Chantal, 1273 58th St. Rev. Patrick J. O'Loughlin, S.P.M.

St. Francis of Assisi, 319 Maple St. Very Rev. Mgr. Francis X. Ludeke.

St. Francis of Paola (Italian), Old Bushwick Road near Skillman Ave. Rev. Leonarda Russo.

St. Francis Xavier's, 225 Sixth Ave. Very Rev. Mons. David J. Hichey, LL.D.

St. Gabriel's, 749 Linwood St. Rev. Thomas J. Fitzgerald.

St. George's (Lithuanian), 207 York St. Rev. Anthony P. Kodis.

St. Gregory's, 1006 Sterling Pl. Rev. Maurice P. Fitzgerald.

St. Ignatius, 1125 Carroll St. Very Rev. Joseph Farrell, S.J.

St. James', Pro-Cathedral, Cathedral Pl. Very Rev. Mgr. Francis J. O'Hara.

St. Jerome's, 2900 Newkirk Ave. Rev. Thomas F. Lynch.

St. John the Baptist, 75 Lewis Ave. Very Rev. J. W. Moore, C.M., LL.D.

St. John Cantius, 477 New Jersey Ave. Rev. Theodore Regulski.

St. John Evangelist, 250 21st St. Rev. Thomas S. Duhigg.

St. Joseph's, 856 Pacific St. Very Rev. Mgr. Wm. T. McGuirl, LL.D.

St. Leonard of Port Maurice (German), 199 Jefferson St. Rev. George D. Sander.

St. Louis (French), 36 Ellery St. Rev. William T. Conklin.

St. Lucy's (Italian), 802 Kent Ave. Rt. Rev. Mgr. Alphonso Arcese.

St. Malachy's, 129 Van Sicklen Ave. Rev. Daniel F. Cherry.

St. Mark's, 2554 East 14th St. Rev. Daniel J. McCarthy.

St. Martin of Tours, 1288 Hancock St. Rev. James H. Lynch.

St. Mary, Mother of Jesus, 2305 85th St. Rev. Henry F. Murray.

St. Mary of the Angels (Lithuanian), 213 South 4th St. Rev. Sylvester Remeika.

St. Mary, Star of the Sea, 467 Court St. Very Rev. Mgr. James J. Corrigan, D.D.

St. Mary the Virgin (Syrian Creek Melchite), 401 Henry St. Very Rev. Mgr. Paul Sanky.

St. Matthew's, 1123 Eastern Pkwy. Rev. William J. Costello.

St. Matthias, 1861 Catalpa Ave. Rev. Nicholas M. Wagner.

St. Michael Archangel (Italian), 230 Concord St. Rev. Joseph R. Agrella.

St. Michael's, Fourth Ave., 352 42d St. Rev. Patrick J. Cherry.

St. Michael's, 225 Jerome St. Rev. Fulgentius Brem, O.M.

St. Nicholas (German), 26 Olive St. Very Rev. Mgr. John P. Hoffman.

St. Patrick's (Kent Ave.), 285 Willoughby Ave. Rev. John F. Cherry.

St. Patrick's (Fourth Ave.), Fourth Ave. and 96th St. Rev. Jeremiah J. Kent.

St. Paul's, 223 Congress St. Rt. Rev. Mgr. Michael G. Flannery.

St. Peter's, 117 Warren St. Rev. Michael A. Fitzgerald.

SS. Peter and Paul's, 71 South 3d St. Rev. John B. Lyle.

St. Rita's, 259 Essex St. Rev. Marco Simonetti, Rev. Leopold Arcess.

St. Roch's (Italian), 216 27th St. Rev. A. de Donatis.

St. Rosalia's, 1359 63d St. Rev. Locksley A. Appo.

St. Rose of Lima's, 269 Parkville Ave. Rev. James McAleese.

St. Saviour's, 611 Eighth Ave. Rev. James J. Flood.

SS. Simon and Jude's, Van Sicklen St. and Avenue T. Rev. John J. McCarron.

St. Stanislaus' (Scandinavian), 289–15th St. Rev. Frederick Lund.

St. Stanislaus' Kostka's (Polish), 607 Humboldt St. Rev. Leo Wysiecki.

St. Stephen's, 108 Carroll St. Very Rev. Mgr. John G. Fitzgerald.

St. Teresa's, 563 Sterling Pl. Rt. Rev. Mgr. Jos. McNamee.

St. Thomas Aquinas, 249 Ninth St. Rev. James Smyth.

St. Thomas Aquinas, 2000 Flatbush Ave. Rev. Edward Dullea.

St. Vincent de Paul, 167 North 6th St. Rev. John F. Geary.

Transfiguration, 263 Marcy Ave. Very Rev. Mgr. William J. Maguire.

Visitation of the Blessed Virgin Mary, 98 Richards St. Rev. Wm. L. Long.

Queens

Blessed Virgin Mary, Help of Christians, 25 Ramsey St., Winifield. Rev. John F. Naab.

Holy Child Jesus, 404 Chestnut St., Richmond Hill. Rev. Thomas A. Nummey.

Holy Cross (Polish), Maspeth. Rev. Adalbert Nawrocki.

Nativity of Our Blessed Lady (Italian), 4312 Jerome Ave., Ozone Park. Rev. John B. Garbottini, S.M.M.

Our Lady of Mt. Carmel, 31 Newtown Ave., L.I.C. Rev. Charles F. Gibney.

Our Lady of Sorrows, Corona. Rev. Wm. K. Dwyer.

Presentation of the Blessed Virgin Mary, 78 Flushing Ave., Jamaica. Rev. John M. Scheffel.

Sacred Heart, Bayside. Rev. Philip T. Brady.

St. Adalbert's (Polish), Elmhurst. Rev. Anthony Witkowski, O.M.C.

St. Bartholomew's, Elmhurst. Rev. Francis J. Uleau.

St. Benedict Joseph, 932 Church St., Morris Park, Richmond Hill. Rev. Wm. T. Kerwin.

St. Camillus, 273 Boulevard, Rockaway Beach. Rev. Joseph P. Brady.

St. Clement, Baldwin Ave., South Ozone Park. Rev. Anthony E. Bourke.

St. Elizabeth, Atlantic Ave. and Digby St. Rev. Gustave E. Baer.

St. Fedelis, College Point. Rev. Ambrose Schumack.

St. Francis de Sales, Washington and Montauk Aves., Belle Harbor. Rev. James F. Foran.

St. Gerard Majella, Hollis. Rev. Edw. Harley.

St. Jean d'Arc, Jackson Heights. Rev. Ward G. Meehan, Rector.

St. Joachim and Anne, Queens. Rev. Fred W. Dotzauer.

St. Josaphat's, Queens. Rev. B. Malinowski.

St. Joseph's (Polish), Jamaica. Rockaway Rd. Rev. Stanislaus Rysiakiewicz.

St. Joseph's (German), 515 Grand Ave., L.I.C. Rev. Peter Henn.

St. Leo's, Corona. Rev. George Caruana.

St. Luke's, 138 South Eleventh Ave., Whitestone. Rev. Francis J. Dillon.

St. Margaret's, 54 Pullis Ave., Middle Village. Rev. John P. Gopp.

St. Mary Gate of Heaven, 4312 Jerome Ave., Ozone Park. Rev. Peter Vaque, S.M.M.

St. Mary Magdalene, Springfield Gardens. Rev. John Tinney.

St. Mary, Star of the Sea, Far Rockaway. Very Rev. Herbert F. Farrel, V.F.

St. Mary's, 118 5th St., L.I.C. Rev. William J. Dunne.

St. Michael's, Flushing. Rt. Rev. Mgr. Eugene J. Donnelly.

St. Monica's, 42 Washington St. Jamaica. Rev. Richard A. Schenck.

St. Pancras, Myrtle Ave. and Deboo Pl., Glendale. Rev. Francis O. Siegelack.

St. Patrick's, 123 Academy St., L. I.C. Rev. Joseph P. McGinley.

St. Pius (Italian), 38 Wyckoff St., Jamaica. Rev. Mario Legnani.

St. Raphael's, 192 Greenpoint Ave., L.I.C. Rev. Edward A. Holley.

St. Rita's, 466 Blvd., L.I.C. Rev. Michael Heffernan.

St. Rose of Lima, 49 South Fairview Ave., Rockaway Beach. Rev. James J. Bennett.

St. Sebastian's, Woodside. Rev. Michael J. Walsh.

St. Stanislaus', Perry Ave., Maspeth. Rev. Joseph A. Bennett.

St. Thomas Apostle, cor. Syosset and 88th Sts., Woodhaven. Rev. Andrew Klarmann.

St. Virgius, Broad Channel (attended from Rockaway Beach, 49 South Fairview Ave.). Rev. James J. Bennett.

Transfiguration (Lithuanian), 94 Hull Ave., Maspeth. Rev. A. M. Miliukas.

Richmond

Blessed Sacrament, West New Brighton, Manor Rd. Rev. Francis J. Heaney.

Immaculate Conception, Stapleton, Tardee St. Rev. Daniel A. Quinn.

Our Lady of Good Counsel, Tompkinsville, Austin Pl. Rev. Michael A. Ryan.

Our Lady, Help of Christians, Tottenville. Rev. James F. Malloy, Rector.

Our Lady of Mt. Carmel, West New Brighton, Castleton Ave. and Columbia St. Rev. Louis Riccio, Rector.

Our Lady, Star of the Sea, Hugue not Park. Rev. James F. Malloy, Rector.

Sacred Heart, West New Brighton, 981 Castleton Ave. Rev. Thos. J. Heafy, Rector.

St. Adalbert, Port Richmond, John St. (Polish). Rev. Joseph Brzoziewski, Rector.

St. Anthony's, Linoleumville, Decker Ave. Rev. A. Jakubowski, Pastor.

St. Clement's, Mariners Harbor, 111 Van Pelt Ave. Rev. James E Goggin, Pastor.

St. Joachim and Ann, Mount Loretto. Rev. Mallick J. Fitzpatrick.

St. John Baptist de la Salles, Stapleton, Jackson St., cor. Beach. Rev. Joseph Kirschoffer, Rector.

St. Joseph's, Rosebank. Rev. Anthony Catoggio, Rector.

St. Joseph's, Rossville, Washington St. Rev. John T. Kelly.

St. Mary's, Rosebank, New York Ave. Rev. Cornelius J. Cronan, Pastor.

St. Mary of the Assumption, Port Richmond, 2232–2236 Terrace. Rev. Joseph C. Campbell.

St. Patrick's, Richmond, 45 St. Patrick's Pl. Rev. Charles J. Parks, Rector.

St. Peter's, New Brighton. Very Rev. Mgr. Charles A. Cassidy.

SALVATION ARMY CORPS

New York

No.

1. 122 West 14th St.
2. 218–220 East 40th St. (Swedish).
3. 426 Central Park West.
4. 157 East 125th St.
5. 329 East 157th St.
6. 156 East 127th St. (Swedish).

7. 1319 Third Ave.
8. 107 West 135th St. (Colored).
9. 145 S. 9th St.
12. 182 East 124th St. (Finnish).
16. 6 Catherine Slip (Swedish).

Brooklyn and Richmond

1. 143 Ashland Place.
2. 1347 Greene Ave.
3. 543 Atlantic Ave. (Swedish).
5. 92 Summit St.
6. 378 Court St. (Swedish).
7. 768 Decatur St.
8. 1224 Eighth Ave. (Finnish).
9. 166 Calyer St.
10. 518 50th St. (Swedish).
11. Stapleton, Port Richmond, S. I. (Swedish).

THEOSOPHICAL

Central Lodge, Broadway and 67th St., Hotel Maria Antoinette.

New York Lodge (Headquarters), 2228 Broadway at 79th St. Mrs. Emilie B. Welton, pres.

Independent, 124 West 58th St. H. W. Percival, pres.

Brooklyn Lodge, 95 Lafayette Ave., near South Portland. Dr. J. N. Wilkie, pres.

UNITARIAN

Manhattan

All Souls', Fourth Ave. and 20th St. See Alphabetical List.

Community, 61 East 34th St. Rev. John Haynes Holmes, Rev. Harvey Dee Brown, Ministers.

Lenox Avenue, Lenox Ave., cor. W. 121st Sts.

West Side, Broadway and 117th St. Rev. Charles Francis Potter, Pastor.

Brooklyn

Church of the Saviour, cor. Pierrepont St. and Monroe Pl.

Fourth, Beverly Rd. and East 19th St.

Second, cor. Clinton and Congress Sts. Rev. Charles H. Lyttle, Minister.

Unity, cor. Gates Ave. and Irving Place.

Willow Place Chapel, Willow Pl. Rev. William J. Greene, Pastor.

Richmond

Church of the Redeemer, New Brighton, Clinton Ave. and Fillmore St.

UNIVERSALIST

Manhattan

Divine Paternity, or Fourth, Central Park West and 76th St. Rev. Joseph Fort Newton, D.D., Pastor See also Alphabetical List.

First Universalist Mission Society, 247 East 53rd St. See Alphabetical List.

Brooklyn

All Soul's, Ocean and Ditmas Aves. Rev. A. Eugene Bartlett, D.D., Minister.

Church of the Good Tidings, Stuyvesant Ave. and Madison St.

Church of Our Father, Grand Ave., cor. Lefferts Pl. Rev. Thomas Edward Potterton, D.D., Minister, 57 Lefferts Pl.

First. See above, CHURCH OF OUR FATHER.

NON-SECTARIAN AND INTERDENOMINATIONAL

Manhattan and Bronx

Beacon Light Gospel Hall, 2350 Third Ave. Wm. A. Blackley, director.

Bowery Mission and Young Men's Home, 227 Bowery. Rev. John G. Hallimond, D.D., supt.

Broome Street Tabernacle, 345 Broome St. Rev. Joseph Brunn, Pastor.

Charlton Street Memorial, 34-40 Charlton St. Rev. Pietro Griglio, Pastor. See also Alphabetical List.

Christ's Mission House, 331 West 57th St. Rev. Patrick Morgan, Pastor.

Church of God, 2132 Grand Ave. Rev. C. J. Blewitt, Pastor.

Church of the Son of Man, 227 East 104th St. Rev. Harry Ely Adriance, Pastor.

Church of the Strangers (Deems Memorial), 309 West 57th St. Rev. Paul Mansfield Spencer, Pastor.

Deems Memorial. See above Church of the Strangers.

Divine Inspiration, Genealogical Hall, 226 West 58th St.

Emmanuel Mission to the Jews, 241 East 120th St.

Ethical Culture Society, Central Park West and 64th St. See Alphabetical List.

Gospel Tabernacle, 692 Eighth Ave.

McAuley Cremorne Mission, 216 West 35th St. Wm. McQuere, supt.

McAuley Water Street Mission, 316 Water St.

Metropolitan Tabernacle, Broadway and 104th St.

Olivet Memorial, 63 Second St. Rev. Harry L. Oldfield (English), Rev. Augustus Roeandt (German), Rev. Louis Ordlie (Italian). See also Alphabetical List.

Parish of All Strangers, 108 West 77th St. Rev. Harry Marsh Warren, Pastor.

Rescue Society, 5-7 Doyers St.

Swedish Bethesda, 138-140 East 50th St.

Union Theological Seminary, Claremont Ave. and 120th St.

Vedanta Society, 117 West 72nd St. Swami Bodhananda, Teacher in charge.

Waldensian, 405 West 41st St. Rev Bartholomew Fron, Pastor.

Young Men's Christian Association, 215 West 23rd St. See Alphabetical List.

Young Women's Christian Association. See Alphabetical List for all branches.

Brooklyn

Brooklyn Spiritualist Society, 28 Irving Place.

Brooklyn Y. M. C. A., 55 Hanson Place. See Alphabetical List.

Grace Gospel, 480 Bainbridge St. Rev. Henri F. Gondret, Pastor.

Life Line Mission, 352 Bridge St. James C. Bogie, Clerk.

Lighthouse Pentecostal Assembly, 1244 Myrtle Ave. Wm. A. Coxe.

Metropolitan, Flushing and Metropolitan Aves.

South Brooklyn Gospel Church, Fourth Ave. and 56th St.

Williamsburgh Rescue Mission, 376 Bedford Ave.

Y. W. C. A. of Brooklyn, 316 Schermerhorn St. See Alphabetical List.

Queens

Church of Forest Hills, Seminole Ave. and Gown St.

Union, 45 Grand Ave.

Richmond

Immanuel, Westerleigh, S. I. Rev. Charles R. Kingsley, Pastor.

Randall Memorial, Sailor's Snug Harbor, New Brighton, S. I.

"HOW TO USE THIS DIRECTORY"

(*See page facing title*)

NAME INDEX

ADVERTISEMENTS

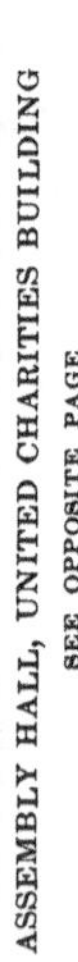

ASSEMBLY HALL, UNITED CHARITIES BUILDING

SEE OPPOSITE PAGE

THE SHELTERING ARMS

INCORPORATED 1864

AMSTERDAM AVENUE AND 129th STREET

For children not orphans from six to twelve years of age. They attend the Public School and are trained to household and other work. Supported by voluntary contributions, income of endowment, and board of children.

TRUSTEES

UNITED HOSPITAL FUND

OF NEW YORK

ORGANIZED 1879 INCORPORATED 1897

105 East 22d Street

ROBERT OLYPHANT .... *President*
GEORGE BLUMENTHAL .... *Vice-President*
JAMES McV. BREED .... *Secretary*
ALBERT H. WIGGIN .... *Treasurer, 57 Broadway*
FREDERICK D. GREENE .... *General Secretary*

DISTRIBUTING COMMITTEE

THE MAYOR OF NEW YORK, *Chairman*
THE PRESIDENT OF THE MERCHANTS' ASSOCIATION
THE PRESIDENT OF THE CHAMBER OF COMMERCE

OTTO T. BANNARD | ARTHUR CURTISS JAMES
CORNELIUS N. BLISS, JR. | JAMES SPEYER

OBJECTS

1. To obtain benevolent gifts for the Hospitals of New York.
2. To further methods of economy and to coordinate and extend the work of the hospitals.

WORTHY OF TESTAMENTARY REMEMBRANCE

The most pathetic, urgent need in the community is that of persons who are seriously ill or injured, and who are too poor to pay for the means of getting well.

A RECENT LETTER

"I enclose my check for $5,000 to the order of the United Hospital Fund of New York, which appeals to me as admirably suited to distribute my contribution widely, impartially, and practically to the aid of the sick and needy ones of our great city."

The Fund reduces duplication of effort in raising money, and distributes the money among the hospitals according to *the actual amount of free treatment which each gives to the poor, irrespective of race or creed.*

This it ascertains through carefully audited reports made by 57 leading hospitals of Greater New York, on *uniform schedules*, which show in detail the "Work Done," "Income," and "Expenses."

Approval by business men is shown by annual contributions of $5 to $5,000 from over 2,000 firms.

Contributors desiring free hospital treatment for proper cases may refer them to *Frederick D. Greene, General Secretary*, 105 E. 22d St.

NEW YORK CITY MISSION SOCIETY

Organized in 1827

OFFICE, UNITED CHARITIES BUILDING
FOURTH AVENUE AND 22d STREET

PROTESTANT AND EVANGELICAL — DOCTRINAL BASIS: THE APOSTLES' CREED

Aims at the evangelization of the city in its more destitute parts.

Has services in English, German, Italian, Spanish, for Jews in Yiddish. Also unit of workers for colored people in Harlem.

Holds property in churches valued at over $900,000.00, all free of incumbrance.

Has Church Schools, Libraries, Reading Rooms, Open-Air Services, Lecture Courses, four large Gymnasiums, and various other instrumentalities for making the Gospel touch the people at all points.

Works where the field is hardest, for people from many lands.

Officers

President: WILLIAM SLOANE COFFIN

Vice-Presidents: A. W. HALSEY, D.D. — F. R. CHAMBERS

Treasurer: STEPHEN BAKER

Secretary: LUTHER H. LEWIS

Board of Directors

Term expires Dec., 1921	*Term expires Dec., 1922*	*Term expires Dec., 1923*
John W. Auchincloss	Stephen Baker	Wm. E. Carnochan
Philip W. Henry	F. R. Chambers	Lincoln Cromwell
A. W. Halsey, D.D.	W. S. Coffin	Thomas Darlington, M.D.
Luther H. Lewis	W. S. Edgar	A. H. Evans, D.D.
Rev. James Palmer, Ph.D.	R. H. Fowler, M.D.	Eugene G. Foster
Robert H. Robinson	W. W. Hall	E. J. Gillies
Fleming H. Revell	W. B. Isham	Rev. Wm. R. Jelliffe
H. M. Sanders, D.D.	J. Henry Lancashire, M.D.	Gates W. McGarrah
A. M. Welch	Paul H. Smart	Wm. P. Merrill, D.D.
		Charles A. Runk

Superintendent: A. H. McKINNEY, D.D.

Director of Extension Work: REV. W. Y. DUNCAN

CHURCHES

Olivet Memorial Church — 59–63 Second Street
DeWitt Memorial Church — 280 Rivington Street
German Work at Olivet and DeWitt Churches
Broome Street Tabernacle — 395 Broome Street
Charlton Street Memorial Church — 34–40 Charlton Street
Jewish Work at 280 Rivington Street
Spanish Work at 109 E. 22d Street and 126 W. 16th Street

FORM OF BEQUEST

I give and bequeath to "New York City Mission Society," instituted in the City of New York, and incorporated by the Legislature of the State of New York, the sum of.. dollars, to be applied to the charitable uses and purposes of said Society.

Help That is Mutual

The Charity Organization Society Laundry is an up-to-date institution for doing the finest kind of work, teaching unskilled women a trade and providing employment. There is no secret process that results in premature decay of the fabric, or scars and gashes from speedy and rough handling. One of the great features of our laundry is the high grade of handwork that we turn out. Delicate pieces of napery are handled only by skilled women. Dainty linen comes home white and smooth—no "stars" in the middle folds of tablecloths, etc. Also, we do the lace curtains of some of the most particular housewives in New York; and great hampers of wash come to us from out-of-town customers.

The Laundry, however, is more than a business for washing clothes. It is a school for training unskilled women to be expert laundresses. They are paid fair wages and given a hot noon-day meal daily. The women are not put on fine work until they have covered every step of the way to doing good work. When their efficiency warrants they are recommended as laundresses in private families.

Let us relieve you of wash day. Standard prices for first-class work.

The Laundry is not self-supporting—but the women are

CHARITY ORGANIZATION SOCIETY LAUNDRY
516 WEST TWENTY-EIGHTH STREET
TELEPHONE 420 CHELSEA

Service That Works Both Ways

When you buy fire wood from the Charity Organization Society Wood Yard you not only get as good wood as you can buy at the regular trade prices, but you also enable some homeless man to earn a decent meal and a good night's sleep in a clean bed, or its equivalent in cash.

A man may be admitted to our yards for a few hours' work on the presentation of a ticket representing the interest of someone in providing him with the means of earning his meal and night's lodging. Books of 10 tickets each are sold at $1.00 to persons interested, either at the Wood Yard (address below) or at the central office of the Charity Organization Society, 105 East 22d Street.

The wood is carried to you by our own trucks and drivers and placed in your cellar without extra charge. The prices are subject to change without notice. January, 1921, they were:

Kindling		*Hickory*		*Pine Knots or Oak*	
¼ Cord	$8.50	¼ Cord	$10.50	¼ Cord	$8.50
½ Cord	16.00	½ Cord	19.50	½ Cord	16.00
1 Cord	32.00	1 Cord	39.00	1 Cord	32 00

We want new customers. *Will you send us an order?*

THE CHARITY ORGANIZATION SOCIETY
WOOD YARD

516 WEST TWENTY-EIGHTH STREET NEW YORK

THE NEW YORK
TRUST COMPANY

M
26

Fr
Ja
H
H
B
E
W

www.ingramcontent.com/pod-product-compliance
Lightning Source LLC
LaVergne TN
LVHW011259110826
845149LV00001B/193

* 9 7 8 1 4 1 8 1 8 8 5 9 7 *